JOBS '94

KATHRYN AND ROSS PETRAS

A FIRESIDE BOOK
PUBLISHED BY

SIMON & SCHUSTER

New York   London   Toronto   Sydney   Tokyo   Singapore

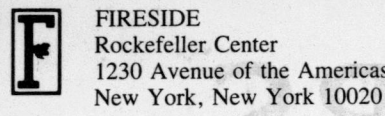

FIRESIDE
Rockefeller Center
1230 Avenue of the Americas
New York, New York 10020

Copyright © 1993 by Kathryn Petras and Ross Petras

FIRESIDE and colophon are registered trademarks
of Simon & Schuster Inc.

Manufactured in the United States of America

10 9 8 7 6 5 4 3 2 1

Library of Congress Cataloging-in-Publication Data is available.

ISBN 0-671-76076-9

IMPORTANT NOTE

This book draws together thousands of careers, companies, and associations from a wide range of sources. In all cases, we've tried to be accurate and up to date, but due to the timely nature of the material, inaccuracies may occur. Also, the inclusion of a company or career in this book does not constitute a recommendation; any recommendations of companies and careers we do make is our own opinion based on the data available to us. The reader must do further research on his or her own to determine if a career or company is the right choice.

CONTENTS

SECTION 3

REGIONAL ROUNDUP 1994

INTRODUCTION

WHAT'S IN THIS BOOK

▶ *Read* **this section, it will enable you to better get your money's worth from the enormous number of sources and material between these covers.**

At last count, by using this book you could access over 40 million jobs. That sounds ridiculously high—but using this book you can call virtually any government employment office at any agency, you can write or call virtually all of the *Fortune* 500, as well as many thousands of smaller companies, you can get a teaching job anywhere on the globe. But this book is most effectively used by those who read what follows.

▶ *Jobs '94* **is divided into three main sections: Career, Industry, and Regional—as well as some special sections devoted to minorities, women, and people with disabilities.**

These sections include major written portions. They describe what you need to know to consider and apply for a job in 1994—and in the near future. Basically, they cover:

- *Job and Industry Descriptions*: what the main jobs are in each area, what qualifications are needed, what you need to know about major career areas from advertising to utilities, what happened in the recent past.

- *Job and Industry Trends and Forecasts*: what the employment prospects are for 1994 and beyond, what is happening now and what will happen next.

- *Best Bets and Employment Spotlights*: which careers have the best long-term potential, seem interesting or unusual; which companies promise the best opportunities.

- *In Demand*: jobs in demand in various industries.

- *Average Salaries*: what to expect when you enter; as you advance.

- *National and Regional Employment Trends*: which parts of the country look good for employment; which areas are weak; predictions.

- *Regional Hotspots*: which cities or regions look particularly good for employment; what types of jobs are opening up, or why economy looks strong.

- *Assorted Top Ten Lists, etc.*: assorted charts, tables, etc., illustrating major employment ideas or trends.

▶ **The employers we list cover most major companies and organizations in the U.S.**

We include:

- *Top corporations in most major industries*: the top employers from advertising to utilities; with addresses and phone numbers.

- *Top companies in each state*: the top employers in each state; with addresses and phone numbers, from Alaska to Florida.

- *Major government employers*: the major government agencies, with addresses, phone numbers, and types of employees being sought.

- *Major international and non profit employers*: the major international organizations and nonprofits, including major employers of teachers overseas.

▶ **The sources we list help you actually contact the people who can get you a job.**

In general, we list several types of sources:

- *Career and industry associations*: useful to join or call to find out more; to meet potential employers; etc. Also: whether the association publishes directories, magazines that include classified ads for jobs, etc.

- *Career and industry directories*: useful directories that can be used in compiling a mailing list for a direct-mail job-hunting campaign.

- *Magazines*: and other periodicals that have job or career information, jobs listings, etc.

- *Other job or career sources*: computer databases, job hotlines, vocational programs, etc.

How To Use This Book

▶ **Now that we've described what's in this book, we'll describe how to use it.**

The textual portions are self-evident—they contain what you need to know to *begin* making a decision about targeting your job hunt. One key point: make certain you read *both* the career and the industry areas; for example, if you're interested in engineering, you should start with the Engineering section, but you should also read the industry areas that interest you, such as Computers and Electronics, Aerospace, and so on. And of course, check the Regional section as well.

▶ **What follows are some suggestions on how to use the source and employer lists in this book.**

These are listed in the approximate order you'll encounter them in the book. One key point: *Try to call these sources to verify addresses.* We live in a fast-moving economy. Names change, addresses change; associations and companies, go out of business or merge, typos occur . . . your best bet is to check.

Associations

These are groups that represent major career or industry areas—from accountants to zoologists, from advertising to utilities.

How to use them in your job hunt:

Associations often publish magazines which contain information of use to a job hunter; sometimes they include job listings and, more importantly, by joining you can meet people in the field who can get you a job. The associations listed here are national associations, but be aware that most have local chapters, which you'll automatically join if you pay your dues to the national chapter.

In the Career section, we've listed hundreds of associations, and in most cases we've told you what particularly useful services they can offer you as a job hunter. Other services include placement or job referral services or career hotlines or electronic job listing. In the Industry section, we've listed the major industry associations—although many of these don't publish as much career information, they can be even more valuable as networking points.

How to contact associations: Call or write them. Be aware that often associations only help those who are members—so you may find it useful to join. Always investigate a little before paying anything to join. Although most associations listed here are large and reputable, you never know . . . And ask about any type of special membership—sometimes you can obtain substantial discounts.

Directories

These are listings of names of people within a functional career area or within an industry, or names of companies within an industry. Some directories, like those for international teachers, are more like listings of job opportunities.

How to use them in your job hunt:

Use them to compile a mailing list for use in a direct-mail campaign during a job hunt, or for a targeted mailing campaign. Note that many associations also publish directories, so when calling always ask if they do, and ask if they are available for purchase. Most sections of the book include directories which can be useful to your job hunt. We didn't list prices in most cases because by the time you read this, the prices will have changed. So call and check prices. But *be aware that directory prices are often very high.* They may not be high on a per-listing basis, but many include thousands of listings and so cost in the hundreds of dollars.

Sometimes you may be pleasantly surprised; association directories, for example, are usually fairly inexpensive. One idea: ask for them at your library or at a nearby college library. And if you decide to buy one, be sure you know what you are getting. For example, some are compiled from telephone Yellow Pages and include little more than names, addresses, and main business—this is fine for some people, but others may want more details.

Magazines and Other Periodicals

We list two basic kinds of periodical—those that are major journals in a field or an industry; and special job-hunting periodicals, which are basically compilations of job listings.

How to use them in your job hunt:

The major journals are an excellent way to get a "feel" for a career or a job—and decide if it's the right one for you. Just by reading a trade journal, you can get ideas on hiring, on what to say at an interview, on whom to write or cold-call for a job lead. In addition, many of these journals have job listings at the back. And the job-hunting periodicals are obviously useful if you want to answer job ads.

Before you subscribe: Call the magazine if you can, see if you can get a sample issue (if you can't find one on the newsstands or in the library).

Government Agency Listings

We've listed government employers in the Government section, some in the International section, some in the Technical, and some elsewhere. In most cases we've included a personnel number, any job hotlines, personnel addresses, and other useful addresses and information. We've also told you how to contact local offices of agencies, so that if you live in Montana and want to stay in Montana, but are still interested in working for the federal government, you can easily find out your options.

How to use them in your job hunt:

You can call or write the personnel departments and the Office of Personnel Management (see page 66). But don't stop with the personnel. We've listed government directories, etc., in an effort to encourage you to contact actual hiring or line officers at an agency—often, networking is the best way to get a government job.

International, Nonprofit, and UN Employers

We've listed, primarily in the International section, major employers in the public and nonprofit sector not affiliated with the U.S. government.

How to use them in your job hunt:

You can call or write them, as per instructions. In some cases, as with the UN, we explain your various options depending on what kind of UN job you're looking for.

Federal and State Employment Offices

These are the federal and state employment offices that usually have federal and state job information, as well as (in some states) other types of job help. They are listed in the Regional section, under each state.

How to use them in your job hunt:

Go to these offices to get postings of federal and state job openings, and the forms you need to apply. Some also offer recorded information.

Computer Databases

Résumé databases are computer databases that generally include either résumés of job hunters, or, sometimes, information about companies *for* job hunters. We list the major résumé and other databases related to careers.

How to use them in your job hunt:
Getting yourself listed can be a useful way of getting yourself a job—more and more recruiters are taking a look at these database services and calling people for interviews. Other services, such as job descriptions, which are sometimes on databases easily accessible by the public, can be useful to the job hunter as well. One example is the interactive job and career database offered by the U.S. government (see page 85). The other major databases are listed in one section, on page 507.

Job Hotlines

Job hotlines are usually phone numbers which offer up-to-date, pre-recorded job information. Many are free; others charge a fee. We list job hotlines underneath the sponsoring organization—whether it is a government organization, a corporation, or an association.

How to use them in your job hunt:
Call them and get an up-to-date listing of *some* jobs that are available; but remember, the informal job market that you open up yourself through networking and so on is often more useful. Most hotlines are run by associations, and of course those run by the U.S. government are reputable. But be careful of disreputable hotlines, which advertise, promise hundreds of jobs (usually just ads from a newspaper), and can charge high fees.

Company Lists

We've listed thousands of the major corporations of the U.S. In each Industry section, we list the major companies of that industry. And in each Regional section, we include the major companies of each state.

How to use them in your job hunt:
Use the listings as a built-in mailing list for a targeted direct-mail campaign. Also, you may want to call the companies directly and ask for any employment material they may have. *A good idea*: if you're interested in a certain major company, call and ask for its *media kit*. Many major firms have these made up for journalists; they include clippings, annual reports, etc. They can be a great way of getting an inside idea of what the company feels about itself—and they give you an edge during an interview.

Other Job or Training Sources

We've also included names and addresses of special publishing programs for those who want training in publishing careers, information on leading vocational programs, how and where to get training in photojournalism, in desktop publishing, etc. These are explained in the text.

Once again, we hope this book is as useful for you as it has been for others, and that it aids you in making your job search quick—and effective.

SECTION 1

CAREER OUTLOOKS 1994

ACCOUNTANTS, AUDITORS, BUDGET ANALYSTS, AND CREDIT SPECIALISTS

BRIEF BACKGROUND

▶ **Accountants and auditors prepare and analyze financial information for governments, businesses, and other organizations.**

Like medicine or law, accounting is self-regulated by its own professional organizations—principally the American Institute of Certified Public Accountants (AICPA). The AICPA sets standards and writes tests that certify accountants in certain areas of the business. Over 40% of the 1 million accountants and auditors are certified—most of them as Certified Public Accountants (CPAs). Another certification, the Certified Management Accountant (CMA), is valuable for accountants who work primarily for corporations.

▶ **There are three main job areas: public accounting, management and government accounting, and internal auditing.**

Public accountants either own their own firms or work in private partnerships. The larger private partnerships form the high-profile sector of the profession, serving large corporate clients. Until a few years ago, this sector was dominated by the so-called Big Eight firms—mergers have reduced them to the Big Six (see names and addresses on page 20).

Management and government accountants work within an organization, preparing financial statements and other financial information. This is the largest area of accounting in terms of employment. Internal auditors analyze and report on corporate financial and information reporting systems. EDP (electronic data processing) auditors, formerly with finance or other backgrounds, increasingly come from information-processing areas.

▶ **Budget analysts develop, manage, and plan company or organization financial plans, while credit specialists focus on one of business's major concerns: Can our loan customers pay us back?**

Budget analysts work in private industry as well as government, with a large percentage in manufacturing, defense, and education. Because of the accounting responsibilities of this type of work, accountants are often employed as analysts; and at large corporations, a CPA is often a requirement.

Credit clerks, checkers, and authorizers work for banks, retailers, wholesalers, and credit card operations and credit agencies—anywhere where credit is granted and loans are made.

For more information on other financial jobs, see Banking on page 267, Financial Services on page 349, and Managers on page 119.

EMPLOYMENT OUTLOOK: Significantly improving over long term.

The good news: estimates are that over 300,000 new jobs in accounting and auditing will be created by the year 2005—according to the U.S. Bureau of Labor Statistics. The *rate* of growth will be faster than average during the next ten years.

Key reason: the complexity of financial transactions is *increasing,* and with that, the need for properly trained accountants and auditors will increase as well. The staid old world of banking and finance has changed radically in recent years, and accountants and auditors will be needed to sort through the complex new ways of borrowing and lending. As the number of new businesses increases, new jobs will be created in these new corporations as well.

That's the good news. And for those in these professions it couldn't come at a better time. Simply put, the past few years were bleaker than normal for accountants and auditors. What happened? Massive changes within the industry—and one of the worst recessions in memory. Both have caused employment jitters.

A brief overview of the changes: once the accounting industry was dominated by eight large accounting partnerships, the Big Eight. They set the tone of the industry—conservative, low-profile, quiet, stable. In terms of employment, job tracks were predictable. Get a job in accounting, and you could pretty much predict where you'd be and what you'd be doing twenty years in the future. Employment wasn't guaranteed, but it came close.

That all changed during the 1980s. During these years, the major accounting firms transformed themselves into hard-charging businesses and diversified into other businesses, such as consulting (Arthur Andersen is the largest consulting firm in the world). Competition increased as well—some firms began cutting prices to win clients, others bought out rival firms. The Big Eight became the Big Six. And then the recession and the Savings and Loan crisis hit.

Firstly, as more and more Savings and Loan institutions went bankrupt, accounting firms were blamed—and sued—for allegedly substandard audits. (However, the rate of negligence has been found to be less than 0.5%—about the same rate as the previous five years.) Regardless of the verity of the allegations, firms began upgrading auditing standards, and had to face costly lawsuits—and these were some reasons for a round of cost-cutting that began in the late '80s and early 1990s. And of course, the recession itself was another major reason. One result: cutbacks in employment. Where a job with a major accounting firm once meant job security and good training, in the recession years it meant the possibility of being fired just before the slow summer season. The firm saved costs during the slow summer, then hired new college grads as replacements in the following fall. Key problem: fired accountants had only a year or so of experience and faced difficulties getting new jobs.

Also: salary increases were reduced, job offers were kept on the table for a shorter period. More firms were offering ninety-day try-out periods for new employees in lieu of permanent offers.

Result: the good old days of virtually guaranteed employment and predictable career paths are over—at least for now.

► **Budget analysts: some good news and some bad news; credit specialists will find that recovery may increase demand for their services—although computerization will cut into job growth to a degree.**

The pool of applicants for budget jobs is increasing, according to the Bureau of Labor Statistics—and computers are replacing many human functions. But on the positive side, increasing complexity and a growing demand for sophisticated analysis point to the continuing need for well-trained, technically competent budget analysts. And analysts are more likely to keep their jobs in a bad economy. Except in the worst of circumstances, the budget cycle keeps on going and analysts are always needed. There are about 60,000 budget analysts today, and the government projects job growth at about the same rate as the economy.

Qualifications required for a good job are increasing. Although some applicants are still promoted out of payroll or accounting clerk positions, MAs or CPAs are preferred at major corporations, along with experience with relevant budgeting programs like Lotus 123 or more. Training is varied—most analysts find the best training is working on the job through the complete budget cycle, from reading projections to implementing procedures.

Employment for credit authorizers, checkers, loan clerks, etc., is expected to grow at the same moderate rate as that for budget analysts. In general, employment prospects tend to improve as interest rates go down—simply because more people tend to borrow; in addition, economic conditions play a strong role in borrowing and lending climate. One problem for employment: retail firms, credit unions, and banks increasingly are centralizing credit operations via more sophisticated computer technology. Where once a branch store made its own credit decisions, today it usually relies on a central credit operation covering an entire region.

The good news for loan and credit clerks, however, is that there is still a personal element in credit decisions—it's still hard to duplicate the intangibles of deciding who will repay a loan on a computer. For example, some small, conservative banks and S&Ls avoided the banking crisis by paying strict personalized attention to their customers and their businesses. That personal touch paid off—they're still in business. And they'll keep on hiring.

WHAT'S NEXT

► **More changes—even as the accounting profession digests all the changes of the 1980s and early 1990s.**

Some major trends to look at:

Technology: The next step will be the use of expert systems and artificial intelligence to solve many complex accounting problems. One possibility, according to the American Institute of Certified Public Accountants (AICPA): the expense of such systems might make some firms specialize in narrow areas of expertise, and network or outsource for areas outside their specialties. Meanwhile, more sophisticated computers are already reducing the numbers of auditors and the time required to do a typical audit—and computer literacy will continue to be emphasized.

Competition: More and more of it, and a trend by firms to offer more nonaccounting and nonauditing services to beat the competition. In addition, greater differentiation and specialization by firms will result in CPA firms increasingly competing with other, non-CPA organizations for the same business. At the same time, look for alliances or associations between CPA and non-CPA firms to increase competitive advantages.

Specialization: Accountants will increasingly concentrate on expertise within certain industries—the rationale being that those who really understand the business will be able to perform better audits and other services. As *Fortune* magazine noted, it was significant that when Big Six firm Peat Marwick announced its new partners last year, it announced not only their functional areas (tax, auditing, or consulting), but also their areas of specific expertise, such as health care, banking, etc.

Standards: Look for even more rigorous hiring, training, and work standards, according to the AICPA. At the same time, the institute is concerned that many of the "best and brightest" graduates are attracted to areas other than accounting.

▶ **Major changes in employment patterns.**

The reduction of partners at some of the Big Six accounting firms—by 5 to 15%—will continue to have repercussions.

The pyramid shape of employment, with many entry- and low-level employees and fewer higher-level employees, will change; the pyramid will flatten. More seasoned personnel will be in demand, as experience in sophisticated areas becomes more crucial. At the same time, more recruits will come from broader, nonaccounting backgrounds.

The AICPA sees new firm mergers on the horizon, as well as an increasing number of start-up firms. More accountants will work as part-time practitioners, more will be from small firms rather than large, and turnover due to life-style considerations will increase. Family and life-style issues will become more important and firms will look to accommodate a more demanding work force. Look for government and environmental employment to increase. Women and minorities will increasingly be hired, training will become more difficult . . . and vital. Accounting firms will offer more training to staff and clients. In other words, most projections point to accounting changing with the economy: greater diversity, more competition, greater complexity . . . and more changes on the horizon.

Bottom line: better employment prospects for educated, computer-literate applicants, especially for those with a broad background, or a specialized background in such areas as international business.

▶ **The outlook for women and minorities is improving.**

The good news for women: in 1992, the *Journal of Accountancy* projected that 57% of new recruits were women in the past year. The problem, of course, is that women are underrepresented in the upper tiers; but even here, surveys show that women are gaining and moving upward in mainstream areas like auditing and consulting.

The bad news for minorities is that their underrepresentation in accounting continues. And while some minorities, including Hispanics and Asians, have increased their presence, black employment actually declined in percentage terms, although the number of black partners has increased. The AICPA has indicated concern over this problem, and has targeted efforts to increase black participation in the profession.

SALARIES

PUBLIC ACCOUNTING: A good rule of thumb: the larger the city and the larger the firm, the higher the salary. The starting salary for accounting graduates was little changed from that of the previous years, roughly $28,000. Low- to mid-level salaries ranged from an average of $26,000 in small cities to about $30,000 in larger regional cities such as Atlanta. Upper mid-level salaries ranged from $30,000 in small towns to about $50,000 in major cities, and up to $75,000 or more in Los Angeles and New York. Higher salaries are found at Big Six firms. Partners at large firms earn from $100,000 on up.

CORPORATE ACCOUNTING: Beginning salaries averaged around $25,000; mid-level from $30,000 to $65,000 for the more experienced. Managers' salaries ranged from $40,000 to $80,000. Above these levels, major corporate financial officers and CEOs with accounting backgrounds received salaries far above $100,000.

GOVERNMENT ACCOUNTANTS: Average salaries were about $36,400 in 1988, the last year reported in surveys; beginning salaries ranged from $15,000 to $20,000; master's degrees candidates from about $24,000. However, this does not take into account very recent salary increases in government, nor the substantial benefits offered to government employees.

BUDGET ANALYSTS: Beginning salaries range from $20,000 to $25,000; more senior analysts earn from $28,000 to $38,000; managers earn from $35,000 to $50,000, depending on the size of the firm. Government analysts earn from about $16,000, with an average salary of about $35,000.

CREDIT WORKERS: Salaries vary widely, depending on experience and type of employment. Credit clerks begin at about $13,500; senior clerks may earn about $26,000.

TOP ACCOUNTING FIRMS: The Big Six
(in order of size)

Arthur Andersen and Co.
69 W. Washington St.
Chicago, IL 60602
312/582-0069
Known for its top-notch training program (most courses are offered at a special training facility in St. Charles, MN), and for its enormous consulting practice (particularly skilled in designing computerized management information systems). Almost merged with Price Waterhouse. It has many oil and gas clients.

Ernst & Young
787 7th Ave.
New York, NY 10019
212/830-6000
Formed from the merger of the old Big Eight firms of Ernst & Whinney and Arthur Young. Specialties include health care and financial services, banking.

Deloitte & Touche
10 Westport Rd.
Wilton, CT 06897
203/761-3000
Formed from the merger of the old Big Eight firms of Deloitte, Haskins & Sells and Touche Ross; specialties include financial services, manufacturing (audits GM, Chrysler), and in particular, retailing. Clients include Sears, Macy's.

KPMG Peat Marwick
5 Chestnut Ridge Rd.
Montvale, NJ 07645
201/307-7000
Formed by the merger of the old Big Eight firm Peat Marwick with KMG Main Hurdman. Specialties include banking, insurance, and computers—strong in Silicon Valley. A semifinalist in the 1990 Malcolm Baldridge quality award.

Coopers & Lybrand
1301 Ave. of the Americas
New York, NY 10020
212/536-2000
Resisted merger mania in the eighties and early nineties; specialties include energy, utilities and particularly communications—its clients include AT&T, BellSouth, Nynex.

Price Waterhouse
1251 Ave. of the Americas
New York, NY 10020
212/819-5000

The oldest Big Six; known as the blue-chip firm, it long boasted more blue-chip clients and more *Fortune* 500 companies than its rivals. Serves multinationals like IBM, Kodak, and Exxon.

OTHER TOP FIRMS:

Altschuler Melvoin and Glasser
30 S. Wacker Dr.
Chicago, IL 60606
312/207-2800

Baird Kurtz & Dobson
P.O. Box 1190
Springfield, MO 65801
417/865-8701

Cherry Bekaert & Holland
3100 1 First Union Center
Charlotte, NC 28202
704/377-3741

Crowe Chizek and Co.
330 E. Jefferson
South Bend, IN 46624
219/232-3992

Richard A. Eisner and Co.
575 Madison Ave.
New York, NY 10022
212/355-1700

Goldstein Golub Kessler and Co.
1185 Ave. of the Americas
New York, NY 10036
212/523-1200

Grant Thornton
1 Prudential Plaza
Chicago, IL 60601
312/856-0001

Clifton Gunderson and Co.
301 SW Adams St.
Peoria, IL 61609
309/671-4560

Kenneth Leventhal and Co.
1633 Broadway
New York, NY 10019
212/790-0500

McGladrey and Pullen
102 W. 2nd St.
Davenport, IA 52801
319/324-0447

Moss Adams and Co.
1001 4th Ave.
Seattle, WA 98154
206/223-1820

George S. Olive & Co.
201 N. Illinois St.
Indianapolis, IN 46204
317/238-4000

Pannell Kerr Forster
P.O. Box 60808
Houston, TX 77205
713/999-5134

Plante.and Moran
P.O. Box 307
Southfield, MO 65801
313/352-2500

WHERE TO GO FOR MORE INFORMATION

ACCOUNTING ASSOCIATIONS

American Accounting Association
5717 Bessie Dr.
Sarasota, FL 34223
813/921-7747
(Publishes *The Accounting Review*.)

American Institute of Certified Public Accountants
Harborside Financial Center
201 Plaza 3
Jersey City, NJ 07311-3881
212/575-5505
(Publishes journal with many listings—see following material.)

American Society of Tax Professionals
P.O. Box 1024
Sioux Falls, SD
605/335-1185

American Society of Woman Accountants
1755 Lynnfield Rd., Suite 222
Memphis, TN 38119
901/680-0470
(Publishes career information, etc.)

American Women's Society of Certified Public Accountants
401 N. Michigan Ave.
Chicago, IL 60611
312/644-6610

Association of Government Accountants
2200 Mt. Vernon Ave.
Alexandria, VA 22301
703/684-6931
(Offers placement service for a fee via phone, publishes periodical with job listings, etc.)

EDP Auditors Foundation
455 E. Kehoe Blvd., Suite 106
P.O. Box 88180
Carol Stream, IL 60188-0180
708/682-1200

Government Finance Officers Association
180 N. Michigan Ave.,
Suite 800
Chicago, IL 60601
312/977-9700
(Publishes periodicals with job listings, etc.)

Institute of Internal Auditors
249 Maitiant Ave.
Altamonte Springs, FL 32701
407/830/7600

National Association of Accountants
P.O. Box 433
10 Paragon Dr.
Montvale, NJ 07645
201/573-9000
703/573-9000

National Association of Credit Management
8815 Centre Park Dr.
Columbia, MD 21045
410/740-5560

(Publishes monthly periodical, job referral service for members, etc.)

National Society of Public Accountants
1010 N. Fairfax St.
Alexandria, VA 22314
703/549-6400
(Publishes periodical with job listings, directory, etc.)

ACCOUNTING DIRECTORIES

Accountant's Directory
American Business Directories, Inc.
American Business Information, Inc.
5711 S. 86th Circle
P.O. Box 27347
Omaha, NE 68127
402/593-4600
(Broken into seven parts; cost of entire U.S. directory is $3,700; each part is less—for example, the Northeast directory of

23,000 addresses is $735, or about 3 cents per name.)

Firm on Firm Directory
American Institute of Certified Public Accountants
Harborside Financial Center
201 Plaza 3
Jersey City, NJ 07311-3881
212/579-6200
1-800/862-4272

(Lists thousands of firms. Phone for information—must be ordered via mail or fax.)

National Directory of Accounting Firms and Accountants by Thomas M. Bachman
Gale Research
835 Penobscot Bldg.
Detroit, MI 48226-4904
1-800/877-GALE
(Costs about $125.)

ACCOUNTING MAGAZINES

Accounting Today
425 Park Ave.
New York, NY 10022
212/371-9400
(Biweekly.)

The California CPA Quarterly
California Society of CPAs

1000 Welch Rd.
Palo Alto, CA 94304

CPA Journal
200 Park Ave., 10th Fl.
New York, NY 10166
212/973-8300
(Monthly journal, mainly New York-oriented.)

CPA Letter
American Institute of Certified Public Accountaints
Harborside Financial Center
201 Plaza 3
Jersey City, NJ 07311-3881
212/596-6200

24   CAREER OUTLOOKS 1994

Florida CPA Today
Florida Institute of
CPAs
P.O. Box 5437
325 W. College Ave.
Tallahassee, FL 32314

Internal Auditor
P.O. Box 1119
Altamonte Springs, FL
32701
407/830-7600
(Bimonthly to
association members.)

*Journal of
Accountancy*
Harborside Financial
Center

201 Plaza 3
Jersey City, NJ
07311-3881
212/575-6200
(Monthly association
magazine; carries job
listings.)

*Management
Accounting*
National Association of
Accountants
P.O. Box 433
10 Paragon Dr.
Montvale, NJ 07645
201/573-9000
(Monthly.)

*National Public
Accountant*
National Society of
Public Accountants
1010 N. Fairfax St.
Alexandria, VA 22314
703/549-6400

*The Practical
Accountant*
Warren, Gorham &
Lamont, Inc.
210 South St.
Boston, MA 02111
617/423-2020

ADMINISTRATIVE ASSISTANTS, CLERICAL WORKERS, AND SECRETARIES

BRIEF BACKGROUND

Over 15 million people work as secretaries, administrative assistants, or in some sort of clerical job—and for the right kind of worker, the general outlook in the 1990s will be fairly bright.

Just as computers are taking away jobs for stenographers, data-entry workers, typists, and some clerks and secretaries, the increasing complexity of business will be creating jobs for others who can manage computers and people in what will be a much more complex organizational environment. And although the *rate* of growth in this area as a whole will be lower during the next ten years, the size of this job area is so large that there will be a large number of new job openings.

NOTE: This section is a general overview of secretarial and hotel jobs. For more information, also see the appropriate industry section.

EMPLOYMENT OUTLOOK: Fair—best for legal and medical secretaries, as well as those with strong computer skills.

▶ **In general, demand for top-notch secretaries is expected to be relatively strong—but a lot depends on the strength of the local economy.**

In many parts of the country in 1993, business growth was slow and unsteady—and competition for secretarial jobs was very keen and salaries were lower than normal.

In the *long run*, however, job openings are expected to be there. Simply put, there are so many secretarial positions—over 3.5 *million*—that each year many jobs open up as secretaries retire or switch jobs or careers. In addition, the number of *new* secretarial jobs is expected to increase, at an average rate, over the next ten years.

One problem: what about office automation? Will computers, voice mail, and a host of other gadgets reduce demand for secretaries in the future? To a certain degree, this is already happening. Many companies have replaced receptionists with voice-mail systems, some executives now prefer to type their own memos, and others prefer to share secretarial services now that computers have increased efficiency. *But,* even with all this innovation, demand should remain relatively strong as the economy improves. Many secretarial functions, such as scheduling, handling the public, etc., call for judgment that is far beyond the reach of computers. In addition, computers themselves need handling! Key point: demand will be strongest for computer-literate, well-trained professionals. One group, Professional Secretaries International, offers certification for secretaries—the Certified Professional Secretary.

One problem with all this is that many secretaries feel the job has become increasingly complex—they do all the work of an executive but get none or few of the perks.

However, this is changing, and will change more rapidly in the 1990s. For example, some companies, such as Morgan Bank, are creating separate departments and special career tracks for secretaries and administrative assistants. An orderly promotion track, and the sense of being recognized for accomplishments, addresses one of the key problems in this area.

▶ **Many traditional clerical jobs are now bad employment bets— computers are doing some of the work human clerks once did. But at the same time, job opportunities are opening for other clerks, particularly those with computer skills. The bottom line? Over the long term, the loss of many clerical jobs to computerization should be offset to some degree by the creation of new clerical jobs for the computer-literate.**

But the Computer Age is here, and many clerical functions are being taken over by computer. This means that many traditional areas for jobs—such as bookkeeping, brokerage house operations, billing and record keeping, etc.—will see only slow increases or declines in the total number of jobs. Of course, replacement jobs will open up, but in general, these will not be dynamic areas of employment growth. Best bet: get computer skills, be flexible, and keep on the lookout for opportunities.

In general, many jobs will be opening because there are already so many people working in these areas—and as they retire or leave, replacements will always be needed.

▶ **Clerical jobs in travel and hospitality: a good way to get your foot in the door.**

Taking a job as a reservation agent, ticket clerk, or passenger service agent is one of the best ways to break into the travel industry—although competition is tough. About 75% of these jobs are with airlines, others with cruise lines and other travel companies.

A brief description of key jobs: *Reservations agents* usually work on computer in centralized offices, booking reservations, answering customer questions. *Ticket clerks* actually sell the tickets at the airports, check baggage and visas, etc.; while *passenger service agents* usually help board passengers, check tickets, make announcements, etc. Sometimes the job duties overlap, but all require a pleasant attitude and an ability to work under pressure. Travel is a twenty-four-hour, fast-moving industry. It's also a growing industry with a strong outlook ahead, which makes this area a good bet for the future.

Hotel work is another good way to break into the hospitality industry. Reason: Hotel work is perceived as glamorous, exciting. The reality? It can also be exhausting and stressful. But perks like free lodging and food make it worthwhile.

And there's an added plus—a clerical entry-level job can be one of the best and fastest ways of making it up the corporate ladder at a major hotel or a chain. Hotels like to promote from within the industry. Best way: find a new hotel opening locally. Hotels like to hire people from the area—and new hotels will often hire inexperienced people. Once inside, many hotels have incentive programs for smart people eager to move up.

There are many job areas, including front office staff (handle reservations, telephones, etc., mostly in contact with guests), as well as food service staff, accounting, and sales and marketing. For more information on the different careers in hotels, write the American Hotel & Motel Association (AH&MA). The AH&MA also has a special educational program for entry-level people interested in the industry. For more information, contact: American Hotel & Motel Association.

NOTE: For information about other careers in the travel industry or hospitality industry, see the industry sections on page 481 and page 381.

WHAT'S NEXT

▶ **Job outlook brightest for legal and medical secretaries and clerks.**

The fastest-growing job machine in America is the local doctor's office. The government predicts that medical secretaries' jobs will skyrocket by 65% by the year 2005, assuming the economy grows moderately; legal secretaries will do almost as well, up 47%.

Why? Both these areas are part of the service economy, and as Americans as a population get older, more and more of us will be using medical and legal services. Other areas, such as medical records technicians, will also increase quickly, as will legal assistants (see page 161).

On the downside, be on the lookout for unforeseen changes due to health care reform. If paperwork declines significantly (possible but doubtful), demand for employees in this area might not increase as rapidly.

SALARIES

SECRETARIAL: Salaries range from $18,000 on up—reaching $70,000 for high-level executive secretaries at top corporations, although top executive secretarial salaries usually are in the $40,000 range.

CLERICAL: Office clerks' salaries vary widely, depending on industry, area, level of employment. The average is about $19,000; supervisory clerks earn much more.

TRAVEL: Reservations agents and ticket clerks make from about $13,000 to $15,000 starting, averaging about $26,000 mid-level. Hotel employees begin from the low; those who work (and study) their way up the ladder into hotel management can make $50,000 to $70,000.

BEST BETS

ADMINISTRATIVE SERVICE MANAGERS: These are employees on the cutting edge of the corporation or government organization, overseeing the day-to-day operations. They may be office managers, managing clerical staff, overseeing administrative functions. They may also supervise administrative functions such as procurement, property disposal, transportation, mail services, inventory control. The job varies with the type of business and the size: at small companies, a manager may supervise almost everything; at large organizations, the job may be more specialized; and a top-level supervisory administrative manager may oversee many lower-level managers.

Demand for these services will grow throughout the 1990s—as organizations grow in size and complexity, and cost-consciousness increases, the need for efficient administrative service managers will increase. Pay reflects this demand, ranging from $20,000 to $75,000: the average starting salary in the federal government was $25,000, with an average salary of $50,700; support services officers earned $45,500.

WHERE TO GO FOR MORE INFORMATION

ADMINISTRATIVE ASSISTANTS, CLERICAL WORKERS, AND SECRETARIES ASSOCIATIONS

Air Line Employees Association
5600 S. Central Ave.
Chicago, IL 60638
312/767-3333

American Hotel and Motel Association
1201 New York Ave., NW, Suite 600
Washington, DC 20005-3931
202/289-3100
(Publishes career brochures, runs special educational program for entry-level applicants.)

American Society of Corporate Secretaries
1270 Ave. of the Americas
New York, NY 10020
212/765-2620

Data Entry Management Association
101 Merritt 7, 5th Fl.
Norwalk, CT 06851
203/846-3777

Executive Women International
Spring Run Office Plaza
965 E. 4800 S. Suite 1
Salt Lake City, UT 84117
801/263-3296
(Women who are in executive secretarial or administrative positions.)

National Association of Executive Secretaries
900 S. Washington St.
Falls Church, VA

22046
703/237-8616

National Association of Legal Secretaries
2250 E. 73rd St., Suite 550
Tulsa, OK 74136
918/493-3540

National Association of Secretarial Services
3637 4th St., N.,
Suite 330
St. Petersburg, FL 33704
813/823-3646

9 to 5—National Association of Working Women
614 Superior Ave., NW,
Suite 852
Cleveland, OH 44113

216/566-9308
(Although a general
women's business
association, does a lot
of work and promotes
legislation for
secretaries and clerical
workers.)

**Professional
Secretaries
International**
10502 NW Ambassador
Dr.
P.O. Box 20404
Kansas City, MO
64195
816/891-6600

(Publishes *The
Secretary Magazine*,
etc.)

ADMINISTRATIVE ASSISTANTS, CLERICAL WORKERS, AND SECRETARIES MAGAZINES

Secretary
2800 Shirlington Rd.
Arlington, VA 22206
703/998-2534
(Monthly association
magazine for career
secretaries.)

*The Secretary
Magazine*
Professional Secretaries
International
10502 NW Ambassador
Dr.
P.O. Box 20404
Kansas City, MO
64195
816/891-6600

Secretary's Update
131 Marpep Publishing
133 Richmond St., W.
Toronto, Ont.
Canada
M5H 3M8
416/869-1177
(Designed specifically
for Canadian
secretaries.)

ARTISTS AND DESIGNERS

[NOTE: For related information, see Advertising, page 225, and Fashion, page 331]

BRIEF BACKGROUND

▶ **The role of design, the importance of visual marketing is now (finally) more appreciated; and ultimately, artists and designers will benefit.**

Despite the ups and downs of the economy, the long-term trend is clear. Art and design are moving into a more central spot in American society—and this means job opportunities.

The trend can be seen in corporate America. Business is moving away from its focus on finance, and instead will pay more attention to product quality and design in the 1990s. More importantly, corporate America is beginning to appreciate the vital role of design in selling products in the world marketplace. Several MBA schools now offer design courses, the role of the creative staff in advertising is paramount, and job opportunities will return there as well. But . . . competition will still be very tough.

EMPLOYMENT OUTLOOK: Good in the long term, but tough competition always. And the next recession, like the last, will take its toll.

A few optimistic numbers from the U.S. government: overall, artists and commercial artists are expected to see jobs increase by 32% to the year 2005—a relatively rapid growth rate; designers can expect a 24% rate, and interior designers a 34% rate—always assuming the economy grows at a moderate pace. These are reassuring numbers; but remember, the competition in the arts is almost always tough.

▶ **In general, *graphic arts* will face the best prospects during the next half of the decade—on the cutting edge of business and art.**

Each year, many more people graduate from the best arts and design schools like Art Center College of Design in Pasadena, California, than there are jobs available. Currently, over 300,000 people are employed in design as a whole—about 40 percent are self-employed.

Competition, particularly at the lower levels, will be extremely tough; but new opportunities, such as computer graphics, will be growing, and the field itself is gaining in importance.

Some good areas:

① Ralston - Hot line
employment
982-2962

② Federal Express
Job Hot line
901-797-6830
2874 - Airport Business
Park, Bldg. D

MAGAZINE DESIGN AND ILLUSTRATION.   It's not too early to begin betting on a resurgence of the magazine, after the great shake-outs of 1991–92. Magazine art staffs will increase, probably in greater proportion to the general staffing level, as magazine design becomes an important part of circulation and positioning. Another trend: as magazines go international, more spin-off business will develop.

For more information, contact: The Graphics Artists Guild (address on page 37). Also check with Graphic Arts Employers of America (listed under the Printing Industries of America).

▶ **Another job option: Working with the design/marketing agencies.**

In many cases, design/marketing agencies are replacing ad agencies as visual positioning and marketing companies. Qualifications: talent, a good portfolio, and a good BFA gets your foot in the door. Another good way—internships with agencies.

For job leads, check the *Design Firm Directory* (address on page 39), which lists hundreds of design firms, as well as listings of advertising agencies and book and magazine publishers. Lists and directories of these employers can be found in the industry sections on pages 331, 225, and 421.

Increasingly important in the field: marketing professionals. As competition increases, it is no longer enough to know a few people and sell a few accounts. Many firms are turning to professionals to sell their services for them. According to employers, what is needed most is marketing expertise, a flair for selling, and a "feel" for arts and design. Actual artistic ability is not necessary, although for sales- and marketing-oriented artists, this can be a lucrative way of making a living.

▶ **Desktop publishing—if you've got the skills and the experience, a good option for employment.**

Desktop publishing is forcing changes in design and publishing—and for the technologically capable and flexible, it is offering job opportunities. Key advantages: speed, savings on production and printing. One problem: by allowing layout to occur on the computer, it is easier for writers and editors to make layout and typographic decisions that were formerly the province of the artist and typographer. And for pre-press employees such as typesetting and page makeup workers, this cuts into employment significantly. Key problem: this may blur the distinctions in the entire field. For example, companies could merge the positions of production artist and a higher-paid designer, keeping more people in lower-paid jobs. Question: Will the technology become *too* user-friendly and affect design employment?

Prediction: Probably not. In fact, the new programs often seem to require more training. Moreover, design is not just a technical skill, it is an art; no computer can mandate good taste. This is evident from some amateur desktop productions. The production values are high, but layout and typefaces may be very wrong.

Employment Prediction: Good for the right professional. In the next few years, as the dust settles, companies will probably have in-house desktop departments, with trained professionals running the programs. Key to a good job: a solid grounding in the technology (both operating system and the actual publishing software), production and typography, and, of course, design. *Getting in*: many universities and schools have now integrated desktop training into their commercial art curricula; on the publishing side, George Washington University in Washington, DC, has recently established a certification program, as has the National Technical Institute for the Deaf (see page 207).

▶ A strong area for the 1990s: *Industrial Design*.

Until recently, U.S. manufacturers for the most part essentially didn't manage design—this is evident just by looking at some products. That's not to say the U.S. is not producing top-rate designers; the problem is they've been underutilized. As the director of design from a major Dutch manufacturer stated: "I have 250 designers working for me in 20 countries and the Americans in that group stand tall. What is wrong is that U.S. companies don't understand the strategic value of design and relegate it to a second-rate position under engineering or marketing."

This is changing now. Witness the interactive children's toys from Texas Instruments, the NeXT computer, the Narrow Aisle Reach Truck (design of the decade by the Industrial Designers Society), Good Grips big-handle utensils (designed by Smart Design, Inc.), the Ford Taurus and the Sable. Key: good designs are essential to international competitiveness—and U.S. business increasingly understands this. *Also*, the importance of design seems to be infiltrating into smaller U.S. firms, which often take greater risks. Best areas in U.S. design: medical, computer, information systems. Some corporate stars: Gillette, Black & Decker, Texas Instruments, Apple Computer.

Qualifications required: usually a BFA (Bachelor of Fine Arts) from an accredited school. Employees usually start at large manufacturing firms, but many are self-employed or, increasingly, work at design/marketing firms.

Another good area: package design. In the 1990s, packaging will be a far more important element in selling consumer items. (Watch for brighter colors, "neckers," "wobblers," shelf talkers, "snipes"—all trade terms, all describing designs intended to do the same thing: stand out from the competition.) According to some in the industry, package designers will reap the benefits.

For general career information in these fields, contact: Industrial Designers Society of America (address on page 38).

▶ Interior Design.

This is a very competitive field that felt the effects of the past recession heavily, as business and personal spending dried up. Long-term outlook good, however, with faster-than-average growth.

Entry into interior design is regulated in some states: Washington, DC, licenses interior designers; five other states regulate use of the title. The Foundation for Interior Design Education Research accredits interior design programs—currently there are about ninety accredited programs across the U.S. (For more information, write them at: 60 Monroe Center NW, Grand Rapids, MI 49503.) After three to four years of professional education and two years of experience, most top designers complete the National Council for Interior Design Exam and are certified as professional interior designers. In many design fields, professional education and certification are increasingly required for higher-level positions.

Top Interior Design Firms

(with headquarter office; ranked by *Facilities Design and Management* on 1991 project square footage)

1. Hellmuth, Obata & Kasenbaum
   St. Louis
2. Gensler and Associates/Architects
   San Francisco
3. Leo A. Daly
   Omaha
4. CRSS, Inc.
   Houston
5. ISD Inc.
   New York
6. Sverdrup Corp.
   St. Louis
7. Architectural Interiors Inc./Interior Design, Inc.
   Chicago/Los Angeles
8. Interior Architects, Inc.
   San Francisco
9. Perkins & Will Group, Inc.
   Chicago
10. Swanke Haydon E. Connell, Ltd.
    New York

SOURCE: *Facilities Design and Management* 1992

Fine Arts

▶ **Most fine artists, painters, sculptors, printmakers, and the like are self-employed, although many work as teachers in universities and schools.**

Outlook: Tough competition as always. One reason: there are few formal entry requirements and a lot of excellent artists. Also, the effects of the recession on the job market. Even with improvements, it takes time. The best way to success is the old way: Assemble a strong, varied portfolio that shows creativity and technical expertise, and then learn how to aggressively market your work to the right gallery owner. A BFA from a good school also helps—both for experience and learning as well as for contacts.

Another option: teaching. Problem: the recession made job hunting tough in most areas, as top artists entered the profession. More recent figures weren't available, but here's an example: According to the College Art Association, in 1991 19 percent fewer college-level job openings were listed—and many of those jobs were temporary or nontenured. On average, about eighty-seven people applied for each opening.

Best areas: according to *The Chronicle of Higher Education*, any high-tech area; "someone who does traditional printmaking and video would be a hot property," according to one expert.

Note: For most of the arts, a significant source of money—and employment—comes in the form of foundation grants. To target the right foundation, check: *Foundation Grants to Individuals*. Also see the regional arts organizations listed at the end of this chapter. They award grants as well as provide assistance to artists. For more on how to pick and apply to foundations, see page 134.

Employment Spotlight: Photojournalists

Technology is coming to the newsroom—and to the darkroom. Digital photography equipment, increased newspaper emphasis on graphics are transforming the role of the photojournalist—according to *presstime* magazine. The jobs: at *New York Newsday*, the photo department comprises a chief photo editor, forty-one photographers, fifteen technicians, a photo researcher, a photo equipment supervisor, three editorial assistants, and twelve photo editors.

Photo editors help plan and coordinate assignments, and understand both the technical aspects of photography and the editorial requirements of the paper. Job potential: problematic. Some see a reduction (usually by attrition) of production staff, and some even see problems for photographers themselves—since the electronic technology can make even the worst photos by an untrained reporter acceptable. This latter scenario, though, is unlikely, since composition and high-quality photos and layouts are essential competitive positioning advantages in the industry.

Prediction: good opportunities for photojournalists who are computer-literate in imaging technology, etc., *and* have experience. With both, demand exceeded supply in 1992.

Ideal candidate: besides computer literacy, a college degree with journalism training, technical knowledge of color printing, etc. Where to go for training: see list below; also the NPPA offers training (919/383-7246), as do the ANPA Technical Dept (703/648-1213), the Society of Newspaper Design (703/648-1308), the Center for Creative Imaging, Eastman Kodak Company (800/428-7400), Rochester Institute of Technology (716/465-5064), and the University of Missouri Electronic Photojournalism Laboratory (314/882-0348).

BEST COLLEGE TRAINING FOR PHOTOJOURNALISTS

(with combined graphics, journalism, and technical curricula, as recommended by veteran photographers; quoted in *presstime*, 1992)

> California Polytechnic State University (San Luis Obispo, CA)
> California State University (Long Beach, CA)
> Ohio University (Athens, OH)
> Rochester Institute of Technology (Rochester, NY)
> San Jose State University (San Jose, CA)
> Syracuse University (Syracuse, NY)
> University of Missouri (Columbia, MO)
> University of Texas (Austin, TX)
> Western Kentucky University (Bowling Green, KY)

Employment Spotlight: Cartoonists

This type of drawing for a living is harder than most arts or design professions—most cartoonists do the gag writing as well. But there are bonuses: creative, recognized work, the attraction of reaching a large audience with your ideas and talent—and making them laugh or see things your way. There are very few full-time cartoonists: probably less than several hundred. Freelancers submit their work to magazines, which usually pay from $50 to $500 per cartoon.

According to one cartoonist interviewed in *The Occupational Outlook Quarterly*, a good cartoonist will sell about one out of every five cartoons drawn. Some may produce up to thirty a week, others less than five. Cartoonists aspiring to the comics have an even harder time; King Features, the main syndicator (a syndicator represents and sells the artist's work to newspapers across the country, in return for a cut of the proceeds, usually 50%), receives thousands of strips each year. For those feeling lucky, contact the Cartoonists Guild (see listing at end of chapter); they offer a placement service. Or try submitting your work to a newspaper syndicator—addresses of syndicators can be found in directories listed on page 435.

WHAT'S NEXT

▶ **Design will become more important and designers will reap the benefits.**

Newest trend: Universal design. The hottest aspect of industrial design. The Americans with Disabilities Act (ADA) of 1990 aims to guarantee the disabled the same access to jobs, transportation, as the rest of us—and this means design challenges as designers try to come up with telephones and office equipment that can be used by the disabled, as well as the rest of the population. Key advantage: it usually works out that the new product is better used by *both* the disabled and nondisabled.

Another example of design's increasing role: The Corporate Design Foundation in Boston is giving grants to major business schools to provide for courses in design for managers. The result: design-oriented future managers who will emphasize creative talent—and pay for it.

Another trend: product designers are foregoing the traditional hourly wage rate and asking instead for performance bonuses of between 1 to 5% of sales. This has been the case with some toy and furniture designers in the past; it is finally coming to other product designers as well.

▶ **The future: the sky's the limit.**

Technology will revolutionize arts and design, creating entirely new creative categories, and new careers. Some guesses: multi-media artforms, a dynamic hybrid of computer, video, holographic imaging, etc., now in its incubation period, will begin to be usable by the mid-1990s—and find incorporation into advertising and entertainment at the same time.

Some designers are already working on interactive books; others are creating a new "computer aesthetic." At the same time, there is a return to classicism by other designers. In all the arts and design, there are cycles of fads, fashions, and major trends. One key aspect of technology: it will speed up these cycles—and at the same time increase their impact. Already, design firms are linking up into worldwide networks, just as advertising agencies are going international. Designers will impact much of the world, not just local regions.

Of course, as technology gives more power to the individual, there will be a countertrend: more designers and artists will be able to link up with their like-minded brethren—and manage to buck the major trends and keep their smaller visions alive.

SALARIES:

GRAPHIC ARTISTS AND DESIGNERS: Beginning salaries in the low to mid-20s, median salaries around $30,000 to $40,000. Design shop owners, top freelancers, and top advertising creatives make considerably more. In general, the best average salaries go to designers working in art/design studios. Industrial designers begin in the mid- to high 20s; average salaries in the 40s. In advertising, salaries range from $25,000 for low-level art directors in small agencies to $90,000 for more senior directors at large agencies. For the politically and artistically talented, there is room at the top for associate creative directors and creative directors, with significantly higher salaries.

COMPUTER GRAPHICS: Beginning from about $25,000 for assistant designers, increasing to an average of about $45,000 for designers, more for senior designers.

FINE ARTISTS, INTERIOR DESIGNERS, CRAFTSPEOPLE: A high number of self-employed, with widely variable incomes. Full-time workers earn median incomes of about $30,000—some much higher, others, particularly those on a part-time basis, much lower.

WHERE TO GO FOR MORE INFORMATION

ARTS AND DESIGN BOOKS

Design Careers
Heller, Steven, and Lita Talarico.
New York: Van Nostrand Reinhold, 1987.
(A complete compendium of career information, with excellent employment sections and advice.)

Graphic Design Career Guide
Craig, James. Watson Guptill Publications, 1983.

Selling Your Graphic Design and Illustration
Crawford, Tad, and Arie Kopelman. New York: St. Martin's Press, 1981.

Supporting Yourself as an Artist
Hoover, Deborah. New York: Oxford University Press, 1989.
(Everyone should have this book; excellent advice, material, and ideas on the practical side of artistic life.)

REGIONAL ARTS ORGANIZATIONS

Arts Midwest
528 Hennepin Ave.
Minneapolis, MN
55403
612/341-0755

Consortium for Pacific Arts and Cultures
2141C Atherton Rd.
Honolulu, HI 96822
808/946-7381

Mid-America Arts Alliance
912 Baltimore Ave.,
Suite 700
Kansas City, MO
64105
816/421-1388

Mid-Atlantic Arts Foundation
11 E. Chase St.,
Suite 2A
Baltimore, MD 21202
410/539-6656

New England Foundation for the Arts
678 Massachusetts Ave.
Cambridge, MA 02139
617/492-2914

Southern Arts Federation
1293 Peachtree St.,
NE,
Suite 500
404/874-7244

Western States Arts Foundation
236 Montezuma Ave.
Sante Fe, NM 87501
505/988-1166

ARTS AND DESIGN ASSOCIATIONS

American Center for Design
233 E. Ontario,
Suite 500
Chicago, IL 60611
312/787-2018

American Council for the Arts
1285 Avenue of the
Americas, 3rd Fl.
New York, NY 10018
212/245-6655
(Publishes career guide, etc.)

American Craft Council
72 Spring St.
New York, NY 10012
212/274-0630

American Institute for the Conservation of Historic and Artistic Works
1400 16th St., NW,
Suite 340
Washington, DC 20036
202/232-6636

American Institute of Graphic Arts
1059 Third Ave.
New York, NY 10021
212/752-0813

American Society of Furniture Designers
P.O. Box 2688
High Point, NC 27261
919/884-4074
(Publishes magazine
with job openings,
placement service,
directories, etc.)

American Society of Interior Designers
608 Massachusetts
Ave., NE
Washington, DC 20002
202/546-3480
(Publishes career
pamphlets, etc.)

Cartoonists Guild of New York
11 W. 20th Street,
8th Fl.
New York, NY 10011
212/463-7759
(Placement service for
members.)

Graphic Artists Guild
11 W. 20th Street,
8th Fl.
New York, NY 10011
212/463-7730
(Publishes periodical,
etc.)

Graphic Communications International
1900 L St., NW
Washington, DC 20036
202/462-1400
(Major graphic arts union; includes many specialties; AFL-CIO-affiliated.)

Industrial Designers Society of America
1142 Walker Rd.,
Suite E
Great Falls, VA 22066
703/759-0100
(Placement service; publishes magazine, directory, etc.)

Institute of Business Designers
341 Merchandise Mart
Chicago, IL 60654
312/467-1950
(Interior designers involved in nonresidential work.)

International Association of Clothing Designers
240 Madison Ave.,
12th Fl.
New York, NY 10016
212/685-6602
(Men's and boy's clothing; directory,

placement service for members.)

National Cartoonists Society
157 W. 57th Street,
Suite 904
New York, NY 10019
212/333-7606

National Computer Graphics Association
2722 Merrilee Dr.
Reston, VA 22031
703/698-9600

National Endowment for the Arts
1100 Pennsylvania Ave., NW
Washington, DC 20506
202/682-5400

National Foundation for Advancement in the Arts
3915 Biscayne Blvd.,
4th Fl.
Miami, FL 33137
305/573-0490

New York Artist's Equity Association
498 Broome St.
New York, NY 10013
212/941-0130

Printing Industries of America
100 Daingerfield Rd.
Alexandria, VA 22314
703/519-8100
(Maintains referral service for members; includes wide variety of jobs in design and printing.)

Professional Photographers of America, Inc.
1090 Executive Way
Des Plaines, IL 60018
708/299-8161
(Publishes periodical with career information, etc.)

Society of American Graphic Artists
32 Union Sq.,
Room 1214
516/725-3990

Women's Caucus for Art
Moore College of Art
20th The Parkway
Philadelphia, PA 19103
215/854-0922

World Computer Graphics Association
2033 M St., NW
Washington, DC 20036
202/775-9556

ARTS AND DESIGN DIRECTORIES

American Art Directory
R. R. Bowker
121 Chanlon Rd.
New Providence, NJ
07974
1-800/521-8110

(Lists thousands of museums, libraries, schools, etc.)

Artist's Market
Writer's Digest Books
1507 Dana Ave.

Cincinnati, OH 45207
1-800-289-0963
(Lists hundreds of markets for art and design work—names, addresses,

requirements, etc. For cartoonists, also publishes *Humor and Cartoon Market*.)

Creative Black Book
Macmillan Creative
Services Group
115 Fifth Ave.
New York, NY 10003
212/254-1330

Design Firm Directory
Wefler & Associates
P.O. Box 1167
Evanston, IL 60204
708/475-1866
(Lists all types of
design firms.)

**Foundation Grants to Individuals;
Foundation Directory;
Corporate Foundation Profiles**
Foundation Center
79 Fifth Ave.
New York, NY
10003-3076
212/620-4230
(The first directory is
particularly valuable to
artists seeking financial
support from
foundations.)

Graphic Artists Guild Directory
Graphic Artists Guild
11 W. 20th St., 8th Fl.
New York, NY 10011
212/463-7730

Graphic Arts Blue Book
A. F. Lewis and Co.,
Inc.
79 Madison Ave.
New York, NY 10016
212/679-0770

ARTS AND DESIGN PERIODICALS

AIGA Journal
American Institute of
Graphic Arts
1059 Third Ave.
New York, NY
212/752-0813

American Artist
BPI Communications
1515 Broadway
New York, NY 10036
212/764-7300

Art Direction
10 E. 39th St.
New York, NY 10016
212/889-6500

Art Forum
65 Bleecker St.
New York, NY 10012
212/475-4000

Artweek
1628 Telegraph Ave.
Oakland, CA 94612
510/763-0422

Communications Arts
410 Sherman Ave.
P.O. Box 10300
Palo Alto, CA 94303
415/326-6040

Computer Graphics World
Penwell Directories
P.O. Box 21278
Tulsa, OK 74121
918/835-3161

Design News
Cahners Publishing
Company
275 Washington St.
Newton, MA 02158
617/964-3030

Graphic Arts Monthly
249 W. 17th St.
New York, NY 10011
212/645-0067
(editorial)
1-800/637-6089
(subscriptions)

Graphic Design: USA
Suite 405
1556 3rd Ave.
New York, NY 10128
212/534-5500
(Monthly magazine for
art directors, etc.)

Graphis
141 Lexington Ave.
New York, NY 10017
212/532-9387

HOW
1507 Dana Ave.
Cincinnati, OH 45207
513/531-2222
(Bimonthly magazine
for graphic artists.)

Industrial Design
250 W. 57th St.
New York, NY 16107
212/956-0535

Interior Design
249 W. 17th St.
New York, NY 10011
212/464-0067
1-800/542-8138
(subscriptions)
(Monthly for designers
and those in the
business of design.)

Personal Publishing
191 S. Gary Ave.
Carol Stream, IL 60188
708/665-1000
(Monthly magazine for
desktop publishers.)

Print
3200 Tower Oaks Blvd.
Rockville, MD 20853
1-800/222-2654

*Professional
Photographer*
1090 Executive Way
Des Plaines, IL 60018
708/299-8161
(Monthly for members
of Professional
Photographers of
America.)

ENGINEERING, COMPUTER, AND HIGH-TECH PROFESSIONALS

BRIEF BACKGROUND

▶ **The pace of technical change continues to increase and, with it, the prospects look good in the long term for professionals in the right areas of computers and engineering. But certain areas look weak in the short term—and even in the long term.**

The key, of course, is to be in the right place at the right time. Many engineers working in the defense industry have suffered from cutbacks in recent years, while those in environmental areas have seen continued strong hiring.

In general, the short term may be very rocky for many engineers, but the future looks brighter. There is simply too much to be done. From ceramic motors to solar technology to hazardous waste clean-up to giant infrastructure projects to moving the mountains of information generated by society, high-tech professionals will be needed. And as we move out from the dampening effects of the recession, we should see more openings, often in areas that were entirely unforeseen. One important point: those who want jobs should keep abreast of the latest technologies.

EMPLOYMENT OUTLOOK: Strong in long run, but pockets of weakness, especially in the short term.

▶ **Engineering and computer professions offer strong long-term prospects—but as defense cutbacks continue, the short-term outlook may be less promising for some.**

For engineers and computer specialists, the end of the Cold War created some bad employment news. Cutbacks in the defense industry have resulted in many layoffs. As many as 127,000 military engineers may lose their jobs by 1995, according to the Office of Technology Assessment. Aeronautical engineers have already faced numerous lay-offs and electrical engineers have been hit with the highest unemployment rate in decades—3%. Engineers in particular face the problem of regearing for a new economic focus—away from defense and into more civilian-oriented industries.

Both engineers and computer specialists also face another employment threat. With the globalization of our economy, many corporations are finding it cheaper and easier to hire foreign employees to do technical work. Wages are lower and quality is high.

So what about the long term?

Best guess: the nonmilitary establishment will pick up some of the slack, as defense engineers retrain. Already, some universities, such as the University of Southern California, have developed programs aimed at aiding defense engineers in switching to environmental engineering, offering a master's degree in the concentration. Some other cause for cautious optimism: most projections point to a continued need for engineers. For example, take a look at electrical engineering: the government projects a 3.1% growth rate to the year 2005 in the enormous electronic and electric equipment industries. This is predicated on strong intermediate demand (using electronic and electric goods such as semiconductors to make other goods), recovering consumer demand and business investment, particularly in the telephone communications industry, and in broadcasting and other communications equipment areas. In fact, the consumer electronic industry itself actually escaped much of the problems of the recession—pulling in a 2.9% increase in the depths of the recession. (However, jobs in these industries as a whole will decline, principally because nonengineering jobs for assemblers, etc., will be automated or exported to low-cost producers overseas.)

One problem: R&D spending fell during the recession—but forecasts point to an increase in the future. Overall prognosis: outlook is still relatively strong for electronic engineers. Similar bright outlooks for other areas as well.

A summary of major engineering areas:

ELECTRICAL AND ELECTRONIC ENGINEERING: accounts for one-third of all engineers, projected to grow 34% by 2005; this is still very high, but remember that recently predictions were that growth would exceed 50%. Prime reason: defense cutbacks. However, this is still a fast-growing major engineering specialty, with strong demand expected by manufacturing as explained above for electronic engineers. Old-style electrical engineers will be in less demand. Another job option: moving into sales and marketing—explaining complex high-tech items to corporate customers.

MECHANICAL ENGINEERING: accounts for almost one-fifth of all engineers; most engineers are in manufacturing. Expected to increase by 24% to 2005, due to increasingly complex manufacturing processes, also more positions in construction. Similar large increases expected in employment for *industrial engineers*, who design and implement production systems, now including robots, computers.

CIVIL ENGINEERING: Civil-structural engineering has been less in demand in recent years. Over the long term, though, the field is expected to increase by 30% to the year 2005; much depends on government plans to rebuild infrastructure— roads, bridges, large-scale construction projects. Over 40% of all civil engineers work for the government—federal, state, or local; another 33% work for private engineering firms. And although the government has allocated an enormous amount of funding for highway reconstruction, etc., don't expect to see thousands of new jobs too soon—except maybe for consulting engineers. Government moves slowly.

Outlook is also good for **chemical engineers, process engineers, computer systems engineers, safety engineers, process engineers, materials engineers** (as industry moves into ceramics, specialty plastics and other synthetics; this is a hot area and the U.S. is a leader), and finally to some degree **mechanical engineers**, reflecting a renewed emphasis on manufacturing, and the large numbers of replacements needed as engineers retire or move into management positions. **Aeronautical engineering** is forecast to see 20% growth to 2005; but 1992 saw worse employment prospects due to defense and aviation cutbacks. For more on this, see page 236.

Prospects for **petroleum** and **mining**? Job growth is projected as low, but particularly with petroleum engineering, prospects could pick up if the economy shifts focus. Also: because fewer students are entering petroleum engineering, there will probably be a growing need for people to fill replacement positions.

And the best bet of all . . .

▶ Environmental engineering—the brightest future.

Some estimate that as many as 5,000 *new* environmental engineering positions will open yearly over the next few years. However, this depends on how quickly and strongly the economy recovers.

The Association of Environmental Engineering Professors estimates that schools are graduating only a third of the engineers needed; another estimate says there are ten jobs per graduate. As Sonia Nazario reported in the *Wall Street Journal*, many government agencies literally go begging for environmental engineers, hiring foreigners and waiving normal immigration requirements.

There are currently between 25,000 to 50,000 environmental engineers. Job duties vary—monitoring pollution, setting standards, running Superfund projects, etc. Various specialties exist, ranging from noise abatement to solid waste management. Jobs can be with government (agencies such as the EPA), with consulting firms, industrial companies.

Bottom line: Long term growth looks strong. See Best Bets, page 48.

Another area of probable growth: environmental jobs abroad, as Eastern Europe and the old Soviet Union start clean-ups. Again, see Best Bets, page 48.

▶ Architects and related positions— long-term outlook mixed.

As very large layoffs hit architectural employees in the early 1990s, it wasn't hard to guess the economy was in recession. The number of jobs in New York dropped by almost 25% in the past three years; major firms like Skidmore, Owings & Merrill cut staffing from 1,600 in 1988 to 700 in 1992. But nothing is forever, and as the economy fully sustains a recovery, the employment outlook will improve. Problems: picking up the slack from the large layoffs in the past. Expect stiff competition, particularly for prestige jobs in major cities. A coming area: environmental architecture. A stronger hiring trend: in elder housing; nursing home design; and other areas geared to this continuing growth market. Also, health care and universities.

For landscape architects: the long-term outlook may prove strong, as cities revamp parks and recreational areas, and in particular, as environmental concerns affect corporations and the public.

▶ **Computers: volatile as always, but demand for computer specialties should be strong.**

The early 1990s were not the best of times for computer workers—but they were worse for almost everyone. That didn't console job hunters, particularly when they looked at rosy government predictions for long-term employment. Bank downsizings, computer production increases at all-time lows, and layoffs at Digital Equipment Corporation (DEC) and other large firms, as well as volatility at firms large and small, increased unemployment and insecurity. But the long-term outlook is a lot better: figures show strong employment growth in many computer specialties to the year 2005—79 for computer systems and other analysts; 56 for computer programmers. These numbers are based on a "moderate growth" assumption for the U.S. economy as a whole; if the economy heats up, growth could be higher.

Of course, as always, the name of the game is flexibility and changing with the times. Easier said than done . . .

▶ **IS—getting more people, business-oriented.**

It's inevitable. As IS (information systems) enters the corporate mainstream, professionals are needed who can communicate effectively with nontech employees. Company recruiters are talking about the need for IS professionals with the social and business skills to implement the technical systems they design, and the people skills to supervise teams of employees—or at least get along with them. Again, this is especially important at the mid- to upper levels.

What about an MBA as a kind of certificate of business and communication skills? The outlook is mixed. In the business world as a whole, in fact, there's some talk of the devaluation of the MBA. It's cheaper to hire non-MBAs and train them on the job—and for higher-level employees, some claim there's little difference in terms of effectiveness. But then again, others claim the opposite, and much of top management in the next twenty years will consist of MBAs.

More important: What are IS recruiters saying? A University of Minnesota survey asked a cross section of IS recruiters what mix of skills they were looking for in a candidate. On a scale of 1 to 10—1 representing only technical skills and a 10 representing an MBA—the average score was 2.3; hardly indicative of a major move toward an MBA. The key is still technical skills and past performance.

But just to make things even; other IS surveys and interviews show the MBA can be very valuable. *Computerworld* quoted managers as suggesting an MBA for those who want to advance out of IS to managing IS or general management (makes sense), for consulting, or in liaison functions. Another good option for movement into management: an IS master's with many business courses.

The major job areas and outlooks:

SYSTEMS ANALYSTS, MANAGERS: going up. Employment will increase up to 79% to the year 2005, according to the Bureau of Labor Statistics. There are currently over 350,000 systems analysts, who help computerize business or scientific tasks, or improve current computer operations. Constant training required, frequent development seminars, etc. Similar outlook and positions for operations research analysts, who primarily use quantitative methods (and computers) to study and streamline corporate or organizational operations.

COMPUTER PROGRAMMERS: currently, there are over 500,000 programmers. Forecasters see a 56% increase between 1990 and 2005. Demand will be strongest for experienced persons with college degrees in programming, with detailed knowledge of newest languages, computer networking, database management, and operating languages. Graduates of two-year programs? Far fewer opportunities. One recruiter's advice: "Go back to school and get a full degree." A potential development: computer jobs could be moving overseas. In order to take advantage of cheaper labor abroad, companies may rely more on overseas computer programmers in the future, according to the director of the Advanced Telecommunications Research Center at the University of Colorado.

Other computer-related jobs: computer design, personal computer design (designing the complex circuit boards that make up the heart of the computer), artificial intelligence programming and development, and research.

▶ **Some good bets for 1994 and beyond—or what to emphasize on your résumé, according to experts . . .**

Best technology specialties to put on your résumé: Networking (LANs, etc.), UNIX, CASE (computer aided software engineering), Windows development, and AS/400, systems integration. Best route for IS jobs in the AS/400 area: either previous experience and facility with the OS/400 operating system and the RPG/400 version of RPG III, or an S/3X background.

In addition to the above, experts highlight these areas as strong prospects in the mid-90s: GUI developer, knowledge engineers, client/server designer (good skill for consulting).

The congressional decision to mandate the ADA in all development and system upgrades at the Department of Defense should make this a fairly potent language specialty—both in government, with government contractors, commercial avionics systems, and in the longer term, outside as well.

Some details:

LAN/WAN/NETWORKING: As downsizing hits the hardware—and companies replace giant systems with networks of micros—and as mid-range and mainframe cooperative processing grows—more LAN experts will be needed. This is a new field—the fastest-growing part of the computer industry, and things are still in a flux. Job duties may range from assisting users and keeping a system up and running to actually designing and installing new systems. As the recession cut into funding, LAN duties expanded in many companies; it's best to be familiar with more than just the network operating system to get employed. And now, managers may get involved in corporate strategy and planning.

In effect, the field will probably break into two—specialists with a particular technology, and managers who can run the whole show and deal with the non-computer side. A good way to break in: work with a network systems integrator. Jobs can be found with banks, insurance and financial services businesses, etc.

▶ **And a few other specialties that look interesting . . .**

CONSULTING: in the height of the recession, while many corporations were cutting IS staff, consulting was still hiring. Long-term outlook probably good, but be ready for the constant change due to short-term assignments; probable high number of travel hours logged. Best way to break in: via skills such as LAN, client/server computing, etc.

MULTIMEDIA PROGRAMMERS AND EXPERTS: multimedia, which unites graphics, text and sound on the computer, is an area that is growing rapidly. Video and software engineering and graphic design are all good areas for employment in this field, according to the Bureau of Labor Statistics.

COMPUTER SECURITY EXPERTS: although the Michelangelo computer virus was (fortunately) a bust, network security in particular will be a major concern, and security experts will be the beneficiaries. Increasing numbers of firms outside of government and banks are hiring these experts, as thieves, hackers, and corporate spies threaten databases. Salaries now range from $50,000 to $90,000.

▶ **Computer employees were battered by the volatility of computer firms, layoffs, bank downsizings in the past few years. Fortunately, things are beginning to bounce back . . .**

What *industries* look good for computer hiring in 1993 and beyond? Banking should be getting better, despite consolidations and downsizings. It seems the worst is over.

A digression: Also on the downswing *for the short term*—as suggested here in previous years—are CIOs (chief information officers), many of them in banking. Corporate downsizings during the recession and a major structural change in corporations have in many cases moved IS out of corporate HQs onto the front lines of the businesses. But wait a bit . . . as banks and insurance firms digest their enormous IS consolidations from mergers and once more need top IS management. Key: IS managers who think like bankers, not IS managers who think like IS managers.

Computerworld forecast good prospects in biotech, health care, and pharmaceuticals, and better prospects in financial services, consumer products, manufacturing, utilities, and education—and insurance. Because many insurance systems are relatively backward technologically, applicants who can manage transitions to mid-range computers and LAN will probably find strong employment prospects.

And don't forget the federal government, which must manage huge amounts of information. At mid-level, the government salary range is competitive, and government managers have been authorized to negotiate starting salaries at the relatively high GS-11 level. Key challenges in the government: managing coming new storage technologies and databases, connecting local area networks into in-house wide area networks. See the Government Careers section on how to apply.

For more information on computer company positions, see the computer industry section on page 298.

WHAT'S NEXT

▶ **Continuing education: a must for most engineers, computer workers.**

Technological change will be rapid in the next half of the 1990s. In response, engineers will have to stay current, or risk losing advancement potential or their jobs. One danger to engineers in specialized fields: in some cases, technology may make their specialty obsolete.

▶ **There will be continued volatility in the computer field, as new technologies spur new employment needs.**

After the micro revolution, the pico revolution with PCs on a chip? What further new technologies and software challenges with portable, palmtop, and handheld technologies, ever more powerful micros, new D-RAMs to best bottlenecks, AI, etc? The best way to weather the volatility is clear: Keep up with the new technologies through continuing education. For example, although 65% of all corporate systems are still running on COBOL and the language is far from dead, COBOL programmers should be ready *now* to branch out and get knowledge of relational databases like DB2, on-line transaction monitors, or UNIX skills.

In all cases, college degrees and further education will also be in demand. For example, most newly hired programmers have college degrees or higher; a recent survey of PC designers found a shift from two-year technical degrees to four-year college degrees.

▶ **Women and minorities are few and far between in engineering and computers—but the percentages will change.**

Only 15% of high-tech professionals are women, they advance more slowly, and are far more likely to be unemployed. Even worse, after peaking in 1986, the number of women entering high-tech fields has leveled off. And some reports show more women are leaving the field, frustrated by sexism and lack of advancement. On the plus side: pay is roughly equal for equivalent experience, age. According to a Cooper Union survey, 70% of women surveyed said they were paid comparable wages for comparable work with men. Also, more women are beginning to appear in the top executive ranks, particularly at small companies.

Some bright spots for women: currently about 21% of Hewlett Packard engineers are women; automotive manufacturers are doing heavy recruitment on college campuses to attract women to their ranks.

The situation for minority engineers is similar. The shrinking labor pool is causing companies to step up recruitment of minorities. The problem? Minorities represent only a small percentage of engineering students, and a very small percentage of professional engineers and computer professionals. For example, only about 7% of all computer professionals are black. One way to combat this: watch for an increase in programs designed to attract minority students to the field. The National Action Council for Minorities in Engineering (see address on page 52) is already beginning a long-term push to increase minority involvement. And the

Black Data Processing Association (215/843-4120) has now topped 3,000 members in 44 chapters nationwide.

The bottom line: Due to shortages of engineers, expect more firms and schools to encourage minority and women's programs. Check "Special Report: Women," page 216, and "Special Report: Minorities," page 209, for names and addresses of associations to contact for more information.

SALARIES

▶ **Key point: engineering and computer science traditionally offer high starting salaries and, on average, relatively high pay throughout a career. But the big money comes from the management and supervisory side of engineering.**

ENGINEERING: higher starting salaries than most graduates, stable pay in mid-levels. Starting salaries in 1992 averaged about $35,000. Every year various surveys show the differentials among various specialties—usually the lowest beginning salaries are for civil and mining engineers by several thousand dollars; highest for chemical, environmental engineers. Engineers with master's degrees usually earn more, from the upper 30s to mid-40s. Mid-level salaries for most engineers range from $38,000 to $45,000, upper-level salaries average from about $60,000–$70,000 up to over $100,000.

ARCHITECTS

LANDSCAPE ARCHITECTS: salaries begin in the 20s; average from the 30s to the 50s for experienced architects.

COMPUTERS: the average salary last year for systems analysts, software specialists, systems planners, etc.—lumped together as "computer systems analysts and scientists"—was $41,000. Starting salaries were in the 30s for software specialists, up to $50,000 for mid-level, over $60,000 for more senior. Systems analysts started in the low 30s; earned up to the mid-60s in 1992. Computer operations personnel averaged about $39,999. Starting pay for computer grads right out of school averaged about $31,500 in 1992, up about 1.8% over 1991, according to preliminary figures. Salary for nonentry-level programmers was about $40,000 in 1992; $50,000–$60,000 for managerial level.

BEST BETS

CONSULTING ENGINEERING: Even nontechnical businesses must often find technical answers to problems, and it is much cheaper to hire an engineer temporarily. Good area for go-getters or individualists because it is made up of small, entrepreneurial firms or one-man shops. *Hottest areas for 1990s*: toxic and hazardous waste control, geotechnical engineering, bridge design and rehabilitation. For more information, contact: The American Consulting Engineers Council, 1015 15th Street NW, Washington, DC 20005.

ENVIRONMENTAL, HAZARDOUS WASTE: Besides consulting, there are jobs in manufacturing firms and waste clean-up companies. Fast-growing field (various fields were growing at a skyrocketing clip of up to 16% per year), with a major shortage of employees. (However, the recession had an unexpected impact in that it may have somewhat slowed this growth rate for the next few years.)

Problem: only about twenty universities offer accredited programs; others are still considering. But demand is there, as Superfund (government-mandated funding for massive clean-ups of hazardous waste sites nationwide) and industrial projects go on line. Few companies involved with hazardous materials will risk going without a full complement of experts. Needed: specialists of all kinds—solid waste engineers, process engineers, environmental engineers in wastewater, industrial waste, engineering geologists, geotechnical engineers. Background required: environmental engineering degree; BS or above.

The American Academy of Environmental Engineers offers short supplementary courses, provides listings of schools offering this environmental engineering. New trend: older engineers are taking courses, learning some aspect of this specialty. Salaries range from the 40s for BS on up to $50,000 for project managers, about $80,000–$100,000 for more senior management. Contact: American Academy of Environmental Engineers, 301/266-3310.

WHERE TO GO FOR MORE INFORMATION

[Note: Also see Aerospace, page 236; Computers and High Tech, page 298]

ENGINEERING, COMPUTER, AND HIGH-TECH PROFESSIONAL ASSOCIATIONS

(For many more computer sources, see "Computers and Electronics" in the "Industry section" on page 298.)

Air and Waste Management Association
P.O. Box 2861
Pittsburgh, PA 15230
412/232-3444
(Publishes periodical with job openings, directory, etc.)

American Association of Cost Engineers
P.O. Box 1557
Morgantown, WV 26507-1557
304/296-8444

(Publishes periodical with some job openings, job referral service for members, etc.)

American Association of Engineering Societies
1111 19th St., NW, Suite 608
Washington, DC 20036
202/296-2237
(An association of many other engineering associations; publishes salary surveys, etc.)

American Ceramic Society
735 Ceramic Pl.
Westerville, OH 43801
614/890-4700
(Publishes periodical, etc.)

American Chemical Society
1155 16th St., NW
Washington, DC 20036
1-800/227-5558

The Top Engineering Employers in the U.S.: Design News Survey

Company		Engineers	Specialties in Demand
1	General Electric	35,000	mechanical, electrical
2	General Motors	32,000	mech., elec., comp., manufacturing
3	IBM	22,000	mech., elec., chem., materials, computing, manufacturing
4	Lockheed	20,000	mech., materials, elec., computers, chem., manufacturing
5	Rockwell International	19,000	elec.
6	Boeing	18,000	mech., elec., computers, aeronautical, manufacturing
7	TRW	18,000	mech., materials, elec., computers, manufacturing
8	General Dynamics	16,158	mechanical, electrical, and computers
9	Hewlett Packard	16,150	mechanical, electrical, materials, computers
10	Motorola	16,000	mechanical, electrical, computers, manufacturing
11	Allied Signal	15,000	materials, chemical, manufacturing
12	McDonnell Douglas	15,000	mechanical, electrical, computers, aerospace
13	Martin Marietta	13,500	mech., elec., computers, manufacturing
14	Digital Equipment	13,000	elec., comp.
15	Texas Instruments	12,000	elec., comp., manufacturing
16	AT&T Bell Labs	12,000	elec., computers, chem.
17	United Technologies	12,000	elec., comp., aerospace
18	Westinghouse	11,350	mech., elec., computers, industrial, manufacturing
19	NASA	11,000	mech., elec., aerospace
20	Ford Motor	11,000	mech., elec., manufacturing
21	GTE	10,100	mech., materials, elec., computers, chemical, manufacturing, industrial
22	Northrop	10,000	mech., elec., manufacturing
23	Du Pont	9,500	mech., elec., chem.
24	Eastman Kodak	9,000	mech., elec., comp., chem.
25	Unisys	9,000	material, elec., comp.

(Publishes various periodicals with job listings—see separate listing for *Chemical & Engineering News*; maintains job bank, listing service, counseling services, etc.)

American Consulting Engineers Council
1015 15th St., NW
Washington, DC 20005
202/347-7474
(Publishes various directories, etc.)

American Institute of Aeronautics and Astronautics
370 L'Enfant Promenade, SW
Washington, DC 20024
202/646-7400
(Newsletter with job listings; special newsletter for students with employment information, etc.)

American Institute of Architects
1735 New York Ave., NW
Washington, DC 20006
202/626-7300
(Publishes periodicals, directories, operates members' referral service.)

American Institute of Chemical Engineers
345 E. 47th St.
New York, NY 10017
212/705-7663
(Publishes periodical with job openings,

placement referral service, etc.)

American Society of Civil Engineers
345 E. 47th St.
New York, NY 10017
212/705-7496
(Publishes periodical with job openings, directories, job service for members, etc.)

American Society of Design Engineers
P.O. Box 931
Arlington Heights, IL 60006
708/259-7120
(Members' placement service, job counseling, etc.)

American Society of Engineering Education
11 DuPont Cir., Suite 200
Washington, DC 20036
202/986-8500
(Publishes periodical with job openings, directories.)

American Society of Heating, Refrigerating, and Air-Conditioning Engineers
1791 Tullie Cir., NE
Atlanta, GA 30329
404/636-8400
(Publishes periodical, etc.)

American Society of Information Science
8720 Georgia Ave., Suite 501
Silver Spring, MD 20910-3602

301/495-0900
(Publishes monthly—sometimes bimonthly—newsletter devoted to careers and job openings.)

American Society of Landscape Architects
4401 Connecticut Ave., NW
Washington, DC 20008
202/686-2752

American Society of Mechanical Engineers (ASME)
345 E. 47th St.
New York, NY 10017
212/705-7722
(Publishes periodical with job listings, etc.)

American Society of Safety Engineers
1800 E. Oakton St.
Des Plaines, IL 60018
708/692-4121
(Publish periodicals with job openings, etc.)

American Welding Society
550 N.W. 42nd Ave.
Miami, FL 33126
305/443-9353
(Publishes periodical, job referral service, etc.)

Association of Energy Engineers
4025 Pleasantdale Rd.
Atlanta, GA 30340
404/447-5083

Association of Groundwater Scientists and Engineers

6375 Riverside Dr.
Dublin, OH 43017
614/761-1711
(Publishes periodical
with job listings, etc.)

**Association of Old
Crows**
1000 N. Payne St.
Alexandria, VA 22314
703/549-1600
(Members are involved
in defense, electrical
engineering, etc.)

**Association for
International Practical
Training**
10400 Little Patuxent
Pkwy.,
Suite 250
Columbia, MD
21044-3501
301/997-2200
(For students in
engineering, sciences,
or agriculture, arranges
overseas exchanges
with on-the-job training
or research for up to a
year.)

**Association for
Systems Management**
1435 W. Bagley Rd.
P.O. Box 38370
Cleveland, OH 44138
216/243-6900

**Environmental
Careers Organization**
286 Congress St.
Boston, MA 02210
617/426-4375
(Publishes special
career publications;
places students and
recent graduates in
short-term professional

positions; career
conferences, etc.)

**IEEE Computer
Society**
1730 Massachusetts
Ave., NW
Washington, DC 20036
202/371-0101
(Publishes
members-only
periodical with job
openings, etc.)

**Institute of Electrical
and Electronics
Engineers (IEEE)**
345 E. 47th St.
New York, NY 10017
212/705-7900
(Publishers periodical
with job openings;
annual directory of
members;
career/employment
guide, etc.)

**Institute of Industrial
Engineers**
25 Technology Pk.
Norcross, GA
30092-2988
404/449-0460
(Publishes periodical
with job openings.)

**Institute of
Transportation
Engineers**
525 School St., SW,
Suite 410
Washington, DC 20024
202/554-8050
(Publishes periodical
with some job listings.)

**Instrument Society of
America**
P.O. Box 12277
67 Alexander Dr.

Research Triangle Park,
NC 277009
919/549-8411
(Offers placement
service, periodical with
job openings, etc.)

**International Society
for Hybrid
Microelectronics**
P.O. Box 2698
1861 Wiehle Ave.,
Suite 260
Reston, VA
22090-2698
703/471-0066
(Offers members-only
newsletter with job
openings, publishes
annual directory.)

**Junior Engineering
Technical Society**
1420 King St.,
Suite 405
Alexandria, VA 22314
703/548-JETS
(A central
clearinghouse for career
information on most
engineering careers,
with various programs,
including guidance, etc.
For information, send a
stamped, self-addressed
envelope and ask to
receive their order
form.)

**National Action
Council for Minorities
in Engineering**
3 W. 35th St.
New York, NY 10001
212/279-2626

**National Society of
Black Engineers**
1454 Duke St.

Alexandria, VA 22314
703/549-2207

National Society of Professional Engineers
1420 King St.
Alexandria, VA 22314
703/684-2800
(Publishes directory, etc.)

National Solid Wastes Management Association
1730 Rhode Island Ave., NW, Suite 1000
Washington, DC 20036
202/659-4613

Operations Research Society of America
1314 Guilford Ave.
Baltimore, MD 21202
3091/528-4146
(Publishes journal with job listings, placement service.)

Robotics International of SME
P.O. Box 930
1 SME Dr.
Dearborn, MI 48121
313/271-1500

Society of American Military Engineers
607 Prince St.
P.O. Box 180

Alexandria, VA 22313-0180
(Publishes directory of defense engineering organizations.)

Society of Automotive Engineers, Inc.
400 Commonwealth Dr.
Warrendale, PA 15096
412/776-4841

Society of Hispanic Professional Engineers
5400 E. Olympic Blvd., Suite 306
Los Angeles, CA 90022
213/725-3970
(Placement service, etc.)

Society of Logistics Engineers
8100 Professional Pl., Suite 211
New Carrollton, MD 20785
301/459-8446
(Publishes directory, etc.)

Society of Manufacturing Engineers (SME)
P.O. Box 930
1 SME Dr.
Dearborn, MI 48121
313/271-1500
(Publishes periodical

Society of Petroleum Engineers
P.O. Box 833836
Richardson, TX 75083
214/669-3377
(Publishes newsletter where members may advertise jobs, educational programs, etc.)

Society of Plastics Engineers
14 Fairfield Dr.
P.O. Box 0403
Brookfield, CT 06804
203/775-0471

Society of Women Engineers
345 E. 47th St.
New York, NY 10017
212/705-7855
(Resource center; publishes periodical with job openings; offers counseling to members.)

Water Pollution Control Federation
601 Wythe St.
Alexandria, VA 22314
703/684-2400
(Publishes periodical with job openings.)

ENGINEERING, COMPUTER, AND HIGH-TECH PROFESSIONAL DIRECTORIES

(for more, check under associations)

CPC Annual, Vol. 3
College Placement Council, Inc.
62 Highland Ave.

Bethlehem, PA 18017
215/868-1421
(Organizations,

including government, with job opportunities.)

Directory of Chemical Engineering Consultants
American Institute of Chemical Engineers
345 E. 47th St.
New York, NY 10017
212/705-7338

Directory of Engineering Societies
American Association of Engineering Societies
415 Second St., NE
Washington, DC 20002
202/296-2237

Directory of Engineers in Private Practice
National Society of

Professional Engineers
1420 King St.
Alexandria, VA 22314
703/684-2882

Engineering, Science, and Computer Jobs
Peterson's Guides, Inc.
P.O. Box 2123
Princeton, NJ
08543-2123
609/243-9111

High Technology Careers
Westech Publishing Co.
4701 Patrick Henry Dr., No. 1901
Santa Clara, CA 95954
408/970-8800

Peterson's Job Opportunities for Engineering, Science and Computer Graduates
Peterson's Guides, Inc.
P.O. Box 2123
Princeton, NJ
08543-2123
609/243-9111
800/338-3282
(Lists hundreds of corporations and government agencies that are hiring; includes detailed information.)

ENGINEERING, COMPUTER, AND HIGH-TECH PROFESSIONAL MAGAZINES

Architectural Record
P.O. Box 564
Hightstown, NJ 08520
1-800/257-9402
(Monthly professional journal; valuable for inside look at industry; some job listings.)

Chemical & Engineering News
345 E. 47th St.
New York, NY 10017
212/705-7663
(Excellent industry roundups are particularly valuable as overviews for entry-level job hunters; classifieds include many job openings.)

Chemical Engineering Progress
American Institute of

Chemical Engineers
345 E. 47th St.
New York, NY 10017
212/705-7663
(Monthly; many job listings.)

Civil Engineering
345 E. 47th St.
New York, NY 10017
212/705-7514
(Monthly for American Society of Civil Engineers; many job listings.)

Engineering News-Record
McGraw-Hill, Inc.
1221 Ave. of the Americas
New York, NY 10020
212/512-2000
1-800/262-4729
(Good help-wanted

section; publishes top companies' listings.)

Engineering Times
National Society of Professional Engineers
1420 King St.
Alexandria, VA 22314
703/684-2800
(Association magazine with some job openings and employment information as well as other information.)

Environment Today
1483 Chain Bridge Rd.
McLean, VA 22101
703/448-0322
(Eight issues per year for environmental engineers, etc.)

**Environmental
Protection**
P.O. Box 2573
Waco, TX 76702
(Nine issues per year;
magazine for specialists
in pollution, hazardous
waste.)

Graduating Engineer
Peterson's/COG
Publishing
16030 Ventura Blvd.,
Suite 560
Encino, CA 91436
818/789-5371
(Career advice; special
issues such as high-tech
careers, women and
minority hiring trends,
etc.)

Hazmat World
800 Roosevelt Rd.
Glen Ellyn, IL 60137
708/858-1888
(Monthly for hazardous
waste specialists.)

**High Technology
Careers**
Westech Publishing
Company
4701 Patrick Henry
Dr., Suite 1901
Santa Clara, CA 95054
(High-tech industry
tabloid with hundreds
of high-tech job
openings listed.)

IEEE Spectrum
345 E. 47th St.
New York, NY 10017
212/705-7016
(With over 500,000
circulation, has many
job listings; note that

this address is for the
magazine, association
address is given above.)

**Journal of Air/Waste
Management**
P.O. Box 2861
Pittsburgh, PA 15230
412/232-3444

Landscape Architecture
4401 Connecticut Ave.,
NW
Washington, DC 20008
202/686-2752
(Main trade journal;
eight issues a year.)

Machine Design
Penton Publishing
1100 Superior Ave.
Cleveland, OH 44114
216/696-7000
Fax: 216/696-0177

**Mechanical
Engineering**
345 E. 47th St.
New York, NY 10017
212/705-7782
(Monthly; carries many
job listings.)

Plant Engineering
1350 E. Touhy Ave.
Box 5080
Des Plaines, IL
60017-5080
708/635-6600

Pollution Engineering
P.O. Box 5080
Des Plaines, IL 60017
708/635-8800
(Monthly.)

PD News (now
incorporating **Captsule**)
P.O. Box 399

Cedar Park, TX 78613
512/250-8127
1-800/678-9724
Fax: 512/331-3900
(Weekly magazine
listing job openings in
electronics,
engineering, computers,
etc.; subscribers can
access BBS for on-line
job listings.)

**Product Design and
Development**
Chilton Way
Radnor, PA 19089
215/964-4355
(Monthly for design
engineers.)

**Progressive
Architecture**
P.O. Box 1361
600 Summer St.
Stamford, CT 06904
203/348-7531
1-800/473-2372 (for
orders)
(Monthly; carries job
listings.)

Waste Age
1730 Rhode Island
Ave., NW
Washington, DC 20036
202/861-0708

**Water
Environment/Technology**
601 Wythe St.
Alexandria, VA 22314
703/684-2400
(Monthly especially for
consulting engineers
and chemists in the
field.)

OTHER JOB SOURCES

See federal job openings and organizations under "Government Jobs," page 66. Also:

InternAmerica
Ford
Ford Careerworks
800/456-7335
(Bimonthly newsletter of intern positions listed by various corporations.)

Office of Personnel Management
P.O. Box 52
Washington, DC 20415
1-900/990-9200 (in Alaska, 912/471-3755)

Palace Acquire
AFCPMC/DCPR
Randolph AFB, TX 78150-6421
800/847-0108
(Air Force intern program for engineers.)

Professional Development Center
Naval Facilities Engineering Command
200 Stovall St.
Alexandria, VA 22232-2300
(Navy engineer intern program.)

GOVERNMENT EMPLOYEES

BRIEF BACKGROUND

▶ **Government employment is a catch-all term for the largest and perhaps the most diverse of employment categories.**

The federal government is the largest single employer in the U.S.—with well over 3 million civilian employees; add to these the millions of teachers, police, and administrators on state, county, or local payrolls. One can see that with such large numbers, despite cutbacks in spending, numerous jobs will open every day, in a wide variety of fields, in most areas of government—and in most areas of the country. Estimates are that the federal government hires more than 300,000 employees a year. And these federal jobs are located nationwide; 86 percent of all federal jobs are outside of Washington, DC.

▶ **Most government employees work for the executive branch, usually as part of the civil service.**

And a quick note for those who have forgotten high school history: the government is divided into three branches—executive, legislative, and judicial. Federal civil service jobs usually fall under the executive branch, although in some cases employees of the judicial and legislative branch are also civil service employees.

This section covers government employment in general, with the most emphasis on federal jobs—and a very comprehensive listing of major federal agencies and organizations. It also covers state and local government jobs, with an emphasis on administrative jobs. Teaching jobs, social work jobs, security jobs, etc., are covered under separate sections—although it's a good idea to read this section as well and to look at the sources at the end.

EMPLOYMENT OUTLOOK: Fair

▶ **Federal government employment levels will rise very slowly if at all; even so, opportunities will be there for the right people.**

The government projects that total federal employment will increase by only 200,000 in the next ten years. Considering it employs over 3 million people, that's a very small number. And meanwhile, deeper-than-expected cuts in the military will cut civilian jobs as well.

But the job outlook for managers, scientists, and computer systems workers, lawyers, and other professionals will be brighter than those numbers suggest. Federal employment is already more managerial or professional than most other employers—nearly 80% of the government is made up of white-collar employees, compared with 25% of the national workforce.

It will be getting more so. Automation, computerization, and the shifting of blue-collar functions to private subcontractors will reduce jobs for drivers, machine operators, and most importantly, clerical staff. Hardest hit by the mid-1990s: data-processing staff in the Social Security Administration and Veteran's Administration as more sophisticated technology comes into use.

Where growth will be: Where one might expect: engineering—up 17%; lawyers—up 15%; management (including contracting and procurement employees, property management workers, and IRS agents)—up 10%, according to a study of the Office of Personnel Management (OPM). Other growth areas will be for medical positions, which should gain 50,000 jobs in the 1990s, for social scientists (particularly economists), and investigators.

▶ **Other positions will be opening up on the other side of government: Congress.**

Even when turnover isn't high among congressional jobs, staff jobs working for those in Congress have a very high turnover. One fairly recent study found that over 78% of people in staff jobs left during an eight-year period. One reason: staff jobs in Washington can be a good route to influential jobs elsewhere in government and outside as lobbyists, etc. One other reason: working conditions can be *very* grueling.

Best route to a job: know your congressperson. If you have the time or money, volunteering can be a good way of getting your foot in the door. Outside of working for a congressperson, staff jobs on various committees and subcommittees are sometimes open—and campaigns are another route. See addresses on page 83 on where to go for staff and campaign openings.

Other jobs can be found in various congressional offices, including the **General Accounting Office** (GAO), which is the legislative watchdog over the executive branch; **the Library of Congress, the Office of Technology Assessment** (OTA); and the **Congressional Budget Office**. (Addresses are listed on pages 74 and 83.)

SPECIAL SECTION: HOW TO APPLY FOR A FEDERAL JOB

It can get complicated. And it's different from applying for a job at the local bank. For starters, instead of a résumé, you'll need a completed SF 171, you'll be looking at GS ratings instead of salary ranges, and you'll be looking at a wealth of job openings.

First, we'll explain how the system is organized, so you'll be familiar with various terms and are able to target, find, and get the federal job you want.

How are jobs filled?

About 80% of government jobs are filled competitively—which means the openings are made public, applicants are evaluated by certain pre-set standards, and of course hiring is nondiscriminatory. Of course, this is the ideal, not necessarily the real. The standards and personnel practices are to a greater or lesser extent set by the Office of Personnel Management (OPM).

The other 20% of government jobs are called "excepted service jobs"—and are filled according to criteria set by the individual agency. The Foreign Service of the State Department, the CIA, etc., are all excepted service jobs.

How do you find job vacancies?

There is no one central government listing of all jobs available—but there's a wealth of resources available to help you find the right job vacancy.

Here are some ways:

1. **Go to the Office of Personnel Management (or Federal Job Information Centers located at OPM area offices, or State Employment Services)**

   These offices will list federal job vacancies by title and GS level—along with instructions whether to apply via the OPM or to the agency and office directly, in which case an address will be given. The state offices will list federal job openings via a computerized listing called the Federal Job Opportunity Listing (FJOL), which is updated monthly or even more frequently.

   Problem: with the Federal centers usually all you'll see are these listings and some instructions; increasingly they don't have employees or counselors to help you out.

   How do you contact the Federal Job Information Centers and OPM offices? Look under the listings of each state. Beginning on page 517, we've listed Federal OPMs and Job Information Centers with phone numbers. Page 66 has the central office.

2. **Visit or call the agency or government office directly**

   This can be the most productive, since you may hear of job openings before they get onto the OPM list, you may make contacts with hiring officials, you may learn what they're looking for in an employee and tailor yourself accordingly.

   Many agencies have special job hotlines or job postings, and so on. Have a good idea of the type of job you're interested in—but be open to other areas, and be aware that most administrative or professional positions with the federal government do not require a specific type of degree.

   How do you contact a federal agency?

   Most main offices of federal agencies and departments are listed beginning on page 66, with instructions on how to find local office numbers as well. Note that the personnel numbers are listed, along with job hotlines, but don't stop there. Try to get the specific numbers of the department heads or supervisors of areas you're interested in and speak with them directly. They, and not personnel, usually determine whom to hire. For more complete listing of offices and addresses and names of the major employees (there are thousands), check the *U.S. Government Manual*. It is in most libraries, or order direct from the Government Printing Office (address on page 74). Other government directories with names and addresses are on page 84.

3. **Buy or subscribe to any of a variety of private newsletters which list federal job openings**

These can be excellent sources. In effect, instead of traveling to an OPM office/Federal Job Information Center, you have the job listings travel to you. The first two periodicals cited below list thousands of federal jobs by title, grade, location, and instructions on how to apply. The next two include job listings along with federal news, etc. Addresses and phone numbers are in the Periodicals section on page 85.

Federal Career Opportunities
Thousands of job listings, from secretarial to engineering

Federal Jobs Digest
(lists thousands of federal jobs, with contacts and addresses to which to apply, grades and salary levels; each issue has over 15,000 job openings)

Federal Employee's News Digest

Federal Times
(a periodical mainly for federal employees; includes many job listings in back)

4. **Call government job hotlines.**

The government now maintains job hotlines which can give you information on careers, jobs, and application information. These are listed under the appropriate agencies, if applicable.

5. **Go to a college placement office.**

Even if it's been years since you graduated, be aware that many college placement offices carry applications, and most importantly, the Federal Job Opportunity Listing—the computerized, updated federal job listing that's issued by the regional OPM offices.

6. **Networking**

An overused word, but with federal employment, it can't be used enough. Employees at the agency you want to work at can target opportunities for you, recommend you, tell you what to say and what not to say—in short, they can get you a job.

7. **Buy the *U.S. Government Manual* and *The Budget of the United States Government***

This is a clever way to get a real headstart on everyone else. Every year the *Manual* is issued; every year it tells the policies and priorities of each federal agency or department. The *Budget* goes one better: it tells where the money is going. Often agencies with increased allocations will be hiring.

8. **If your experience and education warrants it, check on *mid-level opportunities*.** A mid-level rating means a higher GS rating and more responsibility; moreover, many agencies have special programs for qualified applicants in certain areas.

9. **Find out about any special programs via the agency you wish to work for.** Government agencies maintain special hiring programs for women, minorities, veterans, and persons with disabilities. Many have special programs for older job hunters, etc. Each of these can give you an edge.

Where do you apply for a federal job?

There are two basic places to which you send your material when applying for a federal job:

1. The Office of Personnel Management (OPM) itself (or through Federal Job Information Centers at OPM area offices)

The OPM is the central government personnel office—with its main office in Washington, DC, and regional offices and branches nationwide.

In some cases the OPM acts as a sort of job search firm, taking your application, evaluating or rating it, then placing your name on a list for referral to various government agencies—and all you do is wait for them to call you.

How do you know when to go to the OPM directly? You'll be told. When looking through the various magazines or computerized job postings (see page 60), sometimes you'll see the OPM address listed even if the job itself is for another agency. In general, the OPM will fill (some) positions that are common to many agencies, such as accounting positions, and so on.

How do you contact the OPM office? See instructions above.

2. Better yet, apply directly at the federal agency, department, or office where you want to work.

You can do this for many jobs—and above all, for, those where the job is particular to one or a few agencies (air traffic controllers are particular to the FAA, for example), or where the job is one in which there is a critical shortage.

In general, this is the best way to get hired. There is one key advantage with going directly to a federal agency: they make the ultimate hiring decision, so if you don't have to, why go the extra step via OPM?

And by going to the agency, you can learn exactly what they're looking for, make contacts for future positions if you don't get the initial one, and get to understand the *informal* job market—in other words, get to network your way into a job.

What happens when you apply?

If your job indicates you should deal with OPM: After contacting OPM you'll be given a **Standard Form 171**, or as it is more commonly called, an **SF 171,** which is just a long official job application. (And if you have to take some sort of test, you'll be told when and where you may take it.) The SF 171 should be filled out accordingly and returned to OPM.

If the OPM finds that you fulfill the qualifications, you'll be put on a register or listing that is made available to hundreds of government offices. You'll wait until, hopefully, one of them invites you to come in for an interview.

If you've applied directly to a federal agency: you'll be given and will return the SF 171 to the agency directly, and then hopefully be called for an interview.

If you've applied to an excepted agency: you'll learn their specific procedures for application when you apply. In general, you'll still have to fill out an SF 171—but chances are, as with the Foreign Service, you'll have to take a special test or follow some other special procedures. For jobs with some of these agencies—including the CIA, NSA, Foreign Service—see International Careers, page 100.

What types of federal jobs are there?

All types, of course. The government hires for virtually every position—from blue-collar to secretaries and clerks to high-level managerial and technical positions.

Virtually all federal civil service jobs are ranked according to a General Schedule (GS) rating. When you look at a job listing, you'll see a GS rating given. If you then look at a standard GS table (usually posted at a job center), you'll see the standard salary you get if hired at that GS level.

Ratings begin at GS-1; four years of college qualifies you for a GS-5 rating, nine months more of work along with college gives you a GS-7 rating, more experience rates more, on up through GS-18.

Each GS level includes ten "steps," ranging from 1 to 10. Salaries are determined by GS level and step number. Generally speaking, salary ranges can be extensive. Above GS-18 is another scale called Senior Executive Service.

Those are the levels of employment; what types of jobs are there? Recently, the Office of Personnel Management listed a broad breakdown of government job openings:

1. Entry-level administrative and professional jobs (called Administrative Careers with America by OPM):

In many cases there are no specific educational requirements. These jobs are administered via the OPM; or, if you meet various criteria, you can apply directly to the agency in question.

There are two broad categories of jobs within this area;

(a) those in which you can take a written test (Health, Safety, Environmental, Writing, Public Information, Business, Finance, Management, Personnel, Administration, Computers, Benefits Review, Tax, Legal, Law Enforcement, and Investigation). You can apply to the OPM and take the test; or, if you're a college graduate with a GPA of 3.5 or more (based on a 4.0 scale) or have graduated in the top 10 percent of your class, you can go directly to a federal agency without going through the OPM.

(b) those which require completion of **specific college course work** (Archeology, Archival Work, Community Planning, Curatorial Positions, Economics, Educational Programming, Foreign Affairs, General Anthropology, General Education and Training, Geography, History, International Relations, Manpower Research, Psychology, Social Science, and Sociology). With these positions, if you meet the educational criteria above, you may be hired directly by a federal agency; or if (and only if) your local OPM office has posted a job vacancy, you may submit an application to that OPM office for that specific job.

1. Specialized jobs:

These are jobs that require the completion of certain college-level courses. They include: accountants and auditors, biologists, engineers, foresters, mathematicians, and physical scientists.

In most cases, these jobs start at the GS-5 to GS-7 levels, but those with experience, advanced degrees, or both will naturally be hired at higher levels. In many cases, applicants with the skills in these areas are very much in demand.

Best way to contact employers? Contact the agency directly; or for college students and recent grads, try the job hotline for more information, or look for listings in one of the job newsletters.

3. Public safety jobs:

These include: air traffic controllers, Deputy U.S. Marshals, Treasury enforcement agents, U.S. Park Police Officers.

These jobs generally require some sort of bachelor's degree or the right experience, and the passing of a written test. The entry-level grades are between GS-5 and GS-7.

Best way to contact employers? Contact the agency directly, or look for openings in one of the newsletters.

4. Technical jobs:

These include a wide variety of support positions, from paralegals to lab technicians. Usually you should have at least two years of relevant experience, and/or a two-year degree or some combination of the two. In some cases, you'll have to take a written test. Technical jobs usually start at the GS-4 level.

Best way to contact employers? Contact the agency directly, or contact one of the area OPM/Federal Job Information Centers, or find openings in one of the newsletters.

5. Clerical and administrative support:

This is the largest category of government employment. Most start at the GS-2 level and require a high school diploma. These jobs are listed at OPM/Federal Job Centers and by the various newsletters.

IMPORTANT NOTE: After reading about the *formal* procedures for applying for a government job, remember that the *informal* routes are sometimes more important.

Just because a job is listed doesn't mean the hiring is open. Very often, section chiefs within the office already have someone in mind—by listing the job they are merely following OPM requirements.

Conclusion: the best way to get a government job is to network: target the organization where you want to work, get to know the people. Even though you will probably still go through formal procedures, you may have already been pre-selected. Final words from a person who has been in and out of government jobs—"Be persistent."

▶ **State and local government employment: growth tied to economy and rising privatization trend.**

The key is how far will privatization and economic cutbacks extend into the future—and how much if at all will defense spending cutbacks free up money for local projects. Also, in the wake of the L.A. riots look for some increase in targeted programs in the inner city.

Despite the cutbacks we're seeing now, federal labor statistics suggest that state and local government jobs will increase at an average rate—rising from about 15.5 million to around 18.3 million in 2005. Over half of those new jobs will be in public education (for more, see Teachers and Educators, page 170).

Where the other jobs will be:

First of all, don't forget the private sector for government jobs. In other words, as governments privatize—or transfer public functions to the private sector—remember that the jobs don't necessarily go away, they just go somewhere else. For example, Wackenhut Corporation, a giant Florida security company, manages prisons throughout the U.S., manages parking in Alaska, operates huge job-training programs—and expects government service jobs within the company to *increase at an annual rate of over 10% per year for the next decade.*

Few increases are expected in jobs at the very top (usually elected) levels of local city and town administrations. The reason is obvious: only a few new cities or towns will be incorporated in the next ten years. Principal means of employment: job turnover through elections. Average age of top city officials and council members is well over thirty; half are over fifty.

Good areas: social services (although low paying and despite cutbacks), budget and finance, law enforcement.

Another good way to go for a job: Many local governments offer *internships.* In 1992, *Public Management* magazine reported internships in cities and towns ranging from Angel Fire, NM, to Washington, DC. Salaries can range from zero to little above minimum wage to a solid, mainstream income. A good source of internships: *ICMA Newsletter* (address and phone number on page 84).

BEST BET

CITY MANAGER: professional contracted by city, town, or county council to run the local administration; has all the responsibility of a mayor except for being elected. Background: usually an MA in public administration, work as an analyst or assistant in a local government office. Salaries range from $28,000 in municipalities with populations of less than 25,000 to $104,890 in cities of between 500,000 and 1 million. For information and jobs in this and related areas, check *ICMA Newsletter* (address and phone number on page 84).

▶ As for state civil service, opportunities vary widely.

State governments are organized in fifty different ways: some states fill many jobs primarily through patronage (knowing and supporting the right politician gets you the job); other states are well known for professional civil services.

Best way to go for a job: Check with local state employment office or state job center for information and job postings. Addresses for all fifty states are listed by state in the Regional section of this book, beginning on page 499. Also, as with the federal government, target informal ways of getting in. A few best bets in terms of quality administrations: state governments of Michigan, Minnesota, Pennsylvania, Wisconsin. Other jobs at the state level:

LEGISLATIVE STAFF: as state government increases in complexity, staff members have become more professional, far more important—and far more numerous. Between 1979 and 1988 the number increased by 65%, according to the *Journal of State Government*. Best bets: with major states, such as California, Ohio, New York. Some advantages: easy access to jobs—usually few formal hiring requirements such as lengthy applications, background checks, etc. A good way to get an "in" on other state jobs. Best way to get in: Since there are often few formal hiring procedures, contact your legislators directly. On the downside: usually low paying, very high turnover. And then again, you can always run for the state legislature . . .

WHAT'S NEXT

▶ Government will emphasize efficiency.

The mid-1990s will be a period of frugality—emphasis will be on getting more per dollar. This trend will be found not only in the leaner and meaner corporations but in federal, state, and local governments as well. Look for efforts to streamline and maximize efficiency in government, look to efforts at bringing quality control, increased computerization, better and more efficient services.

SALARIES

CITY MANAGERS: Average salary about $60,000; varies according to region, size of city.

OTHER LOCAL GOVERNMENT JOBS: In 1988, the median annual salary of a city or town council member was $2,400; in cities with populations above 500,000, $40,000. According to the Bureau of Labor Statistics, mayors on average earned $8,239; in cities over 1 million the average was $87,751 in the late 1980s.

STATE GOVERNMENT: Legislators earned just expenses in eleven states; in the other thirty-nine states the average salary was $17,700 in 1987.

FEDERAL GOVERNMENT: Salaries ranged in 1991 from GS-1 step 1 (GS1/1) at $11,015, to GS-5/1 at $16,973, to GS-11 step 6 at $36,301, on to Senior Executive Service salaries at $70,000 and above. (With exceptions like $200,000 for the President of the U.S.) Mid-level salaries (GS-8 through 13) range from $23,284 to $57,650. As a rule of thumb, the federal government doesn't pay well on the top scales, but pays very well on the middle level.

FBI AGENT: Out of the approximately 10,000 FBI agents, half will retire by 1995, according to *Fortune* magazine. The FBI itself was under a hiring freeze but by March 1994 the freeze should be lifted, according to sources interviewed at the time of writing. The agency will apparently try to make up for alleged employment infractions in the past, although it says it will not hire on any quota system. Some downsides: relatively low pay compared to the outside (but great benefits), and sometimes dangerous work. Contact your local FBI office, which initiates hiring. Check your local phone book for listings, or contact FBI headquarters, listing on page 77.

PRESIDENTIAL MANAGEMENT INTERN (PMI): For the future best-and-brightest. Sponsored by the Office of Personnel Management, the PMI program selects about 400 graduate students (master's degree) for jobs in various areas of the federal bureaucracy for two to three years. There are many degree areas that qualify—they range from accounting to international relations to urban planning. Starting salary begins at GS-9 (about $25,000) and ends in the mid-$30,000s. Key advantage: high prestige and exposure, a career track that prepares you for eventual high position in the federal bureaucracy. How can you get in? Each year announcements are mailed to graduate schools nationwide—you must be nominated by your dean, director, or chairperson of your graduate program. Or check with OPM; address is below.

SOME MORE BEST BETS:

SOCIAL SECURITY ADMINISTRATION: Not a glamorous government agency, but a well-run, lean agency handling an enormous workload (last year, it served over 46 *million* Americans) with relative efficiency. In a recent survey, over 91% of people questioned rated the agency's performance as fair or better, a stellar record. Key problem: limited administrative budget. The response has been to create an unusually planning-oriented, efficient management structure. On the positive side for potential employees: the average age of SSA employees is forty-six—over half of senior managers will probably retire within the decade.

WHERE TO GO FOR MORE INFORMATION

U.S. GOVERNMENT EMPLOYERS: EXECUTIVE BRANCH

NOTE: Government phone numbers and addresses for employment information are often changed—be certain to double-check all numbers and addresses. Furthermore, the government has been instituting a new telephone system called the Washington Interagency Telecommunications System, which has caused more changes than normal. Sometimes a recorded message will inform you of the new number. If not, remember you can call the government information number at 1-800/347-1997, regular information at 1-202/555-1212 for District of Columbia agencies, 1-703/555-1212 for Virginia agencies, and 1-301/555-1212 for Maryland agencies.

Office of Personnel Management
(OPM)
P.O. Box 52
Washington, DC 20415

202/606-2700
(As mentioned in the text, OPM, in some cases fills the role of a government search firm; it also

oversees the hiring practices of other agencies. *Offices of the regional OPMs/Federal Job Information Centers are listed in each region in the Regional sections. In general, contact the specific OPM nearest where you want to work.)*

ACTION
Personnel Management Division, 5th Fl.
Personnel Staffing Branch
1100 Vermont Ave., NW
Washington, DC 20525
202/606-5108
(Primarily volunteer; administers VISTA, hires all backgrounds.)

Administrative Office of the U.S. Courts
Human Resources Division, Room L701

Washington, DC 20544
202/273-1270
(Provides administration services to federal courts; hires primarily acct., comp. sci, finance, and lawyers; some liberal arts backgrounds; for court positions you must refer to the individual court itself—see U.S. court directory in the Directory section for a listing of federal courts nationwide.)

Agriculture, U.S. Department of
Office of Personnel
Central Employment Unit
Room 1080, South Bldg.
Washington, DC 20520
202/720-2791
(A huge, and for hiring purposes very decentralized agency; hiring is usually done by individual USDA offices.)

OTHER USDA OFFICES:

Agricultural Marketing Service
Field Servicing Office
Attn.: Animal and Plant Health Inspection Service
Butler Sq. W., 5th Fl.
100 N. 6th St.
Minneapolis, MN 55403
612/370-2187 (job hotline and info)
(Most jobs in commodity grading and market reporting; hires primarily ag. backgrounds.)

Agriculture Research Service
Personnel Division
Bldg. 003, BARC-W.
Beltsville, MD 20705
301/344-1124
(Each year employs 100 scientists for full-time research; also employs technicians, etc.)

Agricultural Stabilization and Conservation Service
14th and Independence Ave. SW

Washington, DC 20250
202/720-5237
(Hires acct., ag. bus. admin., etc.)

Animal and Plant Health Inspection Service
Field Servicing Office
Human Resources Division
Butler Sq. W., 5th Fl.
100 N. 6th St.
Minneapolis, MN 55403
612/370-2227
612/370-2187 (jobline)
(Hires mostly agriculture, biology, and lab technology)

Economic Management Staff
Recruitment Coordinator
Personnel Division
Economics Management Staff
Room 1427, S. Bldg.
Washington, DC 20250-3500
202/720-7657
(Hires ag. econ., econ., math.)

Farmers Home Administration
Personnel Division
Room 6900, South Bldg.
Washington, DC 20250
202/720-4323
(Primarily hires ag. business, arch., and civil engin.)

Food and Nutrition Service
Personnel Division
3101 Park Center Dr.
Alexandria, VA 22302
703/305-2351
(Above address is for DC area positions; call for numbers of 7 regional offices; hires home ec., econ., business, and nutritionists.)

Food Safety and Inspection Service
Personnel Division
Room 3143, South Bldg.
14th and Independence Ave., SW
Washington, DC 20250
202/720-6617
(Hires chem, food tech. and vet. backgrounds primarily.)

Forest Service
Washington Office
P.O. Box 96090
Room 906, Rosslyn Plaza E.
Washington, DC 20090-6090
202/205-1760
(Call or write for the address of 9 regional offices and for positions with one of the 8 research stations and 2 labs; hires archeologists, engin., ed., forestry, and various bio. specialties.)

Office of Inspector General (USDA)
Office of Personnel
Personnel Operations
Room 31-W
Washington, DC 20250
202/720-3764
(Employees with legal, comp., etc., skills; audit USDA operations.)

Rural Electrification Division
Personnel Management Division
Room 4031, South Bldg.
14th and Independence Ave., SW
Washington, DC 20250
202/720-9560
(Primarily hires acct., bus. admin., and engin.)

Soil Conservation Service
Personnel Division
P.O. Box 2890
Washington, DC 20013
202/720-4264
(There are also local offices, listed in your local phone directory under "U.S. Government, Agriculture, Soil Conservation Service"; hires engin., soil conservation degrees, etc.)

Board of Governors of the Federal Reserve System
Division of Human Resources Management MS156
20th and Constitution Ave., NW
Washington, DC 20551
202/452-3880
(Primarily hires econ. and attorneys in addition to administrative staff.)

U.S. Department of Commerce
Below we've listed major branches of the Commerce Department and the appropriate personnel addresses. Directly below are the main regional personnel offices. For information on

regional Commerce Department jobs, call or write:

Personnel Officer
Central Administrative Support Center
U.S. Department of Commerce
601 E. 12th St.
Kansas City, MO 64106
816/426-7463

Personnel Officer
Eastern Administrative Support Center
U.S. Department of Commerce
253 Monticello Ave.
Norfolk, Va 23510
804/441-6516

Personnel Officer
Mountain Administrative Support
Center
U.S. Department of Commerce
325 Broadway
Boulder, CO 80303
303/497-6332

Personnel Officer
Western Administrative Support Center
U.S. Department of Commerce
7600 Sand Point Way, NE
BIN C 15700
Seattle, WA 98115
206/526-6053

Office of the Secretary
Office of Personnel Operations
U.S. Department of Commerce
14th and Constitution Ave., NW
H1069
Washington, DC 20230
202/377-5138
(Manage and direct Commerce
Department policy, liaison-type jobs;
hires business/lib. arts/law/comp.
backgrounds.)

Bureau of the Census
Personnel Division
Room 3254, Bldg. Three
Washington, DC 20233
301/763-5780 (for college graduates)

301/763-6064 (vacancy listing)
(Hires stat., comp., and cartographers
primarily.)

Bureau of Economic Analysis
Office of Personnel Operations
14th and Constitution Ave., NW
H1069
Washington, DC 20230
202/377-5138
(Hires econ., stat., comp. sci., and
acct. primarily.)

Bureau of Export Administration
(same address as above)
(Licenses exports; hires tech.,
enforcement, engin., etc.)

Economic Affairs
(same address as above)
(Develops commercial policy; hires
managers, economists.)

**Economic Development
Adminstration**
(same address as above)
(Provides loans and aid to carry our
economic development in the United
States; hires managers, planners.)

**Minority Business Development
Agency**
(same address as above)
(Promotes minority business—hires
bus./marketing, etc.)

**National Institute of Standards and
Technology**
Personnel Officer
Room A-123, Admin. Bldg.
Gaithersburg, MD 20899
301/975-3008
(Formerly the National Bureau of
Standards; tests and studies new
technology and materials; hires engin.
comp. backgrounds, etc.)

**National Oceanic and Atmospheric
Administration**
Personnel Division
6010 Executive Blvd.

WSC No. 5, Room 706
Washington, DC 20852
301/713-0527
(An exciting agency that includes the
National Weather Service and the
National Ocean Service; NOAA
scientists monitor the sea, sky, space,
and sun. Hires scientists, econ., etc.)

**National Technical Information
Service**
Office of Personnel Operations
5285 Port Royal Rd.
Springfield, VA 22161
703/487-4680
(Sales-supported agency that markets
technical reports, etc. Hires marketing
majors, etc.)

**National Telecommunications and
Information Administration**
(same address as above)
(principal U.S. agency advising on

telecom. issues. Hires comm., com.,
and engin. specialists.)

Office of the Inspector General
Personnel Officer
Department of Commerce
14th and Constitution Ave., NW
H-7713
Washington, DC 20230
202/482-4948
(Hires audit., law enforc. primarily.)

Patent and Trademark Office
Office of Personnel
CPK-1, Suite 700
Washington, DC 20231
703/305-8231
Employment hot lines:
1/800/368-3064 (patent examiners)
1/800/327-2909 (attorneys)
703/305-4221 (24-our job vacancies)
(Hires most backgrounds, partic.
engin., sci.)

**Commission on Civil
Rights**
Personnel Officer
1121 Vermont Ave.,
NW
Washington, DC 20425
202/376-8364
(Hires econ., law, etc.,
backgrounds.)

**Commodity Futures
Trading Commission**
Director of Personnel

2033 K St., Room 202
Washington, DC 20581
202/254-3275
(Hires acct.,
investigators, law.,
comp. backgrounds
primarily.)

**Consumer Product
Safety Commission**
Chief of Operations
Division of Personnel

Management
5401 Westbard Ave.,
Room 329
Bethesda, MD 20207
301/504-0100
(Works with industry
and the public; hires
engin. comp., health
sci., lib. arts
backgrounds.)

**Department of the
Army**
Total Army Personnel
Command
ATTN: TAPC-CPS-C
200 Stoval St.
Alexandria, VA
22332-0320
703/325-9653

(Contact for
information on army
employers not
mentioned below, and
for information on the
Army Materiel
Command, which
employs 100,000
military and

civilians—especially
engin., acct., and
librarians—across the
country.)

**Army Corps of
Engineers**
Civilian Personnel
Division

Attn.: CEPE-CS
20 Massachusetts Ave.,
NW, Room 5105
Washington, DC
20314-1000
202/272-0559
(Employs more than
40,000 civilians—hires
mostly engin., acct.,
and mgmt.
backgrounds.)

**Army Finance and
Accounting Center**
Human Resources
Directorate
Attn: FINCU-DF,
Room 220 AA
Indianapolis, IN
46249-0329
317/542-2433
(Hires acct./fin./
admin./econ./comp.
sci., etc.)

**Army Information
Systems Command**
Civilian Personnel

Office
Recruitment and
Placement
Army Garrison-FH
Fort Huachuca, AZ
85613-5000
602/533-2424
or

**Army Information
Systems Command**
Civilian Personnel
Office
Recruitment and
Placement
Army Garrison-FR
Fort Ritchie, MD
21719-5010
301/878-5930
(Hires most college
majors to become
comm. spec., personnel
admin., systems
analysts, etc.)

**Military Traffic
Management
Command**

Career Program
Administrator
Attn.: MT-PEC
5611 Columbia Pike,
Room 735
Falls Church, VA
22041-5050
703/756-1741
(Hires engin.,
transport., lib. arts,
etc.)

**Army Training and
Doctrine Command**
Civilian Intern and
Student Program
Coordinator
Attn.: ATPL-C
Fort Monroe, VA
23651-5000
804/727-3336
(Hires writers, editors,
librarians, engineers,
budget analysts, etc.)

**Department of the
Navy**
Washington, DC
20350-1000
Hires people from most
backgrounds; for
civilian jobs, with any
of the following
commands: **Naval Air
Systems, Naval Sea
Systems, Space and
Naval Warfare
Systems, Medical,
Naval Intelligence,
Naval Security, Naval
Military Personnel,
Naval Supply Systems,
Naval Facilities**

**Engineering, Naval
Telecommunications,
Naval Education,
Military Sealift** and
**Chief of Naval
Research**; for personnel
and Equal Opportunity
jobs contact one of the
**Regional Offices of
Civilian Personnel
Management (OCPM)**
listed below:

Staffing Division
Northeast Region
Office of Civilian
Personnel Management
Bldg. 75-3, Naval Base
Philadelphia, PA

19112-5006
215/897-6521

Staffing Division
Northwest Region
Office of Civilian
Personnel
2890 Main St.,
Suite 301
Walnut Creek, CA
94596-2739
415/944-5608

Staffing Division
OCPM Capital Region
801 N. Randolph St.
Arlington, VA
22203-1927
703/696-4567

Staffing Division
Pacific Region
Office of Civilian
Personnel Management
P.O. Box 119
Pearl Harbor, HI
96860-5060
808/471-3237

Staffing Division
Southeast Region
Office of Civilian
Personnel Management
Bldg. A-67,
Naval Station
Norfolk, VA
23511-6098
804/444-1507

Staffing Division
Southwest Region
Office of Civilian
Personnel Management
880 Front St.,
Room 5-S-29
San Diego, CA
92188-0410
619/532-2912

Administrator, Logistics
Career Intern Program
Navy Career
Management Center
P.O. Box 2010
Mechanicsburg, PA
17055-0787
(For civilian
internships, career
management programs.)

Administrator,
Contracting Career
Intern Program
(same address as
above)

Office of Career
Management
Comptroller of the
Navy
Crystal Mall 3,
Room 119
Washington, DC
20376-5001
904/452-3962
(For financial
management career
intern program.)

Department of the Air Force
hires from most backgrounds, particularly engin., acct., and comp. sci.: for civilian jobs, contact the Central Civilian Personnel

Office at your nearest Air Force base; also check ads, announcements sent to nearby colleges, and check the Air Force Association magazine, listed under Associations above.)

Air Force Civilian Personnel Management Center/DPCR
Randolph AFB, TX
78150-6421
512/652-4948
1/800/847-0108
(For career intern inquiries.)

Defense Communications Agency
Special Programs Unit
Civilian Personnel
Office
8th St. and S.
Courthouse Rd.
Bldg. Two, Room 210
Arlington, VA
20305-2000
703/692-2788
(Employs comp., elec. engin. backgrounds.)

Defense Contract Audit Agency
Nationwide Field
Detachment
Cameron Station
Attn.: CAP,
Room 4A380
Alexandria, VA
22304-6178
703/274-7325
(Hires acct., etc., for auditing jobs. Contact this central office for

addresses of the six regional offices.)

Defense Investigative Service
Resources Directorate
Personnel Operations
Divison
1900 Half St., SW
Washington, DC
20324-1700
202/475-0575
(Conducts security investigations, hires all

majors for investigator and industrial/personnel security jobs; contact one of the 10 local personnel offices nearest you.)

Defense Logistics Agency
Civilian Personnel Service Support Office DCPSO-S
P.O. Box 3990
Columbus, OH
43216-5000
1-800/458-7903
(Provides services —management of supplies and contract admin. for the military. Hires various backgrounds for many areas of management. Contact above for one of the 18 local offices near you.)

Defense Mapping Agency
Personnel Staffing Specialist
Attn.: PRSD
Washington, DC
20315-0030
202/653-0484
(For jobs in DC.)

Defense Mapping Agency
Personnel Staffing Specialist
Aerospace Center
Attn.: POR
3200 S. Second St., Bldg. 37
St. Louis, MO 63118
314/263-4460
(Hires phys. sci., cart.,

geo., math., comp. sci. backgrounds.)

Department of Education
Office of Personnel
Department of Education
400 Maryland Ave., SW, Room 1156
Washington, DC 20202
202/401-0559
(For DC-area jobs—call for numbers of 11 regional offices; hires ed., lib. arts, and poli. sci. backgrounds.)

Department of Energy
Headquarters
Operations Division
1000 Independence Ave., SW, Room 4E-090
Washington, DC 20585
202/586-8558
(Call for the numbers of the more than 17 local offices; hires acct., comp. sci., admin., eng., etc., backgrounds.)

Environmental Protection Agency
Recruitment Center (PM-224)
401 M St, SW
Washington, DC 20460
202/206-3144
(The EPA also has regional offices with employment sections in 10 major cities; call above for addresses; hires most sci. backgrounds, as well as pub. admin., engin., and pol. sci.)

Equal Employment Opportunity Commission
Job Information Center
Equal Employment Opportunity Commission
1801 L St., NW
Washington, DC 20507
202/663-4337
(Hires primarily acct., bus., and law backgrounds.)

Executive Office of the President
Director of Personnel
Office of Administration
725 17th St., NW
Washington, DC 20503
202/395-1088
(Comprises 15 agencies that provide operational staff support to the president; includes the **Office of Management and Budget** and the **Office of Administration**; hires bus., econ., pub. admin., stat. backgrounds.)

Farm Credit Administration
Human Resources Division
1501 Farm Credit Dr.
McLean, VA
22102-5090
703/833-4000
(Banks and credit associations that lend to farmers; hires acct., agribusiness, bus., banking backgrounds.)

Federal Communications Division
Associate Managing Director
Human Resources Management
1919 M St., NW, Room 212
Washington, DC 20544
202/632-7000
(Hires engin., law, econ., comp. spec.)

Federal Deposit Insurance Association
Director of Personnel
550 17th St., NW
Washington, DC 20429
202/898-8890
(Hires all backgrounds, including paralegals.)

Federal Emergency Management Agency
Headquarters, Operations Division
Office of Personnel, Room 816
500 C St., SW
Washington, DC 20472
202/646-2500
202/646-3244 (job hot line)
(Hires acct., bus., educ., pub. admin., comp. sci., law, military backgrounds, etc.)

Federal Maritime Commission
Director of Personnel
1100 L St., NW, Room 10103
Washington, DC 20573-0001
202/523-5773
(Hires acct., bus. econ., law, etc.)

Federal Retirement Thrift Investment Board
Personnel Officer
805 15th St., NW
Washington, DC 20005
202/523-8028
(Hires acct., bus. comp. sci., law, marketing, lib. arts.)

Federal Trade Commission
Division of Personnel
Sixth and Pennsylvania Ave. NW, Room 149
Washington, DC 20580
202/326-2020
(For DC-area jobs; contact for addresses of 10 regional offices; hires acct., bus., paralegals, sec., etc.)

General Accounting Office
Office of Recruitment
441 G St., NW,

Room 4043-OD
Washington, DC 20548
202/275-6092
(Hires acct., bus. admin., comp sci., econ., fin., MIS, pol. sci., soc. sci., etc.)

General Services Administration
Office of Personnel
Central Office
18th and F Sts., NW
Washington, DC 20405
202/501-0398
(Contact for address of field and regional offices; hires arch., comp. sci., law, bus. admin., etc.; note that Kansas City regional office has a job hot line: 816/926-7804.)

Government Printing Office
Chief, Employment Branch
Stop: PSE
N. Capitol and H Sts., NW
Washington, DC 20401
202/512-0000
(Hires acct., chem., comp. sci., engin., printing, mgmt., art and design.)

Department of Health and Human Services
Division of Personnel Operations
330 Independence Ave., SW, Room 1040
Washington, DC 20201

202/619-0146
(For HQ jobs—contact for addresses of regional offices; hires acct., lawyers, most other backgrounds.)

Agency for Toxic Substances and Disease Registry
Personnel Office
1600 Clifton Rd., NE
Atlanta, GA 30333
404/639-3615

(Hires sci. med. backgrounds.)

Alcohol, Drug Abuse, and Mental Health Administration
Personnel Office
5600 Fishers Ln.,
Room 12-95
Rockville, MD 20857
301/443-5407
(Hires med., psych., social workers, etc.)

Centers for Disease Control
Personnel Office
1600 Clifton Rd., NE
Atlanta, GA 30333
404/639-3615
(Hires sci. tech. and admin. primarily.)

Family Support Administration
Division of
Management and
Regional Operations
Department of Health
and Human Services
330 C St., SW
Washington, DC 20201
202/401-9300
(Employees administer family programs; hires acct. and auditors.)

Food and Drug Administration
Division of Personnel
Management
5600 Fishers Ln.,
Room 4B-41
Rockville, MD 20857
301/443-1970
(Hires med., sci., vet., and admin. primarily.)

Health Care Financing Administration
Staffing Branch
E. High Rise Bldg.
6325 Security Blvd.,
Room G-55
Baltimore, MD 21207
410/966-5505
(For regional positions, contact HQ for addresses of regional personnel offices; hires acct., pub. admin., soc. sci., etc.)

Health Resources and Services Administration
Office of Personnel
5600 Fishers Ln.,
Room 14A-46
Rockville, MD 20857
301/443-5460
(Hires acct., admin. primarily; contact HQ for regional office addresses.)

Indian Health Service
Personnel Operations
Branch
5600 Fishers Ln.,
Room 6A-15
Rockville, MD 20857
301/443-6520
(Hires dentists, hygienists, doctors, nurses, etc.)

National Institutes of Health
Division of Personnel
Management
9000 Rockville Pike
Bldg. 31, Room B3C15
Bethesda, MD 20205
301/496-2403
(Hires dent., med., nursing, sci., tech., etc.)

Office of Human Development Services
(Same address as above; hires social service backgrounds for jobs that support state social services programs.)

Public Health Service
Personnel Office
OASH Personnel
Operations Office
5600 Fishers Ln.,
Room 17A-08
Rockville, MD 20857
301/443-1986
(Hires health serv., sci., acct. backgrounds.)

Social Security Administration
Recruitment and
Placement Branch
West High Rise Bldg.
6401 Security Blvd.,
Room G-120
Baltimore, MD 21235
410/965-4506
(Hires comp. sci. and a wide range of other backgrounds.)

Department of Housing and Urban Development
Chief, Staffing and Classification Branch
Office of Personnel and Training, APE
451 Seventh St., SW, Room 2260
Washington, DC 20410-3100
202/708-0408
(Contact for regional and field office addresses;
hires acct., bus., eng., admin. backgrounds.)

Department of the Interior
Personnel Office
Office of the Secretary
Washington, DC 20240
202/208-7150
202/208-4821

Bureau of Indian Affairs
Division of Personnel Management
Headquarters
1951 Constitution Ave., NW
Washington, DC 20240
202/208-7581
(Hires sci. comp., lib. arts, ed., social work backgrounds.)

Bureau of Land Management
Division of Personnel
18th and C Sts., NW
(MIB)
Washington, DC 20240
202/208-3193
(Contact for regional offices; hires sci., animal sci., engin., lib. arts backgrounds, mechanics, etc.)

Bureau of Mines
Headquarters
2401 E St., NW
Washington, DC 20241

202/501-9610
(Contact for regional office addresses; hires econ., engin., sci., comp. sci., tech. backgrounds.)

Bureau of Reclamation
Headquarters
18th and C Sts., NW
Washington, DC 20240
202/208-4662
(Contact for regional addresses; hires sci., engin., electronics, econ. backgrounds primarily.)

Minerals Management Service
381 Elden St.
Herndon, VA
20070-4817
703/787-1414
(Hires sci. and admin.)

National Park Service
Headquarters
Branch of Personnel Operations
18th and C Sts., NW
P.O. Box 37127
Washington, DC 20013
202/208-4649
(Contact for regional offices; hires achaeologists, bus.

admin., hist., lib. arts, foresters, etc.)

Office of Surface Mining Reclamation and Enforcement
Personnel Office
1951 Constitution Ave., NW
Washington, DC 20240
202/208-2953
(Hires accts., bio., engin. primarily.)

U.S. Fish and Wildlife Service
Headquarters
18th and C Sts., NW
Washington, DC 20240
703/358-1743
(Contact for regional offices; hires bio., lib. arts, etc.)

U.S. Geological Survey
USGS National Center
MS-215
12201 Sunrise Valley Dr.
Reston, VA 22092
703/648-4000
(Contact for regional offices; hires sci., engin. mainly; note that USGS Central Regional Office in Denver has a job hot line:
303/236-5846.)

Department of Justice
Personnel Services
Suite 6259, Main Bldg.
10th St. and
Constitution Ave., NW
Washington, DC 20530
202/514-6814
(Hires bus. admin.,
comp. sci., lib. arts
backgrounds,
paralegals, etc.; see
below for lawyers.)

Bureau of Prisons
Chief of Recruiting
Homeowners Loan
Corporation Bldg.
320 First St., NW,
Room 400
Washington, DC 20534
202/307-1304
(Hires criminal justice
backgrounds, accts.,
med., law enforcement,
soc. work, etc.;
increasingly prefers
college grads.)

**Drug Enforcement
Administration**
Office of Personnel
1405 I St., NW
Washington, DC 20537
(Hires accts. chem.,
lib. arts, language
spec.; spec. agents with
acct., pilot/maritime,
language, tech., and
legal backgrounds in
demand.)
202/307-4000

**Executive Office for
U.S. Attorneys**
Security and Personnel

Staff Patrick Henry
Bldg., Room 6200
10th St. and
Pennsylvania Ave., NW
Washington, DC 20530
202/514-2000 (gen.
Treas. no.)
(Supports U.S.
Attorneys' offices; hires
wide variety of
backgrounds for admin.
and legal support
positions.)

**Federal Bureau of
Investigation**
Personnel Resources
10th St. and
Pennsylvania Ave.,
NW, Room 6329
Washington, DC 20535
202/324-4991/2000
(Employment
applications for special
agents are usually
initiated through the
applicant coordinator at
each of the 59 local
FBI field offices—check
your local phone book;
for information and/or
for most support
positions as clerks,
typists, etc., contact
address above.)

**Immigration and
Naturalization Service**
Central Office
Personnel Division

1425 I St., NW, Room
6032
Washington, DC 20536
202/514-2530
(Contact for regional
employment offices;
hires all academic
backgrounds.)

**Office of Attorney
Personnel
Management**
Department of Justice
Main Bldg., Room
4311
10th St. and
Constitution Ave., NW
Washington, DC 20530
202/633-2134
(Hires attorneys.)

**Office of Justice
Programs**
Personnel Office
633 Indiana Ave., NW
Washington, DC 20531
202/724-7725
(Hires accts., stat.,
comp. sci., analysts.)

U.S. Marshals Service
Personnel Management
Division
600 Army-Navy Drive
Arlington, VA 22202
202/307-9600
(Hires all academic
majors, accts., comp.
sci., police admin.;
dep. U.S. marshal
positions require
passing written test.)

Department of Labor
Office of Personnel
Management Services
National Capital Service
Center
Frances Perkins Bldg.,
Room C 5516
200 Constitution Ave.,
NW
Washington, DC 20210
202/523-6677
(Hire most
backgrounds.)

**Bureau of Labor
Statistics**
College
Recruitment/Special
Programs
Department of Labor
441 G St., NW, Room
2827
Washington, DC 20212
202/523-1377
(Hires most
backgrounds, comp.
programmers, econ.,
stats.)

**Employment
Standards
Administration**
Division of Staffing and
Employee Relations
Frances Perkins Bldg.,
Room 53308
200 Constitution Ave.,
NW
Washington, DC 20210

202/523-9064
(Hires most academic
backgrounds.)

**Employment and
Training
Administration**
Division of Staffing and
Employee Relations
Frances Perkins Bldg.,
Room S3308
200 Constitution Ave.,
NW
Washington, DC 20210
202/535-8744
(Hires bud. analysts,
econ., etc.)

**Merit Systems
Protection**
Personnel Division,
Room 850
1120 Vermont Ave.,
NW
Washington, DC 20419
202/653-5916
(Employees are
primarily attorneys and
support staff; hears and
decides federal
employment cases.)

**Mine Safety and
Health Administration**
Human Resources
Division
Personnel Systems and
Services Branch
Department of Labor

4015 Wilson Blvd.
Ballston Tower #3,
Room 500
Arlington, VA 22203
703/235-1352
(Hires hygienists, all
backgrounds as safety
spec.)

**National Aeronautics
and Space
Administration
(NASA)**
**NASA Headquarters
DP**
Washington, DC 20546
202/453-8489
(Employs primarily
engin., comp. sci.,
math., physicists, and
support staff; contact
for regional
employment and
addresses.)

**Occupational Safety
and Health
Administration**
Office of Personnel
Management
Department of Labor
Frances Perkins Bldg.,
Room N3308
200 Constitution Ave.,
NW
Washington, DC 20210
202/523-8013
(Hires all backgrounds
as mgmt. analysts, etc.)

**National Archives and
Records
Administration**
Maintains federal
records nationwide;
hires history, pol. sci.
backgrounds as well as

paper conservation
specialists. Key
employment addresses
below.

**Personnel Operations
Branch**
9700 Page Blvd.

St. Louis, MO 63132
314/263-3901
(General employment
information; contact for
addresses and numbers
of Federal Records
Centers nationwide.)

Office of the National Archives
Eighth St. and
Pennsylvania Ave., NW
Washington, DC 20408
202/501-5402
(Archivist or paper
conservator positions.)

Personnel Office
Office of Federal
Records Centers
Eighth St. and
Pennsylvania Ave., NW
Washington, DC 20408
202/659-6209
(Archives specialists
positions.)

Personnel Office
Office of the *Federal Register*
Eighth St. and
Pennsylvania Ave., NW
Washington, DC 20408
202/523-5240
(Writer-editors.)

National Credit Union Administration
Personnel Management
Specialist
Personnel Office
National Credit Union
Administration
1776 G St., NW
Washington, DC 20456
202/682-9720
(Hires nationwide,
principally credit
examiners.)

National Endowment for the Humanities
Personnel Management
Specialist
Personnel Office, Room
417
1100 Pennsylvania
Ave., NW
Washington, DC 20506
202/606-8415
(Hires arts/hist./lit./
backgrounds as program
spec.)

National Labor Relations Board
Personnel Operations
1717 Pennsylvania
Ave., NW
Washington, DC 20570
202/254-9044
(Investigates unfair
labor practices; hires

acct., bus. admin., law
backgrounds for field
examiner positions.)

National Science Foundation
Staffing Assistant
Division of Personnel
and Management
1800 G St., NW, Room
208
Washington, DC 20550
202/357-9859
(Hires most majors,
pref. w/ acct., sci. to
serve as grants
specialists, etc.)

Nuclear Regulatory Commission
College Recruitment
Coordinator
Office of Personnel
Washington, DC 20555
301/492-9027
(Hires engin., sci.
primarily.)

Office of Personnel Management
Recruitment and Special
Employment Programs
Branch
1900 E St., NW, Room
1469
Washington, DC 20415
202/606-2700
(Hires HR

backgrounds, all majors
to serve in various
personnel specialties.)

Railroad Retirement Board
Bureau of Personnel
844 Rush St.
Chicago, IL 60611
312/751-4580
(Hires acct., audit., all
academic backgrounds
as well as crim. just.
for examiner position.)

Securities and Exchange Commission
Office of Personnel
450 Fifth St., NW
Washington, DC 20549
202/272-2550
202/272-7065 (attorney
recruitment)
(Regulates securities
markets; hires
accountants, finance,
comp. sci., attorneys,
economists, etc.)

Selective Service System
Personnel Services
National Headquarters
Washington, DC 20435
202/724-0435
(Hires acct., comp.
sci., bus., and pub.
admin. primarily.)

Small Business Administration
Central Personnel Office
1441 L. St. NW, Room 300
Washington, DC 20416
202/205-6780
(Call or write for regional office addresses; hires acct., bank., credit, bus. comp., sci., and pub. admin., etc.)

Smithsonian Institution
Chief, Staffing Services Branch
Employment Office
900 Jefferson Dr., Room 1410
Washington, DC 20560
202/357-1354
(Hires curators in various fields, support staff; turnover and hence employment opportunities are limited; easiest for secretaries, etc.)

Tennessee Valley Authority
Employment Services, ET 5C 50 P-K
400 West Summit Hill Dr.
Knoxville, TN 37902
615/632-7746
(Hires engin., comp. sci., etc.)

Department of Transportation
Central Employment Information Office
M-18
400 Seventh St., SW
Washington, DC 20590
202/366-9417
(Hires acct., bus. admin., lib. arts backgrounds.)

U.S. Coast Guard
Civilian Personnel Division
Transpoint Bldg., Room 4100
2100 Second St., SW
Washington, DC 20593
202/267-1706
(Civ. employment for accts., bus. admin., engin., etc.)

Federal Aviation Administration
Headquarters
800 Independence Ave., SW
Washington, DC 20591
202/267-8007
(Hires elec. tech., engin., controllers, etc.; regional employment offices for all regional employment, including air traffic control specialists, are on page 194.)

Federal Highway Administration
Office of Personnel and Training
400 Seventh St., SW, Room 4317
Washington, DC 20590
202/366-0541
(Hires acct., bus., civ. engin., etc.)

Federal Railroad Administration
Office of Personnel
400 Seventh St., SW, Room 8232
Washington, DC 20590
202/366-0584
(Hires acct., econ., lawyers, etc.)

Maritime Administration
Office of Personnel
400 Seventh St., SW, Room 8101
Washington, DC 20590
202/366-4143
(Supports U.S. merchant marine, including training at the Merchant Marine Academy, etc.; hires acct., econ., mech/marine engin., etc.)

National Highway Traffic Safety Administration
Office of Personnel
400 Seventh St., SW, Room 5306
Washington, DC 20590
202/366-2602
(Hires engin., lawyers, math., lib. arts backgrounds.)

Research and Special Programs Administration
Personnel Office
Department of Transportation
400 Seventh St., SW, Room 8401

Washington, DC 20590
202/366-5608
(Analyzes hazardous
material transport; hires
engin. as well as lib.
arts/bus. backgrounds.)

**St. Lawrence Seaway
Development
Corporation**

180 Andrews St.
Massena, NY 13662
315/764-3245
(Hires fin. manag. and
comp. clerks.)

**Urban Mass
Transportation
Administration**

Office of Personnel
400 Seventh St., SW,
Room 7101
Washington, DC 20590
202/366-2513
(Hires bus. admin.,
engin., etc.)

**Department of the
Treasury**
1500 Pennsylvania
Ave., NW
Washington, DC 20220
202/622-2000

**Bureau for Alcohol,
Tobacco, and
Firearms**
Personnel Staffing
Specialist
1200 Pennsylvania
Ave., NW
Washington, DC 20226
202/927-8610
(The ATF hires all
majors; inspects,
investigates, and
enforces federal
firearms, explosives,
alcohol,
violations—hires special
agents, inspectors,
bomb analysts, etc.)

**Bureau of Engraving
and Printing**
Office of Industrial
Relations
14th and C Sts., SW,
Room 202-A
Washington, DC 20228
202/874-2778
(Hires applicants for
printing and engineering

positions as well as
police and office work.)

**Bureau of the Public
Debt**
300 13th St., SW,
Room 446
Washington, DC
20239-1400
202/874-4010
(Hires acct., comp.
analysts, etc.)

Departmental Offices
Office of Personnel
Resources
Employment Section,
Room 1316
Department of the
Treasury
15th St. and
Pennsylvania Ave., NW
Washington, DC 20220
202/566-5411
(Hires economists,
accts., etc.)

**Federal Law
Enforcement Training
Center**
Chief of Staffing
Glynco Facility
Glynco, GA 31524
912/267-2100
(Hires enforcement and
investigative instruc-
tors.)

**Financial Management
Service**
Recruitment
Coordinator
401 14th St., SW,
1st Fl.
Washington, DC 20027
202/566-2000
(Coordinates gov't.
financial operations;
hires mostly acct.,
comp. backgrounds)

**Internal Revenue
Service**
Personnel Office
1111 Constitution Ave.,
NW
Washington, DC 20024
202/566-2000
(For additional
information, college
students may contact
the college recruitment
coordinator at local IRS
offices.)

**Office of the
Comptroller of the
Currency**
490 L'Enfant Plz., SW
Washington, DC 20219
(Charged with
upholding the safety of
the U.S. banking
system—hires
accounting, business,

banking, and econ. majors. There are six district offices nationwide. Below is the Central District address:

Office of the Comptroller of the Currency
1 Financial Pl., Suite 2700
440 S. LaSalle St.
Chicago, IL 60605
312/663-8000

Office of Thrift Supervision
Human Resources Division
1700 G St., NW, 2nd Fl.
Washington, DC 20552
202/906-6060
(Hires accts., bus.

admin., etc., for S&L examiners, comp. prog., econ., lawyers, etc.)

Savings Bonds Division
Personnel Office
1111 20th St., NW, Room 225
Washington, DC 20226
202/377-7663
(Hires managers, comm. spec., lib. arts backgrounds.)

Secret Service
Chief of Staffing
1800 G St., NW, Room 912
Washington, DC 20223
202/435-5800
(Four thousand employees with 65 field offices, hires primarily

from corrections, criminology, or law enforcement backgrounds for special agent positions.)

U.S. Customs Service
OHR-Gelman Bldg.
1301 Constitution Ave., NW
Washington, DC 20229
202/634-5250
(Hires from virtually all disciplines for management, enforcement, and investigative positions.)

U.S. Mint
Chief of Staffing
633 Third St., NW, Suite 655
Washington, DC 20220
202/634-2163
(Hires bus./marketers.)

U.S. Postal Service
General Manager
Headquarters Personnel Division
475 L'Enfant Plz., SW
Washington, DC 20260-4261
202/268-3646
(Also contact your local post office.)

Department of Veterans Affairs
Recruitment and Examining Division (054E)
810 Vermont Ave., NW
Washington, DC 20420
202/872-1151
(Employs applicants from various

backgrounds, for various departments; medical personnel check one of the 172 VA Medical centers located near you—phone and address in local phone directory under "U.S. Government.")

U.S. GOVERNMENT EMPLOYERS: JUDICIAL BRANCH

Personnel Office
U.S. Supreme Court Bldg.
1 First St., NW
Washington, DC 20543
202/479-3404
(For all but

administrative office and claims courts inquiries.)

Personnel Division
Administrative Office of the U.S. Courts, Room

L701
Washington, DC 20544

U.S. Claims Court
717 Madison Pl., NW
Washington, DC 20005

U.S. GOVERNMENT EMPLOYERS: LEGISLATIVE BRANCH

U.S. Senate
Placement Office
Washington, DC 20510
202/224-9167

U.S. House of Representatives
Placement Office
Washington, DC 20515
202/226-6731

Library of Congress
Recruitment and
Placement Office,
Department E
The Library of
Congress
101 Independence
Ave., SE, LM 107
Washington, DC 20540
202/707-5627
202/707-5295
(twenty-four-hr. job hot line)
(Hires librarians, bio., comp. sci., math., soc. sci. backgrounds, wide variety of tech. support and mgmt. positions.)

Office of Technology Assessment
600 Pennsylvania Ave., SE
Washington, DC 20510
202/224-8996
(Evaluates technical and scientific issues for Congress.)

NATIONAL POLITICAL ORGANIZATIONS

Democratic National Committee
430 S. Capitol St., SE
Washington, DC 20003
202/863-8000
(Clearinghouse for applicants for work, primarily voluntary, on political campaigns.)

Democratic Congressional Campaign Committee
same address
202/479-7000

Democratic Senatorial Campaign Committee
same address
202/863-8000

Republican National Committee
310 First St., SE
Washington, DC 20003
202/863-8500
(As with the Democrats above, campaign work is one way of breaking into the Washington scene.)

National Republican Congressional Committee
320 First St., SE
Washington, DC 20003
202/479-7000

National Republican Senatorial Committee
425 Second St., NE
Washington, DC 20003
202/675-6000

GOVERNMENT ASSOCIATIONS

Air Force Association
1501 Lee Hwy.
Arlington, VA
22209-1198
703/247-5800
(Publishes periodical with directory, listings; check Almanac issue in May.)

American Planning Association
1313 E. 60th St.
Chicago, IL 60637
312/955-9100
(Publishes periodical, offers placement service, etc.)

American Society for Public Administration
1120 G St., NW,
Suite 700
Washington, DC 20005
202/393-7878
(Publishes periodical with job listings, etc.)

Capitol Hill Women's Caucus
P.O. Box 599
Longworth House
Office Building
Independence and New
Jersey Aves.
Washington, DC 20515
(Publishes list of jobs
for members.)

Government Finance Officer Association
(Municipal Finance
Officers Association of
the United States and
Canada)
180 N. Michigan Ave.
Chicago, IL 60601
312/977-9700
(Publishes periodical
with job listings.)

International City Management Association
777 N. Capitol St., NE
Washington, DC 20002
202/289-4262
(Publishes directories,
periodical with job
listings, etc.; maintains
internship program for
undergrad. and grad.
students—contact Joy
Pierson, internship
coordinator, at
202/962-3659.)

International Institute of Municipal Clerks
160 N. Altadena Dr.
Pasadena, CA 91107

818/795-6153
(Publishes periodical,
job services.)

Western Governmental Research Association
c/o Graduate Center for
Public Policy and
Administration
California State
University, Long Beach
1250 Bellflower Blvd.
Long Beach, CA 90840
310/985-5419
(Publishes periodical
with job openings in the
West, holds training
programs, etc.)

GOVERNMENT DIRECTORIES

Congressional Yellow Book
Monitor Publishing Co.
104 Fifth Ave., 2nd Fl.
New York, NY 10011
212/627-4140
(Lists members of
Congress, committees,
etc.)

Federal Career Directory
Superintendent of
Documents
U.S. Government
Printing Office
Washington, DC
20402-9325
202/783-3238
(Order number is
006-000-01339-2;
covers federal
employment.)

Federal Personnel Office Directory
Federal Reports, Inc.,
Suite 408
1010 Vermont Ave.,
NW
Washington, DC 20005
202/393-3311
(U.S. government
personnel offices listed
with pertinent
information.)

Federal Regional Yellow Book
Monitor Publishing Co.
104 Fifth Ave.,
2nd Fl.
New York, NY 10011
212/627-4140
(Lists thousands of
local federal offices
nationwide—useful for

the non-DC federal job
hunter.)

Federal Yellow Book
address same as above
(Lists thousands of
major employees of
Executive branch.)

FOCIS: The Federal
Occupation and Career
Information System
National Technical
Information Service
(NTIS)
5285 Port Royal Rd.
Springfield, VA
22161-0001
703/487-4650
(PC-based interactive
expert system that
complements Federal
Career Directory;

guides user through hundreds of federal white-collar positions in hundreds of federal agencies, with descriptions of type of job, description of work, address, qualifications, etc. Current version doesn't include job openings; future versions may. Cost at time of writing was $49.95; updated yearly.)

State and Regional Associations of the United States
Columbia Books
1212 New York Ave., NW, Suite 300
Washington, DC 20005
202/898-0662
(Lists most associations state by state and region by region; useful for the job hunter looking to contact local affiliates

of major associations to use them to help in job hunt.)

U.S. Court Directory
Superintendent of Documents
U.S. Government Printing Office
Washington, DC 20402-9325
202/783-3238
(Lists federal courts nationwide.)

GOVERNMENT PERIODICALS

City & State
740 N. Rush St.
Chicago, IL 60611
312/649-5220
(Biweekly newspaper for state and local officials.)

Community Jobs
ACCESS
50 Beacon St.
Boston, MA 02108
617/720-5627
(Monthly; lists hundreds of jobs in the nonprofit sector.)

Federal Career Opportunities
P.O. Box 1059
Vienna, VA
22185-1089
703/281-0200
(Thousands of job listings.)

Federal Employees' News Digest
P.O. Box 1995
Marion, OH

43305-1995
1-800/347-6969

Federal Jobs Digest
325 Pennsylvania Ave., SE
Washington, DC 20003
800/824-5000
(Lists thousands of federal jobs, with contacts and addresses to which to apply; grades and salary levels.)

Federal Times
6883 Commercial Dr.
Springfield, VA 22159
703/750-8920
(Mainly for federal employees; includes many job listings in back.)

Government Executive
1730 M. St., NW
Washington, DC 20036
202/857-1400
(Ten issues, mainly for federal executives.)

The Government Manager
Circulation
Bureau of National Affairs, Inc.
9435 Key West Ave.
Rockville, MD 20850

The Job Finder
Western Governmental Research Association
c/o Graduate Center for Public Policy and Administration
California State University, Long Beach
1250 Bellflower Blvd.
Long Beach, CA 90840
310/985-5419
(Job listings for local gov't. positions, ranging from police chief to city planner, in western cities and towns.)

Jobs Available
(midwest/eastern edition)
P.O. Box 1222

Newton, IA
50208-1222
515/791-9019
(Biweekly; lists many
public-sector, mostly
local-gov't.
middle-management
jobs.)

Jobs Available (western
edition)
P.O. Box 1040
Modesto, CA 95353
213/498-5419
(Lists job openings in
public administration
and research.)

*Journal of State
Government*
The Council of State
Governments
Iron Works Pike
P.O. Box 11910
Lexington, KY

40578-1910
(Quarterly, professional
journal for state
legislators.)

The National Journal
1730 M St., NW
Washington, DC 20036
202/857-1400
800/424-2921
(subscription)
(Weekly gov't.
magazine; note that the
regular subscription
price is almost eight
times the faculty/student
rate.)

Nation's Cities
1301 Pennsylvania
Ave., NW
Washington, DC 20004
202/626-3040
(Weekly tabloid.)

Planning
1313 E. 60th St.
Chicago, IL 60637
312/955-9100

Public Employee
1625 L St., NW
Washington, DC 20036
202/429-1144
(Huge-circulation
tabloid to members of
American Federation of
State, County, and
Local Employees;
useful in getting a feel
for the major issues and
problems of gov't.
employment.)

State Legislatures
1560 Broadway
Denver, CO 80202
303/830-2200

HEALTH CARE AND MEDICAL SPECIALISTS

BRIEF BACKGROUND

▶ **The big question in health care is, What next? The best guess is that employment trends will remain strong in most sectors.**

This has been a year of controversy and big change in health care—and the uncertainty has made it much more difficult to predict the future.

The industry as a whole is changing rapidly, and new technology will produce even more changes—but the major new employment factor will be probable increased government intervention in the health marketplace. Already in early 1993, presidential complaints about the high price of prescription drugs hammered the drug companies, who announced lower earnings and reduced prospects for the future. Hiring in this sector of the booming health-care market fell.

EMPLOYMENT OUTLOOK: Fairly strong, despite some new uncertainties.

▶ **A few years ago, new jobs were being created in the health care field at the rate of 30,000 a month. This high number has fallen by over 50% in 1993.**

But 14,000 to 15,000 new jobs a month is still healthy growth and still means job opportunities. With President Clinton's new health care proposals, the realization has come that cost escalation must stop, and with it, some hiring will slow down. Does this mean slow times ahead?

Best guess: No. Simply put, whatever the final shape of the Clinton health care package, shortages of many health care workers are still too acute. Registered nurses, physical therapists, pharmacists, dieticians, and nutritionists will still be in relatively short supply. Here are some of the probable best employment bets, based on government projections:

Some of the fastest-growing areas:

MEDICAL ASSISTANTS: work in doctors' offices, hospitals, in both clinical and administrative work. One advantage: applicants can enter without any formal training, although increasingly they are certified by various boards, most commonly by the American Association of Medical Technologists, usually after attending a one-year trade school or a two-year associate degree program. Best bet for a good job:

two-year degree, along with computer expertise. Also in strong demand: dental assistants, nursing aides.

PHYSICAL THERAPISTS: excellent job outlook; as the average American gets older, sports and exercise become more mainstream—and all told, more physical injuries result. Also, improved medicine now can save the severely injured, again increasing the demand for therapists who can help rehabilitate them. Career advantages: autonomy (over 20% are in private practice; this trend will increase as hospitals continue to emphasize outpatient care), relatively high pay, personal satisfaction. Requirements: increasing as field becomes more technical. For entry level: degree or certificate in the field, and license. Some states require continuing education. Also in strong demand: **occupational therapists** (who work with all types of disabled), **physical therapist assistants and aides, recreational therapists.**

MEDICAL TECHNICIANS: many areas are fast growing and in high demand. Some of the fastest growing: EEG technicians (electroencephalograph or, in effect, electric brain scan operators), radiological technicians, medical records technicians (even with administrative cutbacks, the long-term trend in this record-keeping area is strong, particularly for those with extensive computer expertise). One important thing to remember, however: Technology can *reduce* demand for technicians as well. For example, although jobs for laboratory technicians will increase, the rate will not be as fast because improved techniques and laboratory automation reduce the numbers of people needed to make the tests.

NUTRITIONISTS: Now finding employment outside of hospitals, schools, and nursing homes, as food manufacturers and restaurant chains attempt to meet the needs of an increasingly health-conscious public and stringent new federal requirements with food labeling, etc. In addition, jobs can be found with PR and consulting firms, sports medicine and corporate wellness centers. Employment will increase by a strong 24% by the year 2005 according to a government forecast, assuming moderate growth in the economy. An expanding specialty: gerontological nutrition, planning meals for the growing elderly population.

PHARMACISTS: Now finding employment outside hospitals and businesses—more are employed by a wide variety of health care providers, as well as with powerful pharmaceutical manufacturers. Employment is projected to increase by a strong 24% by the year 2005. Pharmacy assistants will also see a very strong job market—government forecasts are for an explosive growth of 57% by 2005.

Other rapidly growing employment areas include: respiratory therapists, speech pathologists and audiologists, opticians, and podiatrists. Although not growing as rapidly as the professions above, there are many opportunities for lab technicians as well, particularly in the expanding (but volatile) biotech labs in San Francisco and other centers.

Also expect a rise in employment of physicians assistants (PAs). These are usually graduates of an AMA-approved school who train for two years, and are certified to take the place of physicians during routine tasks like taking medical histories or making preliminary diagnoses.

▶ **The shortage of nurses: continuing.**

Nurses should have absolutely no trouble finding a job in the 1990s. The American Hospital Association recently estimated that *160,000* nursing positions were vacant. Another study estimated that 600,000 *more* nurses will be needed by the year 2000.

There are approximately 2 million registered nurses in the U.S., of whom 80% are practicing currently. To be a registered nurse, you must graduate from an accredited school and pass a licensing exam.

The nursing shortage is most acute in hospitals, where about half of all nurses work. Why? Although in many cases hospitals offer better pay than the alternatives—insurance companies, home health agencies, etc.—they often can't compete with the better hours, and other life-style benefits.

But why the nursing shortage in the first place? The rising number of aging patients, and better medical care, has increased demand. More important, not enough people were entering the field. For most, the reasons were basic: low pay and high stress, not to mention little autonomy, bad schedules, and often mediocre benefits. Many nurses are bothered by high stress, and many are troubled that they have so little time to spend with patients. As recently as a few years ago, only 25% of nurses had protected benefit plans, and average salaries were under $30,000 in many areas.

That is all changing now, as a shortage drives up wages and adds benefits and the profession rises dramatically in prestige. None too soon, the medical profession is realizing it must do something to attract applicants.

Hospitals are getting much more competitive in an effort to attract and keep nurses. The cost of recruiting nurses is so high that hospitals are transforming the profession. Pay is up significantly; the average starting salary has jumped another $5,000, to somewhere around $35,000. The old pay caps are falling by the wayside. Pay differentials for night shifts, on-call, and weekend shifts are increasing; so is flexibility. Some hospitals are trying to use nurses more efficiently, reducing clerical work and other non-nursing tasks. The shortage has also improved the attitude of other health care workers such as doctors—nurses can no longer be taken for granted. Some other benefits offered at various hospitals include free tuition, bonuses, salary increases, greater flexibility in choosing hours of work, on-site child care, child care payment assistance (currently, 11% of all hospitals have on-site child care; this may sound low, but only 2% of all businesses provide it), and—very significantly— clearer career paths. It's a good time to be looking for a nursing job.

Several other trends: the average age of nursing school graduates is increasing, as older workers in other fields find themselves attracted to the profession as a second career. Part-time traveling "temp" nurses may make double what regular registered nurses make. They are available nationwide, usually for eight- to ten-week shifts. The best known is a New England firm with ten years experience: Travcorp Corporation, Malden, Massachusetts. Another trend continues: nursing certification as a way of recognizing advanced skills—with bonuses of up to $3,000 for certain specialties.

Other career options for nurses: nursing computer programmer, nursing legal consultant (who offers expert testimony in court cases), nursing scientist, medical equipment sales, and insurance expert. Expect nurses to find increasingly more lucrative employment in these specialties, and especially as nurse executives, who supervise nurses and nursing schedules, and earn executive-size salaries, often well into the six figures. Along with registered nurses, or RNs, demand will increase for licensed practical nurses, or LPNs. LPNs work under the direction of RNs or physicians; they must complete a training program of about a year.

▶ Physicians: outlook strong.

Medical technology is making medical care more exacting, more technical—which usually means more specialists are required. Another trend: expect more physicians to move into salaried jobs, particularly in competitive areas like the Northeast. Already, about half of young physicians work as employees for someone else. Salaries will remain very high on the average, but stagnant, with little growth.

Key outlook for the 1990s—good.

A growing shortage: family practice, particularly in rural areas. There are shortages now in many rural areas. These will remain throughout the 1990s, although more doctors are moving into this specialty.

Training note:

For those who can't afford the costs of medical school, the Department of Defense offers a free medical education to qualified college graduates between the ages of eighteen and twenty-seven (or thirty-one if you're already serving). Successful applicants are commissioned as officers, receive a salary in the mid-$20,000s, and agree to serve seven years in the Army, Navy, Air Force—or the Public Health Service.

For details, contact:

> Director of Admissions
> Dept. 9RD
> He'bert School of Medicine
> Uniformed Services University of the Health Sciences
> 4301 Jones Bridge Road
> Bethesda, MD 20814-4799

▶ Dentists: outlook bright.

Spending on dental care has increased by over 4% a year, and because of that spending, Americans have excellent teeth; but enrollment in dental schools has been down—and because of that, Americans need more dentists. The ratio of dentists to the total population is going down from about 60 per 100,000 today to 44.8 in 2020—the lowest since World War I. Meanwhile, an aging population needs more dental care, and pediatric dentistry is also a booming specialty. Another hot spot: cosmetic dentistry for adults.

▶ Health care managers: the odds are this profession will remain strong.

Cost-cutting and greater efficiency will be bywords in the health care industry for the rest of the 1990s, and managers who can deliver will be in demand. One question: will Clinton's streamlining of our health care reduce the need for managers?

Best areas: insurance firms, HMOs, long-term care, and other outpatient areas. Demand for services in these areas will be extremely strong. As hospitals consolidate functions, however, jobs in these traditional settings may decline somewhat.

Best preparation? An advanced degree such as a Masters in Health Administration (or, also applicable in some situations, an MBA).

Another bright spot for women: In 1988, women made up 60% of the master's graduates in health administration from across the country. And 80% of hospital salespeople (who sell their hospital services to physicians and the corporate community) are women.

▶ Veterinarians: high demand, particularly as economic recovery strengthens.

The 1990s will be a good time to enter veterinary medicine. Although the recession may have dampened prospects somewhat, demand is improving and the long-term outlook is excellent. Modern medical technology is entering the field, but, paradoxically, one of the aspects many veterinarians like best about their field is its "old-fashioned" feel; there is still time to deal one-on-one with owners and animal patients.

A few trends: more and more vets are women, and more and more vet school graduates are older people transferring to a second career. Female enrollments to vet school rise each year, male enrollments decline. Vet school itself lasts four years—but unlike human medicine, there is no time-consuming residency afterward. There are currently about 55,000 veterinarians practicing in the U.S., and shortages are predicted by some experts by the mid-1990s. The government projects employment growth to be between 26 and 35%, a strong growth trend, although competition for plum private practices could get tough in the later 1990s especially.

Best areas: specialty veterinary medicine—toxicology, pathology, academics. An interesting new specialty is wildlife veterinary medicine; traditionally, wildlife management has been the domain of ecologists. Two schools offering the program: the University of California, Davis, and the University of Wisconsin, Madison.

WHAT'S NEXT

▶ New job categories as health care becomes more specialized.

The first problem will be to separate some functions from nursing, letting nurses concentrate on the more intensive or technical aspects of patient care. One solution: a new job category, "registered care technician," to perform some of the "easier" tasks—like handling bedpans.

One way to ease the shortage of nurses might be to give nurses more autonomy on the job, make them partners to doctors. However good this idea sounds, it probably won't happen in most cases very soon, at least according to one expert. Reason: physicians are too protective of their status, perks.

▶ **Rise in outpatient facilities and services.**

Although hospitals currently employ the largest number of workers, the fastest-growing employment area will be in outpatient services. Between 1982 and 1988, the jobs in private hospitals rose by 10%, jobs in doctors' offices by 36%—and jobs in outpatient facilities by 81%. The Bureau of Labor Statistics expects this trend to continue, with growth rates of around 5% per year in the 1990s.

▶ **Geriatric medicine and health care: a booming specialty.**

Americans are living longer, and the associated problems of old age will become the focus of geriatricians, doctors who specialize in the medical problems of the elderly. In addition, old-age health care—at home and in nursing homes, hospices, and continuing care facilities—will raise demands for other geriatric health care workers.

Demand is strongest for: nurses, rehabilitation specialists, nursing assistants, and home care workers. Contact: The Gerontological Society of America (address is at the end of this section).

SALARIES

MEDICAL ASSISTANTS: average around $17,000.

PHYSICAL THERAPISTS: average starting salary about $26,000; mid-level, supervisory, and private practice, about $40,000.
Other therapists make similar salaries.

NUTRITIONISTS AND DIETICIANS: starting salaries in the low $20,000s, mid-career salaries from $25,000 to $30,000 average.

MEDICAL TECHNICIANS: salaries vary, beginning in the low 20s, mid-career in the mid-20s, supervisory in the low 30s. Highest salaries: nuclear medicine technologists.

NURSES: the average starting salary has reached over $30,000 in most areas in 1992; in 1989 salaries were $24,000–$26,000, with salaries lowest in the South and Midwest, in the low 20s, and highest in the Northeast and the West, with starting salaries up to the mid-30s, according to the *American Journal of Nursing*. Top average rates ranged from a low of $23,000 in Detroit to a high average of $56,000 in Boston. On the near horizon: higher salaries across the board—up to a $50,000 average for experienced nurses in Pennsylvania, up to $55,000 in Boston. Still lagging: the Midwest and South. Highest average pay for a specialty: Certified Registered Nurse Anesthetists (see Best Bets page 93).

The best and highest pay of all goes to *nurse executives*, who manage nursing care in hospitals. Recent surveys by Olney Associates, Witt Associates, and the American Organization of Nurse Executives reported salaries ranging from $42,000 to $170,000.

PHYSICIANS: Highly paid, but medical school expenses can exceed $100,000—and residential salaries may be less than $10 an hour, taking in account the number of hours worked. The average salary in 1990 was about $164,300. A survey by the AMA from 1992 showed that surgeons had the highest average incomes, $236,400 in 1990 and general practitioners the lowest at $102,700. Health care reform will likely squeeze salaries in the next few years.

DENTISTS: average gross is above $200,000, higher for specialists such as orthodontists.

HEALTH CARE EXECUTIVES: starting salaries in the mid-30s, mid- to upper-level salaries in the 50s, 60s, and 70s. CEOs earn from $100,000 to $300,000—commensurate with top managers in other industries. And salaries have been rising—even exceeding those in other industries.

PHARMACISTS: average salaries range between $40,000 and $45,000.

VETERINARIANS: average income about $45,000, more for those owning a private practice; starting incomes in the mid- to high $20,000s.

PHYSICIAN ASSISTANTS: earn $45,000 to $65,000 a year.

BEST BETS

NURSE ANESTHETISTS: certified nurses trained in anesthesiology. CRNAs are in high demand, receive the highest average pay of all nurses (starting salary about $50,000, rising up to $70,000), and in effect perform the same work as anesthesiologists do prior to surgery. Requirements: BS in nursing or related discipline (more for teaching and management positions), RN license, one-year experience in acute care prior to entry into a CRNA program, which lasts two to three years. Must pass a certifying exam after graduation.

Contact: American Association of Nurse Anesthetists—address is on page 94.

OPTOMETRISTS: Vision declines with age—and our aging population is one reason why this will be one of the fastest-growing careers in the 1990s. Note: optometrists are not MDs, but hold a Doctor of Optometry degree (a four-year professional degree) and are licensed after passing a state board exam. Unlike opthamologists, optometrists do not do eye surgery—but they diagnose eye problems, prescribe glasses, contacts, and work on vision therapy.

Advantages of the profession include reasonable hours, high pay (average salary over $60,000, those in established private practice more than $100,000), flexibility, and often personal autonomy—most are in private practice.

Contact: American Optometric Association—address is on page 95.

Fastest-Growing Health Professions

Career Area	Growth Rate to 2005
Home health aides	91.7
Physical therapists	76.7
Medical assistants	73.9
Radiological technicians/technologists	69.5
Medical secretaries	68.3
Medical scientists	66.0
Physical therapy aides	64.0
Psychologists	63.6
EEG technologists	57
Surgical technologists	55.2
Medical records technicians	54.3
Respiratory therapists	52.1
Podiatrists	46
Registered nurses	43.4
Nursing aides, etc.	43.4
Licensed practical nurses	41.9

WHERE TO GO FOR MORE INFORMATION

HEALTH CARE ASSOCIATIONS

American Academy of Physician Assistants
950 N. Washington St.
Alexandria, VA 22314
703/836-2272
(Publishes employment periodical with job listings, employment information, etc.)

American Association of Dental Assistants
919 N. Michigan Ave.
Chicago, IL 60611
312/664-3327

American Association of Homes for the Aging
901 E St., NW,
Suite 500
Washington, DC 20004

202/783-2242
(Publishes periodical for members with job listings.)

American Association of Medical Assistants
20 N. Walker Dr.,
Suite 1575
Chicago, IL 60606
312/899-1500

American Association of Nurse Anesthetists
216 Higgins Rd.
Park Ridge, IL 60068
708/692-7050

American Association of Occupational Health Nurses
50 Lenox Pt.

Atlanta, GA 30324
800/241-8014
(Publishes periodicals.)

American Association for Respiratory Care
11030 Ables Ln.
Dallas, TX 75229-4593
214/243-2272
(Publishes periodical with job listings.)

American Chiropractic Association
1701 Clarendon Blvd.
Arlington, VA 22209
202/276-8800
(Publishes directory, periodical with job listings, etc.)

American College of Healthcare Executives
840 North Lake Shore Dr., Suite 1103W
Chicago, IL 60611
312/943-0544
(Publishes members-only journal with job listings, directory, etc.)

American College of Sports Medicine
P.O. Box 1440
Indianapolis, IN 46206
317/637-9200
(Publishes career periodical with job listings.)

American Dental Association
211 E. Chicago Ave.
Chicago, IL 60611
312/440-2736
(Publishes periodicals with job listings, career booklets, etc.)

American Dental Hygienists Association
444 N. Michigan Ave., Suite 3400
Chicago, IL 60611
312/440-8900
(Publishes monthly periodical, accredits hygienists, etc.)

American Dietetic Association
216 W. Jackson Blvd., Suite 800
Chicago, IL 60606
312/899-0040
(Publishes periodical, career and educational information, etc.)

American Health Care Association
1201 L St., NW
Washington, DC 20005
202/842-4444

American Health Information Management Association
919 N. Michigan Ave.
Chicago, IL 60611
312/787-2672
(Publishes journal with job listings, directory, referral service, educational programs.)

American Hospital Association
840 N. Lake Shore Dr.
Chicago, IL 60611
312/280-6000
(Primarily for administrators; publishes periodical with openings; publishes directory of thousands of hospitals.)

American Medical Association
535 N. Dearborn St.
Chicago, IL 60610
312/645-5000
(The premier U.S. medical association; many affiliations; numerous services, including job placement; publishes periodicals with job listings, etc.)

American Medical Technologists
Registered Medical Assistant
710 Higgins Rd.

Park Ridge, IL 60068
708/823-5169
(For medical lab. technologists, medical assistants, etc.; offers placement services, various member services.)

American Nurses Association
2420 Pershing Rd.
Kansas City, MO 64108
816/474-5720
(Offers numerous services; operates placement service; publishes periodicals with job openings, etc.)

American Occupational Therapy Association
1383 Piccard Dr.
P.O. Box 1725
Rockville, MD 20852
301/948-9626
(Publishes journal, etc.)

American Optometric Association
243 N. Lindbergh Blvd.
St. Louis, MO 63141
314/991-4100
(Publishes journal with job listings, etc.)

American Osteopathic Association
142 E. Ontario St.
Chicago, IL 60611
312/280-5800
(Publishes directory, etc.)

American Pharmaceutical Association
2215 Constitution Ave., NW

Washington, DC 20037
202/628-4410
(Publishes periodicals
with job openings, etc.)

**American Physical
Therapy Association**
111 N. Fairfax St.
Alexandria, VA 22314
703/684-2782
800/999-2782
(Publishes periodical
with job listings, annual
conference with
placement services,
career information.)

**American
Physiological Society**
9650 Rockville Pike
Bethesda, MD 20814
301/530-7164
(Has career
information.)

**American Podiatric
Medical Association**
9312 Old Georgetown
Rd.
Bethesda, MD
20814-1621
301/571-9200,
(Publishes periodical
with job listings, etc.)

**American Public
Health Association**
1015 15th St., NW
Washington, DC 20005
202/789-5600
(The largest public
health association in the
world; publishes journal
with job listings,
maintains placement
service, directory, etc.)

**American Psychiatric
Association**
1400 K St., NW

Washington, DC 20005
202/682-6250
(Publishes periodicals
with many job listings,
including some for
non-M.D.s.)

**American Public
Health Association**
1015 15th St., NW
Washington, DC 20005
202/789-5600
(Publishes journal,
directory; has placement
service.)

**American Registry of
Diagnostic Medical
Sonographers**
2368 Victory Pkwy.,
Suite 41
Cincinnati, OH 45206
513/281-7111

**American Registry of
Radiologic
Technologists**
1255 Northland Dr.
Mendota Heights, MN
55120
612/687-0048
(Certification board.)

**American School
Health Association**
7263 State Rt. 43
P.O. Box 708
Kent, OH 44240
212/678-1601
(For health workers in
schools; placement
service, etc.)

**American Society of
Allied Health
Professions**
1101 Connecticut Ave.,
NW, Suite 700
Washington, DC 20036
202/857-1150

(Information about
educational/career
paths.)

**American Society of
Clinical Pathologists**
2100 W. Harrison
Chicago, IL 60612
312/738-1336
(Publishes periodical
with job listings, etc.)

**American Society of
Electroneurodiagnostic
Technologists**
204 West 7th
Carroll, IA 51401
712/792-2978

**American Society of
Hospital Pharmacists**
4630 Montgomery Ave.
Bethesda, MD 20814
301/657-3000
(Publishes periodical
with job listings, etc.)

**American Society for
Medical Technology**
2021 L St., NW,
Suite 400
Washington, DC 20036
202/785-3311
(For medical lab.
technicians; has
placement service, etc.)

**American Society of
Radiologic
Technologists**
15000 Central Ave., SE
Albuquerque, NM
87123
505/298-4500
(Publishes periodicals
with job listings, etc.)

**American Veterinary
Medical Association**
930 N. Meacham Rd.

Schaumburg, IL 60196
708/605-8070
(Publishes directory,
periodicals with job
listings, placement
service for members,
etc.)

**Association of
Operating Room
Nurses**
10170 E. Mississippi
Ave.
Denver, CO 80231
303/755-6300
(Publishes journal with
job listings.)

**Gerontological Society
of America**
1275 K St., NW,
Suite 3507
Washington, DC
20005-40006
202/842-1275
(Publishes periodical.)

**Healthcare Financial
Management
Association**
Two Westbrook
Corporate Ctr.
Suite 700
Westchester, IL 60154
708/531-9600
(Publishes periodical
with listings; maintains
job database for
members.)

**Medical Group
Management
Association**
1355 S. Colorado
Blvd., Suite 900
Denver, CO 80222
303/753-1111

**National Association
of Emergency Medical
Technicians**
9140 Ward Pkwy.
Kansas City, MO
64114
816/444-3500
(Offers placement
service, etc.)

**National Association
for Practical Nurse
Education and Service**
1400 Spring St.
Silver Spring, MD
20910
301/588-2491
(Publishes periodical,
career directory, etc.)

**National Commission
on Certification of
Physician Assistants,
Inc.**
2845 Henderson Mill
Rd., NE
Atlanta, GA 30341
404/493-9100
(Certifying body.)

**National Federation of
Licensed Practical
Nurses, Inc.**
P.O. Box 18088
Raleigh, NC 27619
919/781-4791

**National
Rehabilitation
Association**
1910 Association Dr.,
Suite 205
Reston, VA 22091
703/715-9090
(Publishes periodical
with job listings;
placement service, etc.)

**National Rural Health
Association**
301 E. Armour Blvd.,
Suite 420
Kansas City, MO
64111
816/756-3140
(Publishes periodical
with job listings;
placement service, etc.)

**National Society for
Cardiovascular
Technology/National
Society for Pulmonary
Technology**
1101 14th St., NW,
Suite 1100
Washington, DC 20005
202/371-1267
(Publishes periodicals
with job listings;
placement service, etc.)

**National Student
Nurses Association**
555 W. 57th St.
New York, NY 10019
212/581-2211

**Society of Diagnostic
Medical Sonographers**
12225 Greenville Ave.,
Suite 434
Dallas, TX 75243
214/235-7367

**Society of Nuclear
Medicine**
136 Madison Ave.,
8th Fl.
New York, NY 10016
212/889-0717
(Placement service,
etc.)

HEALTH CARE DIRECTORIES

Many of the associations listed above publish directories for various prices. Call for details. Below, we've listed some nonassociation directories.

Hospital Phone Book
Reed Reference
Publishing
121 Chanlon Rd.
New Providence, RI
07974
800/521-8110
(Thousands of numbers, etc., on hospitals nationwide.)

Nursing Career Directory
Springhouse Corp.

1111 Bethlehem Pike
Springhouse, PA 19477
215/646-8700

Nursingworld Journal Professional Career Guide
Prime National
Publishing Co.
470 Boston Post Rd.
Weston, MA 02193
617/899-2702

U.S. Medical Directory
Reed Reference
Publishing
121 Chanlon Rd.
New Providence, RI
07974
800/521-8110
(Extensive listings of health care facilities and practitioners.)

HEALTH CARE PERIODICALS

American Journal of Hospital Pharmacy
4630 Montgomery Ave.
Bethesda, MD 20814
301/657-3000
(Monthly; usually large number of job listings.)

American Journal of Nursing
555 W. 57th St.
New York, NY 10019
212/582-8820
(Monthly for members of the ANA.)

American Nurse
2420 Pershing Rd.
Kansas City, MO
64108
816/474-5720
(Monthly for R.N.s.)

American Pharmacy
2215 Constitution Ave., NW

Washington, DC 20037
202/429-7519
(Monthly.)

AORN Journal
10170 E. Mississippi
Ave.
Denver, CO 80231
303/755-6300
(Association magazine; many job listings for operating room nurses.)

Dental Assistant
919 N. Michigan Ave.
Chicago, IL 60611
312/664-3327
(Bimonthly to ADAA members.)

DVM: The Newsmagazine of Veterinary Medicine
1 E. First St.
Duluth, MN 55802
800/346-0085

(Monthly; includes job listings.)

Emergency: The Journal of Emergency Services
6300 Yarrow Dr.
Carlsbad, CA 92009
619/438-2511
(Monthly journal for EMTs, paramedics, etc.)

Healthcare Financial Management
2 Westbrook Corp. Ctr.
Westchester, IL 60154
708/531-9600
(Monthly for managers and workers in hospital accounting, etc.)

Health Facilities Management
737 N. Michigan Ave.
Chicago, IL 60611

312/440-6800
(Monthly for health
care center products
managers, etc.)

Hospital Pharmacy
E. Washington Sq.
Philadelphia, PA 19105
215/947-1752
(Monthly.)

Hospitals
737 N. Michigan Ave.
Chicago, IL 60611
312/440-6800
(Semimonthly magazine
for hospital
administrators.)

**Journal of the
American Veterinary
Medical Association**
930 N. Meacham Rd.
Schaumburg, IL 60196
708/605-8070

(Bimonthly magazine
with many listings.)

**Journal of the
American Dental
Association**
211 E. Chicago Ave.
Chicago, IL 60611
312/440-2736
(Nine-issue/year
periodical for members
of the American Dental
Association; carries job
listings, etc.)

**Journal of Dental
Hygiene**
444 N. Michigan Ave.
Chicago, IL 60611
312/440-8900

Nursing Management
103 N. 2nd St.
West Dundee, IL 60118
(Monthly magazine for
nurse supervisors.)

Nursing '93
1111 Bethlehem Pike
Springhouse, PA 19477
215/646-8700
(Monthly magazine.)

Nursingworld Journal
470 Boston Post Rd.
Weston, MA 02193
617/899-2702
(Monthly.)

RN
5 Paragon Dr.
Montvale, NJ 07645
312/358-7200
(Monthly magazine for
R.N.s.)

Veterinary Technician
425 Phillips Blvd.
Trenton, NJ 08618
609/882-5600
(Monthly magazine.)

INTERNATIONAL CAREERS

Brief Background

▶ **An international focus will be essential for the rest of the 1990s.**

Along with the increasing political and economic linkages in Europe, the other tremendous changes of the past few years—the collapse of the Soviet Union and the Warsaw Pact nations, the reunification of Germany, the economic revitalization of Mexico and much of South America—are pointing to the urgent need for highly trained, internationally competent employees in government and business and with nonprofit groups.

These changes come at a time when exports have become an increasingly important segment of our GNP, up from 9% of the U.S. economy to 21% today. No longer can many companies casually slough off exports as an afterthought. Ironically, few realize that this "new" globalism is in some senses a return to the years before World War I, when levels of international trade and investment were similarly high. However, the one significant difference between then and now: this time, the odds look good that global interdependence will increase further. This is just the beginning . . .

With these economic and political changes has come a new realization that the world is indeed interconnected and interdependent—we must all learn how to get along. Unlike those years before World War I, one can see the gradual evolution of stronger political, cultural, and technological ties, and (one hopes) a new global sensibility.

So, for those applicants with the right mixture of skills and area expertise, the challenges are there, but the future looks bright.

▶ **"The successful managers of the future will probably be those who speak both Japanese and English, who have a strong base in Brussels and contacts in the Pacific Rim, and who know the cafés and bars of Singapore."**

This description by the Conference Board, an independent association of management executives, summarizes a new reality: mainstream U.S. business is going global, and is beginning to understand the need for internationally trained managers. For years, this wasn't the case, but international assignments are now increasingly seen as a stepping stone to higher jobs. It is still a fact, however, that very often international skills are underrated, language expertise is underused or overlooked—and American business suffers the consequences. A survey of personnel managers at large U.S. multinational corporations reported that over 50% said foreign assignments could hurt or do nothing good for a person's career. This is changing rapidly. At many multinationals, international experience has gone from being a hindrance to being a necessity for top jobs.

Because the range of international jobs is tremendous, this section will cover only some of them—specifically, managerial teaching and government jobs abroad. For other positions, such as technical or medical positions, many of the same ideas apply. See those career sections for specifics.

EMPLOYMENT OUTLOOK: While the long-term outlook is still strong, in the short-term trade wars and local recessions may hinder job growth in some areas, particularly Europe.

▶ **Job seekers interested in international careers should remember one key bit of advice: The best way to get an international job is to already have a skill that can be used just as well at home.**

It's the same advice given year after year (in these pages as well), and it's worth repeating. Whatever you may read about looming shortages and job openings abroad, the best way to approach an international career is to develop a skill—from farming practices to health care management, from sales to economics—and *then* apply for international positions. The reason: most employers look for basics, not language skills, as the primary hiring prerequisite. Take a glance at any of the international job magazines (listed on page 117); you'll find most openings are technical- or business-oriented, with specific required skills listed. Of course, note also that language and cultural skills are often required; *both* are needed for a strong international resume.

▶ **Some good ways to get into a business career abroad: working for a large U.S. multinational, developing an international professional expertise, studying for an MBA abroad.**

Some of the largest international corporations are American—and many offer overseas assignments. *Fortune* magazine's listing of the world's biggest industrial corporations rates General Motors, Ford Motor Company, and Exxon as the three largest world firms—with General Electric as No. 6 and Mobil as No. 8. Yet don't stop there; much growth and employment during the second half of the nineties will be with smaller companies as well.

Most such international firms want their executives to have some overseas experience. A few examples: Merck has internationalized its training program, Dow Chemical wants future CEOs with experience running foreign operations. At least 80% of the top 300 executives at Xerox Corporation have had international experience. *Key to applying to these firms:* apply as a skilled expert *with* international expertise, not vice versa.

Another key trend: Many U.S. firms are now rapidly expanding international operations—with new branches and manufacturing facilities overseas. Increasingly, young MBAs are put right to work overseas—a change from past practices for many corporations.

The key to the next half of the 1990s: foreign trade.

But there are some hitches. Slower growth in Germany and Japan in 1993 meant the reduction of jobs in the U.S. at major exporting corporations. A slow recovery—or worse, a possible deterioration in these major markets—will hinder short-term employment prospects. Second, there's the possibility of continued trade wars, which might hinder employment. Nevertheless, the global economy is here to stay, and with it the long-term prospects for internationally oriented managers, marketers, trade finance experts, etc. will be strong. Second, the role of foreign language teachers and trainers will increase (see Teaching section, page 170, and below, page 106), particularly with corporations, as they recognize the importance of linguistic/cultural knowledge to business success. Third, the role of subsidiary international functions—such as U.S. international consulting, shipping brokers, and the like—will increase . . . along with hiring.

Another area of international jobs: various professions. The same rule of thumb applies—specialize in a professional or business area, along with an international area.

Some good bets:

INTERNATIONAL ACCOUNTING: Probably the best way to the top. According to the chief executive of Arthur Andersen, the next CEO would be "a person with experience outside the borders of the U.S. . . ." Fifty percent of Andersen's revenues were generated abroad last year. See Best Bets section on page 109.

INTERNATIONAL REAL ESTATE: According to a study by the major consulting firm Ferguson Partners, reported in *The New York Times*, the real estate firm of the next half of the nineties will be larger, possibly owned by foreign partners, and often with international branches. Needed: real estate execs with cultural and linguistic abilities to manage in this more international environment.

INTERNATIONAL HEALTH CARE EXECUTIVES: The market will be growing for U.S. health care executives again, after a downturn in the 1980s. Reason: much disillusionment with health care systems overseas, consequent demand for U.S. expertise. Best area: health care consulting (avoids the problem of lack of recent U.S. experience for returnees).

INTERNATIONAL FINANCE: Finance has gone international—better communications and less regulation have increased the flow of investment capital across borders. Problem: international banking has lost much of its luster since the loan problems of the eighties. The days of commercial bankers converging on potential customers in Dar-es-Salaam or Bahrain are over; lending to the Third World and Soviet bloc is more cautious. Best bet: concentrate on Asian financial services, international banking, merchant banking, currency trading. Key to this area: *most* finance is increasingly international, so no matter what area you specialize in, you will at some point be dealing in the international arena.

INTERNATIONAL LAW: Best route is to get a degree, join a top firm—and wait. Few jobs in international law right out of school. One way to utilize foreign language skills: immigration law. Currently an in-demand field. One problem: low prestige among some lawyers, law firms.

INFORMATION SYSTEMS: A potentially strong area—Europe. Particularly for U.S. managers with international experience, Europe will be a strong employer. One drawback: salaries and prestige are lower, but this is changing rapidly.

▶ Some large multinationals hire Americans for international jobs straight out of business school—European business school, that is.

Recruiting at various European business schools is up. One key advantage: getting the inside track in Europe. Recruiters in Europe like these grads because they know the European and world economies, are familiar with cross-cultural marketing; in short, they have firsthand experience in international management.

The competition is tough, partly because of fewer spaces. Only about 3,000 MBAs graduate from leading European schools each year (versus 70,000 in the U.S.). And prices are high. Some of the biggest names: INSEAD (Institut Euro-péan d'Administration) Business School, IMD (International Institute for Management Development), IESE (Instituto de Estudios Superiores de la Empresa), ISA, the London Business School. Also check out U.S. schools: The American Graduate School of International Management (Thunderbird); Wharton, which offers much in international management; Babson (in Wellesley, MA), which sends students on internships abroad.

▶ Where will the growth be in the new worldwide marketplace?

Look south and east. The hottest area in 1993 was Asia and the same will probably be true in 1994 as well. Not only the "Little Tigers" of Hong Kong, Singapore, and Taiwan, but also Malaysia, Thailand, Indonesia, and, most importantly, China itself are experiencing rapid growth. India, whose growth rate suffered a bit with the continued decline of Russia, is expected to do better in 1994 as well.

Latin America is another growth spot for the 1990s as well. U.S. export growth is expected to increase substantially to this region, as reforms continue and economies flourish. One potential problem: if NAFTA, the free-trade agreement, fails, trade levels could drop.

▶ A global economy also has a significant downside for job hunters.

There are many more highly qualified potential employees for American multinational corporations today than there were just a few years ago. The collapse of Communism opened an enormous job market to multinationals; so did the rise of telecommunications, which allows cheap and easy access to factories and employees overseas. Today, many U.S. firms farm out manufacturing and even service functions overseas; for example, an Irish branch of a major U.S. insurance firm handles U.S. insurance claims. This sort of outsourcing is perhaps inevitable—and it pays for *all* job hunters to be aware of the possibility that the job they're looking for in the U.S. may be sent overseas. *Key point:* keep up-to-date, flexible.

Employment spotlight: translators

Translators and interpreters (the first work with the written word, the second with the spoken) will be in demand throughout the 1990s, as borders open and international trade increases. The main areas of employment are government and international organizations (the Department of State and other agencies, the UN and related organizations), and, increasingly, businesses that deal in the international arena. Banks are a major employer—and freelance work, usually arranged through an agency, is another option. Starting salaries range from the mid-20s to the mid-30s.

Requirements: in addition to language proficiency, a BA is helpful, writing or speaking ability a must, a specialized knowledge of business, science, or diplomacy is even more helpful, and accreditation from the American Translators Association (ATA) is helpful and commands respect because the pass rate is a low 35%, according to the *Daily News*. Best areas: Japanese, European languages. Biggest demand: translation of Japanese patent applications into English, according to ATA, but demand is increasing for most positions. The *Wall Street Journal* reports that translators are beginning to organize and lobby—perhaps pointing to better salaries and working conditions in the near future.

For more information, contact: American Translators Association. Address is on page 116.

▶ **Many government agencies, international organizations, and non-profits offer specialized international career tracks.**

There are numerous options: working for U.S. agencies like the Department of State or Commerce, working for international governmental organizations, and working for foreign organizations. Some U.S. government options follow.

DEPARTMENT OF STATE: Most workers are employed as U.S. Foreign Service Officers (FSOs), although some are employed as civil service employees. FSOs work at embassies abroad and in Washington at the department. The news in 1992 was the creation of a slew of new embassies—from Armenia to Uzbekistan. There are four principal specialties or functional areas: political (diplomats in the classic sense, who report on foreign political developments, meet with Foreign Ministry counterparts, negotiate agreements, and brief other officials), economic, administrative, and consular (who issue visas, help U.S. citizens in distress).

If you're a successful applicant, you'll hear a lot about "needs of the service." This means that they, not you, have final say as to what functional and geographic area you'll go to—although you can (and should) learn how to politic well and acquire a good "corridor reputation," and get the postings you want.

Outlook for 1994: tough competition. About 25,000 people take the initial qualifying test, about 250 people eventually enter. In-demand language skills: Arabic, Chinese, Russian, Korean, Japanese, and now, most likely, some of the more exotic languages of Central Asia. Average age of applicants is thirty, but many older mid-career candidates are also entering.

Employment tip: In 1992, State released a paper which spoke of the shortage of—and urgent need for—employees trained in economics and business to master the shift diplomacy is now taking, away from geopolitics toward international commerce.

How to apply: The process is long and grueling; it may take well over a year to get a job. First, a written general knowledge test is given every December across the U.S. Those passing are informed by mail, and invited to select a date for interview. A panel travels the country and you probably will interview when they appear in your area. Or you can travel to Washington, DC, for an interview there. The interviewing process is an all-day affair that includes personal interviews, group exercises, and a written administrative "in-basket" test. You are given a ranking in all the functional areas based on your performance. You also must obtain a medical and security clearance. If all goes well, and your ranking is high enough, you will get an offer. Write: the Foreign Service Recruitment Branch—address is at the end of the section. Note: the application deadline for the annual December written test is in October.

U.S. INFORMATION AGENCY: USIA officers serve in Washington and embassies abroad as press officers, cultural affairs officers, and administrative support staff with a mandate to upgrade the U.S. image abroad. USIA manages exchange programs like the Fulbright; it runs libraries overseas. Newest trends from the previous year: the agency is discussing launching a small business initiative, in effect, to show and promote the success of capitalism in areas such as the old Soviet Union where few positive models exist. The USIA employs about 8,800 people, half of whom work at U.S. embassies in 128 nations. How to apply: see addresses on page 111.

The Voice of America (VOA), which is the official U.S. overseas network, is also under the USIA. It employs over 2,000 people, mostly foreign language specialists and technicians. For most other USIA jobs, taking the Foreign Service test is the first step—see the above address and description. For VOA jobs, contact: Voice of America; address is at the end of this section.

U.S. AGENCY FOR INTERNATIONAL DEVELOPMENT (USAID): AID runs U.S. economic aid abroad—its employees work in the U.S. and in about seventy developing countries worldwide, often out of embassies or field offices. While in many cases other aid groups get the glamour, AID gets the job done, quietly helping to avert famine in various parts of Africa, working to improve agricultural marketing, and so on.

There are two main avenues of employment, via the civil service (usually more limited, often staff positions in computers, etc), or via the Foreign Service. Addresses for both avenues are listed on page 110. AID has recently revamped its internship program, called the IDI (International Development Intern) program. It will be a two-tier system, with one track (75%) for senior candidates with graduate degrees, work and overseas experience, and language ability, and a junior track for those with ability but limited experience. The internship itself will now involve one year in Washington (two for junior interns) and one year overseas.

AID has recently announced that it intends to recruit from a broader background rather than from predetermined areas, although those with accounting, agricultural, economics, health care, urban planning, and engineering degrees and experience are highly represented at AID.

Mid-level hiring of noninterns will continue, but at only about 20% of the year's new hires. Minority recruitment is a priority for the agency. Contact: addresses on page 110.

PEACE CORPS: The ads say it: "The toughest job you'll ever love." And it *is* tough—serving in some of the most undeveloped areas of the world, only basic expenses paid, and at the end, about $200 for every month served, possible college credits, and career help. But looking back, many say it was the best or most transforming part of their lives. Some other advantages: language training, travel, noncompetitive eligibility for government employment.

Some 6,000 Americans work as volunteers in 84 countries nationwide—age range from eighteen to over eighty; most are single and college grads, although neither is a requirement. Terms of service are three months training and twenty-four months abroad—and you must be able to commit to spending all those twenty-seven months, although there is a fairly high dropout rate; 600 other Americans work as Peace Corps staff in Washington, 145 more at recruiting offices nationwide; another 200 or so Americans work as paid staff abroad. For staff positions, see address on page 111 and information on government employment on page 111, for volunteer positions see page 111.

In demand: volunteers with experience or degrees in agriculture, engineering, environment-oriented professions, fisheries, forestry, health, home economics, industrial arts, mathematics, nursing, most sciences, special education, technical (woodworking, metal, etc.), wildlife or resource management. Some 14,000 apply annually, 3,500 or so are chosen.

Employment tip: for those with liberal arts backgrounds, although you are eligible, you are not recruited actively. To enhance your chances—take courses in one of the degree areas above, get English as a second-language experience, learn Spanish, French, or Arabic, or show relevant experience.

DEPARTMENT OF COMMERCE: Overseas staffers include members of the Foreign Commercial Service. FCS officers serve in embassies and work to promote U.S. trade abroad and assist U.S. companies overseas. The application procedures are somewhat similar to those of the State Department.

Best bet: Jobs as commercial officers and counselors are excellent for mid-career business people who are bored, tired of the rat race, and want a change.

Other commerce jobs are in the International Trade Administration (ITA), the U.S. Travel and Tourism Administration (USTAA)—with offices abroad as well as in DC. See page 111.

Other U.S. government departments or agencies with international jobs include the Arms Control and Disarmament Agency (ACDA), the Central Intelligence Agency (CIA), the Defense Intelligence Agency (DIA), the Department of Agriculture (including the Foreign Agricultural Service [FAS]), the International Development Cooperation Agency (IDCA), the National Security Agency (NSA), and the Overseas Private Investment Corporation (OPIC).

Addresses are listed later in this chapter. For domestic agencies, see the Government section on page 57, and read the section on how to find and apply for specific civil service jobs.

Another option: working on congressional committee staffs in foreign affairs areas. The two key staffs are the **House Foreign Affairs Committee** and the **Senate Foreign Relations Committee** (see placement office addresses on page 84). Other staffs also include international orientation. *Requirements*: usually experience and degrees in international affairs, law, or economics. One of the best ways in is to have worked in a congressperson's office. Persons hired tend to be in their late twenties to early forties.

▶ **Outlook for other international jobs: fair, with much competition for the high-prestige areas.**

Rule of thumb: economists, technical specialists, and financial types do best—particularly when armed with an MBA or Ph.D. and significant experience.

Some international organizations:

THE UNITED NATIONS: Probably the toughest international organization to get into—political considerations make it even tougher, and budget tightening in the 1990s will make things harder. The UN offers high pay and perks, along with a large dose of politics.

Many UN jobs are filled through recommendations by the U.S. Department of State (for U.S. citizens). Specific UN agencies should be applied to directly. Addresses are listed at the end of the chapter.

THE WORLD BANK (officially the International Bank for Reconstruction and Development) and subsidiaries: charged with lending in developing countries, primarily infrastructure (dams, bridges, and roads) and agricultural lending, joint ventures, and investment settlement. Excellent pay and perks. *Best way to enter*: Young Professional Program. For experienced people usually in their late twenties, usually with MBA or Ph.D. and business, banking, or development experience. Training program rotates trainees through the Bank and its subsidiary arms; after about a year, trainees join a division. How to get in: applicants submit forms, transcripts, and recommendations, are interviewed several times, then selected. Very competitive.

Other international agency jobs—among many—include the International Monetary Fund (IMF), the General Agreement on Tariffs and Trade (GATT, an organization arising out of multilateral agreements to remove trade barriers), and the Organization of American States (OAS).

▶ **International teaching—for many, it's the only way to teach.**

It's not necessarily easy. Teaching posts can range from American schools in England or Germany to those in China or Central America; but some find it's an enjoyable option from the rigors of teaching in U.S. schools.

By far the largest employer of U.S. teachers is the Department of Defense, which runs the nation's ninth largest school system, with 270 schools in 20 countries with a staff of 13,000. Teachers who are hired work as members of the U.S. Government.

Another option: teaching at American overseas schools. Unlike the Defense schools, these are independent schools that depend on tuition payment—and they are often in more out-of-the-way places, usually in capital cities near U.S. embassies and other government and major corporate offices. The quality is generally high; students tend to be the children of U.S. diplomats. In both cases, salaries and benefits are usually very good, tuition for teacher's children is usually free, housing allowances are usually tax-free, the schools usually pay for storage of your U.S. household effects and/or the duty-free shipping of goods abroad.

Application instructions are on page 114.

▶ **Nonprofit sector: some competition and often low pay make this a tough (although rewarding) area.**

The competition for jobs heated up particularly during the recession—but also due to the increasing desire of many very competent people to do something significant with their lives.

Key problem: With the exception of rich foundations like the Ford Foundation, which has generous salary levels and working conditions, many nonprofits pay lower wages, particularly at low- to mid-level positions. For example, Save the Children advertised in 1990 for field director positions in various African countries at a (tax-free) salary of about $20,000. Upper-level positions sometimes pay considerably more.

The rewards should not be discounted, however. Amnesty International made the difference in the lives of many prisoners, many of whom would literally be dead without the organization's help. Save the Children, the Christian Children's Fund, and other organizations have had the same impact in many undeveloped nations.

Many nonprofits are a lot less lumbering and slow when it comes to action, and so they get things accomplished. There are some career advantages as well: firstly, nonprofits tend to be looser and more fun to work for—and at the same time may be very well run; secondly, they can be good places to get involved with and meet influential people; thirdly, the entire nonprofit area is just beginning to have a real impact now. Nonprofits are more than just secondary organizations—some of them have influence and power in their own right.

For some specific addresses, see the nonprofit organizations listed on page 111, and check *ACCESS* magazine, listed on page 118. This is an invaluable source of job listings for all types of nonprofit jobs.

WHAT'S NEXT

▶ **International jobs will become more of the mainstream.**

The reason is simple: the world is getting smaller. International concerns are everyone's concern—as is evident in the proliferation of individual U.S. state offices in Japan, the large number of foreign companies entering into joint ventures with U.S. companies, the rising levels of (and dependence on) business exports and imports overseas, the increasing interdependence of the world.

The inevitable outcome of this international focus: more jobs will have an international dimension—requiring one to three years in a foreign branch or subsidiary, or at least occasional overseas travel.

▶ Outlook for women: improving

Women make up only about 5% of those employed overseas. According to the Conference Board and a study by Moran, Stahl, & Boyer, these numbers should increase. An overwhelming majority of women working overseas were successful in their assignments, and even more conservative societies accepted their role as business managers.

The trend: increased overseas assignments. Most women are assigned to Europe (the U.K. has the highest percentage) or Canada, but hiring for jobs outside these areas should increase as well.

SALARIES

International salaries are impossible to categorize, as they vary widely according to industry or organization.

A few guidelines:

PRIVATE INDUSTRY: Check appropriate industry or career section.

DEPARTMENT OF STATE: Salaries are ranked similarly to the civil service, but by a Foreign Service rating. The entry-level salary is in the low $30,000 range, depending on qualifications.

PEACE CORPS: Living expenses, including a small stipend, paid during a volunteer's tour of duty; after a two-year tour, a readjustment allowance of $200 per month of duty is paid.

BEST BETS

INTERNATIONAL ACCOUNTING: Multinational business and foreign businesses and individuals in the U.S. have raised the demand for internationally trained accountants. Most of the work is handled by the top accounting firms, mostly the Big Six. Requirements: usually CPA and several years experience. Best languages: Japanese, French, Spanish, Portuguese.

UN GUIDE: For young people in their twenties. Guide jobs are easier to get than most UN jobs, are enjoyable, and can give a person at least a view of UN operations. Requirements: fluency in English and one other UN official language. Contact: see page 115.

WHERE TO GO FOR MORE INFORMATION

U.S. GOVERNMENT ORGANIZATIONS WITH AN INTERNATIONAL FOCUS

(*Important note:* See note on page 66 for important information on DC-area U.S. government agency phone numbers.)

Agency for International Development (AID)
Recruitment Division
PM/R
Washington, DC
20523-0114
202/663-2639
(Overseas development aid agency; above address is for Foreign Service positions; primarily hires accts., economists, development specialists, engineers, etc. Degree, two or more years' appropriate experience.)

Agency for International Development
Office of Personnel Management
Civil Service Personnel Division,
Room 1127, SA-1
Washington, DC
20523-0105
202/663-1491
(For civil service positions with AID; primarily hires acct., bus. admin., econ., and law background.)

Central Intelligence Agency
Personnel Representative (FCD)
P.O. Box 1925
Department S, Room 4N20
Washington, DC 20013
(Hires both operations personnel and analysts.)

Defense Intelligence Agency
Civilian Staffing
Operations Division (RHR-2)
Recruitment Program
Department OP
Washington, DC
20340-3042
202/373-2628
(Hires computer, science, foreign-area-studies specialists, etc.)

Department of State
Recruitment Division
P.O. Box 9317
Rosslyn Station
Arlington, VA 22209
703/875-7247
703/875-7242
(summer clerical)
703/875-7207
(student program inquiries)
703/875-7490 (24-hr. job hot line)
(For Foreign Service employment.)

Department of State
Staffing Services Division
Office of Civil Service Personnel (PER/CSP),
Room 2429
Washington, DC 20520
202/647-7172
703/875-7242 (student program inquiries)
202/647-7284 (24-hr. job hot line)
(Civil service jobs include those for applicants with accounting, banking, business admin.,

computer, finance, management degrees, etc.)

Export-Import Bank of the United States
Personnel Director
811 Vermont Ave., NW
Washington, DC 20571
202/566-8834
(Employees, usually with banking, finance, accounting, or computer backgrounds, work in DC and facilitate export financing of U.S. goods and services overseas.)

Foreign Agricultural Service
Recruitment Officer
FAS Personnel
South Bldg., Room 5627
Washington, DC
20250-1000
202/720-1587
(Employees work as attachés, etc., in U.S. embassies abroad.)

International Trade Administration
Personnel Officer
14th St. and Constitution Ave., NW, H4211
Washington, DC 20230
202/377-1533
(Promotes U.S. exports, advises on policy, hires primarily economics/business/marketing/finance backgrounds.)

International Trade Commission
Office of Personnel
500 E St., SW
Washington, DC 20436
202/377-2000

National Security Agency
Office of Civilian Personnel
Recruitment Branch
Attn: M322
Fort Meade, MD 20755-6000
1-800/255-8415
(Security agency principally concerned with signal intelligence, codes, computer security, foreign intelligence. Hires, linguists, technicians, computer experts, etc. Much testing and interviewing before hiring.)

Peace Corps
Office of Personnel
1990 K St., NW,
Room 7007
Washington, DC 20526
202/254-5170
1-800/424-8580, ext. 225
202/775-2214 (24-hr. hot line)
(For staff positions.)

Peace Corps
Office of Recruitment/Public Response Unit
1990 K St., NW, 9th Fl.
Washington, DC 20526
202/376-2550
1/800/424-8580, ext. 93
(For volunteer positions.)

Travel and Tourism Administration
Office of Personnel Administration
14th St. and Constitution Ave., NW, H-1069
Washington, DC 20230
202/377-5138
(Encourages and supports tourism *to* the United States; hires business/marketing/statistical majors.)

U.S. and Foreign Commercial Service
Office of Foreign Service Personnel,
Room 3226
14th St. and Constitution Ave., NW
Washington, DC 20230
(Employees work in United States and in embassies abroad promoting U.S. goods and services.)

U.S. Information Agency
Office of Personnel
Special Services Branch
301 4th St., SW
Washington, DC 20547
202/619-4665
202/619-4539 (24-hr. hot line)
(Employees work in DC and in embassies abroad promoting U.S. policies, administering programs such as the Fulbright scholarships, etc.)

U.S. Mission to the United Nations
Personnel Office
799 United Nations, Plz.
New York, NY 10017
212/415-4000

Voice of America
Office of Personnel
330 Independence Ave., SW,
Room 1543
Washington, DC 20547
202/619-3117
202/619-0909 (24-hr. job hot line)

NONPROFIT ORGANIZATIONS: INTERNATIONAL AID-ORIENTED

ACCION International
130 Prospect St.
Cambridge, MA 02139
617/492-4930
(Sponsors limited capital small business projects in South America, workshops.)

American Friends Service Committee
1501 Cherry St.
Philadelphia, PA 19102
215/864-0104
(Primarily an overseas development organization.)

American Near East Refugee Aid
1522 K St., NW, No. 202
Washington, DC 20005
202/347-2558

American Organization for Rehabilitation Through Training
American ORT Federation
817 Broadway
New York, NY 10003
212/677-4400
(Originally organized to help Jews in czarist Russia; now the largest nongovernment vocational organization.)

American Refugee Committee
Director, International Programs
2344 Nicollet Ave., Suite 350
Minneapolis, MN 55404
612/872-7060.
(Medical personnel; primarily volunteers.)

Americares Foundation
161 Cherry St.
New Canaan, CT 06840
203/966-5195
(Organizes relief; trains; and sends medical supplies, etc., to Africa, Asia, etc.)

Amideast (American Friends of the Middle East)
American-Mideast

Educational and Training Services
1100 17th St., NW, Suite 300
Washington, DC 20036
202/785-0022

Appropriate Technology International
International Director, Finance and Administration
1331 H St., NW
Washington, DC 20005
202/879-2900
(Engineering, economics, or business background; Spanish or French preferred for applicants for this ''human-sized'' technology development group.)

CARE, Inc.
660 First Ave.
New York, NY 10016
212/686-3110
(One of the largest international/technical assistance organizations; hundreds of employees; experience in developing countries with appropriate degree preferred.)

Catholic Relief Services
209 W. Fayette St.
Baltimore, MD 21201
301/625-2220
(Large development organization operating worldwide.)

Childreach
155 Plan Way
P.O. Box 400
Warwick, RI 02887
401/738-5600
(Provides aid in Asia, Africa, Latin America, etc.)

Christian Children's Fund, Inc.
203 E. Cary St.
Richmond, VA 23251
804/644-4654
(Supports children and their communities in undeveloped areas abroad.)

Church World Service
475 Riverside Dr.
New York, NY 10115-0050
212/870-2061
(Sponsors community development, relief services.)

Compassion International
P.O. Box 7000
3955 Craigwood Dr.
Colorado Springs, CO 70933-7000
719/594-9900
(Relief services primarily for children overseas.)

Food for the Hungry International
7807 E. Greenway Rd.
Scottsdale, AZ 85260
602/951-5090
(Food relief and development abroad.)

Freedom from Hunger Foundation
1644 Da Vinci Ct.

P.O. Box 2000
Davis, CA 95616
916/758-6200

Inter-American Foundation
1515 Wilson Blvd.
Rosslyn, VA 22209
703/841-3868
(Promotes development
in Latin America.)

International Rescue Committee
386 Park Ave. S.
New York, NY 10016
212/679-0010
(Aids in counseling,
resettling refugees.)

Oxfam-America
115 Broadway
Boston, MA 02116
617/482-1211
(Sponsors integrated
rural development, food
aid in poorest parts of
the world; about fifty
U.S. employees,
hundreds abroad.)

Pearl S. Buck Foundation
P.O. Box 181
Perkasie, PA 18944
215/249-0100
(Aids Amerasian
children, etc.; about
200 emloyees.)

Save the Children Federation, Inc.
54 Wilton Rd.
Westport, CT 06880
203/226-7271

Winrock International
Rte. 3
Morriltown, AR
72110-9537
501/727-5435
(Agricultural
development, technical
assistance; about a
hundred employees in
United States and
abroad.)

NONPROFIT ORGANIZATIONS: THINK TANKS, OTHER POLICY-ORIENTED, AND HUMAN RIGHTS

Amnesty International
322 Eighth Ave.
New York, NY 10001
(Premier human rights
organization worldwide;
fights for political
prisoners, etc.)

Asia Foundation
P.O. Box 3223
San Francisco, CA
94119
415/982-4640

Brookings Institution
1775 Massachusetts
Ave., NW
Washington, DC 20006
202/797-6000
(Premier research
organization; one
program is Foreign
Policy Studies, over
200 staff.)

Carnegie Endowment for International Peace
2400 N St., NW
Washington, DC 20037
202/802-7900
(Publishes *Foreign Policy* magazine; about
a hundred employees.)

Center for Strategic and International Studies
Personnel Director
1800 K St., NW, Suite
400
Washington, DC 20006
202/887-0200

Chicago Council on Foreign Relations
Vice President and
Program Director
116 S. Michigan Ave.

Chicago, IL 60623
312/726-3860

Council on Foreign Relations
Personnel Manager
58 E. 68th St.
New York, NY 10021
212/734-0400
(Publishes *Foreign Affairs;* about a hundred
employees, mostly
Ph.D.s, regional
committees.)

East/West Center
1777 East-West Rd.
Honolulu, HI 96848
808/944-7111
(More than 200
employees; founded by
Congress to promote
Asian-American
understanding.)

RAND
1700 Main St.
Santa Monica, CA
90407
213/393-8500
(Premier research
institute; much national
security, public welfare
research; over 500
professionals employed,
mostly Ph.D.s.)

SRI International
333 Ravenswood Ave.
Menlo Park, CA

94205-3493
415/326-6200
1611 N. Kent St.
Arlington, VA 22209
703/524-2053
(Consulting and
technical research on
contract for U.S. gov't.
and international
agencies; one of the
premier think tanks in
the world, with over
three thousand

employees, many
Ph.D.s.)

Tinker Foundation
55 E. 59th St.
New York, NY 10022
212/421-6858
(Promotes better
relations between
Hispanic and
Portuguese-speaking
nations and United
States.)

TEACHING ABROAD

**Fulbright Teacher
Exchange**
U.S. Information
Agency
Teacher Exchange
Branch E/ASX
Washington, DC 20547
1-800/726-0479
(Academic year and
shorter exchange
program for teachers,
grad. students, etc., in
various countries in
Europe, Asia, and
Africa. Deadline for the
next academic year is
usually in mid-October;
information packet
contains application,
host countries, and full
details.)

**International School
Service, Inc.**
P.O. Box 5910
Princeton, NJ 08543
609-452-0990
(This is a major
recruiter for
non-Department of
Defense U.S. overseas

schools worldwide; they
list positions
worldwide, often in
exotic areas such as
Fiji.)

**Office of Overseas
Schools**
Room 234, SA-6
U.S. Department of
State
Washington, DC 20520
(This is the Department
of State office that
handles overseas
schools that the children
of diplomatic and other
personnel attend. These
are *not* official USG
schools—there is no
central "Foreign
Service" of teachers at
State, and unlike
teachers with the
Department of Defense
schools, teachers are
not USG employees.)

**U.S. Department of
Defense Dependents
Schools**

U.S. Department of
Defense
Recruitment and
Assignment Section
2461 Eisenhower Ave.
Alexandria, VA 22331
(Annual listing and
application for teaching
and related jobs at
Department of Defense
schools overseas.)

WorldTeach
Harvard Institute for
International
Development
1 Elliot St.
Cambridge, MA 02138
617/495-5527
(Primarily for
volunteers; successful
applicants teach or
coach abroad for one
year and receive
housing and a small
salary. Teaching
experience and foreign
language are not
necessary.)

PUBLIC INTERNATIONAL ORGANIZATIONS

**International
Monetary Fund**
Recruitment and
Training Division
700 19th St., NW
Washington, DC 20431

**Pan American
Sanitary Bureau**
Pan American Health
Organization
Regional Office of the
World Health
Organization
525 23rd St., NW
Washington, DC 20037

United Nations
General Service Staffing
Section
1 United Nations Plz.
New York, NY 10017
212/963-1234 (general
employment
information)
212/963-8876 (more

specific information;
call between 3 and 5
P.M.)
(For U.N. clerical,
secretarial, U.N. guide
jobs, etc. Call above
numbers; or write with
full details of
background and job
desired; or go to office
Monday to Friday
between 10 A.M. and
noon.)

**U.N. Children's Fund
(UNICEF)**
Division of Personnel
Recruitment and
Placement Section
3 United Nations Plz.
New York, NY 10017

**U.N. Development
Program**
Division of Personnel

1 United Nations Plz.
New York, NY 10017

U.N. Population Fund
220 E. 42nd St.
New York, NY 10017

U.N. Secretariat
Office of Personnel
Services
Recruitment Programs
Section
New York, NY 10017

**World Bank,
International Finance
Corporation (IFC),
and Multilateral
Guarantee Agency
(MIGA)**
Vice President of
Personnel
1818 H St., NW
Washington, DC 20433

OTHER JOB SOURCES FOR WORKING ABROAD: MOSTLY TEMPORARY, SHORT-TERM, OR VOLUNTEER

**Association for
International Practical
Training**
10400 Little Patuxent
Pkwy.,
Suite 250
Columbia, MD
21044-3501
410/997-2200
(For students in
engineering, sciences,
etc.; arranges overseas
exchanges with
on-the-job training or
research; for recent
graduates also offers

exchange programs in
culinary,
hospitality/tourism.)

**CDS International
Internship Program**
300 Seventh Ave.
New York, NY 10001
212/760-1400
(For business, etc.,
college seniors; offers
intensive
German-language
training, then five
months internship with
German firms.)

Exchange Division
The American-
Scandinavian
Foundation
725 Park Ave.
New York, NY 10021
212/879-9779
(For recent graduates
twenty-one to thirty-five
years old, with a few
years' experience in
agriculture, banking,
etc.; provides six- to
eighteen-month training
internships in
Scandinavian countries.

Note: Other foundations may offer similar exchange programs.)

International Christian Youth Exchange
134 W. 26th St.
New York, NY 10001
212/205-7307
(Offers scholarships;

places volunteers abroad for a year in various positions—teacher, literacy, medical, environmental—and provides housing.)

Work, Study, Travel Abroad: The Whole World Handbook

1991–1993
St. Martin's Press, 1992; available at bookstores and libraries (Describes over 1,200 hundred study or work opportunities abroad, including many volunteer work and internships.)

INTERNATIONAL ASSOCIATIONS

American Translators Association
1735 Jefferson Davis Hwy.,
Suite 903
Arlington, VA 22202-3413
703/412-1500
(Accredits translators; publishes periodical

with listings; lists university translation courses; directory)

International Studies Association
216 Herald Clark Bldg.
Brigham Young University
Provo, UT 84602

(Publishes periodical with academic job listings.)

National Foreign Trade Council
1270 Ave. of the Americas
New York, NY 10020
212/399-7128

INTERNATIONAL DIRECTORIES

America's Corporate Families and International Affiliates; Principal International Business; The World Marketing Directory; Latin America's Top 25,000
Dun's Marketing Services
3 Sylvan Way
Parsippany, NJ 07054
1-800/526-0651
201/455-0900

Directory of American Firms Operating in Foreign Countries
World Trade Academy Press
50 E. 42nd St.
New York, NY 10017
212/697-4999

Encyclopedia of Geographic Information Sources,

International Volume
Gale Research, Inc.
835 Penobscot Bldg.
Detroit, MI 48226
800/877-4253

The Fortune World Business Directory
Time Warner
Rockefeller Center
New York, NY 10020
212/586-1212

INTERNATIONAL PERIODICALS

Business International
215 Park Ave.
New York, NY 10003
212/460-0600

Community Jobs
ACCESS
50 Beacon St.
Boston, MA 02108
617/720-5627
(Hundreds of nonprofit
jobs; career centers.)

The Economist
10 Rockefeller Plz.
New York, NY 10020
212/541-5730
(London-based
internationally oriented
general newsmagazine;
carries some job
listings.)

Euromoney
Quadrant Subscription
Services
Oakfield House,
Perrymount Rd.
Haywards Heath, W.
Sussex RH16 3DA
England
(+44) 0444/440421
FAX: (+44)
0444/440619
(Major international
finance magazine.)

Euroweek
c/o Kay Parkinson
Subscription
Department
Euromoney Publications
PLC
Nestor House,
Playhouse Yard
London EC4V 5EX

England
(+44) (0) 71/779-8614
FAX: (+44)
71/779–8617

*Far Eastern Economic
Review*
Review Publishing
Company Ltd.
240 Valley Dr.
Brisbane, CA 94005
415/468-8840
(Influential weekly
business affairs
magazine for the Pacific
basin.)

*Federal Career
Opportunities*
P.O. Box 1059
Vienna, VA
22185-1089
703/281-0200
(Biweekly listing all
types of U.S.
government jobs, in
United States and some
overseas.)

Financial Times
14 E. 60th St.
New York, NY 10022
212/752-4500

Foreign Affairs
58 E. 68th St.
New York, NY 10021
212/734-0400
(Influential policy
journal.)

Foreign Policy
11 DuPont Circle, NW
Washington, DC 20036
202/797-6428

*Foreign Service
Journal*
2101 E St., NW
Washington, DC 20037
202/338-4045
(Monthly; can be useful
background for Foreign
Service test.)

Global Finance
11 W. 19th St.
New York, NY 10011
212/337-5900
(Monthly magazine.)

Global Trade
North American
Publishing
401 N. Broad St.
Philadelphia, PA 19108
215/238-5300

International Business
500 Mamaroneck Ave.
Harrison, NY 10528
914/381-7700
(Monthly; circulation
40,000.)

*The International
Educator*
TIE
P.O. Box 103-EP
West Bridgewater, MA
02379

*International
Employment Hotline*
P.O. Box 3030
Oakton, VA 22124
703/620-1972
(Job listings
overseas—wide range
includes corporations,
U.S. government, and
foreign organizations
and governments.)

*International
Employment Gazette*
1525 Wade Hampton
Blvd.
Greenville, SC 29609
800/882-9188
(Biweekly; contains
hundreds of listings;
many multinational
business jobs, heavy
emphasis for
engineering, education,
and business
backgrounds; some
gov't./U.N.-type jobs
as well; also offers
other services.)

*International Jobs
Bulletin*
University Placement
Woody Hall B-208
Southern Illinois
University at
Carbondale
Carbondale, IL 62901
618/453-2391
(Bimonthly listing of
about a hundred
international
jobs—legal, business,
medical, nonprofit,
etc.)

*International
Management*
McGraw-Hill
1221 Avenue of the
Americas
New York, NY 10020
1-800/262-4729

*Overseas Employment
Services*
P.O. Box 460
Town of Mount Royal
Quebec, H3P 3C7
Canada
514/739-1108

MANAGERS

▶ **How to succeed as a manager in the next half of the 1990s: be multi-lingual, a generalist with technical skills, computer literate, a doer not a follower, a team player—or a team leader.**

That's the ideal, and as corporate America "downsizes" and sheds middle managers, many are contemplating the immense revolutionary changes that have occurred in the past few years. A brief summary:

- **The "lean and mean" corporation is here to stay.** The middle levels of bureaucracy that were cut will stay cut, and more cuts at many firms are in the offing. Bottom line: the managers who are left won't push paper so much as lead people, or supervise technical projects.

- **Low-level managers will deal directly with nonmanagement people.** There won't be layers of supervisors and quasimanagers in between. Company organization charts will become flatter—more people will deal with each other as equals.

- **Competition will be fiercer, faster, and smarter.** Computer technology and the simple faster pace of things means that companies must be fast and flexible to survive.

- **Corporations will compete globally.** It's a cliché, but it bears repeating. Exports have been the engine of our economic growth; and like it or not, our corporations must sell abroad and face down foreign competitors at home to survive.

- **Corporations will be more involved with the public, with government, and with environmental concerns.** In some cases, corporations will take over government functions; in all cases, they must sensitize themselves to the growing diversity of our population, and our growing environmental concerns.

- **Finally and most importantly, the corporation of the 1990s will assume you have technical skills but emphasize "soft" skills—the ability to lead people, think creatively, understand the big picture and relate it to**

technical areas. Already, General Electric management training programs are emphasizing these soft skills, instead of the more technical, "hard" aspects of management traditionally taught in business schools.

This isn't to say the old ways are gone, or that the new ways will be achieved fully. But the consensus is that they will be the key to success in the competitive nineties.

Note: This section covers primarily general managers. For more specifics, see the appropriate section. For example, for managers in finance, see the Financial Services section, Accountants section, and Banking section. For trends and jobs in specific industries or areas, see the appropriate sections in the Industry section.

EMPLOYMENT OUTLOOK: Long-term outlook good for people with the right mix of technical skills and general background; short-term tough as readjustments to corporate downsizing occur. Best for engineers with managerial skills, technically competent applicants with broad backgrounds; health-care professionals

▶ **Management reorganization—from pyramid to pancake.**

This has been *the* organizational change of the past few years—and it looks like for much of U.S. business, it is here to stay. This is not to say that bureaucracies will cease to exist, but watch for continued change, continued "debureaucratization." The key reasons: *Speed.* Companies are emphasizing faster response time and product development, both of which are easier to achieve with fewer layers of managers to go through. *Cost.* The recession prompted a deeper appreciation for the virtues of frugality, which includes keeping staff levels down.

▶ **Don't expect a turnaround in middle management jobs.**

Simply put, the cutbacks are here to stay. Since the mid-1980s, well over 1 million management jobs were cut by corporate America—some experts say that one third of all middle management jobs were eliminated. Some predict that as much as a quarter of the current job force may still face pink slips.

Key point: these cuts are permanent. Behind all the talk of "virtual corporations" and "modular corporations" is a potent trend: corporations have focused on core businesses—and are outsourcing virtually everything else. What does this mean in terms of employment? Fewer middle managers—and those who are chosen will face a different environment. In effect, managers will *ally* themselves with a corporation temporarily, in a sense like contract employes. They will face an average of four or five different jobs during their careers.

But does this mean the long-term employment outlook is grim? Not for the right manager. In fact, the Bureau of Labor Statistics predicts strong employment growth for managers in general—between 20 and 50% to the year 2005, assuming a moderate growth rate. But there's a hitch—you must be a manager with strong "people" skills and be able to work in a team in a highly flexible environment.

Outlook: Tougher competition, more selective hiring practices, more people willing to relocate, more managers working for smaller and mid-size firms, more entrepreneurship.

Corporations will be looking for:

- **Broader responsibility:** Without many layers, managers must take direct responsibility for more projects.

- **More people to supervise:** "First-line managers of the nineties will lead forty to fifty people, not the ten of today," according to J. Stead of Square D Company.

- **Tougher hiring practices:** Be prepared to defend what you can do, and why. Complacency is out.

- **At least lip service to the ideal manager concept of the 1990s:** A "people person," generalist with technical skills, etc.

- **Computer competence:** Forget programming languages, but remember how to use and understand the computer and various key programs. Computers will be an increasingly common communications, thinking, and decision-making tool—a "utility," in the word of one executive.

▶ **Beyond all the advantages (and the hype), the changes are not necessarily for the better—for the employee.**

As organizations lose middle layers of managers, the workload doesn't diminish. It gets larger for the middle managers remaining. A *Wall Street Journal* article described the new regime at a Corning, Inc., plant—managers averaged 70- to 80-hour weeks. Responsibilities are fuzzier: low-level managers, accustomed to following orders, may now be giving them, setting strategy. Another problem: with flatter organizations, it may be harder to get promotions.

But beyond speed, there is another key advantage of this new organizational set-up, whether managers like it or not. Now that they are not insulated from the daily workings of their business by layers of middle managers, they *must* know their business from the bottom up. This should improve American competitiveness.

One increasingly dead-end area in management: *headquarters staff*. It used to be a fast track to the top; now line responsibility carries more weight. According to a survey by *Fortune* magazine, 42% of CEOs say staffs are weaker in power now than five years ago; in terms of size, 36% reported staffs shrinking or stable. Also down: strategic planners.

One trend gaining steam: The hiring of outside managers. Companies will seek motivated leadership, whether from within or outside the corporation.

▶ **What happened to the golden MBA?**

At the time of writing, the debate was in full swing: Is the MBA on a declining trend, or was it just the recession?

Tentative conclusion: The best MBA schools are here to stay, but an economic shake-out will reduce the number of MBA schools. Nevertheless, the MBA has probably depreciated to the extent that it, and its holders, will be scrutinized more carefully than before.

Bottom line: What the managerial applicant can do, MBA or not, will be the key hiring factor. Simply put, there is an enormous pool of qualified MBAs in the employment marketplace. Each year, 75,000 new graduates come on stream. Prediction: According to *Forbes*, more MBA schools will be specializing—MIT in real estate and technology, Northwestern in marketing, Wharton in international management. Duke University has begun a Small-Business Studies section.

▶ **A major trend: self-employment.**

By 2005, one-third of the increase in self-employed workers—*half a million jobs*—will occur among managers, administrators, and executives. Why? Partly from all those layoffs mentioned above. Many executives, realizing their relatively poor chances of matching their previous salaries/responsibilities, are taking their payouts and investing in their own businesses. Another reason: the baby-boom generation wants *control*.

▶ **Strong—some say cutthroat—competition for most top jobs as the baby boomers reach top management ages, and much the same for all jobs for younger job seekers.**

Problem: too many baby boomers chasing too few top management jobs. Adding to the problem: the cutback in middle management positions. There is an increasing number of well-qualified, ambitious employees who are competing for fewer positions.

Probable result: more self-employment, more movement to smaller companies by baby boomers and the generations beneath them. A prediction: Look for an *explosion* of entrepreneurial talent and ideas in the next few years. Baby boomers who want it all may get it after all—on their own terms. And for those who are younger—demographics (and time) is on your side in the long term.

But for the short term, those members of the so-called Generation X or 13 (born after 1961) face the double problem of competing for a smaller number of jobs—as well as competing *within* the workplace with younger baby boomers. They currently earn on average 20 to 30% less than baby boomers did at their age.

▶ **Some career advice for 1994 for younger managers in particular.**

Look at smaller companies. The class of 1992 saw hiring down almost across the board—business/finance degree hiring was down 16%, liberal arts was down 5%—but many of the most successful managerial applicants found jobs with smaller corporations. The Small Business Association found in a study that small businesses of less than 500 employees will create 70% of all new jobs; even if you discount these figures, you can see that opportunities are there.

▶ **What looks good for 1994 and beyond?**

First of all, a warning. After the slump in the early 1980s, very few people predicted that a boom was coming in financial services—and financial services employment. The predictions below are a reflection of what the experts are saying *now*; but unforeseen circumstances, particularly in these days, have a way of cropping up.

Some good bets:

- **Management consulting:** strong during the recession; as companies continue to downsize, corporations may continue to rely on consultants to do what staff is unavailable to do. On the downside: a fairly large number of corporations reported dissatisfaction with consulting services.

- **Wholesaling:** This fragmented industry, employing over 6 million people, is projected to grow about 2.2% per year. According to government projections, significant increases in wholesale exports over the rest of the 1990s will stimulate employment growth in the entire industry.

- **Health care:** Hospitals and health care organizations are predicted to be major growing employers of administrative and executive talent in the next five years. Some good areas: general administration, cost-control jobs.

- **Supermarket chains:** according to industry sources, 680,000 new jobs will be opening in chains—with more challenging managerial and marketing jobs for skilled applicants.

- **Environmental management:** $115 billion will be spent on environmental projects.

- **Pharmaceutical management:** One industry where the U.S. is strong—and strategically minded managers are needed. Regardless of stock market volatility, this area is poised for long term growth, particularly as pharmaceutical corporations strain to squeeze profits out of efficiency and sales growth, rather than price growth, which is now politically unacceptable. (For more information, see Health Care industry section, page 369.)

- **Computer management:** Cutbacks and a changeable environment, particularly in the economic climate now, plus consolidations and shake-outs, have been making employment in this area unstable. Nevertheless, this is still a growth industry with continued enormous potential. Best for the 1990s: marketing managers—particularly hot as companies try to differentiate product. (See Computers and Electronics, page 298.)

- **Restaurant management:** About 500,000 people are currently employed in this field. It is projected as a long-term growth area—one out of two meals is now eaten outside the home. Downside: highly volatile industry. A growing area: international. About seventy U.S. restaurant chains have international outlets, more expected.

- **Financial management:** Financial managers are involved in strategic planning, currency swaps and (increasingly) barters, and more and more with the crucial planning for overseas acquisitions and trade. As the intellectuals in the corporate hierarchy (the average chief financial officer is more apt to have an MBA or even a Ph.D., according to *BusinessWeek*), financial managers can aspire to the number-three spot in the corporation—but increasingly not beyond. The specialty is now often seen as too narrowly focused for visionary leadership.

• **Property management:** The long-term trend is good, particularly because housing, retail stores, etc., are increasingly situated in centralized developments—run by property, mall, apartment, or housing complex managers. Downside: real estate downturns may significantly affect short-term job prospects.

One related area: *golf, country club managers* are in short supply, high demand in some areas. Reason: increasing complexity, broad nature (from maintenance to wine) of responsibility. Salaries are high—from $60,000 to $170,000, according to the *Wall Street Journal*.

• **Facilities management:** A long-term best bet. Facilities managers literally manage the physical structure and assets of a company or organization—from the real estate side to furniture to everyday maintenance. Reasons for growth: increasing cost-consciousness, need for effective cost control and planning. Only now is this area becoming a full-fledged specialty. According to *The New York Times*, training is scarce, confined to less than twenty-five colleges, including MIT, Iona, North Dakota State, and Brigham Young, among others. Best background: BA in facilities management, MBA. For more information: contact International Facility Management Association, page 129.

• **Human resources (HR):** Predicted to grow 32 percent by 2005, according to a moderate economic growth scenario by the government. Fastest-growing area: training. Entry-level jobs as employment interviewers (predicted growth much faster than average), job analyst. A good area: *personnel consulting*—particularly as businesses farm out various human resources functions. Best areas to the top management suites: strategic HR management, succession planning. See Best Bets, page 126.

Other areas:

See Industry, Career sections.

▶ **The impact of technology: some old managerial specialties will show reduced job growth; but for those with the right skills, still a good future.**

Example: buying and purchasing. Buyers purchase manufactured items (clothing, etc.) for retailers; purchasing agents are responsible for buying goods to be used by their corporation—from paperclips to machine tools.

Major trend: computer automation and centralized purchasing or buying operations will lower growth prospects. But both fields employ many people—over 400,000 purchasing managers and workers, over 200,000 wholesale and retail buyers. Although total demand will be less, employment opportunities will be present. And in the past several years, salary levels have risen. Reason: the job is getting more complex, more important. See Best Bets section for one area.

WHAT'S NEXT

▶ **The search for broad-based managers will widen.**

One interesting development: some manufacturing firms are shifting their entry-level hiring focus from the Ivy League to the Big Ten universities of the Midwest, according to *Industry Week* magazine. The reasoning seems to be that these people will be more like "typical" consumers, with a better competitive edge in manufacturing and marketing their products.

▶ **Service and quality—management focus of the 1990s.**

Even with manufacturing firms, product service will become key in selling manufactured goods. Manufacturers will concentrate on building strong dealer-distributor networks—and managers will face the complex task of making certain that lines of communication are strong between the plant, the dealer, and the customer.

U.S. business has accepted one aspect of Japanese business, attention to quality, and realized another current failing, lack of attention to service.

Companies that emphasize both will prosper—from low-end retailers like Wal-Mart to high-end computer giants like IBM. Managers who can motivate a good service attitude in employees will do well.

This is important. In the 1990s there will be a shortage of workers, particularly educated or technically competent entry-level workers. Keeping and motivating good workers will be one of the most crucial functions of a manager. For example, according to Marriott Corporation's senior vice president of human relations, Marriott must sell itself to prospective workers, not vice versa.

▶ **Back to basics mood among U.S. MBAs.**

A good way to predict the future of U.S. business: look at what MBAs are studying now. Major trend on campus: away from investment banking; toward manufacturing, production, and, most of all, international.

SALARIES

According to a recent survey by the National Institute of Business Management, median managerial salaries for top executives at small to mid-sized companies were:

> **Chief executive officers and presidents:** $139,000
> **Marketing executives:** $90,000
> **Manufacturing executives:** $70,750
> **Sales executives:** $75,699
> **Data-processing executives:** $56,258
> **Financial executives:** $75,000
> **Human resources executives:** $55,000

Obviously, top executive salaries at large corporations are usually much higher. Below these levels, salaries vary widely.

HOTEL MANAGEMENT: depending on hotel size, assistant manager $32,000 to $53,000; for a manager, $45,000 to $100,000.

PURCHASING EXECUTIVES: average salary $40,700, median salary $36,000, according to *Purchasing* magazine's December 1989 survey. Salaries range from a low of $27,600 for buyers, up through the mid-30s for more senior buyers. Managers ranged in the mid-40s, materials directors in the high 50s. Highest salaries in New York City (average over $60,000); 2% earned over $100,000.

GENERAL MANAGERS: wide variation. Rules of thumb: higher salaries in larger metro areas, in finance (until recently), large manufacturing and service firms. Median salaries around $40,000. According to the *Wall Street Journal* (special college edition), in 1990, the average management trainee started at $22,080.

FINANCIAL MANAGERS: median salaries in the mid-30s to 40s. Salaries vary widely. Chief financial officers averaged $67,000 base pay in 1987; total compensation was more, including bonuses, stock options, etc.

CONSULTANTS: median salary in the 40s.

HUMAN RESOURCES, PERSONNEL, TRAINING: top salaries reach over $200,000. Average salaries for recruiters were over $35,000 in 1990, more for those in larger cities or with larger firms.

BEST BETS

"SMALL BIG CITIES": Smart job hunters can do well by checking the classifieds or targeting employment opportunities in some of the dynamic smaller cities of America, many of which are seeing much greater economic growth than their larger competitors. Some examples: *Memphis, Tennessee,* which has created over 100,000 jobs in the past ten years by emphasizing distribution businesses; in fact, it calls itself "America's Distribution Center." Nike, Square D, Disney stores, William Sonoma all support such centers here. Also: *Charlotte, North Carolina,* with the 10th busiest airport in the world, and major divisions of headquarters of major corporations from Hearst to Microsoft. And *Cedar Rapids, Iowa,* which attracted hundreds of millions of dollars in factory investments, cutting unemployment from 9.7% to under 4%. One word of caution: last year's "hot city" may not be hot this year, so you'll have to do some checking yourself.

HUMAN RESOURCES: Once on the second tier of American business, human resource managers are moving increasingly to the first. Principal reasons: a new shortage of qualified workers makes retaining employees more important; the rapid changes in our work force make human resource planning more important; the rise in two-income families has resulted in a rise in human resource programs (child care, spouse relocations, etc.); declining loyalty makes it easier for workers to quit;

and finally, telecommunications and computers are making old management-employee structures obsolete—someone has to study, design, and help implement new systems.

Other duties: enhancing employee effectiveness, dealing with unions, enforcing government personnel regulations, developing benefits plans, supervising training. And some duties geared to the late 1990s: managing diversity programs, managing programs to help families within a corporate environment, international training, employee interaction programs. Requirements: usually a college degree, but not necessarily a specialized one, or advanced training (psychology, business, other liberal arts; sometimes an MBA).

In general, there are two tiers to the human resource function—at the top, the high-ranked generalist who supervises various specialists. At the lower levels, in addition to recruiters, demand will grow for compensation and benefits specialists. Also in demand: outplacement counselors and consultants. For the field as a whole, the Bureau of Labor Statistics predicts high% growth in the 1990s.

Human resources is particularly important for women. Because they already occupy many top spots in the field, watch for women to move from high-level human resources positions into other more senior executive positions in the 1990s. Salaries range from $25,000 on up through mid-level and top-level salaries of $40,000–$80,000, more at larger companies. Upper-level vice presidents at large corporations earn over $200,000.

WHERE TO GO FOR MORE INFORMATION

MANAGEMENT ASSOCIATIONS

American College of Physician Executives
4890 W. Kennedy Blvd.,
Suite 200
Tampa, FL 33609
813/287-2000

American Assembly of Collegiate Schools of Business
605 Old Ballas Rd.,
Suite 220
St. Louis, MO 63141
314/872-8481

American Association of Professional Consultants
9140 Ward Pkwy.
Kansas City, MO
64114
816/444-3500
(Publishes directory, etc.)

American Chamber of Commerce Executives
4232 King St.
Alexandria, VA 22303
703/998-0072
(Publishes periodicals.)

American College of Health Care Administrators
325 S. Patrick St.
Alexandria, VA 22314
703/549-5822

American College of Health Care Executives
840 N. Lake Shore Dr.
Chicago, IL 60611
312/943-0544

American Compensation Association
14040 Northsight Blvd.
Scottsdale, AZ 85260
602/951-9191
(For managers associated with compensation packages, etc.; publishes periodical with job listings; holds seminars.)

American Management Association

135 W. 50th St.
New York, NY 10020
212/586-8100
(The major association
for managers; offers
numerous programs,
has many offices in
United States and
worldwide, has
information service,
bookstore, etc.)

**American Planning
Association**
1313 E. 60th St.
Chicago, IL 60637
312/955-9100
(Publishes periodical
with job listings,
referral service, etc., all
for members only.)

**American Society of
Association Executives**
1575 I St., NW
Washington, DC 20005
202/626-2711
(Publish periodical; job
referral service, etc.)

**American Society for
Public Administration**
1120 G St., NW
Washington, DC 20005
202/393-7878

**American Society for
Training and
Development**
1640 King St.
Alexandria, VA 22313
703/683-8100
(Publishes human
resources journal.)

**Association for
International Practical
Training**
10400 Little Patuxent
Pkwy.,

Suite 250
Columbia, MD
21044-3501
410/997-2200
(For recent graduates;
arranges
hospitality/tourism
overseas exchanges
with on-the-job training
or research.)

**Association of
Managing Consultants**
521 Fifth Ave., 35th
Fl.
New York, NY 10175
212/697-8262
(Professional group that
sponsors member
business referral.)

**Cable Television
Administration and
Marketing Society**
635 Slaters Ln.
Alexandria, VA 22314
703/549-4200

**Center for
Management
Development**
135 W. 50th St.
New York, NY 10020
212/586-8100
(Division of American
Management
Association; operates
extension institute, a
home study program,
etc.)

**Employment
Management
Association**
5 W. Hargett St.,
Suite 1100
Raleigh, NC 27601
919/828-6614

**Financial Management
Association**
University of South
Florida
College of Business
Administration
Tampa, FL 33640-5500
813/974-2084
(Publishes periodical
with job listing.)

**Financial Managers
Society**
8 S. Michigan Ave.,
Suite 500
Chicago, IL 60603
312/578-1300

**Institute of
Management
Consultants**
521 Fifth Ave., 35th
Fl.
New York, NY 10176
212/697-8262

**Institute of Real
Estate Management**
430 N. Michigan Ave.,
7th Fl.
Chicago, IL 60611
312/661-1930
(Placement service for
members; certifies
members, etc.)

**International
Association of
Assessing Officers**
1313 E. 60th St.
Chicago, IL
60637-2892
312/947-2064

**International
Association of
Business
Communicators**
870 Market St., Suite
940

San Francisco, CA
94102
415/433-3400
(For managers in
corporate
communications and
public relations.)

**International
Conference of
Building Officials**
5360 S. Workman Mill
Rd.
Whittier, CA 90601
213/699-0541

**International Facility
Management
Association**
One Greenway Plz.,
11th Fl.
Houston, TX 77046
713/623-IFMA

**International Food
Service Executives
Association**
3321 N. Clark St.,
Suite 2900
Chicago, IL 60610
312/644-8989

**International
Personnel
Management
Association**
1617 Duke St.
Alexandria, VA 22314
703/549-7100
(Publishes periodical,
directory, etc.)

**Institute of Real
Estate Management**
430 N. Michigan Ave.,
7th Fl.
Chicago, IL 60611

312/329-6000
(Publishes periodical
for members, with job
listings.)

**National Management
Association**
2210 Arbor Blvd.
Dayton, OH 45439
513/294-0421

**Society for Human
Resource Management**
606 N. Washington St.
Alexandria, VA 22314
703/548-3440
(Publishes periodical
with job listings,
directory; maintains
HRM-net job databank
of jobs listed in its
periodical.)

MANAGEMENT DIRECTORIES

(For much more, see also "General Business Sources," page 504.)

*AMA's Executive
Employment Guide*
Eileen Monahan, Editor
American Management
Association
135 W. 50th St.
New York, NY 10020
FAX: 212/903-8163
(Free to AMA
members; lists search
firms, job registries,
etc.)

*AMBA's MBA
Employment Guide*
Association of MBA
Executives
227 Commerce St.
East Haven, CT 06512
203/467-8870
(For $10 each, sends a

listing of corporations
in three states of choice
for one functional
area.)

*Dun & Bradstreet
Million-Dollar
Directory; Dun &
Bradstreet Reference
Book of Corporate
Managements; Career
Guide*
Dun's Marketing
Services
3 Sylvan Way
Parsippany, NJ 07054
800/526-0651
(Expensive but
extensive listings of
leading U.S.
corporations.)

*Macmillan Directory of
Leading Private
Companies*
Reed Reference
Publishing
P.O. Box 31
New Providence, NJ
07974
800/323-6772
(Expensive but good
source for hard-to-find
private firms.)

*Peterson's Job
Opportunities for
Business and Liberal
Arts Graduates 1993*
P.O. Box 2123
Princeton, NJ
08543-2123
609/243-9111

800/338-3282
(Lists hundreds of
corporations and
organizations that are
hiring; includes detailed
information.)

**Women Directors of
the Top 1,000
Corporations**
National Women's
Economic Alliance
Foundation

1440 New York Ave,
NW,
Suite 300
Washington, DC 20005
202/393-5257

MANAGEMENT PERIODICALS

(For *Forbes, Fortune,* etc., see also "General Business Sources," page 504.)

Across the Board
845 Third Ave.
New York, NY 10022
212/759-0900
(Monthly magazine
published by the
influential Conference
Board.)

**Facilities Design &
Management**
1515 Broadway
New York, NY 10036
212/869-1300
(Monthly for corporate
facilities managers.)

**FE/Financial
Executive**
P.O. Box 1938
Morristown, NJ 07962
201/898-4600
(Bimonthly magazine
for finance executives.)

**Financial Services
Week**
2 World Trade Center
New York, NY 10048
212/227-1200
(Biweekly financial
planning periodical.)

Forty Plus Newsletter
Forty Plus of New York
15 Park Row
New York, NY 10038
212/233-6086

(Four times a year; free
to Forty Plus members,
a group that helps
over-forty managers
find a job.)

**Harvard Business
Review**
Harvard University
School of Business
Administration
Soldiers Field Rd.
Boston, MA 02163
617/495-6182
(Bimonthly; prestigious
journal of business.)

HR Magazine
606 N. Washington St.
Alexandria, VA 22314
703/548-3440
(Monthly for human
resources executives,
particularly those in
compensation, benefits,
training.)

INC.
38 Commercial Wharf
Boston, MA 02110
617/248-8000
(Invaluable for targeting
the fast-moving
corporations that tend to
do the most hiring.)

Industry Week
1100 Superior Ave.
Cleveland, OH 44114
216/696-7000
(Semimonthly; covers
industrial management.)

Journal of Commerce
2 World Trade Center
New York, NY 10048
212/837-7000
(Daily business
newspaper.)

Management Review
135 W. 50th St.
New York, NY 10020
212/903-8063
(Monthly for members
of AMA.)

**National Business
Employment Weekly**
420 Lexington Ave.
New York, NY 10170
212/808-6791

Personnel Journal
ACC Communications
245 Fischer Ave., B-2
Costa Mesa, CA 92626
714/751-4106
subscription address:
P.O. Box 50088
Boulder, CO
80321-0088
(Monthly magazine for
HR pros.)

Traffic Management
275 Washington St.
Newton, MA 02158
617/964-3030
(Monthly magazine.)

Training
50 S. 9th St.
Minneapolis, MN
55402
612/333-0471
(Monthly magazine for

personnel in corporate
and university training
programs.)

PERFORMING ARTISTS

[NOTE: For more information and source material about film and television, see the appropriate industry sections.]

BRIEF BACKGROUND

▶ **For most performing arts professions, you need talent—and then you need luck. There are many more aspiring actors, dancers, and musicians than there are jobs.**

One example of the tight competition: According to the Screen Actor's Guild (SAG), over 80% of all performers who worked under a SAG contract a few years ago earned under $5,000—and less than 6% earned over $25,000.

But then again . . . As with any creative profession, *some* people make it. And to take another example from the acting profession, one actor a few years ago brought home $40 million as salary and bonus—with the added job satisfaction of being critically and popularly acclaimed. Some people have it all . . .

On the other side of the camera—or the lights—film and theatrical production careers will also remain competitive. (For more on film production careers, see Entertainment on page 339.)

NOTE: This section only briefly highlights a few major trends and job reference materials available. For further information, we recommend reading the books mentioned at the end of the chapter, and, most importantly, reading the appropriate magazines for up-to-the-minute employment information. Trends in creative careers change quickly—and hiring opportunities may not even last days, but hours.

EMPLOYMENT OUTLOOK: Poor for most, excellent for the few among performing artists, better for production people, administrative staff; but still intense competition.

Major Employment Areas

ACTORS AND ACTRESSES: Competition is extremely tough, but the number of jobs will increase as the variety of acting venues increases—especially in fast-growing television and film production, but also in industrial films, trade shows, and other less traditional acting areas.

Some major trends for the next half of the 1990s:

- **A widening field for working actors.** Film, videocassettes, theater, cable shows, television commercials, new forms of advertising production, independent television shows, new regional theater (which can now sometimes support full-time actors).

- **More demand for acting talent.** Increasing use of videocassettes and increase in television/cable viewing (the average hours spent watching has gone up consistently) means yet more demand.

- **The pick-up again of regional film and theater.** It may still look bad now, but this is a trend that spans all the arts, despite setbacks during the recession.

- **Regional centers**—regional theater in Texas, San Francisco, Minneapolis, film in Florida, Texas, Georgia, will gain in importance.

A good area for employment: Florida. Number three in film production; and outside of New York and California, the largest number of actors and writers, according to *Emmy* magazine. Some advantages: the powerful presence of two major studios—Universal Studios, Florida, and Disney-MGM.

Best areas for commercials: New York, Los Angeles, Chicago—and Florida, Atlanta, Georgia. The last two are fast-growing regional commercial centers.

DANCERS: As the economy picks up, and as dance companies get back on their feet, employment is expected to grow faster than average, due to an increase in popularity of this art form. On the downside: As with other performing arts professions, the number of applicants will considerably exceed job openings, and economic downturns will always affect employment.

Best areas: regional ballet companies, college and university companies, and teaching. One source for jobs: The American Dance Guild maintains a placement service. Check address under Association listings at the end of the chapter.

MUSICIANS: There are about 200,000 musical jobs in America (and probably more musicians, as the number of part-timers far exceeds the number of jobs). Employment is concentrated in major cities where major orchestras and recording studios are located: Los Angeles, New York, Chicago, Nashville, New Orleans. The cities themselves reflect the diversity of American music, from rock to classical to jazz and country and blues.

Some current trends:

- **In classical music:** Can classical music maintain or build popularity in the 1990s? The current debate in *Musical America* talks about the problems of funding, and keeping, audiences. On the bright side, Young Concert Artists (YCA) in New York has actively encouraged young talent. As a nonprofit, the YCA often manages musicians before they are ready for commercial managerial companies. It has been critical to the success of many famous musicians. Normally, talented young musicians are spotted by local teachers, screened, then the best audition in New York before a panel of judges. Other programs are run by the Boston Symphony and the American Symphony Orchestra League.

• **In opera:** A beneficial trend toward decentralization, plus regional and summer opera companies, points to employment opportunities outside of the East Coast, after the recession's funding effects are over.

• **In contemporary music:** Where the rest of the 1990s will go is anybody's guess. In 1990, *Downbeat* asked prominent insiders their predictions. They ranged from more New Age music to more computers and synthetic to less synthetic to more "bottom-up" control of the industry. Yet in 1994, rap and hip-hop and country have been pulling in most of the dollars. Bottom line for music and other creative careers: Do what you feel is right.

One source for jobs: *Musicians' National Hotline*. The nonprofit hotline finds jobs or gigs for musicians of all types, "from country to folk to rock," and publishes a bimonthly listing of employment opportunities. Contact: Musicians' National Hotline Association; address on page 136.

▶ **How to find a job in the arts: Be persistent.**

It is easy to say—harder to do. Many of the arts associations such as the Dance Guild, maintain job banks. Check the associations listed at the end of the chapter.

Also: The *National Arts Jobbank* is an invaluable weekly listing of current jobs and internships. It covers all arts, but since its merger with the Association of Performing Arts Employment referral service, it can be especially helpful for performing artists, as well as those who want to teach or administer in the fields. Address on page 138.

▶ **Many aspiring artists of any type want to tap into project funding to advance their work. One obvious source is the foundations.**

Some people seem to win many more foundation grants than others. Very often the difference isn't talent, but finding the best foundation for your work. First, check to see if your type of artistic talent matches the type the foundation sponsors.

The best way—check: *Foundation Grants to Individuals* from the Foundation Center; address and information on page 137.

The same publisher also publishes *Foundation Directory* (listing thousands of national and local foundations) and *Corporate Foundation Profiles*. There are no standard application procedures; you'll have to write specific foundations and request instructions. In many cases, foundations only sponsor bona fide arts groups; in this case, the best procedure is to approach a local association or organization familiar with your work and have them apply on your behalf.

SALARIES

ACTING: Most salaries are regulated by the unions; there are many variables, depending on the nature and venue of the work, residuals, and so on. Some representative *minimum* salaries in 1990: TV feature acting (under SAG contract), $414/day; for a TV commercial, $366.60/day. Actors and actresses under AFTRA contracts in 1990 earned a minimum of $1,440/week.

MUSICIANS, DANCERS, ETC.: Highly variable salaries, depending on specific art form, etc. Dancers' minimums ranged around $200/day, musicians, $500–$1500/week. Symphony conductors in 1990 earned a median income of about $28,000, more if extra income from related duties is factored in; much more for those with major symphonies.

BEST BETS

FILM EXTRA: A best bet more for the amateur, or the occasional actor and actress—although sometimes an extra does get noticed and does get a part. What extras do: Film extras form the "people background" to films and commercials. How to become one: In Hollywood, go to Central Casting, an agency that supplies extras to Hollywood films; it works with the Screen Extras' Guild, which extras must usually join. In New York, contact a casting agency like Sylvia Fay (addresses can be found in *Backstage* magazine). Extras in New York are also usually union members, either with the Screen Actors Guild, Actors Equity, or AFTRA (addresses are listed at the end of the chapter). Outside of LA or NY, call the state film commission.

Competition: tough. In LA, a central list is maintained, and when shortages of a specific type occur, newcomers are added to the list. Outside of the major areas, opportunities are easier to find. Guild pay: For extras in a commercial in 1990, for example, $232.37/day; film extras, $86.32/day for members of the Screen Extras' Guild;, for AFTRA members, $64 for a 15-minute show.

WHERE TO GO FOR MORE INFORMATION

PERFORMING ARTS ASSOCIATIONS

Actor's Equity Association
165 W. 47th St.
New York, NY 10036
212/869-8530
6430 Sunset Blvd.
Hollywood, CA 90028
213/462-2334
(Write or call for regional offices and phone numbers.)

Affiliate Artists
37 W. 65th St.
New York, NY 10023
212/580-2000

American Conservatory Theatre Foundation
450 Geary St.
San Francisco, CA 94102
415/749-2200
(Offers M.F.A. and holds auditions for entry; offers placement service, etc.)

American Council for the Arts
1285 Avenue of the Americas,
3rd Fl.
New York, NY 10019
212/245-4510

American Dance Guild
31 W. 21st St.
New York, NY 10019
212/245-4510

American Federation of Musicians—West
1777 N. Vine St.,
Suite 500
Hollywood, CA 90028
213/461-3441

American Federation of Television and Radio Artists
(AFTRA)
250 Madison Ave.
New York, NY 10016
212/532-0800

6922 Hollywood Blvd.,
Suite 900
Hollywood, CA 90028
1-800/367-7966

**American Federation
of Musicians—East**
1501 Broadway
New York, NY 10036
212/869-1330
(Publishes monthly
tabloid with job
listings.)

**American Film
Institute**
John F. Kennedy
Center for the
Performing Arts
Washington, DC 20566
202/828-4000
(Has internship
program; gives grants.)

**American Guild of
Musical Artists**
1727 Broadway
New York, NY 10019
212/265-3687

**American Guild of
Organists**
475 Riverside Dr.
New York, NY 10115
212/870-2310
(Publishes monthly
magazine, etc.)

**American Music
Center**
250 W. 54th St.
New York, NY 10019
212/366-5260

**American Symphony
Orchestra League**
777 14th St., NW
Washington, DC 20005
202/628-0099
(With hundreds of U.S.
orchestras as members,
a valuable contact point
for young conductors
selected by the league.)

**Association of
Independent Video
and Filmmakers**
625 Broadway
New York, NY 10012
212/473-3400

**Dance Theater
Workshop**
219 W. 19th St.
New York, NY 10011
212/691-6500

Dance USA
777 14th St., NW,
Suite 540
Washington, DC 20005
202/628-0144

**International Society
of Performing Arts
Administrators**
6065 Pickerel Dr.
Rockford, MI 49341
616/874-6200

**Musicians National
Hotline Association**
277 E. 6100 S.
Salt Lake City, UT
801/268-2000
(Publishes bimonthly
periodical with listings;
members are helped

finding jobs or gigs in
all areas of music; also
support staff.)

**National Dance
Association**
1900 Association Dr.
Reston, VA 22091
703/476-3436

**National Foundation
for Advancement in
the Arts**
3915 Biscayne Blvd.
Miami, FL 33137
305/573-0490

**New England Theater
Conference**
c/o Dept. of Theater
Northeastern Univ.
360 Huntington Ave.
Boston, MA 02115
617/424-9275

**Producers Guild of
America**
400 S. Beverly,
Suite 211
Beverly Hills, CA
90212
310/557-0807

Screen Actors Guild
7065 Hollywood Blvd.
Hollywood, CA 90028
(Write or call for local
offices.)

Society of Composers
P.O. Box 296
Old Chelsea Station
New York, NY
10011-9998
212/595-3050

PERFORMING ARTS DIRECTORIES

The Academy Players Directories
The Academy of Motion Picture Arts and Sciences
8949 Wilshire Blvd.
Beverly Hills, CA 90211
310-247-3000
(Listing for agented SAG or AFTRA members; distributed to casting directors, etc.)

American Dance Guild Membership Directory
American Dance Guild
31 W. 21st St.
New York, NY 10010
212/627-3790

Foundation Grants to Individuals;
Foundation Directory;
Corporate Foundation Profiles
Foundation Center

79 Fifth Ave.
New York, NY 10003-3076
212/620-4230
(The first directory is particularly valuable to artists seeking financial support from foundations.)

International Motion Picture Almanac;
International Television and Video Almanac
Quigley Publishing Company
159 W. 53rd St.
New York, NY 10019
212/247-3100
(Includes production companies and producers, agencies, affiliated firms and businesses, names and extra information on major film players.)

Regional Theater Directory; Summer Theater Directory
American Theater Works, Inc.
P.O. Box 519
Dorset, VT 05251
802/867-2223
(Theater companies listed by region, hiring information.)

Ross Reports Television
Television Index, Inc.
40-29 27th St.
Long Island City, NY 11101
718/937-3990
(Monthly directory listing major TV employers along with requirements, names of casting personnel, etc.)

PERFORMING ARTS MAGAZINES

American Cinematographer
American Society of Cinematographers
1782 N. Orange Dr.
Los Angeles, CA 90028
213/876-5080
(Monthly.)

Art Search
Theatre Communications Group
355 Lexington Ave.
New York, NY 10017
212/697-5230

(Lists artistic as well as administrative, production, and educational job openings.)

Back Stage
330 W. 42nd St.
New York, NY 10036
212/947-0200
(Weekly tabloid; a major source of ads and information, particularly for the East Coast.)

Billboard
P.O. Box 2011
Marion, OH 43306
1-800/669-1002
(Weekly tabloid of the music industry.)

The Chicago Reader
11 E. Illinois
Chicago, IL 60611
312/828-0350
(Weekly theater magazine listing Chicago theater productions.)

Daily Variety
5700 Wilshire Blvd.
Los Angeles, CA 90036
213/857-6600
(Daily paper covering
film and TV production;
along with *Hollywood
Reporter*, it is *the*
Hollywood source.)

Dance Magazine
33 W. 60th St.
New York, NY 10029
212/245-9050
(Monthly.)

Down Beat
180 W. Park Ave.
Elmhurst, IL 60126
708/941-2030
(Monthly for jazz
players and amateurs.)

Drama-Logue
P.O. Box 38771
Los Angeles, CA
90038-0771
(Major source for
theater, film, and TV
jobs on the West
Coast.)

Emmy
5220 Lankershim Blvd.
N. Hollywood, CA
91601
818/953-7575

Hollywood Reporter
6715 Sunset Blvd.
Hollywood, CA 90028
213/464-7411
(Daily; along with
Daily Variety, it is *the*
major source of
Hollywood TV and film
production
information.)

On Location
P.O. Box 2810
Hollywood, CA 90028
213/541-4363
(Quarterly.)

*Spotlight Casting
Magazine*
P.O. Box 3720
Hollywood, CA 90078
213/462-6775
(Full of help-wanted
ads for many areas.)

Variety
475 Park Ave. S.
New York, NY 10016
212/869-5700
(Weekly; more East
Coast-oriented, more
theater and distribution
rather than the
nitty-gritty daily
production of *Daily
Variety*.)

*Westaf's National Arts
Job Bank (Western
States Arts
Foundation)*
236 Montezuma Ave.
Santa Fe, NM 87501
505/988-1166
(Full of help-wanted
ads for most areas,
including performing
dance, music, theater,
and arts administration;
also grants, etc.,
information. A very
valuable source.)

SALES AND MARKETING PROFESSIONALS

BRIEF BACKGROUND

▶ **Marketing employees position a product or a service—they develop a campaign that includes sales, advertising, and public relations. Then the sales force goes out and sells it. Those are the basics; everything else is changing.**

First, computers are entering the marketplace and are changing the time-worn ways of doing business. They are taking the administrative functions away from the sales force and freeing them to concentrate on sales.

Computers are giving retailers and buyers more information. For example, with computerized sales scanners, they have up-to-date inventory and sales figures. This makes selling more difficult. Today, if a product doesn't sell quickly, it is off the shelves quickly.

Also, more products or services are entering markets, competition is heating up both in the U.S. and abroad, and in many cases products and services are becoming more complex. Once, a salesperson would go out and sell a typewriter; now he or she must make sell a complicated, computerized word-processing system.

That's a big difference. This new complexity is creating a demand for more knowledgeable and technically oriented sales and marketing people. There is more interaction between sales and manufacturing, product development, and other corporate areas. In some areas there's more team selling, in other areas the emphasis is on more targeted sales drawn from sophisticated databases; but in all areas, it is clear that further change is ahead.

▶ **A consulting executive interviewed in *Sales & Marketing Management* put it this way: "Sales management in the 1990s will move from a game of checkers to a game of chess."**

As the corporate chess game intensifies in the nineties, sales and marketing employees will play a key role. Already more top CEOs come from sales or marketing positions than from any other, and salaries average near the top. This is an increasingly open area to women, who make up over 50 percent of some sales categories.

But: recessions and industrial or corporate downturns can hurt sales and marketing people faster and often harder, and tough competition gets tougher. In the words of another sales and marketing executive to a new class of salespeople: "Welcome to the pressure cooker." Someone else, scarred a bit from the recession, put it differently: "It's a roller-coaster ride." [Note: for more specific information, see the various industry sections, and Managerial Careers section.]

EMPLOYMENT OUTLOOK: In general, as economy picks up more steam, job outlook should be good, but expect a lot of competition.

▶ **Three years ago, everything seemed rosy everywhere. Then the recession and a long, sluggish recovery hit. Then . . .**

The key recessionary changes: customers became more cost-conscious, more willing to shop around for a product, more willing to delay a purchase—and competition among sales and marketing forces heightened. New changes: more willingness to go afield, abroad, anywhere to *broaden* sales base. More aggressiveness in *deepening* sales base in home territories—cross-selling, expert consulting with sales, etc.

Employment result: sales and marketing employees felt the pinch. Kodak, GM, and IBM all announced major staff reductions, and although, as *Marketing News* pointed out, no breakdowns were announced, it was clear that sales and marketing staff were involved. But hardest hit were those in other areas, such as media sales, which saw significant downswings as advertisers reduced their presence in magazines and newspapers and on television screens. Also particularly hard hit: independent sales reps—whose responsibilities were easily shed by cost-conscious companies.

▶ **The good news: sales and marketing staff are central to the new market-oriented corporations of today.**

But watch out: some corporations are shedding marketing jobs, preferring to hire outside temporary or consulting marketing staff when the need is there. This is a structural change rather than a legacy of the recession.

However, the bottom line: Business is getting more competitive—and it needs the best marketing and salespeople it can get. Even during the recession, many top sales and marketing staff weathered it well; some said it seemed as if corporations were using the recession as an opportunity to get rid of the newcomers and the poor performers.

Maybe. But sometimes whole departments went—and with them some stars as well. One thing was clear: In today's supercompetitive sales and marketing environment, competence and skills will be more than ever important; and so will luck.

Sales and marketing, particularly sales, are volatile, high-turnover professions. This may intensify in the 1990s, as the pace of business intensifies in the more competitive global environment. According to one study, the average turnover rate was over 25% two years ago. At the same time, salespeople in strong industries will do well.

Remember: The only real way to assess a sales or marketing position's potential is to assess the company *and* the industry *and* the region and your own selling and marketing skills—and then the state of the economy.

▶ **The best way to look for sales jobs: assess the top-performing industries, then look for corporations that have restructured successfully.**

Key point: in today's rapidly changing markets, salespeople will do best to target the corporations that have successfully managed the tough transitions. For example, Hewlett Packard emphasized a decentralized, team approach to sales and marketing long before many other corporations like IBM—and it weathered the storms of the early 1990s far more effectively. In general, look for: concentration on core businesses, strong sales support, lean staffing, a team approach with marketers, salespeople, and service/manufacturing personnel working together closely.

Moving away from specifics, in general, the best broad areas in 1994 and beyond will be: manufacturers' representatives, wholesale representatives. *Key point:* many corporations will rely on these agents to market their goods as a means of cutting costs. Possible advantage for older workers, retirees: some experts are pointing to a trend toward part-time reps—and older, well-trained workers with more experience may find opportunities.

▶ **Financial services: hiring will increase further, but on a selective basis.**

From the crash of 1987 to the hiring miniboom of last year, Wall Street was ahead of the pack in trimming staff, then rehiring to meet new needs.

Key trends: the days of the old-fashioned stockbroker are over. Many firms are looking for salespeople who sell a firm's total financial service package (from insurance to stocks). Somewhat older or more experienced applicants are often preferred. Rationale: they can bring in more moneyed clients faster. Look for more attention to financial planning, etc.—more on *managing* assets as opposed to selling or trading them. Financial salespeople will be called "financial planners," and will sell "wrap-around" services, a complete financial management plan. For details, see Financial Services, page 349.

Employment for insurance agents and brokers: competitive but still good. As with their sales counterparts in brokerage houses, more agents are specializing in financial planning as a way of increasing business. In the long term, the outlook is good, depending on the specific company. There will be strong employment possibilities for people with international experience. A new trend: more emphasis on minority, female hiring. Particularly strong—the relatively wealthy Asian market. One danger: not recognizing the enormous diversity *within* ethnic markets.

▶ **The outlook for real estate salespeople and executives.**

The question is what's happening to the market. There are two broad schools of thought. The first, that things will continue to improve, and at a faster rate. The second, that the real estate downturn was only partly related to the recession, that real estate demand is now at a much lower level, may fluctuate, and will only gradually move up. As for employment, government figures point to a fair growth of 18% in the next fourteen years.

There are currently about 400,000 agents and brokers in the U.S.—but the number is elastic. According to a recent report by *Real Estate Today* and the

National Association of Realtors, real estate companies reported an average turnover of about 20% in one year.

Broad trend: there's a shift in focus away from the technical emphasis on law, finance, and accounting. The need for the future: the ideal real estate candidate should have a broad general education, enabling him or her to tackle the increasingly complex transactions of the future, involving foreign currencies, environmental problems, politics, and so on. Also, according to a major real estate study reported by Elizabeth Fowler in *The New York Times*, the real estate firm of the next half of the nineties will be larger—with larger staffs, possibly international branches, and more services. Needed: the multi-talented, multi-linguistic sales forces and, more particularly, sales managers of the future.

Ideal candidate for a real estate executive position: liberal arts degree, customer experience, and grad degree in urban planning, environmental planning, etc.

Another trend: corporate real estate departments will shrink as U.S. corporations continue to downsize; but this probably means more jobs in outside consulting firms, etc.

▶ **Right now the sales trend is clear: companies are looking for—and getting—the very best.**

In 1992 and 1993, the relatively weak market created the following pattern: just as larger firms were cutting staffs, smaller and mid-sized firms were picking up the very best in a fairly large pool. A buyer's market, to a degree.

Things were a bit different in more technical areas—but better for applicants. Particularly in technical areas, the norm is to hire technically trained sales trainees—for example, a chemical manufacturing firm will hire engineers, a pharmaceutical firm will hire pharmacy grads, nurses. Problem: in many cases, these technical types are in short supply. That's good news for recruits with the right skills.

SOME TOP SALES FIRMS

(In the chemicals, computers, forest products, hotel, pharmaceuticals, property, and casualty insurance industries, ranked by *Sales & Marketing Management*, September 1991, out of 10 possible points in seven different sales functions.)

	Firm	Score
1	Hyatt (hotels)	8.0
2	Dow (chemicals)	7.8
3	Marriott (hotels)	7.7
4	Eli Lilly (pharmaceuticals)	7.6

5	Scott Paper (forest products)	7.3
6	Du Pont (chemicals)	7.3
7	Bayer USA (chemicals)	7.3
8	Boise Cascade (chemicals)	7.2
9	International Paper (forest papers)	7.2
10	Hewlett Packard (food & beverage)	7.1
11	Hilton (hotels)	7.0
12	Merck (pharmaceuticals)	7.0
13	IBM (computers, office equipment)	6.9
14	American-Cyanamid (chemicals)	6.9
15	Progressive (insurance)	6.8
16	Pfizer (pharmaceuticals)	6.8

▶ Best long-term career area: marketing

In the globally supercompetitive world of the 1990s, marketing will play an increasingly important role—differentiating and creating need for product.

Key reasons: more of an emphasis on selling quality products, less on finance. And in the marketplace, there is increasing market segmentation, shorter life cycles for products, increasing demand for new and better-quality items—and more competition. All point to the new role of marketing as the focal point of the corporation in the future.

Be ready for some major changes in the field, including the rise of temporary, consultative marketing. And be ready for more marketers in CEO seats, and much more emphasis on international sales.

Marketing is an enormous field—well over 300,000 Americans work in some aspect of marketing. But growth in the coming years will be very strong—better than 30% by the year 2000, according to the Bureau of Labor Statistics. Competition will be tough, however, in particular for entry-level positions. Many qualified applicants will be competing for the same jobs.

An ideal candidate? Companies are looking for widely skilled, analytical candidates, with proven ability to anticipate trends. Key: no longer will knowledge of technical marketing and products guarantee success—according to the search firm

A good idea: take refresher courses at local schools and universities, get an idea of new ideas, trends . . . buzzwords.

Some interesting recent trends, ideas, people are talking about in the industry:

- **Satisfaction research:** becoming much more important, as quality becomes a byword for corporate America. The most active areas are telecom, airlines, fast food, financial, business services, hotels, health care, oil, and computers.

- **Collaborative marketing returns:** almost unheard of in the 1980s, old foes like IBM and Apple are getting together to survive globally in the 1990s; more usually involves complementary corporations, like the Pathé Entertainment partnership with Bantam Books to promote John LeCarré's *The Russia House.*

- **"Bundled media"** (hitting various advertising and promotion paths simultaneously) becomes a more important ad/marketing tool as power of individual media outlets declines.

- **The "planners":** identified by Ogilvy & Mather's Jane Fitzgibbon, this is a key consumer of the 1990s—the type of person who has a conservative, *strategic* approach to living, who delays, ponders, and studies purchases. Many marketers have not come up to speed with this buyer . . . yet.

- **Anthropological research** instead of market research—why not hire true experts in human behavior? Anthropologists are beginning to revolutionize market research, uncovering some myths of focus groups, learning the real hows and whys of a sales decision. For more, see the magazine listed on page 160.

Good career paths: Product management. Begin as a product specialist, to product manager, to general manager of a product line or area—then on to upper management. And special events marketing—see page 147.

▶ Poised for long-term growth: franchise sales.

According to some experts, salespeople who specialize in selling franchises can expect high pay and strong demand in the rest of the 1990s. Two reasons: franchises will continue to proliferate (in spite of possible temporary lulls in economic downturns and job competition; indeed, and perhaps because of them, as more and more people strike out on their own), and the shortage of qualified, capable salespeople will continue; according to insiders, franchise sales is a tough specialty.

A franchise employer in the *Wall Street Journal* noted that average salaries for 1990 were about $100,000—along with a guaranteed minimum compensation, and in some cases, a high commission of 10 percent.

▶ Retail sales: a growing—and changing—area.

Forget for a moment the mostly sluggish past year. In the long term, retail sales will have one of the *largest* job growth rates in the 1990s. Even better, many of these jobs will have more to offer the motivated worker in the way of job satisfaction, working conditions, and, most importantly, money.

And for upper-level marketers and sales managers, look at this area as the focus of some prime challenges in the second half of the 1990s. MBAs are moving into the Wal-Marts of the country, studying POS (point of sale) strategies, etc.

What's happening? Managers, dissatisfied with, e.g., all-too-typical slow customer service in department stores, are turning to commissions as a way of motivating salespeople. Renaming them "sales associates," and paying a commission on sales (either a straight commission or a base salary and a lower commission), is having its effect on retail morale—and on the bottom line. Already much of the New York retail market is taking the commission route, as have other areas. Watch for this trend to continue throughout the 1990s.

WHAT'S NEXT

▶ Sales will become more complex, more knowledge-oriented.

As a sales manager stated, "There's no longer a sort of homogenous sale. . . . It's no longer just a product and a program. Now it's starting to be product, program, the financial package around it, and how you can deliver it."

Translation: the demand for top-quality salespeople will go up. Markets are growing more competitive, average sales costs are going up, and the need for detailed, up-to-date product or service information is increasing.

In this line, expect:

1. **much greater demand for *specialist* sales representatives**—people with a specialized knowledge and background of products or services. This is already the case in many areas such as computers, banking, and particularly health care, where many salespeople have backgrounds in biology or chemistry.

2. **much greater demand for highly skilled salespeople.** One trend: *IQ and other testing* for sales applicants, increased need for statistical, computer-oriented people, more thorough interviewing process for applicants. Another trend: testing for weaknesses—and specific programs to correct them.

3. **intensified competition for the top sales jobs.** Example: 28,000 people applied for 500 sales positions at Merck.

4. **selling will become more *information-oriented*.** People who can quickly master information in general, statistical data in particular, will prosper.

5. **fewer—but longer—sales calls** (already, average sales calls are down from eight to six a day) as time spent per customer goes up.

6. **hybrid reps**—particularly in media sales, salespeople are representing more than one media area.

7. **more cross-training**—salespeople going into marketing. With a strong background in sales, in knowing what the company wants, they have an edge in making strategic marketing decisions.

But the bottom line: there will always be a demand for top salespeople who can *sell*, with or without the right paper qualifications.

SALARIES

▶ **Sales and marketing middle managers make more** *on average* **than other middle managers. But they earn it with long hours and high pressure.**

Commissions, not base salary, are what motivate most salespeople. Marketing employees are paid on salary—but often with substantial bonuses. In 1988 and 1989, sales and marketing incomes increased, up to 20% over the last year for marketing employees.

But remember: what goes up must come down. A few top earners saw their incomes drop by 50% last year. Volatility is *not* uncommon.

RETAIL: Median salary, $300 per week, lower for certain areas like hardware; $700 and up for certain fields (automotive, boat, and electronics). For salespeople on *straight* commission, the range varies. In a department store, for example, a typical range would be from about 5% for low-ticket goods to 10% for high-ticket items. Partial commission would be around 2%, plus a base salary.

INSURANCE: Begins with base salary of $18,000 to $20,000—lasting usually for a year and a half, provided the agent meets sales targets. Afterward, commissions provide income. Median income for an insurance agent with over five years experience is approximately $50,000, ten years is $70,000. Twenty percent of all agents earn over $100,000.

REAL ESTATE: Agents and brokers usually depend entirely on commission. The *median* income for real estate agents is approximately $25,000. Real estate brokers, who also rent, manage properties, arrange real estate loans, etc., reported a higher median salary of over $35,000. However, in both cases, salaries of $200,000 or more are not uncommon. Many people leave the business each year particularly as real estate suffers from the recession, but in good years, successful real estate brokers can be among the highest paid salespeople in the U.S.

SECURITIES: Salespeople begin in a range from $35,000 to $40,000—usually paid as a base salary until certification requirements are met and commissions reach a certain amount. Experience counts: average earnings increase to $90,000 after several years; institutional account representatives averaged over $200,000 in 1989. Key problem: much greater competition for fewer jobs in 1990.

FINANCIAL SERVICES: For salaries and other information, see the Banking and Financial Services section (pages 267 and 349). Note: Expect large declines in the top incomes paid for Wall Street financial jobs.

SERVICE SALES REPS: earn widely varied salaries, depending on the industry, region, and specific firm and type of payment and commission structure. Advertising salespeople earn a median salary of about $25,000; other business services a median salary of $22,000. Above these medians, salaries can be very high—many advertising salespeople in New York easily earned over $100,000 before the sales slump in 1989.

MANUFACTURING SALES REPS: also vary widely in earnings. Median income is approximately $28,000, the top 10 percent earn over $50,000. Upper-level sales executives averaged $105,000 in base salary last year, or $135,500 in total compensation, according to *Sales and Marketing Management*.

MARKETING: salaries vary widely as well—depending on the firm, the industry, and the individual. In manufacturing, salary increases in the 1990s will probably be higher in nondurables; but again, more depends on the specific industry.

Beginning marketing salaries averaged $21,000 last year; rising to approximately $36,000 after several years. Many firms pay far more: a survey by the National Institute of Business Executives found that the median total compensation of all marketing executives was $90,000 last year. Top sales-and-marketing executives averaged over $180,000 in total compensation, top marketing executives over $130,000, and about $170,000 at larger firms. Often bonuses, stock options, and other nonsalary perquisites like company cars can raise incomes.

BEST BETS

NORTHWESTERN MUTUAL LIFE: a salesperson's dream company. Outdistances all other insurance firms in sales surveys—the best in recruiting, training, reputation. Emphasizes promotion from within, training (over 100 courses per year), and maintaining "personal" attributes of selling in new technical environment. Employs about 7,000 independent agents.

SPECIAL EVENTS MARKETING: The job even sounds fun—putting together everything involved for a special event, usually sports-related, such as a golf or tennis match. It's grueling work, though. Marketers may do everything from selling the concept to corporate sponsors to making sure the lemonade or beer is cold. But the growth is there; this is a fast-growing area and the pay potential is high. Beginning salaries in the 20s, average in the 40s, up to $200,000 and more.

WHERE TO GO FOR MORE INFORMATION

SALES AND MARKETING ASSOCIATIONS

(For advertising associations, directories, and magazines, see Advertising and Public Relations in the Industry section on page 225.)

American Marketing Association
250 S. Wacker Dr., Suite 200
Chicago, IL 60606-5819
312/648-0536
(Publishes periodicals with job listings, directory, placement service.)

Bank Marketing Association
309 W. Washington St.
Chicago, IL 60606
312/782-1442
(Affiliated with American Bankers Association; offers placement service, publishes directory, etc.)

Broadcast Promotion and Marketing Executives
6255 Sunset Blvd.
Los Angeles, CA 90028
213/465-3777

Convention Liaison Council
1575 I St., NW, Suite 1200
Washington, DC 20005
202/626-2764
(Administers the Certified Meeting Professional—CMP—designation; comprises members of many groups in meetings industry.)

Direct Marketing Association
11 W. 42nd St.
New York, NY 10036-8096
212/768-7277
(Publishes directory, periodical with some listings, offers placement service, etc.)

Electronic Representatives Association
20 E. Huron St.
Chicago, IL 60611
312/649-1333
(Covers multiline salespersons of electronic items, including consumer; publishes directory.)

Financial Marketing Association
111 E. Wacker Dr.
Chicago, IL 60601
312/938-2570

Hotel Sales and Marketing Association International
1300 L St., NW, Suite 800
Washington, DC 20005
202/789-0089

International Newspaper Advertising and Marketing Executives
P.O. Box 17210
Washington, DC 20041
703/648-1177

Manufacturers' Agents National Association
P.O. Box 3476
Laguna Hills, CA 92654
714/859-4040
(Publishes magazine, *Agency Sales,* with many job listings, and directory.)

Marketing Research Association
2189 Silas Deane Hwy., Suite 5
Rocky Hill, CT 06067
203/257-4008

Meeting Planners, International
Infomart
1950 Stemmons Fwy., Suite 5018
Dallas, TX 75207-3109
214/746-5222
(Largest professional group in meetings industry.)

National Association of Market Developers
1422 W. Peachtree, NW,
Suite 500
Atlanta, GA 30309
404/892-0244

National Electrical Manufacturers Representatives Association
200 Business Park Dr.
Armonk, NY 10504
914/273-6780
(Association for independent sales reps for electrical manufacturers; sponsors various programs.)

Promotion Marketing Association of America
322 Eighth Ave.
New York, NY 10001
212/206-1100

Sales and Marketing Executive International
Statler Office Tower,
Suite 458
Cleveland, OH 44115
216/771-6650
(Huge group; involved in sales education programs, publishes directory, etc.)

Society of Corporate Meeting Professionals
2600 Garden Rd.,
Suite 208
Monterey, CA 93940
408/649-6544
(Provides scholarship money to members who wish Corporate Meeting Professional certification.)

Society for Marketing Professional Services
99 Canal Ctr. Plz.,
Suite 320
Alexandria, VA 22314
703/549-6117
(Placement and educational services; directory of members.)

United Association Manufacturers Representatives
P.O. Box 6266
Kansas City, KS 66106
913/268-9466
(Publishes monthly journal with many situation listings, etc.)

SALES AND MARKETING DIRECTORIES

(Many associations publish directories, as do some magazines listed below.)

Bradford's Directory of Marketing Research Agencies and Management Consultants in the United States and the World; Bradford's Directory of Marketing Research Agencies
Box 76
Fairfax, VA 22030
703/830-4646

Manufacturers' Agents and Representatives
American Business Directories
5711 S. 86th Cir.
P.O. Box 27347
Omaha, NE 68127
402/593-4600
FAX 402/331-5481
(Twenty thousand names, addresses, and phone numbers nationwide for $660; sells a list of marketing consultants for $330.)

The Salesman's Guide: National Directory of Corporate Meeting Planners
P.O. Box 31
New Providence, NJ 07973
800/323-6772
(Also publishes related directories.)

The 100 Best Companies to Sell For,
by Michael Harkary
John Wiley & Sons
605 Third Ave.
New York, NY 10158

SALES AND MARKETING PERIODICALS

Agency Sales Magazine
P.O. Box 3467
Laguna Hills, CA
92654
714/859-4040
(Monthly for
manufacturers reps.)

**American Agent &
Broker**
408 Olive St.
St. Louis, MO 63102
314/421-5455
(Monthly magazine for
insurance agents and
brokers.)

Business Marketing
Crain Communications
740 N. Rush St.
Chicago, IL 60601
312/649-5200

**Corporate
Meetings/Incentives**
63 Great Rd.
Maynard, MA 01754
508/897-5552
(Monthly for business
meeting planners, etc.)

Direct Marketing
724 Seventh St.
Garden City, NY
11530-5771
516/746-6700
(Monthly; contains
some job listings.)

Industrial Distribution
Cahners Publishing
Circulation Department
44 Cook St.
Denver, CO
80206-5800
303/388-4511
(For sales reps, etc.;
carries some job
listings.)

Insurance Sales
1200 N. Meridian St.
Indianapolis, IN 46206
317/634-1541
(Monthly for life
insurance agents, etc.)

Life Insurance Selling
408 Olive St.
St. Louis, MO 63102
314/421-5445
(Monthly magazine for
insurance agents and
brokers.)

Marketing News
250 S. Wacker Dr.,
Suite 200
Chicago, IL
60606-5819
313/648-0536
(Biweekly association
publication.)

Recreation Resources
50 S. 9th St.
Minneapolis, MN

55402
612/333-0471
(Nine-issue magazine
for recreation
managers.)

**Sales Manager's
Bulletin**
The Bureau of Business
Practice
24 Rope Ferry Rd.
Waterford, CT 06386

**Sales & Marketing
Management**
633 Third Ave.
New York, NY 10017
212/986-4800
(Fifteen issues/yr.,
major magazine for
sales and marketing.)

Successful Meetings
633 Third Ave.
New York, NY 10017
212/986-4800
(Monthly; particularly
for managers who plan
and manage sales and
marketing meetings.)

SCIENTISTS

BRIEF BACKGROUND

▶ **For scientists, the good news is that *in general* there is or will be a shortage of qualified professionals. But the bad news is that a lot depends on what specific specialty you're trained and the state of the economy.**

At first glance, the logic pointing to a shortage seems compellingly simple. The U.S. graduates only 10,000 science Ph.D.s each year, and a proportionally larger (but still small) number of M.S. and B.S. students. Match a small number of graduates with an increasingly technical marketplace. This points to a growing shortage in the coming years—or at least so experts thought. At upper levels, research scientists and workers would be needed for complex new technologies. Science teachers would also be needed as replacements for retiring faculty, and secondary-school teachers would be needed in far greater numbers—one study suggested 300,000 additional science and mathematics teachers would be needed by 1995.

But many scientific job hunters found that all these rosy predictions didn't match realities. Why? There were a number of reasons. First of all, the scientific job market is highly segmented—while there are shortages in one area, another area may be oversupplied. It is also often dependent on government funding, and as funds were reduced with budget cuts and defense cuts, scientific hiring suffered. Also, with the recession many research labs laid off workers—this was particularly noticeable among large computer and telecommunications firms in 1992, and with certain biotech and pharmaceutical firms in 1993. Finally, the collapse of the Soviet Union and the rise of a global economy has opened the doors for many highly qualified applicants from overseas.

EMPLOYMENT OUTLOOK: In general, improving over the long term.

Major areas of employment:

BIOLOGISTS: There are over 100,000 biologists working in the U.S.—half of whom work in colleges and universities. Much job growth in the remaining 1990s will be in private industry, particularly *biotechnology and environmental positions*, as well as with government and universities. Under a "moderate growth" scenario for the economy as a whole, the federal government projects employment to 2005 to increase by a substantial 27%; with medical scientists faring even better—growth approaching 70%. Various studies point to a probable shortage of biological scientists in the 1990s. But there's a hitch. Unemployment is still high—20,000 biomedical scientists lost positions between 1989 and 1992—and the National Institutes of Health (NIH) cut basic research funding just as biotech companies were hit by the recession.

Some more caveats: Biotechnology is entering an unpredictable growth phase; about the only thing that is certain is that *some* areas will be booming in the future. Some estimate that over 1,000 new positions will open each year for the next few years. From engineered plant genes to new medical technologies, job opportunities are available both at small firms and at the giants which have been entering the field in a big way. One drawback: the area is a volatile one, which makes job security often low.

Government hiring will probably also increase in biotech. A lot depends on the direction the NIH takes.

What will be the best qualifications for a new career in this area? According to *Biotechnology* magazine, beyond the right academic background, the key will be laboratory skills—and this does *not* include school laboratory courses. Their recommendations: Get the relevant experience before applying for employment—through work, summer positions, research assistantships.

Environmental positions are becoming mainstream at many companies as they attempt to anticipate the problems of hazardous waste, chemical dumping, and the environmental consequences of industry. In addition, another growing area for the 1990s will be environmental renewal—as people seek to return the environment to its natural condition, with native plants and animals. Again, much depends on the strength of economic recovery.

A good source for *general biology positions:* BioTron, run by the American Institute of Biological Sciences (AIBS), maintains a job bank for biologists. Another job bank is run by the AIBS, and the American Society for Experimental Biology; it is called the FASEB placement service. (See listings and instructions on page 157.)

AGRICULTURAL SCIENTISTS: Good prospects; fairly slow government hiring, but fairly good opportunities in private industry; job growth between 20 and 30 percent in the 1990s, according to the U.S. Government.

CHEMISTS: Job outlook for 1994 and beyond looks fair to good. Key point: a lower number of chem grads coming into the market, along with the probability that the chemical industry will continue to do well. Ph.D.s will probably be in highest demand, along with specialists in polymers and synthetics, analytical chemistry and food chemistry.

There are 85,000 chemists in the U.S. Over half work for manufacturing firms—half of those for firms within the chemical industry. The single largest specialty is pharmaceuticals, which should experience relative strength throughout the 1990s despite current problems within the industry. Key advantage: as biotechnology advances, these firms stand to gain tremendously in the sale of bio-engineered drugs. Another strong growth area should be in materials chemistry.

Best bets: ***Sales:*** companies are turning to science majors for sales positions rather than business majors. Rationale: it is easier to train scientists as salespeople than train salespeople in the sciences. ***Academics:*** best areas include organic chemistry, biochemistry, and analytical chemistry. ***Corporate:*** waste management, environmental firms. Another good area: just as lab scientists complain of poor management, a good area to get into is ***scientific management;*** the Bureau of Labor Statistics rates this area as one of the fastest growing for people with college degrees or higher.

As technical specialties increase, watch for a growth in consulting jobs as well. Already, chemical consulting occupies 3.5–5% of the total U.S. consulting market.

For job openings: check with the American Chemical Society (address on page 156), which operates the Employment Clearing House; want ads in *Chemical and Engineering News* are another good bet.

PHYSICISTS: In general, as the economy improves, so should hiring—particularly as faculty retirements increase and open up some breathing room in the universities. The overall outlook, is however, only fair at best; the government projects a low 5% increase in employment of physicists to the year 2005 under a moderate economic growth scenario; although certain other areas of the physical sciences such as meteorology should fare much better.

A good source of job leads, both academic and nonacademic, is the American Institute of Physics and its various publications, especially *AIP Notice* and *Physics Today*. The address is at the end of this section.

Other physical science areas:

METEOROLOGISTS: Projected job growth between 22 and 34% to the year 2005. These strong job prospects are due to a high projected demand by the National Weather Service, particularly in its expanded field offices, as well as by private industry.

GEOLOGISTS AND GEOPHYSICISTS: Outlook improving as the petroleum industry, which is a major employer, continues recovering from problems in the 1980s. On the downside: competition from overseas firms in exploration (and hiring of foreign nationals), possibility of less oil exploration in U.S. territories in the future. Hot specialties in the 1990s will be in environmental geology. Hydrogeologists, in particular, are in short supply. For job openings, check with the Geological Society of America Matching Service (address is listed on page 158), which is a job bank run by the association listing current geological jobs.

MATHEMATICIANS: The American Mathematical Society reported in 1991 that 12% of new math Ph.Ds. were still seeking work—double the number of previous years. But as the economy recovers further, prospects should improve. Although growth forecasts are at the low end—around 9% in a moderately growing economy—related disciplines are expected to grow very rapidly, namely, mathematical and computer research analysis (upward of 70% employment growth), actuarial work (34%), and statistics (79%). According to Smith Hanley Associates, demand for statisticians with a master's or doctorate doubled between 1985 and 1990, and could double again by 1995. Check for openings with the American Mathematical Society and the Mathematical Association of America—addresses are listed at the end of this section.

WHAT'S NEXT

▶ Although scientists rate high in career satisfaction surveys, various problems surface again and again:

Inadequate career preparation: Many science students are not coached on employment prospects while in college. In many cases, this encourages the "postdoc" syndrome, where graduate students specialize in areas that condemn them to low-paid, low-prestige postdoctoral positions. They aren't steered toward research that will offer rewards once they've got their Ph.Ds. Worst for: physics Ph.D. graduate students; women—who also face lingering discrimination in some areas. The American Physical Society is focusing now on identifying alternative career paths for Ph.D. physicists, while the AIP is studying whether postdocs are having trouble finding permanent employment.

Inadequate use of scientific talent on the job; lack of communication between scientists and management: Some scientists in corporations complain they must sacrifice quick corporate profits for long-term advancement. In other words, the lack of R&D spending—and attention—can be very frustrating. A survey reported in *R&D Magazine* in 1992 found that the problem of inadequate communication was worst in government (66%), next in industry, and least serious in universities and consulting.

Lack of funding for young researchers: This is a major problem—consigning young scientists to post-doc positions.

Academic "inbreeding": Harvard graduates wind up with Harvard jobs, etc. Problem: not enough cross-fertilization, overreliance on "old boy" networks.

Scientists may be vital, but a lot of plumbers make more money: The average scientist with almost twenty years experience makes $45,000 to $50,000 a year. To make substantially more, a scientist must usually leave scientific work and become a manager or an entrepreneur.

▶ Science will become more "international."

Part of it is obvious—more foreign-born U.S. scientists, more and freer communication around the world, better standards of research in more countries. But science is also becoming more expensive. One prediction: the "mega-science" projects, such as the Human Genome Project, the Superconducting Super Collider, and the Space Station, may wind up becoming international projects with costs shared by European and other foreign participants.

SALARIES

BIOLOGISTS: Beginning employees with a bachelor's or master's degree average $20,000 to $25,000; Ph.Ds. $30,000 to $35,000. Experienced biologists average about $40,000 in government, $48,000 in private industry. Biotechnology Ph.Ds. can make over $50,000 starting, $75,000 on up with several years of the right experience.

CHEMISTS: median salaries, according to *C&EN* (*Chemical & Engineering News*), were $45,000 for all chemists; $35,000 for BS degree holders, $41,000 for MS holders, $50,000 for Ph.Ds. In academia, highest salaries were for full professors of Ph.D.-granting schools. The median salary was $50,000, with $63,400 for full professors, $44,600 for associate professors, and $37,000 for assistant professors. Highest salaries for chemists in industrial firms, particularly those working as managers, with a median salary of $68,500.

Chemical engineers received an average starting salary of about $33,000 in 1989.

PHYSICISTS AND OTHER PHYSICAL SCIENTISTS: In 1992, the American Institute of Physics found that starting salaries for physics doctoral recipients in potentially permanent jobs had declined about 4% between 1989 and 1990—the median salary was $42,960; $48,000 for those taking jobs in industry. MAs earn a median salary of approximately $36,000, with those employed by manufacturers earning the most. BS degree holders earned the least, about $32,160. On the bright side, these numbers were higher than those of the previous year. The average salary for **meteorologists** was $40,000. **Astronomy** postdoctoral applicants earned a median salary of $36,000.

MATHEMATICIANS: Starting salaries range from about $25,000$^+$ for BAs to $40,000$^+$ for Ph.Ds. According to the Bureau of Labor Statistics, median salaries for mathematicians with Ph.Ds. ranged from about $42,000 in academics to over $50,000 in business in 1985. **Actuaries** (see page 156) earn from about $25,000 for entry-level positions to $100,000$^+$ for experienced employees.

BEST BETS

ENVIRONMENTAL CAREERS: Depending on the economic recovery, this area should improve, as environmental clean-up (particularly as mandated by Superfund and related legislation), pollution prevention, and environmental management become crucial corporate and government concerns. In-demand areas: hydrogeologists, air-quality engineers, risk assessment specialists, industrial hygienists, and environmental engineers. Best route to a job: an appropriate undergraduate degree (advanced degrees are better, but field is so strong that Ph.Ds. and the like are usually not neccesary). Jobs are available with corporations in chemical, petroleum, and manufacturing industries, and with specialty firms like Waste Management, for the government, or for smaller consulting and engineering firms. However, research prospects carefully; the recession has had its effects in this industry as well.

For more information, contact specialty associations below and in Engineering and High-Tech section on page 41. Particularly for students, note that the Environmental Careers Organization offers careers conferences, special career publications, and other services. It also places students and recent graduates in short-term professional positions, serves as an on-the-job training organization, and gives associates an inside track for employment. For information and applications, see address on page 52.

ACTUARIAL POSITIONS: Where the insurance industry meets science and mathematics. Actuaries are in effect insurance mathematicians, who calculate the odds in life and death (e.g., probabilities that men in their forties will die in that decade) and use these odds in figuring pension plans and insurance benefits for insurance firms and other corporations. Requirements: a strong aptitude for math; must pass a series of examinations over a period of five to ten years. Advantages: high pay, very high demand by industry, growing field (people are living longer, insurance is getting more complex). For more information, contact: the American Academy of Actuaries and the Society for Actuaries—addresses are at the end of this section.

WHERE TO GO FOR MORE INFORMATION

SCIENCE ASSOCIATIONS

American Academy of Actuaries
1720 I St., NW,
7th Fl.
Washington, DC 20006
202/223-8196
(Directory, introductory career guide, etc.)

American Anthropological Association
1703 New Hampshire Ave., NW
Washington, DC 20009
202/232-8800
(Publishes periodical with some job information and listings; sells booklets that list government employment opportunities; members' placement service, etc.)

American Association of Physical Anthropologists
Department of Anthropology
SUNY at Buffalo
365 MFAC
Buffalo, NY 14261
716/636-2414
(Publishes journal, etc.)

American Association of Zoological Parks and Aquariums
Oglebay Park
Wheeling, WV 26003

304/242-2160
(Publishes career guide, directory, periodical with job openings for members.)

American Chemical Society
1155 16th St., NW
Washington, DC 20036
1-800/227-5558
(Publishes various periodicals with job listings, such as the *Journal of Agricultural and Food Chemistry*—see separate listings for *Chemical & Engineering News*—career brochures, and salary surveys; maintains job clearinghouse, listing service, counseling services, etc.)

American Geological Institute
4220 King St.
Alexandria, VA 22302
703/379-2480
(Publishes magazine with job listings, etc.)

American Geophysical Union
2000 Florida Ave., NW
Washington, DC 20009
202/462-6900
800/424-2488
(Publishes weekly newspaper with employment information and listings.)

American Horticultural Society
7931 E. Blvd. Dr.
Alexandria, VA 22308
800/777-7931
(Publishes magazine, offers placement
service for members.)

American Institute of Architects
1735 New York Ave., NW
Washington, DC 20006
202/626-7300
(Publishes periodical with employment
information, directory, etc.)

**American Institute for Biochemistry
and Molecular Biology**
9650 Rockville Pike
Bethesda, MD 20814-3996
301/530-7145
(Offers placement service, etc.)

**American Institute of Biological
Sciences**
730 11th St., NW
Washington, DC 20001
202/628-1500
(Publishes careers brochure,
periodical—*Bio Science*—with job
listing; placement service for
members; directory, etc.; also runs
BioTron, a computerized bulletin
board that includes job opportunities.
Phone number is 202/628-AIBS; may
be accessed by anyone with standard
computer-modem combination. Com
configuration is 300, 1200, or 2400
baud, 8 data bits, 1 stop bit, no
parity, full duplex, Xon, Xoff active,
carriage return, at end of lines. Full
prompts furnished by system.
Received text may be stopped and
started with Control S/Q.)

American Institute of Physics
335 E. 45th St.
New York, NY 10017
212/661-9404
500 Sunnyside Blvd.
Woodbury, NY 11797
(Publishes periodicals with job
listings, surveys, etc.; affiliated
members include American Physical
Society, Acoustical Society,
Association of Physics Teachers, and
Geophysical Union.)

American Mathematical Society
201 Charles St.
Providence, RI 02904
401/455-4000
(Publish periodical with job listings,
directory, etc.)

American Meteorological Society
45 Beacon St.
Boston, MA 02108
617/227-2425
(Publishes journal with employment
listings, educational programs, etc.)

American Society of Agronomy
677 S. Segoe Rd.
Madison, WI 53711
608/273-8080
(Operates placement service for
members, etc.)

American Society for Microbiology
1325 Massachusetts Ave., NW
Washington, DC 20005
202/628-1500
(Publishes periodical with employment
listings; placement service.)

American Statistical Association
1429 Duke St.
Alexandria, VA 22314-3402
703/684-1221
(Publishes periodical with job
openings, directory, etc.)

Archeological Institute of America
675 Commonwealth Ave.
Boston, MA 02215
617/353-9361
(Publishes periodical with dig
information, small directory, etc.)

**Association of American
Geographers**
1710 16th St., NW
Washington, DC 20009-3198

202/234-1450
(Operates placement service;
sometimes expedition announcements,
etc.)

Botanical Society of America
1735 Neil Ave.
Columbus, OH 43210
203/486-4322
(Periodical, etc.)

Center for American Archeology
P.O. Box 366
Kampsville, IL 62503
618/653-4316

Federation of American Societies for Experimental Biology
9650 Rockville Pike
Bethesda, MD 20814
301/530-7020
(Runs job bank, periodical with job openings, directory.)

Geological Society of America
P.O. Box 9140
3300 Penrose Pl.
Boulder, CO 80301
303/447-2020
(Publishes periodical with a few job listings, directory, etc.)

Institute of Mathematical Statistics
3401 Investment Blvd.,
Suite 7
Hayward, CA 94545
510/783-8141
(Publishes periodical with job listings.)

Minerals, Metals, and Materials Society
420 Commonwealth Dr.
Warrendale, PA 15086
412/776-9000
(Publishes periodical with employment listings, etc.)

Society of Actuaries
475 N. Martingale Rd.
Schaumburg, IL 60173-2226
708/706-3500
(Publishes free booklet on careers, etc.)

Society for American Archeology
808 17th St., NW,
Suite 200
Washington, DC 20006
202/223-9774
(Publishes periodicals with some listings.)

Society for Applied Anthropology
P.O. Box 24083
Oklahoma City, OK 73124
405/843-5113
(Three thousand members work in government and business, applying techniques of anthropology to development planning, etc.)

Society for Industrial and Applied Mathematics
3600 University City Science Center
Philadelphia, PA 19104-2688
215/382-9800
(Publishes periodical with job listings, etc.)

Society for Industrial Microbiology
P.O. Box 12534
Arlington, VA 22209
703/941-5373
(Publishes periodical with job listings, directory; offers placement service.)

Society for Mining, Metallurgy, and Exploration
P.O. Box 625002
Littleton, CO 80162
303/973-9550
(Publishes directory, etc.)

SCIENCE DIRECTORIES, DATABANKS

(Many of the associations above publish directories; many are listed under the appropriate association.)

BIOSIS
2100 Arch St
Philadelphia, PA
19103-1399
1-800/523-4806
(Life-science database includes millions of addresses, job listings, etc.)

BioTron
(See listing under American Institute of Biological Sciences.)

Conservation Directory
National Wildlife
Foundation

1400 16th St., NW
Item 79359
Washington, DC 20036
703/790-4402
800/432-6564
(Lists hundreds of state and federal governments, nonprofit organizations, educational institutions, with addresses, names, etc., all involved in conservation.)

Peterson's Job Opportunities for Engineering, Science,

and Computer Graduates
Peterson's
P.O. Box 2123
Princeton, NJ
08543-2123
609/243-9111
800/338-3282
(Lists hundreds of corporations and government agencies that are hiring; includes detailed information.)

SCIENCE MAGAZINES

American Laboratory
P.O. Box 870
Shelton, CT 06484
203/926-9300
(Monthly; particularly for research chemists and biologists.)

American Scientist
P.O. Box 13975
Research Triangle Park,
NC 27709
919/549-0097
(For members of Sigma Xi.)

BioScience
American Institute of
Biological Sciences
730 11th St., NW
P.O. Box 20001
202/628-1500

Chemical & Engineering News
345 E. 47th St.
New York, NY 10017
212/705-7663
(Excellent industry roundups are particularly valuable as overviews for entry-level job hunters; classifieds include many job openings.)

CRM
U.S. Department of the Interior
National Park Service
P.O. Box 37127
Washington, DC
20013-7137
202/343-3395
(News of the Park

Service; gives a feel for the work, sometimes has paid intern information for arch., foresters, etc.)

Federal Archeology Report
Archeological
Assistance Division
National Park Service
P.O. Box 37127
Washington, DC
20013-7127
202/343-4101
(Quarterly; sometimes includes information on volunteer programs, as well as training programs for government workers.)

The Newsletter of Corporate Anthropology
Roger P. McConchie
2400 E. Main St.,
Suite 103-A
St. Charles, IL 606174
708/584-5848
(A small newsletter w/o job listings, but highlights a new and growing and increasingly important area of employment for anthropologists.)

High Technology Careers
Westech Publishing Company
4701 Patrick Henry Dr.,
Suite 1901
Santa Clara, CA 95054
(High-tech industry tabloid with hundreds of high-tech job openings listed.)

Nature
65 Bleecker St.,
12th Fl.
New York, NY 10021
212/477-9600
(Prestigious weekly.)

Physics Today
335 E. 45th St.
New York, NY 10017
212/661-9404
(Monthly association magazine; carries numerous job listings, a few state-of-the-profession articles, etc.)

Science
1333 H St., NW
Washington, DC 20005
202/326-6500
(Prestigious weekly science magazine; carries listings.)

Weatherwise
4000 Albemarle St., NW
Washington, DC 20016
202/362-6445
(Bimonthly.)

SOCIAL SERVICES AND LEGAL PROFESSIONALS

BRIEF BACKGROUND

▶ **Social services and legal services positions are well-poised for growth during the latter half of the 1990s.**

Funding cutbacks and the recession have had their effects, but demographic factors make both areas fairly strong in terms of job growth. The greater demand for legal services and the aging of our population point to job opportunities. Of course, the popularity of many professions in these areas also points to fairly strong competition as well, as do the efforts to trim costs.

EMPLOYMENT OUTLOOK: Mixed. Strongest demand for paralegals, international trade lawyers, and residential and family care social services workers.

▶ **The fastest-growing area: jobs for** *paralegals*—**expected to grow 85% by the year 2005.**

Paralegals will be the second fastest-growing occupation in the U.S. during the next ten years.

Paralegals, or legal assistants, work with lawyers in most areas of legal work, from researching and reporting to preparing legal arguments, helping to draft agreements, and preparing corporate tax returns.

Reason for growth in the 1990s: paralegals are a lower-cost alternative to lawyers, particularly useful as legal services become more generally used in society, and as corporations and individuals become more cost conscious.

Most paralegals are employed by private law firms, where employment prospects will hit new highs. But job turnover will also be fairly high as paralegals leave the profession and move into management—or go on to law school. Jobs in the public sector are expected to increase as well. Reason: the government now provides more legal and related services to the poor and elderly—and paralegals are a low-cost way of maintaining and expanding services.

New trend: Paralegal *firms,* made up of independent paralegals, who offer legal services for lower prices. The number of such firms increased from 200 in 1985 to over 6,000 last year.

Best bet: While paralegals still are not required to be certified, it helps job prospects. The National Association of Legal Assistants (NALA, see address on page 167) sets experience and educational standards for a two-day qualifying exam, after which paralegals who pass are designated Certified Legal Assistants (CLAs). Education for paralegals is varied, from two months to two years, from general to specialized. Contact the NALA for ABA-approved schools and recommended programs; the association also offers a self-teaching cassette course, seminars, and library facilities.

Strong prospects in the field: *trusts and estates*. Reason: high demand, low numbers. According to one recruiter, "Most people want the glamour of litigation, not the more technical work of going through accounts." Paralegals must be familiar with accounting as well as legal issues. *Trademark law*—according to *Legal Professional* magazine, there is a current shortage of adequately trained paralegals. *Employee benefits* is another extremely strong hiring area, with demand expected to stay very high throughout the 1990s.

▶ **Another possible growth area: *legal administration*.**

Law firms are increasingly being run like normal businesses—and are increasingly hiring top business talent to run the nonlegal aspects of the firm. Legal administrators still suffer the stigma of being business people in a nonbusiness arena—lawyers sometimes consider themselves superior within the firm to nonlawyers. But two trends are changing things: law is becoming more competitive—firms are increasingly fighting for the same clients; and law is becoming more businesslike—firms are now routinely being told to justify costs by large corporate clients. Both justify spending top dollars for good administrators. And as a reflection of their new importance, top administrators are now being offered partnerships in some top firms.

▶ **Over the short term, expect a lag in employment growth for lawyers—particularly at the larger law firms. Long term, however, is brighter.**

Like many corporations across the country over the past few years, law firms also fell into a pattern of downsizing—including layoffs and hiring freezes. One reason: As corporations became more cost-conscious, they cut back on their use of outside legal services. As a result, 1993 saw growth at the 500 largest law firms flatter than it had been for over 40 years, according to the survey by legal magazine *Of Counsel.*

This flat growth scenario may continue over the short term, but the long term picture is brighter, with the government predicting a 24% increase in jobs for lawyers to the year 2005. Strongest areas—tax law, international law, and, possibly, such specialties as environmental law. As usual, the top 10% of the best law schools will find the best firms recruiting them.

The bad news: Many people each year enter legal practice as lawyers—around 36,000. And so competition for jobs, particularly good jobs, will be very tough.

Over 500,000 lawyers practice in the U.S. today, around 80% of them in private practice or in legal firms. The percentage choosing this option continues to rise. Change is continuing in the 1990s—where once the majority in private practice were solo practitioners (67% of new law grads chose this option in 1957), today only 2% work alone. Possible reason: as law becomes more complex, it is harder to work on one's own.

About 18% of all private practitioners work in the large, big-name national firms. The majority of the rest work in government or with corporations as in-house counsel. Both areas are expected to increase hiring—particularly as corporations recognize the cost advantages of in-house counsel.

Two trends are affecting employment:

Large legal firms are getting more cost-conscious. For example, in 1992, in an effort to cut costs, major national firms began cutting salaries, which have increased by 460% in the last twenty years. That's not the worst of it: according to a major consulting company quoted in the *Wall Street Journal*: "It is becoming more and more difficult to make partner. For many associates, it is out of their reach entirely. There's just too many lawyers out there." Another result: these mega-firms will be able to pick and choose the best lawyers from the best law schools, reducing the pickings for the rest of the class.

Legal complexity is increasing. This will make lawyers specializing in certain areas more employable. Best bets in the 1990s: tax law, trusts and estates, product liability, environment. Two emerging areas: white-collar crime as a specialty; environmental law. Everyone's talking about the environment and the job opportunities connected with it—and that just means more work for environmental lawyers who defend the public—or corporations and the government—from the consequences of mismanagement. The shortage of environmental lawyers is extremely acute; the laws are complex and new for most lawyers, so those with this specialty will face excellent job prospects. Employment law: rising health care costs, employee litigation, and shifting benefits all point to the strong opportunities in this rapidly changing field.

And, for the near future, good prospects for bankruptcy specialists. Reason: people and companies are more prone to use bankruptcy as a personal, corporate strategy, and the recession itself has spawned enough legal bankruptcies.

But remember a general rule of thumb, according to a top legal recruiter: "Specialize in what you like. That way, you'll be the best, and get the best offer, even in a crowded field."

Two areas that always need law school graduates: public interest groups and government agencies. Reason: it is tough attracting top applicants when all you can offer is an average salary of $27,000 (versus an average starting salary of over $83,600 at top New York law firms). Check with the National Association of Public Interest Law, which sponsors a national job fair.

▶ **A mini-boom in social work and human services jobs may be beginning: from private practice psychotherapy to work in public sector halfway houses.**

The most important thing to remember, however, is that this boom won't translate into high salaries—they'll stay low. And competition will be tough in the more lucrative areas in the private sector, as well as in major cities or metropolitan areas.

In the 1980s, social work was extremely unpopular. In the 1990s, it won't be. For a variety of reasons, from a dissatisfaction with money-centered careers to concern over the social problems of today, many older graduates are returning to school and getting master's degrees in social work (MSWs).

The differences between the 1990s students and those of the 1980s? Today's students are more practical, more grounded in reality, according to one educator. There are currently about 370,000 social workers; about 40% work for state or local government.

Projected employment growth areas: practices centering on children or the elderly (particularly the over-eighty-fives), publicly funded community halfway houses, employee assistance programs, hospitals, Sunbelt states. Rural areas will have continued difficulty attracting social workers, due to low salaries and poorer facilities.

Human services workers—a catchall term referring to the employees who work under professional supervision in health agencies, halfway houses, group homes, prisons, and other organizations—will see their field grow at a very fast rate.

One reason: a high turnover rate as employees "burn out." Another reason: growth in various social programs, such as group counseling, day care for the elderly. The better jobs and advancement potential will go to those with college degrees; almost 500 colleges, institutes, or vocational schools offer courses.

▶ **In the protective and law enforcement professions, the fastest-growing areas will be in the private sector.**

The U.S. is still suffering from a crime wave—in 1991-92, violent crime went up 8%—and corporations and individuals are willing to pay for extra security. But it's not just guard duty. Private security will become increasingly sophisticated, and trained employees will be needed to handle complex problems of computer fraud.

Already, private security companies employ about 1.5 million people and spend over $50 billion a year compared to 600,000 people and $30 billion by government, according to the National Institute of Justice. Look for that number to double by the year 2000—and watch employment figures jump as well.

The best areas: According to insiders, potential applicants should strongly consider specialized enforcement fields like telecommunications, computer security, planning in the private sector.

And what about the public sector? Spending is expected to increase by about a third, and the number of police will increase by about 20 to 25%. One government area, the FBI, looks strong as an employment prospect, although competition is always tough. (See page 65 in the Government section for details.) Also growing fast as a profession: private investigation.

Employment source for all law and security professionals: the NELS job listing. See page 169.

Employment spotlight: Corrections

The numbers keep going up. Highlighted last year, this far from glamorous field—working in the prison system guarding or counseling inmates and offenders, or managing prison staff—will see job growth of by 60%, one of the fastest-growing job categories in America.

Jobs will increase in most areas: for corrections officers, prison social workers and psychologists, and probation officers. According to *Corrections Today* magazine, the greatest growth in the history of the Bureau of Prisons will come in the next five years. Also looking strong: state corrections. In California, the number of corrections officers more than doubled in seven years. On the downside: corrections can be a dangerous profession, and salaries are lower than for others in law enforcement, ranging from $11,000 for entry-level corrections or probation officers, to a high of $35,000–$40,000 in this area; directors of corrections can make $100,000, wardens up to $70,000. For more information, contact: The American Correctional Association, address on page 166.

WHAT'S NEXT

▶ **Legal revolving door: as many people are leaving the law as entering. Most common leavers—new lawyers, corporate lawyers, more women than men.**

This trend will continue, as the thousands who enter law school discover it's not what they thought. Another growing trend: self-help groups for disgruntled, discouraged lawyers who want to switch careers.

▶ **Social workers will turn to the private sector in large numbers.**

Reasons: better pay, more personal autonomy. And a strong feeling that some of the major problems society faces begin with "normal" people. Major employment areas: corporations—employee assistance programs, private practice marriage psychotherapy, and family counseling.

SALARIES

LAWYERS: Average starting salary is about $50,000, more at top firms (up to $80,000), much less at smaller firms. Median salary of all lawyers is about $70,000. Government lawyers average about $55,000; beginning salaries in the 30s.

LEGAL SUPPORT POSITIONS: Legal administrators earn between $35,000 and $100,000, depending on the size of the firm, more for top firms. Accounting managers earn between $30,000 and $60,000; data-processing managers earn between $30,000 and $58,000.

PARALEGALS: starting salaries of around $25,000; with some experience, salaries from $25,000 to $40,000. Supervisors or specialists may earn from $45,000 up to $75,000 supervising a large staff of paralegals.

SOCIAL WORK POSITIONS: beginning salaries average $25,000 (with an MSW); the average for mid-level employees is around $30,000.

HUMAN SERVICES WORKERS: salaries range around $18,000, more for experienced or educated workers.

SOCIAL SCIENTISTS: See "University Faculty," page 177.

POLICE AND PROTECTIVE PERSONNEL: starting salaries in the mid-$20,000s; mid-level in the 30s and 40s. One advantage: liberal benefits; retirement at half-pay after twenty years is common.

BEST BETS

INFORMATION RESOURCE MANAGER (IRM):   A combination computer information specialist, legal librarian, and paralegal. The position will gain importance as law firms rely more and more on computers and become more automated. Good opportunity for computer-minded paralegal.

WHERE TO GO FOR MORE INFORMATION

SOCIAL SERVICES AND LEGAL ASSOCIATIONS AND ORGANIZATIONS

American Association for Counseling and Development
5999 Stevenson Ave.
Alexandria, VA 22304
703/823-9800
800/545-2223
(Major association in certifying counselors; holds workshops, etc., for members; publishes periodical with job openings, educational information, etc.)

American Association of Industrial Social Workers
781 Beta Dr.,
Suite K
Cleveland, OH 44143
216/461-4333

American Association for Marriage and Family Therapy
1100 17th St., NW,
10th Fl.
Washington, DC 20036

202/452-0109
(Publishes periodical with job listings, etc.)

American Association on Mental Retardation
1719 Kalorama Rd., NW
Washington, DC 20009-2783
800/424-3688
202/387-1968
(Publishes periodicals with job listings, etc.)

American Correctional Association
8025 Laurel Lakes Ct.
Laurel, MD 20707
301/206-5100
1-800/ACA-JOIN
(Publishes periodical, directories, etc.)

American Humantics
4601 Madison Ave.
Kansas City, MO 64122
816/561-6415

(For current college students interested in admin., etc., careers in social service attending various colleges, including UCLA, Pepperdine, High Point University (NC), etc. this group offers various orientation and training programs with organizations such as the Red Cross, Boy Scouts, and Girl Scouts.)

American Institute of Certified Planners
1777 Massachusetts Ave., NW
Washington, DC 20036
202/872-0611
(Affiliated with American Planning Association, listed below.)

**American
Occupational Therapy
Association**
P.O. Box 1725
Rockville, MD
20849-1725
800/366-9799
(Offers
educational/career
information.

**American Planning
Association**
1313 E. 60th St.
Chicago, IL 60637
312/955-9100
(Publishes periodical
with listings for
members, directory.)

**American
Psychological
Association**
122 17th St., NW
Washington, DC 20036
202/955-7690
(Publishes periodical
with job listings,
directories, etc.)

**American Society of
Criminology**
1314 Kinnear Rd.,
Suite 212
Columbus, OH 43212
614/292-9027
(Publishes periodical
with job openings,
directory; placement
service for members,
etc.)

**American Society for
Industrial Security**
1655 N. Ft. Myer Dr.,
Suite 1200
Arlington, VA 22209
703/522-5800
(Publishes periodical

with job listings,
placement for members,
etc.)

**American
Speech-Language-
Hearing Association**
10801 Rockville Pike
Rockville, MD 20852
301/897-5700
(Publishes periodical
with job listings,
employment referral,
career/educational
information, etc.)

**American Vocational
Association**
1410 King St.
Alexandria, VA 22314
703/683-3111

**Association for
Curriculum and
Development**
1250 N. Pitt St.
Alexandria, VA
22314-1493
703/549-9110
(Publishes periodical;
educational programs;
sponsors various
members' professional
networks, some of
which publish
newsletters and
directories.)

**Career Planning and
Adult Development
Network**
4965 Sierra Rd.
San Jose, CA 95132
408/559-4946
(Career counselors,
teachers, therapists,
etc.)

**Child Welfare League
of America**
440 First St., NW,
Suite 310
Washington, DC
20001-2085
202/638-2952
(Publishes periodical
with some listings;
placement service.)

**Legal Assistant
Management
Association**
P.O. Box 40129
Overland Park, KS
66204
913/381-4458

**Council on Social
Work Education**
1600 Duke St.
Alexandria, VA
22314-3421
(Publishes journal with
some listings.)

**National Association
of Legal Assistants**
1601 S. Main St., Suite
300
Tulsa, OK 74119
918/587-6828

**National Association
of Social Workers**
750 First St., NE
Washington, DC 20002
202/408-8600
(Publishes periodicals
with job listings, etc.)

**National Court
Reporters Association**
8224 Old Courthouse Rd.
Vienna, VA 22182-3808
703/556-6272
(Publishes employment
periodical with many
job openings,

directories;
computerized job
referral service for
members, etc.)

**National
Rehabilitation
Association**

1910 Association Dr.,
Suite 205
Reston, VA 22091
703/715-9090
(Publishes periodical
with job listings;
placement service, etc.)

**National Shorthand
Reporters Association**
118 Park St., SE
Vienna, VA 22180
703/281-4677
(Publishes monthly
periodical with listings,
for court reporters)

SOCIAL SERVICES AND LEGAL DIRECTORIES

Law Firm Yellow Pages
Monitor Publishing Co.
104 Fifth Ave.
2nd Fl.
New York, NY 10011
212/627-4140

National Paralegal Association
P.O. Box 406
Solebury, PA 18963

215/297-8333
FAX: 215/297-8358
(Publishes and sells many different
directories, salary surveys; rental
mailing lists, placement networks,
etc.)

SOCIAL SERVICES AND LEGAL PERIODICALS

ABA Journal
750 N. Lake Shore Dr.
Chicago, IL 60611
312/988-6003
(Monthly to members
of the American Bar
Association.)

American Lawyer
600 Third Ave.
New York, NY 10016
312/973-2800
(Iconoclastic
"insider's" view of
legal industry—chock
full of ads as well; ten
issues a year.)

*American
Rehabilitation*
Rehabilitation Services
Administration
330 C St., SW
Washington, DC

20202-2531
for subscriptions:
U.G. Government
Printing Office
Washington, DC 20402

Barrister
750 N. Lake Shore Dr.
Chicago, IL 60611
312/988-5990
(Quarterly.)

Business Lawyer
750 N. Lake Shore Dr.
312/988-6056
(Quarterly.)

Community Jobs
ACCESS
50 Beacon St.
Boston, MA 02108
617/720-5637
(Monthly job magazine;
lists hundreds of jobs in
the nonprofit sector.)

Corrections Today
8025 Laurel Lakes Ct.
Laurel, MD 20797
301/206-5100
(Invaluable for anyone
considering a
corrections career.)

Law and Order
1000 Skokie Blvd.
Wilmette, IL 60091
708/256-8555
(Monthly journal for
police, etc.)

NASW News
750 First St., NE
Washington, DC 20002
202/408-8600
(Ten issues/year;
association social
worker magazine; many
job listings.)

National Employment Listing Service
Sam Houston State University
Criminal Justice Center
Huntsville, TX
77341-2296
409/294-1692
(Monthly listing of job openings in all areas of law enforcement and corrections; also social work.)

National and Federal Legal Employment Report
Federal Reports
1010 Vermont Ave., NW
Washington, DC 20005
202/393-3311
(Monthly; lists hundreds of legal jobs, primarily government.)

National Law Journal
111 Eighth Ave.
New York, NY 10011
212/741-8300
(Weekly tabloid for lawyers; many job listings.)

Opportunity in Public Interest Law
ACCESS
50 Beacon St.
Boston, MA 02108
617/720-5627
(Lists hundreds of government legal jobs.)

Police Chief
1110 N. Glebe Rd.
Arlington, VA 22201
703/243-6500
(Monthly.)

Social Service Jobs
10 Angelica Dr.
Framingham, MA
01701
508/626-8644
FAX: 508/626-9389
(Biweekly job listings in social services—counselors, psychologists, etc.)

TEACHERS, EDUCATORS, AND SOCIAL SCIENTISTS

BRIEF BACKGROUND

▶ **Teaching and education are vital to the country's future: only now are we beginning to realize how essential an educated workforce and citizenry really are.**

In a nation where 23 million citizens are estimated to be functional illiterates, and where 40% of one high school class in a major city couldn't identify the U.S. on a map, obviously teaching is something we *should* emphasize.

But there is some good news: people are returning to the profession, and there is at least talk of salary hikes and better conditions for teachers and students. There is some debate as to how many new teachers and professors will be needed—the consensus is that demand will be rising in some areas, but with many new teachers coming into schools, shortages will be relatively rare. Corporations are also getting into the act: already they spend almost as much as public education in training workers. Increasingly they must train workers in the basics since so many students are not learning the basics in school.

One admirable note: Polaroid Corporation, concerned over projected teacher shortages, established Project Bridge, which pays for qualified employees to go into teaching—and pays for teachers to come into the corporation to get hands-on training in their specialties. IBM and other corporations offer other programs that encourage teacher development.

EMPLOYMENT OUTLOOK: Good in general over the long term, particularly as many current teachers retire. Librarians face a tougher job market due to probable continued budget constraints, educational administrators face substantial competition for these prestigious positions. Among social service jobs, psychologists will face the best long-term prospects.

▶ **Some experts are predicting a shortage of over 300,000 teachers by 2001.**

Key point: over half (51.6%) of current teachers are over forty—as many retire over the next ten years, job prospects will open further for applicants. Outlook will be best for mathematics, science and special-education teachers in particular.

Another major factor: teaching is a tough profession (ask any teacher)—and relatively low-paying considering the responsibilities. Some experts are concerned

that not enough highly qualified individuals will be attracted to the profession—
further increasing the potential shortage.

▶ But right now, competition for jobs may be tough.

A few years back, many experts were talking about a teacher shortage *now*. As
of last year, it hadn't really materialized. Why? For one thing, the recession
resulted in budget cuts—which translated into cutbacks in hiring, reduced or non-
existent salary increases, and sometimes actual staff reductions.

And something else seems to be happening as well. Not as many teachers are
leaving the profession as some experts had predicted.

RAND corporation, a major think tank, took a look at trends in Indiana and
found that attrition rates were among the lowest ever. Simply put, fewer teachers
were leaving, job openings were fewer than expected—and the study concluded
that what was happening in Indiana could be applied to the rest of the country as
well. *Key points:* fewer teachers were leaving to have families, more experienced
teachers were returning after starting families, and many older noneducation grads
were coming into the teaching profession for the first time.

So, what's the best guess for employment in the next few years? Prospects will
still improve, but maybe more slowly than many experts are saying. Employment
outlook will then improve more rapidly by the end of this decade as more retirements come on line.

And look for: more government emphasis on teaching. Budgets may start to go
up as we all become more aware of the importance of this profession. Union
officials are lobbying for more pay, less bureaucratic supervision, higher standards.
If more money and attention comes to teaching, look for even better employment
prospects.

And some more good news: Recent Department of Education statistics show
increased immigration and larger families again are pointing to more children in the
school system than previously thought—6% more, to be exact. Employment translation: this means better employment opportunities for many in the long term.

Best geographic areas: rising enrollments in the Southwest point to this as a
growing area. In terms of percentage growth in school enrollments, Arizona is
growing the fastest, followed by New Hampshire, Nevada, Maryland, Hawaii, and
California, Virginia, Washington, Florida, and Georgia. In terms of the largest
increases in absolute numbers of pupils, California and Arizona also top the list,
along with most of the other states above, as well as New York, New Jersey, and
Texas.

▶ There is renewed emphasis on teaching as a career.

As we said above, that's one of the reasons that a teacher shortage hasn't
materialized. And because of this, more people are leaving other careers to enter
teaching. At Columbia's Teachers College, 15% of the entering class came from
other jobs in finance, publishing, and other fields. And in the past few years, the
number of education-degree candidates has jumped by over 60%. This is a far cry
from the times when low pay and stories about lack of fulfillment, crime, and little
autonomy discouraged many people from the profession.

One reason for the change: in at least twenty-six states, there are alternative certification programs, where people with mathematics, business, or other skills can be trained—and then allowed to teach. In New Jersey, whose Provisional Teacher Program has served as a model for other states, prospective teachers must first pass the National Teachers exam, and hold at least a BA or BS in the field they wish to teach. They are then put into the classroom with full pay, taking in addition 200 hours of instruction in teaching and child psychology. They are also rated periodically. After one year, the school principal decides whether to recommend permanent certification. So far, the programs have been extremely successful: the teacher dropout rate is far lower than normal, and the caliber of new teachers is high. For new grads in particular, another option includes signing up with Teach for America, which places grads in schools nationwide, and Recruiting New Teachers, which operates a referral service. Addresses and details on page 182.

Most teachers, however, are graduates of four-year colleges with degrees in education, and most have master's degrees (MATs, master's of arts in teaching, are offered at many colleges) as well. Each state has its own certification programs, usually requiring the applicant to pass the National Teachers exam (required in twenty-two states).

Best bets: minority, bilingual teachers. Math and science. Vocational education (particularly in larger, private, job-training programs). Lesson from the recession: the first areas to be cut are music, art, gifted and remedial programs.

Another good bet: special education. Recent employment numbers showed actual shortages in various areas.

► **Preschool increases—a major trend.**

The fastest-growing area of education involves those who a few years back probably would have stayed at home—the three- and four-year-olds. Enrollment in formal preschool programs has jumped from 2.3 million in 1981 to 3.3 million in 1991, a 44% increase in ten years. According to *American School and University*, this growth rate will increase in the next ten years—pointing to strong job prospects. A good area: business day care centers.

There are currently about 1 million preschool workers. Although many are family day care providers, some are state-certified teachers eligible to teach at any level of public school. Many states require certification for preschool teachers: the CDA, or Child Development Associate. Many public schools require state certification for preschool workers. Contact: the National Association for the Education of Young Children (see page 181) and the Association for Childhood Education International (see page 180); and for more information on the CDA, the Council for Early Childhood Professional Recognition (page 181).

► **The employment outlook for librarians: still cloudy.**

Key point: budget cuts during the recession resulted in "reductions in force"—frequently heard words in many libraries across the country during the past few years. Many of these reductions were accomplished by hiring freezes and attrition—bad news for new job hunters.

There are about 149,000 librarians nationwide (as of 1990), according to the

Bureau of Labor Statistics; 75% of them are women. A master's in library science (MLS) is a requirement for most library jobs. Most librarians work as public and academic librarians, or as special librarians—for corporations, government agencies, or professional associations, and maintaining specialized collections of information. On the cutting edge of the field are database librarians, who manage computer information systems.

In general, the field is split into two main branches: user services (dealing with the public), and technical services (dealing primarily with acquisitions, cataloguing, etc.) In small libraries, these functions may be shared; in larger ones, librarians specialize.

Long-term outlook: Much depends on the strength of economic recovery and government commitment—with, hopefully, more funding getting down to where it is needed. This is vital: libraries are essential to our educational system. In the short term, the outlook is flat. Why? Not only has funding been going down in many cases, but book and journal costs are going up, new technologies (e.g., computerization) are expensive, and many libraries have huge, costly projects to fulfill, such as the preservation of collections. One way they retain enough money to do this: they keep staffing levels low. Note: librarians interested in pursuing government careers, see page 83 for the Library of Congress, and page 66 for the Offices of Personnel Management.

Some good news: Only half as many library students as in the past—pointing to less competition. For Ph.Ds.: Jobs market may be bright. Library school faculty is aging. Over half of all library school deans in a recent survey indicated concern over *"the dearth of Ph.D.-holding professors available to replace an aging professoriate."*

All in all, government statisticians predict employment growth between 3 and 19%. The most likely scenario: presuming a moderately growing economy, by the year 2005 job growth will be at about 11%. Better job prospects will come as the economy strengthens and funding increases can be sustained. Best way to look for jobs: check the many services of the American Library Association—see page 180.

Given the increasingly technical nature of the work, and previous shortages, good areas to specialize in when outlook improves will probably be many technical services, particularly cataloguers, children and young adults, science, engineering, business, and law. Also, bilingual librarians, archivists, and systems analysts, along with graduates in information science.

▶ **University teaching: outlook changes.**

Short-term prospects were hindered by the recession. Public education felt the effects in reduced state appropriations for education, which resulted in funding cuts at many colleges and universities. Private schools saw endowment returns lessening.

College enrollments were down in some areas as well, partly as a result of the recession, but also due to a flattening pool of college-age applicants. For example, a survey by the American Council on Education found that Connecticut showed decreases in all areas of higher education, New York was down in college and university enrollment, while Illinois and Virginia saw fewer students in four-year colleges.

Some good news: The number of college students will increase after 1996, as the first of the baby boomers' children reach college age. Also, a growing number of over-twenty-five-year-olds are entering college. All in all, the Department of Education projects a 16% increase in college enrollments by the year 2000.

But some bad news as well. Continued funding problems, other studies pointing to declining enrollments, and, most importantly, a clogged faculty point to problems for job hunters. The last is key: there are now many tenured professors in their thirties and forties, so the projected retirements of older faculty will not open up all that many positions, particularly as already hired associate professors fill in the slack. Overall, for at least the next five years, the supply of available applicants is expected to exceed the demand in most areas.

Best areas for faculty positions: Health, physical science, and computer science. Engineering and mathematics look weaker in the short term, but may resurge. One interesting trend: a recent study found enrollments in business courses was down by 21%—is this a trend for the future?

▶ Social scientists and historians.

About 200,000 people work as some sort of social scientist—interestingly, about 25% are self-employed as consultants and so on. Outlook: fairly strong competition, best for those with advanced degrees; in the long term probably best for economists (see below). Psychologists will face the best job market—for more on this and similar "helping professions" see page 161.

For other areas, employment prospects are to a greater extent tied to the fate of universities, since many social scientists and historians are employed in academia.

Economists are employed by government, academia, business, financial services firms, and banks. In the short term, outlook is cloudy, particularly for entry-level positions. New economics and finance graduates in 1992 saw a 16% decrease in demand. Long-term employment outlook is good: the government projects 21% growth in employment to 2005, assuming moderate growth of the economy. Areas that look best for employment: consulting, government, manufacturing, teaching, health care, financial services.

Typical career paths: Generally speaking, in academia, a Ph.D. is required— one survey found that over 90% of academic economists had one. The second largest employer of economists is the federal government, which hires a wide range of backgrounds, from BS to Ph.D. See Government, page 57, for employers. *Employment tip:* A good specialty within government: international trade, finance. Vital as government is called upon to support U.S. exports in competitive world economy. See information on U.S. Department of State on page 110; U.S. Dept of Commerce on page 69.

Other areas: business and industry. For more information on a career as a business economist, write the National Association of Business Economists (address on page 181). Banking and finance: a growing area of employment (although

Wall Street analysts saw some job shrinkage recently). Master's degree usually required for analytical jobs—normal specialties include monetary and fiscal policy and theory; business economics and economic development.

Other employers: nonprofits, international organizations (see page 100), and state and local government.

► **Educational administration is expected to grow slowly in total employment, but job openings will be there as older administrators retire.**

There are only about 300,000 educational administrators in the U.S.—ranging from elementary school principals to higher education deans and presidents—so competition will remain strong for the best positions, particularly because many in education meet the requirements.

Requirements for jobs: For public schools, a master's degree or doctorate and a state teaching certificate. For universities and college, usually a doctorate in the appropriate field for deans, and a Ph.D. or Ed.D. for top general administrative posts, although many people enter with BAs and get the advanced degrees on the job.

Demand areas in the future: Principals of school systems, elementary school administrators, medical school deans, hospital med-center administrators, dentistry deans, law deans, administrators of college computer systems, labor relations managers (particularly as college workers unionize), publications administrators, housing officers.

In other auxiliary areas, assessment specialists who test, analyze, and track student performance will probably do well, as school systems become more performance-oriented.

► **Corporate training will be a major growth area in the second half of the 1990s.**

It's happening already. According to experts, corporations train and retrain 10 million people a year—which is very close to the 12 million undergraduates that universities and colleges teach. According to a recent survey of 300 midwestern manufacturing firms, management is shifting emphasis (which means money) from automation to employee training. Reasons: business is becoming increasingly technical. Employees now must be trained how to run complicated machinery—or, in white-collar jobs, to manage complex transactions.

Another major trend of the 1990s: English skills are failing; at the same time, business needs people who can communicate well. According to a survey by the American Society for Training and Development, by 1995, 93% of all major American companies will be teaching employees reading, writing, and arithmetic. Why? Because many new employees are entering the job market without even the most basic skills. Problem: only 10% of all U.S. employees now receive training from their companies—although estimates are that 50 million need it.

Corporate training runs the gamut from factory operations to accounting and computers to basic and remedial English, communication skills and sales training. It can be an excellent—and lucrative—place for teachers in both general and technical fields. In service industries, trainers may specialize in teaching basic business skills, sales techniques, or specialized skills; in manufacturing firms, they may instruct workers on machine or computer use. Generally corporate teachers come out of human resources departments; but former schoolteachers are being hired as well. Technical trainers may be technicians already, or specialists who design manufacturing teaching programs. Many teachers are also hired as consultants (as with many bank-training programs which farm out basic accounting, banking, and finance to local university professors). According to *Money* magazine, this is a good area for entrepreneurs: *Fortune* 500 firms are increasingly hiring small outside training firms to handle many aspects of corporate training.

▶ **In the *long term*, increases in the numbers of jobs for *museum curators, directors*, and *archivists*—and a lot of competition.**

Curators are generally specialists in an academic field who manage museum collections and staff in that area. Major areas are art, archeology, science, technology, botany, zoology. Despite the tough times in recent years, the outlook for museums appears relatively bright, as interest and attendance increase.

In spite of projected increases in jobs, however, there will still be only a very few openings. There are only about 10,000 professional-level museum jobs in the country, and the career is prestigious and interesting to many specialists. The Smithsonian Institution, for example, has one of the lowest turnover rates in government.

One problem is on the rise: "museum director burnout." According to the American Association of Museum Directors and *ARTnews* magazine, it is increasingly common, "almost an epidemic." The problems: not enough money from endowments to meet increasing costs, rising exhibition and fund-raising pressures, and not enough managerial expertise. The result: overworked museum directors— and burnout.

One solution, and a new trend: curators will be getting MBAs or business training along with a specialist degree. Increasingly, museum management is as much financial as curatorial. And so financially astute curators may be ahead of the competition. Already the American Federation of the Arts runs a summer program that trains curators in business administration.

A good source for jobs: Check *Aviso,* the monthly magazine published by the American Association of Museums. Besides general museum news, it lists about fifty openings per issue for museum jobs across the country. See address on page 184.

WHAT'S NEXT

▶ **Empowerment, professionalism, prestige . . . and dollars?**

Calls for school reform, and the realization of the educational crisis facing the U.S., will speed changes in the school system.

Many ideas are already in place. More ease of entry for those with nonteaching backgrounds (in itself controversial with some), more control by teachers, and new "management team" administrative structures are already changing the face of education. The bottom line: administration is becoming more localized, more efficiency-based. Good teachers will increasingly be rewarded—and noticed. The profession itself is at long last gaining the prestige it deserves.

The 1990s will see action replacing talk. The key issue is raising standards—and a major way is to simply encourage teachers to teach. This will mean higher pay as a reward to good teachers (instead of a standardized pay schedule), "mentoring" (where good teachers teach other teachers), less administrative duties, more control over how they do their jobs. The buzzword in teaching is "empowerment"—meaning giving teachers the power to make the critical decisions. The big problem, of course, is getting the money.

▶ **American education: Getting some ideas from Japan?**

Americans typically think of Japanese elementary schools as regimented places, when in fact the opposite is true. In many ways taking their ideas from the famed U.S. scholar John Dewey, the Japanese try to make elementary education exploratory and fun; young students start from the concrete and then move to the theoretical, they have short recesses between class, they are not divided into "tracked" classes of good and poor students, and in general feel less stress.

Some other ideas from the Japanese, as reported in *The New York Times*, which may trickle back to a concerned U.S.:

- **higher pay** for teachers

- **less time teaching;** more time to consult with students and to prepare classes

- **larger classes** (sounds bad, but gives teacher more time for all of the above)

SALARIES

TEACHERS (KINDERGARTEN, PRESCHOOL): The average salary in 1991 was $32,448. Preschool teachers with state certification earned roughly the same amount; much lower for day care workers.

TEACHERS (ELEMENTARY AND SECONDARY): The average salary in 1991 for elementary teachers was about $32,500; the average secondary teacher's salary was $32,880. Average beginning salary about $21,500 in 1991. Best salaries in Alaska (the highest), New York, Connecticut (averaging over $40,000); lowest in South Dakota.

UNIVERSITY FACULTY: According to a salary survey by the American Association of University Professors, the average salary in 1991–92 was $38,969 for an associate professor, $45,312 for an assistant professor, and $61,650 for a full professor.

Much more for top faculty: some professors earn well over $100,000. In keeping with supply and demand, science engineering faculty often earn more than liberal arts faculty; universities and top colleges more than others, four-year colleges more than two-year schools. The highest paid professors are usually found in business schools, where total compensation can reach $120,000 to $200,000. Consulting is the normal way to add-on base salary; the norm in colleges is not to require summer work.

EDUCATION ADMINISTRATORS (ELEMENTARY, SECONDARY SCHOOL): At the top, high school principals in 1989 earned an average of $52,900 (with a high of $86,000); junior and middle school, $49,500; and elementary school, $45,900. Assistant principal salaries averaged between $38,000 and $44,000. Other lower-level salaries range from the mid-20s to mid-30s.

EDUCATION ADMINISTRATORS (COLLEGE, UNIVERSITY): According to the College and University Personnel Association, median salaries for administrators ranged from $21,889 for admissions counselors to $173,287 for medical school deans.

LIBRARIANS: Salary range from $10,000 to $75,000. In a survey of eighteen state library associations, minimum starting salary in 1989–90 ranged from a low of $17,500 to a high of over $27,000. Library directors average between $30,000 for small libraries to $65,000 for large public libraries. Mid-level school and university librarians average salaries between $30,000 and $35,000. Government librarians averaged over $42,000.

CURATORS AND ARCHIVISTS: Salaries vary; much higher for major museums. Average starting salary between $20,000 and $35,000.

CORPORATE TRAINING: The average salary is about $45,000, according to *Training Magazine*. Executive-level training managers average about $60,000, single-person department managers about $40,000. Instructors and evaluators earn between $35,000 and $45,000. Trainers promoted within the human resources department to vice presidents or senior managers can make $100,000 to $200,000.

BEST BETS

LANGUAGE TEACHER: As borders open, and international careers become more important, the basic skill of speaking a foreign language obviously becomes more important. Already, enrollment is up in secondary schools and colleges. According to the Modern Language Association, college student enrollment exceeded 1 million a few years back—for the first time in fourteen years. One major problem for the country is a real advantage for the job hunter: there are far too few foreign language teachers.

According to the National Governors Association, twenty-six states reported shortages of qualified teachers last year. Shortages are worst in elementary and secondary schools, but openings will grow in other areas as business and academia finally address the problem. Some best bets for the 1990s: Japanese, German. On the downside, pay is still often low. And, despite a lot of lip service, many school systems still won't budget funds for language teaching.

Good source for jobs: Check the Job Information List of the Modern Language Association. It lists hundreds of jobs by geographic region, by college and university, by specialty, including related jobs ranging from comparative literature to linguistics, with sections for second-career job hunters. The address is on page 181.

WHERE TO GO FOR MORE INFORMATION

TEACHERS, LIBRARIANS, HISTORIANS, AND SOCIAL SCIENTISTS
ASSOCIATIONS AND
ORGANIZATIONS

Academy for Educational Development
1255 23rd St., NW
Washington, DC 20039
202/862-1900
(Placement service, etc.)

African Studies Association
Credit Union Bldg.
Emory University
Atlanta, GA 30322
(Publishes journal with some job listings, etc.)

American Alliance for Health, Physical Education, Recreation, and Dance
1900 Association Dr.
Reston, VA 22091
703/476-3400
(Publishes periodical with job listings, placement service.)

American Association of Christian Schools
P.O. Box 1088
Fairfax, VA 22030
703/818-7150
(Maintains placement service, certifies teachers, etc.)

American Association for Counseling and Development
5999 Stevenson Ave.
Alexandria, VA 22304

703/823-9800
(Major association in certifying counselors; holds workshops, etc. for members; publishes periodical with job openings, etc.)

American Association for Higher Education
1 Du Pont Circle, Suite 360
Washington, DC 20036
202/293-6440
(Publishes periodical, holds conferences, etc.)

American Association of Law Libraries
53 W. Jackson
Chicago, IL 60604
313/939-4764
(Publishes periodical with job openings, job database, and hot line, directory.)

American Association of Museums
1225 I St., NW
Washington, DC 20005
202/289-1818
(Publishes periodical with job openings, placement service, etc.)

American Association of School Administrators
1801 N. Moore St.
Arlington, VA 22209
703/528-0700

(Publishes periodical with listings, etc.)

American Association of School Librarians
50 E. Huron St.
Chicago, IL 60611
312/944-6780

American Association for State and Local History
172 Second Ave. N., Suite 202
Nashville, TN 37201
615/255-2971
FAX 615/255-2979
(Publishes periodicals with job listings, etc.)

American Association of Teachers of Slavic and East European Languages
Department of Russian
230 Jessup Hall
University of Iowa
Iowa City, IA 52242
319/335-0170
(Publishes periodical with job listings.)

American Association of University Professors
1012 14th St., NW, Suite 500
Washington, DC 20005
(Publishes journal with occasional job listing, etc.)

180   CAREER OUTLOOKS 1994

American Council on Education
1818 R St., NW
Washington, DC 20009
202/939-9300
(Publishes journal, trends, etc.)

American Economic Association
2014 Broadway, Suite 305
Nashville, TN 37203
615/322-2595
(Publishes periodical with job openings, operates placement service, etc.)

American Economic Development Council
9801 W. Higgins Rd.
Rosemont, IL 60018-4726
708/692-9944l
(Publishes periodical, job referrals, etc., for members.)

American Federation of Teachers
555 New Jersey Ave., NW
Washington, DC 20001
202/879-4400

American Historical Association
400 A St., SE
Washington, DC 20003
323/544-2422
(Publishes periodical, etc.)

American Library Association
50 E. Huron Street
Chicago, IL 60611
1-800/545-2455
(Publishes periodicals with job listings.
Important Note: The ALA maintains phone numbers and information on *state library job hot lines*—tape-recorded messages, periodically updated, that list library job openings for some states. Call for specific phone numbers. The ALA also maintains the special Grapevine job database. See also the Guide to Library Placement Sources, under "Directories.")

American Political Science Association
1527 New Hampshire Ave., NW
Washington, DC 20036
202/483-2513
(Publishes periodical for members with job listings; sponsors fellowships, maintains job contacts for members, etc.)

American Society for Information Science
8720 Georgia Ave., Suite 501
Silver Springs, MD 20910
301/495-0900
(Periodical with job openings; members' placement service, etc.)

American Sociological Association
1722 N St., NW
Washington, DC 20036
202/833-3410
(Publishes periodical with job listings, directory, etc)

American Vocational Association
1410 King St.
Alexandria, VA 22314
703/683-3111

Association of American Law Schools
1201 Connecticut Ave., NW,
Suite 800
Washington, DC 20036
202/296-8851
(Publishes *Placement Bulletin,* which lists both faculty and admin. job openings.)

Association of American Universities
1 DuPont Circle, NW,
Suite 730
Washington, DC 20036
202/466-5030

Association for Childhood Education International
11141 Georgia Ave.
Wheaton, MD 20902
301/942-2443

Association of Christian Schools International
P.O. Box 4097
Whittier, CA 90607-4097
213/694-4791
(Placement service, etc.)

Association for School, College, and University Staffing
1600 Dodge Ave.
S-330

Evanston, IL
60201-3451
708/864-1999
(Publishes *Job Search Handbook*, with articles and job listings.)

College and University Personnel Association
1233 20th St., NW,
Suite 503
Washington, DC 20036
202/429-0311
(Major salary survey, professional development programs, etc.)

College Music Society
202 W. Spruce St.
Missoula, MT 59802
406/721-9616

Council for the Advancement and Support of Education
11 Du Pont Circle,
NW, Suite 400
Washington, DC 20036
202/328-5900
(Publishes directory, etc.)

Council for Early Childhood Professional Recognition
1718 Connecticut Ave.,
NW, Suite 500
Washington, DC 20009
202/265-9090

Institute of International Education
809 United Nations,
Plz.
New York, NY 10017
212/984-5412
(Used to publish

directory of international exchange programs and positions; at time of writing institute was unsure if publication would be resumed.)

International Studies Association
216 Herald Clark Bldg.
Brigham Young University
Provo, UT 84602
(Publishes periodical with job listings.)

Modern Language Association
10 Astor Pl.
New York, NY
10003-6981
(Publishes job listings for English- as well as foreign-language teachers.)

National Art Education Association
1916 Association Dr.
Reston, VA 22091
703/860-8000
(Placement service.)

National Association for the Education of Young Children
1834 Connecticut Ave.,
NW
Washington, DC 20009
202/232-8777

National Association for Girls and Women in Sport
1900 Association Dr.
Reston, VA 22091
703/476-3450
(Also HQ of National

Council of Athletic Training.)

National Association of Business Economists
28790 Chagrin Blvd.,
Suite 300
Cleveland OH 44122
216/464-7986
(Publishes periodical with job openings, career booklet, etc.)

National Association of College Admissions Counselors
1800 Diagonal Rd.,
Suite 430
Alexandria, VA 22314
703/836-2222

National Association of College and University Officers
1 Du Pont Circle,
Suite 500
Washington, DC 20036
202/861-2500

National Association of Elementary School Principals
1615 Duke St.
Alexandria, VA 22314
703/684-3345
(Planning at time of writing to operate an electronic bulletin board for job listings, tie-in to state associations, etc.)

National Association of Independent Schools
75 Federal St.
Boston, MA 02110
(Consortium of private schools; has information on teaching careers.)

National Association of Secondary School Principals
1904 Association Dr.
Reston, VA 22091
703/684-0200

National Association for Sport and Physical Education
1900 Association Dr.
Reston, VA 22091
703/476-3410

National Association of Student Personnel Administrators
1875 Connecticut Ave., NW,
Suite 418
Washington, DC 20009
202/265-7500

National Business Education Association
1914 Association Dr.
Reston, VA 22091
703/860-8300

National Council of Teachers of English
111 Kenyon Rd.
Urbana, IL 61801
217/328-3870

National Council of Teachers of Mathematics
1906 Association Dr.
Reston, VA 22091

202/620-9840
(Publishes journal with listings, etc.)

National Science Teachers Association
1742 Connecticut Ave., NW
Washington, DC 20009
202/328-5800
(Publishes periodical with job listings, directory, etc.)

Organization of American Historians
112 N. Bryan St.
Bloomington, IN 47408
812/855-7311
(Publishes periodical with some job listings for members.)

Recruiting New Teachers
395 Concord Ave.,
Suite 100
Belmont, MA 02178-9804
617/45-TEACH
617/489-6000
(Has free referral service.)

Society of American Archivists
600 S. Federal St.,
Suite 504
Chicago, IL 60605

312/922-0140
(Publishes periodical with job listings, information; placement service, etc.)

Special Library Association
1700 18th St., NW
Washington, DC 20009
202/234-4700
(Periodical with job openings, résumé referral service, tape-recorded job openings.)

Teach for America
P.O. Box 5114
New York, NY 10185
800/832-1230
(Well-known new program that encourages and helps place new teachers; submit an application and recommendations, and demonstrate your teaching ability.)

Women Library Workers
c/o Women's Resource Center
University of California
Bldg. T-9,
Room 112
Berkeley, CA 94720
415/642-4786

TEACHERS, LIBRARIANS, HISTORIANS, AND SOCIAL SCIENTISTS DIRECTORIES

American Library Association—Handbook of Organization and Membership Directory
American Library

Association
50 E. Huron St.
Chicago, IL 60611
1-800/545-2433

American Library Directory
R. R. Bowker
P.O. Box 31
New Providence, NJ

07974-9904
1-800/521-8110

*Directory of Federal
Libraries*
Oryx Press
4041 N. Central
Suite 700
Phoenix, AZ
85012-3397
1-800/279-6799

*Directory of Library
and Information
Professional Women's
Groups*
American Library
Association
50 E. Huron St.
Chicago, IL 60611
1-800/545-2455

*Directory of Special
Libraries and
Information Centers*
835 Penobscot Bldg.
Detroit, MI 48226
1-800/877-GALE

*Guide to Library
Placement Sources*
American Library
Association
50 E. Huron St.
Chicago, IL 60611
1-800/545-2433
(This is a valuable,
centralized source that

lists associations and
organizations
nationwide that offer
placement services for
librarians.

*Opportunities Abroad
for Educators:
Fulbright Teacher
Exchange Program*
Teacher Exchange
Program
E/ASX, Room 352
U.S. Information
Agency
Washington, DC 20547
202/619-4555
(Lists countries and
positions available;
includes application and
describes program;
updated yearly.)

*Patterson's American
Education*
Educational Directories,
Inc.
P.O. Box 199
Mount Prospect, IL
60056
312/392-1811

*Requirements for
Certification of
Teachers, Counselors,
Librarians,
Administrators, for*

*Elementary and
Secondary Schools and
Junior Colleges* by
John Tryneski
University of Chicago
Press
5801 Ellis Ave.
Chicago, IL 60637
800/621-2736
312/702-7700
(Before you apply, it
might be best to know
if you can—this guide
lists certification
requirements state by
state.)

*WILSONLINE:
Education Index*
(computer database)
H. W. Wilson
Company
950 University Avenue
Bronx, NY 10452
1-800/367-6770
(On-line database that
extensively lists many
education periodicals.)

*World Guide to
Libraries*
R. R. Bowker
P.O. Box 31
New Providence, NJ
07974-9904
1-800/521-8110

TEACHERS, LIBRARIANS, HISTORIANS, AND SOCIAL SCIENTISTS MAGAZINES

ABA Journal
750 N. Lake Shore Dr.
Chicago, IL 60611
312/988-5000

American Educator
555 New Jersey Ave.,
NW
Washington, DC 20001
202/879-4420
(Quarterly general
magazine.)

American Libraries
50 E. Huron St.
Chicago, IL 60611
1-800/545-2433
312/944-6780
(Monthly association
magazine; job ads can

be obtained three weeks in advance of publication—call for details.)

American School and University
401 N. Broad St.
Philadelphia, PA 19108
(For plant school administrators.)
215/238-5300

American Teacher
555 New Jersey Ave., NW
Washington, DC 20001
202/879-4400
(Monthly tabloid.)

Aviso
American Association of Museums
1225 I St., NW,
Suite 200
Washington, DC 20005
202/289-1818
(General museum news, with job listings.)

Change: The Magazine of Higher Learning
Heldre Publications
4000 Albemarle St., NW
Washington, DC 20016
202/362-6445
(Prestigious journal of higher education.)

Chronicle of Higher Education
1255 23rd St., NW
Washington, DC 20037
P.O. Box 1955
Marion, OH
43306-2055
202/466-1000
(Monthly for college faculty and

administrators; many job listings.)

Current Openings in Education in USA
Education Information Service
P.O. Box 662 D
Newton, MA 02161
617/237-0887

Education Week
Editorial Projects In Education, Inc.
4301 Connecticut Ave., NW
Ste. 250
Washington, DC 20008
202/364-4114

Educational Leadership
1250 N. Pitt
Alexandria, VA 22314
703/549-9110
(Eight-issue magazine for supervisors.)

Instructor
400 Lafayette St.
New York, NY 10003
212/505-4927
(Monthly primarily for elementary school administrators.)

The International Educator
P.O. Box 103-EP
West Bridgewater, MA 02379

Learning
1111 Bethlehem Pike
Springhouse, PA 19477
215/646-8700
(Nine-issue magazine for elementary and junior-high educators.)

Library Administrator's Digest
Administrator's Digest, Inc.
P.O. Box 993
South San Francisco, CA 94080
415/573-5474

Library Journal
249 W. 17th St.
New York, NY 10011
212/463-6822
1-800/669-1002
(Semimonthly magazine; has many job listings.)

NEA Today
1201 16th St., NW
Washington, DC 20036
202/822-7260
(Eight-issue tabloid for association members.)

Phi Delta Kappan
Phi Delta Kappa, Inc.
Box 789
Bloomington, IN
47402-0789
812/339-1156

School Library Journal
249 W. 17th St.
New York, NY 10011
212/463-6759
1-800/842-1669
(subscriptions number; Cahners Publishing in Ohio)
(Monthly journal specializing in school libraries; carries some job listings each month.)

Teacher
4301 Connecticut Ave.,
NW
Washington, DC 20008
202/364-4114
(Monthly.)

Wilson Library Bulletin
950 University Ave.
Bronx, NY 10452
212/588-8400
1-800/367-6770

TECHNICAL CAREERS

BRIEF BACKGROUND

▶ **The number of qualified people for technical support jobs is going down—and that means opportunity.**

The key word is *qualified*. Many corporations and government offices have been swamped with applications; the problem is that very often those applicants don't have the right skills to make the grade. Expect companies now to give more and better support for technical training in high schools, vocational schools, two- and four-year colleges over the next ten years.

The bottom line: business, medicine, law, government are all getting more complex—and more trained technicians are needed to handle this complexity.

The difference between technical work and professional work: in general, technicians have jobs more limited in scope than the professionals overseeing such work. For example, engineering technicians usually work for or under engineers—although others work alone in repairing, servicing, installing, or inspecting positions. But many technicians today rise to managerial positions, supervising staffs of other technicians, or often, with further education, becoming general managers of technical departments.

On-the-job training or two-year associate or vocational degrees is the typical background preparation. In other cases, however, four-year BS degrees are required, particularly for scientific or laboratory positions.

This section focuses on the engineering support positions. For health service and laboratory technicians, see page 87; for paralegals, see page 161.

EMPLOYMENT OUTLOOK: Strong for many fields over the long term. Slow recovery will lessen prospects in short term.

▶ **The government projects that job growth for engineering technicians will be strong during the rest of the 1990s.**

A few numbers: 28% job growth for engineering technicians as a group—this means about 210,000 jobs will be added by the year 2005 if the economy grows moderately, according to the federal government. Also, as many of the 700,000 technicians retire or move into other positions, thousands of replacement jobs will open.

One problem: defense cutbacks in certain areas will reduce prospects.

A *major area of employment*: Computers and engineering.
Engineering technicians work in manufacturing, trade, service industries, and
for schools and universities. Over 40% work in manufacturing, 20% in services,
usually with engineering firms. In many cases, the line is blurring between computer technicians, engineering technicians, and mechanics, as computers become
part of most engineering areas.

Best job areas for the 1990s:

COMPUTER REPAIR TECHNICIANS: It makes sense. As the number of computers
increases, so too the number of technicians needed to install, maintain, trouble-
shoot, repair them. Job prospects recently were good, but not excellent. But if the
economy grows at a moderate pace, the government predicts jobs will grow by 60%
to the year 2005; that's about 50,000 new jobs.

ELECTRICAL AND ELECTRONICS TECHNICIANS: New job openings will increase
moderately in the next fourteen years, according to the government. But take
projected retirements and new jobs together, and you get 280,000 openings for
electronics technicians during the 1990s, according to the Electrical Industries
Association. The key: no matter what the big picture looks like, some areas will be
hiring. One good area: electromedical and biomedical repair. These are the machines in hospitals that can keep us alive—prospects are excellent for specialists
trained in this area.
Key to the best jobs: mathematical skills, technical know-how with latest test
equipment.

CAM (COMPUTER-AIDED MANUFACTURING):   Technicians work maintaining
and installing computerized manufacturing machines, including robots. At higher
levels, engineers supervise entire computerized operations. Most training is still on
the job, at large firms such as General Electric and General Motors, and smaller
innovative firms. Job potential: Good, in many areas a shortage of trained workers.

**MACHINE TOOL WORKERS/NUMERICAL CONTROL TOOL OPERATORS AND PRO-
GRAMMERS:**   Manufacturing machines are computerized and extremely complex,
and technicians who run the electronic controllers on machine tools are in very
short supply. For example, there are only 9,000 numerical control workers in the
U.S. Some advantages in the fields: pay is high (salaries of $30,000 to $40,000 for
young employees with two or three years on the job are not uncommon) and job
security looks good. But—unlike the old days—technicians need to have far more
than a "feel" for machines; they need thinking, analytical, and mathematical skills
to master the new computerized technology.
Because of the shortage, industry and industry associations are encouraging high
school students to get the training and skills to enter the field. In the Chicago area,
one association has begun a foundation to promote the field and provide assistance
to area vocational colleges. For more information, contact: Tooling and Manufacturing Association, 1177 South Dee Road, Park Ridge, IL.

AIRCRAFT MECHANICS: Until the recession, job outlook was excellent—but as airlines merged and the economy got worse, the employment outlook was not as good as expected. Long-term outlook: fair to good. Replacements will be needed for retiring mechanics, and there will be a new demand for technicians who can master increasingly computerized aircraft. According to workers, ''they're not airplanes anymore, they're flying computers.''

CAD (COMPUTER-AIDED DESIGN) DRAFTERS AND RELATED WORKERS: Technicians are literally draftsmen (or women) who draft on specialized computer terminals rather than on paper. Jobs are principally in manufacturing: technicians work on circuit board design, electrical grids, etc. Job potential: Still strong, but there is some debate whether technicians will eventually be replaced by trained engineers.

ENVIRONMENTAL POSITIONS: A hot area for the 1990s, as concern for the environment causes companies to start spending money on clean-up and pollution prevention. Experts forecast over 25% job growth per year. Best opportunities for BS degree holders in chemistry, engineering, geology, etc.—unlike other fields, because demand is so strong, you don't need an advanced degree to get substantial responsibility, and good pay, up front. One problem: the recession seems to have slowed growth to some degree—even as the economy improves further.

▶ **Now for some bad news: sometimes technological advances mean fewer jobs for technicians. In the communications fields, employment is expected to** *fall* **by 35% or so by the year 2005.**

That's almost 2% a year, or a loss of about 223,000 jobs. Why? The break-up of AT&T some years back began the trend, and now better technology is reducing the need for workers. Cable TV for a while boosted some employment in that area, but now that over 50 percent of all U.S. houses are hooked up, technical job growth rates even in this field will grow by a rate of 1% per year—not that bad, but nothing like the 5.6% a year during the late 1970s, 1980s and early 1990s.

Best bet for the 1990s in telecommunications: concentrate on new technologies and education, especially computers. Workers who combine communications experience with computer knowledge will do very well.

An even better bet for the 1990s: with telecom experience, go back to school and get an MBA or a master's degree in information science. According to *Network World*, this is a much faster way up the management pyramid. And consider network management. (See below, and LAN jobs, page 45.)

The key areas in telecommunications:

TELECOMMUNICATIONS TECHNICIANS: Principal responsibility usually maintaining, repairing, and installing voice lines switching equipment. College degree, two-year associate degrees, or significant experience (as with a military background) required. Declines expected—according to the latest government statistics, from 38 to 45% by the year 2005. But, technicians who combine experience with *computer* know-how may do well anyway. Best bets for a job: get an electrical engineering BS or computer BS, or associate, with telecom experience. Technicians can move up into communications managerial positions.

DATA COMMUNICATIONS TECHNICIANS: Principal responsibilities for transmission of computer data over telephone lines, etc. Technicians can move into supervisory positions and average salaries of over $40,000.

1990s TELECOM TECHNICIAN: Expect the above two areas to merge into one position in the 1990s, as sophisticated new technologies allow lines to carry both data and voice communications. Again, the key is to master the new technologies: CASE, etc.

Key employment ideas: Get skills in new high-tech fields in communications, with roughly the same responsibilities as above, such as: fiber-optics technicians— expected to re-revolutionize cable TV; local area network technicians (LAN), who work on communications systems limited geographically (for example, to a corporatewide private communications network), and who are computer communications technicians; and satellite technicians.

Best Bet: Corporate network technicians and managers. As corporations become increasingly communication-oriented, with local area computer networks, phone conferencing, faxing, etc., technicians and managers who can run the show—or part of it—are increasingly being hired.

Other technical fields, and growth prospects for the 1990s:

BROADCAST TECHNICIANS: New technology will offset hiring by new or expanded stations, so job growth will only be slow. Best bet: look for work in nonmetropolitan areas where competition is much less than in major metro areas.

AIR TRAFFIC CONTROLLERS: High competition for jobs, and lowish growth— but still good prospects for qualified applicants in the 1990s. Reason: government is returning to the staffing levels of the early 1980s, when striking controllers were fired. High pay—can range up over $60,000—and good retirement benefits make this an in-demand field. On the downside: very high stress job. Most positions are government positions; to apply, see page 194 for complete details.

AUTOMOTIVE MECHANICS AND RELATED JOBS: There are many car mechanics and body repair workers—and a lot of competition. But this still looks like a good career for the rest of the 1990s, provided you have the *specialist* and *technical* skills to do the job. The government projects job growth to be a strong 22% in most areas. On the repair side, many employers are specialized and prefer to hire people with either a functional specialty (transmissions, etc.) or experience with specific makes. Service employers aren't as picky—but the money isn't usually as good, either.

The key to getting a good job is good training; some of the best training programs are run by Chrysler, Ford, and GM in cooperation with local colleges and technical schools. Advice from an insider: before going to technician school, check to see if the training program is certified and can give you in-depth and up-to-date training; that will make you employable. The National Automotive Technician Foundation has information on these programs. Also, see page 251 for more on the automotive industry.

Finally, most **repair positions** (air conditioning, industrial equipment, etc.) will grow in the next ten years—but not all that quickly. The major exception is in farm equipment mechanics; the number of jobs here is expected to go down substantially. But, in general, this rule of thumb holds: machinery and equipment eventually break down—and people are always needed to fix them.

Important Note: Technical jobs require training—which can be obtained on the job, or at a university, college, two-year college—or trade or technical school. Although many of these trade or technical schools give you your money's worth and are excellent places to learn a trade, others aren't. *Before* enrolling in a school, check with local authorities, a trade association (addresses are listed below), and local employers. To learn what to look for (and look out for), ask for a free pamphlet: *Getting Skills, Getting Ahead.* Contact: Consumer Information Center, Dept. 574W, Pueblo, CO 81009.

WHAT'S NEXT

▶ **Employers are seeing the need for *increased education* for technicians—and are beginning to do something about it.**

There's no time to waste—and finally, people are catching on.

New programs are being offered, old ones revamped. For example: Tech Prep or TPAD, in which high school students take classes designed for them to enter a technical program at a community college. Community colleges are improving curricula—and linking their programs with local and national employers.

Some Department of Education award-winning examples:

Technical Training Winners

1. **Valencia Community College** (Orlando, FL, 407/299-5000)
   (computer training, with placement services; affiliated with major firms like Martin Marietta)
2. **Thief River Falls Technical College** (Thief River Falls, MN, 218/681-5424)
   (aviation maintenance technology, certification training, internships with Northwest)
3. **Longview Community College** (Lee's Summit, MO, 815/763-7777)
   (up-to-date automotive technology program, with partnerships with GM, Ford, Toyota; 95% placement rate)
4. **Spokane Community College** (Spokane, WA, 509/536-7148)
   (fluid power technology—hydraulics, pneumatics, in machinery—program; job placement rate for successful students is near 100%)

▶ **Apprenticeships—a new trend?**

In Europe (and in the U.S. in the past), an apprentice goes to work for a skilled craftsperson, and learns the skills he or she needs on the job. It's a good way for everyone—the craftsperson gets a cheap worker, the apprentice earns a living while learning. Today, only 2% of all U.S. high school grads get their start as apprentices—and this at a time when corporations are *rejecting* applicants in record numbers for not having the right skills.

Apprenticeships are an idea whose time has come again. Grants from the federal government are being provided to help the idea; for example, the Pennsylvania Department of Commerce is working on a program with the metalworking industry.

And giant German manufacturer Siemens AG has indicated it is interested in bringing in an apprenticeship program here in the U.S., where it already employs 30,000 workers.

SALARIES

▶ **General trend: salaries expected to increase for high-demand jobs as competition for scarce workers tightens.**

Salaries for some major areas:

AIR TRAFFIC CONTROLLERS: beginning salaries approximately $25,000; average about $40,000.

AIRCRAFT TECHNICIANS: median salaries $30,000, higher for skilled technicians in avionics. Average salary for *mechanics* in 1989: $15 an hour.

AUTOMOTIVE MECHANICS: highly skilled earned over $15–$20 an hour for a 40-hour work week in 1990.

COMMUNICATIONS TECHNICIANS: varies widely; around $23,000 entry-level, average salaries for those without degrees about $25,000. Several years experience from $33,000 to $38,000; over $40,000 for supervisors or significant experience. Average annual salary increases in past two years: 12%.

COMPUTER SERVICE TECHNICIANS: earnings average around $28,000. Top earners can make over $40,000; more if they own a business.

ENGINEERING TECHNICIANS: earnings average around $27,000; top earners make over $40,000.

ENVIRONMENTAL CAREERS: 1990 starting salaries around $25,000–$35,000, starting in staff positions; supervisory positions up to $50,000; more for project managers.

BEST BETS

COOPERATIVE EDUCATION: Not a technical job, but a means to a full-time technical job; particularly good for those forced out of a profession by layoffs who need to find a new means of making a living. Cooperative education involves job-related classes and paid work, most often in alternating terms for two to four years. Pay is usually low, less than $5,000 (net of tuition and supplies), but the experience can be invaluable. Best area: *Cincinnati, Ohio*, which has five such programs, the most in the U.S. At *Cincinnati Technical College*, a whopping 98% of its co-op graduates found jobs last year; 600 businesses provided co-op jobs, including packaged-goods giant Procter & Gamble. Average age of students is twenty-nine, and students over forty are not uncommon. Students study such fields as engineering technology, nursing, landscape horticulture, medical records technology, etc.

WHERE TO GO FOR MORE INFORMATION

TECHNICAL ASSOCIATIONS AND GROUPS

(See listings also under "Science," page 151, and "Engineering," page 41. Medical specialties are covered on page 87.)

Aeronautical Repair Station Association
121 N. Henry St.
Alexandria, VA 22314
703/739-9543

Air Traffic Control Association
2300 Clarendon Blvd.,
Suite 711
Arlington, VA 22201
703/522-5717
(Publishes periodical, etc.)

American Congress on Surveying and Mapping
5410 Grosvenor Ln.
Bethesda, MD 20814
301/493-0200

American Society for Industrial Security
1655 N. Fort Meyer Dr.
Arlington, VA 22209
703/522-5800

Association of Manufacturing Technicians
7901 Westpark Dr.
McLean, VA 22102
703/893-2900

Computer-Aided Manufacturing International
1250 E. Copeland Rd.,
Suite 500
Arlington, TX 76011-8098
817/860-1654

Corporation for Public Broadcasting
901 E. St., NW
Washington, DC 20004
202/879-6000
0800/582-8220
(Has job hot line: Dial 800 number above for job listings at public radio and TV stations nationwide; includes technical jobs.)

Electronics Technicians Association International
602 N. Jackson St.
Greencastle, IN 46135
317/653-8262
(Publishes periodical with a few job openings and referral service for

members, certification tapes, etc.)

Future Aviation Professionals of America
4959 Massachusetts Blvd.
Atlanta, GA 30337
800/JET-JOBS

International Society of Certified Electronics Technicians
2708 W. Berry
Fort Worth, TX 76109
817/921-9101
(Publishes periodical with job openings, etc.)

National Automotive Technician Education Foundation

13505 Dulles Technology Dr.
Herndon, VA 22071
703/713-0100
(Maintains listing of certified automotive technician schools.)

National Tooling and Machining Association
9300 Livingston Rd.
Fort Washington, MD 20744
301/248-6200

Professional Aviation Maintenance Association
500 Northwest Plz.,

Suite 809
St. Ann, MO 63704
314/739-2580

Society of Motion Picture and Television Engineers
595 W. Hartsdale Ave.
White Plains, NY 10607
914/761-1100
(Publishes *SMPTE* journal.)

Tooling and Manufacturing Association
1177 S. Dee Rd.
Park Ridge, IL 60068
708/825-1120

TECHNICAL PERIODICALS

Aircraft Technician
1233 Janesville Ave.
Ft. Atkinson, WI 53538
414/563-6388
(Bimonthly tabloid covering aircraft maintenance.)

Aviation Equipment Maintenance
Delta Data Center
1020 S. Wabash Ave.
Chicago, IL 60605
312/222-2000

Computer-Aided Engineering
Penton Publishing
1100 Superior Ave.
Cleveland, OH 44114
216/696-700

Professional Surveyor
901 S. Highland St.
Arlington, VA 22204
703/892-0733
(Bimonthly magazine; carries some job listings.)

Tradeswomen
(also *Trade Trax* newsletter)
P.O. Box 40664
San Francisco, CA 94140
415/821-7334
(Both the magazine and the newsletter are devoted to career information for women in "nontraditional"

fields, defined as those that employ fewer than 25 percent women; includes blue-collar jobs. California-based; carries some, mostly local employment listings.)

OTHER TECHNICAL JOB SOURCES

InternAmerica
Ford Careerworks
800/456-7335
(Bimonthly newsletter
with many internships
listed for technical and
vocational grads as well
as liberal arts.)

**Federal Aviation
Administration**
Headquarters
800 Independence
Ave., SW
Washington, DC 20591
202/267-8007
(Employs air traffic
controllers nationwide,
as well as electronics
specialists and
engineers, etc. Regional
offices are listed
below.)

Alaskan Region
Federal Aviation
Administration
701 C. St.
P.O. Box 14
Anchorage, AK 90513
907/271-5747

Central Region (KS,
MO, IA, NE
Federal Aviation
Administration
601 E. 12th St.
Kansas City, MO
64106
816/374-3304

Eastern Region (DE,
MD, NJ, MY, PA,
VA, WV)
Federal Aviation
Administration

JFK International
Airport
Jamaica, NY 11430
718/917-1060

**Federal Aviation
Administration**
Mike Monroney
Aeronautical Center
P.O. Box 25082
Oklahoma City, OK
73125
405/686-4506

**Federal Aviation
Administration
Technical Center**
ACM 110
Atlantic City
International Airport
Atlantic City, NJ 08405

Great Lakes Region
(ND, SD, IL, IN, MN,
MI, OH, WI)
Federal Aviation
Administration
2300 E. Devon
Des Plaines, IL 60018
312/694-7731

New England Region
(CT, ME, MA, NH,
RI, VT)
Federal Aviation
Administration
12 New England
Executive Park
P.O. Box 510
Burlington, MA 01803
617/273-7345

Northwest Mountain
Region (CO, MT, UT,
ID, OR, WA, WY)
Federal Aviation
Administration

17900 Pacific Hwy.
(C-68966)
Seattle, WA 98618
206/432-2014

Southern Region (FL,
AL, GA, KY, MS,
NC, SC, TN, PR, VI)
Federal Aviation
Administration
P.O. Box 20636
Atlanta, GA 30320
404/763-7706

Southwest Region (AR,
LA, NM, OK, TX)
Federal Aviation
Administration
P.O. Box 1689
Ft. Worth, TX 76101
817/624-5014

Western-Pacific Region
(AZ, CA, NV, HI)
Federal Aviation
Administration
P.O. Box 29007
Worldway Postal Center
Los Angeles, CA 90009
213/297-1305

**Office of Personnel
Management**
P.O. Box 52
Washington, DC 20415
202/606-2700
(The federal
government hires many
technicians, and one
place to start is with the
OPM. As mentioned in
the "Government"
section on page 57, the
OPM in some cases fills
the role of a
government search firm;

through its offices nationwide it can offer you information on technical careers in government, and explain what tests, if any, you must pass and where to take them. In general, you're best off contacting the OPM office nearest you—jobs of a technical nature and the requirements will be posted. Check the "Regional" section, for the office nearest you.)

WRITERS, EDITORS, AND JOURNALISTS

▶ **Jobs involved with writing are widely diverse. However, almost all share the same general employment outlook: much competition.**

The problem, of course, is that the number of applicants is expected to more than keep up with the demand in most areas. Each year, colleges graduate thousands of English majors and minors; each year, thousands of people decide to "have more fun out of life" and switch into some "dream job" like freelance writing or editorial work. Each year, the competition stays tough, recession or not; and each year, thousands of dissatisfied applicants switch to other lines of work. But, at the same time, each year sees someone selling or editing a best-selling novel, someone winning a Pulitzer.

There are currently about 250,000 people working as writers, editors, journalists, and in related positions.

EMPLOYMENT OUTLOOK: Fair.

▶ **Overall, tough competition for many writing jobs.**

The early 1990s were not good years to be searching for a job as a journalist or editor, to say the least. But better times are on the horizon, although competition will be fierce as always. In particular, opportunities are expected to be best for technical writers, people who can translate the complex jargon of a technical society into understandable English. In addition, better than average job growth over the long term will be found for public relations writers, as well as for magazine writers and editors, although competition will be particularly keen.

▶ **The rest of the 1990s should be better than the early years, when cost-cutting led to hiring freezes and layoffs.**

Look for a gradual recovery in hiring—and be aware of rapid changes, as various media formats compete.

A brief overview of the major job areas:

BOOK EDITORS: The early 1990s were tough years, and the trends of cost-cutting and much attention to the bottom line will continue. Editors are expected increasingly to understand the marketing aspects of the business, while marketing and financial employees are gaining in importance. On the other hand, a backlash is developing that emphasizes quality books over top-selling books (although sometimes the two are synonymous). Best way to enter the field: attend a publishing program (addresses of some of the most prominent are listed at the end of this section) and learn the basics of the industry, and most importantly, make valuable contacts. *On the bright side:* the book publishing industry is expected to grow substantially in the next five years.

JOURNALISTS: Tough competition as newspaper and magazine journalists come out of recessionary cutbacks in staffing. Currently, over 75,000 people work as journalists—about 55,000 for newspapers, and the rest with magazines, TV, radio, and wire services such as the Associated Press. Outlook is tough, even as the newspaper industry continues recovering. Long-term outlook is fair; most job growth will come from suburban papers, along with some growth from radio and TV. Key point: most openings will come from high turnover in the industry; journalism is a tough, difficult, hectic job and many find the reality far more taxing than the dream.

Many major dailies look for at least five years experience at a good daily; in addition, many require writing and other screening tests. As usual, the best preparation for a journalism career is prior experience. Employment trends, according to a Dow Jones Newspaper Fund survey:

- Almost 85% of new hires have mass communications or journalism degrees.

- Newspapers hire 25% of their staff out of college, 75% from other papers or media.

- 78% of those hired had worked on college newspapers, 83% had worked as interns.

- **Bottom line:** experience counts.

Key point: since no major increase in the number of jobs at major dailies is projected over the next ten years, very tough competition is ahead. For more information on journalism careers, write: The Dow Jones Newspaper Fund, P.O. Box 300, Princeton, NJ 08543-0300.

Ways to get a foot in the door: jobs at community papers, internships (although sometimes they don't offer relevant experience), working initially as a copy editor, outside the field in newsletters, etc. Usual job path for entry-level person: the lucky get hired by a major daily directly; others start at a remote paper with the expectation of waiting five, six, or seven years to make it to a major daily. Many of the major dailies have ''farm'' papers where they do most of their hiring.

MAGAZINES: Competition will still be tough, although prospects should improve as the economy improves. *Key problem:* many magazines closed over the past three years—and understandably many corporations are still hesitant about start-ups, although the next few years should see a resurgence. Probable best employment bets: ''niche'' magazines, those that specialize in certain small areas of interest—

these may be safer bets. And similarly, check "trade magazines," those that cater to a specific industry.

Another good area: association magazines—the magazines put out by various trade and professional associations. For years, these magazines were for the most part stodgy house organs; now the trend is to turn them into competitive profit makers. As they gain ad pages, they're getting glossier and more mainstream; this can mean employment opportunities.

PUBLIC RELATIONS WRITERS: The field itself is increasingly important—in the Information Age of the 1990s, corporations and government will increasingly use public relations professionals to communicate on public and corporate issues. Two important areas: issues management, crisis management. With increasingly fragmented markets (the days of the "one-size-fits-all" press release are long gone), PR writers with specialties will be in demand.

One area with strong potential: environmental communications. As corporations struggle with environmental problems and concerns, the role of PR pros in communicating corporate actions to the public will increase. Another growing PR specialty: legal public relations. Due to increased competition among law firms, PR specialists are being hired to promote firms to clients and to top law school graduates they want to hire. According to an expert quoted in the *Wall Street Journal,* up to 75% of all major law firms may use PR consultants.

COPYWRITERS: a varied field. Some copywriters specialize in print, writing advertising "copy" for promotions (pamphlets, brochures); others focus on direct mail; others work in the biggest print specialty: magazines and newspapers. Copywriters also work in radio, in television, in all or many of these specialties.
Outlook in general: fair, highly variable, problems related to general state of the economy. Agencies with hot clients will pay top dollars for copywriters with experience. For more, see Advertising and Public Relations Section, page 225.

TECHNICAL WRITERS: Demand will increase throughout the 1990s, particularly as the need for well-written computer documentation increases. *Best bet:* jobs on the design side; working hand-in-hand with computer/software designers to create user-friendly machines and programs. On the downside: recent problems in the computer industry, possible defense cutbacks have somewhat affected employment—nevertheless, long-term outlook is very strong. Qualifications: clear writing ability, "feel" for technical side. For more information, contact: the Society for Technical Communication—address on page 202.

▶ **And, among the largely self-employed,**

AUTHORS: The recession caused publishers to attempt to decrease the number of titles released, increase scrutiny of proposals. This resulted in: decreased average advances, decreased number of sales. And, as always, it is hard to break into full-time writing as a career, harder to make money, and almost impossible to make a lot of money. *Best advice*: start by writing for magazines. Check *Writers Digest,*

Writers Guide and *Literary Marketplace*, (which lists virtually every major magazine and book publisher, along with addresses, requirements)—addresses are listed at the end of this section. Also check such industry bibles as *Publishers Weekly*, which gives you an inside view of what publishers are buying, and current trends and fads in the industry.

SCREENWRITERS: Most screenwriters have other jobs—the odds of seeing a screenplay you write produced on the silver screen are close to zero. But then again—the rewards are there if you make it. One screenplay by a first-time author sold for $500,000, before "points" or a percentage of the profits. As a result of the recession, prices are down substantially—but then again, in Hollywood that may mean $250,000 up front against another $250,000 or so if it goes into production. And there's always the thrill of seeing your work on the screen.

Best avenue to success? Comedy is king (and usually the hardest to write), television is usually the easiest place to start. Start by writing a complete script (story ideas or treatments are rarely bought from first-timers, according to insiders), then write another and another. Then meet with anyone you can, in order to sell it. The best way to get the right people interested is to find an LA agent who likes your script enough to push it—or *anyone* producing, directing, or acting in similar projects. Check the *LMP* for a listing of agents.

Other jobs in the field include **story editors** (who also usually double as writers) and **script readers**, who work for large studios reading and evaluating scripts submitted by agents and writers. Both can give you an inside track on contacts— and a good income while you learn and write. The name of the game in Hollywood, more than anywhere else, is just that: contacts. From several insiders: "And if you haven't read *Screenplay* [New York: Delta, 1982] by Syd Field, read it soon: sooner or later someone in The Business will recommend it."

WHAT'S NEXT

▶ **Turbulent change: As technology improves, new opportunities and ways of working will open, and other avenues will close.**

In magazines: Continued shake-outs and ever fiercer competition will dominate. Only 20% of new magazines survive for more than four years—and the recession killed many promising ones. Look for more start-ups as the recession becomes more and more a bad memory.

• The proliferation of specialty magazines and ever more specific trade magazines will resume, and so will opportunities for writers with background or experience to write about such topics as Hawaiian scuba diving, fine embroidery—or hog futures (one award-winning trade magazine is entitled *Pork 1993*).

• Consider this: by the year 2000, over 60% of the population of the U.S. will be over thirty-five. Look for magazines which specialize in this market—and think about this as a hot area. One prediction by *Folio*: the special interest magazines owned by the Reader's Digest Association may be a surprisingly big success.

- More decentralization, smaller offices, writers and editors working at home and "commuting" electronically with the home office via computer modems and networks.

- Readers may break the "printed-page barrier" and pick and choose types of articles from a computer at home, in effect creating their own magazines—according to F. Jill Charboneau, speaking at the Magazine Publishing Conference.

In newspapers: an acceleration of the big changes in the past fifteen years: computers will dominate the newsrooms even more than today.

- Better databases (and better ways of accessing them) will speed story and court research; voice-activated computers may change the way stories are written.

- More new beats: reporters will be assigned more special areas to focus coverage, e.g., ethics, family life, elderly, taxes—and journalists with such specialties will experience excellent employment prospects.

- Hiring of minorities, elderly, and the disabled will increase.

In general: For all writers, *increased* opportunities coupled with competition. Just as literacy is going down, the need for writers is going up. Some sources of jobs:

- Large corporations. From in-house corporate newsletters and video presentations, corporate speechwriting, corporate reports and public relations, corporate America will absorb a large number of writers each year.

- Television, video, film media. With all the lamenting about the decline of the written word, it is easy to forget that writers are busy *writing* the spoken word for actors, newspeople, and the like. As entertainment and news keeps rising in importance, so will the role of entertainment and news writers. On the horizon: computers for screenwriters which actually "picture" scenes for the writer on the screen—according to Syd Field, author of *Screenplay*.

SALARIES

BOOK AND MAGAZINE EDITORS: Variable. *Publishers Weekly* salary survey of 1992 showed 1991 salaries for editors as ranging from $14,000 to $32,000 for an entry-level editorial assistant/secretary, with an average of about $19,000. Copy editors averaged $24,000; editors about $35,000; managing editors about $38,000; editors-in-chief about $50,000. Those at large firms earned more—averaging from $20,000 for an editorial assistant to about $70,000 for an editor-in-chief. Presidents of larger firms earned an average of $165,000; the highest salary was $750,000.

JOURNALISTS: Beginning salaries in the high teens to low 20s. According to a 1987 survey by Ohio State University and Dow Jones, college graduates received $13,900. Mid-level salaries are in the $30,000 range—over 50% of journalists have incomes over $40,000, according to a *Los Angeles Times* poll. A recent survey in the *Columbia Journalism Review* showed that salaries increased by about 7.6% in the past three years for newspaper reporters, and by 11.4% for TV journalists in one year alone. Rule of thumb: outside of TV, you shouldn't be in reporting for the money.

BOOKS, MAGAZINES, AND OTHER FREELANCE WRITING: Highly variable. Magazines may pay anywhere from zero to thousands of dollars. In general, small magazines pay from $250 to $1,000 for articles; some small fiction magazines pay 3–5 cents a word, more for experienced authors. Major magazines pay more. Book authors are usually paid an advance—a payment against projected royalties—generally half on acceptance and half on receipt. Often, the author is represented by an agent (who negotiates for and represents the author to the publisher); in return, the agent receives 10–15% of the advance and future royalties. Royalties for first-time novelists are usually several thousand dollars—on up to six figures and more for major authors or authors with hot ideas. In 1990, according to *Publishers Weekly,* first-time mystery novelists earned advances between $3,000 and $7,500; more experienced novelists with wider audiences between $10,000 and $25,000—more for major writers.

SCREENWRITING: The Writers Guild lists current minimums for screenplays, teleplays, rewrites, etc. Most film screenwriters are employed by the project; television writers are often employed by the production company. The money varies according to type of film or television feature, type of writing, and so on. According to the Writers Guild, in 1990, the minimum for the purchase of a screenplay was $21,585 for a low-budget (under $2.5 million) feature film; the purchase of a high-budget screenplay (over $2.5 million) was $44,181. For employment to write a screenplay adapted from an already existing work, the minimums in 1990 were: for a low-budget film, $17,566; for a high-budget film, $36,148.

The Guild also has minimums for rewrites, etc.—which can add more money to the totals. And writers may negotiate for more. Television writers earned median incomes from the mid- to high 20s to the high 30s—with major writers on major programs earning far more. In related fields: Story editors make about $2,000 a week; script readers for major studios usually earn about $40,000 a year.

BEST BETS

SPEECHWRITER: "The better you are, the more unnoticed you are," unless it is by the people who count, said one writer in *BusinessWeek* magazine. Speechwriting can be risky (if your boss is fired, you may go, too), annoying (often the speaker gets the credit), and boring (it's more fun writing novels). But it can also be lucrative—top corporate speechwriters can make over $100,000, freelancers even more. And it is important. Rhetoric is coming back into vogue. Speechwriters can make the difference between a win and a loss in elections, and can help set corporate agendas by the power of their writing. Speechwriters don't just make speeches, they write editorials, scripts for executives, and coach them as well. Way to break into the field: usually through corporate or government public relations.

WHERE TO GO FOR MORE INFORMATION

SPECIAL PUBLISHING PROGRAMS

Dow Jones Newspaper Fund
P.O. Box 300
Princeton, NJ
08543-0300
609/452-2820
(Offers various programs for young people interested in journalism; publishes career guides.)

The New York University Summer Publishing Institute
48 Cooper Sq.,
Room 108
New York, NY 10003
212/998-7219

The Radcliffe Publishing Procedures Course
77 Brattle St.
Cambridge, MA 02138
617/495-8678

Rice University Publishing Program
Office of Continuing Studies
P.O. Box 1892
Houston TX 77001
713/520-6022

University of Denver Publishing Institute
2199 S. University Blvd.
Denver, CO 80208
303/871-2570

WRITERS, EDITORS, AND JOURNALISTS ASSOCIATIONS

For more associations, directories, and periodicals, see the appropriate industry section; including "Advertising and Public Relations," and "Publishing."

Editorial Free-lancers Association
P.O. Box 2050
Madison Sq. Sta.
New York, NY 10159
212/677-3357
(For annual fee, members may use listing service which lists full time, part time jobs for editors, writers, indexes, etc.)

Investigative Reporters and Editors
P.O. Box 838
Columbia, MO 65205
314/882-2042

National League of American Pen Women
1300 17th St., NW
Washington, DC 20036
202/785-1997

Small Press Writers and Artists Organization
1210 Greer Ave.
Holbrook, AZ 86205
(For writers and artists

interested in publishing via small—not subsidy—presses.)

Society for Technical Communication
901 N. Stuart St.,
Suite 304
Arlington, VA 22203
703/522-4114

Writers Guild of America, West
8955 Beverly Blvd.
Los Angeles, CA 90048

WRITERS, EDITORS, AND JOURNALISTS DIRECTORIES

Children's Writers and Illustrator's Market; Guide to Literary Agents and Art/Photo Reps; Novel and Short Story Writer's Market; Poet's Market; Songwriter's Market; Writer's Market
Writer's Digest Books
1507 Dana Ave.
Cincinnati, OH 45207
1-800/289-0963
(All books are lists of prime markets for free-lance sale of written work, with names, addresses, requirements, etc.)

The Editor & Publisher Syndicate Directory
11 W. 19th St.
New York, NY 10011
(This is the prime source of information about syndicates—the companies that syndicate writers' work to papers across the country. The directory includes contact names, etc.)

Foundation Grants to Individuals; Foundation Directory; Corporate Foundation Profiles
Foundation Center
79 Fifth Ave.
New York, NY
10003-3076
212/620-4230
(The first directory is particularly valuable for those seeking financial support from foundations.)

Literary Market Place; International Literary Market Place
B. B. Bowker

245 W. 17th St.
New York, NY 10011
212/645-9700
800/521-2222
(*LMP* and *ICMP* are the "bibles" of the writing trade, with names, addresses of publishers, agents, etc.)

PRSA Register Issue, Public Relations Journal
331 Irving Pl.
New York, NY
10003-2376
212/995-2230
(Lists all PRSA members, etc.)

Writer's Guild Directory
Writer's Guild of America, West
8955 Beverly Blvd.
Los Angeles, CA 90048
213/205-2502

WRITERS, EDITORS, AND JOURNALISTS PERIODICALS

(For more, see "Publishing," page 421.)

Columbia Journalism Review
700A Journalism Bldg.
Columbia University
New York, NY 10027
212/854-2716
(Bimonthly magazine devoted to bettering journalism.)

Editor & Publisher
11 W. 19th St.
New York, NY 10011
(Weekly magazine for newspaper editors; valuable in giving a "feel" for what editors want.)

PC Publishing and Presentations
503 Fifth Ave.
New York, NY 10036
212/768-7666
(Bimonthly for desktop publishers.)

The Writer
120 Boyleston St.
Boston, MA 02116
617/423-3157
(Monthly magazine designed primarily for free-lance writers; also useful for agents, editors, etc.)

Writer's Digest
1507 Dana Av.
Cincinnati, OH 45207

513/531-2222
(Monthly magazine designed primarily for free-lance writers. Includes monthly "markets" section, which lists currently buying magazines and book publishers and describes requirements.)

SPECIAL REPORT: DISABLED WORKERS

EMPLOYMENT OUTLOOK: Should be improving.

Technological breakthroughs and labor shortages in certain areas should have increased employment opportunities. But until recently, employment of the disabled was still lagging—and opportunities were not growing as fast as hoped. The major question: Will the Americans with Disabilities Act (ADA) change all this? The hope is that it will, although the recession has kept it from having an immediate positive impact.

WHAT'S NEXT

▶ **The Americans with Disabilities Act (passed in 1990, implemented in 1992), still isn't changing the hiring of the disabled as much as was hoped. But with an easing of the recession, there is room for cautious optimism.**

There are many Americans with disabilities—about 43 million at last count; and about 67% of them are unemployed. According to *American Rehabilitation* magazine, most of them want to work, and the ADA was designed to enable them to do so.

Briefly put, the ADA mandates that people with disabilities receive equal treatment in the workplace. On January 26, 1992, it went into effect for employers with twenty-five or more workers; and for those with fifteen to twenty-five workers, it goes into effect in July 1994; there are, of course, certain exceptions.

Obviously, this doesn't guarantee the disabled a job, but it does ensure that an employer must now make certain its employment practices don't discriminate against a person with a disability.

The problem? Hiring slowed across the board with the recession, so the ADA didn't have the impact many hoped. However, with an economic rebound and a rise in hiring, the ADA should help persons with disabilities gain access to *mainstream* jobs.

▶ **New technology is aimed at assisting disabled workers—and making it easier for employers to hire them.**

A number of products have been developed to help the disabled at the workplace. One of the newest? A computer system developed by IBM to help deaf people communicate by telephone. The premise: a person types a message into the computer; the computer translates the message into a synthesized voice, which is transmitted over the phone. The listener types out a response using the push buttons on the telephone. This response appears on the deaf person's computer screen.

As for other products, they include: Telesensory System's VersaBraille II Plus, which converts letters on a computer screen to Braille, and Optacon, a non-Braille reader; Verbal Operating System (VOS), an electronic voice which says what is on a screen, from Computer Conversations; IBM's PS/2 ScreenReader, another program equipping computers with a voice; Kurzweil's Personal Reader, a reading machine that converts text into synthetic speech . . .

The list goes on and on. Light-sensitive keyboards, keyboard emulators, speciality keyboards, voice-controlled robots: these, and other programs and systems, are being produced by a range of major computer vendors, some of which offer discounts to handicapped users.

The computer devices are making it possible for the disabled to work in a range of fields. For example, the New York City Bar Association Library has installed telecommunications devices that type out telephone communications for deaf lawyers, and voice-equipped reading devices for the visually impaired.

Companies are teaming together to train disabled people in computers and other high-tech areas. For example, a group of twenty companies including IBM, General Foods, and Xerox has formed BIPED, Business Information Processing Education—which offers training at two centers, one in Stamford, Connecticut, and another in White Plains, New York.

In addition, IBM maintains the National Support Center for Persons with Disabilities, a clearinghouse and library for products and agencies for the disabled; and Apple offers Trace Software and Listing of Programs Adapted for Rehabilitation Applications with Microcomputers.

For more information about computer systems and programs for the disabled, contact: Special Needs Informational Referral Center, page 207.

► **A good area for the disabled: desktop publishing.**

It's far from certain, but it looks like desktop publishing might be a growing employment area for the next number of years. Desktop publishing is the term coined for computerized layout, design, and typesetting of newsletters, books, magazines, etc. The publisher must know one or more desktop publishing programs such as Aldus. Most users are only partly trained: one estimate is that only 40 to 60% of the potential power of an average program is utilized. Some estimates are that corporations will increase hiring of publishers to produce in-house documents, magazines, newsletters and advertising. On the downside: others feel that the programs will become so user-friendly that demand for trained professionals will not increase as predicted.

Contact: The National Institute for the Deaf is planning to establish a High Technology Center at its School for Visual Communications. According to a professor at the school, "with the state-of-the-art equipment we'll have, we'll be able to train young deaf adults to enter the field immediately upon graduation."

BEST BETS

► **There are a wide range of other good areas for disabled employees.**

The federal government has been a major employer of the handicapped—employing about 170,000 people. And since 1986, legislation requiring that all office equipment purchased by the federal government be adaptable for disabled workers makes it clear the government has a headstart on other employers.

For employment: The government maintains special hiring authorities for those with disabilities. Contact the federal agency for which you wish to work directly (see Government, page 57) and ask about Selective Placement Programs for persons with disabilities.

And several companies have been hiring the handicapped for years. Among them are Sears, Roebuck; McDonald's; Du Pont; and IBM.

Other companies, such as Metropolitan Life Insurance, have flexible work arrangments, which allow disabled computer programmers and other technical workers to work out of their own homes.

In general, computers and other high-tech positions offer good opportunities for the disabled, particularly because computer equipment is adaptable.

WHERE TO GO FOR MORE INFORMATION

ASSOCIATIONS FOR THE DISABLED

American Foundation for the Blind
15 W. 16th St.
New York, NY 10011
212/620-2000
(Publishes various publications on employment for the visually impaired.)

National Center for Persons with Disabilities
201 I.I. Willets Rd.
Albertson, NY 11507
516/747-5400

Mainstream International
1200 15th St., NW,
Suite 403
Washington, DC 20005
202/775-9004

Special Needs Information Referral Center
P.O. Box 2150
Atlanta, GA
30301-2150
800/426-2133
(IBM affiliate that provides information on IBM and IBM-compatible programs and adaptive devices.)

DIRECTORIES FOR THE DISABLED

Career Planning and Placement Strategies for Postsecondary Students with Disabilities
Higher Education and Adult Training of People with Handicaps
1 DuPont Circle, NW,
Suite 800
Washington, DC 20036
202/939-9320

(Career placement programs for handicapped students past high school; publishes directory that lists schools, organizations, information resources—available on computer or audio diskette.)

College and Career Programs for Deaf Students
Gallaudet Research Institute
800 Florida, Ave.,
House 4
Washington, DC 20002
202/651-5575

(Publishes directory listing colleges, universities, and other postsecondary institutions providing special programs and services including career programs for deaf students.)

PERIODICAL FOR THE DISABLED

Careers and the
Disabled
Equal Opportunity
Publications
44 Broadway
Greenlawn, NY 11740
516/261-8899

SPECIAL REPORT: MINORITIES

EMPLOYMENT OUTLOOK: Mixed—as always, certain industries and companies offer better opportunities than others.

WHAT'S NEXT

▶ Minorities are becoming an increasingly important force in the labor market.

The reason? Changing demographics and a shrinking labor market. The result? By the year 2000, there will be a higher percentage of nonwhites entering the labor force, and a smaller percentage of white males—29 to 15%.

This shift is already beginning to happen as the number of minority workers steadily increases each year. According to the Bureau of Labor Statistics, in about twelve years, black employment is projected to increase 32%; Asian, Native American, and other, 74%; and Hispanic, 75%. The result: a truly diverse work force, including 18 million African-Americans, representing about 11.8% of the total work force; 17 million Hispanics, or 11.1% of the total work force; and 7.2 million Asians, Native Americans, and others, or 4.8% of the work force.

▶ What does this mean for *today's* employment picture?

The changing demographics of the labor market are causing more companies and industries to begin laying the groundwork for this more culturally diverse work force. In other words, many are beginning actively to recruit minority workers and are setting up programs to help encourage minority advancement.

▶ On the flip side: the percentage of minority employees reaching management positions is still relatively low.

To put it bluntly, the glass ceiling hasn't been broken yet. Relative to their numbers in the labor market, there are few minority workers who have made it to the upper ranks. For example, according to the Equal Employment Opportunity Commission (EEOC), in 1990, only 5.9% of all managers in the U.S. were black, and only 3% of those were in corporate management.

Some companies are better than others when it comes to minority advancement. For example, Xerox posts a better-than-average percentage of minorities in high-ranking positions. One reason: an enlightened affirmative action program. In addition, it has caucus groups of minority and female workers who meet, share problems, advice, and the like, as well as offer suggestions to management on

minority issues. At insurance company Equitable Life, over 13% of its managers
are minorities, 6% in upper management; at Federal Express, 13% are black.
The list goes on—which means that the picture is improving.

▶ **To help minorities break the glass ceiling, there will be a rise in the**
number of minority employee support groups or mentor pro-
grams—and in informal networking.

Mentor programs, in which minority managers work with lower-level employees
and help them in career development, have proven highly successful in encouraging and increasing minority advancement into higher management positions. For
example, Bell regional company Nynex has set up a Minority Management Association to aid in the recruitment and career advancement of minority workers.
Expect to see more programs such as this.

A less structured way of getting ahead is informal networking. As the number of
minorities in the workplace keeps increasing, more of them will be creating an "old
boy" network of their own. One good way of accessing this: alumni groups, trade
associations.

▶ **A growing trend as more minorities enter the labor force: diversity**
management.

Diversity management, multi-cultural training—whatever the specific name
given to this trend, the bottom line is a simple one: As corporations become more
ethnically and racially diverse, they must make sure that their managers know how
to manage the wide range of workers. The goal: to break down any communication
barriers, iron out misunderstandings, and eliminate racist or sexist discrimination.

For example, cosmetics giant Avon Products, Inc., has a middle management
development program—with courses on how to manage a diverse work force. They
also have support groups for black, Hispanic, and Asian workers, all of whom are
involved in the diversity task force. UAL Corp., the parent company of United
Airlines, offers similar programs in multi-cultural training and has minority focus
groups. Digital Equipment Corporation has a program called "Valuing Differences," in which small core groups meet monthly to talk about problems, stereo-
types, and assumptions based on ethnic group and gender.

There are numerous other examples, and over the next few years a growing
number of companies will institute multi-cultural training or diversity training
along these lines.

An employment note: The growth of diversity management has led to the growing need for cultural diversity managers—a position that appears to be an interesting opportunity for minority human resources professionals. In brief, diversity
managers create and oversee the corporate strategies and special programs centering on a multi-cultural work force. This may include setting up focus groups;
establishing a diversity panel of top management and minority members to open the
lines of communications and encourage minority advancement and hiring; developing diversity management training for managers; and more. Best background?
Human resources experience, an advanced degree in sociology or organizational
development.

BEST BETS

▶ **Crucial for success: basic skills. An added plus: computer or other technical ability.**

This is the case for workers across the board, and it's especially true for minority workers.

The reason: A growing skills gap. Put simply, the job categories where there are labor shortages require people with certain skills, yet the people looking for jobs are those without the needed skills.

The answer: Training. Competition will be heating up for skilled jobs candidates. Computer skills are becoming especially necessary—for entry-level and lower-level positions in areas such as the hospitality or travel industries (both of which are traditionally strong in minority hiring), as well as for more skilled management positions.

▶ **There are specific industries that will be actively targeting minorities.**

With the changing demographics of the labor market, more industries and occupational fields are focusing on recruiting minorities. In some cases, as with accounting, this is primarily due to the current underrepresentation of minorities in the field. In fact, while the employment of Hispanics and Asians has increased, the percentage of blacks has declined. (One bright note, however: the number of black partners in accounting firms has increased.) The result? The American Institute of Certified Public Accountants (AICPA) is instituting recruitment efforts to increase minority hiring, and many accounting firms are stepping up their hiring of minorities.

Two other fields offering better-than-average opportunities for minorities are **engineering** and **computer science.** Both are hot areas for the future in general, and for minorities in particular. A key reason for the increased efforts in minority recruitment—the low number of minority students in this area. To encourage higher participation, a range of programs has been developed. One of the leading established programs is the National Consortium for Graduate Degrees for Minorities in Engineering—the GEM program—which offers scholarships for minority students seeking master's degrees in engineering, fellowships for those seeking Ph.Ds. in engineering and science. (For more on engineering and science, see Engineers, page 41, and Scientists, page 151; Computers, page 298.) Similarly, the low number of minority teachers is resulting in stepped-up recruitment.

Also a good bet: Insurance. The better to sell to and service their increasingly diverse customers, insurance companies have been actively recruiting minority members for work as agents and brokers. (For more on this field, see Insurance, page 391.)

▶ **Another good idea: Be on the lookout for companies offering specific programs and recruitment drives for minority workers.**

A number of companies have a reputation for specifically emphasizing minority hiring. Others offer special programs and training to aid career development of minority employees. As such, they are generally good bets for employment.

A good source for information on these areas: *Black Enterprise* puts out an annual issue covering the best places for blacks to work. In its company profiles, the magazine includes information on the variety of programs these different companies run.

THE TOP 25 COMPANIES FOR BLACK EMPLOYEES

**American Telephone
& Telegraph (AT&T)**
550 Madison Ave.
New York, NY 10022
212/605-5500

Ameritech
(Bell Regional Holding
Company)
30 S. Wacker Drive
Chicago, IL 60606
312/750-5000

Avon Products, Inc.
9 W. 57th St.
New York, NY 10019
212/546-6015

Chrysler Corp.
1200 Chrysler Drive
Highland Park, MI
48288-1919
313/956-5741

The Coca-Cola Co.
One Coca-Cola Plaza
NW
Atlanta, GA 30313
404/676-2121

Corning, Inc.
Houghton Park
Corning, NY 14830
607/974-9000

Du Pont Company
1007 Market St.
Wilmington, DE 19898
302/774-1000

**Equitable Life
Assurance Society**
787 7th Ave.
New York, NY 10019
212/554-1234

Federal Express
2005 Corporate Ave.
Memphis, TN 38194
901/369-3600

Ford Motor Co.
Renaissance Center
Detroit, MI 48242
313/446-3800

Gannett Co., Inc.
1100 Wilson Blvd.
Arlington, VA 22209
703/284-6000

General Mills, Inc.
Number One General
Mills Blvd.
Minneapolis, MN
55426
612/540-2311

General Motors
3044 W. Grand Blvd.
Detroit, MI 48202
313/556-5000

**International Business
Machines Corp.
(IBM)**
Old Orchard Rd.
Armonk, NY 10504
914/765-1900

Johnson & Johnson
1 Johnson & Johnson
Plaza
New Brunswick, NJ
08933
201/524-0000

Kellogg Co.
1 Kellogg Square
P.O. Box 3599
Battle Creek, MI 49016
616/961-2000

Marriott Corporation
10400 Fernwood Rd.
Bethesda, MD 20817
301/380-9000

McDonald's Corp.
McDonald's Plaza
Hinsdale, IL 60521
708/575-3000

Merck & Co., Inc.
P.O. Box 100
Whitehouse Station, NJ
08889
908/423-1000

Nynex Corp.
(Bell Regional Holding
Company)
335 Madison Ave.
New York, NY 10017
212/370-7400

**Pepsi-Cola
Metropolitan Bottling
Co.**
(div. of Pepsico, Inc.)
Rts. 35 and 100
Somers, NY 10589
914/253-2000

Philip Morris Cos., Inc.
120 Park Ave.
New York, NY 10017
212/880-5000

Teachers Insurance & Annuity Association College Retirement

Equities Fund
730 Third Ave.
New York, NY 10017
212/490-9000

UAL
1200 East Algonquin
Elk Grove Village, IL

60007
312/952-4000

Xerox Corp.
800 Long Ridge Rd.
Stamford, CT 06904
203/968-3000

SOURCE: *Black Enterprise*, February 1992.

WHERE TO GO FOR MORE INFORMATION

MINORITY TRADE AND PROFESSIONAL ASSOCIATIONS

African Studies Association
Credit Union Bldg.
Emory University
Atlanta, GA 30322
(Publishes journal with some academic job listings, etc.)

American Association of Black Women Entrepreneurs
909 Pershing Dr., Suite 207
Silver Spring, MD 20910
301/565-0258
(Publishes periodical; helps members find business opportunities within government corporations)

Asian American Journalists Association
1765 Sutter St.
San Francisco, CA 94115
415/346-2051
(Publishes yearly directory listing members; maintains

special twenty-four hour employment hot line for job seekers:
415/346-2261.)

Interracial Council for Business Opportunity
51 Madison Ave.
New York, NY 10010
212/779-4360

National Association of Black Accountants
7249A Hanover Pkwy
Greenbell, MD 20770
301/474-6222
(Publishes career information.)

National Association of Black Journalists
11600 Sunrise Valley Dr.
Reston, VA 22091
703/648-1270

National Association of Negro Business and Professional Women's Clubs
1806 New Hampshire Ave., NW

Washington, DC 20009
202/483-4206

National Bankers Association
1802 T St., NW
Washington, DC 20009
202/588-5432
(For minority bankers and banks; operates placement service, publishes directory.)

National Black M.B.A. Association
180 N. Michigan Ave., Suite 1825
Chicago, IL 60601
312/236-2622
(Publishes periodical with listings, etc.)

National Conference of Black Lawyers
126 W. 119th St.
New York, NY 10026
212/864-4000

National Hispanic Business Group
960 Southern Blvd.
New York, NY 10549
212/589-5000

214

CAREER OUTLOOKS 1994

National Minority Supplier Development Council
15 W. 39th St., 9th Fl.
New York, NY 10018
212/944-2430
(Publishes periodical and directories—with over 15,000 minority business members, can be a possibly valuable networking source.)

National Network of Minority Women in Science
c/o American Association for the Advancement of Science
Education & Human Resource Department

1333 H St., NW
Washington, DC 20005
202/326-6670
(Central office of group that promotes and aids women in science.)

National Organization of Black Law Enforcement Executives
908 Pennsylvania Ave., SE
Washington, DC 20003
202/546-8811

National Society of Black Engineers
1454 Duke St.
Alexandria, VA 22314
703/549-2207

Native American Communication and Career Development
P.O. Box 1281
Scottsdale, AZ
85252-1281
602/483-8212
(Job referrals for Native Americans.)

United Indian Development Association
9650 Flair Dr.
El Monte, CA 91731
818/442-3701
(Assists Native American business owners and those starting a business.)

MINORITY BUSINESS DIRECTORIES

Directory of Special Programs for Minority Group Members; Career Information Services, Employment Skills Banks, Financial Aid Sources
Garrett Park Press
P.O. Box 190F
Garrett Park, MD 20896
301/946-2553

Guide to Obtaining Minority Business Directories
Try-Us Resources, Inc.
2105 Central Ave., NE
Minneapolis, MN 55418
612/781-6819

MINORITY BUSINESS PERIODICALS

Black Careers
P.O. Box 8214
Philadelphia, PA 19101
215/387-1600
(Bimonthly: job guidance.)

The Black Collegian
Black Collegiate Services, Inc.
1240 S. Broad St.

New Orleans, LA
70125
504/821-5694
(Career and job information for students and recent grads.)

Black Enterprise
Subscription Service, Ctr.
P.O. Box 3011

Harlan, IA 51593
editorial offices:
130 Fifth Ave.
New York, NY 10011
212/242-8000
(Business and job advice, forecasts.)

Career Focus, for Today's Professional; AIM: A Resource

Guide for
Vocational/Technical
Graduates
Communications
Publishing Group
3100 Broadway,
Suite 225
Kansas City, MO
64111
816-756-3039
(Career guidance for
black, Hispanic young
adults.)

Equal Opportunity
Equal Opportunity
Publications

44 Broadway
Greenlawn, NY 11740
516/261-8917
(Career advice, listings
for minorities.)

J.O.B.: The Job
Opportunities Bulletin
for Minorities and
Women in Local
Government
ICMA
777 N. Capitol St., NE
Washington, DC
20002-4201
202/962-3620

Minority Business
Entrepreneur
924 N. Market St.
Inglewood, CA 90302
213/673-9398
(Bimonthly; business
advice.)

The Minority Engineer
Equal Opportunity
Publications
44 Broadway
Greenlawn, NY 11740
516/261-8917

OTHER MINORITY JOB SOURCES

HispanData: National Hispanic
Résumé Database
360 S. Hope Ave.,
Suite 300C
Santa Barbara, CA 93105
805/682-5843
(A database of résumés from which
employers can pick applicants.)

Teacher Recruitment Internship
Project for Success
American Federation of Teachers

555 New Jersey Ave., NW
Washington, DC 20001
202/879-4400
(Recruits minority math and science
college grads for teaching internships
in urban public schools.)

SPECIAL REPORT: WOMEN

EMPLOYMENT OUTLOOK: Improving slowly.

There is still a long way to go until women reach the same levels as men in the labor market. A good example: according to a 1993 study conducted by the Women's Research and Education Institute, it will take 75 to 100 years for women to reach equal pay and equal representation at all management levels, if things progress at the current rate. One reason for the pessimistic outlook where women in management is concerned: the cutbacks in middle management jobs due to the poor economic climate of the early '90s. On the other hand, there have been improvements. In 1981, of the total number of senior placements made by Korn/Ferry recruiters, only 5% were women; in 1991, that figure had more than tripled, to 16%. As one executive put it: "The glass ceiling is still there, but at least there are cracks."

WHAT'S NEXT

▶ **While a large number of women will continue dropping out of the labor force, the overall number of working women will be increasing.**

By the year 2005, the number of women in the labor force will have increased 26%—slower than the huge 51% increase between 1975 and 1980, but faster than the growth of the labor market as a whole.

But why is the rate slowing at all? So far there's only speculation; suggestions that more women are choosing to return to the home, and so on. But there has also been one compelling statistic: more women are quitting; then entering into business for themselves.

▶ **First the glass ceiling, now glass walls.**

Despite some of the good news you've been hearing about women making it to the corporate boardrooms, there's a significant problem that bodes ill for the future. *Women are far more likely to be found in corporate staff functions rather than in line functions.* Women tend to find or be placed in positions in corporate communications, human resources, finance, legal, marketing research, public relations, and systems. Problem: To make it into senior management, it's usually neccessary to have line experience in core areas like marketing, production, and sales.

What to do: Find out what experience is needed to get into the executive suite—and then plan on ways to get it. Ask for the assignments you need, seek out corporations which offer women lateral experience, or those which place women in line positions.

And some good news: as corporations transform themselves into more flexible organizations, "cross-functional" training is being offered to more executives at more corporations.

▶ **Women are networking to advance in corporate ranks.**

Recognizing that the "old boy" networks can prove vital to advancement, women are increasingly creating formal networks of their own. For example, Dow, McDonnell Douglas, and CBS are the sites of company-based networks; the Financial Women's Association in New York and New England Women in Real Estate are two functional networks.

▶ **Here's something to ponder: across the board, in virtually every field, women earned and still earn higher school and college grades; yet this educational superiority is not rewarded in the job market.**

A study by the U.S. Department of Education found significant differences between women and men, of all races, in both high school and college. The news was that women of all races, in every field including science, math, engineering, computer science and business, scored higher on average than men. In fact, it was in these technical fields that women did relatively better. Key problem: women are not rewarded for this in the marketplace. Their pay matched that of men in only seven (or twelve, using different criteria) out of thirty-three major occupations surveyed. Another interesting finding: women were nevertheless more enthusiastic, more satisfied with their work than men.

Key idea: women are a major—and still underutilized—productive force in our society.

▶ **Perhaps in response, more women are becoming entrepreneurs.**

Today, 6 million businesses are owned by women, with an extremely strong success rate; 75% of female-owned businesses succeed, compared with 20% of all businesses.

Key: women are seeing the advantages of being in business for themselves, and finally have the business experience, confidence, knowledge—and right environment—to do something about it.

Note: Some organizations, including the National Association of Female Executives (NAFE; see page 220), offer programs to help new businesswomen. In addition to informational programs, NAFE operates a venture capital fund for small businesses.

BEST BETS

▶ **Financial services: women are gaining.**

In general, according to the nonprofit organization Catalyst for Women, financial services industries like insurance, banking, and brokerage are more likely to offer women senior management positions. Twenty-eight percent of all financial services companies reported that 11% of their senior managers were women. By contrast, other industries average about 5%.

More good news: more large pension funds are moving money into the hands of minority- and female-owned money management firms. The trend began back in 1989, when California passed into law a bill requiring the state to put 20% of its pension investments into these firms; since then, other organizations and corporations have followed suit. Result: the number of investment management firms has gone up by 50% in the past year. The bad news: most of these firms are small; the best way to get a job here is to have had one or more jobs already managing money at one of the giants.

▶ **Some high-tech jobs are among the best employers of women.**

Key advantage: in many areas, the jobs are gender-blind. No one cares what sex you are; the key is whether you can use the technology. And the pay gap is less than average; women earn 82.7% of male salaries.

Best areas: information systems jobs with financial services firms, pharmaceutical firms. Some top employers: Merck, McNeil Pharmaceutical, and Smithkline Beacham Corporation.

In many cases, other high-tech areas employ few women; but according to women in the field, many areas look strong as employment possibilities in the future. Key problems: women in general are still not in the highest positions; women face barriers to high-tech employment in manufacturing, retailing.

Corporations in the News

Corporations mentioned recently that offer programs or better opportunities for women:

American Airlines (AMR Corporation)
(stresses cross-functional training)
Arthur Andersen & Co.
(40% of new hires are women; runs awareness workshops, etc.)
Baxter International
(over one-third of all managers, officials are women)
Chubb
(mentoring program)
Du Pont Corporation
(cross-functional rotations, which give employees experience in several functions)
Gannnett
(33.5% of management are women, including 20% of general management jobs; good promotion program)
Johnson Wax
(mentoring program)

Tenneco
(sophisticated promotion analysis; promotes women to major line positions)

WHERE TO GO FOR MORE INFORMATION

WOMEN'S TRADE AND PROFESSIONAL ASSOCIATIONS

Advertising Women of New York
153 E. 57th St.
New York, NY 10022
212/593-1950

9 to 5—National Association of Working Women
614 Superior Ave., NW,
Suite 852
Cleveland, OH 44113
800/245-9T05
(Focuses on helping working women in job-related areas; lobbies and publishes books and pamphlets; has Job-Problem hot line: (1-800/522-0925.)

American Association of Black Women Entrepreneurs
909 Pershing Dr., Suite 207
Silver Spring, MD 20910
301/565-0258
(Publishes periodical; helps members find business opportunities within government corporations.)

American Association of University Women
2401 Virginia Ave., NW

Washington, DC 20037
202/785-7726

American Business Women's Association
9100 Ward Pkwy.
Kansas City, MO 64114
816/361-6621
(Publishes periodical with career advice, etc.)

American Medical Women's Association
801 N. Fairfax St.
Alexandria, VA 22314
703/838-0500

American Society of Professional and Executive Women
1511 Walnut St.
Philadelphia, PA 19102
215/563-4415
(Executive recruitment service.)

American Society of Woman Accountants
1755 Lynnfield Rd.,
Suite 222
Memphis, TN 38119
901/680-0470

American Women's Economic Development Corporation
641 Lexington Ave., 9th Fl.
New York, NY 10022

212/688-1900
800/222-AWED
800/442-AWED
(Telephone hot line and counseling service for women with business problems and questions; management training and technical support for women entrepreneurs.)

American's Women's Society of Certified Public Accountants
401 N. Michigan Ave.
Chicago, IL 60611
312/644-6610

American Women in Radio and Television
1101 Connecticut Ave., NW,
Suite 700
Washington, DC 20036
202/429-5102

BPW/USA The National Federation of Business and Professional Women's Clubs, Inc.
2012 Massachusetts Ave., NW
Washington, DC 20036
202/293-1100
(Advocacy group for working women; operates Clairol scholarship program, which allows women

from diverse backgrounds—such as a thirty-five-year-old mother of two—to go back to school and study for a degree in a work-related field; also offers grants, etc.)

Capitol Hill Women's Caucus
P.O. Box 599
Longworth House Office Bldg.
Independence and New Jersey Aves.
Washington, DC 20515
(Publishes lists of jobs for members.)

Catalyst National Network of Career Resource Centers
250 Park Ave.
New York, NY
212/777-8900
(Promotes change for women in the workplace; researches and publishes findings on women's issues; directories and career information.)

Families and Work Institute
330 Seventh Ave.
New York, NY 10001
212/465-2044
(Deals with work/family issues: helps companies set up child-care centers; publishes annual guide to work-family programs in corporations.)

International Fashion Group
9 Rockefeller Plz.
New York, NY 10020
212/247-3940
(Women executives in the fashion industry.)

National Association of Bank Women
500 N. Michigan Ave., Suite 1400
Chicago, IL 60611
312/661-1700

National Association for Female Executives
127 W. 24th St., 4th Fl.
New York, NY 10011
212/645-0770
(Publishes magazine; offers career workshops, résumé guide, and writing service, discounts on career books, aptitude testing.)

National Association of Insurance Women
P.O. Box 4410
1847 E. 15th St.
Tulsa, OK 74159
918/744-5195

National Association of Women Business Owners
600 S. Federal St., Suite 400
Chicago, IL 60605
312/922-0465
(Publishes newsletter, directory; holds annual conference.)

National Association for Women in Careers
P.O. Box 81525

Chicago, IL 60681-0525
312/938-7662
(Provides support, networking, skills development services for members.)

National Federation of Business and Professional Women's Clubs, Inc.
2012 Massachusetts Ave., NW.
Washington, DC 20036
202/293-1100
(One hundred thousand members; publishes periodical provides discounts, scholarships.)

National Federation of Press Women
P.O. Box 99
Blue Springs, MO 64105
816/229-1666

National Foundation for Women Business Owners
1001 Pennsylvania Ave., NW,
Suite 435, N. Concourse
Washington, DC 20004
202/347-0978
(Provides training, research for business owners.)

National League of American Pen Women
1300 17th St., NW
Washington, DC 20036
202/785-1997

National Women's Economic Alliance Foundation
1440 New York Ave., NW,
Suite 300
Washington, DC 20005
202/393-5257
(Places women executives on corporate boards: publishes directory.)

National Women's Economic Development Foundation
1440 New York Ave., NW,
Suite 300
Washington, DC 20005
202/393-5257

Ninety-Nines
Will Rogers Airport
P.O. Box 59965
Oklahoma City, OK 73159
405/685-7969

(Publishes directory; career information.)

Older Women's League
66 11th St., NW,
Suite 700
Washington, DC 20001
202/783-6686
(Publishes career information on job discrimination, counseling, etc.)

Society of Women Engineers
345 E. 47th St.
New York, NY 10017
(Resource center; publishes periodical with job openings; offers counseling to members.)

Wider Opportunities for Women
1325 G St., NW,
Lower Level

Washington, DC 20005
202/638-3143
(Sponsors Women's Work Force Network, national network of 350 employment programs and advocates.)

Women in Film
6464 Sunset Blvd.
Hollywood, CA 90028
213/463-6040

Women Library Workers
c/o Women's Resource Center
University of California
Building T-9, Room 112
Berkeley, CA 94720
415/642-4786

Women in Sales Association
8 Madison Ave.
P.O. Box M
Valhalla, NY 10595
914/946-3802

WOMEN'S BUSINESS DIRECTORIES

A Directory of Nontraditional Training and Employment Programs Serving Women
U.S. Department of Labor
Women's Bureau
P.O. Box NT
200 Constitution Ave., NW
Washington, DC 20210
202/523-6666
(Lists programs offering apprenticeships, etc.)

Directory of Special Opportunities for Women
Garrett Park Press
P.O. Box 190F
Garrett Park, MD 20896
301/946-2553

Women Directors of the Top 1,000 Corporations
National Women's Economic Alliance Foundation
1440 New York Ave., NW,
Suite 300
Washington, DC 20005
202/393-5257

WOMEN'S BUSINESS PERIODICALS

CareerWoman
Equal Opportunity
Publications
44 Broadway
Greenlawn, NY 11740
516/261-8899
(Primarily for college
women; usually
distributed via
placement offices.)

Executive Female
127 W. 24th St.,
4th Fl.
New York, NY 10011
212/645-0770

*Financial Woman
Today*
500 N. Michigan Ave.,
Suite 1400
Chicago, IL 60611
312/661-1700

*J.O.B. The Job
Opportunities Bulletin
for Minorities and*

*Women in Local
Government*
ICMA
777 N. Capitol St., NE
Washington, DC
20002-4201
202/962-3620

Tradeswomen
(*also Trade Trax*
newsletter)
P.O. Box 40664
San Francisco, CA
94140
415/821-7334
(Both the magazine and
the newsletter are
devoted to career
information for women
in ''nontraditional''
fields, defined as those
that employ fewer than
25 percent
women—which
includes blue-collar

jobs. California-based;
carries some, mostly
local employment
listings.)

Woman Engineer
Equal Opportunity
Publications
44 Broadway
Greenlawn, NY 11740
516/261-8917
(Quarterly career
guidance magazine.)

Working Mother
WWT Partnership
230 Park Ave.
New York, NY 10169
212/551-9412

Working Woman
Working Woman, Inc.
342 Madison Ave.
New York, NY 10173
212/309-9800

SECTION 2

INDUSTRY

FORECASTS 1994

ADVERTISING AND PUBLIC RELATIONS

INDUSTRY OUTLOOK: Still weaker than in the past, but expect improvement tied to economic recovery, along with increased competition.

As the national economy improves, so should the well-being of the advertising industry. One challenge, however—agencies will continue to be forced to prove their effectiveness to clients as consumer brand loyalty keeps eroding. Other key trends: increased interest in small agencies by large clients; the resulting increase in competition for midsize clients by large agencies. Bottom line? Hot competition ahead.

Public relations is in for a similar future—improving business in pace with a recovering economy, but tight competition for clients.

A LOOK BACK

▶ **Merger mania was the name of the game in the '80s; then came the '90s and shakeups, shakedowns, and extremely bumpy times.**

The 1980s were characterized by mega-mergers, which formed mega-agencies. Much of the merger activity centered around advertising giants taking over other advertising giants. The result was the growing dominance of agency mega-groups— advertising/marketing communications conglomerates. The other chief result was industry volatility, as accounts switched agencies and staffers followed accounts to different agencies. By the end of the '80s, however, some of the mega-agencies began having problems, including Saatchi & Saatchi, the agency that many believe started the merger trend.

Then came the recession, which hit the advertising and public relations industries hard. Business grew tougher—companies slashed advertising budgets and put accounts up for review; a number of agencies lost long-standing accounts, agencies had to cut back on staffing, and the industry slid into a slump. An example of how tough it has been: In two years (June 1989 to June 1991) advertising employment dropped 5.5%—and kept going down.

WHAT'S NEXT

▶ **Continued shakeups—and continued competition.**

This has become a way of life in the advertising industry, and it doesn't look like it will change in the near future. Experts expect more of the same, even as advertising expenditures rise again. The old days when an agency with a long-standing account could relax a bit are over. Expect clients to continue the practice of using "shadow agencies"—agencies that aren't officially assigned an account but do backup or project work on the account even while another agency is still the agency of record. Similarly, expect continuing account reviews and shifts.

▶ Look for the "smaller is better" trend to continue.

It began as a backlash movement against the mega-agencies formed by the mergers. Now it has become an industry trend—and one that looks like it will continue. Witness the success of such boutiques as Weiden & Kennedy (the Portland, Oregon–based agency that won attention for its Nike ads, then won the plum Subaru automotive account).

Where employment is concerned, this points to potential opportunities at the smaller shops. Of course, keep in mind that competition for spots at small agencies is very tight, and positions may not be secure, as they depend upon the account.

▶ On the flip side, don't write off integrated services yet.

Even though the day of the mega-agencies seems to be over, the concept of offering integrated communications services to clients isn't dead. Many agencies will continue to offer a battery of communications services—from advertising to marketing, sales promotion, and public relations.

The effect of this on employment: Some agencies are now looking for different types of account executives—people with more than straight ad experience, but with experience in a related field such as public relations, sales promotion, or packaging.

▶ Expect a growing focus on targeted advertising and marketing.

It's a way to break through the clutter—more agencies are and will be focusing on very specific markets and methods.

Niche markets will become more important than ever to agencies—especially small agencies. Among the areas that will see growth: foreign-language programming and advertisements; advertising aimed at distinct ethnic groups; advertising aimed squarely at the over-fifty market. For example, Spanish language advertisements; ads aimed directly at the growing Asian population; etc.

Along these lines, there should be growth at small agencies that specialize in specific markets—which may translate into job opportunities.

▶ The old New York/San Francisco dominance of the ad industry will continue to decline.

Expect to see more agencies succeeding outside of the New York/San Francisco axis. One reason—the nationwide trend for businesses to move away from traditional urban areas to the outlying exurbs. Another reason—the shakeups in the ad industry, which led to smaller, less well known agencies winning high-visibility accounts.

This trend, which began in the '80s, will continue in the '90s. Agencies outside of New York and San Francisco have now established themselves and are coming on strong—winning awards, major clients, a great deal of attention, and a great deal of business. The leaders of the pack: Chiat/Day/Mojo in Los Angeles, Hill Holiday in Boston, The Martin Agency in Richmond, and Earle Palmer Browne in Maryland.

Where employment is concerned, this trend is good news. The industry is clearly becoming more regionally diverse, which means that job hunters may find opportunities springing up in different parts of the country.

EMPLOYMENT OUTLOOK: Fair—and highly competitive.

It's an obvious cause-and-effect situation: With a rise in ad spending by corporate America there comes a rise in advertising agency employment. This means that the long-term employment picture should be a fairly bright one. As the economy recovers, ad agency billings will rise—which means that fewer small and midsized agencies will close, and more larger agencies will be hiring once again. The U.S. government forecasts an increase of more than 4% in employment over the next decade.

A good bet for employment? Smaller (and usually newer) "hot shops" or "creative boutiques." While these agencies usually have fewer staffers than the more established older shops, they are also raking in billings lately and adding new clients. One word of warning: Competition is *extremely* intense. A strong portfolio (of actual or spec work) is a must for creatives seeking employment in these agencies. On the account side, experience on their accounts or similar accounts is important.

As for Public Relations: As always, the employment picture is dependent on the economic health of the specific business or industry an agency services, or (for corporate PR specialists) the health of a specific company or industry sector.

A rule of thumb: Corporate public relations staffers are often among the first cut when companies slide into earnings slumps. When earnings recover, however, public relations staff is added once again. It's a similar situation at PR agencies: Clients cut back on public relations expenditures during a recession, resulting in agency streamlining; after the recession, agency billing goes back up.

The bottom line where employment is concerned? Improvement is ahead, and opportunities will be there through the '90s. Some areas will be stronger than others.

Strong qualifications are a help in terms of employment. The best bet? Expertise, experience, or educational credentials beyond straight public relations. An MBA is especially helpful as is a background in areas like finance, marketing, international business, law, or science. Governmental experience can also be a help, depending on the particular company or agency clients.

JOBS SPOTLIGHT

Advertising

SALES PROMOTION STAFFERS: From the account side to the creative side, the need for sales promotion experts has been heating up. The key reason? More companies have been pumping up their promotion budgets in an effort to keep their products selling. This has translated into higher demand for promotion staffers, particularly at the larger agencies that offer a range of communications services. Salaries vary, depending on the size of the agency.

Public Relations

ENVIRONMENTAL PUBLIC RELATIONS SPECIALIST: This is a relatively new specialty and one that is going to boom in the long term. Reasons: Growing environmental awareness is forcing corporations to deal publicly with their environmental records, both negative (handling press and public relations after an environmental disaster, such as the Exxon Valdez oil spill) and positive (notifying press and public about company-sponsored "green" campaigns, projects, or products). Best preparation: a background in science as well as in public relations, English, or journalism.

LEGAL PUBLIC RELATIONS SPECIALIST: This is a specialty that is growing swiftly at a number of agencies because the legal field has become more crowded and more competitive—and law firms want to win clients without resorting to advertising. To do this, they hire agencies to promote a law firm or its partners. The PR specialist must tread a fine line, promoting the firm without making it appear "pushy." Legal experience or a background in a related area is a big plus.

BEST BETS

Warwick Baker & Fiore Inc.
100 Ave. of the Americas
New York, NY 10013
212/941-4200

This agency is committed to making communications-services integration work—and to do so, is offering interesting employment opportunities. Chairman and CEO Wilder D. Baker wrote in a "Forum" piece in a 1992 *Advertising Age* that he feels strongly about hiring "a different kind of account executive"—that is, one with experience in areas other than straight account management, but a background in a marketing communications area related to advertising. Among the backgrounds he mentions: public relations, sales promotion, packaging, corporate identity experience. This type of flexibility speaks well for the direction in which the company is headed—and spells out possible employment for those people interested in advertising, but with a non-traditional background.

Leo Burnett
Prudential Plaza
Chicago, IL 60602
312/565-5959

A Best Bet for the past three years, Leo Burnett continues to be a good choice for employment in the usually volatile ad industry. It is known for its traditional client, traditional ways, and successful advertisements and, as such, keeps coming on strong in an understated way. One of the main reasons it's known as a good place to work: stability. Leo Burnett believes in long-term relationships—both with clients and with staff members.

TOP ADVERTISING AGENCIES

AC&R Advertising, Inc.
16 E. 32nd St.
New York, NY 10016
212/685-2500

Admarketing, Inc.
1801 Century Park E.
Los Angeles, CA 90067
213/203-8400

Ally & Gargano, Inc.
805 Third Ave.
New York, NY 10022
212/688-5300

Ammirati & Puris, Inc.
100 Fifth Ave.
New York, NY 10011
212/206-0500

N. W. Ayer, Inc.
825 Eighth Ave.
New York, NY 10019
212/474-5000

Backer Spielvogel Bates Worldwide
405 Lexington Ave.
New York, NY 10174
212/297-7000

BBDO Worldwide, Inc.
1285 Ave. of the Americas
New York, NY 10019
212/459-5000

Bloom FCA, Inc.
3500 Maple Ave.
Dallas, TX 75219
214/443-0901

Bozell, Inc.
40 W. 23rd St.
New York, NY 10010
212/727-5000

Leo Burnett Co.
35 W. Wacker Dr.
Chicago, IL 60601
312/220-5959

Campbell-Mithun-Esty, Inc.
222 S. 9th St.,
22nd Fl.
Minneapolis, MN 55402
612/347-1000

Cato Johnson Worldwide
675 Ave. of the Americas
New York, NY 10010
212/941-3700

Chiat/Day/Mojo Advertising
320 Hampton Dr.
Venice, CA 90291
213/314-5000

Dailey International Group
3055 Wilshire Blvd.
Los Angeles, CA 90010
213/386-7823

Darcy Masius Benton & Bowles
1675 Broadway
New York, NY 10019
212/468-3622

DDB Needham Worldwide, Inc.
437 Madison Ave.
New York, NY 10022
212/415-2000

W. B. Doner & Co.
25900 Northwestern Hwy.
Southfield, MI 48075
313/354-9700

Doremus & Co., Inc.
200 Varick St.
New York, NY 10014
212/366-3000

Earle Palmer Brown Cos.
6935 Arlington Rd.
Bethseda, MD 20814
301/986-0510

Fahlgren Martin
Rosemar Rd. and Seminary Dr.
Parkersburg, WV 26102
304/424-3591

FCB/Leber Katz Partners, Inc.
767 Fifth Ave.
New York, NY 10153
212/705-1000

Grey Advertising, Inc.
777 Third Ave.
New York, NY 10017
212/337-6400

Griffin Bacal, Inc.
130 Fifth Ave.
New York, NY 10011
212/337-6400

GSD&M
1250 S. Capitol of
Texas Hwy.
Austin, TX 78746
512/327-8810

Hill Holiday Connors
Cosmopulos
200 Clarendon St.
Boston, MA 02116
617/437-1600

Bernard Hodes
Advertising
555 Madison Ave.
New York, NY 10022
212/758-2600

Jordan McGrath Case
& Taylor
445 Park Ave.
New York, NY 10022
212/326-9100

Kallir, Phillips, Ross,
Inc.
333 E. 38th St.
New York, NY 10016
212/878-3700

Keller-Crescent Co.,
Inc.
1100 E. Louisiana St.
Evansville, IN 47711
812/464-2461

Ketchum
Communications, Inc.
6 PPG Pl.
Pittsburgh, PA 15222
412/456-3500

Kobs & Draft
Advertising
142 E. Ontario
Chicago, IL 60611
312/944-3500

Laurence Charles Free
& Lawson
260 Madison Ave.

New York, NY 10016
212/213-4646

Lavey Wolff Swift,
Inc.
488 Madison Ave.
New York, NY 10022
212/593-3630

Lintas:Worldwide
1 Dag Hammarskjold
Plz.
New York, NY 10017
212/605-8000

Lord Dentsu &
Partners
810 Seventh Ave.
New York, NY 10019
212/408-2100

Lowe & Partners, Inc.
1345 Ave. of the
Americas
New York, NY 10105
212/708-8800

The Martin Agency
500 N. Allen Ave.
Richmond, VA 23220
804/254-3400

McCann-Erickson,
Inc.
750 Third Ave.
New York, NY 10017
212/697-6000

McCaffrey & McCall
Partners
575 Lexington Ave.
New York, NY 10022
212/350-1000

Medicus Intercon
International
1675 Broadway
New York, NY 10019
212/468-3100

Nationwide
Advertising Service
1228 Euclid Ave.
Cleveland, OH 44115
216/579-0300

Ogilvy & Mather
Worldwide
309 W. 49th St.
New York, NY 10019
212/237-4000

Richards Group, Inc.
10000 N. Central Expy.
Dallas, TX 75231
214/891-5700

Hal Riney & Partners
735 Battery St.
San Francisco, CA
94111
415/981-0959

Ross Roy, Inc.
100 Bloomfield Hills
Pkwy.
Bloomfield Hills, MI
48034
313/433-6000

Saatchi & Saatchi
Advertising
375 Hudson St.
New York, NY 10014
212/463-2000

Scali McCabe Sloves,
Inc.
800 Third Ave.
New York, NY 10022
212/735-8000

Sudler & Hennessey,
Inc.
1633 Broadway
New York, NY 10019
212/265-8000

Tarlow Corp.
950 Third Ave.
New York, NY 10022
212/826-0399

Tatham, RSCG
980 N. Michigan Ave.
Chicago, IL 60611
312/337-4400

TBWA Advertising, Inc.
292 Madison Ave.
New York, NY 10018
212/725-1150

J. Walter Thompson Co.
466 Lexington Ave.
New York, NY 10017
212/210-7000

Tracy-Locke, Inc.
200 Crescent Ct.
Dallas, TX 75201
214/969-9000

Warwick Baker & Fiore, Inc.
100 Ave. of the
Americas
New York, NY 10013
212/941-4200

Wells Rich Greene BDDP, Inc.
9 W. 57th St.
New York, NY 10019
212/303-5000

Wunderman Worldwide
575 Madison Ave.
New York, NY 10022
212/752-9800

Wyse Advertising, Inc.
24 Public Sq.
Cleveland, OH 44113
216/696-2424

Young & Rudicam, Inc.
285 Madison Ave.
New York, NY 10017
212/210-3000

TOP PUBLIC RELATIONS AGENCIES

(*—advertising agency affiliate)

Ayer Public Relations*
1345 Ave. of the
Americas
New York, NY 10105
212/708-6650

BmC Strategies, Inc.
18 Muzzey St.
Lexington, MA 02173
617/862-3384

Burson-Marsteller*
230 Park Ave. S.
New York, NY 10003
212/614-4000

Cerrell Associates, Inc.
320 N. Larchmont
Blvd.
Los Angeles, CA 90004
213/466-3445

Charles Ryan Associates
1021 Kanawha Blvd. E.
Box 2464
Charleston, WV 25329
304/342-0161

Clarke & Co.*
380 Stuart St.
Boston, MA 02116
617/536-3003

CMF&Z Public Relations (Creswell, Munsell, Fultz, & Zirbel)*
600 E. Court Ave.
Box 4807
Des Moines, IA
50309-4807
515/246-3500

Cohn & Wolfe*
225 Peachtree Rd.
Atlanta, GA 30303
404/688-5900

Cone Communications
90 Canal St.
Boston, MA 02114
617/227-2111

Cunningham Communications, Inc.
2350 Mission College
Blvd., No. 900
Santa Clara, CA 95054
408/982-0400

Aaron D. Cushman & Associates, Inc.
35 E. Wacker Dr.
Chicago, IL 60601
312/263-2500

DeVries Public Relations
30 E. 60th St.
New York, NY 10022
212/881-0400

Dewe Rogerson, Inc.
(U.S. office)
850 Third Ave.
New York, NY 10022
212/688-6840

Dix & Eaton
1010 Euclid Bldg.
Cleveland, OH 44115
216/241-0405

Dragonette, Inc.
303 E. Wacker Dr.
Chicago, IL 60601
312/565-4300

Dye, Van Mol, & Lawrence
126 Second Ave. N.
Nashville, TN 37201
615/244-1818

Earle Palmer Browne Public Relations*
6935 Arlington Rd.
Bethesda, MD 20814
301/657-6000

Edelman Public Relations Worldwide
211 E. Ontario St.
Chicago, IL 60611
312/280-7000

Financial Relations Board
675 Third Ave.
New York, NY 10017
212/661-8030

Fleishman-Hillard, Inc.
200 N. Broadway
St. Louis, MO 63102
314/982-1700

Foote Cone & Belding Communications
101 E. Erie St.
Chicago, IL 60611
312/751-7000

Franson, Hartery, & Associates
181 Metro Dr.,
No. 300
San Jose, CA 95110
408/298-1221

GCI Group*
777 Third Ave.
New York, NY 10017
212/546-2200

Gibbs & Soell
126 E. 38th St.
New York, NY 10016
212/481-4488

Gross Townsend Frank Hoffman, Inc.*
114 Fifth Ave.
New York, NY 10011
212/886-3100

E. Bruce Harrison Co.
1440 New York Ave.,
NW
Washington, DC 20005
202/638-1200

Hill & Knowlton*
420 Lexington Ave.
New York, NY 10017
212/697-5600

Holt, Ross & Yulish, Inc.
2035 Lincoln Hwy.
Edison, NJ 08877
908/287-0045

Edward Howard & Co.
1021 Euclid Ave.
Cleveland, OH 44115
216/781-2400

The Kamber Group
1920 L St., NW
Washington, DC 20036
202/223-8700

KCS&A Public Relations
820 Second Ave.
New York, NY 10017
212/682-6300

Ketchum Public Relations*
1133 Ave. of the Americas
New York, NY 10036
212/536-8800

Lobsenz-Stevens, Inc.
460 Park Ave. S.
New York, NY 10016
212/684-6300

Makovsky & Co.
245 Fifth Ave.
New York, NY 10016
212/532-6300

Manning, Selvage & Lee*
72 Madison Ave.
New York, NY 10016
212/213-0909

Morgan-Walke Associates, Inc.
420 Lexington Ave.
New York, NY 10170
212/986-5900

MWW/Strategic Communications, Inc.
70 Grand Ave.
Grand Four Office Center
River Edge, NJ 07661
201/342-9500

Nelson Communications Group

125 E. Baker St.,
No. 180
Costa Mesa, CA 92626
714/957-1010

**Ogilvy Public
Relations Group***
140 W. 57th St.
New York, NY 10019
212/977-9400

**Omnicom PR
Network***
120 Broadway
New York, NY 10271
212/964-0700

**Pacific-West
Communications
Group**
3435 Wilshire Blvd.
Ste. 2850
Los Angeles, CA 90010
213/487-0830

**Padilla Speer
Beardsley**
224 Franklin Ave. W.
Minneapolis, MN
55404
612/871-8877

PRx, Inc.
255 W. Julian St.,
No. 100
San Jose, CA
95110-2406
408/287-1700

**Public
Communications, Inc.**
35 E. Wacker Dr.
Chicago, IL 60601
312/558-1770

**Robinson, Lake,
Lerer, &
Montgomery***
75 Rockefeller Plz.
New York, NY 10019
212/484-7700

The Rockey Co.
2121 Fifth Ave.
Seattle, WA 98121
206/728-1100

Rowland Worldwide*
415 Madison Ave.
New York, NY 10017
212/527-8800

Ruder Finn
301 E. 57th St.
New York, NY 10022
212/593-6400

Shandwick PLC
61 Grosvenor St.
London WIX 90A
England
011/44-1-403-2232

**M. Silver Associates,
Inc.**
1120 Ave. of the
Americas
New York, NY 10036
212/704-2020

**Stoorza, Ziegaus, &
Metzger**
801 12th St.
Sacramento, CA 95814
916/446-6667

**Bob Thomas &
Associates, Inc.***
228 Manhattan Beach
Blvd., No. 300
Manhattan Beach, CA
90266
213/376-6978

WHERE TO GO FOR MORE INFORMATION

ADVERTISING/PUBLIC RELATIONS ASSOCIATIONS

**Advertising Research
Foundation**
3 E. 54th St.
New York, NY 10022
212/751-5656

**Affiliated Advertising
Agencies International**
2280 South Xanadu
Way
Aurora, CO 80014
303/671-8551

**American Advertising
Federation**
1400 K St., NW
Washington, DC 20005
202/898-0089
(Sponsors a special
competition for
students.)

**American Association
of Advertising
Agencies**
666 Third Ave.

New York, NY 10017
212/682-2500

**Association of
National Advertisers**
155 E. 44th St.
New York, NY, 10017
212/697-5950

**International
Advertising
Association**
342 Madison Ave.,

Suite 2000
New York, NY 10017
212/557-1133

**Public Relations
Society of America**
33 Irving Pl.

New York, NY 10003
212/995-2266
(Provides a job hot
line—212/995-0476—
with listings of job

opportunities and
information on résumé
forwarding for these
jobs.)

ADVERTISING/PUBLIC RELATIONS DIRECTORIES

*AAAA Roster and
Organization*
American Association
of Advertising Agencies
666 Third Ave.
New York, NY 10017
212/682-2500

*Directory of Minority
Public Relations
Professionals*
Public Relations Society
of America
33 Irving Pl.
New York, NY 10003
212/995-2266

*Macmillan Directory of
International
Advertisers and
Agencies*
National Register
Publishing Company

3004 Glenview Rd.
Wilmette, IL 60091
708/441-2210
800/323-6772

*O'Dwyer's Directory of
Corporate
Communications*
271 Madison Ave.
New York, NY 10016
212/679-2471

*O'Dwyer's Directory of
Public Relations
Executives*
271 Madison Ave.
New York, NY 10016
212/679-2471

*O'Dwyer's Directory of
Public Relations Firms*
271 Madison Ave.

New York, NY 10016
212/679-2471

*Public Relations
Consultants Directory*
American Business
Directories, Inc.,
Division
American Business
Lists, Inc.
5707 S. 86th Cir.
Omaha, NE 68127
402/331-7169

*Standard Directory of
Advertising Agencies*
National Register
Publishing Company
3004 Glenview Rd.
Wilmette, IL 60091
800/323-6722
708/441-2210

ADVERTISING/PUBLIC RELATIONS PERIODICALS

Advertising Age
220 E. 42nd St.
New York, NY 10017
212/210-0100
(Weekly tabloid
covering the advertising
industry. Excellent
help-wanted section.)

Adweek
49 E. 21st St.
New York, NY 10010

212/529-5000
(Weekly magazine
covering the advertising
industry. Like *Ad Age*,
this publication has a
strong help-wanted
section.)

Madison Avenue
17 E. 48th St.
New York, NY 10017

212/688-7940
800-223-1245

*O'Dwyer's PR
Marketplace*
271 Madison Ave.
New York, NY 10016
212/679-2471
(Biweekly newsletter
listing job opening and
business opportunities
for PR practitioners.)

PR Reporter
PR Publishing
Company, Inc.
Box 600
Exeter, NH 03833
603/778-0514
(Weekly newsletter sent
to PR practitioners.)

**Public Relations
Journal**
Public Relations Society
of America

33 Irving Pl.
New York, NY 10003
212/995/2230
(Monthly magazine sent
free to PRSA members
but available at a yearly
subscription price to
nonmembers; annual
Register issue lists
members, affiliations,
addresses.)

Public Relations News
127 E. 80th St.
New York, NY 10021
212/879-7090
(Weekly newsletter sent
to corporate
public-relations
executives, PR
agencies, etc.)

AEROSPACE

INDUSTRY OUTLOOK: Continued challenges—defense still feeling the effects of budget cuts; commercial coping with the effects of the worldwide economy and hot competition.

Defense aerospace manufacturers will continue to face tough times. Expect industry consolidation, shifts in product focus, and less spending on R&D. Layoffs should continue, but at a slower rate than in the recent past.

In general, commercial aerospace should improve in pace with the worldwide economy. However, decreased demand and stiff competition from international companies will continue having an impact, forcing many domestic manufacturers to continue restructuring and streamlining.

A LOOK BACK

▶ **The late '70s and early '80s were a boom time for defense aerospace manufacturers—then matters took a sharp downturn.**

Heavy peacetime buildup of weapons and high defense budgets gave the aerospace and defense electronics industry a series of good years. For about eleven years, defense budgets kept increasing, and the defense aerospace industry kept winning new orders and posting higher earnings. Defense spending peaked in 1985—and then, the defense aerospace industry began its downhill slide.

Cuts in defense budgets in the United States and other developed countries took their toll on the industry. Cost-cutting measures, discontinued programs, and a lack of new orders (in spite of a brief flurry during the Gulf War) have hammered aerospace companies.

▶ **In the '80s, commercial aerospace manufacturers were flying high, as well. But the recession took its toll on the industry.**

Deregulation, increasing air traffic, and a strong economy were all factors in the success of commercial aerospace manufacturers. Airlines were on a buying spree, which gave commercial manufacturers a run of banner years in earnings and a dizzying growth rate. In 1989 U.S. and European manufacturers received the most aircraft orders since 1947—which was the beginning of the jet age.

But the good times didn't last as the recession took its toll on airlines. Air travel slumped, a number of airliners went bankrupt or out of business, and orders for new planes fell. Result: Drops in aircraft and parts orders from 1990 to 1993—and slumping sales for commercial aerospace manufacturers.

WHAT'S NEXT

▶ **Ups and downs in the short term for commercial aerospace as airlines regroup, but the long term looks good.**

While the past three years were grim ones for the commercial aerospace industry, marked by order cancellations and delayed orders, it looks like all systems are go where the long-term outlook is concerned.

The key reason? World air-traffic growth is expected to resume its upward climb, with some predicting that air traffic will *triple* by the year 2010. In addition, a high number of planes are due to be retired. The bottom line—a surge in new-plane orders. This will translate into employment opportunities in the long term, as aircraft manufacturers staff up to meet the production demands.

▶ **Expect tougher competition from foreign companies as they continue to grow in strength.**

European and Asian countries are beginning to take a bite out of U.S. exports of aircraft. Aerospace is the number-one U.S. export, responsible for $38 billion in overseas sales annually. The commercial aerospace sector has been particularly strong in exports, but foreign competition is beginning to weaken this strength. For example, in 1991 Boeing and McDonnell Douglas exported more than 50% of their combined output of commercial aircraft. These sales gave them 67% of the world aircraft market, a drop from 1987, when they had 78% of the market.

Watch as foreign companies, particularly European ones, cut even more deeply into U.S. aerospace sales in the years ahead. One of the toughest competitors is Airbus Industries, the European consortium that is number two, behind Boeing, in worldwide orders. Airbus is boosting its annual production rate from 95 aircraft to 200 aircraft this year. Other competitors include British Aerospace and Fokker Aircraft.

▶ **Along similar lines, watch as the U.S. aerospace industry becomes increasingly globalized.**

The globalization trend that is sweeping the rest of U.S. industry will affect aerospace as well. Some of the results: Expect to see more foreign investment in U.S. companies. In some cases, this will be a way of getting the funding that used to come from government contracts. For example, in November 1991, McDonnell Douglas announced that it was working on a deal to sell up to 40% of its commercial aircraft business to the Taiwan Aerospace Corporation (which has been partially underwritten by the Tawainese government).

Also expect to see more U.S. companies turn to foreign companies for subcontract work and others team up with foreign manufacturers. There is already a rising number of international team arrangements in the aircraft engine area: General Electric is working with European and Japanese manufacturers on advanced engines such as the CFM56, CF6-80, and GE90; Pratt & Whitney is doing the same with the V2500, the JTD-8-200, and the PW4000. This trend should continue.

▶ **On the defense side of the industry, the difficult times will continue for manufacturers, forcing them to refocus their businesses.**

It's an inevitability—cutbacks in the defense budget will keep defense aerospace manufacturers in a slump. By 1995 defense spending may be cut to roughly 50 percent of what it was during the Reagan years. As a result, defense companies will be forced to rethink their business and focus on their core capabilities. For example, in a recent *Aviation Week and Space Technology*, Northrop said it would focus on advanced composites and stealth technologies, TRW on modular avionics and software development. In short, defense companies will be sticking with the areas in which they have the most experience.

▶ **Watch defense aerospace manufacturers target themselves for nondefense projects, sometimes teaming up with former competitors to gain them.**

In many cases, this is the only way of recapturing earnings. More manufacturers will seek different areas of business to compensate for the defense projects that have been cut. Some companies have a headstart: For example, Hughes Aircraft Co. formed a subsidiary in 1990 called Hughes Information Technology Co. to begin exploring opportunities in technology markets other than defense. TRW's Space and Defense Sector is producing tax-processing equipment for the IRS and is planning nuclear-waste disposal equipment for the Energy Department. Martin Marietta has begun managing research laboratories for the Energy Department and computer systems for the Department of Housing and Urban Development. Expect to see more actions like this as companies struggle to find new lines of business. One area that should see stiff competition is the space sector.

Similarly, watch as more companies team up to share expertise in an attempt to win new defense and nondefense government contracts. An example: In 1990, airframe manufacturers Rockwell International, General Dynamics, and McDonnell Douglas and engine manufacturers Pratt & Whitney and Rocketdyne (a Rockwell division) switched from being competitors to being partners in the development of the hypersonic NASP (National Aerospace Plane).

Expect more companies to aim their sights at projects unconnected with the government. For example, McDonnell Douglas has been exploring the market for and profitability of building bullet trains—high-speed rail transports, which are already widely used in Japan. Westinghouse Electronics Systems is making (among other products) security gear for home and commercial use and radar equipment.

The effect on employment? Limited at this time, as companies shop around for new work. The key to uncovering employment opportunities is keeping abreast of any developments and contracts awarded. However, don't expect miracles. According to a recent *BusinessWeek*, experts say that over the short term, switching to nondefense projects will replace only 25 to 30% of the defense work that was cut.

▶ **Keep an eye on: Commercial space business.**

It's an interesting area with long-term potential. Even while NASA's budget stays fairly level, the commercial space sector is growing. The U.S. Commerce

Department has forecast annual growth rates of about 20%. Particularly hot: the light satellite industry, remote sensing data, Global Positioning System receivers.

EMPLOYMENT OUTLOOK: Both commercial and defense feeling the impact of industry streamlining. Short term looks fair to poor; expect improvement over the long term, however.

The employment picture in the aerospace industry in general has been very poor in the recent past. An example: the Bureau of Labor Statistics reported that, between December 1989 and May 1992, total aerospace employment dropped an average of about 6,200 jobs per month. This type of job fallout hit both the commercial and defense sectors, although defense suffered most. Commercial giant Boeing announced plans to lay off employees—estimates range from 10,000 to 20,000—while defense manufacturers including McDonnell Douglas, Lockheed, Grumman, General Dynamics and Northrop also eliminated jobs or announced plans to do so.

As for the future? The long-term outlook shows some improvement, especially if the worldwide economy shows a strong recovery. Where commercial aerospace is concerned, the key problem, as mentioned earlier, will be increased competition. Expect stabilized employment over the next few years, with some areas showing stronger employment possibilities than others. For example, as aging aircraft need to be replaced, general aircraft manufacturers (such as Boeing) should resurge, probably after 1994. In the defense sector, the picture remains shakier. According to the Office of Technology Assessment, from 530,000 to 920,000 private-sector defense jobs will be cut by 1995. The key to employment opportunities in defense? Keeping abreast of new developments and projects. The companies that will eventually be hiring again will be those that find a means of replacing earnings lost in the defense cutbacks.

On the other hand, the employment picture is poor in the defense aerospace industry. The severe cutbacks in defense have led to layoffs and company streamlinings, and it is unlikely that these jobs will reappear. According to the Office of Technology Assessment, from 530,000 to 920,000 private sector defense jobs will be cut by 1995. Most of the major companies have announced plans to eliminate jobs or have already done so, including McDonnell Douglas, Lockheed, Grumman, General Dynamics and Northrop. The key to employment opportunities in this sector of aerospace is keeping abreast of new developments and projects. The companies that will eventually be hiring again will be those that find a means of replacing earnings lost in the defense cutbacks.

JOBS SPOTLIGHT

SOFTWARE ENGINEERS: Demand has been high in this area, particularly for engineers who can model physical systems. Many aerospace companies cite this as a strategic need.

BEST BETS

B/E Avionics
P.O. Box 22008
Santa Ana, CA 92701
714/835-6575

A relatively young small company, BEAvionics is coming on strong even while larger competitors are struggling. The key to its success? A very specific niche. The company makes systems for plane interiors, such as passenger control units (the overhead buttons used to signal the flight attendant, etc.) and recently acquired an airline galley manufacturer and a seat manufacturer. A new area it is getting into: video systems for individual seats. This appears to be a growing field, especially as airlines try to come up with special amenities to attract travelers. For this reason, BEAvionics should continue to be a growing concern.

Harris Corp.
1025 West NASA Blvd.
Melbourne, FL 32919
407/727-9100

Actively seeking to move away from defense business, Harris has been making strides in other areas. For example, at the end of 1991, it won a Federal Aviation Administration contract—to overhaul the air traffic control system—away from AT&T. In addition, Harris is hoping to expand overseas, selling air-traffic control, weather forecasting, and communications systems to foreign clients. This type of vision and activity make Harris look like a fairly good bet, even in these difficult times for aerospace.

TOP AEROSPACE AND DEFENSE ELECTRONICS COMPANIES

(For related companies, also see "Top Electronics Companies," page 307.)

Alliant Techsystems, Inc.
5901 Lincoln Dr.
Edina, MN 55436
612/939-2000

Allied-Signal Aerospace Co.
2525 W. 190th St.
Torrance, CA
90504-6099
213/321-5000

The Boeing Company
Box 3707
7755 E. Marginal Way S.
Seattle, WA 98124
206/655-2121

Coltec Industries, Inc.
430 Park Ave.
New York, NY 10022
212/940-0400

Delco Electronics Corp.
(Subdivision of GM

Hughes Electronics Corp.)
1 Corporate Center
Kokomo, IN
46904-9005
317/451-2353

E-Systems, Inc.
P.O. Box 660248
Dallas, TX 75266-0248
214/661-1000

The Fairchild Corporation
300 W. Service Rd.

Box 10803
Chantilly, VA 22021
703/478-5800

**Garrett Engine
Division**
(Division of
Allied-Signal Aerospace
Co.)
111 S. 34th St.
Phoenix, AZ 85034
602/231-1000

**General Dynamics
Corp.**
Pierre Laclede Center
St. Louis, MO 63105
314/889-8200

GE Aerospace
(Subsidiary of General
Electric Co.)
Box 8555
Philadelphia, PA 19101
215/354-1000

GE Aircraft Engines
(Division of General
Electric Co.)
1 Neumann Way
Cincinnati, OH 45215
513/243-2000

Gencorp, Inc.
175 Ghent Rd.
Fairlawn, OH 44333
216/869-4200

**GM Hughes
Electronics Corp.**
(Subsidiary of General
Motors Corp.)
GM Building
3044 W. Grand Blvd.
Detroit, MI 48202
313/556-2025

Grumman Corp.
1111 Stewart Ave.
Bethpage, NY

11714-3580
516/575-0574

**Grumman Aircraft
Systems Division**
(Division of Grumman
Corp.)
Bethpage, NY
11714-3580
516/575-0574

Harris Corp.
1025 W. NASA Blvd.
Melbourne, FL 32919
407/727-9100

**The Henley Group,
Inc.**
Liberty Ln.
Hampton, NH 03842
603/926-5911

Honeywell, Inc.
Honeywell Plz.
Minneapolis, MN
55408
612/870-5200

Hughes Aircraft Co.
(Subsidiary of GM
Hughes Electronics
Corp.)
7200 Hughes Ter.
Los Angeles, CA 90045
310/568-7200

ITT Defense
(Subsidiary of ITT
Corp.)
1000 Wilson Blvd.
Arlington, VA 22209
703/247-2942

Kaman Corp.
Blue Hills Ave.
Bloomfield, CT 06002
203/243-8311

Kollsman
(Division of Sequa
Corp.)

220 Daniel Webster
Hwy.
Merrimack, NH 03054
603/889-2500

Litton Industries
360 N. Crescent Dr.
Beverly Hills, CA
90210
310/859-5000

Lockheed Corp.
4500 Park Granada
Blvd.
Calabasas, CA 91399
818/876-2000

Loral Corp.
600 Third Ave.
New York, NY 10016
212/697-1105

The LTV Corp.
2201 Ross Ave.
Dallas, TX 75265-5003
214/979-7711

**Martin Marietta
Corp.**
6801 Rockledge Dr.
Bethesda, MD 20817
301/897-6000

**McDonnell Aircraft
Co.**
(Division of McDonnell
Douglas Corp.)
P.O. Box 516
St. Louis, MO 63166
314/232-0232

**McDonnell Douglas
Corp.**
P.O. Box 516
St. Louis, MO 63166
314/232-0232

**McDonnell Douglas
Space Systems**
(Division of McDonnell
Douglas Corp.)

5301 Balsa Ave.
Huntington Beach, CA
92647
714/896-3311

Northrop Corp.
1840 Century Park E.
Century City
Los Angeles, CA
90067-2199
310/553-6262

Parker Hannifin Corp.
17325 Euclid Ave.
Cleveland, OH 44112
216/531-3000

**Pratt & Whitney
Group**
(Division of United
Technologies Corp.)
400 Main St.
East Hartford, CT
06108
203/565-4321

Raytheon Co.
141 Spring St.
Lexington, MA 02173
617/862-6600

**Rockwell International
Corp.**
2201 Seal Beach Rd.
Box 4250

Seal Beach, CA 90740
310/797-3311

**Rockwell International
Corp.**
Defense Electronics
Division
3370 Miraloma Ave.
P.O. Box 3105
Anaheim, CA 92803
714/762-8111

Rockwell International
North American
Aircraft Operations
P.O. Box 92098
Los Angeles, CA 90009
310/647-1000

Rockwell International
Space Systems Division
12214 Lakewood Blvd.
Box 7009
Downey, CA 90241
310/922-2111

Rohr Industries, Inc.
P.O. Box 878
Chula Vista, CA 92012
619/691-4111

Sundstrand Corp.
P.O. Box 7003
4949 Harrison Ave.
Rockford, IL 61125
815/226-6000

Teledyne, Inc.
1901 Ave. of the Stars
Los Angeles, CA 90067
310/277-3311

Textron, Inc.
40 Westminster St.
Providence, RI 02903
401/421-2800

Thiokol Corp.
2475 Washington Blvd.
Ogden, UT 84401
801/629-2000

**United Technologies
Corp.**
United Technologies
Bldg.
Hartford, CT 06101
203/728-7000

**Westinghouse
Electronics Systems**
(Division of
Westinghouse Electric
Corp.)
Box 1693
Baltimore-Washington
International Airport,
MD 21203
301/765-1000

WHERE TO GO FOR MORE INFORMATION

(For more information sources relating to the aerospace industry, also see "Engineering," page 41, "Aviation," page 260, and "Computers and Electronics," page 298.)

AEROSPACE ASSOCIATIONS

**Aerospace Industries
Association**
1250 I St., NW

Washington, DC 20005
202/371-8500

**American Institute of
Aeronautics and
Astronautics**
370 L'Enfant

Promenade, SW
Washington, DC 20024
202/646-7400
(Among other
publications, puts out
the *AAIA Bulletin,*
which includes
employment listings,
and the *AIAA Student
Journal,* which is aimed

at aerospace students
and includes articles on
job hunting and
entry-level career
opportunities.)

**Aviation Distributors
and Manufacturers
Association**
1900 Arch St.
Philadelphia, PA 10103
215/564-3484

**General Aviation
Manufacturers
Association**
1400 K. St., NW
Washington, DC 20005
202/393-1500

AEROSPACE DIRECTORIES

*Aerospace Facts &
Figures*
Aerospace Industry
Association
1250 I St., NW
Washington, DC 20005
202/371-8400

**Aerospace Consultants
Directory**
Society of Aerospace

Engineers
400 Commonwealth Dr.
Warrendale, PA 15096
412/776-4841

*International ABC
Aerospace Directory*
Jane's Information
Group
1340 Braddock Pl.
Ste. 300

P.O. Box 1436
Alexandria, VA
22313-2036

**World Aviation
Directory**
Aviation Week Group
McGraw Hill, Inc.
1156 15th St., NW
Washington, DC 20005
202/822-4600

AEROSPACE PERIODICALS

Aerospace Daily
1156 15th St., NW
Washington, DC 20005
202/822-4600
(Daily newsletter
circulated to
government officials
and aerospace
executives.)

Aerospace Engineering
400 Commonwealth Dr.
Warrendale, PA 15096
412/772-7114
(Monthly publication

put out by the society
of Aerospace Engineers;
geared to design
engineers, technical
managers, etc.)

*Aviation Week and
Space Technology*
1221 Ave. of the
Americas
New York, NY 10020
212/512-3660
(Weekly magazine;
considered by many to
be the industry

"bible"; covers all
phases of the aerospace
industry—commercial
defense, space, etc.
Includes classified ads.)

Defense News
and *Space News*
6883 Commercial Dr.
Springfield, VA 22159
703/658-8400
(Magazines covering the
defense industry and
space industry.)

AGRICULTURE

INDUSTRY OUTLOOK: Depends upon trade agreements and governmental policies, among other factors—but probably fair.

General prospects for agriculture look fair. The plus side—low farm debt, low interest rates, and strong exports, particularly to Mexico. Potential problems—cuts in imports by cash-poor China, Russia, and Eastern Europe if U.S. government financing slows. As for agricultural suppliers? Outlook is directly tied to farmers' attitudes—which may remain cautious. One note: As of this writing, however, the full impact of the flooding of the Midwest was not certain. Possible repercussions? Increased reliance on imports, surges in ag-supply prices.

A LOOK BACK

▶ **The two major forces that affected agriculture: in the past decade the "Farm Belt Depression" of 1982 and the increasing subsidies from the federal government.**

Agriculture went into a steep decline in the early 1980s. A key cause was the fact that farmers had been expanding rapidly, buying land and equipment, taking on a heavy debt load in the process (about $183 billion at its peak in 1983). Next exports dropped consistently, reaching a low in 1986. At the same time, crop prices were declining, land prices were declining—and many farms failed.

To help farmers out of their financial straits, the government began to beef up its federal farm subsidy program. Payments to farmers skyrocketed, hitting $27.5 billion in 1986. The problem? Payments were often highest to the farms and farmers who needed them least. So even with the subsidy program, large numbers of smaller farms continued to fail or to lose money.

But by the late '80s, the farm depression ended. Debt declined, incomes began to rise once again, and the subsidies were scaled back. Farmers closed the decade with a new, cautious outlook, streamlined operations, and the ability to weather any downturn that would come next. And it paid off: In 1990, farmers reaped a record $61.3 billion in cash income, and 1992 and 1993 were similarly profitable, helped by low debt and even lower interest rates.

WHAT'S NEXT

▶ **Look for the impact of the "new world order" on agriculture, specifically, on grain growers.**

The collapse of communism in Eastern Europe is already translating into an increase in the amount of grain grown and sold to Russia and Eastern Europe. This trend should continue in the short term as demand remains high and the region remains unsettled.

▶ **A growing trend: fewer—but larger—farms.**

This has been happening for the past few years. Each year, the number of U.S. farms drops by about 30,000. This has resulted in a 61% decline in the number of farms over the past forty years. Department of Agriculture figures show 5,399,437 working farms in 1950 and only 2,104,560 in 1991.

But the amount of land used for agriculture hasn't dropped by the same degree. The reason? While the number of farms is decreasing, the size of farms is *increasing*.

Expect this to continue as the agriculture industry polarizes, with small "hobbyist" farms run by people whose primary sources of incomes are in nonfarming areas at one end, and large farms, with sales of more than $250,000 annually, dominating the picture. These larger farms are better equipped to stay financially sound without government help; they tend to be more profitable and so can invest in the machinery and other capital improvements that are becoming increasingly vital to modern farming.

▶ **In line with the trend toward larger farms, midsized farms will fade out of the U.S. agriculture picture.**

This, too, has been happening for the past few years. Farms with annual sales ranging from $40,000 to $250,000 have been unable to keep up with the financial realities of agriculture in the '80s and '90s. In short, their sales and profits aren't high enough to maintain their high equipment costs, and to endure marginal crops and weak prices, bad weather and possible natural disasters, or no subsidies. In addition, when farm land credits don't keep pace with inflation, banks tighten credit—which means lack of financing and possible failure. Over the next few years, watch for the continuing decline of the midsized farm.

▶ **Expect more farms to take advantage of technological breakthroughs.**

It's a growing trend: Large farms, in particular, are introducing high-tech methods to farming and are automating their cycle of crop production. The result? Farms that are run similarly to factories and are very profitable.

The use of technology has changed the employment picture at many of the larger farms. Employees, especially farm managers, must have some degree of technical skills and even better, experience with the new methods.

▶ **Farms will be adjusting their output to meet changing consumer demands.**

As with other industries, the agricultural industry will become more market-driven, tracking demographics and customer preferences to determine what will sell best. The key factor: a growing health-consciousness that is sweeping the nation. Given this, expect a growing number of organic and natural farms to keep up with the increasing demand for foods produced without the use of chemical pesticides. Similarly, there should be a growth in production of livestock that haven't been treated with hormones.

Also getting a great deal of attention: Genetic engineering and other facets of agriculture biotechnology. This is still a relatively young area in agriculture, but it will be taking off, as current research and development evolve into actual breakthroughs that can be adopted by more farmers. Keep an eye on this area—in the long term, it will have a huge impact on the agriculture field. For more information on ag biotech; see Chemicals, page 290.

EMPLOYMENT OUTLOOK: Fair.

According to the U.S. Bureau of Labor Statistics, farming is the occupational category with the largest projected job decline over the next twelve years: 20.9%. This translates into a loss of about 224,000 jobs for farmers, 92,000 for farm workers.

In spite of these figures, job opportunities will remain. For example, in 1988, about 1,272,000 jobs were held by farm operators and managers. Of these, roughly three out of five managed crop production; more than two out of five managed livestock production. The bottom line? While the field is shrinking, the slack is being taken up, in part, by the larger farms.

JOBS SPOTLIGHT

FARM MANAGERS: A position that has become more important as, on the one hand, farms grow larger and more technologically complex and, on the other, absentee ownership rises. Salary levels depend upon the type and size of farm managed, and cover a wide range—typically from $20,000 to $40,000.

BEST BETS:

"BRAND NAME" FARMS: There is a growing presence of brand-name farms— that is, farms that market their product like other manufacturers. For example, J.G. Boswell Company, a cotton farm, sells Boswell Cotton—at a higher price than the competition because of high quality and brand identification. Brand-name farms will continue to be a growing trend and should offer growing employment opportunities.

LEADING AGRICULTURE COMPANIES

(For related companies, also see listing under "FOOD," page 357.)

A & B-Hawaii, Inc.
820 Bishop St.
Honolulu, HI 96813
808/525-6611
(Sugar, molasses, etc.)

Ag Processing, Inc.
11717 Burt St.
Omaha, NE 68154
402/496-7809
(Soybean oil, cake, meal, etc.)

Bud Antle, Inc.
(Subsidiary of Dole Co.)
639 S. Sanborn
Salinas, CA 93901
408/422-8871
(Vegetables.)

C. Brewer & Co. Ltd.
827 Fort St. Mall
Honolulu, HI 96813
808/536-4461
(Nuts, sugar cane, etc.)

Alfred Brubaker
21700 SW 252nd St.
Homestead, FL 33031
305/246-9969
(Produce.)

Cal-Maine Foods, Inc.
3320 Woodrow Wilson Ave.
Jackson, MS 39209
601/948-6813
(Eggs, etc.)

Joseph Campbell Co.
Campbell Pl.
Camden, NJ 08103
609/342-6029
(Produce.)

Campbell's Fresh, Inc.
Maiden Creek Rd.
Blandon, PA 19510
215/926-4101
(Mushrooms.)

Castle & Cooke, Inc.
10900 Wilshire Blvd.
Los Angeles, CA 90024
213/824-1500
(Fruits, vegetables.)

Central Soya Company, Inc.
1300 Ft. Wayne National Bank Bldg.
Ft. Wayne, IN 46802
219/425-5100
(Livestock and poultry feeds, soybean meal, etc.)

DeKalb Genetic Corp.
3100 Sycamore Rd.
DeKalb, IL 60115
815/758-3461
(Corn, etc.)

Diamond Walnut Growers, Inc.
1050 Diamond St.
Stockton, CA 95205
209/467-6000
(Walnuts.)

A. Duda & Sons
1975 W. State Rd.
Oviedo, FL 32765
407/365-2111
(Produce.)

Durbin Marshall Food Corp.
3125 Independence Dr.
Birmingham, AL 35209

205/870-5800
(Broiler, fryer, and roaster chickens.)

Foster Poultry Farms
1000 Davis St.
Livingtons, CA 95334
209/394-7901
(Poultry hatchery.)

Fresh International Corp.
1020 Merrill St.
Salinas, CA 93901
408/422-5334
(Crops.)

Gilroy Foods, Inc.
(Subsidiary of McCormick & Co.)
1350 Pacheco Pass Hwy.
Gilroy, CA 95020
408/847-1414
(Dehydrated garlic, onion, etc.)

Granada Corp.
10900 Richmond Ave.
Houston, TX 77042
713/783-1310
(Livestock services.)

Harris Farms, Inc.
I-5 and Highway 145
Coalinga, CA 93210
209/884-2435
(Crops.)

Hudson Foods, Inc.
1225 Hudson Rd.
Rogers, AR 72756
501/636-1100
(Poultry.)

Lykes Brothers, Inc.
215 E. Madison St.
Tampa, FL 33602
813/223-3981
(Fruits, cultivation
services.)

**Maui Land &
Pineapple Co., Inc.**
120 Kane St.
Kahului, HI 96732
808/877-3351
(Fruits.)

**Mid-America
Dairymen, Inc.**
3253 E. Chestnut
Expwy.
Springfield, MO 65802
417/865-7100
(Dairy products.)

**Monterey Mushrooms,
Inc.**
1500 41st Ave.
Capitola, CA 95010
408/475-1955
(Mushrooms.)

Murphy Farms, Inc.
Hwy. 117 S.
P.O. Box 759
Rose Hill, NC 28458
919/289-2111
(Hogs.)

Pilgrims Pride Corp.
110 S. Texas
Pittsburg, TX 75686
903/856-7901
(Broiler, fryer, and
roaster chickens.)

**Prairie Farms Dairy,
Inc.**
1110 N. Broadway
Carlinville, IL 62626
217/854-2547
(Milk processing.)

Riceland Foods
2120 Park Ave.
Stuttgart, AR 72160
501/673-5500
(Milled and polished
rice, vegetable
shortenings and oil
—except corn oil—etc.)

**Sun World
International, Inc.**
5544 California Ave.,
No. 280
Bakersfield, CA 93309
805/833-6460
(Crop preparation
services for market
fruits, vegetables.)

Townsend Farms, Inc.
Rte. 24
P.O. Box 468

Millsboro, DE 19966
302/934-9221
(Broiler, fryer, and
roaster chickens.)

Tyson Foods, Inc.
2210 W. Oaklawn Dr.
Springdale, AR 72764
501/756-5000
(Broiler, fryer, and
roaster chickens.)

**United States Sugar
Corp.**
111 Ponce de Leon
Ave.
Clearwater, FL 33340
813/983-8121
(Sugar, vegetables,
etc.)

**Wisconsin Dairies
Co-op, Inc.**
Rt. 3, Hwy. 12 W.
P.O. Box 111
Baraboo, WI 53913
608/356-8316
(Dairy products.)

Zacky Farms, Inc.
2000 N. Tyler
El Monte, CA 91733
818/443-9351
(Broiler, fryer, and
roaster chickens.)

WHERE TO GO FOR MORE INFORMATION

AGRICULTURE ASSOCIATIONS

**Agriculture Council of
America**
1250 I St., NW,
Suite 601
Washington, DC 20005
202/682-9200

**Agricultural Research
Institute**
9650 Rockville Pike
Bethesda, MD 20814
301/530-7122

**American Farm
Bureau Federation**
225 Touhy Ave.
Park Ridge, IL 60068
312/399-5700

American Feed Industry Association
1501 Wilson Blvd.,
Suite 1100
Arlington, VA 22209
703/524-1921

American Society of Agricultural Engineers
2950 Niles Rd.
St. Joseph, MI 49085
616/429-0300

American Society of Agronomy
677 S. Segoe Rd.
Madison, WI 53711
608/272-8080
(Puts out monthly magazine—also available to nonmembers for a low subscription price—that

includes a help-wanted section; also offers a résumé bank/job placement service—free for members; low cost to nonmembers.)

American Society of Farm Managers and Rural Appraisers
950 S. Cherry St.
Denver, CO 80222
303/758-3513

Future Farmers of America
P.O. Box 15160
Alexandria, VA 22309
703/360-3600

National Corn Growers Association
201 Massachusetts

Ave., NE,
Suite CO4
Washington, DC 20002
202/546-7611

National Council of Agricultural Employers
499 S. Capitol St., SW,
Suite 411
Washington, DC 20003
202/488-1100

National Grain and Feed Association
1201 New York Ave.,
NW,
Suite 830
Washington, DC 20005
202/289-0873

AGRICULTURE DIRECTORIES

Directory of Information Resources in Agriculture and Biology
U.S. National Agriculture Library
U.S. Government Printing Office
Washington, DC 20402
202/783-3238

Directory of State Departments of Agriculture
U.S. National Agriculture Library
U.S. Government Printing Office
Washington, DC 20402
202/783-3238

Farms Directory
American Business Directory
5711 S. 86th Circle
Omaha, NE 68127
402/593-4600

AGRICULTURE PERIODICALS

(There are a number of agricultural magazines and newspapers focusing on specific regional areas and specific crops or livestock. To find the appropriate names, check a periodicals directory at the public library, such as *Business Publication Rates & Data,* published by Standard Rates & Data Service.)

Ag Consultant
37733 Euclid Ave.
Willoughby, OH 44094
216/942-2000

(Nine-issue magazine on the agricultural field, aimed at agricultural advisers, agri-fieldmen,

researchers, and schools.)

250

*Agribusiness
Worldwide*
4800 Main St.
Kansas City, MO
64112
816/756-1000
(Bimonthly magazine
for those involved in
agribusiness in Asia,
Africa, and Latin
America.)

Agri Finance
6201 W. Howard
Niles, IL 60648
708/647-1200
(Nine-issue magazine
on agricultural
financing, designed for

bank officers, farm
credit agencies,
management and
loan/mortgage firms,
etc.)

Feed Management
122 S. Wesley Ave.
Mt. Morris, IL 61054
815/734-4171
(Monthly magazine for
executives, managers,
manufacturers, etc., in
the feed industry.)

Successful Farming
1716 Locust St.
Des Moines, IA 50336

515/284-2897
(Monthly magazine
covering farming,
aimed at a wide range
of readers, including
farmers, managers,
opertors, bankers, and
business managers.)

Top Producer
230 W. Washington Sq.
Philadelphia, PA 19106
215/829-4700
(Monthly magazine for
farmowners and farm
managers.)

AUTOMOTIVE

INDUSTRY OUTLOOK: Gaining steam as the economy strengthens.

It looks like the worst is over, and the outlook for the auto industry should be improving. Competition will remain tight, but automakers and dealers should begin seeing a rise in demand. Other factors on the plus side: Expect a growth in exports of both vehicles and parts over the next few years. A protectionist stance by the Clinton administration could help the Big Three fight Japan. Potential problems? The often-present threat of strikes, the impact of changes in fuel-economy standards and other new environmental legislation requiring extensive R&D to meet new standards and, over the short term, overcapacity.

A LOOK BACK

▶ **1989–91 were grim years. But the industry turned the corner in late 1992 and 1993.**

Like much of the nation, the auto industry was swept up in the go-go '80s. It experienced six years of consecutive growth in every market segment, from small subcompacts to luxury cars. Expansion was the name of the game—from manufacturers to auto dealers. Then the market went south. Sales in 1991 were the lowest in eight years. And the Big Three automakers continued to lose market share to the Japanese importers.

And it wasn't only U.S. automakers that were feeling the financial pinch. The Japanese automakers also saw their profit margins squeezed—to the point where serious debates were ongoing in Japan about the cost of obtaining market share.

By 1992 even the market segments thought invulnerable to swings in the marketplace were being affected. Luxury-car sales dropped, which was unusual. In past recessions this segment usually weathered the storm, but thanks to a new federal tax on cars costing over $30,000, potential buyers stayed away.

Automakers initiated major cost-cutting measures that continued throughout 1992. These included closing factories and laying off both factory workers and middle-management staff. General Motors alone announced the closing of eleven factories and the eventual loss of 80,000 jobs.

Manufacturing wasn't the only sector of the industry that was hard-hit. In 1991 645 dealers closed their doors, bringing the total up to 1,588 closed dealers since 1989.

Dealers that survived were often forced to institute their own cost-cutting efforts, laying off staff and closing unprofitable operations. But the picture began to improve by 1993, when consumers began buying again, Detroit began gaining on the Japanese—and automakers and dealers faced the future with cautious optimism.

WHAT'S NEXT

▶ Competition will continue to be intense.

The bottom line, according to industry insiders: The Big Three and their primarily Japanese competition will continue to be locked in a battle for market share. U.S. car makers will reduce the number of models they manufacture, and some will drop unprofitable car lines altogether. Unlike previous years, however, the Japanese are also reevaluating their positions. They will also make adjustments because the pressure to increase profits is intense.

▶ Look for an increase in joint ventures between U.S. auto makers and their foreign counterparts. However, the day of the transplant is just about over.

For all the competition, both U.S. manufacturers and their import counterparts realize they actually need one another. In 1992, Ford increased its interest to 50 percent in the Flat Rock, Michigan, factory it launched with Mazda. (The plant produces the Ford Probe.) It also linked up with Nissan to produce a minivan marketed by both companies under the Mercury and Nissan badges. General Motors has no intention of loosening its ties with Toyota, which led to the production of the Geo Prizm and the Toyota Corolla. Nor will it change the ventures that led to the Geo Metro and Geo Tracker, produced with Suzuki.

Saturn, the company started by General Motors, is completely on stream and powering its way into the marketplace.

The big change will be in the expansion of the so-called "transplants"—Japanese manufacturers that build in the United States. Nissan, Honda, Toyota, Mazda, Subaru, and Isuzu operate factories in the United States. Don't expect to see more Japanese building factories or expanding their operations. There is, however, a strong possibility that some European automakers may start assembly operations in the United States. For them, it is more cost effective to build in the United States than in their home countries, as labor costs are lower here. But if the Europeans do assemble here, it will not be on the scale of the Japanese.

▶ Watch Japanese transplants increase their sourcing of U.S. parts and components.

The Japanese transplants are under intense political pressure to increase their use of U.S.–made parts and components in cars and trucks built in this country. As such, they will work closely with U.S. suppliers, particularly in systems engineering, development, and production. Expect to see more contracts given to U.S. suppliers, which will result in more jobs.

The big winners will be the super suppliers—giants like Dana Corp. and TRW, which can offer complete services. The key to working with the Japanese, however, is to understand their culture. This means it can be a wide-open area for even midsized suppliers.

Employment in the supplier area: There should be job opportunities as the Japanese start ordering both on the engineering and the production side. But don't expect to see suppliers overstaffing. The lessons of the '80s are still too fresh in their memories.

▶ Watch U.S. manufacturers look for more overseas sales.

U.S. auto manufacturers have made no secret of the fact that they want to export their products overseas. General Motors reorganized its overseas sales units. Ford already plans to increase its export business as does Chrysler. They are looking at both Europe and Japan.

The overseas markets are projected to grow faster than the U.S. market. Eastern Europe is especially promising: According to a forecast by Ford Europe, this market will account for about 7 million car sales in 2008. Add to this the 16 million projected for the Western European markets and the result is a strong market.

Japanese transplants are also looking hard at exporting. Honda already exports its Accord to Japan; expect to see others doing the same thing. This will enable them to free up their Japanese factories for other models and avoid duplication of effort. But the real exporting opportunity for the transplants will be Europe. Unlike the United States, Europe is not a totally free market. There are restrictions on Japanese automakers there. But the U.S. exports will receive more favorable treatment. On the employment side: If the Japanese succeed in exporting more products, they will have to expand their production, perhaps not by building new plants but by adding more shifts.

▶ Expect increased emphasis on—and budgets for—research and development.

Domestic automakers are spending more on R&D. They must, to meet the competition as well as to comply with today's stiff environmental laws.

Japanese auto manufacturers have a shorter new-product cycle—about four years to design and build a new car. American manufacturers are on an eight-year cycle, although GM is trying to put a five-year product cycle in place.

U.S. automakers have invested heavily in new-product development. Buick alone introduced five new cars over two model years. Chrysler launched four.

While U.S. automakers are looking hard to cut their cycles, the Japanese have started to rethink their philosophy as well. In 1992 the unmentionable was finally mentioned: The Japanese product cycle doesn't do much for the bottom line. Several manufacturers, including Toyota, have said that they would like to see longer cycles. Expect the Japanese to meet the U.S. automakers somewhere in the middle.

But it's more than product cycle that is spurring R&D—it is also the need for new technology. Stricter air-pollution laws have pressured both U.S. and import automakers to rethink the automobile. Watch for new technology that will mean more electric cars and cars powered by alternative fuels such as natural gas.

Greater effort will also be put into the use of recyclable materials. New technologies will have to be developed, so expect to see expanded development and production of composite polymer materials and development of applications.

Car makers will also attempt to target specific markets for their products—for example, by manufacturing cars with features for older people in an effort to capitalize on the aging population.

The shift to R&D across the board to meet the changing demands of the market points to opportunities for design engineers.

▶ Auto dealers will continue to retrench.

Even with sales picking up, dealers are not going to be anxious to increase their sales staffs—and when they do hire, they will be looking for experience and dedication. The biggest opportunity, however, remains in the service department. Service will be the name of the game in the '90s—and as such, dealers will want skilled service personnel more than ever.

EMPLOYMENT OUTLOOK: Better than in the recent past; improving over the long term.

Layoffs and factory shutdowns have always been commonplace in the auto industry. Employment in the auto industry dropped in 1991 and 1992. The Big Three alone cut nearly 40,000 jobs.

Over the short term, factory workers will continue to feel the pinch. GM's announcement that it will cut 80,000 jobs by 1995 came in late 1991 after both Ford and Chrysler announced cutbacks. Suppliers, including TRW and Allied-Signal, are also cutting jobs.

Engineering and design positions will open, and hiring will be done for the most part at the entry level. Requirements are fairly basic: a B.S. degree, grade-point average above 3.0, and work or co-op experience at a major manufacturer.

Demand for higher-level engineering positions tends to be stable. The automakers, after all, are trying to gain a competitive edge.

Another area that looks good is purchasing. With manufacturers becoming extremely cost conscious, they want stable prices.

JOBS SPOTLIGHT

DESIGN/SYSTEMS ENGINEERS: These individuals are particularly valuable to original equipment suppliers. This is not a huge market, but suppliers who develop long-term relationships with manufacturers will continue to need design/systems engineering.

AUTOMOBILE SERVICE PERSONNEL: As people hold onto their cars longer, these cars need maintenance. Dealers are also putting more emphasis on their service departments. The dealership and repair shops should enjoy a rise, and long-term prospects look good.

MIS/FACTORY AUTOMATION PERSONNEL: This is not a huge market, but there is a constant need in the industry. Domestic manufacturers are focusing on automated systems, just as their Japanese and transplant counterparts have done, and they need trained people to operate those systems.

QUALITY CONTROL PERSONNEL: Producing a high-quality product is a key to success these days. Domestic manufacturers, transplants, and suppliers all need skilled manufacturing managers and other personnel skilled in this area.

BEST BETS

Buick Motor Division
General Motors
902 E. Hamilton Ave.
Flint, MI 48550
313/236-5000

One domestic nameplate that has been going strong even while the rest of the industry suffered, Buick has seen improving sales and has been gaining market share. A key reason? After fishing around for new customers with new car designs, Buick has gone back to its roots with "mature" cars, like the Park Avenue. The result—Buick is attracting an older consumer (a strong market segment these days), sales are going strong, and corporate image is improving. This makes Buick one of the best bets among the domestic manufacturers.

Toyota Motor Sales U.S.A., Inc.
19001 S. Western Ave.
Torrance, CA 90509
213/618-4000

Chosen a "Best Bet" in the past four years of the *Jobs* series, Toyota remains a good choice. U.S. sales have stayed strong, its Lexus division has posted gains when the rest of the luxury market stayed stagnant, and, most importantly, Toyota looks the strongest of all the import companies. In 1992, when other automakers were closing plants, Toyota kept adding them. In the U.S. alone, it is planning to double the size of its Georgetown, Kentucky, plant and is thinking about opening a new plant for assembly of its new pickup truck. An added note: It has been beefing up minority hiring.

LEADING AUTOMOTIVE COMPANIES

Acura Division
American Honda Motor Co.
1919 Torrance Blvd.
Torrance, CA
90501-2746
213/783-2000

Alfa Romeo Distributors of North America
8259 Exchange Dr.
P.O. Box 598026
Orlando, FL
32859-8026
407/856-5000

American Honda Motor Co., Inc.
1919 Torrance Blvd.
Torrance, CA

90501-2746
213/783-2000

American Isuzu Motors, Inc.
13181 Crossroads
Pkwy., N.
City of Industry, CA
91746
310/699-0500

American Suzuki Motor Corp.
3251 E. Imperial Hwy.
Brea, CA 92621-6722
714/996-7040

Audi of America, Inc.
3800 Hamlin Rd.
Auburn Hills, MI
48326
313/340-5000

BMW of North America, Inc.
300 Chestnut Ridge Rd.
Woodcliff Lake, NJ
07675
201/307-4000

Buick Motor Division
General Motors
902 E. Hamilton Ave.
Flint, MI 48550
313/236-5000

Cadillac Motor Car Division
General Motors
2860 Clark St.
Detroit, MI 48232
313/554-5067

Chevrolet Motor Division
General Motors
30007 Van Dyke Ave.
Warren, MI 48090
313/492-8846

Chrysler Corp.
12000 Chrysler Dr.
Highland Park, MI
48288-1919
313/956-5741

Daihatsu America, Inc.
4422 Corporate Center
Dr.
Los Alamitos, CA
90720
714/761-7000

Dodge Car & Truck Division
Chrysler Motors Corp.
12000 Chrysler Dr.
Highland Park, MI
48288-1919
313/956-5741

Ferrari North America, Inc.
250 Sylvan Ave.
Englewood Cliffs, NJ
07632
201/871-1234

Ford Division
Ford Motor Co.
P.O. Box 43301
300 Renaissance Center
Detroit, MI 48242
313/446-3800

Hyundai Motor America
10550 Talbert Ave.
Fountain Valley, CA
92728
714/965-3508

Infiniti Division
Nissan Motor Co.
18071 S. Figueroa St.
Carson, CA 90248
213/532-3111

Jaguar Cars, Inc.
555 MacArthur Blvd.
Mahwah, NJ 07430
201/818-8500

Jeep/Eagle Division
Chrysler Motors Corp.
12000 Chrysler Dr.
Highland Park, MI
48288-1919
313/956-5741

Lamborghini U.S.A., Inc.
7601 Centurion Pkwy.
Jacksonville, FL 32256
904/565-9100

Lexus Division
Toyota Motor Sales
U.S.A., Inc.
19001 S. Western Ave.
Torrance, CA 90509
213/618-4000

Lincoln
Lincoln-Mercury
Division
Ford Motor Co.
300 Renaissance Ctr.
P.O. Box 43322
Detroit, MI 48243
313/446-4450

Lotus Cars U.S.A.
1655 Lakes Pkwy.
Lawrenceville, GA
30243
404/822-4566

Maserati Automobiles, Inc.
1501 Caton Ave.
Baltimore, MD 21227
301/646-6400

Mazda Motors of America, Inc.
7755 Irvine Center Dr.
Irvine, CA 92718
714/727-1990

**Mercedes-Benz of
North America, Inc.**
1 Mercedes Dr.
Montvale, NJ
07645-0350
201/573-0600

Mercury
Lincoln/Mercury
Division
Ford Motor Co.
300 Renaissance Center
Detroit, MI 48243
313/446-4450

**Mitsubishi Motor
Sales of America, Inc.**
6400 W. Katella Ave.
Cypress, CA
90630-0064
714/376-6000

Nissan Motor Corp.
18501 Figueroa St.
Carson, CA 90248
213/532-3111

Oldsmobile Division
General Motors
920 Townsend St.
Lansing, MI 48921
517/377-5000

Plymouth
Chrysler/Plymouth
Division

Chrysler Motors Corp.
12000 Chrysler Dr.
Highland Park, MI
48288-1919
313/946-5741

Pontiac Division
General Motors
1 Pontiac Plz.
Pontiac, MI
48058-3484
313/857-5000

**Porsche Cars North
America, Inc.**
100 W. Liberty St.
Reno, NV 89501
702/348-3000

**Range Rover of North
America, Inc.**
4390 Parliament Pl.
P.O. Box 1503
Lanham, MA 20706
301/731-9040

**Rolls-Royce Motor
Cars, Inc.**
120 Chubb Ave.
P.O. Box 476
Lyndhurst, NJ 07071
201/460-9600

Saab Cars USA, Inc.
Saab Dr.
Orange, CT 06477
203/795-1326

Saturn Corp.
General Motors
1420 Stephenson Hwy.
Troy, MI 48007-7025
313/524-5000

**Subaru of America,
Inc.**
Subaru Plz.
P.O. Box 6000
Cherry Hill, NJ 08034
609/488-8660

**Toyota Motor Sales
U.S.A., Inc.**
19001 S. Western Ave.
Torrance, CA 90509
213/618-4000

**Volkswagen of
America, Inc.**
3800 Hamlin Rd.
Auburn Hills, MI
48326
313/340-5000

**Volvo Cars of North
America**
1 Volvo Dr.
Rockleigh, NJ 07647
201/768-7300

WHERE TO GO FOR MORE INFORMATION

AUTOMOTIVE INDUSTRY ASSOCIATIONS

**American
International
Automobile Dealers
Association**
1128 16th St., NW
Washington, DC 20036
202/659-2561

**American Society of
Body Engineers**
Wilshire Office Center,
Suite 3031
24634 Five Mile
Redford, MI 48239
313/533-2600

**Autobody Supply and
Equipment
Manufacturers
Council**
300 Sylvan Ave.
Englewood Cliffs, NJ
07632
201/894-6810

Auto Internacional Association
11540 E. Slauson Ave.
P.O. Box 4967
Whittier, CA 90606
213/692-9402
(People and companies involved in the important automotive aftermarket industry.)

Automobile Importers of America
1725 Jefferson Davis Hwy.
Arlington, VA 22202
703/979-5550

Automotive Affiliated Representatives
111 E. Wacker Dr.
Chicago, IL 60601
312/644-6610
(Automotive aftermarket manufacturers' representatives.)

Automotive Electric Association
(Division of Autmotive Service Industry

Association)
444 N. Michigan Ave.
Chicago, IL
60611-3975
312/836-1300

Automotive Parts and Accessories Association
4600 E. West Hwy.
3rd Fl.
Bethesda, MD 20814
301/654-6664

Automotive Service Industry Association
444 N. Michigan Ave.
Chicago, IL 60611
312/836-1300

Motor Vehicle Manufacturers Association of the U.S., Inc.
7430 Second Ave.
Detroit, MI 48202
313/872-4311

Motor Vehicle Manufacturers Organization U.S.A., Inc.

2100 NW 93rd Ave.
Miami, FL 33172
305/593-0493

National Automobile Dealers Association
8400 Westpark Dr.
McLean, VA 22102
703/821-7000

National Automotive Parts Association
2999 Circle 75 Pkwy.
Atlanta, GA 30339
404/956-2200

National Independent Automobile Dealers Association
600 Los Colinas Blvd.
Irving, TX 75039
214/586-0044

Society of Automotive Engineers
400 Commonwealth Dr.
Warrendale, PA 15096
412/776-4841
(Puts out monthly magazine, *Automotive Engineering,* for members.)

AUTOMOTIVE INDUSTRY DIRECTORIES

Automotive Marketing Annual Buyer's Guide
Chilton Book Co.
Chilton Way
Radnor, PA 19089
800/345-1214
215/964-4000

Automotive News Market Data Book
Automotive News
1400 Woodbridge Ave.
Detroit, MI 48207

313/446-6000
(Annual, special issue of *Automotive News;* in addition to statistics, includes extensive listings of auto manufacturers, suppliers, etc., that include addresses, contact names.)

Ward's Automotive Yearbook
Ward's
Communications, Inc.
28 W. Adams St.
Detroit, MI 48226
313/962-4433

AUTOMOTIVE INDUSTRY MAGAZINES

Auto Age
6633 Odessa Ave.
Van Nuys, CA 90406
818/997-0644
(Monthly magazine for
dealership owners and
managers, and
suppliers.)

Automotive Executive
National Auto Dealers
Association
8400 Westpark Dr.
McLean, VA 22102
703/821-7150
(Monthly paper sent to
members of NADA, as
well as financial
personnel.)

Automotive Industries
2600 Fisher Bldg.
Detroit, MI 48202
313/875-2090
(Monthly magazine for
design, management,
manufacturing, and
sales personnel.)

Automotive Marketing
201 King of Prussia
Rd.
Radnor, PA 19089
215/964-4395
(Monthly magazine for
parts/accessories
retailers,
manufacturers.)

Automotive News
1400 Woodbridge Ave.
Detroit, MI 48207

313/446-6000
(Weekly newspaper
considered the industry
"bible"; covers all
phases of the
industry—manufacturing,
marketing, sales, etc.;
includes extensive
help-wanted section.)

Ward's Auto World
28 W. Adams St.
Detroit, MI 48226
313/962-4433
(Monthly magazine
aimed at
manufacturers.)

AVIATION

INDUSTRY OUTLOOK: Heightened competition with long-term improvement ahead.

As the economy strengthens, aviation will head for better times. But there's still a long way to go. Expect continued industry consolidation and cost-cutting, with possible problems ahead for smaller carriers. Larger carriers, however, should be stronger. The troubles that could derail the airlines? Prolonged fare wars, high fuel costs, and attempts by other countries to restrict U.S. airlines' overseas routes.

A LOOK BACK

▶ **The '80s were turbulent, taking the industry from deregulation, to heavy competition, to a frenzy of mergers and acquisitions.**

Deregulation brought about an increase in the number of airlines, including small upstarts that shook the larger established airlines. Competition was cutthroat as airlines entered into price slashing to attract passengers, and profits sank.

Then came consolidation: the upstarts were bought out; large airlines snapped up regional carriers; commuter airlines were swallowed.

▶ **Next it was high flying—as the emergence of the hub system and mergers ended the price wars—then a slump as the country entered a recession.**

By the end of the '80s, airlines were ringing up record profits, as mergers cut down on the number of competing airlines and the institution of the hub system (in which one or two airlines become primary carriers at an airport) eliminated route duplication.

But the recession caused a sharp downturn in air traffic, and in 1991 the industry went through the worst year it had faced since deregulation. The triple whammy of the Persian Gulf War, high fuel prices, and plunging tourism rates sent airlines into a tailspin. Some airlines, including Pan Am, Eastern, and Midway, went belly up, others filed for bankruptcy protection, and others just waited for the better times to return. Airlines had a grim year in 1992, as traffic dropped further, leading to industry losses of up to $1.7 billion. And a lukewarm 1993 saw airline industry leaders hoping the worst was over—but still facing numerous challenges, including supply in excess of demand.

WHAT'S NEXT

▶ Competition will remain heated.

The weapons airlines will use? Fluctuating fares and customer service. Expect periods of price wars, as airlines try to woo passengers away from one another with new fare structures and promotional deals. But the industry focal point will be customer service, especially as airlines try to corner the lucrative business-travel market.

Along these lines, expect a wide range of customer-service offerings, from such amenities as passenger-seat video monitors, and new in-flight entertainment, to services like express check-in, the use of fax machines, and special business-class offerings.

This renewed attention to customer service will be felt in the employment area, as service personnel such as flight attendants and airport gate staffers will be given increased responsibility. This also may translate into opportunities for marketing and promotion specialists.

▶ Expect continued consolidation, with larger airlines growing and expanding and smaller ones losing ground.

This will come about as a result of the heavy competition and the financial difficulties many airlines have faced. Watch the financially strong carriers pull ahead, pumping their money into competitive programs, while the weaker ones fall behind—and perhaps fall prey to their stronger competitors.

In some cases, expansion will be necessary to stay alive. The larger companies will be expanding abroad, which may lead some of the smaller carriers to serve as domestic "feeder airlines," in effect funneling passengers to the larger airlines' airports.

▶ The newest arena of competition: the international market.

Consolidation is shaking out the weaker players in the domestic airline industry. But now the winners of this battle are facing new competitors in foreign airlines. The international market has been of increasing importance to U.S. airlines, with the giants like American, Delta, and United snapping up international routes.

Now competition is increasing, especially with the opening up of Europe's borders and the growing importance of the Asian market. Expect U.S. airlines to go head to head with their foreign counterparts, battling for customers, market share, and routes. Among their moves: the addition of European and Pacific Rim flights; improved passenger service to rival the service of foreign carriers.

This new internationalization of the airline industry is pointing to increased career opportunities for people with international business backgrounds and foreign-language ability.

▶ Watch for continued industry globalization, marked by joint ventures, marketing agreements, and other team arrangements.

Increased cooperation between companies is one way of coping with increased global competition. While early 1992 talks between British Airways, KLM Royal Dutch Airlines, and Northwest Airlines concerning a merger to form a global carrier went nowhere, the issue is far from dead. This remains an interesting long-term event to watch for.

Already, more carriers are becoming interdependent to maintain a competitive edge. For example, KLM owns 49% of Northwest; as a result, Northwest now has a European route system. Expect to see more companies enter into joint marketing arrangements, enabling them to offer their customers better service, enhanced routes, and the like.

EMPLOYMENT OUTLOOK: Fair.

On the down side, the airline employee shortages are over. There is now in-creased competition for fewer jobs. The reason? The problems of the past two years, which saw airlines such as Pan Am, Eastern, and Midway going out of business, and layoffs at such airlines as USAir and TWA.

But the bad times are over as well. The long-term employment picture looks fairly bright, especially as the aviation industry regroups for the future. The U.S. government predicts that 276,000 new jobs will be added in the aviation industry over the next twelve years. International opportunities may be stronger than those in other areas because of the international expansion so many domestic airlines have been going through.

JOBS SPOTLIGHT

APPLICATIONS DEVELOPERS: More airlines are switching applications that don't require a centralized database (like crew scheduling, airport check-in, and dis-patching) to PC local-area networks (LANs). Due to this, airlines are using ap-plications developers with networking backgrounds to facilitate this changeover. Requirements: computer experience, network experience, general business skills, and airline experience (it is difficult to break in with experience from another industry).

BEST BETS

Southwest Airlines
8008 Aviation Place
Dallas, TX 75235
214/902-1100

An airline that has carved out a niche for itself by offering frequent short-hop flights at low prices, Southwest looks like a winner. The past few years have seen it through a period of growth: It was one of the few airlines to pull out a profit in 1990; it has been expanding routes and adding flights; it keeps a tight rein on operating costs. Southwest also has an excellent reputation as an employer. Em-ployee morale is consistently high; staffers talk about the camaraderie they feel between themselves and management. (It's so strong that a third of the employees actually took voluntary pay cuts to cover the high cost of airline fuel during the

Gulf War.) One reason for this loyalty is job security. Management keeps staffing lean, so there is no need for layoffs. Finally, Southwest is well known for a sense of fun that runs through the company, from the CEO (who dropped in on maintenance hangars at 2:00 A.M. dressed like Klinger from "MASH") to flight personnel (who entertain passengers with skits, contests, and the like). The one drawback? Southwest is reportedly selective in its hiring practices.

TOP NATIONAL AND REGIONAL AIRLINES

Air Wisconsin, Inc.
203 Challenger Dr.
Appleton, WI 54915
414/739-5123

Alaska Airlines
Box 68900
Seattle, WA 98168
206/433-3200

Aloha Airlines
P.O. Box 30028
Honolulu, HI 96820
808/836-1111

America West
4000 E. Sky Harbor
Blvd.
Phoenix, AZ 85034
602/693-0800

American Airlines
Box 619616
Dallas Ft. Worth
Airport, TX

75261-9616
817/967-1234

Continental Airlines
P. O. Box 4607
Houston, TX
77210-4607
713/834-2950

Delta Airlines
Hartsfield-Atlanta
International Airport
Atlanta, GA 30320
404/715-2600

Northwest Airlines
Minneapolis-St.Paul
Airport
St. Paul, MN 55111
612/726-2111

Southwest Airlines
2702 Love Field Dr.
Dallas, TX 75235
214/904-4000

Tower Air
JFK International
Airport
Hangar 8
Jamaica, NY 11432
718/917-4300

United Airlines
P.O. Box 66919
Chicago, IL 60666
708/952-4000

USAir
2345 Crystal Dr.
Crystal Park Four
Arlington, VA 22227
703/418-7000

Worldcorp and World Airways
13873 Park Center Rd.
Herndon, VA 22071
703/834-9200
(Contract flight, charter passenger, and cargo.)

TOP AIR FREIGHT AND FREIGHT FORWARDING COMPANIES

Airborne Freight Corp.
3101 Western Ave.
P. O. Box 662
Seattle, WA 98111
206/286-4600

Air Express International Corp.
120 Tokeneke Rd.

Darien, CT 06820
203/655-7900

Amerford International Corp.
21801 Merrick Blvd.
Jamaica, NY 11413
718/528-0800

Burlington Air Express
(Subs. of Pittston)
18200 Von Karman
Ave.
Irvine, CA 92715
714/752-4000

**Coastal Express
International Airways**
P. O. Box 6920
Ontario International
Airport
San Bernadino, CA
92412
714/889-2758

**Continental Airlines
Cargo Division**
Gateway II, Suite 300
15333 JFK Blvd.
Houston, TX 77032
713/987-6661

Danzas-Northern Air
330 120th Ave., NE
Bellevue, WA 98008
206/646-7171

DHL Airways
(Subsidiary of DHL
Corp.)
333 Twin Dolphin Dr.

Redwood City, CA
94065
415/593-7474

**Emery Air Frieght
Corp.**
(Subsidiary of
Consolidated
Freightways)
3350 W. Bayshore Rd.
Palo Alto, CA
94303-0986
415/855-9100

**Evergreen
International Airlines**
3850 Three Mile Ln.
McMinnville, OR
97128-9496
503/472-0011

Federal Express
2005 Corporate Ave.
Memphis, TN 38132
901/369-3600

Fritz Air Freight
735 Market St.
San Francisco, CA
94103
415/541-8318

**Southern Air
Transport**
P. O. Box 52-4093
International Airport
Miami, FL 33152
305/871-5171

United Parcel Service
Greenwich Office Park
No. 5
51 Weaver St.
Greenwich, CT 06830
203/862-6000

United Van Lines
One United Dr.
Fenton, MO 63026
314/326-3100

WHERE TO GO FOR MORE INFORMATION

(For more information sources relating to the Aviation industry, check listings under "Aerospace," page 236; "Technical Careers," page 186; and "Engineers," page 41. For information related to air cargo, also see listings under "Transportation," page 472.)

AVIATION INDUSTRY ASSOCIATIONS

**Aeronautical Repair
Station Association**
1612 K St., NW,
Suite 1400
Washington, DC 20006
202/293-2511

**Air Line Employees
Association**
5600 S. Central Ave.
Chicago, IL
60638-3797
312/767-3333
(Puts out *Job
Opportunity Bulletin,* a
monthly publication
listing job openings in
all areas of aviation.)

**Air Traffic Control
Association**
2300 Clarendon Blvd.,
Suite 711
Arlington, VA 22201
703/522-5717

Air Transport Association of America
1709 New York Ave., NW
Washington, DC 20006
202/626-6000

American Association of Airport Executives
4212 King St.
Alexandria, VA 22302
703/824-0500
(Puts out publications including *Airport Report* and *Airport Report Express,* which contain help-wanted ads.)

Future Aviation Professionals of America
4959 Massachusetts Blvd.
Atlanta, GA 30032
404/538-5627
(Offers a range of career assistance for members, including putting out publications that include job listings, including *Pilot Job Reports* and *Flight Attendant Job Reports,* and maintaining computerized job banks for mechanics/technicians, etc., and for pilots.)

General Aviation Manufacturers Association
1400 K St., NW, Suite 801
Washington, DC 20005
202/393-1500

National Air Carrier Association
1730 M St., NW
Washington, DC 20036
202/833-8200

National Air Transportation Association
4226 King St.
Alexandria, VA 22302
703/845-9000

National Business Aircraft Association
1200 18th St., NW
Washington, DC 20036
202/783-9000

Regional Airline Association
1101 Connecticut Ave., NW
Washington, DC 20036
202/857-1170

AVIATION INDUSTRY DIRECTORIES

Annual Report of the Computer Regional Airline Industry
Regional Airline Association
1101 Connecticut Ave., NW
Washington, DC 20036
202/857-1170

Aviation and Aerospace White Pages
P. O. Box 8286
Saddle Brook, NJ 07662
201/794-6725
800/543-6725
(Low-cost directory.)

Official Airline Guide: North American Edition; Official Airline Guide: Worldwide Edition
Official Airlines Guides, Inc.
2000 Clearwater Dr.
Oak Brook, IL 60521
312/654-6000
800/323-3537

Travel Weekly's World Travel Directory
Travel Weekly
500 Plaza Dr.
Secaucus, NJ 07096
201/902-2000

World Aviation Directory
McGraw-Hill
1156 15th St.
Washington, DC 20005
202/822-4600

AVIATION INDUSTRY MAGAZINES

Air Cargo News
P.O. Box 777
Jamaica, NY 11431
718/479-0716
(Monthly publication
for those involved in
cargo—freight
forwarders, cargo
airline personnel,
customs brokers, etc.)

Air Jobs Digest
P.O. Box 70127
Department JF
Washington, DC 20088
301/984-4172
(Monthly publication of
job listings in all areas
of aviation.)

Airline Executive
6255 Barfield Rd.
Atlanta, GA 30328
404/256-9800
(Monthly magazine for
airline executives in
sales, marketing,
finance, technology,
etc.)

Air Line Pilot
P.O. Box 1169
Herndon, VA 22070
703/689-4182
(Monthly magazine sent
to members of the Air
Line Pilots
Association.)

Airport Press
P.O. Box 879
Jamaica, NY 11430
718/244-6788
(Monthly aimed at
airline officials, airport
personnel, freight
forwarders, etc.)

Air Transport World
1030 15th St., NW
Washington, DC 20005
202/659-8500
(Monthly magazine
designed for air
transport executives and
supervisors.)

*Aviation Employment
Monthly*
Box 8286
Department A
Saddle Brook, NJ
07662
800/543-5201
(Lists job openings
worldwide for pilots,
engineers, technicians,
A&Ps.)

*Business &
Commercial Aviation*
4 International Dr.
Rye Brook, NY 10573
914/939-0300
(Monthly publication
for airline owners and
operators, aviation
managers, operations
and maintenance
personnel, etc.)

Commuter Air
6255 Barfield Rd.
Atlanta, GA 30328
404/256-9800
(Monthly magazine for
commuter and charter
airline executives and
supervisors.)

Professional Pilot
3014 Colvin St.
Alexandria, VA 22314
703/370-0606
(Monthly publication
for pilots in all
phases of
aviation—commercial,
commuter, corporate,
charter, and
military—as well as
airport operators.)

BANKING

INDUSTRY OUTLOOK: Should continue to improve, but weak banks will continue to decline.

For many banks, the worst years are over. Even though loan problems aren't over, many banks are through the worst of cost-cutting, layoffs and structural changes. And the banking industry was lucky—the low interest rates of last year made it easier to make much needed profits. But the challenges for 1994 will be there; namely, what to do about nonbank competition in the same marketplace.

Note: There are currently about 12,000 banks in this country—9,000 of them small (under $1 billion), the other 3,000 ranging upward in size to giants like Citicorp and Bank of America. In addition, there is also the troubled savings and loan industry, whose thrift institutions take in savings deposits and engage in mortgage lending.

A LOOK BACK

▶ **Over the past decade, banks have been battered by a series of losses in various lending markets, resulting in an industrywide crisis.**

First came the so-called oil-patch loans, in which banks financed oil well drillers on the assumption that increasing oil prices made these loans relatively prudent. But instead prices dropped, and many banks, particularly Texas banks, suffered from the sudden increase in bad loans. Banks also initiated increased lending to farmers, expecting that crop and land prices would rise, virtually insuring loan repayments. Needless to say, by 1981 and 1982, prices went down, defaults went up, and banks suffered the consequences. Another problem: In the '70s and '80s OPEC petrodollar deposits began pouring into U.S. banks; bankers took these deposits and dramatically increased lending abroad. Far too many of these loans were to Third World nations and projects whose ability to repay proved quite illusory. The result? Defaults and reschedulings. Finally, during the "go-go" years of real estate in the United States, banks began lending heavily in commercial real estate and in LBOs (leveraged buyouts, whereby a buyer borrows the bulk of the money to purchase a company and promises to repay the loan out of revenues from the company). As real estate prices began to drop, and as many LBOs faltered, unable to handle the enormous debt loads they had taken on, banks once again suffered the consequences. Bad debt on bank books rose dramatically. Bank failures increased—up to 1,500 by mid 1992.

These numbers say it all: Every year now, banks write off more than $20 billion in bad loans, the consequences of the events outlined above.

▶ Mergers change the face of banking.

Bank mergers were (and still are) a feature of the 1980s and 1990s, from the Wells Fargo purchase of Crocker, to the Chemical Bank saga—first taking over Texas Commerce Bancshares, and then Horizon Bancorp, and finally, in 1991 announcing its merger with Manufacturers Hanover Trust. Meanwhile, down South, powerhouse NCNB merged with C&S Sovran, itself the product of mergers, to form Nationsbank. And giant Bank of America merged in 1992 with rival Security Pacific Corporation, consolidating its position as the second largest U.S. bank. The dollar value of private-sector bank mergers in 1991 was five times that of 1990.

Rationale for the mergers: economies of scale—banks can increase capital and simultaneously eliminate costly duplicate branches and functions; diversification of assets and increase in market share—banks can enter more markets and spread their risks. In other words, mergers are expected to help banks position themselves better for much tougher competition in the next half of the 1990s.

Problem for jobseekers: most mergers are accompanied by layoffs.

▶ Trouble for S&Ls.

A brief look back: In the 1980s federal regulations loosened considerably on thrift institutions. But at the same time, the Feds backed up these institutions with deposit and loan guarantees. As a result, many S&L executives felt free to lend to almost anyone (and collect fat profits); after all, the Feds were right behind them, backing them up. As the 1980s ended and the 1990s began, more and more of these loans went bad, and the scope of the problem became clear.

Suddenly, tough new savings-and-loan regulations came into being, which (of course) shifted the burden for the wasteful practices of others to the taxpayer. One important note: Far from all S&Ls were profligate. Most of those that survived the 1980s and early 1990s had executives with the old-fashioned virtues bankers once prized: solid analytical skills, good instincts, and a conservative attitude toward lending.

WHAT'S NEXT

▶ Leaner, meaner, and more competitive banks.

The watchword is: cut costs, increase capital. Despite the bad news of the past years, banks have been doing something about it, transforming themselves into more competitive businesses.

Some are succeeding. In 1992, with the revitalization of Latin American economies, Third World debt increased in value and liquidity, reducing banks' bad loan exposures and problems, particularly for those who wrote down loans.

The top fifty banks have increased their capital from 5.5% of assets in 1988 to 6.25% in early 1993, reserves against loan losses were up from 2.3% of borrowings to about 4.8%. Consolidations have resulted in reduced costs at some banks, and most are reducing costs by cutting where it hurts. According to the Bureau of Labor Statistics, 22,000 jobs, from tellers through executive positions, were lost at commercial banks in 1991, and most industry experts felt this was just the beginning.

▶ Mergers will continue—and banks will get bigger—and smaller.

Some predict that by the end of the 1990s mergers will have reduced the number of banks to a dozen or so huge national banks, and a larger number of regional and community banks.

The big players will operate—and advertise—nationwide, seeking, like a McDonald's or a Wendy's, to establish a national identity. The super-regionals will operate on a slightly smaller scale—but don't forget the community banks. Some of these small banks, run by conservative old-line bankers, will do surprisingly well. Key: Making loans is a personal business. And local bankers, who *know* the local marketplace and local personalities, will more than likely weather any economic storms and benefit from economic recoveries of the future.

▶ The major problem banks face is reduced—and declining—demand for many basic bank services.

Banks used to be the major lenders to major corporations. Today that has changed. Healthy large corporations can raise money directly on the capital markets, bypassing banks and bypassing bank fees.

So what will banks do? Answer: go where the business is. Some banks are now specializing in niche markets. For example, Bankers Trust has transformed itself into something of a Wall Street firm, emphasizing wholesale banking and securities and derivatives trading. Others are focusing on retail mortgage lending, or an entire new range of retail services, going against finance companies in their quest for new business. And others are focusing on transactions processing—or in other words, the basic job of moving money. One prime player in this area is State Street Boston, which handles billions of dollars of mutual fund money.

And of course, banks are also beginning to move into the mutual fund business themselves, banking on their customers' desire for convenience—being able to have both an account and investments under one roof. One key advantage for bank mutual funds: a built-in distribution network. So far, this foray into the mutual fund business appears to be working well.

▶ Estimates are that almost half of the 2,900 savings and loan institutions in the United States will be gone by the mid-1990s.

The S&L industry as we know it is disappearing. The reason is obvious in light of the events of the past few years. At the time of writing, Washington was in the midst of an election-year stalemate on the S&L bailout, with some arguing that it might be best to keep large insolvent S&Ls open instead of closing them and selling assets. Bottom line: The sick will disappear, sooner or later, and taxpayers will foot the bill—sooner or later.

▶ Look for new regulations as the FDIC struggles to deal with the debt crisis and banks reposition themselves.

The government—and all of us—have a problem. Many feel a taxpayer bailout of banking is all but inevitable. It has been estimated that upward of $180 billion may be required. And another potential problem is lurking on the horizon: the popularity of home equity loans, coupled with the still-shaky economy in some areas has raised the prospect of defaults—and, of course, the need for a bailout.

Obviously, it is in the interests of all that banking become more profitable, in order to reduce this burden. Although cause and effect rarely operate in Washington, look for the government to lift further barriers from banking—and erect others. The net result? Banks will participate more fully in the securities business (they already do to some extent, through various legal artifices), the insurance business, etc.

On a different note, watch for deposit insurance regulations to change. In 1992 a not-so-subtle policy change took place, resulting in a stricter FDIC outlook on the $100,000 maximum. Expect more changes in the next year or so. For example, banks could offer both insured and uninsured deposits, perhaps reducing the FDIC burden.

▶ **More competition from nonbank financial services firms.**

It almost goes without saying. Banks are entering a phase of heavy competition with insurance companies, financial services firms, and corporations. No area of banking seems safe—AT&T, GM, GE, Ford, Prudential, and Fidelity have entered the lucrative credit-card market—and many banks may end up selling off this business. Some mutual-fund companies, like Fidelity, also offer services such as check writing and loans against fund balances, which, barring some differences in terminology and mechanics due to law, sound very much like regular banking services. Even businesses that have been banking focal points, such as payment processing, are being invaded by nonbank companies.

EMPLOYMENT OUTLOOK: Fair.

▶ **A streamlined industry facing challenges doesn't mean that jobs won't be there.**

First the bad news. Many jobs in banking were shed in the past few years. As of 1993, Citicorp had cut its work force by 18,000, or 18%. The big merger between Chemical and Manufacturers Hanover resulted in job cutbacks of 4,500. And those cutbacks aren't over yet, as banks seek to continue to streamline operations and cut costs. In fact, according to Andersen Consulting and the Bank Administration Institute, by 2000 the number of bank jobs will drop by 250,000 from the current level of about 1.49 million. Half of these cuts will involve tellers and administrators, the other half will be certain technicians and managers.

Now the good news. Since the banking industry is so huge, many jobs will open as workers simply retire or transfer to other jobs; moreover, certain areas are projected to grow substantially: these include computer, mathematical and operations research specialists, which the government projects will grow by a substantial 63% by the year 2005. Best general area: mortgage banking and personal credit. Best nontechnical specialties: financial managers, loan officers.

▶ **Key question: What do banks want?**

As stated before, banks are looking for sales- and marketing-oriented people. Since the culture of banking will change, so too will the ideal candidates. According to *Banker's Monthly*, the old idea of a "tenure track" at a bank—safe, stable working conditions in exchange for loyalty and a "don't rock the boat" attitude—will change.

Look for an emphasis on more aggressive sales-oriented personalities, and greater flexibility, a willingness to learn new techniques and services.

One advantage for liberal arts graduates: Banking is a field in which entry-level employees can get free training that almost matches a financial MBA. Competition is expected to remain extremely tough, however, as many people meet entry-level qualifications for banking positions. For example, according to *The New York Times*, the Bank of New York recently received 3,000 applications for 35 positions in its training program.

Bankers with strong credit experience will be increasingly in demand. Reason: When problems hit, banks become more concerned with credit worthiness.

JOBS SPOTLIGHT

SALES AND MARKETING SPECIALISTS: Increased competition and new services will make this area relatively strong for the long term, particularly after banks regain strength. As financial service companies enter the banking area, banks must aggressively compete to increase—or maintain—market share. Key areas: brokerage and mutual-fund sales, as banks compete with mutual funds and brokerage houses; marketing research; product development.

PRIVATE BANKING: This niche focuses on developing bank relationships with well-heeled individuals, entrepreneurs, principal stockholders, and others who may have specialized banking needs and large balances. So far this area has not grown as predicted, probably because the specialty is relatively new. This is a profitable and potentially high-growth area. Some advantages: retail bank clients typically generate about $1000 in annual revenue to a bank; private banking clients generate $5000; it is not capital intensive but more fee-income oriented—and it's very customer-service oriented. Most major banks have now established private banking groups, which provide a good source of income and a targeted market for new bank services. Best for people with strong personal as well as banking skills.

BEST BETS:

In these times of flux, it's tough to pick the winners in terms of employment and growth. Some likely winners include: Wells Fargo (profitable, with good benefits and a strong record in minority hiring and training); Republic (long a stodgy bank, now breaking out into mutual funds and other financial services areas); National Bank of Detroit (consistantly profitable, very service-oriented); and among global giants, Banker's Trust, Citicorp (even with layoffs and problems, some experts are betting it will pick up in the later '90s), and Morgan.

TOP MULTINATIONAL BANKS

BankAmerica
Box 37000
San Francisco, CA
94137
415/622-3456

Bank of Boston
100 Federal St.
Boston, MA 02110
617/434-2200

Bankers Trust NY
280 Park Ave.
New York, NY 10017
212/250-5000

Chase Manhattan
1 Chase Manhattan Plz.
New York, NY 10081
212/552-2222

Chemical Banking
270 Park Ave.
New York, NY 10017
212/270-6000

Citicorp
399 Park Ave.
New York, NY 10043
212/559-1000

Continental Bank
231 S. LaSalle St.
Chicago, IL 60697
312/828-2345

First Chicago
1 First National Plz.
Chicago, IL 60670
312/732-4000

J. P. Morgan
60 Wall St.
New York, NY
10260-0060
212/483-2323

TOP BANKS—EAST

Bank of New York
48 Wall St.
New York, NY 10286
212/495-1784

Baybanks
175 Federal St.
Boston, MA 02110
617/482-1040

CoreStates Financial
Broad & Chestnut Sts.
Philadelphia, PA 19101
215/973-3100

Dauphin Deposit
213 Market St.
Harrisburg, PA 17105
717/255-2121

First Empire State
1 M&T Plz.
Buffalo, NY
14203-2399
716/842-4200

First Fidelity
Bancorporation
1009 Lenox Dr.

Lawrenceville, NJ
08648
609/895-6800

Fleet Financial Group
50 Kennedy Plz.
Providence, RI 02903
401/278-5800

Integra Financial
Corp.
4 PPG Pl.
Pittsburgh, PA 15222
412/644-7669

KeyCorp
30 S. Pearl St.
Albany, NY 12207
518/486-8000

Mellon Bank
Mellon Bank Ctr.
Pittsburgh, PA 15258
412/234-5000

Merchantile
Bankshares
2 Hopkins Plz.

Baltimore, MD 21201
410/237-5900

Meridian Bancorp
P.O. Box 1102
Reading, PA 19601
215/655-2000

Midlantic
499 Thornall St.
Edison, NJ 08818
908/321-8000

National Community
Banks
385 Rifle Camp Rd.
W. Paterson, NJ 07424
201/357-7600

Northeast Bancorp
Church and Elm St.
New Haven, CT 06510
203/929-5552

PNC Financial
Fifth Ave. & Wood St.
Pittsburgh, PA 15265
412/762-2000

Republic New York
452 Fifth Ave.
New York, NY 10018
212/525-6000

Shawmut National
777 Main St.
Hartford, CT 06115
203/728-2000

State Street Boston
225 Franklin St.
Boston, MA 02101
617/786-3000

Summit
Bancorporation
One Main St.
Chatham, NJ 07928
201/701-6200

UJB Financial
301 Carnegie Ctr.
Princeton, NJ 08543
609/987-3200

U.S. Trust
114 W. 47th St.
New York, NY 10036
212/852-1000

Wilmington Trust
1100 N. Market St.
Wilmington, DE 19890
302/651-1000

TOP BANKS—MIDWEST

Ameritrust
900 Euclid Ave.
Cleveland, OH 44115
216/737-5000

Banc One
100 E. Broad St.
Columbus, OH 43271
614/248-5800

Boatmen's Bancshares
800 Market St.
St. Louis, MO 63102
314/466-6000

Comerica
211 W. Fort St.
Detroit, MI 48275
313/222-3300

Commerce Banshares
1000 Walnut St.
Kansas City, MO
64106
816/234-2000

Fifth Third Bancorp
38 Fountain Sq. Plz.
Cincinnati, OH 45263
513/579-5300

First of America Bank
211 S. Rose St.
Kalamazoo, MI 49007
616/376-9000

First Bank System
601 Second Ave. S.
Minneapolis, MN
55402
612/973-1111

Firstar
777 E. Wisconsin Ave.
Milwaukee, WI 53202
414/765-4321

Huntington
Bancshares
Huntington Ctr.
Columbus, OH 43287
614/476-8300

INB Financial
1 Indiana Sq.
Indianapolis, IN 46266
317/266-6000

Manufacturers
National
100 Renaissance Ctr.
Detroit, MI 48243
313/222-4000

Marshall & Illsley
770 N. Water St.
Milwaukee, WI 53202
414/765-7801

Mercantile
Bancorporation
721 Locust St.
St. Louis, MO 63101
314/425-2525

Merchants National
One Merchants Plz.
Indianapolis, IN 46255
317/267-7000

National City
1900 E. 9th St.
Cleveland, OH 44114
216/575-2000

NBD Bancorp
611 Woodward Ave.
Detroit, MI 48226
313/225-1000

Northern Trust
50 S. LaSalle St.
Chicago, IL 60675
312/630-6000

Norwest
Norwest Ctr.
Minneapolis, MN

55479
612/667-1234

Old Kent Financial
One Vanderberg Ctr.
Grand Rapids, MI
49503
616/771-5000

Society
127 Public Sq.
Cleveland, OH 44114
216/689-3000

Trustcorp
3 Seagate
Toledo, OH 43604
419/259-8598

**United Missouri
Bankshares**
1010 Grand Ave.
Kansas City, MO
64141
816/860-7000

TOP BANKS—SOUTH

AmSouth Bancorp
1900 Fifth Ave.
Birmingham, AL 35288
205/320-7151

Bank South
55 Marietta St., NW
Atlanta, GA 30303
404/529-4111

Barnett Banks
50 N. Laura St.
Jacksonville, FL 32202
904/791-7720

Central Fidelity Banks
1021 E. Cary St.
Richmond, VA 23219
804/782-4000

Crestar Financial
919 E. Main St.
Richmond, VA 23219
804/782-5000

Dominion Bankshares
231 S. Jefferson St.
Roanoke, VA 24040
703/563-7000

**First Alabama
Bancshares**
P.O. Box 10247
Birmingham, AL 35202
205/326-7060

First American Corp.
First American Ctr.
Nashville, TN 37237
615/748-2000

First Florida Banks
P.O. Box 31265
Tampa, FL 33631
813/224-1455

**First Tennessee
National**
165 Madison Ave.
Memphis, TN 38103
901/523-4444

First Union
One First Union Ctr.
Charlotte, NC 28288
704/374-6565

First Virginia Banks
6400 Arlington Blvd.
Falls Church, VA
22042-2336
703/241-4000

Hibernia
313 Carondelet St.
New Orleans, LA
70130
504/586-5552

NationsBank
One Nations Bank Plz.
Charlotte, NC 28255
704/386-5000

Signet Banking
7 N. Eighth St.
Richmond, VA 23219
804/747-2000

**South Carolina
National**
1426 Main St.
Columbia, SC 29226
803/765-3000

Southeast Banking
1 Southeast Financial
Ctr.
Miami, FL 33131
305/375-7500

SouthTrust
420 N. 20th St.
Birmingham, AL 35290
205/254-5000

SunTrust Banks
25 Park Pl., NE
Atlanta, GA 30303
404/588-7711

Wachovia
301 N. Main St.
Winston-Salem, NC
27101
919/770-5000

TOP BANKS—WEST

Bancorp Hawaii
130 Merchant St.
Honolulu, HI 96813
808/537-8111

City National Bank
400 N. Roxbury Dr.
Beverly Hills, CA
90210
310/550-5400

**First City
Bancorporation of
Texas**
P.O. Box 2557
Houston, TX 77252
713/658-6011

First Hawaiian
165 S. King St.
Honolulu, HI 96813
808/525-7000

**First Interstate
Bancorp**
633 W. Fifth St.
Los Angeles, CA 90071
213/614-3001

Puget Sound Bancorp
1119 Pacific Ave.
Tacoma, WA 98411
206/593-3600

Union Bank
350 California St.
San Francisco, CA
94104-1476
415/445-0200

U.S. Bancorp
111 SW Fifth Ave.
Portland, OR 97204
503/225-6111

Valley National
241 N. Central Ave.
Phoenix, AZ 85001
602/221-2900

Wells Fargo
420 Montgomery Ave.
San Francisco, CA
94163
415/477-1000

TOP THRIFT INSTITUTIONS

H. F. Ahmanson & Co.
4900 Rivergravd Rd.
Irwindale, CA 91706
818/960-6311

**American Capital
Asset Management,
Inc.**
2900 Post Oak Blvd.
Houston, TX 77056
713/993-0500

Anchor Bancorp
Anchor Savings Bank
1420 Broadway
Hewlett, NY 11557
516/596-3900

CalFed
5700 Wilshire Blvd.
Los Angeles, CA 90036
213/932-4200

**Coast Savings
Financial**
1000 Wilshire Blvd.
Los Angeles, CA 90017
213/362-2222

Commercial Federal
2120 S. 72nd St.
Omaha, NE 68124
402/554-9200

**Dime Savings Bank
FSB**
1225 Franklin Ave.
Garden City, NY 11530
516/351-1550

FirstFed Michigan
1001 Woodward Ave.
Detroit, MI 48226
313/965-1400

GlenFed
700 N. Brand Blvd.
Glendale, CA 91203
818/500-2000

**Golden West Financial
Corp.**
1901 Harrison St.
Oakland, CA 94612
510/446-6000

**Great Western
Financial**
9200 Oakdale Ave.
Chatsworth, CA 91311
818/775-3411

HomeFed
625 Broadway
San Diego, CA 92101
619/699-7679

Northeast Federal
50 State House Sq.
Hartford, CT 06103
203/280-1000

People's Bank
850 Main St.
Bridgeport, CT 06604
203/338-7171

**Standard Federal
Bank**
2600 W. Big Beaver

Rd.
Troy, MI 48084
313/643-9600

**The Talman Home
Federal Savings &
Loan Assn. of Illinois**
30 W. Monroe St.
Chicago, IL 60603
312/726-8915

TCF Financial Corp.
801 Marquette Ave.
Minneapolis, MN
55402
612/370-7000

**Washington Mutual
Savings Bank**
1201 Third Ave.
Seattle, WA 98101
206/461-2000

WHERE TO GO FOR MORE INFORMATION

BANKING INDUSTRY ASSOCIATIONS

**American Bankers
Association**
1120 Connecticut Ave.,
NW
Washington, DC 20036
202/663-4000
(Publishes *American
Banker* magazine; see
below for more
information.)

**American League of
Financial Institutions**
1709 New York Ave.,
NW,
Suite 801
Washington, DC 20006
202/628-5624
(Offers career
placement assistance.)

**Association of Bank
Holding Companies**
730 15th St., NW,
Suite 820
Washington, DC 20005
202/393-1158

**Bank Administration
Institute**
60 Gould Ctr.

Rolling Meadows, IL
60008
312/228-6200
(Publishes monthly
magazine *Bank
Management*.)

**Bank Marketing
Association**
309 W. Washington St.
Chicago, IL 60606
312/782-1442

**Credit Union
Executives Society**
P.O. Box 14167
Madison, WI 53714
608/271-2664
800/252-2664
(Puts out *Credit Union
Management*, also
available to
nonmembers.)

**Financial Institutions
Marketing Association**
111 E. Wacker Dr.
Chicago, IL 60601
312/938-2570

**Independent Bankers
Association of
America**
1 Thomas Cir., NW,
Suite 950
Washington, DC 20005
202/659-8111
(Publishes monthly
magazine *Independent
Banker*.)

**Mortgage Bankers
Association of
America**
1125 15th St., NW
Washington, DC 20005
202/861-6500
(Publishes monthly
magazine *Mortgage
Banking* for members.)

**National Association
of Federal Credit
Unions**
3138 N. 10th St.,
Suite 300
Arlington, VA 22201
703/522-4770
(Publishes monthly
Jobs/OPS, which lists

job opportunities;
available, free, to
members only.)

**National Bankers
Association**
122 C. St., NW,
Suite 580

Washington, DC 20001
202/783-3200
(Operates job referral
service for members.)

**National Council of
Savings Institutions**
1101 15th St., NW

Washington, DC 20005
202/857-3100

**U.S. League of
Savings Institutions**
111 E. Wacker Dr.
Chicago, IL 60601
312/644-3100

BANKING INDUSTRY DIRECTORIES

*American Banker
Directory of U.S.
Banking Executives*
American Banker, Inc.
525 W. 42nd St.
New York, NY 10036
212/563-1900

*American Banker
Yearbook*
American Banker, Inc.
1 State St. Plz.
New York, NY 10004
212/943-6700

*American Financial
Directory*
McFadden Business
Publications
6195 Crooked Creek
Rd.
Norcross, GA
30092-9986
800/247-7376
404/448-1011

*American Savings
Directory*
McFadden Business
Publications
6195 Crooked Creek
Rd.
Norcross, GA
30092-9986
800/247-7376
404/448-1011

Business Week—Top
**200 Banking
Institutions Issue**
McGraw-Hill, Inc.
1221 Ave. of the
Americas
New York, NY 10020
212/512-4776

*Directory of American
Savings & Loan
Associations*
T. K. Sanderson

Organization
1115 E. 30th St.
Baltimore, MD 21218
301/235-3383

*Moody's Bank and
Financial Manual*
Moody's Investors
Services, Inc.
99 Church St.
New York, NY 10007
212/553-0300

Polk's Bank Directory
R. L. Polk & Co.
P.O. Box 3051000
Nashville, TN
37230-5100
615/889-3350
800/827-2265
(Two different editions:
North American edition
and International
edition.)

BANKING INDUSTRY MAGAZINES

ABA Banking Journal
345 Hudson St.
New York, NY 10014
212/620-7200
(Monthly for bank and
S&L officers, financial
executives, insurance
firm executives, etc.)

American Banker
1 State St. Plz.
New York, NY 10004
212/943-6700
(Daily newspaper for
senior executives and
bank officers; often has
good help-wanted
section.)

Bankers Monthly
200 57th St.
New York, NY 10019
212/399-1084
(Monthly magazine
aimed primarily at
commercial bank and
trust company senior
management.)

United States Banker   (Monthly magazine for   including securities,
10 Valley Dr.   managers in banking   insurance, brokerages.)
Greenwich, CT 06831   and other finance fields,
203/869-8200

BROADCASTING

INDUSTRY OUTLOOK:
Improving as the economy strengthens, but each segment marked by heavy competition.

Television: Still fighting the turf wars against cable and home videos. One bright spot: increasing advertising revenues as the economy picks up.

Cable: Still picking up viewers from networks, but facing challenges due to high rates and legislative woes. Watch cable turn to new technology to pick up steam. Over the long term, look for more channels, introduction of interactive game shows and the like, and other on-line services. In line with this, expect more cooperative ventures between cable companies and telecommunications companies (such as the 1993 pairing of Time-Warner and US West), retail giants (such as Macy's), and others eager to get into the interactive field. Also expect to see more local telephone companies take advantage of late 1993 legislature and enter the cable business.

Radio: Smaller stations will continue losing ground to group-owned stations. Hot competition will lead to continued consolidation.

A LOOK BACK

▶ **In the '80s, network television was feeling the pinch of increased competition from cable television, independent, and home videos; cable TV was going strong. But 1992 brought about a change in fortunes.**

In the 1980s network television started losing command of its traditional pool of viewers. Competition from outside sources (cable, independent programmers, and video cassette recorders) cut into network viewership. Plus the formation of a fourth network—Fox—sent tremors through the industry, and caused advertisers to cut back.

Cable TV, on the other hand, was a broadcasting success story. The '80s was a period of rapid growth. Subscribers skyrocketed, advertising revenues followed suit—and cable was on a roll, leaving the networks worrying that their day was over.

But in mid-1992 the networks started seeing a rebound in their viewership figures. The fifteen-year prime-time viewer decline ended when the September–April 1992 season officially ended. For the first time since 1976–77, networks saw an increase in share of audience over the previous year.

► **It has been a run of bad times and industry consolidation for radio.**

Stagnant audience numbers and dropping advertising dollars caused the industry to slump. AM stations were especially hurt. As a result, the radio industry went through a period of consolidation; similarly, the number of group-owned stations increased.

WHAT'S NEXT

► **Competition will still be setting the scene for television broadcasters.**

The upward blip in network audience share doesn't spell an end to the tight competition between networks, cable TV, and independent programmers. It's still going to be business as usual—which means hot competition as usual.

One trend to keep an eye on: The networks will be trying to maintain—and build—audience share by playing to their strengths. Along these lines, expect to see more divergent programming with the different networks aiming at distinct audience segments. For example, Fox will build on its youth-oriented audience, CBS on its older audience, etc.

► **Along the same lines, watch the growth of niche networks in cable.**

With fierce competition for advertising dollars, the broad-based cable networks will be spending more money for original programming, sports, series development, and the like.

The winners may well be the cable networks that aim at a very targeted audience or that offer "narrowcasted" programming, such as MTV, CNN, and Court TV. Expect the continued success and growth of these networks—and possibly the development of spin-off networks, similar to MTV's development of VH-1 for older viewers. This area will be ripe for employment opportunities in the long term as the number of narrowcast cable networks increases.

► **It will be a two-tier picture for radio: The larger stations will continue to hold their own; the smaller will be falling by the wayside.**

A 1992 FCC report on the state of the radio business cited in *Broadcasting* magazine summed it up by saying that radio is a world of "large haves and little have-nots." It backed up the statement with these telling statistics: one-half of 1% of the 10,000-plus stations on the air accounted for 11% of 1990 industry revenues and 50% of the profits, while 75% of all stations on average lost money. This trend will continue.

Expect the largest radio stations to continue performing fairly well but the smaller stations to fall victim to low audience numbers and intense competition.

One probable result? The number of "robot" stations will increase—that is, stations that act, in effect, as transmitters for larger stations instead of offering up their own programming.

Adding to the picture: the FCC changed rules in 1992. One company can now own up to six stations in one city and sixty stations nationwide. This replaces the old rule that allowed single ownership of only one AM and one FM station per city, and twelve each nationwide, and it means that the strength of the larger broadcasters will increase, as they snap up smaller stations that couldn't make it alone.

Where employment is concerned, this means fewer jobs across the board as the number of stations decreases. Opportunities will continue to be found at the larger stations, however, especially in programming, as broadcasting companies beef up original programming to be played on their group stations.

▶ A question mark: Will satellite-to-home broadcasting catch on?

Satellite-to-home broadcasting (or direct satellite broadcasting) is a simple idea: High-powered direct broadcast satellites orbit the earth, beaming television programming directly into viewers' homes.

Althogh the few attempts to make direct satellite broadcasting a competitor in the home viewing industry didn't pan out, it's an idea that won't die—and some industry experts are predicting that it will eventually catch on. The newest planned DBS system is Hubbard Broadcasting's, which would offer two free advertiser-supported channels, pay-per-view movies, and a premium subscription channel, all planned for a launch date in summer 1994. If this, or another DBS program, gets off the ground, it will mean new competition for network and cable television—and a new broadcasting medium that could offer employment opportunities.

EMPLOYMENT OUTLOOK: Like the industry itself, very competitive.

Broadcast is historically a tough field to break into and stay afloat in, and this won't change.

As network fortunes go up and down, expect periodic hiring freezes depending upon business at the moment. As always, the easiest way to break into television is to work at a local independent station. Hiring in news, especially at local stations, should remain stable. Best qualifications: a B.A. or B.S. in science, political science, or other specialty area. Undergraduate journalism degrees are not necessary or even desirable at many stations. In addition, many executives don't think internships are all that valuable, but work experience is always a plus.

As for sales, the outlook is varied. Expect ups and downs depending upon the specific time, but in general the outlook is favorable.

JOBS SPOTLIGHT

DIRECTOR OF MARKETING/ASSISTANT DIRECTOR (in radio): These two promotion department positions are of increasing importance at radio stations as competition remains high. Most radio stations have a two-person promotion department, consisting of a director and an assistant. Among the areas that radio promotion staffers are involved in, depending on the size of the station and of the department: advertising, direct mail, promotional copy, public relations (in terms of developing an image for the station), special events, publicity, promotional events such as on-air contests. Experience in radio is a definite plus, as are writing, promotion, and marketing experience or skills. Salaries depend on the station size and market.

The Top 20 Radio Groups
(ranked by ratings)

1. CBS
2. Group W
3. Capcities/ABC
4. Infinity
5. Emmis
6. Cox
7. Bonneville
8. Gannett
9. Malrite
10. Viacom
11. Great American
12. Greater Media
13. Summit
14. Susquehanna
15. EZ Communications
16. Nationwide
17. Shamrock
18. Noble
19. Booth American
20. Evergreen Media Corp.

SOURCE: *Broadcasting*

BEST BETS

Turner Communications
1 CNN Center
Atlanta, GA 30348
404/827-1500

Owner and operator of three of the top commercial cable stations in the United States—CNN, TBS, and TNT—Turner is also a company with a conscience, devoting programming time and corporate backing to many environmental issues. In addition, CNN has a longstanding reputation for being a great place for people wanting to start out in television news. Pay tends to be lower than at the networks, but it is often easier to break in here, and training is reportedly excellent. A Best Bet in *Jobs '92* as well, Turner remains a good choice for employment.

TOP TELEVISION COMPANIES

(including networks, group television station owners)

A. H. Belo Corp.
400 S. Record St.
Dallas, TX 75202
214/977-6600

Bonneville International Corp.
Broadcast House
55 N. Third W.
Salt Lake City, UT
84110
801/575-7500

Capital Cities/ABC
77 W. 66th St.
New York, NY
10023-6298
212/456-7777
West Coast office:
2040 Ave. of the Stars
Century City, CA
90067
310/577-7777

CBS
51 W. 52nd St.
New York, NY 10019
212/975-4321
West Coast office:
7800 Beverly Blvd.
Los Angeles, CA 90036
213/852-2345

Chris-Craft Industries
600 Madison Ave.
New York, NY 10022
212/241-0200

Cox Enterprises
1400 Lake Hearn Dr.,
NE
Atlanta, GA 30319
404/843-5000

Fox Broadcasting Company
10201 W. Pico Blvd.
Los Angeles, CA 90035
213/203-3266
East Coast office:
205 E. 67th St.
New York, NY 10021
212/452-5555

Gannett Broadcasting Group
1100 Wilson Blvd.
Arlington, VA 22209
703/276-3400

Great American Communications Corp.
1 E. Fourth St.
Cincinnati, OH 45202
513/579-2121

King Broadcasting Co.
333 Dexter Ave. N.
Seattle, WA 98109
206/448-5555

LIN Broadcasting Corp.
5295 Carillon Pt.
Kirkland, WA 98033
206/828-1902

Multimedia Broadcasting Co.
1000 Market St.
St. Louis, MO 63101
314/444-5266

NBC
30 Rockefeller Plz.
New York, NY 10112
212/664-4444
West Coast office:
3000 Alameda Ave.

Burbank, CA 91523
818/840-4444

Park Communications, Inc.
Terrace Hill
Ithaca, NY 14850
607/272-9020

Post/Newsweek Stations, Inc.
1150 15th St., NW
Washington, DC 20071
202/334-4600

Providence Journal Broadcasting Co.
(subs. of Providence
Journal Co.)
75 Fountain St.
Providence, RI 02902
401/277-7000

Pulitzer Broadcasting Co.
515 N. Sixth St.
St. Louis, MO 63101
314/231-5950

Schurz Communications, Inc.
225 W. Colfaz Ave.
South Bend, IN 46626
219/287-1001

Scripps-Howard Broadcasting Co.
1100 Central Trust
Tower
Cincinnati, OH 45202
513/977-3000

Telemundo Group, Inc.
1740 Broadway

New York, NY 10019
212/492-5500

Time Warner
75 Rockefeller Plz.
New York, NY 10019
212/484-8000

Tribune Broadcasting
435 N. Michigan Ave.
Chicago, IL 60611
312/222-3737

Univision Station Group
330 Madison Ave.,
26th Fl.
New York, NY 10017
212/983-8500

Viacom
1515 Broadway
New York, NY 10036
212/258-6000

Westinghouse Broadcasting Co.
(Group W)
888 Seventh Ave.
New York, NY 10106
212/307-3000

TOP CABLE NETWORKS AND PAY TV SERVICES

A&E—Arts & Entertainment Cable Network
555 Fifth Ave.
New York, NY 10017
212/661-4500

ACTS Satellite Network
6350 W. Fwy.
Fort Worth, TX 76150
817/737-4011

American Movie Classics; Bravo Rainbow Programming Service
150 Crossways Pk. W.
Woodbury, NY 11797
516/364-2222

BET—Black Entertainment Television
1232 31st St., NW
Washington, DC 20007
202/337-5260

CNBC Consumer News and Business Control
2200 Fletcher Ave.

Ft. Lee, NJ 07024
201/585-2622

CNN; CNN Headline News
Box 105366
CNN Ctr.
Atlanta, GA
30348-5366
404/827-1500

Country Music Television
704 18th Ave. S.
Nashville, TN 37203
615/255-8836

C-SPAN (Cable Public Affairs Network)
400 N. Capitol St.,
NW, Suite 650
Washington, DC 20001
202/737-3220

The Discovery Channel
8201 Corporate Dr.,
Suite 1260
Landover, MD 20785
301/577-1999

The Disney Channel
3800 W. Alameda Ave.
Burbank, CA 91505
818/569-7701

E! Entertainment Television
1800 N. Vine St.,
3rd Fl.
Hollywood, CA 90028
213/960-5800

ESPN—Entertainment and Sports Programming Network
ESPN Plz.
Bristol, CT 06010
203/585-2000

EWTN—Eternal Word Television Network
5817 Old Leeds Rd.
Birmingham, AL 35210
205/956-9537

Family Channel
1000 Centerville Tpke.
Virginia Beach, VA
23463
804/523-7301

Home Box Office, Inc.
(includes HBO and
Cinemax)
1100 Ave. of the
Americas
New York, NY 10036
212/512-1000

**Home Shopping
Network, Inc.**
Box 9090
Clearwater, FL
34618-9090
818/572-8585

Lifetime
36-12 35th Ave.
Astoria, NY 11106
718/482-4000

MTV Networks, Inc.
(inc. MTV,
Nickelodeon, Nick at
Nite, VH-1)
1515 Broadway
New York, NY 10038
212/258-7800

The Nashville Network
Group W. Satellite
Communications
Box 10210
250 Harbor Plz. Dr.
Stamford, CT
06904-2210
203/965-6000

The Nostalgia Channel
Royal Commerce Ctr.
2144 Royal Ln., Suite
150

Dallas, TX 75229
214/243-0877

NuStar
1332 Enterprises Dr.
West Chester, PA
19380
215/692-5900

**Playboy; Playboy at
Night (pay-per-view)**
Playboy Enterprises,
Inc.
8560 Sunset Blvd.
Los Angeles, CA 90069
213/659-4080

QVC Network, Inc.
Goshen Corporate Pk.
1365 Enterprise Dr.
West Chester, PA
19380
215/430-1000

Request Television
(pay-per-view)
Box 10210
250 Harbor Dr.
Stamford, CT
06904-2210
203/965-6000

**Showtime/The Movie
Channel, Inc.**
1622 Broadway,
37th Fl.
New York, NY 10019
212/708-1600

**SportsChannel
America**
3 Crossways Pk.
Woodbury, NY 11797
516/921-3764

**TNT—Turner
Network Television**
1 CNN Ctr.
Atlanta, GA 30348
404/827-1647

The Travel Channel
1370 Ave. of the
Americas,
27th Fl.
New York, NY 10019
212/603-4500

**Trinity Broadcasting
Network, Inc.**
Box A
Santa Ana, CA 92711
714/832-2950

USA Network
1230 Ave. of the
Americas
New York, NY 10020
212/408-9100

Viewer's Choice.
(pay-per-view)
909 Third Ave.,
21st Fl.
New York, NY 10022
212/486-6600

The Weather Channel
2600 Cumberland Pky.
Atlanta, GA 30339
404/434-6800

TOP RADIO COMPANIES

ABC Radio Networks
New York office:
125 W. End Ave.
New York, NY 10023
212/887-5200

ABC Radio Networks
Chicago office:
360 N. Michigan Ave.
Chicago, IL 60601
312/899-4050

ABC Radio Networks
Los Angeles office:
2040 Ave. of the Stars
Century City, CA

90067
213/557-7100

ABC Radio Networks
Detroit office:
3000 Town Center,
Suite 2910
Southfield, MI 48075
313/354-1260

ABC Radio Networks
Dallas office:
600 E., Las Colinas
Blvd.
Irving, TX 75039
214/869-4455

**Associated Press
Radio Division**
1825 K St., NW
Washington, DC
20006-1253
202/955-7200

**Business Radio
Network**
888 Garden of the Gods
Rd.
Colorado Springs, CO
80907
719/528-7040

Cadena Radio Centro
(CRC Radio Network)
12655 N. Central
Expy.,
Suite 525
Dallas, TX 75243
214/991-9761

CBS Radio Division
New York office:
51 W. 52nd St.
New York, NY 10019
212/975-4321

CBS Radio Division
Los Angeles office:
7800 Beverly Blvd.
Los Angeles, CA 90036
213/852-2345

**Chancellor
Broadcasting Network**
Union Plaza Hotel
1 Main St.
Las Vegas, NV 89101
702/385-7212

CNN Radio Network
1 CNN Ctr.
Box 105366
Atlanta, GA
30348-5366
404/827-1400

**Gear Broadcasting
International, Inc.**
Box 23172
Weybosset St.
Providence, RI 02903
401/331-6072

**Moody Broadcasting
Network**
820 N. LaSalle Dr.
Chicago, IL 60610
800/621-7031

National Public Radio
2025 M St., NW
Washington, DC 20036
202/822-2000

NBC Radio Network
1755 S. Jefferson Davis
Hwy.
Arlington, VA 22202
703/685-2000

**Satellite Music
Network**
12655 N. Central
Expy.,
Suite 600
Dallas, TX 75243
800/527-4892

**Sheridan Broadcasting
Networks**
1 Times Sq. Plz.,
18th Fl.

New York, NY 10036
212/575-0099

**Unistar Radio
Networks**
660 Southpointe Ct.,
Suite 200
Colorado Springs, CO
80906
719/576-2620

UPI Radio Network
1400 I St., NW,
9th Fl.
Washington, DC 20005
202/898-8111

USA Radio Network
2290 Springlake Rd.,
Suite 107
Dallas, TX 75234
214/484-3900

**Wall Street Journal
Radio Network**
200 Liberty St.,
14th Fl.
New York, NY 10281
212/416-2381

Westwood One, Inc.
9540 Washington Blvd.
Culver City, CA 90232
310/840-4000

Westwood One, Inc.
New York office:
1700 Broadway
New York, NY 10019
212/237-2500

Westwood One, Inc.
Washington, DC,
office:
1755 S. Jefferson Davis
Hwy.
Arlington, VA 22202
703/685-2000

Westwood One, Inc.
Chicago office:
111 E. Wacker Dr.
Chicago, IL 60601
312/938-0222

Westwood One, Inc.
Dallas office:
10000 N. Central Expy.

Dallas, TX 75231
214/373-0022

Westwood One, Inc.
Detroit office:
3250 W. Big Beaver
Troy, MI 48084
313/649-6300

Westwood One, Inc.
Toronto office:
260 Richmond St. W.
Toronto, Ont. M5V
1W5 Canada
416/597-8529

WHERE TO GO FOR MORE INFORMATION

BROADCASTING INDUSTRY ASSOCIATIONS

Academy of Television Arts & Sciences
3500 W. Olive Ave.,
Suite 700
Burbank, CA 91505
818/953-7575

Broadcast Promotion and Marketing Executives
6255 Sunset Blvd.
Los Angeles, CA 90028
213/465-3777
(Operates job referral bank for members.)

Corporation for Public Broadcasting
901 E St., NW
Washington, DC 20004
202/876-9600
(Maintains a computerized job referral service for public television and radio stations nationwide—Employment Outreach Project Talent Bank. Also provides a toll-free job hot line that explains job openings:
1-800/582-8220.)

International Radio and Television Society
420 Lexington Ave.,
Suite 1714
New York, NY 10170
212/867-6650
(Sponsors summer internships for college communications majors.)

International Television Association
6311 N. O'Connor Rd.
LB51
Irving, TX 75039
214/869-1112

National Academy of Television Arts and Sciences
111 W. 57th St.
New York, NY 10019
212/586-8424

National Association of Black-Owned Broadcasters
1730 M St., NW
Washington, DC 20036
202/463-8970
(Maintains placement service and offers workshops. Puts out

annual *Black-Owned Station Directory.*)

National Association of Broadcasters
1771 N St., NW
Washington, DC 20036
202/429-5300
(Publishes career brochures; *Careers in Radio* and *Careers in Television;* maintains placement service for minorities and job clearinghouse.)

National Association of Business & Educational Radio
1501 Duke St.
Alexandria, VA 22314
703/739-0300

National Association of Public Television Stations
1350 Connecticut Ave.,
NW
Washington, DC 20036
202/887-1700

National Association of Television Program Executives
10100 Santa Monica

Blvd.,
Suite 300
Los Angeles, CA 90067
213/282-8801

**National Cable
Television Association**
1724 Massachusetts
Ave., NW
Washington, DC 20036
202/775-2550

**Radio Advertising
Bureau**
304 Park Ave.

New York, NY 10010
212/254-4800

**Radio-Television News
Directors Association**
1717 K St., NW
Washington, DC 20006
202/659-6510
(Puts out a newsletter
listing job opportunities
free to members, but
also available to
nonmembers for a
subscription price.)

**Satellite Broadcasting
& Communications
Association**
225 Reinekers Ln.,
Suite 600
Alexandria, VA 22314
703/549-6990

**Television Bureau of
Advertising**
477 Madison Ave.
New York, NY 10022
212/486-1111

BROADCASTING INDUSTRY DIRECTORIES

*Broadcasting & Cable
Marketplace*
P.O. Box 31
New Providence, NJ
07974-9903
800/521-8110

Broadcasting Yearbook
Broadcasting
Publications, Inc.
1705 DeSales St., NW
Washington, DC 20036
202/659-2340

*Gale Directory of
Publications and
Broadcast Media*

Gale Research, Inc.
835 Penobscot Bldg.
Detroit, MI 48226-4094
800/877-4253

*International
Television and Video
Almanac*
159 W. 53rd St.
New York, NY 10019
212/247-3100

*Standard Rate & Data
Service*
*Spot Radio Rates &
Data*

and
*Spot Television Rates
& Data*
SRDS
3004 Glenview Rd.
Wilmette, IL 60091
708/256-6067

*World Radio TV
Handbook*
Billboard Publications,
Inc.
1515 Broadway
New York, NY 10036
212/764-7300

BROADCASTING INDUSTRY MAGAZINES

Broadcast Engineering
P.O. Box 12901
Overland Park, KS
66212
913/888-4664
(Monthly magazine
covering radio,
television, and cable
broadcasting; for

engineers, operators,
managers, etc.)

Broadcasting
1735 DeSales St., NW
Washington, DC 20036
202/638-1022
(Weekly magazine
covering the broadcast
industry; aimed at
network and station

personnel, broadcast
advertisers, etc. Good
help-wanted section.)

Electronic Media
740 N. Rush St.
Chicago, IL 60611
312/649-5200
(Weekly publication on
all aspects of the
broadcast industry; for

personnel at stations, networks, manufacturers, etc.)

Television Broadcast
2 Park Ave.
New York, NY 10016
212/779-1919
(Monthly publication covering radio and television broadcasting; for engineering and production staffs, management.)

Video Week
Television Digest, Inc.
1836 Jefferson Pl., NW
Washington, DC 20036
202/872-9200
(Weekly publication covering the television industry.)

VideoNews International
1680 Vine St.
Hollywood, CA 90028
213/462-6350
(Publication covering international video.)

CHEMICALS

INDUSTRY OUTLOOK: Signs of growth ahead, as the economy improves.

The long-term outlook is a positive one for the chemical industry. Organic chemicals will improve in step with the world economy; inorganic chemicals in step with the U.S. economy. For petrochemicals, over the short term growth should be steady, with faster growth predicted after 1995. Strongest probable chemical sectors? Fuel oxygenates and biotechnological applications of agricultural chemicals.

A key factor in the long-term outlook for the chemical industry is the "greening" of American industry. This will force the industry to choose new plant sites, change manufacturing processes and increase R&D expenditures.

A LOOK BACK

▶ **The chemical industry experienced a series of good years in the '80s, so confident companies spent their profits on expansion.**

The '80s brought high demand, strong sales, and peak earnings to the chemical industry. Buoyed by their success, companies turned their profits back into business and began spending heavily on expansion. They announced plans to build new plants and facilities and beefed up research-and-development budgets. Reasons: to hedge against overcapacity of traditional chemicals and to diversify into new markets, such as specialty chemicals, biotechnology, and other emerging areas.

▶ **The heavy expense of expansion, plus overcapacity and slow demand due to a slumping economy, led to an industry downturn.**

The good times didn't last. The chemical industry is a cyclical one, and the 1990s opened with chemical companies facing the low end of their cycle. In 1991 earnings dropped about 15%. Hardest hit were the commodity chemicals producers. One bright spot remained chemical exports, which continued to grow—up 10% in 1991. As recession hit, chemical companies went through downsizing, restructuring, cost-cutting and debt control. And, when domestic demand increased as the economy began recovering, companies were poised for a brighter future.

WHAT'S NEXT

▶ **Of key importance for the continuing growth of the U.S. chemical industry: International competitiveness.**

Strong international sales have kept many areas of the U.S. chemical industry strong, even through domestic economic downturns. (The U.S. chemical industry is the largest in the world, responsible for about 30 percent of the worldwide chemical markets.)

This won't change in the future, but there are several challenges and changes on the horizon. Chief among them: the changing chemical investment policies of much of the world. This will result in a rise in the number of new companies, partnership agreements between existing companies, and the like, which will create more competition in the world markets. Among the specific areas that should show increased competition in the near future are South Korea, Taiwan, and Mexico. Asia, in general, is gearing up for competition. Over the next few years, a number of new facilities should begin production. In addition, Japan has been making inroads into the U.S.–dominated advanced composites industry.

On the plus side where the international markets are concerned are Eastern Europe and the former Soviet Union. The emerging nations in these areas have already signed contracts with U.S. companies, which will mean increased business.

Where employment is concerned, this international focus points to an increasing need for people with backgrounds in international business.

▶ **Expect continued restructuring.**

This is a trend that should continue through the next few years as the industry remains cost conscious.

Also watch as small and midsize chemical companies increase their production of both specialty and commodity chemicals for the domestic market and for export.

▶ **Look for increased environmental awareness to continue having a strong impact on the chemical industry, helping some companies, hurting others.**

Companies that have already developed chemicals that can replace those that deplete the ozone layer will benefit from this "greening of America." Among them are Allied-Signal, Dow, and Du Pont. Similarly, expect to see a push in R&D in environment-friendly chemicals, especially fuel additives such as methanol and methyl tertiary butyl ether.

This points to employment opportunities over the long term, as companies are forced to increase production of these chemicals, either through development of new processing technologies or through plant expansion. Keep in mind, however, that there will also be strong competition emerging from foreign companies, which may directly affect the U.S. companies' health.

▶ **On the same note, watch for more chemicals companies to move into environmental services.**

It's already a hot area and will continue to be so in the future. Du Pont, Dow, and Monsanto are among the large chemicals companies already moving heavily into environmental services. Expect more to follow suit. Also watch for linkups between larger, established environmental services firms and chemical companies, as well as buyouts of smaller environmental services firms by chemical companies.

The impact of this concentration on employment opportunities? Increased demand for chemists and chemical engineers with an environmental specialty, with the possibility of job growth up to 25 percent over the next few years. Also looking strong: geochemists, environmental consultants.

▶ **There will be a continued emphasis placed on research and development.**

It's the keystone to the long-term success of the chemical industry—and chemical producers are aware of it. So they are making sure that they stay technologically in step with their competitors, both domestic and overseas. Adding to the renewed focus on R&D are the new environmental regulations and concerns.

A positive outcome of this emphasis where workers are concerned: The heavy focus on technology has translated into higher salaries paid to nonproduction workers, including technicians, chemists, and engineers.

▶ **Keep an eye on agricultural biotechnology.**

This is the less-noticed side of biotechnology—biotech aimed at agricultural and industrial usage—but it's slowly beginning to make inroads. Ag biotech research is being conducted in a number of areas, including development of BST (a milk-production hormone), PST (a lean pork hormone), and insect and herbicide–resistant cotton.

Among the companies involved in ag biotech are industry giants American Cyanamid, Ciba-Geigy, and Monsanto, as well as the lesser-known DNA Plant Technology, Ecogen, Biotechnical International, and Calgene.

EMPLOYMENT OUTLOOK: Fair; stronger in some areas than in others.

The chemical industry remains a large employer—employing over 850,000 people as of 1993. About five percent of all U.S. manufacturing workers and about ten percent of all U.S. scientists and engineers work for chemical companies. Most of these jobs should remain fairly stable as the U.S. government has forecast that the chemical industry should continue growing slightly faster than the U.S. economy as a whole.

More specifically: Petrochemical producers, which account for roughly 30% of the total chemical industry employment, should continue to offer job opportunities, especially as the automotive, electronic, and construction materials industries improve.

The inorganic chemicals industry is headed for flat times, according to the U.S. Department of Commerce. The long-term employment picture shows little growth, perhaps even losses. As for organic chemicals, the picture is a bit brighter as new plants are being added on line, particularly to keep up with demand for ethanol.

Jobs Spotlight

Chemical Engineers with B.S. Degrees: Because of the dwindling number of students, chemical engineers holding B.S. degrees were in great demand in recent years. And salaries have been reflecting that demand: In 1990 the average starting salary was $35,084. The average salary at a basic chemicals or plastics industry company is $46,200. This area looks strong for the short term, with company spokesmen citing increases of at least 10% in demand.

Best Bets

Du Pont
1007 Market Street
Wilmington, DE 19898
302/774-1000

Du Pont has gone through layoffs and restructurings, but it offers good employment prospects in the long term. One area to keep an eye on: Environmental services. Du Pont has been very bullish on this hot area and is planning to continue emphasizing and expanding its business in environmental services. Among its areas of interest: wastewater management, soil and groundwater cleanup, and consulting. A good choice for those in the environmental field, such as industrial hygienists and the like.

H. B. Fuller
2400 Energy Park Drive
St. Paul, MN 55108
612/645-3401

Chosen as a Best Bet in *Jobs '93* as well, Fuller, a specialty chemicals maker, is considered a corporate leader in terms of its environmental consciousness. It has established an environment, health, and safety policy that all of its plants and labs must adhere to; it follows strict recycling and pollution-control procedures; and its Willow Lake research and development lab is a model of energy efficiency.

TOP CHEMICAL COMPANIES

Air Products and Chemicals, Inc.
7201 Hamilton Blvd.
Allentown, PA 18195
215/481-4911

American Cyanamid Co.
1 Cyanamid Plz.
Wayne, NJ 07470
201/831-2000

American International Chemical, Inc.
27 Strathmore Rd.
Natick, MA 01760
508/655-5805

Arcadian Corp.
6750 Poplar Ave.
Memphis, TN 38138
901/758-5200

Arco Chemical Co.
3801 W. Chester Pike
Newton Square, PA
19073
215/359-2000

**Aristech Chemical
Corp.**
600 Grant St.
Pittsburgh, PA 15230
412/433-2747

**Ashland Chemical,
Inc.**
P.O. Box 2219
Columbus, OH 43216
614/889-3333

Baroid Corp.
3000 N. Belt E.
Houston, TX 77032
713/987-4000

BASF Corporation
Chemicals Div.
100 Cherry Hill Rd.
Parsippany, NJ 07054
201/316-3000

BASF Corp.
8 Campus Dr.
Parsippany, NJ 07054
201/397-2700

**Betz Laboratories,
Inc.**
4636 Somerton Rd.
Trevose, PA 19053
215/355-3300

Cabot Corp.
75 State St.
Boston, MA 02109
617/345-0100

Cargill
P.O. Box 9300
Minneapolis, MN
55440
612/475-7575

CF Industries, Inc.
1 Salem Lake Dr.
Long Grove, IL 60047
708/438-9500

Dexter
1 Elm St.
Windsor Locks, CT
06096
203/627-9051

Dow Chemical USA
2030 Willard H. Dow
Ctr.
Midland, MI 48674
517/636-1000

Dow Corning Corp.
Box 994
Midland, MI 48686
517/496-4000

Du Pont Company
Engelhard Corp.
Menlo Park
CN 40
Edison, NJ 08818
908/205-6000

Engelhard Corp.
101 Wood Ave.
Iselin, NJ 08830
201/205-6000

Ethyl Corp.
P.O. Box 2189
Richmond, VA 23217
804/788-5000

Ferro Corp.
1000 Lakeside Ave.
Cleveland, OH 44114
216/641-8580

First Chemical Corp.
(subs. of First
Mississippi Corp.)
700 North St.
Jackson, MS 39202
601/949-0246

First Mississippi Corp.
700 North St.
Jackson, MS 39215
601/948-7550

FMC Corp.
Chemical Products
Group
2000 Market St.
Philadelphia, PA 19103
215/299-6000

**Freeport
McMoRan-Agrico**
1615 Poydras St.
New Orleans, LA
70112
504/582-4000

H. B. Fuller Co., Inc.
2400 Energy Pk. Dr.
St. Paul, MN 55108
612/645-3401

**GAF Chemicals
Corporation**
1361 Alps Rd.
Wayne, NJ 07470
201/628-3000

**Georgia Gulf
Corporation**
400 Perimeter Ctr.
Terr.
Atlanta, GA 30346
404/395-4500

**B. F. Goodrich
Company**
3925 Embassy Pkwy.
Akron, OH 44333
216/374-2000

W. R. Grace
One Town Center Rd.
Boca Raton, FL 33486
407/362-2000

**Great Lakes Chemical
Corp.**
P.O. Box 2200
West Layfayette, IN
47906
317/497-6100

M. A. Hanna
1301 E. Ninth St.
Cleveland, OH 44114
216/589-4000

Hercules, Inc.
Hercules Plz.
1313 N. Market St.
Wilmington, DE 19894
302/594-5000

**Hoechst Celanese
Corp.**
Rte. 202–206
Somerville, NJ 08876
908/231-2000

**IMC Fertilizer Group,
Inc.**
2100 Sanders Rd.
Northbrook, IL 60062
708/272-9200

Loctite Corp.
Ten Columbus Blvd.
Hartford, CT 06106
203/520-5000

The Lubrizol Corp.
29400 Lakeland Blvd.
Wickliffe, OH 44092
216/943-4200

**Monsanto Chemical
Co.**
800 N. Lindbergh Blvd.
St. Louis, MO 63167
314/694-1000

**Morton International,
Inc.**
100 N. Riverside Plz.
Chicago, IL 60606
312/807-2000

Nalco Chemical Co.
1 Nalco Ctr.
Naperville, IL 60563
708/305-1000

Olin Chemicals
(div. of Olin Corp.)
120 Long Ridge Rd.
Stamford, CT 06904
203/356-2000

**PPG Industries
Chemicals Group**
1 PPG Pl.
Pittsburgh, PA 15272
412/434-3131

**Quantum Chemical
Corp.**
99 Park Ave.
New York, NY 10016
212/949-5000

Rexene Corp.
5005 LBJ Fwy.
Occidental Tower
Dallas, TX 75244
214/450-9000

**Rohm and Haas
Company**
Independence Mall W.
Philadelphia, PA 19105
215/592-3000

A. Schulman, Inc.
3550 W. Market St.
Akron, OH 44313
216/666-3751

Sherwin-Williams Co.
101 Prospect Ave., NW
Cleveland, OH 44115
216/566-2000

**Sterling Chemicals,
Inc.**
1200 Smith St.
Houston, TX 77002
713/365-3700

Union Carbide Corp.
39 Old Ridgebury Rd.
Danbury, CT 06817
203/794-2000

Valhi, Inc.
3 Lincoln Ctr.
5430 LBJ Fwy., Suite
1700
Dallas, TX 75240
214/233-1700

Valspar Corp.
1101 S. Third St.
Minneapolis, MN
55415
612/332-7371

Vista Chemical Co.
P.O. Box 19029
900 Threadneedle
Houston, TX 77079
713/588-3000

Wellman, Inc.
1040 Broad St.
Shrewsbury, NJ 07702
908/542-7300

Witco Corp.
520 Madison Ave.
New York, NY 10022
212/605-3800

WHERE TO GO FOR MORE INFORMATION

CHEMICAL INDUSTRY ASSOCIATIONS

American Association of Textile Chemists and Colorists
P.O. Box 12215
Research Triangle Park, NC 27709
919/549-8141
(Publishes *Textile Chemist & Colorist*—free to members, also available at a subscription price for nonmembers—which contains help-wanted ads.)

American Chemical Society.
1155 16th St., NW
Washington, DC 20036
202/872-4600
(Publishes *Chemical & Engineering News*, listed below, as well as *Environmental Science & Technology*, both of which contain help-wanted ads; also offers helpful employment-related programs—including career counseling and a job clearinghouse—to members.)

American Institute of Chemists
7315 Wisconsin Ave., NW
Bethesda, MD 20814
801/652-2447
(Publishes *The Chemist*—free to members, available for $25/yr. to nonmembers—which includes employment listings; also maintains a job placement service.)

Chemical Manufacturers Association
2501 M St., NW
Washington, DC 20037
202/887-1100

Chemical Specialties Manufacturers Association
1913 I St., NW
Washington, DC 20006
202/872-8110

National Association of Chemical Distributors
1200 17th St., NW
Suite 400
Washington, DC 20036
202/296-9200

CHEMICAL INDUSTRY DIRECTORIES

Chem Sources—International
and
Chem Sources—USA
Chemical Sources International
Box 1824
Clemson, SC 29633
904/673-1241

Chemical Industry Directory
State Mutual Book and Periodical Service
521 Fifth Ave.
New York, NY 10017
212/682-5844

Chemicals Directory
275 Washington St.
Newton, MA 02158
617/964-3030
(Relatively low-cost—$40 in 1992—making this a good basic source for a résumé mailing list.)

Directory of Chemical Producers U.S.A.
Stanford Research Institute International
333 Ravenswood Ave.
Menlo Park, CA 94025
415/859-3627

CHEMICAL INDUSTRY PERIODICALS

(Also see listings under "Scientists," page 151.)

Chemical Engineering
1221 Ave. of the
Americas
New York, NY 10020
212/512-2849
(Monthly magazine for
chemical engineers and
technical executives.)

**Chemical &
Engineering News**
1155 16th St., NW
Washington, DC 20036
202/872-4600
(Weekly magazine put
out by the American
Chemical Society.
Annual jobs outlook
coverage is especially
helpful for the recent
graduate.)

Chemical Processing
301 E. Erie St.
Chicago, IL 60611
312/644-2020

(Fifteen-issue magazine
aimed at executives and
managers in chemical
processing. Puts out
annual Directory issue.)

Chemical Week
810 Seventh Ave.
New York, NY 10019
212/586-3430
(Weekly magazine for
chemical processing
executives and technical
managers.)

Modern Plastics
1221 Ave. of the
Americas
New York, NY 10020
212/512-6241
(Monthly magazine
covering the plastics
industry; for engineers,
developers, designers,
technicians, etc.)

Plastics Technology
633 Third Ave.
New York, NY 10017
212/884-2289
(Monthly magazine for
plastics industry
personnel, including
engineers, managers,
and factory
supervisors.)

Plastics World
275 Washington St.
Newton, MA 02158
617/964-3030
(Monthly magazine on
the plastics industry;
aimed at a range of
professionals, including
those in engineering,
technical areas, design,
production, and
management.)

COMPUTERS AND ELECTRONICS

INDUSTRY OUTLOOK: Continued competition and restructuring, but calmer times may be ahead over the long term.

The changes aren't over for the computer and electronics industry—and neither are the challenges. Expect to see a repeat of the past few years: industry volatility and hot competition, including price wars. The upshot? An industry split between winners and losers—with weaker companies falling behind and possibly going out of business; stronger companies grabbing market share and possibly taking over the weaker ones; an increase in manufacturing, research and marketing joint ventures. Hottest areas: work stations, portables, LANs, software. Improving fortunes: midrange systems, electronic components, semiconductors.

A LOOK BACK

▶ **With the end of the '80s and the beginning of the '90s came shake-out time for the computer industry, with an industrywide downturn, restructuring, consolidation, and downsizing.**

Shrinking sales and lower-than-expected consumer demand took a toll on the industry. Announcements of layoffs and job cutbacks became common news. In 1989 alone, the computer industry cut more than 40,000 jobs from the U.S. work force. It was more of the same in 1990, 1991, and 1992. The giants posted dismal sales records and responded by restructuring and slashing work forces. In 1991 Apple cut 1,000 jobs; Compaq 1,700. In 1992 IBM announced that it was cutting another 20,000 jobs. And in 1993, Big Blue broke with its long-held tradition and began instituting layoffs for the first time.

There were some bright spots, however, as several smaller companies took the industry by storm. Among them: Sun Microsystems, which rode to success on the strength of work-station demand; AST Research, with high sales of IBM clones; and mail-order companies. But the overriding trend was one of upheaval and competition.

What's Next

▶ **The bywords of the computer industry:** *Tougher, meaner, and leaner.*

In other words, competition will stay hot; companies will continue fighting to maintain customer bases; and the industry will continue to restructure.

Expect the price-cutting warfare that computer and electronics manufacturers have been engaged in for the past year or so to continue. A key reason: the commoditization of the computer and electronics industry. That is, computer systems, parts, semiconductors, and other products on the market appear interchangeable to the consumer—which means that brand names mean less and less and price and value mean more.

In addition to fighting by price slashing, companies will be trying to come up with ways to distinguish their products from the competition. Among the methods they will use: added features, software, and intensive marketing. This will have repercussions where employment is concerned. Product and software development will be highlighted by many companies, which points to opportunities in product development and software engineering. Also, the emphasis on marketing has made marketing and product management staffs crucial employees. This points to opportunities for product managers and marketing experts.

▶ **Competition in worldwide markets will also increase.**

In the past few years, as the U.S. market slowed, attention turned abroad. And even with a resurgence in domestic sales, companies—both hardware and software—will continue to target worldwide markets, especially as the Asian and European markets keep growing.

The U.S. and Japan in particular will be competing head-to-head for the upper hand in the world market, especially Europe. One problem that will continue to hammer at U.S. producers: the low-cost, high-volume capability of many foreign computer companies.

▶ **There will be a rising number of joint agreements between companies and industry consolidation.**

This is a way of boosting competitive edge and gaining access to new technology, R&D funding, and marketing muscle. One notable example: In 1992, Apple teamed up with Sony Corp. to build one of Apple's PowerBook notebook computers.

Joint ventures and consolidation will have a particularly strong impact on software companies because of the high number of small companies (those with one hundred employees or less). While teaming up will give smaller companies access to capital they would otherwise lack, or broaden the products they can offer, those that are unable to link up or gain the backing of a larger company will be unable to keep up. The possible result? A shakeout and eventual industry consolidation.

Joint ventures will also be used to maintain U.S. competitive edge in relation to foreign computer companies. As such (according to the U.S. Department of Commerce Office of Computers and Business Equipment) they may go beyond linkages between computer companies into broader associations between computer companies, telecommunications companies, semiconductor producers, and other parts and subassembly suppliers.

▶ **Also expect an increase in relationships between U.S. and foreign companies, particularly Japanese.**

Joint ventures between U.S. computer companies and their foreign counterparts have been increasing over the past few years.

Tandy has already formed a joint venture with Japan's Matsushita Electric Industrial Co. Ltd. to make notebook and laptop PCs for the U.S. market and has expressed its desire to enter into agreements with other Japanese companies. Similarly, in 1992 Apple and Microsoft announced their intentions to develop relationships with Japanese high-tech firms.

One area that is particularly open to Japan-U.S. ventures is notebook PCs.

▶ **Software: Still one of the hottest industry segments, but facing new challenges.**

Software has been one of the fastest-growing segments of the computer industry, and this explosive growth will continue—with the U.S. government forecasting double-digit growth through the '90s. The hottest areas will be applications tools and system software and utilities. As with other areas of the computer industry, there will be a push into international markets to increase sales.

And as with the rest of the computer industry, software companies will be facing competition, not only from other software companies but also from systems suppliers trying to beef up sales by selling software. The other key factor affecting the software industry is the move toward standards and open systems (like UNIX), which are especially prevalent in Europe. While both the United States and Japan will hold back in backing open systems, in the long term expect use to increase as globalization backs this move.

▶ **The '90s will be the decade in which network computing evolves.**

There will be action both on the LAN front and in the area of larger, enterprise-wide networks. Industry experts see LAN vendors growing as much as 20 to 30% a year. Similarly, there should be growth in wide-area networks (WANs) and integrated network management.

In terms of employment, this points to good opportunities for (IS) (information systems) staffers in industries such as insurance and banking, as well as employees of network companies, such as software engineers and designers.

▶ **A growing trend: offering comprehensive services, including training, setup information, and field support.**

This is part of the overall shift from being a technology-driven industry to being a service-driven one—and is another way that companies worried about commoditization hope to attract and keep customers.

Among the services companies will be offering: system setups, consulting, training, and general support. Even IBM is getting into the act, setting up a nationwide toll-free customer hot line for people needing help and for direct sales.

This trend will open up a range of increased field-support positions, from computer trainers, to customer service experts, to technical support staffers, to technicians skilled in systems setup.

▶ Keep an eye on the growing importance of computer-services companies.

This is partly due to the increasing use of computerized networks by companies. The result? A growing number of companies that work with corporations to help with the network in a range of areas, including data transmission, retrieval, coordination, and general consulting work. This translates into a growth area where jobs are concerned.

EMPLOYMENT OUTLOOK: Improving after the recent shakeouts; long term looks positive.

The recession rocked the computer and electronics industry where employment was concerned. As the Department of Commerce noted in 1993, *Workplace Trends* newsletter reported that the computer industry was hit by layoffs more than defense, aerospace and automobile manufacturers—laying off nearly 192,000 workers from 1988 to only the first months of 1992. And the layoffs continued through 1993.

But the overall picture is beginning to improve. And, even in the worst of times, job opportunities in certain areas in the computer and electronics industry stayed strong—and will remain so.

Best bets? *Software companies*—both large and small. This area has been the hot spot for hiring in the computer industry, and should continue to perform well over the long term. Even during the period of heaviest layoffs, employment in the U.S. software industry rose—up 7% in prepackaged software, 6% in integrated systems design, and 3% in programming services. The software sector accounted for over 400,000 employees in July 1992 (the latest government data available) and should continue to add workers.

Computer services companies specializing in outsourcing (also called facilities management). In 1992 alone, this area added 29,000 new jobs. And it looks like it will stay hot as more companies interested in keeping costs down outsource their data-processing operations to computer-service companies. In particular, keep an eye on smaller and midsize companies that often specialize in specific industries and are beginning to steal business away from giants like EDS or Computer Sciences.

Information services—both at specific information-services companies, such as database providers, and at general corporations with information-service departments. On-line information services are growing in importance, with more companies relying on computerized information sources. As such, there should be job opportunities in this field in all areas, including technical, customer service and sales and marketing.

Also showing some signs of hiring activity: computer-equipment and chip manufacturers.

As for specific career areas, the long-term outlook looks strongest for software designers, programmers (specifically those with business-applications expertise and those with experience programming multimedia systems), data-communications analysts (also called systems analysts or systems integrators) and, more generally, for computer workers specializing in imaging technology—including programmers, technicians and software designers.

JOBS SPOTLIGHT

SOFTWARE ENGINEER: A field that has been hot for the past few years, software engineering remains strong. Salaries cover a wide range—from about $30,000 for entry-level workers up to the mid-$60,000s at the top of the scale.

BEST BETS

Hewlett-Packard Co.
3000 Hanover St.
Palo Alto, CA 94304
415/857-1900

Hewlett-Packard began coming on strong in 1993—especially with the introduction of its new subnotebook, the OmniBook 300, which tapped into the hottest computer sales segment and introduced new technology. And it's a good bet in other ways as well. Well known for its team orientation and "management by walking around" policies, H-P has long had an excellent reputation as a place to work. One example of how highly it is regarded by executives and business experts: In both 1992 and 1993, H-P was voted most admired corporation in the Computers and Office Equipment Industry in Fortune magazine's annual survey. All in all, H-P is a great place to work . . . but, of course, competition for a job here is usually quite tough.

Novell Inc.
122 E. 1700 S.
South Provo, UT 84606
800/453-1267

Novell has been coming on strong—expanding and adding workers—as it steps up new-product development. This, coupled with the recent licensing agreement it signed with IBM allowing IBM to market, service, and support Novell's products, exemplifies the company's aggressive stance in the marketplace. Novell should continue to grow and to offer strong employment opportunities.

TOP COMPUTER COMPANIES

Amdahl Corp.
1250 E. Arques Ave.
Sunnyvale, CA 04088
408/746-6000
(Computer peripherals.)

**American
Management Systems**
1777 N. Kent St.
Arlington, VA 22209
703/841-6000
(Systems integration.)

**American Telephone
& Telegraph Co.**
(human resources)
100 Southgate Dr.
Morristown, NJ 07960
212/387-5400 (HQ)
(Personal computers,
data communications,
software.)

Andersen Consulting
69 W. Washington St.
Chicago, IL 60602
312/580-0069
(Systems integration.)

Apple Computer, Inc.
20525 Mariani Ave.
Cupertino, CA 95014
408/996-1010
(Computers, software,
peripherals.)

Ashton-Tate Corp.
20101 Hamilton Ave.
Torrance, CA 90509
310/329-8000
(Software.)

**ASK Computer
Systems, Inc.**
2440 W. El Camino
Real
Mountain View, CA

94039
415/969-4442
(Software.)

AST Research, Inc.
16215 Alton Pkwy.
Irvine, CA 92713
714/727-4141
(Computers.)

Atari Corp.
1196 Borregas Ave.
Sunnyvale, CA 94088
408/745-2000
(Computers, software.)

Autodesk, Inc.
2320 Marinship Way
Sausalito, CA 94965
415/332-2344
(Software.)

**Automatic Data
Processing, Inc.**
1 ADP Blvd.
Roseland, NJ 07068
201/994-5000
(Computer services.)

**Bell Atlantic Business
Systems Services**
50 E. Swedesford Rd.
Frazer, PA 19355
215/296-6000
(Computer services.)

**Boeing Computer
Services**
2810 160th Ave., SE
Bellevue, WA 98008
206/655-1131
(Computer services.)

**Bolt Beranek and
Newman, Inc.**
70 Fawcett St.
Cambridge, MA 02138
617/873-2000

(Computers, software,
etc.)

**Cadence Design
Systems, Inc.**
555 River Oaks Pkwy.
San Jose, CA 05134
408/943-1234
(Software.)

Cincom Systems, Inc.
2300 Montana Ave.
Cincinnati, OH 45211
513/662-2300
(Software.)

**Commodore
International Ltd.**
1200 Wilson Dr.
West Chester, PA
19380
215/431-9100
(Computers, etc.)

**Compaq Computer
Corp.**
20555 State Hwy.
Houston, TX 77070
713/370-0670
(Computers.)

**Computer Associates
International, Inc.**
1 Computer Associates
Plz.
Islandia, NY
11788-7000
516/342-5224
(Software.)

**Computer Sciences
Corp.**
2100 E. Grand Ave.
El Segundo, CA 90245
310/615-0311
(Systems integration.)

Computer Task Group, Inc.
800 Delaware Ave.
Buffalo, NY 14209
716/882-8000
(Consulting, systems integration, computer services.)

Concurrent Computer Corporation
106 Apple St.
Tinton Falls, NJ 07724
908/758-7000
(Computer systems.)

Conner Peripherals, Inc.
3081 Zanker Rd.
San Jose, CA 95134
408/456-4500
(Disk drives.)

Control Data Corp.
8100 34th Ave. S.
Bloomington, MN 55425
612/853-8100
(Computers, systems integration.)

Convex Computer Corp.
3000 Waterview Pkwy.
Richardson, TX 75080
214/497-4000
(Computers.)

Cray Research, Inc.
655A Lone Oak Dr.
Eagan, MN 55121
612/683-7100
(Mainframes, minisupercomputers, etc.)

Data General Corp.
4400 Computer Dr.
Westborough, MA 01580

508/366-8911
(Computers.)

Dell Computer Corp.
9505 Arboretum Blvd.
Austin, TX 78759
512/338-4400
(Computers.)

Diebold, Incorporated
818 Mulberry Rd., SE
Canton, OH 44711
216/489-4000
(Automated transaction systems, security equipment.)

Digital Equipment Corp.
146 Main St.
Maynard, MA 01754
508/493-5111
(Computers, workstations, peripherals, software, data communications, computer services, maintenance.)

Dun & Bradstreet Software Services, Inc.
299 Park Ave.
New York, NY 10171
212/593-6800
(Software.)

Electronic Data Systems Corp.
7171 Forest Ln.
Dallas, TX 75230
214/661-6000
(Computer services.)

Everex Systems, Inc.
48431 Milmont Dr.
Fremont, CA 94538
510/498-1111
(Peripherals, computer systems.)

General Electric Information Systems
401 N. Washington St.
Rockville, MD 20850
301/340-4000
(Computer services.)

HBO & Co.
301 Perimeter Ctr. N.
Atlanta, GA 30346
404/393-6000
(Software.)

Hewlett-Packard Co.
3000 Hanover St.
Palo Alto, CA 94304
415/857-1501
(Computers, workstations, peripherals.)

IBM—International Business Machines Corp.
Old Orchard Rd.
Armonk, NY 10504
914/765-1900
(Computers, workstations, peripherals, data communications, maintenance, software.)

Information Builders, Inc.
1250 Broadway
New York, NY 10001
212/736-4433
(Software.)

Intel Corp.
3065 Bowers Ave.
Santa Clara, CA 95052
408/765-8080
(Microchips.)

Intergraph Corp.
Rte. 20
Huntsville, AL 35894
205/730-2000

(Workstations and applications.)

Lotus Development Corp.
55 Cambridge Pkwy.
Cambridge, MA 02142
617/577-8500
(Software.)

MAI Systems Corp.
14101 Myford Rd.
Tustin, CA 92680
714/731-5100
(Software.)

Maxtor Corp.
211 River Oaks Pkwy.
San Jose, CA 95134
408/432-1700
(Disk drives.)

McDonnell Douglas Systems Integration Co.
J. S. McDonnell Blvd.
and Airport Rd.
St. Louis, MO 63166
314/232-0232
(Systems integration services.)

Mentor Graphics Corp.
8005 SW Boeckman Rd.
Wilsonville, OR 97070
503/685-7000
(Computer program and software services.)

Micropolis Corp.
21211 Nordhoff St.
Chatsworth, CA 91311
818/709-3300
(Disk drives.)

Microsoft Corp.
1 Microsoft Way
Redmond, WA 98052

206/882-8080
(Software.)

NCR Corp.
1700 S. Patterson Blvd.
Dayton, OH 45479
513/445-5000
(Computers, peripherals.)

Novell, Inc.
122 E. 1700 S.
South Provo, UT 84606
801/429-7000
(Software.)

Oracle Corp.
500 Oracle Pkwy.
Redwood Shores, CA 90465
415/506-7000
(Software.)

Pansophic Systems, Inc.
2400 Cabot Dr.
Lisle, IL 60532
708/505-6000
(Software.)

Pyramid Technology Corp.
1295 Charleston Rd.
Mountain View, CA 94039
415/965-7200
(UNIX systems.)

Quantum Corp.
500 McCarthy Blvd.
Milpitas, CA 95035
408/894-4000
(Disk drives.)

Recognition Equipment, Inc.
2701 E. Grauwyler Rd.
Irving, TX 75061
214/579-6000
(Imaging processing, software.)

Reynolds & Reynolds Company
115 S. Ludlow St.
Dayton, OH 45402
513/443-2000
(Computer systems and system supports.)

SAS Institutes, Inc.
SAS Campus Dr.
Cary, NC 27513
919/677-8000
(Software.)

SCI Systems, Inc.
5000 Technology Dr.
Huntsville, AL 35805
205/882-4800
(Computers.)

Science Applications International Corp.
10260 Campus Pt. Dr.
San Diego, CA 92121
619/546-6000
(Software, computer services.)

Seagate Technology
920 Disc Dr.
Scotts Valley, CA 95066
408/438-6550
(Disk drives, storage devices.)

Shared Medical Systems Corp.
51 Valley Stream Pkwy.
Malvern, PA 19355
215/296-6300
(Computer-based information processing service.)

Silicon Graphics, Inc.
2011 N. Shoreline Blvd.
Mountain View, CA

94039
415/960-1980
(Workstations,
software.)

Software AG of North America, Inc.
11190 Sunrise Valley Dr.
Reston, VA 22091
703/860-5050
(Software.)

Sterling Software, Inc.
11050 White Rock Rd.,
Suite 100
Rancho Cordova, CA 95670
916/635-5535
(Software.)

Storage Technology Corp.
2270 S. 88th St.
Louisville, CO 80028
303/673-5151
(Storage devices.)

Stratus Computer, Inc.
55 Fairbanks Blvd.
Marlboro, MA 01752
508/460-2000
(Computers.)

Sun Microsystems, Inc.
2550 Garcia Ave.
Mountain View, CA 94043
415/960-1300
(Workstations.)

Systematics, Inc.
4001 Rodney Parham Rd.
Little Rock, AR 72212
501/223-5100
(Data processing services, software.)

Tandem Computers, Inc.
19333 Vallco Pkwy.
Cupertino, CA 95014
408/285-6000
(Multiple processor computer systems.)

Tandon Corp.
301 Science Dr.
Moorpark, CA 93021
805/523-0304
(Computers.)

Texas Instruments, Inc.
13500 North Central Expy.
Dallas, TX 75243
214/995-2011
(Computers, software, semiconductors.)

Textronix, Inc.
P.O. Box 500
14150 SW Karl Braun Dr.
Beaverton, OR 97077
503/626-7111
(Computer peripherals, workstations.)

3Com Corp.
3165 Kifer Rd.
Santa Clara, CA 95052
408/562-6400
(Global data networking systems.)

TRW, Inc.—Information Systems and Services
1900 Richmond Rd.
Cleveland, OH 44124
216/291-7000
(Computer services, systems integration.)

The Ultimate Corp.
717 Ridgedale Ave.
E. Hanover, NJ 07936

201/887-9222
(Software, computer systems and services.)

Unisys Corp.
Townshipline and Union Meeting Rds.
Blue Bell, PA 19424
215/986-4011
(Computers, software, data communications, computer services.)

Wang Laboratories, Inc.
1 Industrial Ave.
Lowell, MA 01851
508/459-5000
(Computers, software.)

Western Digital Corp.
2445 McCabe Way
Irvine, CA 92714
714/863-0102
(Storage management, communication and video controller products, intelligent disk drives, core logic.)

Word Perfect Corp.
1555 N. Technology Way
Orem, UT 84057
801/225-5000
(Software.)

Wyse Technology
3471 N. First St.
San Jose, CA 95134
408/433-1000
(Computers, terminals, workstations.)

Xerox Corp.
800 Long Ridge Rd.
Stamford, CT 06904
203/968-3000
(Workstations, software, etc.)

TOP ELECTRONICS AND PRECISION INSTRUMENTS COMPANIES

(For related companies, also see "Top Aerospace Companies," page 240.)

Advanced Micro Devices, Inc.
901 Thompson Pl.
Sunnyvale, CA 94086
408/732-2400

Ametek, Inc.
Station Sq. Two
Paoli, PA 19301
215/647-2121

AMP, Inc.
470 Friendship Rd.
Harrisburg, PA 17111
717/564-0100

Analog Devices
1 Technology Way
Norwood, MA 02062
617/329-4700

Applied Magnetics Corp.
75 Robin Hill Rd.
Goleta, CA 93117
805/683-5353

Avnet, Inc.
80 Cutter Mill Rd.
Great Neck, NY 11021
516/466-7000

AVX Corp.
750 Lexington Ave.
New York, NY 10022
212/935-6363

Beckman Instruments, Inc.
2500 Harbor Blvd.
Fullerton, CA 92634
714/871-4848

Chips & Technologies, Inc.
3050 Zenker Rd.
San Jose, CA 95134
408/434-0600

Cypress Semiconductor Corp.
3901 N. First St.
San Jose, CA 95134
408/943-2600

Dynatech Corp.
3 New England Executive Pk.
Burlington, MA 01803
617/272-6100

Eastman Kodak Co.
343 State St.
Rochester, NY 14650
716/724-4000

EG&G, Inc.
45 William St.
Wellesley, MA 02181
617/237-5100

Fasco Industries, Inc.
1 Westminster Pl.
Lake Forest, IL 60045
708-295-7600

Fujitsu Microelectronics, Inc.
3545 N. First St.
San Jose, CA 95134
408/922-9000

Imo Industries, Inc.
3450 Princeton Pike
Lawrenceville, NJ 08648
609/896-7600

Intel Corp.
3065 Bowers Ave.
Santa Clara, CA 95054
408/765-8080

Johnson Controls, Inc.
5757 N. Green Bay Ave.
Milwaukee, WI 53209
414/228-1200

LSI Logic Corp.
1551 McCarthy Blvd.
Milpitas, CA 95035
408/433-8000

M/A-Com, Inc.
7 New England Executive Pk.
Burlington, MA 01803
617/272-9600

Memc Electronic Materials, Inc.
501 Pearl Old Hwy.
O'Fallon, MO 63376
314/279-5000

Millipore Corp.
80 Ashby Rd.
Bedford, MA 01730
617/275-9200

Molex, Inc.
2222 Wellington Ct.
Lisle, IL 60532
708/969-4550

Motorola, Inc.
1303 E. Algonquin Rd.
Schaumburg, IL 60196
708/576-5000

National Semiconductor Corp.
2900 Semiconductor Dr.
Santa Clara, CA 95052
408/721-5000

Perkin-Elmer Corp.
761 Main Ave.
Norwalk, CT 06859
203/762-1000

Polaroid Corp.
549 Technology Sq.
Cambridge, MA 02139
617/577-2000

Raychem Corp.
300 Constitution Dr.
Menlo Park, CA 94025
415/361-3333

Sprague Technologies, Inc.
4 Stamford Forum
Stamford, CT 06903
203/964-8600

Tektronix, Inc.
14150 SW Karl Braun Dr.
Beaverton, OR 97077
503/627-7111

Thermo Electron Corp.
81 Wyman St.
Waltham, MA 02254
617/622-1000

Thomas & Betts Corp.
1001 Frontier Rd.
Bridgewater, NJ 08807
908/685-1600

Varian Associates
3050 Hansen Way
Palo Alto, CA 94301
415/493-4000

Vishay Intertechnology, Inc.
63 Lincoln Hwy.
Malvern, PA 19355
215/644-1300

VLSI Technology, Inc.
1109 McKay Dr.
San Jose, CA 95131
408/434-3000

Western Digital Corp.
2445 McCabe Way
Irvine, CA 92714
714/863-0102

WHERE TO GO FOR MORE INFORMATION

(For more information sources related to the computers/electronics industry, see "Engineers," page 41; "Technical Careers," page 186; "Aerospace," page 236; and "Telecommunications," page 459.)

COMPUTER/ELECTRONICS INDUSTRY ASSOCIATIONS

American Electronics Association
P.O. Box 54990
Santa Clara, CA 95056
408/987-4200

Association for Computing Machinery
11 West 42nd St., 3rd Fl.
New York, NY 10036
212/869-7400
(Runs résumé databank for members.)

Computer and Automated Systems Association of SME
1 SME Dr.
Dearborn, MI 48128
313/271-1500

Computer & Business Equipment Manufacturers Association
311 First St., NW
Washington, DC 20001
202/737-8888

Computer & Communications Industry Association
666 11th St., NW
Washington, DC 20001
202/783-0070

Computer Dealers and Lessors Association
1212 Potomac St., NW
Washington, DC 20007
202/333-0102

Electronics Industries Association
2001 I St., NW
Washington, DC 20006
202/457-4900

IEEE Computer Society
1730 Massachusetts Ave., NW
Washington, DC 20036
202/371-0101

Information Industry Association
555 New Jersey Ave., NW
Washington, DC 20001
202/639-8262

Information Technology Association of America
1616 N. Ft. Myer Dr.,
Suite 1300
Arlington, VA 22209
703/522-5055

Robotics International of SME
P.O. Box 930

1 SME Dr.
Dearborn, MI 48121
313/271-1500

Semiconductor Equipment and Material Institute
805 E. Middlefield Rd.
Mountain View, CA

94043
415/764-5111

Semiconductor Industry Association
4300 Stevens Creek Blvd.,
Suite 271
San Jose, CA 95129
408/246-2711

COMPUTERS/ELECTRONICS INDUSTRY DIRECTORIES

Directory of Public High Technology Corporations
American Investor, Inc.
311 Bainbridge St.
Philadelphia, PA 19147
215/925-2761

Directory of Top Computer Executives
Applied Computer Research
P.O. Box 9280
Phoenix, AZ 85068
602/995-5929

Who's Who in Electronics Regional Source Directory
2057 Aurora Rd.
Twinsburg, OH 44087
216/425-9000
800/888-5900

COMPUTERS/ELECTRONICS INDUSTRY PERIODICALS

Computer Systems News
600 Community Dr.
Manhasset, NY 11030
516/562-5000
(Weekly tabloid for systems personnel, engineers, manufacturers, etc.)

Computer World
375 Cochituate Rd.
Framingham, MA 01701
617/879-0700
(Weekly tabloid covering all phases of the computer industry.)

Corporate Computing
1 Park Ave.
New York, NY 10016
(Monthly magazine sent to corporate computer executives.)

Data Communications
1221 Ave. of the Americas
New York, NY 10020
212/512-3139
(Monthly magazine for professionals involved in computer network integration and implementation.)

Datamation
875 Third Ave.
New York, NY 10022
212/605-0400
(Semimonthly magazine aimed at IS managers, manufacturers, etc. Annual *Datamation 100* issue lists the top companies in the field and includes addresses as well as company profiles. This may be useful in a résumé mailing campaign.)

Digital News
33 West St.
Boston, MA 02111
617/482-8470
(Biweekly publication for hardware and software manufacturers, dealers, retailers, etc.)

ECN Electronic Component News
Chilton Way
Radnor, PA 19089
215/964-4347
(Monthly publication for design engineers,

engineering managers, etc.)

EDN
275 Washington St.
Newton, MA 02158
617/964-3030
(Biweekly for electronics engineers, product designers, systems designers, etc.)

Electronic Business
275 Washington St.
Newton, MA 02158
617/964-3030
(Semimonthly magazine covering the computer and electronics industry. Annual *Electronic Business 200* issue runs down the top companies in the industry.)

Electronic Design
611 Rte 64 W.
Hasbrouck Heights, NJ 07604
(Biweekly magazine for engineers and design managers.)

Electronic Engineering Times
600 Community Dr.
Manhasset, NY 11030
516/562-5000
(Weekly publication aimed at engineers, managers, supervisors, and marketing and research staffers.)

Electronic News
825 Seventh Ave.
New York, NY 10019
212/887-8323
(Weekly newspaper for computer/electronics industry professionals, including engineers and sales and marketing managers.)

Infoworld
1600 Marsh Rd.
Menlo Park, CA 94025
415/328-4602
(Weekly tabloid covering all aspects of the computer industry; aimed at a wide range of people, including manufacturers, designers, programmers, and students. Often includes helpful articles on job-hunting, areas that are hot, etc. Good help-wanted section.)

CONGLOMERATES

INDUSTRY OUTLOOK: Track individual companies to see strengths and weaknesses.

Because conglomerates are holding companies, with interests in four or more industries, each company faces a different outlook, completely dependent on the health of the different industries it is involved in and the management of the units making up the company. In other words, there is no one track that conglomerates automatically follow. For more specific forecasts, see the various industry chapters to find outlooks and trends for the different areas of business held by a conglomerate.

A LOOK BACK

▶ **The past years were changeable ones for most conglomerates as the economy went up—then down.**

As with many other industries, the '80s brought refocusing, restructuring, and change to conglomerates. The most important change: The number of conglomerates continued shrinking. Some companies (such as Insilco, Amfac, and Pullman) fell victim to the mergers-and-acquisition fever that swept the country. Others refocused on one area or a group of related areas instead of maintaining holdings in a broad range of industries. The prime example: Gulf & Western, long the epitome of a traditional U.S. conglomerate, shed its noncommunications holdings to become Paramount Communications.

The remaining conglomerates were then hit by the recession. This further increased the trend toward refocusing corporate aims to center around a single industry or group of related industries. In addition, some larger conglomerates began to look for suitors for unprofitable subsidiaries. For example, in 1992 LTV put its aerospace and missile divisions up for sale.

WHAT'S NEXT

▶ **The general trend affecting conglomerates: Like the U.S. economy as a whole, expect to see continued cost cutting, streamlining, and close attention to the bottom line.**

As the economy continues its recovery, conglomerates will remain somewhat cautious, careful to avoid the excesses of the '80s. Expansion will be balanced by consolidation; conglomerates will avoid taking on the heavy debt that characterized the "go-go" years in the past.

▶ **Single-industry or related-industry holding companies will continue to replace the traditional conglomerates.**

The years ahead should bring more of the same activity that marked the past few. The days of the old-fashioned conglomerate with holdings in a range of industries appear to be over for the time being. Instead, it looks like there will be an increase in the number of industry-specific conglomerates, like Paramount Communications and other communications giants.

Along these lines, expect to see sell-offs of subsidiaries unrelated to core businesses, consolidation activity, and a refocusing of business among some of the giants.

▶ **As for the conglomerates that remain, their overall performance will depend on the strengths and weaknesses of their subsidiaries.**

It's the obvious rule of thumb: A conglomerate is as strong or as weak as the sum total of its parts. Certain conglomerates may be vulnerable in the short term if their subsidiaries are involved in slumping or excessively competitive industries.

EMPLOYMENT OUTLOOK: Varies according to the specific company and subsidiaries.

Employment opportunities at conglomerates are directly related to the particular industries the company is involved in. For forecasts, then, check the specific industry section that correlates with the company or subsidiary that interests you. Also check the Occupations section, such as Managers (page 119) or Sales and Marketing Professionals (page 139).

BEST BETS

General Electric
3133 Easton Turnpike
Fairfield, CT 06431
203/373-2211

One of the biggest and the best, General Electric is consistently a best bet for employment. Among the reasons? Its extensive training programs and attention to continued employee development. Entry-level employees get immediate attention and intensive training, and it continues all the way up the ladder to upper-level seminars for managers. Another strong point for GE is its recent push for innovation. Even though the company has a reputation for being traditional, its managers are open to flexible working methods, like team manufacturing. Even better, GE isn't forcing the issue. It lets each plant decide what methods it wants to use.

3M (Minnesota Mining & Manufacturing)
3M Center
St. Paul, MN 55144
612/733-1110

3M is known as a company that believes in career employees. As such, it is big on promoting from within. And to help new employees, it has developed a mentor program, in which new employees can go to a mentor who will help them, answer work-related questions, and so forth. Another 3M trait: rewarding employees for jobs well done, with everything from parties to pizza to bonuses. This type of attention to employees is one of the reasons 3M was chosen (in a 1990 *Fortune* magazine survey) one of the three most admired companies in the United States in terms of its ability to attract, develop and keep talented people. The company has long had a reputation for providing job security for workers and a history of maintaining a no-layoff policy even in tough times. The downside? Lagging sales have been plaguing the industry giant. If sales don't increase, 3M may be forced to trim its work force. However, in line with its corporate policy, it will try to avoid layoffs and rely instead on early retirement and attrition. The bottom line? While hiring activity might not be hot, this is a great bet if you can land a job here.

TOP CONGLOMERATES

(Also see company listings in other industries.)

Alco Standard Corporation
P.O. Box 834
Valley Forge, PA 19482
215/296-8000

Allied-Signal, Inc.
Columbia Rd.
Morristown, NJ 07962
201/455-2000

Delaware North Cos.
438 Main St.
Buffalo, NY 14202
716/858-5000

Dial Corp.
Dial Tower
Phoenix, AZ 85077
602/207-4000

Figgie International, Inc.
4420 Sherwin Rd.
Willoughby, OH 44094
216/953-2700

Fuqua Industries, Inc.
4900 Georgia-Pacific Ctr.
Atlanta, GA 30303
404/658-9000

General Cinema Corp.
27 Boylston St.
Newton, MA 02167
617/232-8200

General Electric Co.
3135 Easton Tpke.
Fairfield, CT 06431
203/373-2211

Itel Corp.
2 N. Riverside Plz.
Chicago, IL 60606
312/902-1515

ITT Corp.
1330 Ave. of the Americas
New York, NY 10019
212/258-1000

MacAndrews & Forbes Holdings
36 E. 63rd St.
New York, NY 10021
212/688-9000

National Intergroup, Inc.
20 Stanwix St.
Pittsburgh, PA 15222
412/394-4100

Ogden Corporation
2 Pennsylvania Plz.
New York, NY 10121
212/868-6100

The Penn Central Corp.
1 E. Fourth St.
Cleveland, OH 45202
513/579-6600

Philip Morris Cos., Inc.
120 Park Ave.
New York, NY 10017
212/880-5000

Pittway Corp.
333 Skokie Blvd.
Northbrook, IL 60065
708/498-1260

Premark International, Inc.
1717 Deerfield Rd.

Deerfield, IL 60015
708/405-6000

Sequa Corp.
200 Park Ave.
New York, NY 10166
212/986-5500

Tenneco, Inc.
Tenneco Bldg.
Houston, TX 77002
713/757-2131

TRW, Inc.
1900 Richmond Rd.
Cleveland, OH 44124
216/291-7000

Valhi Group, Inc.
5430 LBJ Fwy., Suite 1700
Dallas TX 75240
214/233-1700

Whitman Corp.
3501 Algonquin Rd.
Rolling Meadows, IL 6008
708/818-5000

Wickes Cos., Inc.
3340 Ocean Park Blvd.
Santa Monica, CA 90405
213/452-0161

CONSUMER PRODUCTS

INDUSTRY OUTLOOK: Extremely competitive.

Package goods: This area will still be affected by the 1993 consumer move away from brand names. As such, expect hot competition for market share, and a rush to develop new products to meet changing consumer needs. Over the long term: Keep a lookout for an increase in mergers and acquisitions as companies try to increase market share the least expensive way—by taking over other companies instead of investing in developing and marketing new products.

Cosmetics: Expect long-term growth, an increase in mergers and acquisitions, and tighter competition in foreign markets. In addition, as a result of changing consumer demand and increased environmental awareness, cosmetics companies will be pumping more into R&D to come up with new products that are environmentally safe and that meet the needs of specific consumer niches. Hot areas: Products aimed at aging baby boomers, minorities.

Appliance manufacturers: This sector will rebound with the economy. Positive trends that point to a bright long-term outlook? Expected increases in home building and buying, an aging population, a high level of two-income families, and increases in spending.

A LOOK BACK

▶ **The '80s brought merger-and-acquisition fever to the consumer products industry; the first years of the '90s brought hot competition—and a sales lag due to the recession.**

The '80s was a changeable decade, filled with reshufflings, reconsolidation, restructuring, and rapid events. The Big 5 appliance manufacturers (General Electric, Whirlpool, White/Electrolux, Maytag, and Raytheon) remained intact, but many of their smaller competitors were swallowed up.

Package-goods companies were also hit by merger activity. One of the most noteworthy mergers was Procter & Gamble's takeover of Noxell, followed in the early '90s by its purchase of Max Factor. The outcome of this activity? The industry was getting smaller and the giants were getting larger.

The '90s opened with aggressive repositionings, as companies sought to find footing in the restructured industry. Then came the recession and with it a decline in sales—and increased competition for the shrinking market.

WHAT'S NEXT

▶ **Cutthroat competition will continue to have a marked effect on all areas of the consumer products industry.**

The days of hot competition are far from over. One problem that will be concerning both package goods and consumer electronics manufacturers is the erosion of brand loyalty. The past few years of stiff competition have made consumers more price conscious and less inclined to stick with the same brands. Expect the next few years to bring a continuation of price wars, promotional activity, and new-product introduction.

Where the employment picture is concerned, this competition should increase opportunities in product development, marketing, and product management.

▶ **Consolidation—of domestic and foreign companies—will be changing the face of the industry.**

It's been happening for several years: Companies merge or take one another over. One chief reason: competition. By merging with or acquiring another company, a company can expand market reach, add products, and increase global market share. This activity will continue over the long term, with larger companies continuing to dominate the industry.

▶ **Similarly, keep an eye out for consolidation *within* companies.**

Industry giant Procter & Gamble started the trend toward consolidation and streamlining. The recession made it look more attractive to other companies, and it looks like this trend will keep going strong. Specifically, more companies will be setting up smaller teams within their operations and focusing on working closely with their retail customers. These teams will be made up of specialists from different areas, including logistics, finance, information, and sales. In many cases, salespeople will have responsibility for an entire sector or category, as opposed to just one or two brands.

Problems: Some manufacturers will be relying increasingly on distributors, wholesalers, and retailers for sales and marketing while they concentrate on production. Moverover, in an effort to streamline and make systems more efficient for retailers, more manufacturers may begin to use electronic ordering systems—which may result in cuts in sales jobs. But in the long term, this trend points to opportunities in broad-based product management, customer support, and logistics.

▶ **A long-term trend that will keep growing: industry globalization.**

In some cases, this is one of the by-products of industry consolidation. The new, larger companies are better able to gain foreign market share. In addition, an increase in the number of joint-venture agreements between U.S. and foreign companies is aiding the internationalization of the consumer products industry.

More companies will be setting up international marketing networks to penetrate different parts of the world. U.S. companies are particularly interested in penetrating Eastern Europe, the Pacific Rim, and Latin America.

There's a flip side to this as well: Foreign companies, particularly European ones, are entering into joint ventures with U.S. companies to gain a toehold in the American marketplace. The long-term bottom line? By the year 2000, expect to see multinational giants dominate the worldwide consumer products industry.

In general, this attention to world markets points to employment opportunities for people with international experience, especially product managers and international marketing experts.

▶ **Keep an eye on efforts to target and reach niche markets.**

It's one way of reaching new customers and getting a foothold in a new market. More companies will be targeting specific consumer sectors—such as blacks, Hispanics, and Asians—not only by introducing advertising and promotion directly aimed at these groups but also by introducing new products developed especially for them.

Cosmetics and health and beauty aids manufacturers have already made inroads in this area. Product lines such as Estee Lauder's Prescriptives All Skins and Maybelline's Shades of You are selling strong. Expect more companies to enter this field with complete lines. This should translate into employment opportunities both in new product development and sales and marketing.

▶ **Watch for more industry developments and changes due to environmental issues.**

Environmental issues will continue to have a strong impact on consumer products companies. Soap and detergent manufacturers will continue to come out with products that are environmentally sound—such as concentrated detergents, products with less packaging, and natural (as opposed to petrochemical-based) soaps and detergents. The R&D area will heat up as tougher environmental regulations are instituted and manufacturers look for new ways to produce products that conform to the new laws. This means opportunities for scientists and chemical engineers.

Appliance manufacturers will also be developing new products in response to concerns about environmental and health issues—such as chlorofluorocarbons (CFCs) and their impact on the ozone layer, electromagnetic fields (EMFs) and their effects on health, and appliance disposal and recycling. The result: the necessity for more R&D. In certain ways, concerns about the environment will have a positive impact on the appliance industry. With increased environmental awareness and new legislation, watch for refrigerator and air-conditioner companies to reap the rewards. Why? To combat a depleted ozone layer, consumers and industries will have to replace their existing appliances for new, environment-friendly ones.

EMPLOYMENT OUTLOOK: Fair to good in the long term.

The consumer products industry, while competitive, is headed for a fairly stable future. A key area for opportunities is sales and marketing. As competition stays hot, this area is of vital importance. Appliance manufacturers should be in for stable growth. This will translate into fairly stable employment opportunities. Best areas—new-product development, purchasing.

On the technical side, logistics engineers will be in demand. A key reason: "Just-in-time" manufacturing—whereby factory orders are received at the time they are needed, rather than weeks or months in advance—is making the logistics of factory work a more vital concern. People with strong organizational and computer skills should do well.

JOBS SPOTLIGHT

PRODUCT MANAGERS: The backbone of most consumer products companies and as such always needed. Lately, with more brands on the shelves competing head to head, this area is becoming more visible—and more competitive. Salaries generally begin in the low $40s and can reach well over $90,000, with salaries in the six-figure range not uncommon at some of the larger companies.

CATEGORY MANAGERS: The newest twist on product and brand managers, they are becoming more common—and, as competition grows, more in demand. Category managers (also called trademark managers) are responsible for an entire category of products (such as soaps or laundry detergents) as opposed to a specific brand. They create long-term marketing plans for that category and work closely with retailers. Salaries are similar to those paid to product managers, ranging from the low $40s up to the mid-six figures, depending on experience, category, and company.

BEST BETS

Elizabeth Arden
1345 Ave. of the Americas
New York, NY 10105
212/261-1000

This prestige cosmetics manufacturer is coming on strong after years of going downhill. According to *Fortune* magazine, since 1989 sales have grown about 25% a year, and it looks like this strong performance will continue. Since the company was taken over by Unilever, it has been coming up with best-selling products, like its Ceramide Time Complex Capsules. One problem: if rumors regarding Unilever's plan to sell off the division turn out to be true, Arden will be in for some changes and shakeouts. Even so, this is a good company to keep an eye on.

Procter & Gamble
1 P&G Plaza
Cincinnati, OH 45202
513/983-1100

The ubiquitous package goods company, Procter & Gamble has been making a number of changes to face the 90s—including partnerships with retailers, a revamped brand management system, and streamlined product development. And, on the employment side, it announced plans to reduce its work force by 12% within four years. However, especially at the entry levels, P&G is still a good bet. Even during the recession, it continued college recruitment for its well-known training programs. Competition, as always, is high for a spot at P&G, but if you've got the right combination of skills, it's a good spot for the future.

TOP CONSUMER PRODUCTS COMPANIES
(PERSONAL PRODUCTS, COSMETICS, SOAP AND DETERGENTS, ETC.)

Alberto-Culver Co.
2525 Armitage Ave.
Melrose Park, IL 60160
708/450-3000

Avon Products, Inc.
9 W. 57th St.
New York, NY 10019
212/546-6015

Carter Wallace, Inc.
1345 Ave. of the
Americas
New York, NY 10105
212/339-5168

**Church & Dwight
Co., Inc.**
469 N. Harrison St.
Princeton, NJ
08543-5297
609/683-5900

Clairol, Inc.
345 Park Ave.
New York, NY 10154
212/546-5000

Clorox Co.
1221 Broadway
Oakland, CA 94612
510/271-7000

Colgate-Palmolive Co.
300 Park Ave.
New York, NY 10022
212/310-2000

Cosmair, Inc.
30 Terminal Ave.
Clark, NJ 07066
908/382-7000

Helene Curtis, Inc.
325 N. Wells St.
Chicago, IL 60610
312/661-0222

Dial Corp.
Dial Tower
Phoenix, AZ 85077
602/207-4000

Estée Lauder, Inc.
767 Fifth Ave.
New York, NY 10153
212/572-4200

Gillette Co.
Prudential Tower Bldg.
Boston, MA 02199
617/421-7000

**International Flavors
& Fragrances**
521 W. 57th St.
New York, NY 10019
212/765-5500

Andrew Jergens Co.
2535 Spring Grove
Ave.
Cincinnati, OH 45214
513/421-1400

Johnson & Johnson
1 Johnson & Johnson
Plz.
New Brunswick, NJ
08933
908/524-0400

S.C. Johnson Wax
1525 Howe St.
Racine, WI 53403
414/631-2000

**Mary Kay Cosmetics,
Inc.**
8787 Stemmons Fwy.
Dallas, TX 75247
214/630-8787

Maybelline Co.
3030 Jackson Ave.
Memphis, TN 38112
901/320-2011

Mennen Co.
Hanover Ave.
Morristown, NJ 07960
201/631-9000

NCH Corp.
2727 Chemsearch Blvd.
Irving, TX 75062
214/438-0211

Noxell Corp.
11050 York Rd.
Hunt Valley, MD

21030
301/785-7300

Proctor & Gamble Co.
1 Procter & Gamble Plz.
Cincinnati, OH 45202
513/983-1100

Revlon, Inc.
767 Fifth Ave.
New York, NY 10153
212/572-5000

Tambrands
777 Westchester Ave.
White Plains, NY

10604
914/696-6000

Unilever US, Inc.
390 Park Ave.
New York, NY 10022
212/888-1260

TOP APPLIANCE/CONSUMER ELECTRONICS COMPANIES

Amana Refrigeration, Inc.
Main St.
Amana, IA 52203
319/622-5511

Bissell, Inc.
2345 Walker Rd., NW
Grand Rapids, MI 49504
616/453-4451

Conair Corp.
150 Milford Rd.
Hightstown, NJ 08520
908/426-1300

Electrolux Corp.
2300 Windy Ridge Pkwy.
Marietta, GA 30067
404/933-1000

Matsushita Electronic Corporation of America
1 Panasonic Way
Secaucus, NJ 07084
201/348-7000

Maytag Corp.
1 Dependability Sq.
Newton, IA 50208
515/792-8000

North American Philips Corp.
100 E. 42nd St.

New York, NY 10017
212/850-5000

Philips Consumer Electronics
(subs. of North American Philips)
1 Philips Dr.
Knoxville, TN 37914
615/521-4316

Remington Products, Inc.
60 Main St.
Bridgeport, CT 06602
203/367-4400

Royal Appliance Manufacturing
650 Alpha Dr.
Cleveland, OH 44143
216/449-6150

Scott & Fetzer Company
28800 Clemens Rd.
Cleveland, OH 44145
216/892-3000

Sharp Electronics Corp.
Sharp Plz.
P.O. Box 650
Mahwah, NJ 07430
201/529-8200

Sony Corp. of America
1 Sony Dr.
Park Ridge, NJ 07656
201/930-1000

SSMC, Inc.
200 Metroplex Dr.
Edison, NJ 08817
908/287-0707

Sunbeam Corp.
2 Oliver Plz.
Pittsburgh, PA 15230
412/562-4000

Thomson Consumer Electronics
600 N. Sherman Dr.
Indianapolis, IN 46201
317/267-5000

Toshiba America, Inc.
375 Park Ave., Suite 1705
New York, NY 10152
212/308-2040

Whirlpool Corp.
2000 M63 N.
Benton Harbor, MI 49022
616/923-5000

White Consolidated Industries, Inc.
11770 Berea Rd.

Cleveland, OH 44111
216/252-3700

Zenith Electronics Corp.
1000 N. Milwaukee

Ave.
Glenview, IL 60025
708/391-7000

WHERE TO GO FOR MORE INFORMATION

CONSUMER PRODUCTS INDUSTRY ASSOCIATIONS

Association of Home Appliance Manufacturers
20 N. Wacker Dr.
Chicago, IL 60606
312/984-5800

Cosmetic Toiletry and Fragrance Association
1101 17th St., NW,
Suite 300
Washington, DC 20006

Independent Cosmetic Manufacturers and Distributors
1230 W. Northwest

Hwy.
Palatine, IL 60067
708/991-4499

Electronic Industries Association
2001 Pennsylvania
Ave., NW
Washington, DC
20006-1813
202/457-4900

National Housewares Manufacturers Association
6400 Shafer Ct., Suite
650

Rosemont, IL 60018
708/292-4200

Soap and Detergent Association
475 Park Ave. S.
New York, NY 10016
212/725-1262

Society of Cosmetic Chemists
1995 Broadway, Suite
1701
New York, NY 10023
212/874-0600
(Offers job placement
service to members.)

CONSUMER PRODUCTS INDUSTRY DIRECTORIES

Appliance Manufacturer Annual Directory
Corcoran
Communications, Inc.
29100 Aurora Rd.,
Suite 310
Solon, OH 44139
216/349-3060

Electronic Market Data Book
Electronic Industries
Association

2001 Pennsylvania
Ave., NW
Washington, DC
20006-1813
202/457-4900

Household and Personal Products Industry Buyers Guide
Rodman Publishing
Corp.
26 Lake St.
Ramsey, NJ 07446
201/825-2552

Soap Blue Book
MacNair-Dorland Co.
101 W. 31st St.
New York, NY 10001
212/279-4457

Soap/Cosmetics/Chemical Specialties Blue Book
MacNair-Dorland Co.
101 W. 31st St.
New York, NY 10001
212/279-4457

CONSUMER PRODUCTS INDUSTRY MAGAZINES

Appliance
Dana Chase
Publications
1110 Jorie Blvd.
Oak Brook, IL 60522
708/990-3484

*Appliance
Manufacturer*
Corcoran
Communications, Inc.
29100 Aurora Rd.,
Suite 310
Solon, OH 44139
216/349-3060

*Cosmetic Insiders
Report*
Edgell Communications
7500 Old Oak Blvd.
Cleveland, OH 44130
216/243-8100

*Drug & Cosmetic
Industry*
Edgell Communications

7500 Old Oak Blvd.
Cleveland, OH 44130
216/243-8100

*Household and
Personal Products
Industry*
Box 555
Ramsey, NJ 07446
201/825-2552
(Monthly magazine
covering the soap,
detergent, cosmetics,
toiletries, and fragrance
industries. Good
help-wanted section.)

Housewares
Harcourt Brace
Jovanovich
1 E. First St.
Duluth, MN 55802
714/231-6616

*Product Design and
Development*
Chilton Book Co.
Chilton Way
Radnor, PA 19089
800/345-1214
215/964-4000

*Soap/Cosmetics/Chemical
Specialties*
445 Broad Hollow Rd.
Melville, NY 11747
516/845-2700
(Monthly magazine for
professionals involved
in all aspects of the
soap, cosmetics, and
chemicals
industry—including
production,
management,
formulation,
purchasing, marketing,
and packaging.)

ENERGY

INDUSTRY OUTLOOK: Varied.

Three main factors will be affecting the overall energy industry: foreign oil, the amount of domestic exploration, and the environment. More specific outlooks for each sector:

Coal: Probable long-term steady growth ahead—but only if there are no changes in current laws or regulations. If, however, environmental legislation cuts back on coal usage, expansion plans or costs, the industry will pay the price.

Natural Gas: A bright long-term outlook, with long-term growth in this industry sector expected to be higher than other energy sources. Key reasons: Environmental concerns and the desire to rely less on foreign oil.

Oil: As always, the outlook for oil depends upon OPEC actions and world crude-oil production. Probable long-term scenario? Slow growth. As for refiners, expect industry restructuring, including plant modifications and other changes, especially in reaction to environmental regulations.

A LOOK BACK

▶ A changeable few years for the oil industry.

The past few years have been volatile ones. In the late '80s, as a result of the combined effect of slow growth in demand, a decline in drilling and exploration, and excess production capacity, the petroleum industry went through a flurry of mergers, acquisitions, and reshuffling. The industry consolidated: The number of operating rigs dropped, and about 40% of the independent companies in the United States closed. The one bright area was "downstream" operations, or refining and marketing, which profited from the low prices for crude oil.

But the '90s brought about a change in focus. Refining and marketing slumped, petrochemicals declined, and the industry regrouped. Crude prices rose again and oil companies began putting money into exploration—chiefly targeting overseas areas, especially Canada. Then came the recession, and with it a drop in oil consumption. This, combined with the successful push for world market share by OPEC nations, brought about a drop in the price of crude oil—and a bleak beginning to the '90s.

▶ Natural gas went through a series of disappointing years.

The key problem: Too much gas and not enough demand, which has been termed the "natural gas bubble." For a short time, the bubble burst—in a good way.

Demand increased due to environmental concerns and a resurgence in manufacturing activity. But the turnaround was short lived, and the industry sector began sputtering again.

▶ Coal, too, had a disappointing performance.

The combination of lower-cost foreign competitors, declining exports, falling prices, and costly environmental standards hammered coal producers in the '80s.

Matters got worse in the early '90s, as the recession cut into electric power consumption. Since electric utilities are the prime buyers of coal, this forced coal prices downward. The situation improved slightly in 1992.

WHAT'S NEXT

▶ Keep a closer eye than usual on: OPEC production of oil.

It's a rule of thumb: OPEC actions directly affect the outlook for U.S. oil producers. But with the return of Kuwaiti and Iraqi facilities on line, there may be more of an impact than usual. The concern? Over the next three years or so, this added capacity might ultimately lead to overproduction. In the past, OPEC members were bound by mandatory production quotas. But now these quotas are voluntary, so overproduction can occur. If oil production exceeds world demand, the price of crude drops—and oil companies suffer. In light of this, OPEC production will be making the energy industry even more uncertain than usual.

▶ Expect to see a continuing drop in domestic crude petroleum production.

This has been happening for the past few years and should continue. Companies are doing two things: buying proven reserves (as opposed to drilling); and shifting their exploration and development to other areas, such as Canada and Mexico. Among the reasons: low crude and gas prices have reduced the profitability of drilling and exploration; governmental limits have been placed on domestic offshore exploration and drilling due to environmental concerns; there is a better chance of locating a substantial reserve overseas; operating costs are lower when production of a large reserve is kept in one place. Areas that should see heavier exploration activity in the future: Latin America, the Pacific Basin.

The drop in drilling will result in a short-term drop in oil-field services employment and will bring about a period of volatility in oil-field services companies. Expect to see more companies engage in asset sell-offs, smaller independents driven out of business, and an increase in the number of mergers between companies. The ultimate outcome? A more consolidated industry.

▶ One way to keep domestic production up is through technological breakthroughs and increased usage of high-tech methods.

New methods of exploration and extraction are vital to companies trying to continue domestic oil and gas production. The energy industry is relying more on high-tech exploration to locate oil in U.S. reserves. Among the new methods and equipment: computer software that simulates oil-fields; specially designed high-speed computers and seismic gauges to locate oil; horizontal drilling (as opposed to standard vertical drilling), which reaches a much larger percentage of a reservoir. These new methods will be used overseas as well.

An employment note: The increased importance of technological developments and equipment may point to a growing demand in the industry for software and research engineers.

▶ **Over the long term, natural gas will see a resurgence.**

One key reason: Environmental concerns. Natural gas has so-called clean fuel characteristics. Sulfur, which helps cause acid rain, can be removed from it easily, and it releases fewer toxic emissions like sulfur dioxide (which contributes to the greenhouse effect) than do either coal or oil.

Another reason: The U.S. and other countries are trying to break away from heavy consumption of oil from OPEC nations because of volatile prices. At the same time, U.S. dependence on foreign oil has been growing. In 1990 24% of the total amount of oil consumed in the U.S. was from a foreign source. The government projects that this percentage will rise by 16% over the next decade—up to 40%. The best way to break this dependence is to increase the use of natural gas.

Once the current surplus of natural gas is depleted, there will be more action in this area.

▶ **Environmental legislation will continue to change much of the energy industry—particularly oil refining and coal.**

The entire energy industry will feel the impact of environmental concerns and legislation such as the Clean Air Act, but these two sectors will be particularly affected.

Oil refiners will be forced to spend money on reconfiguring their refineries to produce the new, cleaner types of gasoline, in line with government regulations. This may translate into problems for smaller companies with simpler refineries and financial resources. Upgrading may be too expensive for them, yet if they don't upgrade, they will fall behind—and possibly go out of business. The probable outcome, then, will be the further consolidation of the refining industry.

As for coal: While coal production will be increasing over the next few years, the industry will be forced to deal with the environmental side effects of coal use. One probable outcome will be increased use of low-sulfur coal. This will mean increased output from the low-sulfur coal reserves in Central Appalachia and the Powder River Basin in Wyoming; decreased output from high-sulfur reserves, primarily those in the Midwest.

▶ **Environmental concerns—and the push to move away from volatile oil—will bring about renewed emphasis on developing new energy products.**

An area that has been seeing a great deal of action is the development of alternative fuels, such as methanol, to replace gasoline. As more companies devote time, effort, and funding to developing replacement fuels, this may translate into opportunities for chemical engineers and others involved in the research and development of these fuels. In addition, many refiners will be setting up distribution systems for the new fuels, which may point to sales and marketing opportunities. On the down side, however, it may cut deeply into the earnings of petroleum refiners and even bring about the collapse of independents and smaller companies.

EMPLOYMENT OUTLOOK: Varied.

Like the industry itself, the employment outlook in the petroleum industry depends on the price and availability of foreign oil.

The overall picture isn't that bright. According to the U.S. Bureau of Labor Statistics, the crude oil and petroleum industry is in for a period of slow job growth. One key reason: As mentioned above, reliance on foreign oil will be increasing, which means that domestic producers will be forced to cut back.

But if the price of foreign crude rises, this could translate into renewed job opportunities, especially in the oil-field services area. Why? Rising prices will cause a resurgence of domestic exploration and drilling activity—which in turn will mean hiring opportunities in a range of job categories, including petroleum engineers, geologists, and geophysicists. Similarly, when natural gas finally takes off, there may be a resulting creation of job opportunities.

Draftspeople, science technicians, engineering technicians, and surveyors, as well as other exploration jobs, look strong in the long term but are subject to sporadic ups and downs.

Where oil refining and gas processing are concerned, the future looks fairly bright for chemical engineers. The number hired has nearly doubled since 1986. Job growth should continue in this field.

As for the coal industry: Increased use of labor-saving machinery will cut into the employment numbers. As such, the government forecasts a drop in employment over the next decade—from about 148,000 employees to 113,000. The bottom line? Not the best of job outlooks.

JOBS SPOTLIGHT

PETROLEUM ENGINEER: Employment growth in this field is projected at about 1% to year 2005, up to 3% if the economy is strong. But where actual hiring is concerned, the outlook may be brighter. The key reason? Since 1983 the number of students enrolled in petroleum engineering has dropped 80%, according to the Society of Petroleum Engineers. This means that as people retire or leave the field, the pool of qualified replacements is small.

BEST BETS

Consolidated Natural Gas
CNG Tower
Pittsburgh, PA 15222
412/227-1000

A leading natural-gas producer with a healthy amount of gas reserves, CNG should have a bright long-term future, once natural gas starts taking off as has been predicted . . . and perhaps before. One reason: "co-firing"—a new technology it is developing that reduces environmentally damaging emissions from coal-burning plants by burning gas with coal. With environmental legislation plus heightened awareness, this can be a winner for CNG.

Lyondell Petrochemical
1221 McKinley
#1600
Houston, TX 77010
713/652-7200

Oil refinery and petrochemical producer Lyondell is a small, scrappy company that looks like it is headed for a relatively bright future in the often-troubled energy industry. Among the reasons—technological advances have made the refinery capable of processing any crude oil at all, making it perhaps the only refinery in the world able to do so. In addition, the company is run with an open management style. Teams of managers and workers work together on projects and ideas. If a new proposal is instituted, the entire team gets a bonus. Another plus: The majority of its employees are shareholders in the company—something that aids both productivity and morale. Adding to the morale is the anonymous hotline via which employees are encouraged to make complaints or suggestions. Each month, these are printed in a newsletter along with the corresponding management reaction. All of this adds up to a best bet for employment in the energy industry.

TOP COAL COMPANIES

Amax Coal Industries, Inc.
251 N. Illinois St.,
Suite 600
Indianapolis, IN 46206
317/266-1500

Consolidation Coal Co.
Consolidation Plz.
Pittsburgh, PA 15241
412/831-4000

Cyprus Minerals Corp.
9100 E. Mineral Cir.
Englewood, CO 80155
303/643-5000

Drummond Co., Inc.
530 Beacon Pkwy.
Birmingham, AL 35209
205/387-0501

Island Creek Coal Co.
250 W. Main St.
Lexington, KY 40507
606/288-3000

Nerco, Inc.
500 NE Multnomah St.
Portland, OR 97232
503/731-6600

Peabody Coal Co., Inc.
1951 Barrett Ct.
Box 1990
Henderson, KY 42420
502/827-0800

The Pittston Company
100 First Stamford Pl.
Stamford, CT 06912
203/978-5200

Westmoreland Coal Co., Inc.
200 S. Broad St.
Philadelphia, PA 19102
215/545-2500

TOP OIL & GAS COMPANIES

Amerada Hess Corp.
1185 Ave. of the
Americas
New York, NY 10036
212/997-8500

American Petrofina Holding Co.
P.O. Box 2159
Dallas, TX 75221
214/750-2400

Amoco Corp.
200 E. Randolph Dr.
Chicago, IL 60601
312/856-6111

Ashland Oil, Inc.
P.O. Box 391
Ashland, KY 41114
606/329-3333

Atlantic Richfield Co.
515 S. Flower St.
Los Angeles, CA 90071
213/486-3511

BP America, Inc.
200 Public Sq.
Cleveland, OH 44114
216/586-4141

Chevron Corp.
225 Bush St.
San Francisco, CA
94104
415/894-7700

Citgo Petroleum Corp.
P.O. Box 3758
Tulsa, OK 74102
918/495-4000

Coastal Holding Corp.
9 Greenway Plz.
Houston, TX 77046
713/877-1400

Conoco, Inc.
600 N. Dairy Ashford
Rd.
Houston, TX 77079
713/293-1000

**Crown Central
Petroleum Corp.**
1 N. Charles St.
Baltimore, MD 21203
301/539-7400

**Diamond Shamrock,
Inc.**
PO Box 696000
San Antonio, TX
78269-6000
210/641-6800

**E. I. DuPont
DeNemours & Co.**
1007 Market St.
Wilmington, DE 19898
302/774-1000

Exxon Corp.
225 E. Carpenter Fwy.
Irving, TX 75062
214/444-1000

Kerr-McGee Corp.
Kerr-McGee Ctr.
Oklahoma City, OK
73125
405/270-1313

**Lousiana Land &
Exploration Co.**
909 Poydras St.
New Orleans, LA
70112
504/566-6500

Mapco, Inc.
1800 S. Baltimore Ave.
Tulsa, OK 74119
918/581-1800

Marathon Oil Co.
P.O. Box 3128
Houston, TX 77253
713/629-6600

Maxus Energy Corp.
717 N. Harwood St.
Dallas, TX 75201
214/953-2000

Mobil Corp.
3225 Gallows Rd.
Fairfax, VA 22037
703/846-3000

Murphy Oil Corp.
200 Peach St.
El Dorado, AR 71730
501/862-6411

**Occidental Petroleum
Corp.**
10889 Wilshire Blvd.
Los Angeles, CA 90024
310/208-8800

Oryx Energy Co.
Box 2880
Dallas, TX 75221-2880
214/715-4000

Pennzoil Co.
700 Milam St.
Houston, TX 77002
713/546-4000

Phillips Petroleum Co.
Fourth & Keeler Sts.
Bartlesville, OK 74004
918/661-6600

Quaker State Corp.
255 Elm St.
Oil City, PA 16301
814/676-7676

Shell Oil Co.
1 Shell Plz.
Houston, TX 77001
713/241-6161

Sun Company, Inc.
1801 Market St.
Philadelphia, PA
19103-1699
215/977-3000

Texaco, Inc.
2000 Westchester Ave.
White Plains, NY
10650
914/253-4000

**Union Texas
Petroleum Holdings,
Inc.**
1330 Post Oak Blvd.
Houston, TX 77252
713/623-6544

Unocal Corp.
Unocal Ctr.
Los Angeles, CA 90017
213/977-7600

USX-Marathon Group
600 Grant St.
Pittsburgh, PA 15219
412/433-1121

TOP PETROLEUM SERVICES COMPANIES

Baker Hughes, Incorporated
3900 Essex Ln.
Houston, TX 77027
713/439-8600

Cameron Iron Works, Inc.
P.O. Box 1212
Houston, TX 77251
713/939-2211

CBI Industries
800 Jorie Blvd.
Oak Brook, IL 60521
708/572-7000

Dresser Industries, Inc.
1600 Pacific Bldg.

Box 718
Dallas, TX 75221
214/740-6000

Halliburton Co.
500 N. Akard St.
Dallas, TX 75201
214/978-2600

Helmerich & Payne, Inc.
1579 E. 21st St.
Tulsa, OK 74114
918/742-5531

Noble Affiliates, Inc.
110 W. Broadway
Ardmore, OK 73401
405/223-4110

Noble Drilling Corporation
10370 Richmond Ave.
Houston, TX 77042
713/974-3131

Rowan Company, Inc.
2800 Post Oak Blvd.
Houston, TX 77056
713/621-7800

Schlumberger Ltd.
277 Park Ave.
New York, NY 10172
212/350-9400

WHERE TO GO FOR MORE INFORMATION

ENERGY INDUSTRY ASSOCIATIONS

American Gas Association
1515 Wilson Blvd.
Arlington, VA 22009
703/841-8600

American Petroleum Institute
1220 L St., NW, Suite 900
Washington, DC 20005
202/682-8000

National Coal Association
1130 17th St., NW
Washington, DC 20036
202/463-2625

National Petroleum Council
1625 K St., NW
Washington, DC 20006
202/393-6100

Petroleum Marketers Association of America
1120 Vermont Ave., NW
Washington, DC 20005
202/331-1198

ENERGY INDUSTRY DIRECTORIES

Brown's Directory of North American & International Gas Companies
1 E. First St.
Duluth, MN 55802
218/723-9200

Oil & Gas Directory
P.O. Box 130508
Houston, TX 7729
713/529-8789

Refining, Natural Gas Processing and Engineering Contractors
Midwest Register
601 S. Boulder, No. 1001
Tulsa, OK 75105
918/582-2000

West Coast Petroleum Industry Directory
Pacific West Oil Data
14621 Nordhoff St.

Panaroma City, CA 91402
818/892-1121

Whole World Oil Directory
National Register Publishing Company, Inc.
3004 Glenview Rd.
Wilmette, IL 60091
800/323-6772
708/441-2210

ENERGY INDUSTRY PERIODICALS

Coal
29 N. Wacker Dr.
Chicago, IL 60606
312/726-2802
(Monthly magazine for coal industry executives in all areas, including administrative, engineering, and operating.)

Oil and Gas Journal
P.O. Box 1260
Tulsa, OK 74101
918/835-3161
(Weekly magazine for those involved in oil production, exploration, and marketing.)

Petroleum Engineer International
P.O. Box 1589

Dallas, TX 75221
214/691-3911
(Monthly magazine for oil industry engineers, contractors, and drillers as well as managers and executives.)

Petroleum Marketer
P.O. Box 507
West Haven, CT 06516
203/934-5288
(Bimonthly aimed at those involved in petroleum marketing, including managers and operations personnel, jobbers, etc.)

Petroleum Marketing Management
1801 Rockville Pike
Rockville, MD 20852

301/984-7333
(Bimonthly for petroleum marketing professionals, including major company executives, independent marketers, distributors, etc.)

World Oil
P.O. Box 2608
Houston, TX 77252
713/529-4301
(Monthly magazine covering the oil industry; for company owners, operating managers, geologists, production engineers, and drilling contractors.)

FASHION

INDUSTRY OUTLOOK: Improving—certain areas stronger than others.

As always, the health of the fashion industry is directly linked to the retail industry. But generally, the outlook will improve as a stronger economy and higher consumer confidence translate into stronger sales for the fashion industry. A key trend: Watch more apparel manufacturers jump on the outsourcing bandwagon—allowing their products to keep pace with consumer demand and changing tastes.

A LOOK BACK

▶ **Slumping—and failing—retailers, increased competition, poor interpretation of consumer needs, and, finally, the recession battered the fashion industry.**

First came a period of slow growth. The reasons: a sluggish retail environment; heated-up competition due to a surge in new apparel companies plus an increase in the number of retailers producing private lines; and, most important, disinterested consumers. The latter problem resulted from a mismatch between clothing designs and demographics. Women's clothing in particular suffered, as designers and manufacturers failed to provide what the typical working woman—one of the strongest customers—wanted. The result? In addition to lagging sales, roughly one in four apparel companies lost money and had to institute cost-cutting measures and tighter production.

Things improved for only a year or two. Then retailers began having troubles, which led to cutbacks on orders, late—or no—payment on delivered goods, and a general malaise in the industry. The Gulf War and the recession came on the heels of this. Consumer confidence dipped, sales dropped, retailers cut back even more on inventory, and the fashion industry suffered. The situation began to improve in 1992, especially as the fashion industry began seeking new ways of keeping customers interested in their merchandise.

WHAT'S NEXT

▶ **Designers and manufacturers have learned the lessons of the last few years. The result? They're following demographic trends, trying different approaches to market research, and sticking close to what the consumer wants.**

Apparel manufacturers and designers have learned the hard way—people won't buy whatever the fashion world dictates. Those days are long over. So now the fashion industry is closely tracking consumer preferences and demographics through a variety of market research methods.

Among them is the focus-group method used by other marketing-driven manufacturers (especially package-goods companies). In this case, manufacturers are developing satellite research operations, pulling together a selection of styles, and then showing the different styles to test subjects around the country. One result: this is creating employment opportunities for market research personnel.

Another method that will be growing in use: Producing limited runs of items as a test to gauge consumer reaction. These runs are often sold in outlet stores or in stores chosen as test-market labs. It's a way of testing different styles, colors, and price points while avoiding disastrous overruns of unwanted merchandise. Items that sell well are then mass-produced; those that don't are cut from production.

► **Technological changes will continue to affect the manufacturing process.**

It's the best way to keep costs down, productivity up, and excessive inventory (especially unfinished products) in check. An increasing number of apparel manufacturers have been automating, investing in new equipment and computer systems to design products, to determine how to cut costs in fabric by making pattern layout more efficient, and, ultimately, for use in sales presentations, to enable buyers to see the product. To accommodate the new equipment, companies are updating old factories or building new ones, and switching over to new production methods, such as modular manufacturing systems.

By switching from the traditional labor-intensive methods to robotics and automation, apparel manufacturers can react more quickly to changes in style based on consumer demand. (For more on this, see the section on Quick Response below.) In addition, automation enables domestic manufacturers to compete with the low-cost foreign producers.

In the short term, however, there is a high price to pay for these changes. Because modernization is so expensive, small and midsized companies are being forced to merge. The outcome? A shift in the makeup of the industry. Once comprised of a large number of small, specialized companies, the apparel industry is switching to one comprised of larger, more diverse corporations. The end result, clearly, is a consolidated industry of fewer manufacturers with larger product lines.

Technological breakthroughs are also affecting the employment picture. Traditional production jobs are being cut and will probably not be replaced. On the other hand, however, there is an increasing demand for people skilled in advanced manufacturing techniques.

► **An important trend: the growing use of "Quick Response," which allows designers and manufacturers to respond quickly to customer preferences.**

This may be one of the most important factors affecting the apparel industry. Basically, Quick Response is a production concept that allows manufacturers to quickly produce and deliver products that are in high demand, at the same time that they avoid producing products that are in low demand. In so doing, QR allows manufacturers and designers to react to changing customer demand. Color, style, trim—virtually any aspect of a garment or accessory can be swiftly changed in line with what is selling most.

QR typically relies on computerization—automated checkouts with bar-code scanners. The system allows retailers to track inventory, identify strong sellers, and know when to replenish stock. QR can cut the time between the order of goods and delivery of those goods from an average of sixty-six weeks to as little as twenty-one weeks.

Expect the use of QR to continue—and increase—as the need for shorter lead times, coupled with a rising consumer demand for quality and an increasing concern for trend tracking, make automation more necessary.

▶ Foreign sourcing and foreign production will continue—and increase.

It's partially a reaction to the high cost of automation, partially a way of keeping costs down. Even as the Made in the USA sentiment remains high, manufacturers and designers will continue looking overseas for low-cost production.

As such, expect increased competition between U.S. and foreign manufacturers as those domestic manufacturers continue to fight for higher market share.

Another interesting development to keep an eye on: U.S. companies are targeting overseas markets for their products, especially men's outerwear and home furnishings. The biggest markets so far have been Southeast Asia, Latin America, and Japan, but there is also increasing activity in South Korea, Hong Kong, Taiwan, and even Europe. This may translate into interesting international sales and marketing opportunities. Expect to see stepped-up efforts to increase market share abroad as this trend continues.

▶ The result of increased attention to customers? Interesting shifts in focus for designers and apparel manufacturers.

In the short term, expect to see the continued strength of "bridge lines." Also called secondary lines or diffusion lines, these are lower-priced lines of designer clothing. The trend began to a great degree when consumers started to cut back on higher-priced purchases, and it also cashed in on the growing number of affluent baby boomers. Among the names: Donna Karan's DKNY, Giorgio Armani's A/X, Ellen Tracy's Company, Anne Klein's A-Line.

In the longer term, expect to see the continued growth of lines aimed at aging baby boomers. Environmental awareness is getting a push, with lines such as Esprit, Susie Tompkins (owner of Esprit), catalog house Smith & Hawken, and others offering natural-dyed clothing and the like. Manufacturers are also eager to tap the growing market of older Americans, many of whom will have high disposable incomes. Another hot target is children's wear, because of the mini–baby boom that has been happening.

The target markets may be different, but the bottom line is clear: Designers and companies that track demographic trends and come up with the product lines that meet the demands of a changing marketplace will be the winners. The losers? Those that don't change with the times.

EMPLOYMENT OUTLOOK: Competitive.

The apparel industry is traditionally a very labor-intensive one, employing about 6% of all employees in the U.S. manufacturing industry while accounting for only about 2% of the products. But in the recent past, the industry shrank. According to the Bureau of Labor Statistics, 1,000 apparel manufacturers closed since 1986—for a loss of about 20,000 jobs. But the worst seems over: in 1992, employment grew 2% to about 986,000 employees—the first increase since 1977. On the production side, the growing use of automation is cutting back on jobs, which account for about 85% of all jobs in the industry. The keys to securing a job in today's apparel industry are computer skills, and computerized manufacturing experience.

On the nonproduction side, the fashion industry has always been competitive. Skills, contacts, and just plain luck are, to a great degree, the key factors in landing a design job. Several interesting employment trends: While New York remains the seat of the U.S. fashion industry, its dominance is less strong than in the past. Los Angeles, in particular, is growing in importance as a fashion capital, as are San Francisco and Chicago.

JOBS SPOTLIGHT

PRODUCT MANAGER: A growing area as retailers switch to centralized marketing. Product managers in the fashion industry work with buyers from retail stores to determine what the store wants; then they do "sourcing"—finding producers and production areas (often overseas) to make the item. Product managers sometimes offer design input. Salaries range from the low to mid $20s for assistant product managers to the mid $60s for senior product managers.

BEST BETS

Donna Karan Co.
770 7th Ave.
New York, NY 10018
212/398-0616

A star of the sportswear field, Donna Karan is one of the driving forces behind the trend toward bridge lines. The key to her success? Understanding her customer and aiming her clothing directly at the 30 + woman. Bridge line DKNY has been a brilliant success since it was introduced—and her forays into other areas seem equally profitable. The only question: Can this success be sustained against hotter competition?

Levi Strauss & Co.
1155 Battery St.
San Francisco, CA 94111
415/544-6000

Levi Strauss has a reputation for having its workers participate in the management process. The management sponsors a number of programs designed to promote positive change in the company, such as CORE Curriculum, a training program covering such subjects as leadership, ethics, and diversity. This type of attention to employees, and a product line that has been evolving to keep up with its customers, make Levi Strauss a positive bet for the future.

TOP FASHION COMPANIES

Aileen, Inc.
1411 Broadway
New York, NY 10018
212/398-9770

Argenti, Inc.
512 Seventh Ave.
New York, NY 10018
212/221-1840

**Benetton
Manufacturing Corp.**
501 English Rd.
Rocky Mount, NC
27804
919/937-6883

Harve Bernard Ltd.
225 Meadowlands
Pkwy.
Secaucus, NJ 07094
201/319-0909

Bill Blass Ltd.
550 Seventh Ave.
New York, NY 10018
212/221-6600

Bon Jour Group Ltd.
1411 Broadway
New York, NY 10018
212/398-1000

**Bugle Boy Industries,
Inc.**
2900 N. Madera Rd.
Simi Valley, CA 93065
805/582-1010

Byer California
66 Potrero Ave.
San Francisco, CA

94103
415/626-7844

Z. Cavaricci Inc.
2535 E. 12th St.
Los Angeles, CA 90221
213/629-1988

Bernard Chaus, Inc.
1410 Broadway
New York, NY 10018
212/354-1280

Cherokee, Inc.
9545 Wentworth St.
Sunland, CA 91040
818/951-1002

Liz Claiborne, Inc.
1441 Broadway
New York, NY 10018
212/354-4900

Donkenny, Inc.
1411 Broadway
New York, NY 10018
212/730-7770

Esprit
600 Minnesota
San Francisco, CA
94107
415/648-6900

Evan-Picone, Inc.
7801 Tonnelle Ave.
North Bergen, NJ
07047
201/869-9200

Gant Corp.
2645 Mitchell Ave.
Allentown, PA 18103
215-797-6200

Guess, Inc.
1444 S. Alameda St.
Los Angeles, CA 90021
213/765-3100

Hartmarx Corp.
101 N. Wacker Dr.
Chicago, IL 60606
312/372-6300

J. G. Hook, Inc.
1300 Belmont Ave.
Philadelphia, PA 19104
215/477-9600

Jantzen, Inc.
411 NE 19th Ave.
Portland, OR 97232
503/238-5000

JH Collectibles
1411 Broadway
New York, NY 10018
212/944-6644

Jones Apparel Group
250 Rittenhouse Cir.
Bristol, PA 19007
215/785-4000

**Jordache Enterprises,
Inc.**
226 W. 37th St.
New York, NY 10018
212/643-8400

Joujou Designs, Inc.
525 Seventh Ave.
New York, NY 10018
212/997-0230

Donna Karan Co.
770 Seventh Ave.
New York, NY 10018
212/398-0616

Kenar Enterprises, Inc.
530 Seventh Ave.
New York, NY 10018
212/944-5300

Anne Klein & Co.
205 W. 39th St.
New York, NY 10018
212/221-7880

Calvin Klein Co.; Calvin Klein Sport, Inc.
205 W. 39th St.
New York, NY 10018
212/719-2600

Michael Kors, Inc.
119 W. 24th St.
New York, NY 10011
212/620-4677

Ralph Lauren Womenswear
550 Seventh Ave.
New York, NY 10019
212/212-0675

Leslie Fay Companies, Inc.
1400 Broadway
New York, NY 10018
212/221-4000

Levi Strauss Associates, Inc.
1155 Battery St.
San Francisco, CA 94111
415/544-6000

Maggy London International Ltd.
530 Seventh Ave.
New York, NY 10018
212/944-7199

Necessary Objects Ltd.
524 Broadway
New York, NY 10012
212/334-9888

Philips-Van Heusen Corp.
1290 Ave. of the Americas
New York, NY 10104
212/541-5200

Polo Ralph Lauren
650 Madison Ave.
New York, NY 10022
212/318-7000

Russ Togs, Inc.
1411 Broadway
New York, NY 10018
212/642-8500

Ellen Tracy, Inc.
575 Seventh Ave.
New York, NY 10018
212/944-6999

VF Corp.
1047 N. Park Rd.
Reading, PA 19610
215/378-1151

Warnaco Group, Inc.
90 Park Ave.
New York, NY 10016
212/661-1300

Woolrich, Inc.
Mill St.
Woolrich, PA 17779
717/769-6464

Yes Clothing Co.
1360 E. 17th St.
Los Angeles, CA 90021
213/742-0201

TOP TEXTILE MANUFACTURING AND HOME FASHIONS COMPANIES

Albany International
1 Sage Rd.
Menands, NY 12204
518/445-2000

Belding Hemingway
1430 Broadway
New York, NY 10018
212/944-6040

Burlington Industries, Inc.
3330 W. Friendly Ave.

Greensboro, NC 27410
919/379-2000

Celanese Corporation
1211 Ave. of the Americas
New York, NY 10036
212/719-8000

Collins and Aikman
210 Madison Ave.
New York, NY 10016
212/578-1200

Concord Fabrics
1359 Broadway
New York, NY 10018
212/760-0300

Dan River, Inc.
111 W. 40th St.
New York, NY 10018
212/554-5531

Delta Woodside
233 N. Main St.
Greenville, SC 29601
803/232-8301

Fieldcrest Cannon
326 E. Stadium Dr.
Eden, NC 27288
919/627-3000

Liberty Fabrics
200 E. 42nd St.
New York, NY 10017
212/867-0300

**Milliken and
Company**
P.O. Box 1926
Spartanburg, SC 29304
803/573-2020

Shaw Industries
616 E. Walnut Ave.
Dalton, GA 30720
706/278-3812

Springs Industries
205 N. White St.
Fort Mill, SC 29715
803/547-3650

**J. P. Stevens
Company, Inc.**
1185 Ave. of the
Americas
New York, NY 10036
212/930-2050

**United Merchants and
Manufacturers**
1407 Broadway
New York, NY 10018
212/930-3900

West Point-Pepperell
400 W. 10th St.
West Point, GA 31833
404/645-4000

WHERE TO GO FOR MORE INFORMATION

(For more information sources in related areas, also see "Designers," page 30, and "Retailing," page 448.)

FASHION INDUSTRY ASSOCIATIONS

**Affiliated Dress
Manufacturers**
1440 Broadway
New York, NY 10018
212/398-9797

**American Apparel
Manufacturers
Association**
2500 Wilson Blvd.,
Suite 301
Arlington, VA 22201
703/524-1864

**Clothing
Manufacturers
Association of the
USA**
1290 Ave. of the

Americas
New York, NY 10104
212/757-6664

**Federation of Apparel
Manufacturers**
225 W. 34th St.
New York, NY 10122
212/594-0810

**Footwear Industries of
America**
1420 K St., NW,
Suite 600
Washington, DC 20005
202/789-1420

**International
Association of
Clothing Designers**

240 Madison Ave.
New York, NY 10016
212/685-6602

**Men's Fashion
Association of
America**
240 Madison Ave.
New York, NY 10016
212/683-5665

**National Association
of Fashion and
Accessory Designers**
2180 E. 93rd St.
Cleveland, OH 44106
216/231-9375

FASHION INDUSTRY DIRECTORIES

AAMA Directory
American Apparel
Manufacturers
Association
2500 Wilson Blvd.
Arlington, VA 22201
703/524-1864

Apparel Trades Book
Dun & Bradstreet, Inc.
1 Diamond Hill Rd.

Murray Hill, NJ 07974
201/665-5000

**The Fashion Guide:
International Designer
Directory**
Fairchild Publications
7 E. 12th St.
New York, NY 10003
212/630-3880
800/247-6622

**The Fashion Resource
Directory**
Fairchild Publications
7 E. 12th St.
New York, NY 10003
212/630-3880
800/247-6622

FASHION INDUSTRY PUBLICATIONS

**Apparel Industry
Magazine**
180 Allen Rd., NE
Atlanta, GA 30328
404/252-8831
(Monthly magazine for
staffers in all aspects of
the apparel
industry—designers,
manufacturers,
contractors, suppliers.)

Bobbin
P.O. Box 1986
Columbia, SC 29202
803/771-7500
(Monthly magazine for
executives in apparel
manufacturing, textile
milling, retailing.)

**California Apparel
News**
110-R Ninth St.

Los Angeles, CA 90079
213/627-3737
(Weekly covering
California-based fashion
industry.)

Daily News Record
7 E. 12th St.
New York, NY 10003
212/741-4280
(Daily newspaper for
apparel manufacturers,
wholesalers, buyers,
retailers, and jobbers.)

Footwear News
7 W. 34th St.
New York, NY 10001
212/630-4000
(Weekly newspaper
covering the footwear
industry; for designers,
buyers, wholesalers,
suppliers, etc.)

Needle's Eye
1 Union Special Pl.
Huntley, IL 60142
708/659-5101
(Bimonthly magazine
covering the
textile/apparel industry,
including
manufacturers,
wholesalers, retailers,
mill executives, and
more.)

Women's Wear Daily
7 E. 12th St.
New York, NY 10003
212/741-4280
(Daily newspaper,
women's clothing
industry ''bible,'' for
designers, wholesalers,
retailers, etc.)

FILM AND ENTERTAINMENT

INDUSTRY OUTLOOK: Picking up steam with an improved economy—but, as always, highly competitive.

Film: A strong overseas market and improved economy add up to a positive picture over the long term. A continuing challenge: coping with trade barriers imposed by foreign governments to restrict the flow of U.S. film exports.

Music: Competition will heat up as recent technological breakthroughs, such as digital audio tape machines, MDs (mini discs) and digital compact cassettes, become more widely available to consumers.

A LOOK BACK

▶ **It was a five year run of record earnings for the film industry—winding up with record earnings of more than $5 billion in 1989.**

The film industry had been hitting box office pay dirt, with movies like *Batman* fueling the charge. But then earnings slumped slightly, when 1990 saw a drop of 2% in box-office receipts. 1991 brought a drop also—making it the third-best year in the movie industry but still not up to the peak of 1989.

During this period, the film industry was also going through a number of changes, chief among them, an industry shakeout that forced several independents to go out of business. In addition, the slight drop in viewership caused studios to cut back on various costs. A flat 1992 gave way to a brighter 1993, a resurgence in optimism—and the expectation that an upswing was on the way.

▶ **The music industry has been going through a series of changes.**

Over the past three years, the industry has gone through a volatile period marked by a flurry of mergers and acquisitions. A sign of the times: according to *Billboard*, the large companies (including Polygram and MCA) paid a total of almost $1.5 billion for three independents: Island, A&M, and Geffen. Numerous new labels emerged during this period, many of them cashing in on the giant success of rap music. But these new entrants also heightened competition. Then came the recession and a corresponding drop in sales, the end result being a slump. Companies were forced to cut back on both their staffing and their artist rosters and to streamline operations. For example, Thorn EMI combined three labels—SBK, Chrysalis, and EMI—into one operation. They kept their individual names and talent-scouting operations but centralized all other departments. In early 1992 there was one more large deal—Thorn EMI bought Virgin Music Group—and experts started believing that industry consolidation was dropping. In 1993 companies were still belt-tightening but expecting an improvement with the lifting of the recession.

WHAT'S NEXT

▶ Foreign markets will continue to be of vital importance to the film industry.

This is due partly to the new international focus of U.S. business and partly to simple economics: About 80% of all films don't earn enough to cover their costs through U.S. distribution. Producers count on ancillary markets—cable, broadcast television, video cassettes, and especially foreign distribution—to make more money. Demand is high overseas for American films—high enough to make film one of the country's most successful exports—and should stay high.

A key reason for the lucrative foreign market is the fact that cable and broadcast television are being expanded overseas. The results? More U.S. companies will be producing shows with foreign sales potential firmly in mind. And shows that may pull only fair ratings domestically can stay in production due to a strong foreign showing.

There is one problem, however: the growing backlash against American film exports. Some foreign governments, primarily European Community members, have instituted quotas limiting both television broadcast and theater screen time of foreign films, as well as restrictions on imports. This situation may worsen as the U.S. seeks to penetrate the international market further.

▶ Independents will continue struggling to fight with the big players, and some will fall by the wayside.

It's an inevitability, especially in a high-cost industry like film. Independents have been facing various problems: a run of "marginal" performers (aka bombs), spiraling production costs, an extremely high number of releases, and movie-theater chains that focus on blockbusters.

How to compete? Some independents find that market niches are the path to success. Others, like Castle Rock, which produced *When Harry Met Sally* and *City Slickers,* and Morgan Creek, which produced *Robin Hood,* gamble on bigger, high-visibility projects and hope for a winner.

But many indies will be battered by the studios and will either be bought out or go belly-up. The result? Continued consolidation in the industry, with the giants getting larger and the smaller companies being squeezed out of the picture.

▶ "Vertical integration"—entertainment companies occupying several different niches in the entertainment business—will still play a major role in the industry, even as mergers slow down.

It's connected with the general trend that swept American industry—a movement away from traditional conglomerates to newer ones formed of subsidiaries in related areas. Some examples of vertically integrated entertainment companies include Viacom, which is involved in television production, cable TV, and syndication; Fox, which has a film studio, television stations, and television production units; and Sony, which has a film studio, recording labels, and more.

While mergers between companies won't be occurring as rapidly as in the past, these companies will still make their mark on the industry. The key reason? They can dominate through sheer size and diversity. In the case of a Viacom or Fox, they can produce shows, distribute them, then broadcast or syndicate them. A Sony or an MCA can promote new music artists by recording a music video, then running the video as an opener to a movie. The possibilities are numerous—and, in these days of hot competition, they give the large companies an edge over their smaller competitors.

Watch for continued linkages and periodic spurts of merger activity as the industry goes through its usual ups and downs.

▶ **Technological advances will have a major impact on the future of the music industry—causing growth in some areas, decline in others.**

CDs and digital cassettes are taking over the prerecorded music business. The losers? Analog cassettes and, of course, LPs. Cassette shipments have been dropping each year, down about 12 to 17% in both 1991 and 1992. (An interesting note: There is one area of cassette production that is seeing growth—audio books on tape.) LPs have dropped even more, down 66.2% in 1990 alone.

But there is competition ahead for the newer forms of prerecorded music. CDs are ahead, for the time being, but their hot sales have leveled off. And with the introduction of DCCs (digital compact cassettes) and recordable CDs, the technology picture will keep changing. The outlook? Digital cassettes may catch on, but the jury is most definitely out. It's been a long time coming, chiefly because of the fight between the music industry and the consumer electronics industry about making digital audio tape (DAT) machines available to the public. Because DAT machines make perfect copies, music companies were concerned that this would encourage tape pirating. But the two industries have made an agreement, and DAT machines will become available. Even so, many insiders are placing their bets on recordable CDs, citing the high cost of digital tapes.

The bottom line? Things will keep changing, even as some industry insiders worry that all the breakthroughs will confuse consumers over the short term and cause them to sit back and wait until an industry standard emerges.

▶ **Changing consumer buying habits and heated competition are forcing music companies to try new ways of attracting attention and customers.**

The two main reasons for this trend? First, music-buying consumers are older than in the past and are less likely to buy a new release automatically or to walk into a music store at all. Second, it's harder to get radio airplay for a new (or even an old) act because of the intense competition. As a result, companies will be exploring new ways of marketing and promoting their wares.

The biggest push will be in direct marketing. Expect to see increased use of such methods as direct-mail catalogs from which a consumer can order by mail or by calling an 800 number; advertisements of new releases that include an 800 number; mail-order advertising in consumer magazines. An example of how far it may go: According to *Billboard* magazine, Time Warner Direct Entertainment (a subsidiary of the Warner Music Group) even offers a 900 number that consumers who receive their catalog can call to hear three selections from any album included in the catalog.

Other methods record companies will be using to reach more consumers: increased television advertising, particularly on cable; mass-transit and outdoor advertising; and (more common with labels that are part of a larger entertainment conglomerate) showing music videos in movie theaters before the main feature; arranging promotional tours of in-store appearances for new artists.

This activity in promotion and advertising points to *increased employment opportunities for sales and promotional staffers,* especially those with direct mail backgrounds, and advertising personnel.

▶ **The outlook for another area of the entertainment field: An aging population will mean bright days ahead for leisure companies— sporting goods manufacturers, recreational services, and the like.**

An older population means more money will be spent on leisure activities. Sporting goods companies, amusement parks, playgrounds, and other recreational services companies are all poised for a run of good years.

What does this mean in terms of employment? There may be opportunities in a range of areas, from recreational services to health clubs to sporting goods companies. Looking particularly strong: those companies or services that target families. This is a result of the large number of baby boomers having children themselves. The focus is now on family entertainment. In light of this, there may be a number of employment opportunities in companies that offer goods or services directly aimed at families, such as playground or "play-care" service franchisers and companies, amusement parks, and the like.

EMPLOYMENT OUTLOOK: Competitive, as always.

Entertainment companies are always competitive—but they're also always hiring. The trick, of course, is managing to land a job in spite of the intense competition. Generally, it's a combination of timing and luck.

More specifically: Film production jobs generally depend on specific companies and shows. However, given the recent influx of competition in television production, expect more of a squeeze than ever in this area.

A good bet: Because of growing competition and a blockbuster focus in the film industry, prerelease publicity and marketing are becoming more important. These areas will offer employment opportunities in the short term, but competition will be stiff.

An Employment Tip: The best way to get a job in Hollywood is to know someone. But for those who don't have that in, there is another way to break into

directing. The Directors Guild offers a formal training program for assistant directors, for individuals with a BA or a minimum of three years' experience. Applicants must take an all-day written test and oral exam. An example of how competitive it is: Only a little more than 1% of the applicants pass.
Contact:

> Assistant Director's Training Program
> Directors Guild of America
> 14144 Ventura Blvd.
> Sherman Oaks, CA 91423
> 213/289-2000

BEST BETS

HBO
1100 Avenue of the Americas
New York, NY 10036
212/512-1000

More than just a cable company, HBO is moving strongly into production—producing shows such as ''Roc'' (on Fox-TV), as well as a number of pilots, specials, and made-for-TV movies. In a crowded field, HBO Productions is carving out a niche for itself and looks headed for a bright future. An additional plus: HBO has a reputation for being a ''family-friendly'' company and was chosen one of the best companies for parents in a 1991 *Working Mother* ranking.

New Line Cinema Corp.
575 8th Ave.
New York, NY 10018
212/239-8880

From its successes with niche films like *Teenage Mutant Ninja Turtles* and the *Nightmare on Elm Street* films, New Line is now expanding at a rapid pace. Among its recent ventures: It has launched a new film division called Fine Line Features, has formed a television distribution division, obtained domestic video rights to independent Castle Rock's films, and has entered into a home-video sales agreement with RCA Video. This flurry of activity points to one thing: New Line looks like it's on a fast track to success.

TOP FILM & VIDEO PRODUCTION COMPANIES

Buena Vista Home Video
500 S. Buena Vista St.
Burbank, CA 91521
818/560-0044

Stephen J. Cannell Productions
7083 Hollywood Blvd.
Los Angeles, CA 90028
213/465-5800

Cannon Pictures
8200 Wilshire Blvd.
Beverly Hills, CA 90211
213/966-5600

Carolco Pictures, Inc.
8800 Sunset Blvd.
Los Angeles, CA 90069
213/850-8800

Carson Productions, Inc.
100 University
N. Hollywood, CA 91608
818/840-3690

Castle Rock Entertainment
335 N. Maple Dr., No. 135
Beverly Hills, CA 90210
213/285-2300

Dick Clark Productions, Inc.
3003 W. Olive Ave.
Burbank, CA 91505
818/841-3003

Columbia Pictures—TV
3400 W. Riverside Dr.

Burbank, CA 91505
818/972-8512

Corday Productions, Inc.
Columbia Plaza E.
Burbank, CA 91505
818/954-2637

Walt Disney Co.
500 S. Buena Vista St.
Burbank, CA 91521
818/560-1000

Walt Disney Pictures & TV
500 S. Buena Vista St.
Burbank, CA 91521
818/560-6455

Fries Entertainment, Inc.
6922 Hollywood Blvd.
Los Angeles, CA 90028
213/466-2266

Group W Productions, Inc.
3801 Barham Blvd.
Los Angeles, CA 90068
213/850-3800

Hanna Barbera Productions, Inc.
3400 W. Caheunga Blvd.
Los Angeles, CA 90068
213/851-5000

Hemdale Film Corp.
7966 Beverly Blvd.
Los Angeles, CA 90048
213/966-3700

Heritage Entertainment, Inc.
7920 Sunset Blvd.
Los Angeles, CA 90046
213/850-5858

Imagine Films Entertainment, Inc.
1925 Century P. E., No. 2300
Los Angeles, CA 90067
213/277-1665

Kings Road Entertainment, Inc.
1901 Ave. of the Stars
Los Angeles, CA 90067
213/552-0057

Kushner-Locke Co.
11601 Wilshire Blvd.
Los Angeles, CA 90025
213/445-1111

Lorimar Productions; Lorimar Telepictures Corp.
4000 Warner Blvd.
Burbank, CA 91522
818/954-6000

Lucasfilm Ltd.
5858 Lucas Valley Rd.
Nicasio, CA 94946
415/662-1700

MCA, Inc.
100 Universal City Plz.
N. Hollywood, CA 91608
818/777-1000

MGM-Pathé Communications Co.
8670 Wilshire Blvd.
Beverly Hills, CA 90211
213/280-6000

New Line Cinema Corp.
575 Eighth Ave.
New York, NY 10018
212/239-8880

New World Entertainment Ltd.
14400 S. Sepulveda Blvd.
Los Angeles, CA 90025
310/444-8100

Orion Pictures Corp.
1325 Ave. of the Americas
New York, NY 10019
212/956-3800

Paramount Pictures Corp.
5555 Melrose Ave.
Hollywood, CA 90038
213/956-5000

Prism Entertainment Corp.
1888 Century Pk. E., 10th Fl.
Los Angeles, CA 90067
213/277-3270

Republic Pictures Corp.
12636 Beatrice St.
Los Angeles, CA 90066
213/306-4040

Aaron Spelling Productions
5700 Wilshire Blvd.
Los Angeles, CA 90036
213/860-2413

Twentieth Century-Fox Film
10201 W. Pico Blvd.
Los Angeles, CA 90035
213/277-2211

Universal City Studios, Inc.
100 Universal City Plz.
N. Hollywood, CA 91608
818/777-1000

Vestron, Inc.
1010 Washington Blvd.
Stamford, CT 06901
203/978-5400

Warner Brothers, Inc.
4000 Warner Blvd.
Burbank, CA 91522
818/954-6000

TOP RECORD COMPANIES

A&M Records
1416 North La Brea
Hollywood, CA 90028
213/469-2411
New York office:
595 Madison Ave.
New York, NY 10022
212/826-0477

Arista Records, Inc.
6 W. 57th St.
New York, NY 10019
212/489-7400

Atlantic Recording Corp.
75 Rockefeller Plz.
New York, NY 10019
212/484-6000

BMG Music (RCA Records)
1133 Ave. of the Americas
New York, NY 10036

212/930-4000
Los Angeles office:
6363 Sunset Blvd.
Los Angeles, CA 90028
213/468-4000
Nashville office:
1 Music Circle N.
Nashville, TN 37203
615/664-1200

Capitol-EMI Music, Inc.
1750 N. Vine St.
Hollywood, CA 90028
213/462-6252
Nashville office:
Liberty Records
3322 West End Ave.
11th Fl.
Nashville, TN 37203
615/269-2000

Columbia Records
(c/o Sony Music Entertainment Inc.)

Elektra Entertainment
962 North LaCienaga Blvd.
Los Angeles, CA 90069
310/288-3800
New York office:
75 Rockefeller Plz.
New York, NY 10019
212/275-4000

EMI Music Worldwide
152 W. 57th St.
New York, NY 10019
212/603-8600

EMI Records Group
(Chrysalis & SBK)
1290 Ave. of the Americas

New York, NY 10104
212/492-1200

Epic Records
(c/o Sony Music
Entertainment Inc.)
51 W. 52nd St.
New York, NY 10019
212/975-4321
Los Angeles office:
1801 Century Pk. W.
Los Angeles, CA 90067
213/556-4700
Nashville office:
49 Music Sq. W.
Nashville, TN 37203
615/329-4321

Island Records, Inc.
14 E. Fourth St.
New York, NY 10012
212/477-8000

MCA Records
70 Universal City Plz.
N. Hollywood, CA
91608
818/777-1000

Motown Records
6255 W. Sunset Blvd.
Los Angeles, CA 90028
213/468-3500

**Polygram Records,
Inc. (Mercury and
Polydor)**
825 Eighth Ave.
New York, NY 10019
212/333-8000
Los Angeles office:
11150 Santa Monica
Blvd.
Ste. 1100
Los Angeles, CA 90025
310/996-7200

Sire Records
(c/o Warner Brothers
Records)
75 Rockefeller Plz.
New York, NY 10019
212/484-6800

**Sony Music
Entertainment, Inc.**
P.O. Box 4450
New York, NY
10101-4450

Attn: Recruitment 51/3
212/445-4321
Los Angeles office:
1801 Century Pk. W.
Los Angeles, CA 90067
310/556-4700
Nashville office:
34 Music Sq. E.
Nashville, TN 37203
615/742-4321

Sun International
3106 Belmont Blvd.
Nashville, TN 37212
615/385-1960

**Warner Brothers
Records**
3300 Warner Blvd.
Burbank, CA 91505
818/846-9090
New York office:
75 Rockefeller Plz.
New York, NY 10019
Nashville office:
1216 17th Ave. S.
Nashville, TN 37212
615/320-7525

WHERE TO GO FOR MORE INFORMATION

ENTERTAINMENT INDUSTRY ASSOCIATIONS

**Academy of Motion
Picture Arts and
Sciences**
8949 Wilshire Blvd.
Beverly Hills, CA
90211
213/859-9619

**American Film
Marketing Association**
12424 Wilshire Blvd.
Los Angeles, CA 90025
213/447-1555

**American Society of
Cinematographers**
P.O. Box 2187
Los Angeles, CA 90213
213/876-5080
800/448-0145

**Association for
Independent Video
and Film**
625 Broadway
New York, NY 10012
212/473-3400

**Directors Guild of
America**
7920 Sunset Blvd.
Hollywood, CA 90046
213/289-2000

**International
Association of
Independent
Producers**
P.O. Box 2801
Washington, DC 20013
202/775-1113

(Has placement service for members and supports on-the-job training programs and apprentice programs.)

Motion Picture Association of America
1133 Ave. of the Americas
New York, NY 10036
212/840-6161

National Academy of Recording Arts and Sciences
303 N. Glen Oaks Blvd.
Burbank, CA 91502
213/849-1313

Producers Guild of America
400 S. Beverly Dr.
Ste. 211
Beverly Hills, CA 90212
213/557-0807

Recording Industry Association of America
1020 19th St., NW
Washington, DC 20036
202/775-0101

Society of Motion Picture and Television Engineers
595 W. Hartsdale Ave.
White Plains, NY 10607
914/761-1100

ENTERTAINMENT INDUSTRY DIRECTORIES

Billboard International Recording Studio & Equipment Directory
Billboard Publications, Inc.
1515 Broadway
New York, NY 10036
212/764-7300

Cash Box Annual World Wide Directory
Cash Box
330 W. 58th St.
New York, NY 10019
212/586-2640

International Film Guide
Zoetrope, Inc.
80 E. 11th St.
New York, NY 10013
212/254-8235

International Motion Picture Almanac
Quigley Publishing Co.
159 W. 53rd St.
New York, NY 10019
212/247-3100

Nationwide Music Record Industry Toll-Free Directory
CDE
Box 310551
Atlanta, GA 30331
404/344-7621

On Location: National Film and Videotape Production Directory
6777 Hollywood Blvd.
Los Angeles, CA 90028
213/467-1268

Radio & Records Ratings Report & Directory
Radio and Records, Inc.
1930 Century Pk. W.
Los Angeles, CA 90067
213/553-4330

Recording Engineer/Producer Black Book
Intertec Publishing Corp.
9221 Quivira Rd.
Overland Park, KS 66215
913/888-4664

Who's Who in the Motion Picture Industry
Packard Publishing
P.O. Box 2187
Beverly Hills, CA 90213
213/854-0276

ENTERTAINMENT INDUSTRY MAGAZINES

Back Stage
330 W. 42nd St.
New York, NY 10001
212/947-0020
(Weekly newspaper
covering film
production,
entertainment, and
television commercial
production. Includes
help-wanted ads.)

Billboard
Billboard Publications,
Inc.
1515 Broadway
New York, NY 10036
212/536-5002
(Covers the music
industry.)

Box Office
1800 N. Highland Ave.
Hollywood, CA 90028
213/465-1186
(Aimed at theater
owners, managers,
operators, etc.—people
involved in film
production and
distribution.)

Cash Box
157 W. 57th St.
New York, NY 10019
212/586-2640
(Music industry
magazine aimed at
record manufacturers
and distributors, music
publishers, store
owners, and recording
artists.)

Daily Variety
5700 Wilshire Blvd.
Los Angeles, CA 90036
213/857-6600

Film Journal
244 W. 49th St.
New York, NY 10019
212/246-6460

Hollywood Reporter
6715 W. Sunset Blvd.
Hollywood, CA 90028
213/464-7411

**Recording Engineer &
Producer**
Box 12901
Overland Park, KS
66212
913/888-4664
(Aimed at professionals
involved in music
recording—professional
recording studios,
production units, sound
personnel and
engineers, etc.)

Variety
475 Park Ave. S.
New York, NY 10016
212/779-1100

FINANCIAL SERVICES

INDUSTRY OUTLOOK: Fair to good.

Financial services firms cover a broad spectrum and market that serve the financial and investment needs of the public.

Securities firms, which are the main focus of this section, perform various functions. They act as agents for buyers on securities exchanges like the New York Stock exchanges; as dealers, by making markets (buying or selling on their own accounts to preserve liquidity); as underwriters, by marketing and selling new stock and bond issues to finance clients; as lenders to giant institutional customers (and to individuals via margin accounts); and as advisors in mergers and acquisitions (particularly during the 1980s).

There are about 8,000 security firms today, ranging from giants like Merrill Lynch, which carries out virtually every function, to medium-and small-size specialty firms.

A LOOK BACK

▶ **The 1980s were one of the longest and strongest "up cycles" in the history of the business, and although it's all memory, it's important to understanding the business today.**

The '80s started slow but built momentum, as investors—both private and institutional—poured money into stocks, bonds, and other securities. Wall Street firms changed. The industry moved away from small partnerships to large corporations, hiring increased dramatically, and branch offices opened here and abroad. New investment vehicles were created or marketed more aggressively, including mortgage-backed securities (Fannie Maes, Freddie Macs, etc.) and junk bonds (bonds rated Ba or less, offering higher yields). Meanwhile, an unprecedented wave of mergers and acquisitions revolutionized the marketplace—and earned investment bankers fat fees.

Then, in October 1987, the stock market plunged. The result? A drop in earnings and the beginning of layoffs. But the economy, contrary to predictions, remained strong, and merger activities, which had slowed briefly, picked up. Late '80s' mergers brought large fees to some big players, including Morgan Stanley, Bear Stearns.

In 1989, however, two of Wall Street's major money-makers turned sour. Merger activity slowed and junk-bond financing stopped almost completely, culminating in the closure of Drexel Burnham Lambert, the junk-bond king. Liquidity problems at other firms, which occurred as business dried up, prompted a Street-wide cost-cutting purge. Layoffs dominated the news. It has been estimated that over the next three years, 70,000 employees were laid off; one-fifth of the total pre-1987 crash work force.

But by 1991, as the recession made front-page news, things started looking up on Wall Street (except for the investment firm Salomon Brothers, which admitted to bidding illegally on the U.S. Treasury markets). The stock market entered into another long bull market, and it became evident that Wall Street was on a different cycle from the rest of the economy. It had entered into the recession first, trimmed its fat earlier, and resumed hiring earlier. But there were changes. Wall Street emerged a bit more conservative, a bit less wildly optimistic. And by 1993, as the bull market wavered, there was talk once more about retrenchment.

WHAT'S NEXT

▶ The key in the next years: fierce competition for the same customer.

The financial marketplace is becoming crowded, as banks, insurance firms, and other giants seek to offer the same services to the same customer. Expect more competition in the near future—and various changes.

General Electric and Sears have already acquired securities subsidiaries, while the weakening of regulatory barriers has brought banks such as Citicorp into the mutual-fund business.

Three major results: pricing pressures, emphasis on sales, and emphasis on service.

Responding to these challenges, securities firms are postioning themselves in various ways. Giant brokerage houses like Merrill Lynch are transforming their retail arms into full-service financial planners, moving their emphasis away from individual securities transactions and into "wraparound" accounts that take care of all of a client's financial needs. Other firms are focusing differently. Various investment banks are transforming themselves into old-line merchant banks, much like the classic British ones such as Baring Brothers. Other investment firms are beefing up their trading arms, reducing customer contacts, and trading their own accounts. The key strategy is concentration on "core" areas—where they do business best.

▶ Companies will continue to expand geographically or into businesses that relate to core areas.

The places to watch are the traditional money centers of Europe, Japan, and East Asia. Key: Telecommunications advances and declining regulatory barriers have increased the flow of investments across international borders. U.S. firms have expanded abroad, where their branches buy foreign investments for U.S. portfolios as well as participate in foreign domestic market—giving others access to U.S. sources of finance. At the same time, foreign firms will further increase their presence in this country. One example of this trend: In 1981, 3.4% of total capital in U.S. securities markets was from foreign-controlled securities firms. In 1989 this amount skyrocketed to 12.4%. The bottom line? Finance has become truly global, and U.S. investment and securities firms realize it.

▶ **To some degree, the investment banking mission of the 1990s will be to continue to undo the 1980s.**

Even with the ups and downs of the market, watch for debt-equity swaps as corporate America deleverages itself. Expect more investment banks to act as merchant banks, taking an equity stake in the companies they take public—and earning large profits.

Another trend is a move toward private partnerships, away from the 1980s' ideal of public ownership. Combine the two trends and you see a return, to some degree, of the old investment banking days. With their own partnership money on the line, investment bankers will be conservative, not flamboyant.

Along the same lines, look for more investment boutiques—small firms that tend to specialize in one financial area. Look for local investment banks to pick up more business—the feeling is, it's better to do business with a financial firm down the street that really knows you. Also watch the number of true investment banks diminish—perhaps by 25 to 33% by the end of the 1990s.

Key factor: Be prepared for virtually anything. The increasing volatility and worldwide size of the markets makes calling the shots on Wall Street very tricky . . . but potentially very lucrative.

EMPLOYMENT OUTLOOK: Good in long term.

Key long-term trend: more money into the financial services industry will generate demand for more financial salespeople and advisors. Rationale: as baby boomers age (the 45–64 age group saves the most of any group on average), even more money will come into the securities markets as their incomes rise, they inherit money, and they save for retirement. Also, with the increasing array of investment products and options, more investment advisors will be needed to guide investors through a bewildering array of options—from IRAs, SEPs and Keoghs to REITs, annuities and mutual funds.

Best area for employment: financial sales. After cutbacks stemming from the financial recession, in 1991 hiring began again, and by early 1993 salaries and bonuses were once again approaching the heights of precrash Wall Street. One warning: jobs on Wall Street and related areas are highly dependent on the state of the economy. Regardless of long-term trends, short-term hiring outlook can be variable.

Employment tips: look for a greater emphasis on hiring of older applicants. For example, in 1990, the average age of a Dean Witter recruit was twenty-six, by 1991 thirty-six. Why? Older recruits bring business experience (often in unrelated industries), maturity, drive—and contacts with money to invest. Also look for an emphasis on "softer skills"—less a hard sell than the ability to get and *keep* clients. Reason: many firms are now looking to get clients to place *all* their money with a broker, from banking accounts to insurance to investments—for a fee. The broker, or financial advisor, now serves more as a hand-holder and front man, passing on the management of his or her client's money to various experts within the firm.

JOBS SPOTLIGHT

REORGANIZATION SPECIALISTS: The more experience one has in this area the better, but this is one Wall Street specialty that is attractive to newly minted MBAs as well. The job: These individuals often work with mergers-and-acquisition specialists and merchant bankers. They target potential candidates, act in advisory roles to companies, and arrange for the purchase of company debt. In effect, they design and/or implement strategies for troubled companies. Because of the complexity of the job, there is a shortage of experts in the field.

PRIVATE-PLACEMENT SPECIALISTS: These individuals help companies sell debt or stock directly to institutional investors through private placement. Though it's not considered a "glamour" area by many on Wall Street, this should be a good employment bet. Typical salary is $250,000; those structuring more complex deals earn more.

BEST BETS

Merrill Lynch
World Financial Center
New York, NY 10080
212/449-1000

As the premier retail house, it is still expanding into such quasi-banking practices as business lending and insurance. According to an insider, "anyone contemplating a career at Merrill should expect that an increasing share of his income will be derived from nontraditional investment areas, such as insurance, and business lending, instead of the traditional stocks and bonds."

A. G. Edwards & Sons
1 N. Jefferson St.
787 Seventh Avenue
St. Louis, MO 63103
314/289-3000

This is the broker's brokerage house. It consistently wins accolades from brokers as *the* place for ethics and honesty as well as quality work. It has a conservative approach to the business, it doesn't pressure its brokers to sell the latest hot investment product but rather lets them pick what *they* feel objectively suits their clients' investment objectives. It has high payouts for brokers, and possibly the best retirement package in the business. Branches in New York, New Jersey, Washington, DC, Colorado, California and Florida.

Another best bet is the premier investment firm **Goldman Sachs.**

TOP SECURITIES COMPANIES

Bear Stearns Cos., Inc.
245 Park Ave.
New York, NY 10167
212/272-2000

Dean Witter Financial Services Group
2 World Trade Ctr.
New York, NY 10048
212/392-2222

Donaldson Lufkin & Jenrette
140 Broadway
New York, NY 10005
212/504-3000

A. G. Edwards & Sons
1 N. Jefferson St.
St. Louis, MO 63103
314/289-3000

Equitable Investment Corp.
787 Seventh Ave.
New York, NY 10019
212/554-2555

First Boston Corp.
55 E. 52nd St.
New York, NY 10055
212/909-2000

Goldman Sachs Group
85 Broad St.
New York, NY 10004
212/902-1000

Kidder Peabody Group, Inc.
10 Hanover Sq.
New York, NY 10005
212/510-3000

Legg Mason, Inc.
111 S. Calvert St.
Baltimore, MD 21203
301/539-3400

Merrill Lynch & Co.
North Tower
World Financial Ctr.
New York, NY 10281
212/449-1000

Morgan Stanley Group
1251 Ave. of the Americas
New York, NY 10020
212/703-4000

Oppenheimer Group
Oppenheimer Tower
World Financial Ctr.
New York, NY 10281
212/667-7000

PaineWebber Group
1285 Ave. of the Americas
New York, NY 10019
212/713-2000

Piper Jaffrey & Hopwood Incorporated
222 S. Ninth St.
Minneapolis, MN 55402
612/342-6000

Prudential-Bache Securities
1 Seaport Plz.
New York, NY 10292
212/776-1000

Salomon, Inc.
7 World Trade Ctr.
New York, NY 10048
212/747-7000

Charles Schwab Corp.
101 Montgomery St.
San Francisco, CA 94104
415/627-7000

Shearson Lehman Hutton
American Express Tower
World Financial Ctr.
New York, NY 10285
212/298-2000

Smith Barney, Harris Upham & Co.
1345 Ave. of the Americas
New York, NY 10105
212/399-6000

TOP CREDIT AGENCIES, ETC.

American Express
American Express
Tower
World Financial Ctr.
New York, NY 10285
212/640-2000

Beneficial Corp.
4000 Bellevue Pkwy.
Wilmington, DE 19809
302/798-0800

H&R Block
4410 Main St.
Kansas City, MO
64111
816/753-6900

**The Dreyfus
Corporation**
200 Park Ave.
New York, NY 10166
212/922-6000

Equifax
1600 Peachtree St.,
NW
Atlanta, GA 30309
404/885-8000

**Federal Home Loan
Mortgage Corp.**
8200 Jones Branch Dr.
McLean, VA 22102
703/903-2000

**Federal National
Mortgage Association**
3900 Wisconsin Ave.,
NW
Washington, DC 20016
202/752-7000

Fidelity Investments
82 Devonshire St.
Boston, MA 02109
617/570-7000

Franklin Resources
P.O. Box 7777
San Mateo, CA
94403-7777
415/570-3000

GATX Corp.
120 S. Riverside Plz.
Chicago, IL 60606
312/621-6200

**Household
International, Inc**
2700 Sanders Rd.
Prospect Heights, IL
60070
708/564-5000

MBIA, Inc.
113 King St.
Armonk, NY 10504
914/273-4545

MBNA Corp.
400 Christiana Rd.
Newark, DE 19713
302/453-9930

Primerica
65 E. 55th St.
New York, NY 10022
212/891-8900

**Student Loan
Marketing Association
(Sallie Mae)**
1050 Jefferson St., NW
Washington, DC 20007
202/333-8000

WHERE TO GO FOR MORE INFORMATION

(For more information sources in related areas, also see "Banking," page 267.)

FINANCIAL SERVICES INDUSTRY ASSOCIATIONS

**Association for
Investment
Management and
Research**
P.O. Box 3668
Charlottesville, VA
22901
804/977-5724
(Operates free
twenty-four-hour job

opportunities hot line,
for members only.)

**Commercial Finance
Association**
225 W. 34th St.,
Suite 1815
New York, NY 10122
212/594-3400

**Financial Analysts
Federation**
5 Boar's Head Lane
Charlottesville, VA
22903
804/980-3688
(Operates free
twenty-four-hour job
opportunities hot line,
for members only.)

Financial Executives Institute
10 Madison Ave.
Morristown, NJ 07960
201/898-4600
(Offers members free job-hunting services, including career counseling and job referrals.)

Financial Managers Society
111 E. Wacker Dr.

Chicago, IL 60601
312/938-2576

National Association of Real Estate Investment Trusts
1129 20th St. NW
Washington, DC 20036
202/785-8717

International Credit Association
243 N. Lindbergh Blvd.

St. Louis, MO 63141
314/991-3030

National Association of Credit Management
8815 Centre Park Dr.
Columbia, MD 21045
410/740-5560

Securities Industry Association
120 Broadway
New York, NY 10271
212/608-1500

FINANCIAL SERVICES INDUSTRY DIRECTORIES

Bankers Monthly Roster of Major Finance Companies
Bankers Monthly
601 Skokie Blvd.
Northbrook, IL 60062
312/498-2500

Corporate Finance Sourcebook
National Register Publishing Company
3004 Glenview Rd.
Wilmette, IL 60091

708/441-2210
800/323-6772

Directory of American Financial Institutions
McFadden Business Publications
6195 Crooked Creek Rd.
Norcross, GA 30092
404/448-1011

Moody's Bank and Finance Manual
Moody's Investor

Service
99 Church St.
New York, NY 10007
212/553-0300

Securities Industry Yearbook
Securities Industry Association
120 Broadway
New York, NY 10271
212/608-1500

FINANCIAL SERVICES INDUSTRY MAGAZINES

Barron's National Business and Financial Weekly
200 Liberty St.
New York, NY 10281
212/416-2700
(Weekly newspaper for finance executives, investors, etc.)

Financial Planning
Macmillan Information Company, Inc.

910 Sylvan Ave.
Englewood Cliffs, NJ 07632
800/562-0245

Financial Services Report
Philips Publishing
7811 Montrose Rd.
Potomac, MD 20854
301/340-2100

Financial World
Financial World Partners
1328 Broadway
New York, NY 10001
212/594-5030

Futures: The Magazine of Commodities and Options
219 Main St.
Cedar Falls, IA 50613
800/221-1271

(Monthly magazine
aimed at commodity
and options traders.)

Institutional Investor
488 Madison Ave.
New York, NY 10022
212/303-3300
(Monthly magazine for
a range of people
involved in the
investment area,
including brokers,
portfolio managers,

bankers, financial
consultants, and
professional investors.)

Pension World
6255 Barfield Rd.
Atlanta, GA 30328
404/256-9800
(Monthly publication
for institutional
investors as well as
accountants, trust
officers, etc.)

***Pensions & Investment
Age***
220 E. 42nd St.
New York, NY 10017
212/210-0121
(Biweekly newspaper
for pension plan
managers, executives,
and administrators.)

FOOD & BEVERAGE

(including Food Processing, Beverage Processing, and Food Retailing)

INDUSTRY OUTLOOK: Changeable, as competition heats up and consumer demands shift.

Food Processing: Still coping with changes brought about by the recession, the resulting cost-consciousness and consumer disloyalty to brand names that rocked them in 1992–93. Expect to see more companies relying less on marketing than in the past, and paying more attention to efficient manufacturing and distribution. Also: watch for the impact of the new FDA food labeling laws (announced in December 1992, but not required until May 1994), which lay out what, where and how processors tell consumers about nutritional and health information. One possible result—a decrease in food imports from other countries.

Beverages: Hot competition ahead, as soft-drink companies try to tap into changing consumer demands. Smaller firms may be squeezed as the large companies muscle in on their turf—such as "New Age" drinks.

Alcoholic Beverages: Not a promising outlook, as the industry faces a number of key challenges—such as a drop in consumer demand, intensifying competition at home, and problems arising in the international marketplace.

Food Retailers: Slow, steady growth forecast over the long term. Key challenge: hot competition, especially from new entries such as warehouse clubs.

Food retailers are also in for hot competition as they try to regain ground lost during the recession. One dark cloud: stronger competition from non-supermarket chains, price discounters, and warehouse clubs.

A LOOK BACK

▶ **The mergers-and-acquisitions binge that swept the country in the 1980s had a strong effect on the food industry. Then it was straight into a recession—and a period of slowed growth and flatter sales.**

The past decade was a volatile time: companies changed hands; brands switched from company to company; and industry giants swallowed other industry giants. Some big deals: Phillip Morris Companies' purchase of Kraft Foods; Tyson's purchase of Holly Farms, PepsiCo's purchase of General Cinema's buying operations.

Then came the '90s, and with it a slowdown in sales and growth and an increase in promotions and price cutting. The result? Cost cutting, including several plant closings and a flurry of layoffs. At the same time, companies began to experiment with new products in an attempt to regain growth.

▶ **A battery of changes had a strong impact on the food retailing business.**

The changes were as follows: a shifting marketplace with fewer housewives, more working women, and a bulge of aging baby boomers; increasing operational costs; stronger competition from smaller regional stores. The result of these changes was a round of mergers and takeovers, and restructuring and refocusing as companies tried to adapt to their changing customers. The recession hit food retailers fairly hard, leading to a period of low sales. In a double whammy, supermarkets also faced hotter competition from such competitors as warehouse clubs and other discount stores.

WHAT'S NEXT

▶ **The two key trends of the future: new-product development and overseas expansion.**

These two areas are where the action will be in the long term. Companies will be trying to come up with new products to cling to market share and at the same time will be trying to find new avenues of growth by seeking new marketplaces overseas.

▶ **New product development will center around the needs of a changing marketplace.**

It's the only way to keep—and grow—market share. Expect to see competitive lines introduced by most major companies that are directly targeted to distinct niches in the marketplace: working parents, aging baby boomers, ethnic groups, and the like.

For example, one new product line, frozen food for kids, is designed to ease the burden of working parents. Foods that are lower in sodium, calories, or carbohydrates are aimed at newly health-conscious baby boomers and their elders. Ethnic packaged and frozen foods are aimed at the diverse ethnic groups in the country. Look for more product developments along these lines—and more head-to-head competition between companies eager to cash in on the different markets. Still continuing to be the hottest area for new products: "light" foods and drinks.

The impact on employment? More action—and possibly more job opportunities—in R&D in particular, as competing companies work to develop new products. There should be similar emphasis on product management and brand development. And finally, sales and marketing staffers will be needed to push the new products.

▶ **One aspect of heated-up competition: Watch supermarket house brands and other small brands take away sales from the big brand names.**

It's part of the erosion of brand loyalty. During the recession, consumers became more cost conscious—and thus began leaving their usual brands and switching to whatever was the least expensive. Often, the least expensive comparable product was a store brand or a smaller, lesser-known brand. But with the recession easing, customers haven't been as quick to switch back as the larger companies hoped. Expect this trend to continue. This will result in increased promotional activity, a stronger presence in the marketplace by store brands and small brands, and, of course, hotter competition between the big and the small players. Also expect to see more action in niche areas—to avoid head-to-head competition, companies, especially smaller ones, will be bringing out products to fit into a narrow niche (health food, gourmet foods, international foods, etc.).

On the employment side, this trend away from brand loyalty means higher visibility for promotion staffers—and possibly increased employment opportunities. In addition, smaller companies may offer better employment opportunities than in the past, as they continue to grow.

▶ With competition so strong in the U.S., food and beverage companies will keep pushing aggressively overseas.

Foreign markets should prove to be the hottest arena for the domestic food and beverage industry. Expect to see more companies trying to establish brand presence and market share in Europe, in particular, as well as in Japan.

Along the same lines, watch for an increase in joint ventures between U.S. companies and their foreign counterparts—one of the safest ways for domestic companies to expand overseas. A common scenario: A U.S. company supplies the technology or product formulation, and the foreign company supplies sales distribution, warehousing, production facilities—and, most important, marketing.

The effect of this on employment? An increased demand for food marketing specialists with international experience. For more information, see Jobs Spotlight, page 360.

▶ Expect to see a rise in joint ventures between beverage companies.

This trend has already begun. In 1991, for example, Coke and Pepsi joined in what they termed "strategic alliances" in an effort to come up with non-cola brands. And each of them has also teamed up with other companies in other ventures: Pepsi with Thomas J. Lipton Co. to develop tea-based drinks, and with Ocean Spray for fruit-based drinks; Coca-Cola with Nestle Beverage Co. to market tea-based drinks. Look for more developments like these.

▶ Alcoholic beverage producers will be facing strong competition and a continuing drop in demand.

With the national interest in health and fitness still going strong, alcohol companies will continue to suffer a decline in consumer demand. This will result in stronger competition, as companies fight for a piece of the shrinking market. As with food products, "light" will be the focus of most new alcoholic beverages—light and dry beers, alcoholic cooler-type drinks, etc.

▶ Food retailers will be trying to keep up with the demands and desires of the changing marketplace.

This is the chief way of beating the competition and keeping customers coming in. With the population growing more slowly than in the past, food retailers will be carefully focusing their products and promotional efforts to fit the specific demographics of their customers. An aging, health-conscious population will mean that many food retailers will be paying special attention to produce. Also coming on strong: organic and natural foods supermarkets. This looks like an area with hot growth prospects.

▶ **Another major trend in the food industry: the emergence of a new relationship between food processors and food retailers.**

This is a trend that should be growing in the long term. Advances in technology and competitive pressures will be forcing retailers and suppliers to work more as partners than in the past. This will mean different things to different companies. For example, as mentioned in a 1992 *Progressive Grocer* article, food processors and distributors may ship directly to a supermarket; in other cases they will set up Electronic Data Interchange (EDI) programs to reduce paperwork and allow better inventory control; in other case they will arrange special promotion deals or the like.

This may change the employment picture to some degree, as field salespeople may have more responsibility in terms of working out alliances with the supermarkets to which they sell. Customer support services will become a hotter area. Another probability: the growth of "category managers," people responsible for an entire category of product as opposed to one or two brands. This is an interesting area to keep an eye on.

EMPLOYMENT OUTLOOK: Fair, but like the industry itself, competitive.

As the food and beverage industry steels itself for stiff competition, many companies are cutting back on jobs, trying to streamline operations and restructure. This should stabilize in the long term, however.

With more new-product introductions expected as companies try to keep attracting new customers, employment opportunities may be found in product management. Another area that looks good in the long term is advertising.

With so much attention turned toward overseas expansion, employment opportunities should be stronger for people with international backgrounds.

JOBS SPOTLIGHT

FOOD MARKETING SPECIALISTS: A growing field that hasn't peaked yet, food marketing is looking hot. A key reason for this is the internationalization of the U.S. food industry. Now that fast food has made inroads abroad and (literally) whet the appetites of a huge new market, food-processing companies are moving in to sell their products to that overseas market. Requirements vary, but a marketing degree and related experience are a definite plus. Best—a degree in food service or food marketing.

FOOD SCIENTISTS: New-product development—especially fat-free, sugar-free, and other "nutrition-sensitive" products—will create a long-term need for food scientists. The career track for food scientists (especially those involved in product R&D) often leads to managerial positions. Salaries reach the high $50s for people with B.S. and M.S. degrees, higher for those with Ph.Ds.

BEST BETS

Ben & Jerry's Homemade Inc.
Route 100
P.O. Box 240
Waterbury VT 05676
802/244-5641

Well known as a company that cares about its employees and about social causes, Ben & Jerry's is an innovative firm that truly seems to try to keep its employees happy and motivated. One strong point: The company maintains a seven-to-one salary ratio—that is, no one in the company can make more than seven times what another employee makes, even a top manager. It also offers what it calls "joy grants." These are grants of $500 given to work groups to pay for improvements as they see fit. Other policies: tuition reimbursements, evaluate-your-boss polls, maternity, paternity, and adoption leaves, child-care centers, wellness programs, paid health club fees. For these and other reasons, the esprit de corps at Ben & Jerry's is reportedly very high, making it a great place to work.

PepsiCo, Inc.
700 Anderson Hill Rd.
Purchase, NY 10577
914/253-2000

Chosen one of Fortune's most admired corporations in 1990, one of the best companies for blacks by *Black Enterprise* in 1992, and a Best Bet in *Jobs '93*, PepsiCo has a reputation for being a good place to work, with an ability to attract, develop, and keep talented people. The key reason for this? Policies that treat employees well. For example, in 1989 Pepsico began the practice of giving each employee stock options equal to 10% of his or her salary. It operates a mentor program for minority employees and has a good reputation for hiring and promoting minorities and women.

RJR Nabisco Inc.
1301 Ave. of the Americas
New York, NY 10019
212/258-5600

This snack-food and cigarette company offers a number of excellent benefits for employees. One of the newest—and one that is attracting a great deal of attention—is its education initiative package, which includes a child education assistance program. Under this, RJR Nabisco helps employees pay for their children's secondary education, offering such things as payment of fees and/or interest on school loans and payments up to $4,000 per employee to go toward tuition and other school expenses. Other benefits include skills training programs, a matched savings plan to go toward a child's education, assistance in applying for and securing student loans, and more. This focus on education and assistance for employee's children makes RJR Nabisco a good choice for workers with families.

TOP FOOD COMPANIES

Agway, Inc.
333 Butternut Dr.
P.O. Box 4933
Syracuse, NY 13221
315/449-6127

American Crystal Sugar Co.
101 N. Third St.
Moorhead, MN 56560
218/236-4400

American Maize-Products Co.
250 Harbor Dr.
Stamford, CT 06904
203/356-9000

Archer-Daniels-Midland Co.
4666 Faries Pkwy.
Decatur, IL 62526
217/424-5200

Beatrice Co.
2 N. LaSalle St.
Chicago, IL 60602
312/558-4000

Beatrice/Hunt–Wesson Foods
1645 W. Valencia Dr.
Fullerton, CA 92634
714/680-1000

Borden, Inc.
277 Park Ave.
New York, NY 10172
212/573-4000

Campbell Soup Co.
Campbell Pl.
Camden, NJ 08103
609/342-4800

Chiquita Brands International, Inc.
250 E. Fifth St.
Cincinnati, OH 45202
513/784-8000

ConAgra, Inc.
1 ConAgra Dr.
Omaha, NE 68102
402/595-4000

CPC International, Inc.
International Plz.
P.O. Box 8000
Englewood Cliffs, NJ 07632
201/894-4000

Dean Foods Co.
3600 N. River Rd.
Franklin Park, IL 60131
312/625-6200

Del Monte Foods
1 Market Plz.
San Francisco, CA 94105
415/442-4000

Doskocil Companies, Inc.
321 N. Main St.
S. Hutchinson, KS 67505
316/663-1005

DWG Corp.
6917 Collins Ave.,
Drawer K
Miami Beach, FL 33141
305/866-7771

Erly Industries Inc.
10990 Wilshire Blvd.,
Suite 500
Los Angeles, CA 90024
213/879-1480

Flowers Industries, Inc.
200 U.S. Hwy. 19 S.
Thomasville, GA 31799
912/226-9110

General Mills, Inc.
1 General Mills Blvd.
Minneapolis, MN 55426
612/540-2311

Gerber Products Co.
445 State St.
Fremont, MI 49413
616/928-2000

Gold Kist, Inc.
244 Perimeter Ctr.
Pkwy., NE
Atlanta, GA 30346
404/393-5000

Grand Metropolitan PLC Pillsbury
(subs. of Grand Metropolitan PLC)
200 S. Sixth St.
Minneapolis, MN

55402
612/330-4966

H. J. Heinz Co.
600 Grand St.
Pittsburgh, PA 15219
412/456-5700

Hershey Foods Corp.
100 Crystal A. Dr.
Hershey, PA 17033
717/534-4000

George A. Hormel & Co.
501 16th Ave., NE
P.O. Box 800
Austin, MN 55912
507/437-5611

IBC Holdings Corp.
12 E. Armour Blvd.
P.O. Box 419627
Kansas City, MO 64111
816/561-6600

IBP, Inc.
IBP Ave.
Dakota City, NE 68731
402/494-2061

Imperial Holly Corp.
8016 Hwy. 90-A
Sugarland, TX 77487
713/491-9181

International Multifoods Corp.
Multifoods Tower
33 S. Sixth St.
Minneapolis, MN 55402
612/340-3300

Kellogg Co.
1 Kellogg Sq.
Battle Creek, MI 49016
616/961-2000

Kraft General Foods, Inc.
Kraft Ct.

Glenview, IL 60025
708/998-2000

Lance, Inc.
8600 S. Blvd.
Charlotte, NC 28273
704/554-1421

Land O'Lakes, Inc.
4001 Lexington Ave. N.
Arden Hills, MN 55112
612/481-2222

Thomas J. Lipton, Inc.
(subs. of Unilever PLC Lipton)
800 Sylvan Ave.
Englewood Cliffs, NJ 07632
201/567-8000

Mars
6885 Elm St.
McLean, VA 22101
703/821-4900

McCormick & Co., Inc.
18 Loveton Circle
Sparks, MD 21152
410/771-7301

Michael Foods
5353 Wayzata Blvd.
Minneapolis, MN 55416
612/546-1500

Morningstar Foods, Inc.
5956 Sherry Ln., Suite 1100
Dallas, TX 75225
214/360-4700

National Grape Co-op Association, Inc.
2 S. Portage St.
Westfield, NY 14787
716/326-3131

Nestlé Chocolate and Confection Co., Inc.
100 Manhattanville Rd.
Purchase, NY 10377
914/251-3000

Nestlé Food Company
800 N. Brand Blvd.
Glendale, CA 91203
818/549-6000

Philip Morris Cos., Inc.
120 Park Ave.
New York, NY 10017
212/880-5000

The Procter & Gamble Co.
1 Procter & Gamble Plz.
Cincinnati, OH 45202
513/983-1100

The Quaker Oats Co.
321 N. Clark St.
Chicago, IL 60610
312/222-7111

Ralston Purina Co.
Checkerboard Sq.
St. Louis, MO 63164
314/982-1000

RJR Nabisco, Inc.
1301 Ave. of the Americas
New York, NY 10019
212/258-5600

Sara Lee Corp.
3 First National Plz.
Chicago, IL 60602
312/726-2600

Savannah Foods & Industries, Inc.
2 E. Bryan St.
Savannah, GA 31402
912/234-1261

Seaboard Corp.
200 Boylston St.
Newton MA 02167
617/332-8492

Smithfield Foods, Inc.
501 N. Church St.
P.O. Box 447
Smithfield, VA 23430
804/357-4321

J. M. Smucker Co.
Strawberry Ln.
P.O. Box 280
Orrville, OH 44667
216/682-0015

Thorn Apple Valley, Inc.
18700 W. Ten Mile Rd.
Southfield, MI 48075
313/552-0700

TLC Beatrice International Holdings
9 W. 57th St.
New York, NY 10019
212/756-8900

Universal Foods Corp.
433 E. Michigan St.
Milwaukee, WI 53202
414/271-6755

WLR Foods, Inc.
P.O. Box 228
Hinton, VA 22831
703/867-4001

Wm. Wrigley Jr., Co.
410 N. Michigan Ave.
Chicago, IL 60611
312/644-2121

TOP BEVERAGE COMPANIES

American Brands, Inc.
1700 E. Putnam Ave.
P.O. Box 0811
Old Greenwich, CT 06870
203/698-5000

Anheuser-Busch Companies, Inc.
1 Busch Pl.
St. Louis, MO 63118
314/577-2000

Bacardi Imports
2100 Biscayne Blvd.
Miami, FL 33137
305/573-8511

Brown-Forman Corp.
850 Dixie Hwy.
P.O. Box 1080
Louisville, KY 40210
502/585-1100

The Coca-Cola Co.
1 Coca-Cola Plz., NW
Atlanta, GA 30313
404/676-2121

Coca-Cola Bottling Co. of Chicago
7400 N. Oak Park Ave.
Chicago, IL 60648
708/775-0900

Coca-Cola Bottling Co. Consolidated
1900 Rexford Rd.
Charlotte, NC 28211
704/551-4400

Coca-Cola Bottling Co. of New York
20 Horseneck Ln.
Greenwich, CT 06830
203/625-4000

Coca-Cola Enterprises
(bottling company group)
1 Coca-Cola Plz., NW
Atlanta, GA 30313
404/676-2100

Adolph Coors Co.
311 Tenth St.
Golden, CO 80401
303/279-6565

Dr Pepper/Seven UP Companies, Inc.
8144 Walnut Hill Ln.
Dallas, TX 75231
214/ 360-7000

E&J Gallo Winery
600 Yosemite Blvd.
Modesto, CA 95353
209/579-3111

G. Helleman Brewing Co.
100 Harborview
LaCrosse, WI 54601
608/785-1000

Johnston Coca-Cola
600 Krystal Bldg.
Union Sq.
Chattanooga, TN 37402
615/756-1202

John Labatt Ltd.
451 Ridout St. N.
P.O. Box 5870
London, Ont. N6A 5L3
Canada
519/667-7612

Miller Brewing Company
(subs of Philip Morris Co.)
3939 W. Highland Blvd.
Milwaukee, WI 53201
414/931-2000

The Molson Companies Ltd.
40 King St. W.
Rexdale, Ont. M5H 3Z5
Canada
416/360-1786

Ocean Spray Cranberries, Inc.
1 Ocean Spray Dr.
Lakeville-Middleboro, MA 02360
508/946-1000

PepsiCo, Inc.
Anderson Hill Rd.
Purchase, NY 10577
914/253-2000

Joseph E. Seagram & Sons
375 Park Ave.
New York, NY 10152
212/572-7000

The Stroh Brewing Co.
100 River Pl.
Detroit, MI 48207
313/446-2000

Vintners International
800 S. Alta St.
Gonzales, CA 93926
408/675-2481

Whitman Corp.
(Pepsi-Cola General Bottlers)
3501 Algonquin Rd.
Rolling Meadows, IL 60008
708/818-5000

TOP FOOD RETAILERS

Acme Markets, Inc.
75 Valley Stream Pkwy.
Malvern PA 19355
215/889-4000

Albertson's, Inc.
250 Parkcenter Blvd.
Boise, ID 83726
208/385-6200

American Stores Co.
709 E. South Temple
Salt Lake City, UT 84102
801/539-0112

Bruno's, Inc.
800 Lakeshore Pkwy.
Birmingham, AL 35211
205/940-9400

Circle K Corp.
1601 N. Seventh St.
Phoenix, AZ 85006
6023/253-9600

Dominick's Finer Foods
505 Railroad Ave.
Northlake, IL 60164
708/562-1000

Food Lion, Inc.
2110 Executive Dr.
Salisbury, NC 28144
704/633-8250

Furr's Inc.
1708 Ave. G.
Lubbock, TX 79408
806/763-1931

Giant Eagle, Inc.
101 Kappa Dr.
Pittsburgh, PA 15238
412/963-6200

Giant Food, Inc.
P.O. Box 1804
Washington, DC 20013
301/341-4100

Grand Union Co.
201 Willowbrook Blvd.
Wayne, NJ 07470
201/890-6000

Great Atlantic & Pacific Tea Co.
2 Paragon Dr.
Montvale, NJ 07645
201/573-9700

Hannaford Bros. Co.
145 Pleasant Hill Rd.
Scarborough, ME 04074
207/883-2911

HEB Grocery
646 S. Main Ave.
San Antonio, TX 78204
512/246-8000

Hy-Vee Food Stores
1801 Osceola Ave.
Chariton, IA 50049
515/774-2121

Kroger Co.
1014 Vine St.
Cincinnati, OH 45202
513/762-4000

Lucky Stores, Inc.
6300 Clark Ave.
Dublin, CA 94568
510/833-6000

Fred Meyer, Inc.
3800 SE 22nd Ave.
Portland, OR 97202
503/232-8844

**The Penn Traffic
Company**
319 Washington St.
Johnstown, PA 15901
814/536-9900

Publix Super Markets
1936 George Jenkins
Blvd.
Lakeland, FL 33802
813/688-1188

**Ralph's Supermarkets
Inc.**
1100 W. Artesia Blvd.
Compton, CA 90220
213/637-1101

**Red Apple Companies
Inc.**
823 11th Ave.
New York, NY 10019
212/956-5770

Safeway Stores, Inc.
201 Fourth St.
Oakland CA 94660
510/891-3000

Shaw's Supermarkets
140 Laurel St.
East Bridgewater, MA
02333
617/378-7211

**Stop & Shop
Companies**
60 Campanelli Dr.

Braintree, MA 02184
617/380-8000

**Supermarkets General
Corp.**
301 Blair Rd.
Woodbridge, NJ 07095
908/499-3000

**The Vons Companies,
Inc.**
618 Michillinda Ave.
Arcadia, CA 91007
818/821-7000

Weis Markets
1000 S. Second St.
Sunbury, PA 17801
717/286-4571

**Winn-Dixie Stores,
Inc.**
5050 Edgewood Ct.
Jacksonville, FL 32205
904/783-5000

WHERE TO GO FOR MORE INFORMATION

FOOD AND BEVERAGE INDUSTRY ASSOCIATIONS

**American Bakers
Association**
1111 14th St., NW
Washington, DC 20005
202/296-5800

**American Frozen
Food Institute**
1764 Old Meadow Ln.
McLean, VA 22102
703/821-0770

**Biscuit & Cracker
Manufacturers
Association**
888 16th St., NW
Washington, DC 20006
202/898-1636

**Distilled Spirits
Council of the United
States**
1250 I St., NW, Suite
900
Washington, DC 20005
202/628-3544

**Grocer Manufacturers
Association**
1010 Wisconsin Ave.,
NW,
Suite 800
Washington, DC 20007
202/337-6233
(Puts out free annual
directory.)

**International Frozen
Food Association**
1700 Old Meadow Rd.
McLean, VA 22102
703/821-0770

**Milk Industry
Foundation**
888 16th St., NW
Washington, DC 20006
202/296-4250

**National Food Brokers
Association**
1010 Massachusetts
Ave., NW
Washington, DC 20001
202/789-2844

**National Food
Processors Association**
1010 Wisconsin Ave.,
NW,
Suite 800

Washington, DC 20005
202/639-5900

**National Soft Drink
Association**
1101 16th St., NW
Washington, DC 20036
202/463-6732

FOOD AND BEVERAGE INDUSTRY DIRECTORIES

*American Frozen Food
Industry Directory*
American Frozen Food
Institute
1764 Old Meadow Ln.
McLean, VA 22102
703/821-0770

*Food Engineering's
Directory of U.S. Food
and Beverage Plants*
Chilton Book Co.
Chilton Way
Radnor, PA 19089
215/687-8200

*Hereld's 5000: The
Directory of Leading
U.S. Food,
Confectionary,
Beverage and Petfood
Manufacturers*
The Hereld Org.
200 Leeder Hill Dr.
Ste. 341
Hamden, CT 06517
203/281-6766

Jobson's Handbook
**Jobson Publishing
Corp.**
325 Park Ave. South
New York, NY 10010

212/685-4848
(Covers the alcoholic
beverage industry.)

*Prepared Foods
Industry Sourcebook*
Prepared Foods
8750 W. Bryn Mawr
Ave.
Chicago, IL 60631
312/693-3200

*Progressive Grocer's
Marketing Guidebook*
4 Stamford Forum
Stamford, CT 06901
203/325-3500

FOOD AND BEVERAGE INDUSTRY PERIODICALS

Beverage Industry
7500 Old Oak Blvd.
Cleveland, OH 44130
216/243-8100
(Monthly publication
for those involved in
the bottling and
distribution of soft
drinks, beer, and wine.)

Beverage World
150 Great Neck Rd.
Great Neck, NY 11021
516/829-9210
(Monthly magazine for
beverage industry
executives. Puts out
annual leading
companies issue, which

may be useful for
targeting a résumé
mailing list.)

*Convenience Store
News*
7 Penn Plz.
New York, NY 10001
212/594-4120
(Tabloid for executives
in the convenience store
industry, as well as
suppliers and
distributors.)

Food Business
301 East Erie Street
Chicago, IL 60611
312/644-2020

(Monthly magazine
covering food industry.)

Food Engineering
Chilton Way
Radnor, PA 19089
215/964-4448
(Monthly magazine for
food industry personnel,
including food
processors, equipment
manufacturers and
distributors, retailers,
etc.)

Food Processing
301 E. Erie St.
Chicago, IL 60611
312/644-2020

(Monthly magazine, plus annual special issue, covering all aspects of food processing industry.)

Frozen Food Age
230 Park Ave.
New York, NY 10017
212/697-4727
(Monthly tabloid for frozen food executives and managers, distributors, and suppliers.)

Health Foods Business
567 Morris Ave.
Elizabeth, NJ 07028
908/353-7373
(Monthly publication for health food industry personnel as well as wholesalers and retailers.)

Meat Processing
1 First St.
Duluth, MN 55802
218/723-9870
800/346-0085
(Monthly magazine covering the meat processing industry, including meat packing,

sausage manufacture, etc.)

Natural Foods Merchandiser
New Hope Communications Inc.
328 S. Main St.
New Hope, PA 18938
215/862-9414

Poultry Processing
1 E. First St.
Duluth, MN 55802
218/723-9870
800/346-0085
(Monthly magazine covering the poultry processing industry, including egg production.)

Prepared Foods
8750 W. Bryn Mawr Ave.
Chicago, IL 60631
312/693-3200
(Monthly publication for those involved in the prepared food industry, including distributors, retailers, and sales and production personnel.)

Progressive Grocer
4 Stamford Forum
Stamford, CT 06901
203/325-3500
(Monthly magazine for grocery/supermarket executives, owners, operators, etc.)

Snack Food
1 E. First St.
Duluth, MN 55802
218/723-9870
800/346-0085
(Monthly magazine covering the snack food industry.)

Supermarket Business
342 Madison Ave.
New York, NY 10173
212/867-2350
(Monthly magazine for supermarket executives, owners, etc.)

Supermarket News
7 W. 34th St.
New York, NY 10001
212/630-3759
(Weekly tabloid for food store executives, managers, owners, etc.)

HEALTH SERVICES & PHARMACEUTICALS

INDUSTRY OUTLOOK: Long-term changes ahead linked to national policy.

The jury is still out as to how much the health services and pharmaceutical industries will change. But one thing is certain: changes—brought about by the Clinton administration's drive to bring down high health care costs—are inevitable.

Where health services companies are concerned, the probable winners of national health care reform will be managed care groups, such as HMOs. Probable losers? Hospitals.

Governmentally imposed price restraints will be the major challenge for drug companies. Over the short term, watch for continued cost-cutting—with R&D being the last to feel the pinch. At the same time, expect increased competition. A key reason—over the next five years, over 150 top-selling drugs will lose their patent exclusivity. Major manufacturers and generic producers will be going head-to-head, producing lower-cost versions of these.

A LOOK BACK

▶ **The past few years have brought a number of changes to the health services industry, new competition, and growth.**

The biggest change has been the emergence of health maintenance organizations (HMOs) as major players in the healthcare industry. Many individuals and employers, concerned about the high cost of health care, have opted for HMOs over other forms of medical care. As a result, the HMO industry took off, while hospitals started to feel the pinch.

HMOs went through rapid growth—but also through rapid changes: Intense competition and overexpansion led to mergers and industry consolidation as smaller or mismanaged plans were squeezed out of the picture. Hospitals, in the meantime, went through a period of restructuring as well, to counteract several years of slumping profits and dwindling patient admissions. They cut back on beds, beefed up outpatient services, and began trying to learn how to compete with their new rivals.

▶ **Strong growth was the byword for pharmaceutical companies.**

The past few years were good ones for pharmaceutical companies. A run of successful drug introductions, heavy investment in R&D, and a growing number of older Americans combined to make the late '80s and early '90s high-earning years for drug companies. Among the key trends of the period: the emergence of small biotechnology companies as industry growth spots; and, on the other hand, a rash of mergers that resulted in a number of mega-companies dominating the industry. But 1993 brought a new change to the industry: a governmental push to cut drug costs. In response, drug companies started cutting costs (and employees)—and began preparing for leaner times.

WHAT'S NEXT

▶ **Depending upon the specifics of national health care reform, there may be increased competition among health care providers.**

The competition may occur in all levels of the industry. HMOs, currently the industry leaders, will be facing competition from modified HMOs called Preferred Provider Organizations (PPOs), which allow a patient to see a doctor outside of the network; from hospitals that have jumped on the managed-care bandwagon; and from corporations that are setting up their own health network plans.

As for hospitals, they are competing not only with HMOs or PPOs but also with specialized health care providers, such as psychiatric institutions or institutions offering care to substance abusers.

The result of this competition? More mergers and consolidations in the managed-care industry and possible polarization in the hospitals industry—with larger hospitals surviving but smaller hospitals, those in poorer areas, and teaching hospitals facing financial problems.

Another result of the competition will be changes in the services HMOs and hospitals offer. A few trends for HMOs: shifting away from flat fee coverage and charging for such items as prescriptions or office visits; offering "open-ended plans" that allow patients to receive partial reimbursement when receiving treatment outside the HMO.

▶ **As for hospitals, competition may cause them to emphasize outpatient services.**

In a recent *Hospitals* survey, more than two-thirds of those polled believed that outpatient services would account for at least 40% of a hospital's income by the year 2000. As a result, watch hospitals continue to add and expand outpatient and specialty services—such as home health services, freestanding outpatient surgery centers and diagnostic centers, physical rehabilitation, industrial medicine, women's medicine, skilled nursing, and cardiac rehabilitation. They will also be setting up HMOs or PPOs themselves.

These developments will clearly affect employment opportunities. Expect increased opportunities in the fields listed above and other health services.

▶ **Home health care: the hottest industry growth spot.**

This area of health services has been coming on strong for the past decade and will continue to do so. In fact, it may grow even more rapidly than before. As the population ages and as health costs rise, watch home health care take off. As mentioned above, hospitals are adding home health care services to the outpatient services they offer. In addition, the number of home health care companies, many with specific specialties such as brain rehabilitation, is growing.

The impact on the employment picture: Home health aides will be in increasing demand, with growth rates predicted up to 96% over the next twelve years. There will also be increased opportunities for nurses, health consultants, physical therapists, health managers, and others involved in the field.

▶ **The factors having the greatest impact on the pharmaceutical industry are high R&D costs, generic drugs, government regulation, and globalization. First, a look at R&D.**

The entire drug industry is struggling to come up with new products. But this push in product development also means a corresponding rise in R&D costs. Added to this is the cost of clinical drug trials, the increasing expense of high-tech equipment, and the fact that many diseases the drug companies are trying to treat are extremely complex. The result? Drug companies are spending ever-increasing amounts. But even while companies try to cut costs, they will be forced to keep up R&D—as their financial health depends upon developing new drugs.

As for employment, this attention to R&D means job opportunities for chemists, biologists, science technicians, R&D managers, and, ultimately, for marketers and salespeople to sell the new products.

▶ **The growing sales of generic drugs are adding to the already competitive nature of the drug industry.**

As with health services, the drug industry is headed for a period of heightened competition. Domestic pharmaceutical companies will be competing with one another, with foreign manufacturers, and with the newest competitors—generic drug producers.

Generic drug producers are posing new challenges for traditional pharmaceutical companies. One is the fact that generic drug producers have been advertising directly to consumers. As a result, the traditional pharmaceutical companies are stepping up their marketing efforts to stem the flow away from their competitors' products. The outcome? Opportunities in both areas, for pharmaceutical advertising staffers and pharmaceutical marketing professionals.

Another challenge posed by generic drugs is their lower cost. The rising cost of drugs has already upset a great number of consumers—and state and federal government legislators. One development: as patents expire on important drugs, pharmaceutical companies will come out with their own lower-cost generic version to compete with the generic producers—and with their own higher-priced brand-name version.

▶ **U.S. companies will continue their push overseas, especially in Europe.**

The U.S. already has a strong stake in the international market, accounting for about 42% of the major drugs sold worldwide, according to the U.S. Department of Commerce, Office of Chemicals and Allied Products. But competition from foreign companies is increasing, and factors such as price controls and foreign regulations are making things even more difficult for U.S. drug manufacturers. In addition, U.S. government regulations in the pharmaceutical industry are often considered the toughest in the world, a fact that is affecting U.S. pharmaceutical companies' performance in the international market.

Even so, expect to see increased attention to worldwide markets. Also probable: an increase in joint ventures and licensing agreements with European and Japanese companies. This will help both parties gain new products without the usual high development costs.

▶ **Now past its infancy, biotechnology will continue to grow but will face certain challenges.**

Individual companies will have their ups and downs depending on the results of research and drug testing, but the industry sector as a whole will keep booming. Several factors, however will continue to affect the industry.

One of the most important: the time lag between product development and product introductions. Only after a product is brought to market does it generate any income for the company. But because biotechnology is still relatively young and is research driven, a large number of biotech firms have no sales at all—all of their work is currently centered around R&D. The result: The need to raise capital to meet high R&D costs will probably push some firms into mergers or joint ventures with larger, established pharmaceutical companies.

This is a beneficial arrangement to both parties: The large companies get the benefit of innovative products and cutting edge technology; the small companies get financial benefits, and, once the products have been tested and are ready for commercial use, a stronger marketing push and preestablished sales and distribution networks.

EMPLOYMENT OUTLOOK: Has been brighter than most other industries, but may weaken in the short term depending upon national health care legislation.

Health care has been strong—with over 240,000 new jobs created in 1992 alone—but the employment outlook depends to a great degree upon the outcome of the national health care debate. As such, expect fluctuations as the entire industry comes to grips with the changes imposed by health care reform.

The long-term outlook, however, should remain positive. The health care and pharmaceutical fields have been great sources of employment over the past few years, and it looks as though this will continue through the long term.

The key reason? The aging population. This has brought about a higher demand for health care services and products.

More specifically, the picture for health services: According to recent federal government studies, employment in the health services area should grow by about 3.9 million over the next twelve years. Of this total, 1.3 million will be in hospitals, 900,000 in physician's offices, and 700,000 in nursing and personal-care facilities. One of the strongest growth areas will be home health care. For example, according to a 1992 article in *BusinessWeek,* Caremark Inc., a home health care subsidiary of Baxter International, increased its nursing staff by 40%. The U.S. government projects employment growth for home health aides at about 96% by 2005. Other fast-growing employment areas include physical therapists (87%), medical scientists (87%), and medical assistants (77%). There will also be substantial employment growth for occupational therapists, speech-language pathologists, and general managers. For more information on health care occupations, see Health Care and Medical Specialists, page 87.

As for the pharmaceutical industry: while a number of companies have cut costs by cutting employees (like Bristol-Myers, which announced plans to cut its work force by 6% in 1993), the downsizing should ease once the industry adjusts to the new profit margins, probably by 1995. In addition, as mentioned before, R&D will remain a crucial area to drug companies and so should continue to offer opportunities.

Biotechnology will remain hot as well, with opportunities depending upon the particular companies. Many biotech companies are small, employing few people, but more of them are being swallowed by larger companies, and others are entering into joint agreements. This all points to the possibility of job creation. Employment opportunities in this area will range from scientists (biologists, chemists) to lab technicians.

Finally, the medical instruments and supplies industry also looks good where employment is concerned. The Bureau of Labor Statistics forecasts an industry employment growth rate of about 35%.

JOBS SPOTLIGHT

CLINICAL RESEARCH ASSOCIATE: The boom in drug research is causing a boom in this area. CRAs are employed by pharmaceutical and biotech companies to work with the medical centers that are conducting tests of new drugs. Generally, a B.S. degree in a related area (chemistry, biology, pharmacy, nursing, etc.) is required, as is experience in a laboratory, hospital, or related field, although specific requirements may vary. Pay ranges from the mid-$20s for entry-level workers, up to the high $60s for upper-level positions.

NURSING HOME/LONG-TERM CARE FACILITIES MANAGEMENT: As the population of the country ages, demand grows for managers of facilities aimed at senior citizens. This area should show long-term opportunity. The downside? Salaries are often lower than those paid to management at hospitals. But the pluses are definitely there, including the opportunity for rapid career advancement, as well as career stability.

NURSE: The demand has been very high for nurses. Registered nurses, practical nurses, nurse-anesthetists—virtually all types of nurses are needed. The shortage of nurses didn't ease during the recession. Especially hot: Community health nurses are particularly in demand, a function of the increasing number of hospitals offering outpatient and home health services. In general, the overall need for nurses has resulted in higher salaries, better hours and shifts, the elimination of rote duties, and in some cases sign-on bonuses as high as $10,000. For more information see Health Care and Medical Specialists, page 87.

BEST BETS

Amgen
1900 Oak Terrace Lane
Thousand Oaks, CA 91320
805/499-5725

This biotechnology firm has been growing at a rapid pace—as of April 1992, it employed 1,900 people and was growing at the rate of 50% a year. But it's not just a good bet because of the job prospects. It's also reportedly a great place to work because of the work style. Projects are developed and introduced through a team system. Product Development Teams (PDTs) are responsible for R&D; task forces handle other aspects of work. Both deal directly with upper management and have members from all departments in the company. This type of work environment, plus an emphasis on building a family atmosphere through cook-offs, whale-watching and other trips, and the like, make Amgen an excellent choice.

American Home Products Corp.
685 Third Ave.
New York, NY 10017
212/878-5000

American Home Products is entering an aggressive phase—moving into biotech, and getting actively involved in R&D of a number of products, including an in-home blood cholesterol test and an anti-depressant to compete with Lilly's Prozac. The bottom line? This is a company that in the past was content to sit back but is now expanding at a rapid pace. While the results aren't in yet, American Home Products may shape up to be a major player in the '90s. A good bet.

TOP HEALTH SERVICES COMPANIES

American Healthcare Management, Inc.
14160 Dallas Pkwy.
Dallas, TX 75240
214/385-7000

American Medical International, Inc.
8201 Preston Rd.
Dallas, TX 75225
214/360-6300

Beverly Enterprises, Inc.
P.O. Box 3324
Fort Smith, AR 72913
501/452-6712

Care Enterprises
2742 Dow Ave.
Tustin, CA 92680
714/544-4443

Charter Medical Corp.
577 Mulberry St.
Macon, GA 31298
912/742-1161

Community Psychiatric Centers
24502 Pacific Pk. Dr.
Laguna Hills, CA

92656
714/831-1166

FHP International Corp.
9900 Talbert Ave.
Fountain Valley, CA 92708
714/963-7233

Foundation Health Corp.
3400 Data Dr.
Rancho Cordova, CA 95670
916/631-5000

Health Care & Retirement Corp.
1 Seagate
Toledo, OH 43666
419/247-5000

Health Trust
4525 Harding Rd.
Nashville, TN 37205
615/383-4444

Hillhaven Corporation
1148 Broadway Plz.
Tacoma, WA 98401
206/572-4901

Hospital Corp. of America
1 Park Plz.
Nashville, TN 37202
615/327-9551

Humana, Inc.
500 W. Main St.
Box 1438
Louisville, KY 40201
502/580-1000

Lifetime Corp.
75 State St.
Boston, MA 02109
617/330-5080

Manor Care, Inc.
10750 Columbia Pike
Silver Spring, MD 20901
301/681-9400

National Health Laboratories, Inc.
7590 Fay Ave.
La Jolla, CA 92037
619/454-3314

National Healthcare, Inc.
300 Galleria Pkwy.
Atlanta, GA 30339
404/933-5500

National Medical Enterprises, Inc.
P.O. Box 4070
Santa Monica, CA 90411-4070
310/998-8000

Nu-Med, Inc.
16633 Ventura Blvd.
Encino, CA 91436
818/990-2000

PacificCare Health Systems
5995 Plaza Dr.
Cypress, CA 90630-5028
714/952-1121

Republic Health Corporation
15303 Dallas Pkwy.
Dallas, TX 75248
214/851-3100

Summit Health Ltd.
2600 W. Magnolia Blvd.
Burbank, CA 91505
310/201-4000

United HealthCare
9900 Bren Rd. E.
Minnetonka, MN 55343
612/936-1300

Universal Health Services, Inc.
367 S. Gulph Rd.
King of Prussia, PA 19406
215/768-3300

U.S. Healthcare, Inc.
980 Jolly Rd.
Box 1109
Blue Bell, PA 19422
215/628-4800

TOP PHARMACEUTICAL COMPANIES

Abbott Laboratories
1 Abbott Park Rd.
North Chicago, IL 60064
708/937-6100

Allergan, Inc.
2525 DuPont Dr.
Irvine, CA 92715
714/752-4500

ALZA Corp.
950 Page Mill Rd.
Palo Alto, CA 94303
415/494-5725

American Home Products Corp.
685 Third Ave.
New York, NY 10017
212/878-5000

Amgen
1840 DeHavilland Dr.
Thousand Oaks, CA 91320
805/499-5725

Baxter Healthcare Corp.
(Subs. of Baxter International)
1 Baxter Pkwy.
Deerfield, IL 60015
312/948-2000

Baxter International, Inc.
1 Baxter Pkwy.
Deerfield, IL 60015
708/948-2000

Beecham, Inc.
1 Franklin Plz.
Philadelphia, PA 19102
215/751-4000

Block Drug Company, Inc.
257 Corneilson Ave.
Jersey City, NJ 07302
201/434-3000

Boehringer Ingleheim Corp.
90 E. Ridge Rd.
Ridgefield, CT 06877
203/798-9988

Bristol Myers-Squibb Co.
345 Park Ave.
New York, NY 10154
212/546-4000

Burroughs Wellcome Co.
3030 Cornwallis Rd.
Research Triangle Park, NC 27709
919/248-3000

Ciba-Geigy Corp.
444 Saw Mill River Rd.
Ardsley, NY 10502
914/478-3131

DuPont-Merck Pharmaceutical Co.
Barley Mill Plz.
Wilmington, DE 19880
302/992-5107

Genentech, Inc.
460 Pt. San Bruno Blvd.
South San Francisco, CA 94080
415/225-1000

Glaxo, Inc.
5 Moore Dr.
Research Triangle Park, NC 27709
919/248-2100

Hoechst Corp.
1041 U.S. Rte.
202–206 N.
Somerville, NJ 08807
201/231-2000

Hoffman-LaRoche, Inc.
340 Kingsland St.
Nutley, NJ 07110
201/235-5000

Imcera Group, Inc.
2315 Sanders Rd.
Northbrook, IL 60062
708/564-8600

Eli Lilly & Co.
Lilly Corporate Ctr.
Indianapolis, IN 46285
317/276-2000

Marion Merrell Dow, Inc.
9300 Ward Pkwy.
Kansas City, MO 64114
816/966-4000

Merck & Co., Inc.
P.O. Box 100
Whitehouse Station, NJ 08889
908/423-1000

Miles, Inc.
1127 Myrtle St.
Elkhard, IN 46515
219/264-8111

Ortho Pharmaceutical Corp.
Rte. 202
P.O. Box 300
Raritan, NJ 08869
201/218-6000

Pfizer, Inc.
235 E. 42nd St.
New York, NY 10017
212/573-2323

Rhone-Poulenc-Rorer
P.O. Box 1200
Collegeville, PA 19426
215/454-8000

Richardson-Vicks, Inc.
1 Procter & Gamble Plz.
Cincinnati, OH 45202
513/983-1100

A. H. Robins Co., Inc.
1407 Cummings Dr.
Richmond, VA 23220
804/257-2000

Sandoz Corp.
608 Fifth Ave.
New York, NY 10020
212/307-1122

Sandoz Pharmaceuticals Corp.
(Subs. of Sandoz Corp.)
Rte. 10
East Hanover, NJ 07936
201/503-7500

Schering-Plough Corp.
1 Giralda Farms
Madison, NJ 07940
201/822-7000

G. D. Searle & Co.
5200 Old Orchard Rd.
Skokie, IL 60077
708/982-7000

SmithKline Beecham Corp.
1 Franklin Plz.
Philadelphia, PA 19101
215/751-4000

Sterling Drug, Inc.
90 Park Ave.
New York, NY 10016
212/907-2000

Syntex USA, Inc.
3401 Hillview Ave.
Palo Alto, CA 94304
415/855-5050

Upjohn Co.
7000 Portage Rd.
Kalamazoo, MI 49001
616/323-4000

Warner-Lambert Co.
201 Tabor Rd.
Morris Plains, NJ 07950
201/540-2000

Whitehall Laboratories Division
(American Home Products Corp.)
685 Third Ave.
New York, NY 10017
212/878-6000

Wyeth-Ayerst Laboratories Division
(American Home Products Corp.)
Lancaster Ave.
P.O. Box 8299
Radnor, PA 19087
215/688-4400

TOP MEDICAL SUPPLY COMPANIES

Acuson Corp.
1220 Charleston Rd.
Mountain View, CA 94043
415/969-9112

C. R. Bard, Inc.
730 Central Ave.
Murray Hill, NJ 07974
908/277-8000

Bausch & Lomb, Inc.
1 Lincoln First Sq.
Rochester, NY 14604
716/338-6000

Baxter International, Inc.
1 Baxter Pkwy.
Deerfield, IL 60015
708/948-2000

Beckman Instruments, Inc.
2500 Harbor Blvd.
Fullerton, CA 92634
714/871-4848

Becton Dickinson & Co.
1 Becton Dr.
Franklin Lakes, NJ 07417
201/847-6800

Biomet, Inc.
Airport Industrial Pk.
Warsaw, IN 46580
219/267-6639

Henley Group
Liberty Ln.
Hampton, NH 03842
603/962-5911

Hillenbrand Industries, Inc.
Hwy. 46 E.
Batesville, IN 47006
812/934-7000

Johnson & Johnson
1 Johnson & Johnson Plz.
New Brunswick, NJ 08933
908/524-0400

Medtronic, Inc.
7000 Central Ave., NE
Minneapolis, MN 55432
612/574-4000

Perkin-Elmer Corp.
761 Main Ave.
Norwalk, CT 06859
203/762-1000

St. Jude Medical, Inc.
1 Lillehi Plz.
St. Paul, MN 55117
612/483-2000

U.S. Surgical Corp.
150 Glover Ave.
Norwalk, CT 06856
203/845-1000

WHERE TO GO FOR MORE INFORMATION

HEALTH CARE INDUSTRY ASSOCIATIONS

American Association of Homes for the Aging
1129 20th St. NW,
Suite 400
Washington, DC 20036
202/296-5960

American Health Care Association
1201 L St., NW
Washington, DC 20005
202/842-4444

American Hospital Association
737 N. Michigan Ave.
Chicago, IL 60611
312/440-6836
800/621-6902

American Medical Association
515 N. State St.
Chicago, IL 60610
312/464-0183

American Pharmaceutical Association
2215 Constitution Ave.,
NW
Washington, DC 20037
212/628-4410

Drug, Chemical and Allied Trades Association
2 Roosevelt Ave.,
Suite 301
Syosset, NY 11791
516/496-3317

Group Health Association of America
1129 20th St., NW,
Suite 600
Washington, DC 20036
202/778-3247

Health Industry Distributors Association
225 Reinekers Ln.,
Suite 650
Alexandria, VA 22314
202/452-8240
(Puts out low-cost—$35
in 1992—annual
directory.)

Health Industry Manufacturers Association
1030 15th St., NW,
Suite 1100
Washington, DC 20005
202/452-8240

Healthcare Financial Management Association
2 Westbrook Corporate
Ctr.,
Suite 700
Westchester, IL 60154
800/252-4362

800/821-6459 (in
Illinois)

National Association for Home Care
591 C St., NE
Washington, DC 20002
202/547-7424

National Association of Pharmaceutical Manufacturers
747 Third Ave.
New York, NY 10017
212/838-3720

National Association of Private Psychiatric Hospitals
1319 F. St., NW
Washington, DC 20004
202/393-6700

National Pharmaceutical Association
College of Pharmacy
and Pharmacal Sciences
Howard University
Washington, DC 20059
202/636-6544/6530
202/328-9229

National Pharmaceutical Council
1894 Preston White Dr.
Reston, VA 22091
703/620-6390

Nonprescription Drug Manufacturers Association
1150 Connecticut Ave., NW

Washington, DC 20036
202/429-9260

Pharmaceutical Manufacturers Association

1100 15th St., NW
Washington, DC 20005
202/835-3400

HEALTH CARE INDUSTRY DIRECTORIES

AHA Guide to the Health Care Field
American Hospital Association
840 N. Lakeshore Dr.
Chicago, IL 60611
312/280-6000

Billian's Hospital Blue Book
2100 Powers Ferry Rd.
Atlanta, GA 30339
404/955-5656
(Affordable price; possibly useful for mailing lists.)

Biotechnology Directory
Stockton Press
15 E. 26th St.
New York, NY 10010
212/481-1334

Blue Book Digest of HMOs
National Association of

Employers on Health Care Alternatives
P.O. Box 220
Key Biscayne, FL 33149
305/361-2810

Directory of Public High Technology and Medical Corporations
American Investor Information Services, Inc.
311 Bainbridge St.
Philadelphia, PA 19147
215/925-2761

Drug Topics Red Book
Medical Economics Co.
5 Paragon Dr.
Montvale, NJ 07645
201/358-7200

Dun's Guide to Healthcare Companies
Dun's Marketing

Services
3 Sylvan Way
Parsippany, NJ 07054-3896
201/605-6000

Medical and Health Information Directory
Gale Research Co.
Book Tower
Detroit, MI 48226
800/223-GALE
313/961-2242

National Directory of Health Maintenance Organizations
Group Health Association of America
1129 20th St., NW, Suite 600
Washington, DC 20036
202/778-3247

HEALTH CARE INDUSTRY PERIODICALS

Biomedical Products
Box 650
Morris Plains, NJ 07950
201/292-5100
(Monthly tabloid for those involved in biopharmaceutical

research and development.)

Biotechniques
154 E. Central St.
Natick, MA 01760
508/655-8282
(Monthly magazine for bioresearch scientists.)

Contemporary Long Term Care
Box 3599
Akron, OH 44320
216/867-4401
(Monthly magazine for professionals in the long-term care health-services industry,

covering hospitals, nursing homes, retirement and assisted living centers, etc.)

Drug Topics
680 Kinderkamack Rd.
Oradell, NJ 07675
201/262-3030
(Twenty-three issue magazine aimed at professionals in all phases of the pharmaceutical industry—manufacturers, pharmacists, retailers, distributors, etc.)

Healthcare Executive
840 N. Lake Shore Dr.
Chicago, IL 60611
312/943-0544
(Bimonthly publication for healthcare industry executives.)

Healthweek
600 Community Dr.
Manhasset, NY 11030
516/562-5000

(Biweekly publication for health service professionals—personnel at hospitals, nursing houses, HMOs, suppliers, nurses, physicians, etc.)

Long-Term Care News
1419 Lake Cook Rd.
Deerfield, IL 60015
708/945-0345
(Monthly publication for nursing home personnel—administrators, managers, nursing directors, etc.)

Modern Healthcare
740 Rush St.
Chicago, IL 60606
312/649-5341
(Biweekly magazine for healthcare professionals—including healthcare administrators, purchasing agents, medical staffs.)

Pharmaceutical Processing
Box 650
Morris Plains, NJ 07950
201/292-5100
(Monthly magazine for people in pharmaceutical production, research & development, quality control, engineering, etc.)

Pharmaceutical Technology
Box 10460
Eugene, OR 97401
503/343-1200
(Monthly magazine for people in pharmaceutical production, research & development, quality control, and related areas.)

HOSPITALITY

(including Hotels and Restaurants)

INDUSTRY OUTLOOK: Improved, but challenges still ahead.

Hotels: With an end to the recession over and a resurgence in travel, the hotel industry will rebound . . . slowly. It still faces troubles from other problems of the past—an oversupply of rooms due to overbuilding, high operating costs, and over-segmentation of markets.

Restaurants: Highly competitive. Chains will continue battling for market share, relying on increased service, low prices. Independent restaurants, still getting back on their feet after the recession, may be caught in the crunch competing against the wealthier chains. Midsize chains, however, should continue gaining on the larger chains.

A LOOK BACK

▶ **Over the past decade, the hotel and motel industry went from boom to bust.**

Appreciating real estate values, high growth rates, increasing occupancy rates, and, most importantly, the Economic Recovery Tax Act of 1981, which gave tax incentives for building, pushed hotel companies into expanding. And expand they did, in the largest building boom in recent history.

But the boom went bust. Hotels overbuilt, and with too many rooms and not enough demand, they slumped. Declining real estate values, the Gulf War, and the recession made matters worse. Vacation travel and business travel were cut, and hotel companies were stuck paying high operating costs for empty rooms. Occupancy rates dropped from 71% in 1979 to 60.9% in 1991.

▶ **The restaurant industry's fortunes also went through a sharp up-and-down cycle.**

For much of the '80s, the restaurant industry was in high gear—eating out was in vogue, fast-food chains were raking in money, new restaurants were opening and prospering. But the number of restaurants ultimately grew faster than demand. Added to the oversupply were a labor shortage, high food costs, and a sudden rise in stay-at-home consumers. The '90s—and the recession—brought about the beginnings of a shakeout. Weaker restaurants were forced out of business by the heavy competition; stronger ones began seeking new ways to increase market share.

WHAT'S NEXT

▶ **In the short term, oversupply of rooms and intense competition will remain the two greatest challenges facing the hotel industry.**

Even with a resurgence in travel, the problems that plagued the hotel industry for the past few years won't go away. First of all, the industry rule of thumb is that hotels need about a 66 percent occupancy rate just to break even. The average occupancy rate in 1991 was only 61.9%. According to an industry expert quoted in *Fortune* magazine, only about 32% of the full-service hotels in this country were able to break even. While the numbers weren't in for 1992 at the time of publication, they were projected to be not much better. On the whole, the industry is holding its breath, treading water, and waiting for 1995—which is when the turnaround in occupancy is finally expected to take place.

In the meantime, most hotel companies will be struggling to keep costs in check, and offering promotional packages and special rates to attract customers. Where employment is concerned, this trend means fewer job opportunities. Some of the large chains, including Marriott and Hilton, have downsized their corporate and headquarters staffs as a cost-cutting measure. But on the bright side, this corporate belt-tightening will eventually give way to business as usual—and hiring as usual—when customer demand and room supply finally balance out.

▶ **The combination of competition and oversupply will result in continuing consolidation, some business failures (especially among independents), and a growth in consortiums.**

The winners? The large chains who, because of size, marketing power, and financial strength, can weather the competition even while facing the pinch from overbuilding. The losers? The smaller independents who won't be able to continue operating.

This scenario is being played out overseas as well. International hotel companies are getting hammered by the 1991–92 drop in American travel and a shaky world economy—and are trying price slashing, promotions, and anything else they can think of to woo back customers.

But consolidation is an industry inevitability: About 50% of all rooms worldwide are already controlled by the top 25 chains, while independent hotels are falling flat. As a result, expect more independents to be swallowed by the healthier and wealthier chains and other independents to follow the lead of travel agencies and form networks with their fellow independents. These consortiums of hotels can then act like chains by combining marketing strengths and budgets, instituting centralized reservation systems, and doing cooperative advertising.

▶ **Over the long term, expect increasing specialization in the hotel/ motel industry.**

In an effort to keep up with changing demographics and to differentiate themselves from the competition, hotel companies will be seeking out market niches and clearly positioning their hotels to meet the needs of the markets they have targeted. Categories that will continue strong are corporate meeting/convention, budget, and luxury.

For the short term, a new area that looks promising is the "short stay" market. With a growing number of working couples, more people are taking mini-vacations of three to seven days. Watch more hotels offer special promotional packages to tap this market.

Market specialization and the development of promotional packages should translate into some limited employment opportunities for sales, marketing, and promotions staffers.

▶ **Increased international travel is translating into increased internationalization of U.S. hotels.**

In other words, U.S. hotels are offering special amenities and services to make foreign guests feel at home. This is another example of the niche marketing that is taking hold of the industry. One way of beating the competition where international travelers are concerned is to "internationalize"—which includes serving international foods, and offering more visible concierges, multilingual staffers, and room directories and information in different languages. Especially hot: offering services to attract Pacific Rim travelers.

Employment note: Excellent opportunities exist for people with language skills and those with foreign experience. As hotels rush to prove how international they are, they will be seeking people who can promote this global image. Best language skill: Japanese.

▶ **Also increasing: the use of technology at hotels.**

Even through the recession and the corresponding cost cuts, hotels were introducing technological methods and equipment to their properties. In many cases, they help keep costs down and enhance customer service. The innovations already catching on include "smart card" room keys; televisions allowing in-room checkout. On the horizon are computerized services that will allow for remote check in; robotic cleaning.

▶ **A growing segment of the hospitality industry: communities and food services aimed at the elderly.**

As Americans age, the hospitality industry is keeping up with them. One key way it is doing so is through the development of life-care communities: living complexes that offer full service (housing, meals, and, in some cases, nursing care) to senior citizens. Marriott has announced plans to invest $1 billion in life-care community development and hopes to have 150 such communities by 1995.

This developing area will offer wide employment opportunities—from nutritionists to geriatric care specialists to hotel managers or nursing home managers.

▶ **Heavy competition in the restaurant industry will lead to a flurry of new-product introductions and increased attempts by restaurants to position themselves for the changing (and shrinking) marketplace.**

The recession cut into profits as consumers who were suddenly very price conscious began cutting back on their restaurant going. In addition, customers became more health conscious than in the past and began staying away from restaurants altogether. These trends haven't died down. And at the same time, restaurants are facing competition from new players: gourmet take-out shops, supermarkets offering take-home food, delis, and food delivery companies (especially common in urban areas).

Restaurants will be responding by offering new products that fit in with the changing marketplace and stepping up advertising and marketing campaigns that position them as price or value leaders. Where products are concerned, more restaurants will be leaping on the nutrition-conscious bandwagon, offering lower-fat foods, salads—anything that seems likely to appeal to older baby boomers and their families. Also looking hot: "gourmet" products (international foods and the like), as fast-food restaurants try to get away from the "burgers only" image. In addition, there may be an increase in regional fare, with national chains offering certain foods only in specific regions.

At the same time, expect periodic resurgences in the price wars between the big chains, and numerous short-run promotions, tied in to new-product introductions, as well as general promotions.

All of this activity points to opportunities in sales and marketing and promotion, as new products and new campaigns become vital to restaurant companies trying to regain their customer base.

▶ **The fast-food industry will be expanding into more overseas markets.**

From Paris to Moscow to Beijing, American fast-food restaurants are attracting attention and customers. This is a growing area for U.S. restaurant companies and one that is proving very profitable. Watch for a continued push, especially into Eastern Europe, Southeast Asia (especially Vietnam, once relations are normalized), Canada, and Mexico.

International marketing specialists will be in increased demand, due to this attention.

EMPLOYMENT OUTLOOK: Short-term opportunities are fair; long-term opportunities look better.

Managerial hiring at hotels will be slower in the short term, but the long-term picture is brighter. The Bureau of Labor Statistics projects a job-growth rate for managers in the industry of about 33% over the next twelve years. It's a similar story for marketing personnel. Marketing is becoming more important to hotel companies as they try to combat competition. As a result, the long-term outlook points to increasing employment opportunities. Nonmanagerial positions—desk and reservation clerks, other administrative positions, housecleaning, etc.—should remain fairly tight, with most openings occurring when employees retire or resign. Again, the long-term picture is better than the short-term outlook.

The long-term outlook is also good for the restaurant and food service industries. For example, an additional 449,000 jobs for waiters and waitresses are expected to be added by 2005. The food service portion of the industry—hospitals, schools, and other institutions—should be offering employment opportunities, particularly in areas catering to the older population. Food service companies with contracts at nursing homes, retirement communities, and the like should provide increasing employment opportunities. See the Jobs Spotlight below for more information.

Lower-level positions at chain restaurants have been available even through the recession as the labor pool of young workers (sixteen to twenty-four) shrinks and salary levels stay lower than in many other industries. (Average weekly pay in 1990 was $220.) At the same time, the Bureau of Labor Statistics projects that there will be a 30% increase in jobs between now and 2005. The result? Increasing attempts on the part of fast-food restaurants to target nontraditional employees such as senior citizens and the disabled.

On the managerial level, restaurant hiring should remain fair to good, primarily because of the high turnover in the industry. The BLS estimates that the number of jobs should grow about 33% by 2005. Best background: experience or degree in restaurant management or food service. As for cooks, the long-term outlook is good with the number of jobs projected to grow about 42% by 2005.

Hiring at independent restaurants will depend primarily on the specific region of the country in which they are located and the type of food/service offered. In general, expect an improvement over the past two years, as the economy strengthens and people begin to eat out more.

JOBS SPOTLIGHT

FOOD SERVICE DIRECTORS/MANAGERS (also called Food Distribution Managers): A growing area, primarily because of the increase in nursing homes, retirement communities, and senior citizens centers offering food services, as well as programs such as Meals on Wheels. Food service directors are employed by food service companies to work with the nursing home, social welfare program, or retirement community that has contracted the food service company. A food service director will often work on site at the nursing home, retirement community, etc. Best background? A degree and/or experience in hotel/restaurant management, dietetics/nutrition, or, in some cases, general business administration. Salaries range from the low $20s for entry-level staffers up to the high $40s for upper-level employees.

BEST BETS

Marriott Corp.
1044 Fernwood
Bethesda, MD 20817
301/897-9000

The past few years have brought about tough times for this hotel giant resulting in layoffs and cost-cutting, but the long-term outlook for Marriott is a good one. Two reasons: its focus on niche markets in its domestic business, and its international expansion. These, plus its heavy investment in and development of senior-citizen life-care communities, make Marriott look well poised for the future. Add to this the fact that Marriott has a reputation as a good employer. It offers such things as "fast-track" management development programs to encourage career advancement for minorities and women, day-care discounting for working parents, elder-care programs, and other family-friendly benefits.

TOP HOTEL, MOTEL, AND CASINO COMPANIES

Aztar Corp.
2390 E. Camelback Rd.
Phoenix, AZ 85016
602/381-4100
(Casino hotels.)

Best Western International
P.O. Box 10203
Phoenix, AZ 85064
602/957-5700
(Hotels, motels.)

Caesars NJ, Inc.
2100 Pacific Ave.
Atlantic City, NJ 08401
609/348-4411
(Casino hotel.)

Caesars World, Inc.
1801 Century Park E.,
No. 2600
Los Angeles, CA 90067
310/552-2711
(Resort hotels, casinos.)

Carlson Hospitality Group, Inc.
Carlson Pkwy.
P.O. Box 59159
Minneapolis, MN 55459
612/540-5275
(Hotels/motels—Radisson Hotels International; Colony Hotels & Resorts; Country Lodging by Carlson.)

Choice Hotels International
10750 Columbia Pike

Silver Springs, MD 20901
301/593-5600
(Hotels/motels—Comfort Inns/Suites; Quality Inns/Hotels/Suites; Clarion Hotels/suites/resorts—Carriage House Inns; Sleep Inns; Rodeway Inns; Econo Lodges; Friendship Inns.)

Circus Circus Enterprises
2880 Las Vegas Blvd. S.
Las Vegas, NV 89109
702/734-0410
(Casino hotel.)

Days Inns of America
2751 Buford Hwy.
Atlanta, GA 30324
404/329-7466
(Motels—Days Inn; Daystop.)

Desert Palace, Inc.
3570 Las Vegas Blvd. S.
Las Vegas, NV 89109
702/731-7110
(Casino hotel.)

Embassy Suites, Inc.
(subs. The Promus Companies, Incorporated)
1023 Cherry Rd.
Memphis, TN 38117
901/762-8600
(All-suite hotels.)

Forte Hotels, Inc.
1973 Friendship Dr.
El Cajon, CA 92020
619/448-1884
(Hotels/motels—Travelodge; Travelodge Hotels; Thriftlodge; Forte Hotels.)

Golden Nugget, Inc.
129 Fremont St.
Las Vegas, NV 89101
702/385-7111
(Casino hotel.)

Harrah's
300 E. Second St.
Reno, NV 89501
702/786-3232
(Casinos, hotels.)

Hilton Hotels Corp.
9336 Civic Ctr. Dr.
Beverly Hills, CA 90209
310/278-4321
(Hotels—Hilton Hotels; Hilton Inns; Hilton Suites; Conrad Hotels—overseas.)

Hilton International Co.
605 Third Ave.
New York, NY 10158
212/973-2200
(International hotels.)

Holiday Inns
3796 Lamar Ave.
Memphis, TN 38195
901/369-5895
(Hotels/motels—Holiday

Inn Hotels; Holiday Inn Crowne Plaza; Holiday Inn Express; Holiday Inn Garden Court.)

Hyatt Hotels Corp.
200 W. Madison St.
Chicago, IL 60607
312/750-1234
(Hotels—Hyatt Hotels; Hyatt International.)

Inter-Continental Hotels Corp.
100 Paragon Dr.
Montvale, NJ 07645
201/307-3300
(Hotels.)

ITT—Sheraton Corporation
60 State St.
Boston, MA 02109
617/367-3600
(Hotels/motels—Sheraton Hotels; Sheraton Inns; Sheraton Resorts; Sheraton Suites.)

Kyo-Ya Co. Ltd.
2255 Kalakaua Ave.
Honolulu, HI 96815
808/924-5170
(Hotels.)

La Quinta Motor Inns, L.P.
10010 San Pedro Ave.
San Antonio, TX 78216
512/366-6030
(Motels.)

Marriott Corporation
1 Marriott Dr.
Washington, DC 20058
301/380-9000
(Hotels/motels—Marriott Hotels/Resorts/Suites; Residence Inns;

Fairfield Inns; Courtyard.)

Mirage Resorts
3400 Las Vegas Blvd. S.
Las Vegas, NV 89109
702/791-5627
(Casino hotel.)

Motel 6, LP
14561 Dallas Pkwy., Suite 500
Dallas, TX 75240
214/386-6161
(Motels.)

Omni Hotels Management Corp.
500 Lafayette Rd.
Hampton, NH 03842
603/926-8911
(Hotels.)

Penta Hotels, Inc.
401 Seventh Ave.
New York, NY 10001
212/736-5000
(Hotels.)

Prime Motor Inns, Inc.
400 Rte. 46 E.
Fairfield, NJ 07007
201/882-1010
(Motels.)

The Promus Companies, Inc.
1023 Cherry Rd.
Memphis, TN 38117
901/762-8600
(Hotels, motels—Embassy Suites; Hampton Inns; Homewood Suites; Harrah's.)

Radisson Hotels International, Inc.
701 Carlson Pkwy.

Minneapolis, MN 55459
612/540-5526
(Hotels.)

Ramada International Hotels & Resorts
3838 E. Van Buren St.
Phoenix, AZ 85008
602/273-4000
(Hotels/motels.)

Red Lion Hotels and Inns, L.P.
4001 Main St.
Vancouver, WA 98663
206/696-0001
(Hotels/motels.)

Red Roof Inns, Inc.
4355 Davidson Rd.
Hilliard, OH 43026
614/876-3200
(Motels.)

Stouffer Hotel Company.
29800 Bainbridge Rd.
Solon, OH 44139
216/248-3600
(Hotels—Stouffer Hotels; Stouffer Resorts; Stouffer Presidente Hotels/Resorts.)

Super 8 Motels, Inc.
1910 Eighth Ave., NE
Aberdeen, SD 57401
605/225-2272
(Motels.)

Trump Plaza Associates
Boardwalk and Mississippi Ave.
Atlantic City, NJ 08401
609/441-6000
(Casino hotel.)

**Trump Taj Mahal
Associates, Inc.**
1000 Boardwalk
Atlantic City, NJ 08401
609/449-1000
(Casino hotel.)

**Westin Hotel &
Resorts**
Westin Bldg.
2001 Sixth Ave.

Seattle, WA 98121
206/443-5000
(Hotels.)

TOP RESTAURANT/FOOD SERVICE COMPANIES

ARA Services, Inc.
ARA Tower
1101 Market St.
Philadelphia, PA 19107
215/238-3000

Arby's, Inc.
10 Piedmont Ctr.
Atlanta, GA 30305
404/262-2729

**Baskin-Robbins USA
Co.**
31 Baskin-Robbins Pl.
Glendale, CA 91201
818/956-0031

**Big Boy Family
Restaurants**
Marriott Corp.
Marriott Dr.
Washington, DC 20058
202/897-9000

**Burger King
Corporation**
1777 Old Cutler Rd.
Miami, FL 33157
305/378-7011

**Caterair International
Corporation**
7811 Montrose Rd.,
Suite 400
Potomac, MD 20854
301/309-2800

**Al Copeland
Enterprises, Inc.**
(Popeye's Chicken)
1333 S. Clearview

Jefferson, LA 70121
504/733-4300

Denny's, Inc.
3345 Michelson,
Suite 200
Irvine, CA 92715
714/251-5000

Domino's Pizza, Inc.
30 Frank Lloyd Wright
Dr.
Ann Arbor, MI 48105
313/668-4000

**Dunkin' Donuts,
Incorporated**
P.O. Box 317
Randolph, MA 02368
617/961-4000

Foodmaker
P.O. Box 783
San Diego, CA 92112
619/571-2121
(Jack in the Box,
Chi-chi's)

**General Mills
Restaurants, Inc.**
(Red Lobster Inns, etc.)
6770 Lake Ellenor Dr.
Orlando, FL 32809
407/851-0370

**Hardee's Food
Systems, Inc.**
1233 Hardee's Blvd.
Rocky Mount, NC
27804
919/977-2000

**International Dairy
Queen, Inc.**
P.O. Box 35286
Minneapolis, MN
55435
612/830-0020

**Kentucky Fried
Chicken Corp.**
P.O. Box 32070
Louisville, KY 40232
502/456-8300

**Little Caesar
Enterprises, Inc.**
2211 Woodward Ave.
Detroit, MI 48201
313/983-6000

Long John Silver's
101 Jerrico Dr.
Lexington, KY 40579
606/263-6000

McDonald's Corp.
McDonald's Plz.
Oak Brook, IL 60521
708/575-3000

Morrison, Inc.
4721 Morrison Dr.
Mobile, AL 36625
205/344-3000

Pizza Hut, Inc.
9111 E. Douglas
Wichita, KS 67207
316/681-9000

Shoney's, Inc.
1727 Elm Hill Pike
Box 1260
Nashville, TN 37202
615/391-5201

Taco Bell Corp.
17901 Von Karman
Ave.

Irvine, CA 92714
714/863-4500

TW Services, Inc.
203 E. Main St.
Spartanburg, SC 29302
803/597-8000

**Wendy's
International, Inc.**
4288 W.
Dublin-Granville Rd.
Dublin, OH 43017
614/764-3100

WHERE TO GO FOR MORE INFORMATION

HOSPITALITY INDUSTRY ASSOCIATIONS

American Hotel and Motel Association
1201 New York Ave.,
NW
Washington, DC 20005
202/289-3162
(Publishes monthly
Lodging Magazine,
which includes
help-wanted listings.)

Hotel Sales and Marketing Association
1300 M. St., NW,
Suite 800
Washington, DC 20005
202/789-0089

International Food Service Executives Association
1100 S. State Rd. 7,

Suite 103
Margate, FL 33068
305/977-0767

National Restaurant Association
1200 17th St., NW,
Suite 800
Washington, DC 20036
800/424-8156

HOSPITALITY INDUSTRY DIRECTORIES

Chain Restaurant Operators; High Volume Independent Restaurants
Lebhar-Friedman, Inc.
425 Park Ave.
New York, NY 10022
212/371-9400, ext. 306

Directory of Hotel and Motel Systems; Hotel and Motel Red Book
American Hotel
Association Directory
Corp.
1201 New York Ave.,
NW
Washington, DC 20005
202/289-3162

Directory of Hotel/Motel Management Companies
Edgell
Communications, Inc.
7500 Old Oak Blvd.
Cleveland, OH 44130
216/243-8100

Foodservice Industry Directory
National Restaurant
Association
1200 17th St., NW,
Suite 800

Washington, DC 20036
800/424-8156

Who's Who in the Lodging Industry
American Hotel and
Motel Association
1201 New York Ave.,
NW
Washington, DC 20005
202/289-3162
(This relatively
low-cost annual
directory—$39.95 in
1992—
is also available printed
on address labels.)

HOSPITALITY INDUSTRY PERIODICALS

*Cornell Hotel and
Restaurant
Administration
Quarterly*
Cornell University
School of Hotel
Administration
327 Statler Hall
Ithaca, NY 14853
607/255-2093

*Hotel and Motel
Management*
7500 Old Oak Blvd.
Cleveland, OH 44130
216/243-8100
(Twenty-one issue
magazine aimed at
hotel/motel industry
executives.)

*Hotel & Resort
Industry*
488 Madison Ave.
New York, NY 10022
212/888-1500
(Monthly publication
for hotel/motel/resort
industry managers and
buyers.)

Hotels
1350 E. Touhy Ave.
Des Plaines, IL 60018
708/635-8800
(Monthly magazine
aimed at hotel industry
executives, developers,
management firms,
etc.)

Lodging Hospitality
1100 E. Superior Ave.
Cleveland, OH 44114
216/696-7000
(Monthly magazine for
lodging/food service
managers, owners, etc.)

*Nation's Restaurant
News*
425 Park Ave.
New York, NY 10022
212/371-4000
(Weekly tabloid for
restaurant owners and
food service managers.)

*Opportunities in
Hospitality*
21250 Box Springs
Rd.,
Suite 215
Moreno Valley, CA
92557
714/788-9099
(Biweekly publication
listing hospitality
industry jobs, including
those in hotels,
restaurants, resorts.)

Restaurant Business
633 Third Ave.
New York, NY 10017
212/986-4800
(Eighteen-issue
magazine for food
service organization

executives,
manufacturers, and
restaurant food
distributors.)

Restaurant Hospitality
1100 E. Superior Ave.
Cleveland, OH 44114
216/696-7000
(Monthly magazine for
restaurant owners,
managers, etc.; aimed
chiefly at table-service
establishments.)

*Restaurant
Management*
HBJ Publications
7500 Old Oak Blvd.
Cleveland, OH 44130
216/243-8100

*Restaurants and
Institutions*
1350 E. Touhy Ave.
Des Plaines, IL 60603
312/635-8800
(Biweekly publication
for hospitality industry
managers.)

*Vacation Industry
Review*
Worldex Corp.
P.O. Box 431920
South Miami, FL 33243
305/667-0202

INSURANCE

INDUSTRY OUTLOOK: Changes—and long term improvement—ahead.

Life Insurance: As the population ages, demand for life insurance and annuity products should increase—pointing to a positive long-term outlook for life insurance companies. But expect increased competition for these markets from banks, mutual funds and other financial firms, and from foreign insurers. Also watch more life insurance companies, chiefly through holding companies, compete with financial firms by moving into other financial services, such as securities and real estate. In addition, expect more U.S. life insurers to tap expanding foreign markets. Health insurance will be facing changes when the Clinton national health care program takes shape.

Property/Casualty Insurance: Still dealing with the effects of the swift sequence of catastrophes in 1992—Hurricane Andrew, Hurricane Iniki, and the Los Angeles riots, as well as the Midwestern flooding of 1993. Expect industry restructuring, with stronger companies grabbing market share and weaker companies streamlining, merging with their better-off competitors, or going belly up.

A LOOK BACK

▶ **Since the early 1980s, it has been a roller-coaster ride for property and casualty companies.**

It started with rates competition in which companies cut premiums to gain more corporate clients. Then came some heavy losses which, in turn, led companies to raise prices, cut coverage, or cut back on types of insurance offered. It was smooth sailing for a while. But at the end of the '80s competition heated up again, income started sliding again, prices started getting cut again, and the cycle appeared to be starting all over.

Added to this activity was the swift succession of natural disasters—such as Hurricane Hugo, the San Francisco earthquake, Hurricane Andrew, Hurricane Iniki, as well as the nameless nor'easters that battered the East Coast in 1992—the recession, and a string of insolvencies in the P/C insurance industry, primarily brought about by mismanagement. The bottom line? Not the best of times.

▶ **Over the past few years, a growth surge for life insurance companies was followed by a drop leading to consolidation, brought about by poor real estate investments, lagging income, and consumer concern about financial stability.**

In the '80s, life insurance companies felt the benefit of nervous investors turning to life insurance policies and annuities as investments. It was a period of booming sales and double-digit growth. Then, confident life insurance companies decided to get more business by introducing a range of low-margin, interest-sensitive products. The upshot? They sold more but earned less.

Then came the bad times: heated-up competition brought about by a high number of new entrants, a flurry of financial difficulties and restructurings, and industry-wide consolidation. Poor real estate investments and lagging income from premiums in the early '90s brought about a new problem: consumer concerns about the financial stability of insurers.

WHAT'S NEXT

▶ **Expect to see more competition in the life and health insurance industry over the next few years.**

Not only will insurers be competing with one another, they will also be facing increased competition from nontraditional sources. Regulations may allow banks to sell and underwrite insurance. Already, banks and other financial institutions, such as mutual funds, are offering investment and savings vehicles that compete head-to-head with insurance offerings. As for health insurance providers (often life insurers), with the increase in managed-care services, employer-funded health plans, and, possibly, the introduction of a government health plan, demand may drop and the market for private health insurance shrink.

The outcome? A competitive push to hold on to old customers and win new ones.

▶ **To keep earnings up, watch more companies target the needs of the changing (aging) population.**

Insurance companies are focusing on two key areas: senior citizens and aging baby boomers.

As the American population grows older and senior citizens control about 50 percent of all U.S. discretionary income, it's no wonder that insurance companies will be emphasizing products and services aimed directly at this market segment. These include long-term care policies that pay for nursing homes or in-home medical assistance, "last-to-die" life insurance policies that can be used to pay off estate taxes; "living benefits" policies that allow holders to receive a portion of their benefits before death.

Along the same lines, aging baby boomers represent a huge bulge in the population. Insurance companies will therefore be targeting them with products such as health insurance and services such as financial planning and retirement planning.

Employment note: This points to increased opportunity for agents with specialized retirement or financial planning training, as well as certified financial planners. An offshoot of this: Since agents moving into retirement and financial planning need upgraded training, this will also mean increased opportunities for trainers and other human-resources personnel in this area.

▶ **Another growing trend: Life insurance companies will be moving into other financial services fields.**

New regulations on insurance, increased competition, and diminished returns on life insurance will force insurance companies to come up with new ways of making money. Watch for an increase in the number of life-insurance holding companies entering other financial services areas, such as banking, real estate, and securities.

▶ **Expect life insurance companies to try new sales and marketing methods.**

Belt-tightening on the part of life insurers will lead to the exploration of different ways of selling insurance. Watch for an increase in joint ventures between insurers and banks, brokers or, as mentioned earlier, foreign insurers. Also increasing: using direct mail to reach customers, and establishing marketing ties with funeral directors, financial advisers and consultants, etc.

The effect on employment? In the short term, insurance agents may face increased competition, but these changes also point to new employment opportunities as the industry expands its sales and marketing efforts. New jobs may be created—in direct mail or sales and marketing at insurance companies, for example.

▶ **Consolidation and competition ahead for independent agencies.**

Independent agencies have already been forced in increasing numbers to consolidate so they can better compete with the larger agencies. Consolidation also enables them to afford the usually expensive automation that agencies need to keep up. Another problem for independent agents: Compensations are being cut.

▶ **Both life and personal/casualty insurance companies will be expanding their international business.**

Watch as American companies continue their push into overseas markets, through branches, subsidiaries, joint ventures, and reinsurance. Companies will be offering straight insurance packages, as well as claims processing, investment services, actuarial services, and information services. In addition to Canada, Europe, and Japan, South Korea, Taiwan, and other Asian markets are seeing a great deal of action.

Employment note: This trend points to increasing opportunities for people with international backgrounds. Foreign-language ability is a definite plus. Companies will also be looking for people who understand the cultural differences involved in working in a foreign country, as well as the political and economic situation there—in other words, anything that will enable them to meet the client's needs more easily.

▶ **Insurance companies will be cutting back on their offerings and seeking more specialized niches.**

To a great degree, this will be occurring as a result of problems with automobile insurance, worker's compensation, and health care. More specifically: More states will be reducing automobile insurance rates; similarly, worker's compensation insurance is becoming increasingly unprofitable as medical costs rise and pressure to keep rates down increases. In addition, increased competition makes cutting back more cost-effective. As a result, expect to see more companies cut back and concentrate on core businesses. For example, The Continental Corporation has dropped life and health insurance to concentrate on P/C to midsized manufacturers and shipping companies; Cigna, Aetna, and Travelers scaled back and are moving heavily into managed care. This type of activity will continue.

One negative outcome: The move away from multiline insurance companies has led to employment cuts. But on the plus side, lower-cost/high-volume companies may be expanding to pick up the slack—and will be adding workers, as well.

▶ **The P/C insurance industry will be in for a shakeout.**

Larger, financially strong companies will win larger and larger market shares, while smaller, weaker companies will lag behind. Their only chance for survival will be to find other capital sources—very possibly from foreign investors—or to link up with one of the stronger companies.

This type of activity should continue for the next few years, resulting in a more streamlined industry. Depending on the particular company, this may affect employment opportunities. The key to a stable job outlook? Sticking with the larger companies that will weather the shakeout.

EMPLOYMENT OUTLOOK: Fair to good over the long term.

Things haven't been great lately. In 1992 alone, 33,000 jobs were lost in the insurance industry. The upshot? Competition remains tough and won't let up in the short term. But the long term looks brighter. About 240,000 new jobs are projected to be created over the next twelve years at insurance carriers, bringing the total to almost 1.7 million. Only one negative trend is affecting job opportunities: An increasing use of computers and other technology may keep hiring of claims processors from increasing as quickly as it could.

As for insurance agents and brokers, employment in this area seems to be headed for growth. According to the U.S. Bureau of Labor Statistics, by 2005 about 221,000 new jobs will be added in this area.

JOBS SPOTLIGHT

INSURANCE SALESPEOPLE: For information on insurance sales, see Sales and Marketing Professionals, page 139.

INFORMATION SYSTEMS (IS)/TECHNOLOGY EXPERTS: As the insurance industry becomes more technology-driven—and as existing technologies used in the industry are replaced by newer ones—there is a growing need for information systems personnel in the industry. Insurance companies are shifting from the use of older mainframe systems to a number of new technologies—including LANs, CASE (computer-aided software engineering) tools, laptop and pen-based computers, open systems, client/server environments, image processing, even artificial intelligence. Along these lines, opportunities are opening up for people with expertise in these areas—and, in many cases, people with the ability to integrate the older systems with the new ones. The best qualifications—technological skills, as well as knowledge of (or even better, experience in) the insurance industry.

BEST BETS

Equitable Life Assurance Society
787 7th Ave.
New York, NY 10019
212/554-1234

This insurance giant has a record for enlightened hiring and advancement policies. For example, Equitable has a career-development track to encourage the advancement of women and minorities. It also runs a number of training programs. While recent restructurings have cut back on the number of positions, Equitable remains a good bet for employment.

Northwestern Mutual Life
720 E. Wisconsin Ave.
Milwaukee, WI 53202
414/271-1444

(For information on this company, see Sales and Marketing Professionals, page 147.)

TOP INSURANCE COMPANIES

Aetna Life & Casualty Co.
151 Farmington Ave.
Hartford, CT 06156
203/273-0123

Allstate Insurance Co.
Allstate Plz.
Northbrook, IL 60062
708/402-5000

American Bankers Insurance Group, Inc.
11222 Quail Roost Dr.
Miami, FL 33157
305/253-2244

American Family Corp.
1932 Wynnton Rd.
Columbus, GA 31999
706/323-3431

American Financial
1 E. Fourth St.
Cincinnati, OH 45202
513/579-2121

American General Corp.
2929 Allen Pkwy.
Houston, TX 77019
713/522-1111

American International Group, Inc.
70 Pine St.
New York, NY 10270
212/770-7000

American National Insurance Co.
1 Moody Plz.
Galveston, TX 77550
409/763-4661

Aon Corp.
123 N. Wacker Dr.
Chicago, IL 60606
312/701-3000

W. R. Berkley Corp.
165 Mason St.
Greenwich, CT 06836
203/629-2880

Berkshire Hathaway, Inc.
1440 Kiewit Plz.
Omaha, NE 68131
402/346-1400

Broad, Inc.
11601 Wilshire Blvd.
Los Angeles, CA 90025
213/312-5000

Capital Holding Corp.
680 Fourth Ave.
Louisville, KY 40202
502/560-2000

Chubb Corp.
P.O. Box 1615
Warren, NJ 07061
908/580-2000

Cigna Corporation
1 Liberty Pl.
Philadelphia, PA 19192
215/761-1000

**Cincinnati Financial
Corp.**
6200 S. Gilmore Rd.
Fairfield, OH 45014
513/870-2000

CNA Financial Corp.
CNA Plz.
Chicago, IL 60685
312/822-5000

Conseco
P.O. Box 1911
Carmel, IN 46032
317/573-6100

**Equitable Life
Assurance Society**
787 Seventh Ave.
New York, NY 10019
212/554-1234

**Equitable of Iowa
Cos.**
P.O. Box 1635
Des Moines, IA 50306
515/245-6911

**Fireman's Fund
Insurance Co.**
777 San Marin Dr.
Novato, CA 94498
415/899-2000

**Foremost Corp. of
America**
5800 Foremost Dr., SE
Box 2450
Grand Rapids, MI
49506
616/942-3000

Geico Corp.
Geico Plz.
Washington, DC 20076
301/986-3000

General Re Corp.
695 E. Main St.
Stamford, CT 06904
203/328-5000

**Hanover Insurance
Co.**
100 N. Pkwy.
Worcester, MA 01605
508/853-7200

**Hartford Steam Boiler
Inspection &
Insurance Co.**
1 State St.
Hartford, CT 06102
203/722-1866

**Independent Insurance
Group**
1 Independent Dr.
Jacksonville, FL 32276
904/358-5151

Jefferson-Pilot Corp
100 N. Greene St.
Greensboro, NC 27401
919/691-3000

Kemper Corp.
Kemper Ctr.
Long Grove, IL 60049
708/540-2000

**Leucadia National
Corp.**
315 Park Ave. S.
New York, NY 10010
212/460-1900

Liberty Corp.
Wade Hampton Blvd.
Greenville, SC 29602
803/268-8111

**Lincoln National
Corp.**
1300 S. Clinton St.
Fort Wayne, IN 46801
219/455-2000

**Metropolitan Life
Insurance Co.**
1 Madison Ave.
New York, NY 10010
212/578-2211

**Mutual of Omaha
Insurance Cos.**
Mutual of Omaha Plz.
Omaha, NE 68175
402/342-7600

Nationwide Corp.
1 Nationwide Plz.
Columbus, OH 43216
614/249-7111

**Northwestern Mutual
Life Insurance Co.**
720 E. Wisconsin Ave.
Milwaukee, WI 53202
414/271-1444

**NWNL Companies
Inc.—
Northwestern National
Life Insurance Cos.**
20 Washington Ave. S.
Minneapolis, MN
55401
612/372-5432

Ohio Casualty Corp.
136 N. Third St.
Hamilton, OH 45025
513/867-3000

**Old Republic
International Corp.**
307 N. Michigan Ave.
Chicago, IL 60601
312/346-8100

Orion Capital Corporation
30 Rockefeller Plz.
New York, NY 10112
212/541-4646

Primerica Holdings, Inc.
65 E. 55th St.
New York, NY 10022
212/891-8900

Progressive Corp.
6000 Parkland Blvd.
Mayfield Heights, OH 44124
216/464-8000

Provident Life & Accident Insurance Co.
Fountain Sq.
Chattanooga, TN 37402
615/755-1011

Prudential Insurance Co. of America
213 Washington St.
Newark, NJ 07101
201/802-6000

Reliance Group Holdings, Inc.
55 E. 52nd St.

New York, NY 10055
212/909-1100

Safeco Corp.
Safeco Plz.
Seattle, WA 98185
206/545-5000

St. Paul Companies, Inc.
385 Washington St.
St. Paul, MN 55102
613/221-7911

Torchmark Corp.
2001 Third Ave. S.
Birmingham, AL 35233
205/325-4200

Transamerica Corp.
600 Montgomery St.
San Francisco, CA 94111
415/983-4000

The Travelers Corp.
1 Tower Sq.
Hartford, CT 06183
203/277-0111

USF&G Corp.
100 Light St.
Baltimore, MD 21202
410/547-3000

USLife Corp.
125 Maiden Ln.
New York, NY 10038
212/709-6000

Unitrin, Inc.
1 E. Wacker Dr.
Chicago, IL 60601
312/661-4600

UNUM Corp.
2211 Congress St.
Portland, ME 04122
207/770-2211

Uslico Corp.
4401 Fairfax Dr.
Box 3700
Arlington, VA 22203
703/875-3600

Wausau Insurance Companies
2000 Westwood Dr.
Wausau, WI 54401
715/845-5211

WHERE TO GO FOR MORE INFORMATION

INSURANCE INDUSTRY ASSOCIATIONS

Alliance of American Insurers
1501 Woodfield Rd.
Schaumburg, IL 60173
708/330-8500
(Members are property and casualty insurance companies, not individuals.)

American Council of Life Insurance
1001 Pennsylvania Ave., NW, Suite 500-S
Washington, DC 20004
202/624-2000

American Insurance Association
85 John St.

New York, NY 10038
212/669-0400

Health Insurance Association of America
1025 Connecticut Ave., NW,
Suite 1200

Washington, DC 20036
202/223-7780

Insurance Information Institute
110 William St.
New York, NY 10038
212/669-9200
(Members are property and liability insurance companies. This group provides information services to the public, schools, etc.; sponsors seminars; and has a library.)

Life Insurance Research & Marketing Association
8 Farm Springs Rd.

Farmington, CT 06032
203/677-0033

Life Office Management Association
5770 Powers Ferry Rd.
Atlanta, GA
30327-4308
404/951-1770

National Association of Independent Insurers
2600 River Rd.
Des Plaines, IL 60018
708/297-7800

National Association of Mutual Insurance Companies

3601 Vincennes Rd.
P.O. Box 68700
Indianapolis, IN 46268
317/875-5250

Reinsurance Association of America
1301 Pennsylvania Ave., NW,
Suite 900
Washington, DC 20036
202/638-3690

Risk and Insurance Management Society
205 E. 42nd St.
New York, NY 10017
212/286-9292

INSURANCE INDUSTRY DIRECTORIES

Best's Insurance Reports
(See listing for *Best's Review* in "Insurance Industry Periodicals.")

Insurance Almanac
Underwriter Printing & Publishing Co.
50 E. Palisade Ave.
Englewood, NJ 07631
201/569-8808
(Lists more than three thousand insurance companies; national, state, and local insurance associations; and agents, brokers, etc.)

Insurance Field Directories
Insurance Field Company
P.O. Box 24244
Louisville, KY 40224
502/491-5857
(Directories for eleven different states or regions.)

Insurance Phone Book & Directory
U.S. Directory Service
655 NW 128th St.
Miami, FL 33168
305/769-1700

Who's Who in Insurance
Underwriter Printing & Publishing Co.
50 E. Palisade Ave.
Englewood, NJ 07631
201/569-8808
(Lists more than five thousand individuals involved in the insurance industry, such as officials, brokers, etc. Includes title, company affiliation and address, biographical information, and more. May be useful to prepare for interviews.)

INSURANCE INDUSTRY PERIODICALS

American Agent & Broker
408 Olive St.
St. Louis, MO 63102
314/421-5445
(Monthly magazine for insurance agents, brokers, department heads, and adjusters.)

Best's Review
Ambest Rd.
Oldwick, NJ 08858
908/439-2200
(Monthly magazine; there are two different editions, *Life and Health* and *Property and Casualty*. Both are aimed at insurance executives and often include good help-wanted sections. The annual *Best's Insurance Reports* is a directory of companies.)

Business Insurance
740 Rush St.
Chicago, IL 60611
312/649-5200
(Weekly tabloid for those involved in corporate property, casualty, and employee insurance protection.)

Insurance Review
110 William St.
New York, NY 10038
212/669-9200
(Monthly magazine for insurance industry managers and executives.)

National Underwriter
43–47 Newark St.
Hoboken, NJ 07030
201/963-2300
(Weekly tabloid; there are two editions, *Property & Casualty* and *Life & Health Insurance*, both aimed at management.)

MANUFACTURING

INDUSTRY OUTLOOK: Depends on the performance of other industries and on foreign economic development.

Overall, it looks as though manufacturing isn't in for any great shakeups, but it isn't in for a huge surge either. The industry as a whole appears streamlined and prepared to grow as the economy picks up. The key trends: continuing cost consciousness, increased attention to international markets, and tough competition from foreign competitors.

A LOOK BACK

► **Tough times were followed by a mini-boom, then the hammer fall of the recession.**

Manufacturers went through several straight years of plunging revenues, but the picture became brighter in the late '80s. The weakened dollar led to a rise in exports. Industrial sales increased as demands for products rose. Real spending for industrial equipment hit 9% in 1989—higher than for computers—as companies from a wide range of industries, from pulp and paper to construction to food and beverages, began buying machinery. The result? Order backlogs and confident manufacturing companies. Manufacturing jobs, which had been cut year after year, started to increase again. For the first time in years, large manufacturing companies began recruiting, and staffs grew.

But there were problems as the industry entered the '90s, among them a continued automotive slump and a continued lag in American productivity in comparison with foreign manufacturers. Then came the recession. Industries began to cut back and manufacturing suffered.

WHAT'S NEXT

► **Continued restructuring, streamlining, and expansion ahead as manufacturers fight to be competitive.**

Some trends: shifting management styles, cutbacks in layers of management, refocused corporate direction, and, most important, reconfigured and upgraded facilities. In general, U.S. manufacturers are striving to improve productivity through these changes. Some companies, particularly in the metalworking sector, will be cutting back product lines and focusing instead on specific product groups.

In addition, there will be an increase in joint ventures between companies, particularly in the research and development areas. Linking up with another company helps a manufacturer defray the high cost of research while still allowing the benefit of innovation. Similarly, there will be some merger activity and increased industry consolidation.

▶ **Expect an increased push into international markets.**

Already, U.S. manufacturers are expanding overseas. Many have set up foreign subsidiaries or have entered into joint-venture agreements with a manufacturer from the area. Among the reasons for establishing a physical presence in a foreign market: companies gain a market advantage by being able to adapt their products more easily to the market's specific needs; they can avoid trade barriers and negative fallout from a fluctuating dollar.

Construction machinery companies will be targeting the former Soviet Union, Asia, and Eastern Europe, in particular, to capitalize on the development that will be occurring in these areas. Machine tool companies will be focusing more on Thailand, where machine tool exports nearly doubled in 1991, South America, as well as on European countries.

▶ **A growing trend: the use of team manufacturing.**

This method is called by many names—including worker participation, employee involvement (EI), and self-managed team manufacturing—but whatever the name used, it describes the same method, and it is a rapidly growing trend in the manufacturing industry.

A brief explanation: With self-managed team manufacturing, a group of workers forms a team that is responsible for the production of an entire product, not just a single part. Every team member is trained in every step of the manufacturing process; in some cases, members rotate through each position. Members are also trained to handle problems such as production bottlenecks and equipment failures and to do their own production scheduling. At many companies, teams elect a team leader who, along with a plant supervisor, represents the only management at the facility.

The team manufacturing method has been credited with improving productivity—with increases up to 30 percent, according to some reports. In addition, workers often report higher morale and improved working conditions.

The impact on employment? A need for more skilled workers. Companies that use the team method generally seek highly motivated individuals and say that attitude is important. On the down side, the team method may point to cutbacks in lower-management and supervisory positions.

▶ **Another growing trend, and one that fits in with team management: increased use of automation.**

Automation has become crucial to maintain a competitive edge. For example, many manufacturers have instituted concurrent engineering (also called design-integrated manufacturing or simultaneous engineering). This method relies on the use of integrated networks of personal computers, mainframes, and other systems—in effect, a web of computerized systems. Some of the individual automated systems that can be linked up through the network include expert systems (ES) software, used to streamline the manufacturing process; computer-aided design and manufacturing (CAD/CAM) systems; and electronic data interchange (EDI) systems, often used in ordering materials.

By using concurrent engineering, manufacturers can raise productivity, cut costs (after the initial capital outlay), and reduce time lags in product development and production. In some cases, it dovetails into a version of team manufacturing, as a team of workers from different departments—design, manufacturing, purchasing, etc.—work together to develop the specific concurrent engineering program for a new project.

In line with automation, there is also an increased use of "just-in-time" manufacturing, in which manufacturing supplies reach the factory as needed, rather than in prescheduled shipments, and "small batch" manufacturing, in which manufacturers customize products to meet specific customer needs and demands.

These changes in manufacturing methods are having a major impact on employment. First of all, there is a growing need for IS (Information Systems) staffers to develop the software and hardware used in the manufacturing process (although a number of companies use outside firms for this). There are also employment opportunities for workers skilled in computerized manufacturing, CAD/CAM technicians, mechanical engineers, software engineers, and skilled craftspeople.

▶ **One result of the streamlining that has been going on in manufacturing: There has been an increase in the use of outside contractors to supply part-time and temporary workers.**

This is a way of keeping costs down and permanent staffing lean.

And manufacturers have found that relying on a part-time or temporary work force to meet demands when orders are high means they can avoid layoffs and furloughing of workers during slack periods. One result—higher productivity and higher morale among permanent employees.

Employment note: Typically, a company uses a contractor to provide temporary workers. Agencies specialize in different fields and often make efforts to keep their temp employees working year-round, by finding them positions at different companies when one company doesn't need them.

EMPLOYMENT OUTLOOK: Affected by automation and other corporate innovations. As such, expect increased hiring in some areas, decreased in others.

Over the past five years, manufacturers slashed over 1.4 million jobs. And technological breakthroughs, automation and a shift in the economy will continue to result in a long-term drop in manufacturing jobs. The federal government predicts a decline of about 3% over the next decade—a loss of about 600,000 jobs.

Generally speaking, this is part of the overall trend shifting employment from goods-producing to service-producing areas. For example, in 1920, manufacturing accounted for about 27% of those working; in 1990, the number dropped to 17%. And by 2005, experts predict the number will drop even lower, to about 12%.

Some of the results: According to the federal government's Bureau of Labor Statistics, machine builder and metal fabricator jobs will decline about 10% by the year 2000.

But there will be employment opportunities. First, increased automation is actually *increasing* the demand for skilled workers and engineers. Projections show that there may be a shortage of these people, so training programs for machinists and craftspeople are increasing. In addition, about 7 million people will land jobs that replace workers who retire or otherwise leave manufacturing. Certain areas look stronger in terms of job creation and employment opportunity than others. More specifically, the government figures from 1990 to 2005: Jobs for sales and marketing staffers at manufacturing companies are projected to increase about 27%; technicians about 9%.

Finally, certain industry segments are headed for better performance than others, which will result in strong hiring activity. For example, the construction machinery industry should be heating up over the long term as a result of the need for repair and replacement of infrastructure and public utility plants.

JOBS SPOTLIGHT

"GENERALIST" ENGINEERS: Companies employing the team manufacturing method often need "generalist" engineers—that is, manufacturing engineers who understand an entire manufacturing process. These engineers often lead teams and must be able to supervise a variety of operations and maintenance workers. As such, both technical and strong interpersonal skills are a necessity.

TECHNICAL TRAINERS: This is a growing area as companies increase automation and workers need to upgrade skills or learn new skills to work with the new technologies. Technical trainers often work in the human resources department of a company, although some are contracted on a per-project basis and, as such, work for a training firm. Requirements vary but may include manufacturing experience, a degree in engineering or another technical area, and course work in education. Salaries range from about $30,000 for an entry-level position up to the six figures for senior management.

BEST BETS

Herman Miller, Inc.
8500 Byron Rd.
Zeeland, MI 49464
616/772-3300

An office furniture manufacturer with a strong emphasis on employee welfare as well as profits, Herman Miller offers a "silver parachute" of one year's severance pay to *all* employees with more than two years' service in event of a hostile takeover. It has a reputation as a good employer and is poised for long-term growth.

Rubbermaid Inc.
1147 Akron Rd.
Wooster, OH 44691
216/264-6464

Consistently on the top of "Best Companies" lists, Rubbermaid has been chosen a Best Bet for the last three years and was the second most admired corporation in America in *Fortune*'s 1993 survey. It has a reputation for being a tough but fair place to work. Considered a key to the company: close attention to quality and fierce pride in the goods manufactured—attitudes that come from the CEO on down. With strong sales and a fine reputation, Rubbermaid looks like a good bet for the long term.

TOP GENERAL MANUFACTURING COMPANIES

Avery Dennison Corp.
150 N. Orange Grove Blvd.
Pasadena, CA 91103
818/304-2000

Blount, Inc.
4520 Executive Pk. Dr.
Montgomery, AL 36116
205/244-4000

Corning, Inc.
Houghton Pk.
Corning, NY 14830
607/974-9000

Crane Co.
757 Third Ave.
New York, NY 10017
212/415-7300

Duracell International
Berkshire Industrial Pk.
Bethel, CT 06801
203/796-4000

Exide Corp.
P.O. Box 14205
Reading, PA 19612
215/378-0500

First Brands Corp.
83 Wooster Heights Rd.
Danbury, CT 06813
203/731-2300

Great American Management & Investment, Inc.
2 N. Riverside Pl.
Chicago, IL 60606
312/648-5656

Harsco Corp.
350 Poplar Church Rd.
Camp Hill, PA 17011
717/763-7064

Hillenbrand Industries, Inc.
Hwy. 46 E.
Batesville, IN 47006
812/934-7000

Illinois Tool Works, Inc.
3600 W. Lake Ave.
Glenview, IL 60625
708/724-7500

Jostens, Inc.
5501 Norman Ctr. Dr.
Minneapolis, MN 55437
612/830-3300

Mark IV Industries, Inc.
501 Audubon Pkwy.
Amherst, NY 14228
716/689-4972

Minnesota Mining & Manufacturing Co. (3M)
3M Center
St. Paul, MN 55144
612/733-1110

Rubbermaid, Inc.
1147 Akron Rd.
Wooster, OH 44691
216/264-6464

Trinova Corp.
3000 Strayer
Maumee, OH 43537
419/867-2200

TOP INDUSTRIAL MACHINERY, MACHINE, AND HAND TOOLS MANUFACTURING COMPANIES

Black & Decker Corp.
701 E. Joppa Rd.
Baltimore, MD 21286
410/716-3900

Briggs & Stratton Corp.
12301 W. Wirth St.
Wauwatosa, WI 53222
414/259-5333

Caterpillar, Inc.
100 NE Adams St.
Peoria, IL 61629
309/675-1000

Cincinnati Milacron, Inc.
4701 Marburg Ave.
Cincinnati, OH 45209
513/841-8100

Clark Equipment Co.
100 N. Michigan St.
South Bend, IN 46634
219/239-0100

Cummins Engine Co.
500 Jackson St.
Columbus, IN 47202
812/377-5000

Danaher Corp.
1250 24th St., NW
Washington, DC 20037
202/828-0850

Deere & Co.
John Deere Rd.
Moline, IL 61265
309/765-8000

Dover Corp.
280 Park Ave.
New York, NY 10017
212/922-1640

FMC Corp.
200 E. Randolph Dr.
Chicago, IL 60601
312/861-6000

General Signal Corp.
1 High Ridge Pk.
Stamford, CT 06904
203/357-8800

Harnischfeger Industries, Inc.
13400 Bishops Ln.
Brookfield, WI 53005
414/671-4400

Ingersoll-Rand
200 Chestnut Ridge Rd.
Woodcliff Lake, NJ 07675
201/573-0123

Interlake Corp.
550 Warrenville Rd.
Lisle, IL 60532
708/852-8800

Nacco Industries, Inc.
12800 Shaker Blvd.
Cleveland, OH 44120
216/752-1000

Pall Corp.
2200 Northern Blvd.
East Hills, NY 11548
516/484-5400

Parker Hannifin Corp.
17325 Euclid Ave.
Cleveland, OH 44112
216/531-3000

Pentair, Inc.
1700 W. Hwy. 36
St. Paul, MN 55113
612/636-7920

Snap-On Tools Corp.
2801 80th St.
Kenosha, WI 53141
414/656-5200

SPX Corp.
100 Terrace Plz.
Muskegon, MI 49443
616/724-5011

Stanley Works, Inc.
1000 Stanley Dr.
New Britain, CT 06053
203/225-5111

Tenneco, Inc.
1010 Milam St.
Houston, TX 77002
713/757-2131

Terex Corp.
201 W. Walnut St.
Green Bay, WI 54305
414/435-5322

Timken Co.
1835 Dueber Ave., SW
Canton, OH 44706
216/438-3000

Trinity Industries, Inc.
2525 Stemmons Fwy.
Dallas, TX 75207
214/631-4420

Tyco Laboratories, Inc.
1 Tyco Pk.
Exeter, NH 03833
603/778-9700

WHERE TO GO FOR MORE INFORMATION

(For more information sources in related areas, also check listings under "Engineers," page 41, and "Technical Careers," page 186.)

MANUFACTURING ASSOCIATIONS

American Hardware Manufacturers Association
801 N. Plz. Dr.
Schaumburg, IL 60173
312/605-1025

American Production and Inventory Control Society
500 W. Annandale Rd.
Falls Church, VA 22046
703/237-8344

Construction Industry Manufacturers Association
111 E. Wisconsin Ave.
Milwaukee, WI 53202
414/272-0943

Fabricators & Manufacturers Association International
5411 E. State St.

Rockford, IL
61108-2376
815/399-8700

Industrial Research Institute
1550 M St., NW
Washington, DC 20005
202/872-6350

Institute of Industrial Engineers
25 Technology Park
Norcross, GA 30092
404/449-0460
(Puts out monthly publication *Industrial Engineering.*)

Machinery & Allied Products Institute
1200 18th St., NW
Washington, DC 20036
202/331-8430

National Association of Manufacturers
1331 Pennsylvania Ave., NW,
Suite 1500, North Lobby
Washington, DC 20004-1703
202/637-2000

Society of Manufacturing Engineers
P.O. Box 930
1 SME Dr.
Dearborn, MI 48121
313/271-1500

Tooling & Manufacturing Association
1177 S. Dee Rd.
Park Ridge, IL 60068
708/825-1120
(Offers job referral information and résumé bank service.)

MANUFACTURING DIRECTORIES

American Manufacturers Directory
American Business Directories
5711 S. 86th Cir.
Omaha, NE 68127
402/593-4600

MacRAES' Blue Book, Inc.
Business Research Publications, Inc.
817 Broadway
New York, NY 10003
212/673-4700
800/622-7237

Moody's Industrial Manual
Moody's Investors Service, Inc.
99 Church St.
New York, NY 10007
212/553-0300

Thomas Register of American Manufacturers; Thomas Register

Catalog File
Thomas Publishing Company

1 Penn. Plz.
New York, NY 10119
212/290-7310

MANUFACTURING MAGAZINES

American Machinist
826 Broadway
New York, NY 10003
212/477-6420
(Monthly magazine for manufacturing personnel, engineers, plant managers, research/developers, etc.)

Automation
1100 E. Superior Ave.
Cleveland, OH 44114
216/696-7000
(Monthly magazine for manufacturer production executives and staffers in process/handling.)

Design News
275 Washington St.
Newton, MA 02158
617/964-3030
(Semimonthly magazine for design and technical engineers, managers, etc.)

Machine Design
1100 E. Superior Ave.
Cleveland, OH 44114
216/696-7000
(Primarily biweekly magazine aimed at design and technical engineers, managers, etc.)

Manufacturing Engineering
Box 930
Dearborn, MI 48121
313/271-1500
(Monthly magazine put out by the Society of Manufacturing Engineers; aimed at manufacturing engineers as well as plant managers, designers, technicians, and researchers.)

Material Handling Engineering
1100 E. Superior Ave.
Cleveland, OH 44114
216/696-7000
(Thirteen-issue magazine for executives, chief engineers, technicians, foremen, etc.)

Plant Engineering
P.O. Box 5080
Des Plaines, IL 60017
708/635-8800
(Twenty-two-issue magazine for personnel in plant engineering.)

Plant Services
301 E. Erie St.
Chicago, IL 60611
312/644-2020
(Monthly magazine for plant personnel in a range of fields, including maintenance, engineering, materials handling, environment, sites.)

Quality
191 S. Gary Ave.
Wheaton, IL 60188
708/665-1000
(Monthly magazine for manufacturing/engineering managers, quality assurance managers and inspectors, etc.)

Quality Progress
310 W. Wisconsin Ave.
Milwaukee, WI 53203
414/272-8575
(Monthly magazine for quality assurance/quality control engineers, inspectors, etc.)

METALS AND MINING

INDUSTRY OUTLOOK: Rebounding as the economy improves; some sectors weaker than others.

Steel will see a pickup as consumer demand for products made of steel (appliances, cars, etc.) increases. But competition will be the byword over the long term. The large steel companies will be in for hot competition—both from foreign competitors and from domestic mini-mills. And steel in general will be competing with lighter-weight materials such as aluminum and plastic.

Aluminum may see sluggish short-term results but is headed for long-term growth, especially as it makes inroads into markets previously dominated by steel.

As for metals, the picture, as always, is mixed. Looking strongest over the long term: copper.

A LOOK BACK

▶ **Grim times in the early '80s, a turnaround in the late '80s, then the recession of the early '90s hammered the metals and mining industry.**

1981 to 1983 were bad years for the metal industry, particularly for steel producers. More than 200,000 workers were laid off. The top steel producers lost nearly $6 billion. The downhill spiral forced an industrywide restructuring. Companies closed plants, rebuilt, and modernized—and it looked like everything was set for good times again.

But, spearheaded by a lag in automobile sales, demand began dropping. Steel shipments declined and producers edged into overcapacity. Similarly, prices of other metals began dropping as supply exceeded demand. Companies began streamlining again, cutting costs and workers. When the recession hit, metals companies, especially steel, suffered. A key reason? Construction and motor vehicles are steel's biggest markets, and they were the two industries hardest hit by the recession. Aluminum was also hit hard, with prices falling to their lowest levels in almost five years.

While there were a few bright spots, including a 1991 export boom and a growing container market, the overall mood was grim as the industry waited for a nationwide economic recovery to pull it out of the slump.

WHAT'S NEXT

▶ **A key challenge ahead for big steel: Raising enough money for necessary capital investments.**

While the picture for the integrated steel companies has been improving, times won't be completely perfect. A major problem: the amount of money the big steel makers owe in pension and retirement benefits has made lenders and investors leery of investing in the companies. And the steel makers need capital to stay afloat—for new equipment, to keep pace technologically with competitors and to meet environmental legislation demands. This may hurt big steel—and help mini-mills.

▶ **Watch for the increased use of aluminum in motor vehicles.**

This, clearly, points to a very positive development for aluminum producers. Aluminum is already being used more and more in cars—for example, more than 30% of the 1991 Acura NSX's weight, or 941 pounds, is aluminum—and its use is expected to increase dramatically in the future. Experts predict that over the next five years, Japan's use of aluminum in its cars will more than double. Similar developments may occur with U.S. car manufacturers and Japanese transplants in the U.S. One result? Watch for joint ventures and agreements between steel companies and aluminum companies.

▶ **Mini-mills will continue to come on strong.**

While they may face short-term downslides, mini-mills (low-cost steel producers using smaller furnaces and, usually high-tech methods) are in for a very promising future. The reasons for their strength? An emphasis on cost-efficiency—instead of more costly iron ore, they usually use scrap, labor costs are lower, etc.; and streamlined operations typically utilizing technologically advanced methods and equipment. These efficient and low-cost mini-mills have been able to successfully compete head-to-head with the larger integrated steel producers. As such, expect to see further growth in the area.

▶ **On the horizon: aluminum mini-mills.**

The use of continuous casting to produce sheet aluminum for beverage cans may make aluminum mini-mills another success story. While the recent poor performance of aluminum has slowed the industry down, this is an area that may see growth over the long term. A leading proponent of the mini-mill is Golden Aluminum in San Antonio, Texas. If this method of producing sheet aluminum works efficiently, it should have far-reaching effects on the industry.

▶ **Increased automation and the use of manufacturing methods such as "just in time" will be key to staying competitive.**

Like most other manufacturers, metals producers will try to remain cost-efficient by using "just in time" manufacturing, keeping finished-goods, in-process goods, and raw-material inventory in check. Similarly, more mills and service centers will be computerizing, linking systems by computer networks to keep track of all phases of production. Another trend to watch for is the development of strategic partnerships between producers and customers.

▶ **Similarly, watch for continued technological breakthroughs to change the industry.**

Companies will follow in the path of the mini-mills and continue to come up with new methods of producing metals. For example, in early 1992 MicroMet Technology Inc. introduced Rhondite, a new type of steel with a different structure than that of regular steel. The key pluses? It is stronger than conventional steel, and it reportedly can be produced at the same or lower cost than mini-mill–produced steel. Another example: Republic Engineered Steels, a bar and specialty steel manufacturer, has come up with a quality-verification system called the Quality Verification Line. According to *Industry Week,* this is an integrated system that inspects and verifies the quality of bar steel and so assures customers of high quality.

These types of breakthroughs will bring about shifts in the industry power balance—and may, in the long term, result in a shakeout among companies. Those unable to keep up technologically due to the high cost of modernizing will risk failure.

▶ **Expect the mining industry to move toward further globalization.**

This will occur in a number of ways. First of all, watch as more companies step up global activity. As a result, the number of joint ventures between domestic and foreign companies will increase. One reason? Joint ventures will enable companies to get involved in expensive overseas mining projects without taking on too much of a financial burden. With the rise in joint ventures, there also will be an increase in multiple-country ownership of companies.

▶ **A growing trend: Metals companies are developing new markets and new products.**

They are doing so to help the cyclical industry cope with the inevitable drops in demand. The different segments of the industry will continue to search for new areas in which to market their traditional products and will be developing new products as well.

A few examples: Aluminum producers are making efforts to sell aluminum packaging for products not traditionally packaged in aluminum. They also are modernizing and developing new products. One of the most promising is a composite incorporating aluminum but reinforced with lightweight, high-strength materials, which increases its applications.

Titanium producers, facing cutbacks in a prime market, the defense sector, are exploring alternative industrial markets, including hole oil drilling applications and tubing for desalinization plants. Lead producers are researching and testing different uses for lead-acid batteries, including using them as computer and communication systems backup and as a power source for industrial trucks and electric cars. Copper producers, facing a decrease in demand from telecommunications companies due to the growth of fiber optics, are targeting the construction, roofing, and automotive electronics industries.

In short, the metals industry is staying as flexible as possible to ensure strong performance in the years ahead.

EMPLOYMENT OUTLOOK: Fair to poor.

Between 1979 and 1992, there was a 50.6% drop in employment in mining. Although the pace may slow, this trend should continue over the long term. The key reason? Technological breakthroughs. Today's labor-saving equipment doesn't require the same number of hourly production workers as in the past. At the same time, the new technology has created a greater need for administrative and managerial personnel. The result? An increase in the number of supervisors and engineers. This trend should continue as technological breakthroughs continue to effect the industry.

JOBS SPOTLIGHT

METALLURGISTS/METALLURGIC ENGINEERS: With the government forecasting growth in this area from 10 to 20% between now and 2005, this area appears promising. One reason for the bright outlook—the industry's push to develop new ways of processing low-grade ores.

BEST BETS

Allegheny Ludlum Corp.
1000 Six PPG Pl.
Pittsburgh, PA 15222
412/394-2800

Allegheny Ludlum is setting its sights on R&D and technology to keep going strong. Some examples: more than fifteen years before its competitors, Allegheny Ludlum began computerizing; its Natrona Heights, PA, technology center employs 430 scientists and technicians; it pumps more than $30 million annually into R&D, and it has been spending on capital improvements as well, investing in an efficient cold-rolling mill, among other things. CEO Robert Bozzone explains that the company is "technology-driven." For this reason, it appears poised for a strong future—and may, in fact, turn out to be *the* hot post in the steel industry.

Chaparral Steel
300 Ward Rd.
Midlothian, TX 76065
214/775-8241

This mini-mill looks like a performer well-suited for the '90s. According to a 1992 *Fortune* article, Chaparral appears to be able to weather the shakeout most experts see coming in the steel industry. In addition to its reputation for customer service, it's known as a company with an entreprenuerial management style. Employees schedule their own lunch hours and breaks. Salaries and bonuses are calculated by merit, job performance, company performance and, perhaps most interestingly, new skills learned. This emphasis on education is strong at Chaparral. Employees take courses, and are cross-trained in a range of areas. The bottom line—the open management style is paying off for Chaparral. It has become the world's lowest cost producer of steel and should keep coming on strong.

Nucor
4425 Randolph Rd.
Charlotte, NC 28211
704/366-7000

A leading high-tech mini-mill company, Nucor was chosen a Best Bet in *Jobs '93*, as well as one of the companies to watch in the '90s by the *Wall Street Journal*. A key reason? Its Crawfordville, Indiana, plant, which makes flat-rolled sheet steel more quickly and cheaply than other larger plants. Where the large integrated steel producers would take about three man-hours to produce a ton of sheet steel, Nucor's new plant can turn it out in forty-five minutes. It is currently building another such plant. There's still a fight ahead competing with Big Steel, but it looks like a real winner.

TOP METALS & MINING COMPANIES

Alcan Aluminum Corp.
100 Erieview Plz.
Columbus, OH 44114
216/523-6800

ALCOA—Aluminum Co. of America
1501 Alcoa Bldg.
425 Sixth Ave.
Pittsburgh, PA 15219
412/553-4545

Allegheny Ludlum Corp.
1000 Six PPG Pl.
Pittsburgh, PA 15222
412/394-2800

Amax, Inc.
200 Park Ave.
New York, NY 10166
212/856-4200

Armco, Inc.
300 Interpace Pkwy.
Parsippany, NJ 07054
201/316-5200

Asarco, Inc.
180 Maiden Ln.
New York, NY 10038
212/510-2000

Bethlehem Steel Corp.
1170 Eighth Ave.
Bethlehem, PA 18016
215/694-2424

Cyprus Minerals Co.
9100 E. Mineral Cir.
Englewood, CO 80112
303/643-5000

Engelhard Corp.
101 Wood Ave.
Iselin, NJ 08830
908/205-6000

Freeport McMoRan Copper Co.
1615 Poydras St.
New Orleans, LA 70112
504/582-4000

Handy & Harman
850 Third Ave.
New York, NY 10022
212/752-3400

Homestake Mining Co.
650 California St.
San Francisco, CA 94108
415/981-8150

Inco United States, Inc.
1 New York Plz.

New York, NY 10004
212/612-5690

Inland Steel Industries
30 W. Monroe St.
Chicago, IL 60603
312/346-0300

Kennecott Corp.
10 E. S. Temple St.
Salt Lake City, UT
84147
801/322-7000

**Magma Copper Co.,
Inc.**
Hwy. 76
San Manuel, AZ 85631
602/575-5670

Maxxam, Inc.
5847 San Felipe
Houston, TX 77057
713/975-7600

Newmont Gold
1700 Lincoln St.
Denver, CO 80203
303/863-7414

**Newmont Mining
Corp.**
1700 Lincoln St.
Denver, CO 80203
303/863-7414

Nucor Corp.
2100 Rexford Rd.
Charlotte, NC 28211
704/366-7000

Phelps Dodge Corp.
2600 N. Central Ave.
Phoenix, AZ 85004
602/234-8100

Reynolds Metals
6601 W. Broad St.
Richmond, VA 23261
804/281-2000

USX-U.S. Steel Group
600 Grant St.
Pittsburgh, PA 15219
412/433-1121

Weirton Steel Corp.
400 Three Springs Dr.
Weirton, WV 26062
304/797-2000

**Wheeling-Pittsburgh
Steel Corp.**
1134 Market St.
Wheeling, WV 26003
304/234-2400

**Worthington
Industries, Inc.**
1205 Dearborn Dr.
Columbus, OH 43085
614/438-3210

WHERE TO GO FOR MORE INFORMATION

METALS AND MINING INDUSTRY ASSOCIATIONS

**American Institute of
Mining, Metallurgical,
and Petroleum
Engineers**
345 E. 47th St.,
14th Fl.
New York, NY 10017
212/705-7695

**American Iron & Steel
Institute**
1101 17th St., NW,
13th Fl.
Washington, DC 20036
202/452-7100

**American Mining
Congress**
1920 N St., NW

Washington, DC 20036
202/861-2800

**ASM International
(American Society for
Metals)**
9639 Kinsman
Materials Park, OH
44073
216/338-5151
(Publishes *Advanced
Materials and
Processes* and *ASM
News* magazines, which
include help-wanted
ads.)

**Association of Iron
and Steel Engineers**
3 Gateway Ctr., Suite
2350
Pittsburgh, PA 15222
412/281-6323

**Association of Steel
Distributors**
401 N. Michigan Dr.
Chicago, IL 60611
312/644-6610

**Minerals, Metals and
Materials Society**
420 Commonwealth Dr.
Warrendale, PA 15086
412/776-9080

**Society of Mining
Engineers**
Caller No. D
Littleton, CO 80127
303/973-9550
(Puts out monthly

Mining Engineering
magazine.)

**Steel Manufacturers
Association**
815 Connecticut Ave.,

NW, Suite 304
Washington, DC 20006
202/342-1160

METALS AND MINING INDUSTRY DIRECTORIES

*Directory of Iron and
Steel Plants*
Association of Iron and
Steel Engineers
3 Gateway Ctr., Suite
2350
Pittsburgh, PA 15222
412/281-6323

*Directory of Steel
Foundries in the
United States, Canada
and Mexico*
Steel Founders' Society
of America
455 State St.
Des Plaines, IL 60016
312/299-9166

*Dun's Industrial
Guide: The
Metalworking Directory*
Dun's Marketing
Services
3 Sylvan Way
Parsippany, NJ
07054-3896
201/455-0900

*Iron & Steel Works of
the World*
Metal Bulletin Inc.
220 Fifth Ave.
New York, NY 10001
212/213-6202

*Iron and Steel Works
Directory of the United
States and Canada*

American Iron and
Steel Institute
1000 16th St., NW
Washington, DC 20036
202/452-7100

*Western Mining
Directory*
Howell Publishing
Company
Box 1030
Castle Rock, CO 80104
303/688-8982
(Lists about fourteen
hundred firms and
organizations involved
in the mining industry
in the West.)

METALS AND MINING INDUSTRY PERIODICALS

*American Metal
Market*
825 Seventh Ave.
New York, NY 10019
212/887-8560
(Daily newspaper
covering the metals
industry; aimed at
executives, managers,
etc.)

*Engineering & Mining
Journal*
29 N. Wacker Dr.
Chicago, IL 60606

312/726-2802
(Monthly magazine
covering the mining
industry; for mining and
processing production
and engineering staffs,
executives, etc.)

Iron Age
191 S. Gary Ave.
Carol Stream, IL 60188
708/462-2286
(Monthly magazine
covering the iron
industry.)

Mining World News
90 W. Grove St.
Reno, NV 89505
702/827-1115
(Monthly tabloid for
professionals involved
in mining, including
mining engineers,
geologists,
geophysicists,
metallurgists, etc.)

PAPER AND FOREST PRODUCTS

INDUSTRY OUTLOOK: Improving in step with the economy.

Paper: Watch for intensified competition, increased spending to stay in step with environmental demands and a push into overseas markets.

Forest Products: Still feeling the effects of environmental legislation, but will see improvement as housing starts increase with the rebounding economy.

A LOOK BACK

▶ **A three year run of high demand and high profits led to mergers and acquisitions and increased capital spending.**

The late '80s was a record-setting period for the industry. Demand surged domestically and exports of paper and wood products jumped due to a weak dollar. The result? Prices increased, contributing to record-high industry profits in 1988 and 1989.

A flurry of mergers followed by consolidations and restructuring followed. Two of the leaders in the acquisition game were Jefferson Smurfit and Stone Container, although Georgia-Pacific was responsible for the single largest merger when, in 1990, it took over Great Northern Nekoosa.

The same period saw a jump in capital spending as companies began expanding—investing in new facilities and equipment. But when the '90s opened with a downhill slide, the capital investments damaged a number of companies. One problem—overcapacity coupled with sluggish demand. Forest products companies also slumped, due to a drop in construction. Overall industry profits dove, dropping about 35% in 1990, another 12% in 1991, with 1992 and 1993 showing less improvement than hoped for.

WHAT'S NEXT

▶ **Expect to see a growing push into international markets.**

Increasing exports and international market share help paper companies deal with lags in domestic demand. As such, more companies will be expanding overseas or emphasizing their international operations.

There will be increased international opportunities for paper companies due a number of factors, among them the unification of Western Europe, the democratization of Eastern Europe, and the U.S.-Canada Free Trade Agreement. In addition, in spite of tough competition, paper and paperboard manufacturers will be targeting Japan and other Pacific Rim countries.

Expect to see activity in a number of different ways. Some companies will enter the international marketplace as general paper and paperboard producers, others with more specialized products targeted to niche markets. Competition should be intense as U.S. manufacturers already entrenched go head to head with new arrivals, as well as with their foreign competitors. In many cases, companies are entering into joint ventures with their foreign counterparts—and in so doing, have the advantage of in-country facilities, distribution networks, and market position. Others are buying local operations or building new plants.

Another outgrowth of the growing internationalism of the paper industry will be increased competition from foreign companies in the domestic marketplace. One example: Low-cost producers and suppliers from South American companies are already putting the squeeze on U.S. pulp companies.

▶ Paper and pulp companies will increasingly rely on automation and technological advancements to keep costs down and productivity high.

Like most other U.S. industries, the paper and pulp industry is increasingly automating and computerizing. Plant automation will be one of the most significant technological changes for the industry. Expect to see the development and implementation of systems that will allow for a completely automated mill—from setting production schedules to measuring and controlling quality.

But like other manufacturing industries, the paper industry may be feeling the results of the skilled labor shortage and will be setting up retraining programs to prepare workers to use the new high-tech equipment.

▶ Dealing with environmental issues will be a key challenge for the paper industry.

As in the past, preventing water pollution will be a prime focus for the paper industry. New legislation from the Environmental Protection Agency regarding waste limitations and industry standards under the Clean Water Act is pending. The proposed guidelines will be released in 1993, and put into effect by 1995. Expect to see continued heavy cash outlays by companies to upgrade plants to meet more stringent pollution levels.

Concern about air pollution will also be affecting numerous paper and pulp mills. Under the Clean Air Act Amendments, mills in areas that do not meet national standards for clean air will have to demonstrate either that they are in compliance with air standards or that the benefits of having the mill in the area outweigh the pollution concerns. The possible outcome in these cases? Costly renovations or plant closings.

More generally, expect to see paper and pulp companies do further research into wastewater management, emissions control, waste recycling, and energy recovery. More plants will increase their use of recycled materials as part—or all—of their raw materials. Along related lines, expect to see more research into and development of paper products in synch with environmental consciousness: more biodegradable paper products, more recyclables, etc.

Environmental awareness is also leading to *new employment opportunities,* specifically for environmental specialists at paper and pulp companies, and in the areas of R&D and product development and management.

▶ **Along the same lines, forest products companies will also be coping with pressure from environmental groups and changes in federal legislation.**

Expect continued efforts on the part of environmentalists and preservationists to stop or modify lumber-cutting in the Pacific Northwest. The U.S. Fish and Wildlife Service has designated 8.1 million acres as proposed critical habitat areas due to the presence of the northern spotted owl, an endangered species. Timber harvesting will probably be severely cut back or eliminated in these areas.

More developments like this are expected, especially as environmentalists continue to win an increasing number of forest protection cases. For example, in 1991 the Seattle Audobon Society won a case barring the U.S. Forest Service from offering timber sales on about 66,000 acres. The result? Tight log supplies and the closing of more than fifty lumber and panel mills.

EMPLOYMENT OUTLOOK: Fair to poor.

Employment in the paper industry—estimated at about 627,000 in 1992—has remained relatively flat for five years. And this should continue. Over the long term, the trend toward automation will continue to cut into employment prospects. Hiring will be centering primarily around filling replacement positions.

A few brighter areas: With international expansion so strong, there may be more positions in sales and marketing. Furthermore, the push for new product development at many paper companies may translate into product management and marketing positions. As for wood products, even as demand for timber rises, the employment picture will remain flat.

BEST BET

Kimberly-Clark Corp.
545 Carpenter Fwy.
Irving, TX 75062
214/830-1200

Kimberly-Clark is known for product innovation and aggressive marketing. One of its most recent successes is Huggies Pull-Ups, disposable pants for toddlers. Now it is aggressively targeting Europe. According to *BusinessWeek,* it has invested $980 million in European facilities and has been expanding its European sales force, distribution network, and information systems. This type of activity makes Kimberly-Clark look like a good bet for employment.

TOP PAPER & FOREST PRODUCTS COMPANIES

Boise Cascade Corp.
1111 W. Jefferson St.
Boise, ID 83702
208/384-6161

Bowater, Inc.
1 Parklands Dr.
Darien, CT 06820
203/656-7200

Champion International Corp.
1 Champion Plz.
Stamford, CT 06921
203/358-7000

Chesapeake Corp.
1021 E. Cary St.
Richmond, VA 23219
804/697-1000

Consolidated Papers, Inc.
231 First Ave. N.
Wisconsin Rapids, WI 54495
715/422-3111

Federal Paper Board Co.
75 Chestnut Ridge Rd.
Montvale, NJ 07645
201/391-1776

Ft. Howard Corp.
1919 S. Broadway
Box 19130
Green Bay, WI 54307
414/435-8821

Gaylord Container Corp.
500 Lake Cook Rd.
Deerfield, IL 60015
708/405-5500

Georgia-Pacific Corp.
133 Peachtree St., NE
Atlanta, GA 30303
404/521-4000

P. H. Glatfelter Co.
228 S. Main St.
Spring Grove, PA 17362
717/225-4711

International Paper Co.
2 Manhattanville Rd.
Purchase, NY 10577
914/397-1500

ITT Rayonier, Inc.
1177 Summer St.
Stamford, CT 06904
203/348-7000

James River Corp. of Virginia
120 Tredegar St.
Richmond, VA 23219
804/644-5411

Jefferson-Smurfit Corp.
8182 Maryland Ave.
St. Louis, MO 63105
314/746-1100

Kimberly-Clark Corp.
545 E. Carpenter Fwy.
Irving, TX 75062
214/830-1200

Louisiana-Pacific Corp.
111 SW Fifth Ave.
Portland, OR 97204
503/221-0800

Mead Corp.
Ten W. Second St.
Dayton, OH 45463
513/222-6323

Potlatch Corp.
1 Maritime Plz.
San Francisco, CA 94111
415/576-8800

Scott Paper Co., Inc.
1 Scott Plz.
Philadelphia, PA 19113
215/522-5000

Union Camp Corp.
1600 Valley Rd.
Wayne, NJ 07470
201/628-2000

Westvāco Corp.
299 Park Ave.
New York, NY 10171
212/688-5000

Weyerhaeuser Co.
Weyerhaeuser Bldg.
Tacoma, WA 98477
206/924-2345

Willamette Industries, Inc.
1300 SW Fifth Ave.
Portland, OR 97201
503/227-5581

TOP PACKAGING COMPANIES

Bemis Co., Inc.
222 S. Ninth St.
Minneapolis, MN
55402
612/376-3000

Owens-Illinois
One Seagate
Toledo, OH 43666
419/247-5000

Longview Fibre Co.
End of Fibreway
Longview, WA 98632
206/425-1550

Sonoco Products Co.
1 N. Second St.
Hartsville, SC 29550
803/383-7000

St. Joe Paper Co.
1650 Prudential Dr.
Jacksonville, FL 32207
904/396-6600

Stone Container Corp.
150 N. Michigan Ave.
Chicago, IL 60601
312/346-6600

Temple-Inland, Inc.
303 S. Temple Dr.
Diboll, TX 75941
409/829-2211

WHERE TO GO FOR MORE INFORMATION

PAPER AND FOREST PRODUCTS ASSOCIATIONS

**Forest Products
Research Society**
2801 Marshall Ct.
Madison, WI 53705
608/231-1361
(Puts out *Forest
Products Journal.*)

**National Forest
Products Association**
1250 Connecticut Ave.,
NW, Suite 200
Washington, DC 20036
202/463-2700

**National Hardwood
Lumber Association**
P.O. Box 34518
Memphis, TN 38184
901/377-1818

**National Paper Trade
Association**
111 Great Neck Rd.
Great Neck, NY 11021
516/829-3070

**Paper Industry
Management
Association**
2400 E. Oakton St.
Arlington Heights, IL
60005
312/956-0250
(Publishes *PIMA
Magazine*, which
includes good
help-wanted section.)

**Paperboard Packaging
Council**
1101 Vermont Ave.,
NW
Washington, DC 20005
202/289-4100

**Technical Association
of the Pulp and Paper
Industry**
15 Technology
Pkwy. S.
Norcross, GA 30092
404/446-1400
(Puts out monthly
magazine *TAPPI.*)

PAPER AND FOREST PRODUCTS INDUSTRY DIRECTORIES

Crow's Buyers and Sellers Guide of the Forest Products Industries
C. C. Crow Publications
Box 25749
Portland, OR 97225
503/297-1535

Directory of the Forest Products Industry
Miller Freeman
Publications, Inc.
P.O. Box T
Gilroy, CA 95021-9968
408/848-5296

International Pulp and Paper Directory
Miller Freeman
Publications, Inc.
P.O. Box T
Gilroy, CA 95021-9968
408/848-5296

Lockwood-Post's Directory of the Paper, Pulp, and Allied Trades
Miller Freeman
Publications, Inc.
P.O. Box T
Gilroy, CA 95021-9968
408/848-5296

Walden's ABC Guide and Paper Production Yearbook
Walden-Mott Corp.
475 Kinderkamack Rd.
Oradell, NJ 07649
201/261-2630

Who's Who in Paper Distribution
(special issue of *Management News*)
National Paper Trade Association
111 Great Neck Rd.
Great Neck, NY 11021
516/829-3070

PAPER AND FOREST PRODUCTS INDUSTRY PERIODICALS

American Papermaker
6 Piedmont Ctr.
Atlanta, GA 30305
404/841-3333
(Monthly publication to papermaking industry executives.)

Forest Industries
600 Harrison St.
San Francisco, CA 94104
415/905-2200
(Monthly magazine for forest industry executives, logging managers, superintendents, manufacturers, and processors.)

Logger and Lumberman
P.O. Box 489
Wadley, GA 30477
912/252-5237
(Monthly magazine for forest industry professionals, including manufacturers, loggers, pulp and paper mills personnel, lumber fabricators, processors, etc.)

Paper Age
400 Old Hook Rd.
Westwood, NJ 07675
201/662-2262

(Monthly tabloid for pulp and paper mill executives, marketing personnel, technicians, superintendents, etc.)

Pulp & Paper
600 Harrison St.
San Francisco, CA 94107
415/905-2200
(Monthly magazine for pulp and paper industry managers, technicians, supervisors, etc.)

PUBLISHING

(including Books, Magazines, and Newspapers)

INDUSTRY OUTLOOK: Marked by intense competition and the need to meet changing consumer demands.

Books: Good long-term outlook due to demographic trends, including the aging population and increasing school enrollments. Watch for increased emphasis on electronic products (books on tape, CD-ROMS, etc.).

Magazines: Improving as the economy picks up, but extremely competitive—between different magazines and between magazines and other media—in battling for audience and for advertisers. To attract readers (and in so doing, attract advertisers), watch more magazines aim at a clearly identified audience or narrowly defined interest area. Expansion into electronic forms (CD-ROMS, videos, etc.) also expected over the long term.

Newspapers: Hot competition from other media will force newspapers to emphasize meeting both advertisers' and consumers' wants and needs. Watch for new electronic products, newspaper coverage aimed at specific groups (such as women, minorities, young adults). Also expect some companies to explore foreign markets.

A LOOK BACK

▶ **Mergers, shakeouts, and a new emphasis on the bottom line were the key factors in the recent past for book publishers.**

The volatile period began with a series of mergers in the media industry. A number of large companies went on a buying spree, scooping up other media companies and growing into even larger conglomerates.

The outcome? A consolidated industry, in which many publishers were owned by a single larger company; and, more importantly, a new industry outlook, in which the bottom line became more important than ever.

This new emphasis led to management changes, restructurings, and wide shifts in company focus. Now parts of mega-companies, book publishers were pressed to show profitability. To do this, they cut back on the number of titles printed, changed top executives, and cut staff—or, in some cases, entire departments and imprints. This trend will continue in the short term, as book publishers continue to feel the pressure to stay lean.

▶ **For magazines, it was a decade of strong growth—then a sharp slump, as the Gulf War and recession cut deeply into ad revenues.**

Magazines had been going through a period marked by explosive growth, a high number of new magazine launches, and skyrocketing ad revenues, but it all ground to a sharp halt in 1990. Ad pages dropped. Circulation flattened. And it got worse in 1991, when the full-fledged recession and the Gulf War cut even deeper into already-falling ad pages and circulation rates. Added to this was the rise in postal rates. This combination of events brought about a period of cutbacks, streamlinings, and shakeouts. The magazine company Family Media went belly-up, leaving more than 250 employees jobless. Cahners Magazine company laid off 200 people. Time Warner laid off more than 600 employees, from both the business and editorial sides. The list of casualties continued to grow as budget cuts streamlined departments and new magazines and weaker magazines shut down. But with 1992 came a guarded optimism as publishers felt they had weathered the worst.

▶ **Newspapers were plagued by declining ad pages, declining readership, and intense competition.**

It has been a run of bad years for newspapers. First, competition from other media cut into circulation and advertising. Then the consolidation of the retail industry cut into advertising even more. Add to these problems the fact that their traditional readership was aging and the customer base was drying up, and the picture looked pretty grim. But then, in 1990, it got worse. As industry bible *Editor & Publisher* put it, it was "two years of what has been the worst recession for newspapers since at least World War II."[1] A number of papers, including the *Dallas Times Herald* and the *Arkansas Gazette,* folded. Advertising plummeted. Circulation stagnated. But by 1992 executives were hoping that the worst was behind them and that all the streamlining and refocusing would make them ready to spring back once the economy—and the advertising—did.

WHAT'S NEXT

▶ **Intense competition will keep newspapers on the ropes.**

Although the industry is improving, it's not going to be easy street for a while where newspaper publishing is concerned. Competition for advertising revenues will come from the traditional sources—radio, television, magazines, the yellow pages, and direct mail—and from some newer sources, like electronic yellow pages, targeted cable programming, interactive telemarketing, and home shopping.

To fight back, newspapers will take a number of moves. A few to keep an eye out for: To attract both readers and advertisers, many newspapers will be redesigning, trying more sophisticated layouts and increasing the use of color and graphics. This will mean opportunities for layout specialists, graphic designers, and design consultants.

Newspapers will also be targeting growing ethnic groups by adding coverage or

---

[1] "Newspaper Financial Reports," *Editor & Publisher,* March 7, 1992.

special sections. This will attract both new readers and advertisers eager to reach a targeted market—and may increase employment opportunities, both on sales and editorial staffs.

Similarly, some newspaper publishers will try to gain both new readership and increased ad revenues by putting out publications in addition to their regular newspapers—covering such subjects as health care, business, hobbies, and lifestyle. This may point to increased employment opportunities in a range of positions, as newspaper companies may need to add staff to put out these publications.

► **Another growing trend for newspaper companies: moving into a variety of electronic media.**

It's another way of generating new revenues. Expect to see a number of newspaper companies expand into nonprint areas, from the traditional, such as cable television, to the less traditional. Among the latter are audiotex—telephone voice-information services covering different areas of interest for caller; videotex—information accessible to subscribers via their computers; and newspapers, newspaper abstracts, and summaries delivered over fax machines. These will grow over the long-term and will generate new employment opportunities.

► **A growing trend: treating magazines as brands and developing a variety of spin-off businesses around them.**

It began during the recession when magazines started to suffer from lower ad revenues. Publishers wanted to come up with ways of generating income from a specific magazine other than the two traditional sources: circulation and ad revenues. The result? A number of large companies started looking into other ways of maximizing the profitability of magazines, and they came up with a several workable ideas.

Among the related areas magazines are already trying: movies and television shows, audiotapes, international editions, books, home videos, spin-off titles (for example, *Ladies' Home Journal* developed *Ladies' Home Journal Parents Digest*, first as an insert, then as an individual magazine), subscriber clubs, even mail-order merchandise (such as Times-Mirror's hats, T-shirts, and other items bearing the *Golf* magazine or *Salt Water Sportsman* logo).

► **Specialization: the name of the game in magazine publishing.**

It's a growing trend—magazines that are aimed at a narrow audience—and it will continue growing. One reason for this move: The ad revenue slump that came with the 1991 recession made many publishers refocus their priorities on readership as opposed to advertising. Narrow-focus magazines can attract strong newsstand sales, a devoted readership, and an advertiser pool that is targeted to that specific market niche.

A related note: Publishers will remain cautious. As a result, expect to see most new magazines start out as inserts in an existing magazine, as spin-offs of popular titles, or as quarterlies as opposed to monthlies.

► **The two groups most affecting the direction magazines will be taking are aging baby boomers and senior citizens.**

It's part of the old rule of thumb: Give the public what it wants. In this case, the reading public is getting older, and a traditionally prime magazine audience— young adults (ages eighteen to thirty-four) should shrink about 11% by the end of the decade.

As a result, watch more magazines redirect their editorial content to appeal to an older audience. Similarly, in line with the specialization trend, expect to see the continued success of new magazines aimed directly at the interests of older readers. *Walking, Longevity,* and *Mirabella* are good examples of magazines that have skewed a basic area—in this case, sports, health, and fashion, respectively— toward an older audience. Areas that should stay popular are parenting and grand-parenting, health care, hobbies, travel, and the home.

▶ The aging marketplace will also have a strong impact on book publishers.

And it appears that it will be a positive impact. The strongest book-buying segment of the population is people aged thirty-five to fifty-four—a segment that is forecast to increase by 9.5 million (bringing the total to 75.1 million) by 1996. The result? A huge surge in potential book buyers. As such, expect book publishers to continue focusing their sights on this market and on senior citizens. Watch for trends in book topics that parallel the interests of both aging baby boomers and their parents. Probable winners: child rearing, children's books, retirement planning.

Also growing in popularity, perhaps as a function of the number of older Americans and two-income families with less time to read, is the audio book. This area will stay red-hot.

▶ A growing internationalization will mean different things to the different publishing industries.

In general, the print media industries have been increasing their international focus. One reason for this is the fact that many U.S. publishing companies have become part of larger multinational media companies. For example, German giant Bertelsmann owns the book publishing group Bantam Doubleday Dell, among others; French-owned Hachette Filipacchi Communications owns a number of magazines including *Elle* and *Woman's Day,* and Maxwell Communications Corp, owns book publisher Macmillan, among other U.S. companies. This trend, clearly, has encouraged a global emphasis among publishing companies.

The international picture in each area of publishing:

Book publishers will continue to expand their push into international markets. Over the past twenty years, the percentage of exports has nearly doubled. Watch for increased emphasis on international markets, which will create stronger visibility for staffers in the foreign rights areas, as well as agents with foreign experience.

Magazine publishers aggressively targeted international markets in the past few years, in part to compensate for the lagging business in the United States. Examples of successful international penetration include McGraw-Hill's *BusinessWeek,* which was recently launched in Hungarian and Russian language editions; *Forbes,* which is now published in a Chinese language edition; and the International Data Group's corral of more than one hundred computer magazines, which are now distributed in more than forty countries. This activity will continue in a number of different ways. Some magazine companies will establish foreign-language editions of U.S. magazines on their own; to do this, a number may set up separate international divisions. But expect to see the majority of magazine companies enter into joint ventures with foreign publishers or set up licensing agreements.

As for *newspaper publishers:* Several of the larger newspapers will continue a global orientation, hoping to cash in on the rising number of Americans abroad (due to other industries' globalizing efforts) as well as capture foreign readers interested in U.S. coverage. A number are already pushing international editions, including *USA Today International,* the *Wall Street Journal,* as well as the more established *Asian Wall Street Journal* and the *Herald Tribune.* Depending on the global economy, there may be a rise in new entrants in the international newspaper field. On the other side, expect to see an increase in foreign ownership of U.S. newspapers.

Top Ten Small Magazines

1. *Compute*
2. *Country America*
3. *Walking*
4. *Cooking Light*
5. *Midwest Living*
6. *Longevity*
7. *Spin*
8. *Soap Opera Digest*
9. *Entrepreneurial Woman*
10. *Backpacker*

SOURCE: *Adweek,* 2/17/1992

(Note: Magazines are ranked according to adjusted advertising page increases, weighted percentage of revenue increases, gain or loss in Audit Bureau of Circulation figures. grade from *Adweek* editors and panel of media buyers)

EMPLOYMENT OUTLOOK: Mixed—book publishing and magazines look better than newspapers.

Book Publishing

Book publishing employment has been improving. While the industry cut 2,600 jobs during the 1990–91 recession, it began adding them again by the beginning of 1992. Over the long term, the picture should improve even more, especially as book publishers begin to reap the benefits of an aging, book-buying population. The field is always competitive, however, and this will continue. Another drawback: The historically low salaries paid by publishers, especially to entry-level employees.

Magazine Publishing

A varied employment outlook: Large, established magazines continue to offer a range of opportunities, but, as always, competition will be tough. As the industry improves, new magazine launches will increase, which will lead to the creation of new jobs. The drawback? These jobs may be risky in terms of job security, as many magazine launches fail. Also increasing employment as the economy improves: Trade publications. The recession took a toll on trade publications, but as different industry segments improve, the publications covering that industry also pick up. These are often good stepping-stone positions to consumer publications.

Newspaper Publishing

As the newspaper industry suffered, so, too, did employment. For example, according to the Bureau of Labor Statistics, the number of newspaper jobs fell from an all-time high of 479,000 in June 1990 to 458,700 in October 1991. And this doesn't include the jobs lost when the *Knoxville Journal*, the *Arkansas Gazette*, and the *Dallas Times-Herald* closed. In addition, newspapers kept trimming after that date—laying people off, offering early retirement, and the like. But it looks like the employment picture has stabilized. Newspapers are now running leaner; the staff layoffs of the past shouldn't be returning soon. But some experts say that staff won't be added as quickly as in the past either. In some cases, when a worker leaves, a newspaper is splitting up the job between other staffers instead of hiring a replacement. The bottom line? While it has always been relatively tough to get a job in newspapers due to competition, it will be even harder in today's climate.

For more information on jobs in the editorial side of publishing, see Writers, Editors, and Journalists, page 196; on graphic artists, see Artists and Designers, page 30; and on advertising space sales, see Sales and Marketing Professionals, page 139.

JOBS SPOTLIGHT

CIRCULATION STAFFERS: This is becoming a hot area at magazines recently and will become more so. The reason? As ad revenues began dropping in the early '90s, more emphasis has been placed on circulation. As such, circulation is becoming a high-visibility department. In fact, *Folio* magazine predicts that circulation directors will eventually be considered more important than ad sales directors.

BEST BETS

Gannett Co., Inc.
1100 Wilson Blvd.
Arlington, VA 22209
703/284-6000

Gannett, the largest U.S. newspaper company, has long had a reputation for being committed to equal opportunity for its workers and for treating employees fairly. And the reputation is well-founded. Chosen as one of the best places to work by *Black Enterprise*, Gannett offers a number of programs that encourage nondiscrimination and push for advancement of women and minorities, such as the Partners in

Progress program. In addition, it provides all workers with extensive seminars and training, and has instituted a "management-by-objective" program, under which managers are judged by merit and goal-achievement. Another promising sign: Even while the newspaper industry slumped terribly, Gannett did not institute the massive layoffs many other companies in the industry did. Instead of layoffs, they chose not to hire replacements when a job fell empty and, in this way, preserved the jobs of existing employees. This newspaper giant is a good choice for the '90s.

McClatchy Newspapers
200 Q St.
Sacramento, CA 95813
916/321-1000

Even with the slump in newpapers, McClatchy is a good choice for employment. The reasons? This newspaper chain is big on promotion from within and emphasizes management training. To coordinate promotion between the different papers, it has developed a Management Development Plan, in which top managers meet semimonthly to discuss who has executive potential and what training he or she will need to advance. Their chosen executives will take different positions at the different papers, working their way to the top. It's this type of program that makes McClatchy a good choice for fast-trackers on the business side of newspapers.

TOP BOOK PUBLISHING COMPANIES

Addison-Wesley
Publishing Co., Inc.
1 Jacob Way
Reading, MA 01867
617/944-3700

Avon Books
The Hearst
Corporation
1350 Ave. of the
Americas
New York, NY 10019
212/261-6800

Ballantine—Del
Ray—Fawcett—Ivy
(div. of Random
House)
201 E. 50th St.
New York, NY 10022
212/572-2677
(Imprints: Ballantine
Books, Del Ray Books,
Fawcett, Ivy Books.)

Bantam Books
Bantam Doubleday
Dell Publishing
Group, Inc.
1540 Broadway
New York, NY 10036
212/354-6500

Basic Books
(div. of HarperCollins)
10 E. 53rd St.
New York, NY 10022
212/207-2000

The Berkley
Publishing Group
200 Madison Ave.
New York, NY 10016
212/951-8800
(Imprints: Berkley,
Berkley Trade
Paperbacks, Jove,
Charter, Diamond,

Pacer, Ace Science
Fiction.)

Carol Publishing
600 Madison Ave.
New York, NY 10022
212/486-2200
(Imprints: Lyle Stuart,
Birch Lane Press,
Citadel Press,
University Books.)

Collins Publishers San
Francisco
(div. of HarperCollins)
50 Osgood Pl.,
Suite 400
San Francisco, CA
94133
415/788-4111

Contemporary Books
180 N. Michigan Ave.
Chicago, IL 60601
312/782-9181

The Crown Publishing Group
201 E. 50th St.
New York, NY 10022
212/572-2568
(Imprints: Crown Publishers, Inc., Clarkson Potter/Publishers, Orion Books, Harmony Books, Bell Tower, Living Language, Prince Paperbacks.)

Dell Publishing
(div. of Bantam Doubleday Dell)
1540 Broadway
New York, NY 10036
212/354-6500
(Imprints: Delacorte Press, Delta, Laurel.)

Doubleday
(div. of Bantam Doubleday Dell)
1540 Broadway
New York, NY 10036
212/354-6500
(Imprints: Dolphin Books, Double D Western, Spy Books, Zephyr Books.)

HarperCollins Publishers
10 E. 53rd St.
New York, NY 10022
212/207-2000
(Imprints: Harper Business, Harper Perennial, Harper References, Collins Publishers San Francisco.)

Houghton Mifflin Company
2 Park St.
Boston, MA 02108
617/725-5000
(Imprints: Clarion Books)

Little, Brown and Company
34 Beacon St.
Boston, MA 02108
617/277-0730
New York office:
205 Lexington Ave.
New York, NY 10016
212/522-8700

Macmillan Publishing Company
866 Third Ave.
New York, NY 10022
212/702-2000
(Imprints: Atheneum, Collier, Charles Scribner's Sons.)

McGraw-Hill, Inc.
1221 Ave. of the Americas
New York, NY 10020
212/512-2000

William Morrow & Company, Inc.
1350 Ave. of the Americas
New York, NY 10019
212/889-3050

W. W. Norton & Company, Inc.
500 Fifth Ave.
New York, NY 10010
212/354-5500

Paramount Publishing
1230 Ave. of the Americas
New York, NY 10020
212/698-7000
(Imprints: Simon & Schuster, Touchstone Books, Fireside Books, Meadowbrook Press, Washington Square Press.)

Penguin USA
375 Hudson St.
New York, NY 10014
212/366-2000
(Imprints: E. P. Dutton, Plume/Meridian.)

Pocket Books
Paramount Publishing
1230 Ave. of the Americas
New York, NY 10020
212/698-7000

G. P. Putnam's Sons
200 Madison Ave.
New York, NY 10016
212/951-8400

Random House, Inc.
201 E. 50th St.
New York, NY 10022
212/751-2600
(Imprints: Alfred A. Knopf, Pantheon Books, Vintage Books, Villard Books, Times Books, Schocken Books, Random House Reference.)

St. Martin's Press Inc.
175 Fifth Ave.
New York, NY 10010
212/645-5151

Viking
Penguin USA
375 Hudson St.
New York, NY 10014
212/366-2000

Warner Books, Inc.
666 Fifth Ave.
New York, NY 10103
212/484-2900

John Wiley & Sons, Inc.
605 Third Ave.
New York, NY 10158
212/850-6000

TOP NEWSPAPER COMPANIES

Affiliated Publications
135 Morrisey Blvd.
Boston, MA 02107
617/929-2000

American Publishing Co.
111–115 S. Emma St.
West Frankfort, IL 62896
618/932-2146

Capital Cities/ABC, Inc.
77 W. 66th St.
New York, NY 10023
212/456-7777

Central Newspapers, Inc.
307 N. Pennsylvania St.
Indianapolis, IN 46204
317/231-9201

The Chronicle Publishing Co.
901 Mission St.
San Francisco, CA 94103
415/777-7444

Cooke Media Group
21221 Oxnard St.
Woodland Hills, CA 91367
818/713-3800

Copley Newspapers
7776 Ivanhoe Ave.
P.O. Box 1530

La Jolla, CA 92038
619/454-0411

Cowles Media Company
329 Portland Ave.
Minneapolis, MN 55415
612/673-7100

Cox Newspapers
P.O. Box 105720
Atlanta, GA 30348
404/843-5000

Donrey Media Group
920 Rogers Ave.
P.O. Box 1359
Fort Smith, AR 72902-1359
501/785-7798

Dow Jones & Co., Inc.
200 Liberty St.
New York, NY 10281
212/416-2000

DTH Media, Inc.
1101 Pacific Ave.
Dallas, TX 75202
214/720-6620

Freedom Newspapers, Inc.
17666 Fitch
Irvine, CA 92714
714/553-9292

Gannett Co., Inc.
1100 Wilson Blvd.
Arlington, VA 22234
703/284-6000

Harte-Hanks Communications
P.O. Box 269
San Antonio, TX 76291
512/829-9000

Hearst Newspapers
Hearst Magazine Bldg.
959 Eighth Ave.
New York, NY 10019
212/649-2000

Howard Publications
P.O. Box 570
Oceanside, CA 92054
619/433-5771

Journal Register Company
State St. Sq.
50 W. State St.
Trenton, NJ 08608-1298
609/396-2200

Knight-Ridder, Inc.
1 Herald Plz.
Miami, FL 33132
305/376-3800

Landmark Communications, Inc.
150 W. Brambleton Ave.
Norfolk, VA 23501
804/446-2030

Lee Enterprises, Inc.
130 E. 2nd St.
Davenport, IA 52801
319/383-2100

Macromedia, Inc.
150 River St.
Hackensack, NJ 07601
201/646-4545

McClatchy Newspapers
200 Q St.
Sacramento, CA 95813
916/321-1850

Media General, Inc.
P.O. Box 32333
Richmond, VA 23293
804/649-6000

Media News
4888 Loop Central Dr.
Houston, TX 77081
713/295-3800

Morris Communications Corp.
725 Broad St.
Augusta, GA 30913
404/724-0851

Multimedia Newspapers
305 S. Main St.

P.O. Box 1688
Greenville, SC 29602
803/298-4373

New York Times Co.
229 W. 43rd St.
New York, NY 10036
212/556-1234

Newhouse Newspapers
485 Lexington Ave.
New York, NY 10017
212/697-8020

News America Publishing, Inc.
1211 Ave. of the Americas
New York, NY 10036
212/852-7056

Park Communications, Inc.
Terrace Hill
P.O. Box 550
Ithaca, NY 14851
607/272-9020

Pulitzer Publishing Co.
900 N. Tower Blvd.
St. Louis, MO 63101
314/622-7000

Scripps Howard
1100 Central Trust Tower
Cincinnati, OH 45202
513/977-3000

Seattle Times Co.
P.O. Box 70
Seattle, WA 98111
206/464-2329

Thomson Newspapers
3150 Des Plaines Ave.
Des Plaines, IA 60018
708/299-5544

Times Mirror Co.
Times Mirror Sq.
Los Angeles, CA 90053
213/237-3700

Tribune Company
435 N. Michigan Ave.
Chicago, IL 60611
312/222-9100

Washington Post Co.
1750 15th St., NW
Washington, DC 20071
202/334-6000

TOP MAGAZINE PUBLISHING COMPANIES

The Condé Nast Publications, Inc.
(subs. of Advance Publications)
Condé Nast Bldg.
350 Madison Ave.
New York, NY 10017
212/880-8800
(Publishes *Vogue, Glamour, Mademoiselle, GQ,*

Self, Vanity Fair, Bride's & Your New Home, Gourmet, etc.)

Enquirer/Star Group
600 S.E. Coast Ave.
Lantana, FL 33462
407/586-1111
(Publishes *National Enquirer, Star Magazine.*)

Forbes, Inc.
60 Fifth Ave.
New York, NY 10011
212/620-2200
(Publishes *Forbes.*)

General Media International
1965 Broadway
New York, NY 10023
212/496-6100

(Publishes *Penthouse*, etc.)

Hachette Magazines, Inc.
1633 Broadway
New York, NY 10019
212/767-5800
(Publishes *Elle*, *Woman's Day*, *Popular Photography*, etc.)

Hearst Magazine Division
The Hearst Corporation
1700 Broadway
New York, NY 10019
212/903-5000
(Publishes *Cosmopolitan*, *Good Housekeeping*, *Harper's Bazaar*, *Popular Mechanics*, *House Beautiful*, *Redbook*, *Country Living*.)

Johnson Publishing Co.
820 S. Michigan Ave.
Chicago IL 60605
312/322-9200
(Publishes *Ebony*, *Jet*, etc.)

K-III Magazine Corporation
717 Fifth Ave.
New York, NY 10022
212/745-0100
(Publishes *Seventeen*, *Soap Opera Digest*, *New York*, *New Woman*.)

Knapp Communications Corp.
3900 Wilshire Blvd.
Los Angeles, CA 90036

213/965-3700
(Publishes *Architectural Digest*, *Bon Appétit*.)

McGraw-Hill, Inc.
McGraw-Hill Bldg.
1221 Ave. of the Americas
New York, NY 10020
212/512-2000
(Publishes *Business Week*, *Byte*.)

Meredith Corp
1716 Locust St.
Des Moines, IA 50336
515/284-3000
(Publishes *Better Homes & Gardens*, *Metropolitan Home*, *Ladies' Home Journal*.)

Murdoch Magazines
200 Madison Ave.
New York, NY 10016
212/447-4600
(Publishes *Mirabella*, etc.)

National Geographic Society
1145 17th St., NW
Washington, DC 20036
202/857-7000
(Publishes *National Geographic*.)

The New York Times Company Magazine Group
110 Fifth Ave.
New York, NY 10011
212/556-1234
(Publishes *Family Circle*, *McCalls*, *Golf Digest*.)

News Corp.
Four Radnor Corporate Ctr.

100 Matsonford Rd.
Box 500
Radnor, PA 19088
215/293-8500
(Publishes *TV Guide*.)

Newsweek, Inc.
444 Madison Ave.
New York, NY 10022
212/350-4000
(Publishes *Newsweek*.)

Playboy Enterprises, Inc.
919 N. Michigan Ave.
Chicago, IL 60611
312/751-8000
(Publishes *Playboy*.)

Reader's Digest Association
Reader's Digest Rd.
Pleasantville, NY 10570
914/238-1000
(Publishes *Reader's Digest*.)

Rodale Press
33 E. Minor St.
Emmaus, PA 18098
215/967-5171
(Publishes *Prevention*, etc.)

Straight Arrow Publishers
745 Fifth Ave.
New York, NY 10151
212/758-3800
(Publishes *Rolling Stone*, *US*.)

Time, Inc., Magazine Company
Time-Warner
Time & Live Bldg.
Rockefeller Ctr.
New York, NY 10020-1393
212/522-1212

(Publishes *People,*
Sports Illustrated,
Time, Fortune, Money,
Southern Living, Life.
etc.)

Times-Mirror
Magazines
380 Madison Ave.
New York, NY 10017

212/687-3000
(Publishes *Outdoor*
Life, Popular Science,
Field & Stream, Golf
Magazine.)

U.S. News & World
Report
2400 N St., NW
Washington, DC 20037

202/955-2000
(Publishes *U.S. News &*
World Report.)

Ziff Communications
1 Park Ave.
New York, NY 10016
212/503-5100
(Publishes *PC, PC*
Week, MACuser, etc.)

(*Note:* In many cases, specific magazines have addresses or telephone numbers different from those of their parent company. It's often best to call to check what the address and number of the particular magazine is. Another way: Check the masthead—the staff listings—in an issue of the magazine.)

WHERE TO GO FOR MORE INFORMATION

PUBLISHING ASSOCIATIONS

American Business
Press
201 E. 42nd St.,
Suite 400
New York, NY 10017
212/661-6360
(Puts out monthly
Employment Roundup
listing employment
opportunities for
members.)

American Newspaper
Association
11600 Sunrise Valley
Dr.
Reston, VA 22091
703/648-1072
(Formed by merger of
American Newspaper
Publishers Association

and Newspaper
Advertising Bureau;
offers special
twenty-four-hour job
hot line: 800/562-2672.)

Association of
American Publishers
220 E. 23rd St.
New York, NY 10010
212/689-8920

Association of
Business Publishers
675 Third Ave.,
Suite 400
New York, NY 10017
212/661-6360

International
Newspaper
Advertising and

Marketing Executives
P.O. Box 17210
Dulles International
Airport
Washington, DC 20041
703/648-1177

Magazine Publishers
Association
575 Lexington Ave.
New York, NY 10022
212/752-0055

National Newspaper
Association
1627 K St., NW,
Suite 400
Washington, DC 20006
202/466-7200

PUBLISHING DIRECTORIES

American Book Trade
Directory
R. R. Bowker Co.
245 W. 17th St.

New York, NY 10011
212/645-9700
800/521-8100

Bacon's Publicity
Checker
Bacon's Publishing
Company

332 S. Michigan Ave.,
Suite 900
Chicago, IL 60604
312/922-2400
(Lists newspapers and
magazines)

*Burelle's New England
Media Directory; New
Jersey Media
Directory; New York
State Media Directory;
Pennsylvania Media
Directory*
Burelle's Media
Directories
75 E. Northfield Ave.
Livingston, NJ 07039
201/992-7070

*Editor & Publisher
International Yearbook*
11 W. 19th St.
New York, NY 10011
212/675-4380

*Editor & Publisher
Market Guide*
Editor & Publisher
Company, Inc.
11 W. 19th St.
New York, NY 10011
212/675-4380

*Gale Directory of
Publications and
Broadcast Media*
Gale Research, Inc.
835 Penobscot Bldg.

Detroit, MI 48226-4094
800/877-4253

*Journalism Career and
Scholarship Guide*
The Dow Jones
Newspaper Fund
Box 300
Princeton, NJ 08543
609/452-2820

*Literary Marketplace:
The Directory of
American Book
Publishing;
International Literary
Marketplace*
R. R. Bowker Co.
245 W. 17th St.
New York, NY 10011
212/645-9700
800/521-8110

*Magazine Industry
Marketplace*
R. R. Bowker Co.
245 W. 17th St.
New York, NY 10011
212/645-9700

*National Directory of
Magazines*
Oxbridge
Communications
150 Fifth Ave.
New York, NY 10011
212/741-0231 (in New
York)
800/955-0231

Publishers Directory
Gale Research, Inc.
835 Penobscot Bldg.
Detroit, MI 48226-4094
800/877-4253

*Standard Periodical
Directory*
Gale Research, Inc.
835 Penobscot Bldg.
Detroit, MI 48226-4094
800/877-4253

*Standard Periodical
Directory*
Oxbridge
Communications
150 Fifth Ave.
New York, NY 10011
212/741-0231 (in New
York)
800/955-0231

*Standard Rate & Data
Service: Business
Publications Rates and
Data*
Standard Rate & Data
Service
3004 Glenview Rd.
Wilmette, IL 60091
800/323-4588

*Ulrich's International
Periodicals Directory*
R. R. Bowker Co.
P.O. Box 31
New Providence, NJ
07974-9903
800/521-8100

PUBLISHING PERIODICALS

Editor & Publisher
11 W. 19th St.
New York, NY 10011
212/675-4380
(Weekly magazine with
in-depth coverage of the

newspaper industry;
extensive help-wanted
section.)

*Folio: The Magazine
for Magazine
Management*
P.O. Box 4949
Stamford, CT 06907
203/358-9900

434

(Monthly magazine for magazine publishing managers and editors.)

Magazine & Bookseller
322 Eighth Ave.
New York, NY 10001
212/620-7330
(Monthly magazine for people in magazine and book retailing and wholesaling.)

Publishers Weekly
245 W. 17th St.
New York, NY 10011
212/463-6752
(Weekly magazine, considered the industry "bible," covering all phases of book publishing, including production and design, book selling, rights, new book forecasts, and more; good help-wanted section.)

Publishing News
P.O. Box 4949
Stamford, CT 06907
312/226-5600
(Bimonthly tabloid for magazine executives; focuses on the noneditorial side of magazine publishing.)

REAL ESTATE AND CONSTRUCTION

INDUSTRY OUTLOOK: Improvement ahead—certain sectors stronger than others.

Real estate and construction companies should be bouncing back from the problems caused by commercial overbuilding, the recession, and the credit crunch, but there will still be challenges to face. Among them: growing foreign competition, high liability insurance.

More specifically, commercial real estate will finally start to improve as the economy picks up, but there's a long way to go. Housing should see improvement, especially in the regions that emerge first from the recession but the short term looks less than bright for construction in general. In the long term, expect increased demand in industrial construction, as the manufacturing sector recovers and as facilities are renovated to keep in line with technological breakthroughs and environmental legislation.

A LOOK BACK

▶ **In the late '80s commercial builders and real estate companies experienced a slump, industrial builders a mini-boom. Then came the '90s, a recession, and the worst period for the industry as a whole since World War II.**

Commercial building slumped earlier than other areas because of overbuilding in the '80s. An oversupply of office buildings led to a decline in commercial construction, a drop in property values, empty office space, and a slow commercial real estate market. It wasn't the best of times for the housing market, either. But at the same time, the industrial market was growing. The renewed health of manufacturing and other industrial sectors led to expansion and to a healthy jump in construction billings. International construction was even stronger.

Then came the '90s, and the construction and real estate industries slumped. The key problems? A three-year credit crunch that made it difficult to get funding from banks and other financial institutions; a drop in consumer confidence that kept people from buying houses; corporate cutbacks that kept commercial buildings empty. The results were grim: 477,000 construction jobs were lost from July 1990 to January 1992—the largest drop in construction spending since 1944. Real estate prices plummeted. But there was a light at the end of the tunnel. 1992 saw slight improvement, and industry experts began to believe that the worst was over. But 1993 failed to deliver the sharp upturn in fortunes many hoped for.

WHAT'S NEXT

▶ Ups and downs in the different areas of real estate are still ahead.

While times aren't as bad as they were, the industry is still feeling the results of the past few years. Along these lines, expect to see continued consolidation. Many industry experts predict a drop in the number of real estate developers and the emergence of two tiers in the industry. The top tier will be the larger, well-financed firms that were best able to weather the recent slump and can take the downturns in the cyclical industry best because of size, geographic diversity, and access to capital. The other tier will consist of smaller developers that are attuned to local markets and can be more flexible because of their size. Squeezed out of the picture? Midsized developers.

▶ The real estate industry will continue to seek new ways of attracting investment capital.

New infusions of capital are necessary to continue rebuilding the industry. Damaged by the credit crunch—the inability to get bank loans—and the recession, real estate developers and builders will be exploring other areas of financing. For example, some large builders, including The Presly Cos. (a large California builder), went public with stock offerings to raise money. A number of already public builders, including Arizona-based Dell Webb Corp, made additional stock offerings. Pension funds have already stepped up their real estate investments; expect to see an increase in this trend. Over the short term, there should also be a rise in real estate investment trusts (REITs), which work like mutual funds, except that the assets held are mortgages instead of stocks or bonds.

Keep an eye on the National Association of Realtors' plans to organize a secondary market for commercial real estate loans. Under the plan, lenders would pool and sell mortgages on existing buildings to investors. If successful, this could help the commercial real estate industry avoid a repeat of the early '90s by lessening its reliance on its traditional finance sources (banks, thrifts, and insurance companies) and so encourage long-term stability.

The bottom line of all this activity: The real estate industry will be coming up with ways to rebuild and come back strong, in spite of recent downturns.

▶ Foreign investment will continue to play a role in real estate and construction.

The past five years have seen substantial foreign real estate investment. Japan, West Germany, Canada, and France have been the most visible foreign presences, scooping up property in such cities as Boston, New York, and Los Angeles.

In 1992 Japanese investors began to pull back from the U.S. real estate market, but there's still a great deal of interest and investment coming from foreign sources—other Pacific Rim countries such as Taiwan, Hong Kong, Singapore, and South Korea, in particular, as well as European pension funds. A key reason for the continued interest? The weak real estate market of the past few years led to bargain prices, often as low as 35% of replacement cost. Even so, the influx of foreign investment acts as a safety net against a larger drop in real estate value (like the one that hit Texas in the '80s).

Similarly, expect to see increased foreign investment in U.S. engineering and construction firms. As of 1990, foreign companies owned 15% of the top 400 U.S. construction companies. This percentage will increase, especially as Japanese and European companies attempt to penetrate the U.S. market in terms of winning contracts. The outcome? Increased competition between U.S. and foreign firms for domestic nonresidential projects.

▶ **On the flip side, there will be new opportunities and challenges ahead for U.S. companies in international engineering and construction.**

Changes in the global economy—such as the democratization of Eastern Europe and the former Soviet Union, the U.S.-Canada Free Trade Agreement, developments in the European Community (EC), and growing opportunities in Asia and other developing areas—are creating new opportunities for U.S. engineering and construction firms.

Billings have already been increasing annually. The reason for this success? Providing quality service and staying technologically ahead of foreign competition. But for future success, these companies must actively promote and market their services.

One way to maintain their position in the international marketplace is to enter into joint ventures with local (foreign) companies. This strategy has worked successfully for Japanese companies, in particular, as have their other strategies: investing in other countries, and allowing subsidaries to operate independently. The outcome of these strategies? Stronger ties with local experts and the ability to identify potential projects.

As the U.S. construction industry tries to become more international, expect to see it take similar tacks. Watch for a rise in the number of joint ventures between U.S. firms and their foreign counterparts, especially in developing countries, where U.S. firms can share their technological expertise.

The following areas look especially strong for U.S. business abroad: environmental projects; industrial construction—such as chemical plants amd refineries; infrastructure. The countries that should remain strong prospects include Hong Kong, South Korea, Taiwan, Malaysia, Indonesia, and Thailand, Saudi Arabia, and Kuwait. Over the long term, opportunities should be developing in Eastern Europe and the former Soviet Union.

This overall trend toward internationalization points to *expanded employment opportunities,* particularly for those with international experience. Foreign language skills are a help.

▶ **Infrastructure renovation and replacement will mean long-term activity for construction and engineering firms.**

Aging infrastructure will be creating opportunities over the long term for heavy construction and engineering firms. While many projects are pending due to legislation, expectations in this industry sector are high, chiefly because so many roads, bridges, and other infrastructure are in such urgent need of repair or replacement that it is unlikely that projects can be put off. For example, financially strapped New York City is currently repairing the Williamsburg Bridge—a ten-year project.

This type of activity will have positive effects on employment. As outlined below in Employment Outlook, heavy construction should offer strong employment opportunities over the long term.

▶ A restructuring in the real estate agency business is ahead.

It's already happening, and as with developers, the midsized firms are falling by the wayside. The industry is shaping up into a top tier of large national agencies that primarily service institutions, and a lower tier of small agencies specializing in local markets.

EMPLOYMENT OUTLOOK: Better than in the recent past.

The real estate employment picture appears to be improving. After a number of soft years, things should start looking up, with-long term job opportunities growing. The reason? Even though the number of first-time home buyers (typically people between twenty-five and thirty-four) is shrinking, the bulge of the population will now be aged thirty-five to fifty-four—people who typically have higher incomes and so can spend money on new houses.

As for construction: According to the U.S. Bureau of Labor Statistics, construction is a field with a good long-range outlook. About 1 million new jobs are projected by 2005, bringing employment totals up to 6.1 million. The key reason for this projected growth, as mentioned before, is the need to replace aging infrastructure, such as bridges and roads. This will also bring about an increase in job opportunities for civil and consulting engineers.

Similarly, as industrial businesses replace or add plants and facilities, employment opportunities will increase for industrial construction staffers, engineers, and those in architectural services. Also adding to the employment picture: environmental legislation that will force manufacturers to retrofit plants and facilities to stay in line with new legislation will result in an increase in repair and renovation work.

Housing should also be picking up, but hiring in the commercial area will probably be slower, as the overbuilding in the late '80s and early '90s continues to take its toll on the industry as a whole.

The engineering and architectural area in general is headed for a bright future, with job growth projected to rise faster than the average: nearly 300,000 new jobs by 2005.

JOBS SPOTLIGHT

REAL ESTATE SALESPEOPLE: For information on real estate sales, see Sales and Marketing, page 139.

CONSTRUCTION MANAGERS: The federal government predicts a faster-than-average growth rate in construction management. Construction managers oversee different aspects of a construction project—they determine construction methods, do time estimates, determine labor requirements, and, in some cases, supervise workers, including engineers, designers, clerks, estimators, and equipment operators. During a project, construction managers supervise construction supervisors and monitor all construction activities. In other words, it's their job to keep the construction job going smoothly. Starting salaries range from the mid-$20s to the mid-$30s. Salaries for experienced construction managers cover a wider range: from the low $40s to over $100,000. For more information, contact:

> Construction Management Association of America
> 12355 Sunrise Valley Drive
> Reston, VA 22091

BEST BETS

BE&K, Inc.
2000 International Park Drive
Birmingham, AL 35201
205/969-3600

An industrial construction company that actively recruits women, BE&K has a lot going for it. One big plus where working parents are concerned: It has opened BEKare, movable day-care centers housed in trailers located on-site at projects, which are open during regular work hours and close when the workday is over. The program is designed to work with the construction workers' schedules and has won praise from women's groups.

Ryland Group
P.O. Box 4000
Columbia, MD, 21044
301/730-7222

Chosen a Best Best in *Jobs '93* as well as one of the companies best prepared to face the '90s by *Forbes* magazine, residential construction company Ryland looks like a good bet for the future. It's a company that has been on a roll, making money even when the housing market has been flat. A key reason? It targets customers interested in trade-ups—older baby boomers who are a growing demographic segment. Add to this the fact that the region Ryland specializes in—Texas and other south central states—is expected to show an increase in housing starts. All in all, Ryland looks like a winner for both the short and the long term.

TOP REAL ESTATE DEVELOPERS

The Alter Group
3000 Glenview Rd.
Wilmette, IL 60091
708/256-7700

Barker-Patrinely Group, Inc.
5151 San Felipe,
Suite 1400
Houston, TX 77056
713/961-5780

Betawest, Inc.
1999 Broadway,
Suite 2000
Denver, CO 80202
303/292-7000

Breslin Realty Development Corp.
500 Old Country Rd.
Garden City, NY 11530
516/741-7400

Bronson & Hutensky/Monitor Mgt.
185 Asylum St., 34th Fl.
Hartford, CT 06103
203/275-6600

The Cafaro Co.
2445 Belmont Ave.
Youngstown, OH 44504
216/747-2661

The Oliver Carr Co.
1700 Pennsylvania Ave., NW
Washington, DC 20006
202/624-1700

Carter
1275 Peachtree St., NE
Atlanta, GA

30367-1801
404/888-3000

Catellus Development Corp.
201 Mission St.
San Francisco, CA 94105
415/974-4500

CBL & Associates, Inc.
1 Park Pl.
6148 Lee Hwy.
Chattanooga, TN 37421
615/855-0001

Cousins Properties, Inc.
2500 Windy Ridge Pkwy.,
Suite 1600
Marietta, GA 30067
404/955-2200

Crown American Corp.
Pasquerilla Plz.
Johnstown, PA 19901
814/536-4441

The Edward J. DeBartolo Corp.
7620 Market St.
Youngstown, OH 44513
216/758-7292

Donahue Schriber
3501 Jamboree Rd.,
Suite 300, S. Tower
Newport Beach, CA 92660
714/854-2100

Duke Associates
8888 Keystone Crossing,

Suite 1200
Indianapolis, IN 46240
317/846-4700

Leo Eisenburg & Co., Inc.
1101 Walnut St.,
Suite 800
Kansas City, MO 64106
816/221-8000

Forest City Enterprises, Inc.
10800 Brookpark Rd.
Cleveland, OH 44130-1199
216/267-1200

The Galbreath Co.
180 E. Broad St.
Columbus, OH 43215
614/460-4444

General Growth Cos.
215 Keo Way
Des Moines, IA 50309
515/281-9140

Gosnell Builders
2728 N. 24th St.
Phoenix, AZ 85008
602/956-4300

J. J. Gumberg Co.
1051 Brinton Rd.
Pittsburgh, PA 15221-4599
412/244-4000

The Hahn Co.
4350 La Jolla Village Dr.,
Suite 700
San Diego, CA 92122-1233
619/546-1001

Hillman Properties
450 Newsport Center Dr.,
Suite 304
Newport Beach, CA 92660
714/640-6900

Hines Interests Limited Partnership
2800 Post Oak Blvd.
Houston, TX 77056-6110
713/621-8000

Homart Development Co.
(subs. of Sears, Roebuck & Co.)
55 W. Monroe St.,
Suite 3100
Chicago, IL 60603-5060
312/875-6666

Industrial Developments International, Inc.
950 E. Paces Ferry Rd.,
Suite 875
Atlanta, GA 30326
404/233-6080

Kornwasser & Friedman Shopping Center Properties
145 S. Fairfax Ave.
Los Angeles, CA 90036
213/937-8200

The Kroenke Group
1001 Cherry St. Centre,
Suite 308
Columbia, MO 65201
410/449-8323

The Landmarks Group
1 Concourse Pkwy.,

Suite 600
Atlanta, GA 30328
404/698-2200

Lefrak Organization
97–77 Queens Blvd.
Rego Park, NY 11374
718/459-9021

Lincoln Property Co.
500 N. Akard,
Suite 3300
Dallas, TX 75201
214/740-3300

Maguire Thomas Partners
1299 Ocean Ave.,
Suite 1000
Santa Monica, CA 90401
213/394-7620

Manulife Real Estate
250 Bloor St. E.
Toronto, Ont.
M4W 1E5
Canada
416/926-5500

The McGuire Group
212 S. Tryon St.,
Suite 800
Charlotte, NC 28281
704/334-9735

Melvin Simon & Assocs., Inc.
P.O. Box 7033
Indianapolis, IN 46207
317/636-1600

Metropolitan Structures
111 E. Wacker Dr.,
Suite 1200
Chicago, IL 60601
312/938-2600

The Morris Cos.
535 Secaucus Rd.
Secaucus, NJ 07094
201/863-0900

New England Development
1 Wells Ave.
Newport, MA 02159
617/965-8700

New Market Cos.
950 E. Paces Ferries Rd.,
Suite 2800
Atlanta, GA 30326
404/231-9333

Opus Cos.
9900 Bren Rd. E.
Minnetonka, MN 55343
612/936-4444

Prentiss Properties Limited, Inc.
1717 Main St.,
Suite 5000
Dallas, TX 75201
214/761-1440

The Prudential Property Co.
751 Broad St.
Newardk, NJ 07102
201/802-4990

The Pyramid Cos.
The Clinton Exchange
4 Clinton Sq.
Syracuse, NY 13202-1078
315/422-7000

Edward Rose Building Enterprise
23999 W. Ten Mile Rd.
P.O. Box 937
Southfield, MI 48037
313/352-0952

**Richard I. Rubin &
Co., Inc.**
200 S. Broad St.
Philadelphia, PA 19102
215/875-0700

Charles E. Smith Cos.
2345 Crystal Dr.
Arlington, VA 22202
703/920-8500

Spaulding and Slye Co.
25 Burlington Mall Rd.
Burlington, MA 21803
617/270-9595

Stein & Co.
227 W. Monroe St.,
Suite 3400

Chicago, IL 60606
312/372-4240

Trammel Crow Co.
2001 Ross Ave.,
Suite 3500
Dallas, TX 75201-2997
214/979-5100

**Trammel Crow
Residential**
2859 Paces Ferry Rd.,
Suite 2100
Atlanta, GA 30339
404/433-2000

Westcor Partners
11411 N. Tatum Blvd.
Phoenix, AZ 85028
602/953-6200

**Western Development
Corp.**
3000 K St., NW
Washington, DC 20007
202/965-3600

**Wright Runstad &
Co.**
1201 Third Ave.,
Suite 2000
Seattle, WA 98101
206/447-9000

TOP CONSTRUCTION COMPANIES

**Apogee Enterprises,
Inc.**
7900 Xerxes Ave. S.
Minneapolis,MN 55431
612/835-1874
(Commercial
construction.)

**Ashland Engineering
and Construction**
3340 Peachtree Rd.
Atlanta, GA 30326
404/261-2610
(Engineering services.)

Guy F. Atkinson Co.
10 W. Orange Ave.
S. San Francisco, CA
94080
415/876-1000
(Industrial and heavy
construction.)

Bechtel Group, Inc.
50 Beale St.
San Francisco, CA
94119

415/768-1234
(Heavy construction.)

B E & K, Inc.
2000 International Park
Dr.
Birmingham, AL 35243
205/969-3600
(Industrial construction,
engineering, etc.)

Blount, Inc.
4520 Executive Park Dr.
Montgomery, AL
36116
205/244-4000
(Commercial
construction.)

Brown & Root, Inc.
4100 Clinton Dr.
Houston, TX 77020
713/676-3011
(Heavy construction,
engineering, etc.)

**Butler Manufacturing
Co.**
BMA Tower
Kansas City, MO
64108
816/968-3000
(Commercial
construction.)

CBI Industries, Inc.
800 Jorie Blvd.
Oak Brook, IL 60521
708/572-7000
(Commercial
construction.)

Centex Corp.
3333 Lee Pkwy.
Dallas, TX 75219
214/559-6500
(Residential and
nonresidential
construction.)

Ebasco Services, Inc.
(subs. of Enserch)
2 World Trade Ctr.
New York, NY 10048
212/839-1000
(Heavy construction,
engineering services.)

Fluor Corp.
3333 Michelson Dr.
Irvine, CA 92730
714/975-2000
(Nonresidential
construction.)

Foster Wheeler Corp.
Perryville Corporate Pk.
Clinton, NJ 08809
908/730-4000
(Engineering services.)

**Granite Construction,
Inc.**
P.O. Box 900
Watsonville, CA 95077
408/724-1011
(Heavy civil
construction.)

ICF Kaiser Engineers
1800 Harrison St.
Oakland, CA 94612
510/268-6000
(Engineering, design,
and construction.)

**Jacobs Engineering
Group, Inc.**
251 S. Lake Ave.
Pasadena, CA 91101
818/449-2171

**Kaufman & Broad
Home Corp.**
10877 Wilshire Blvd.
Los Angeles, CA 90024
213/443-8000
(Operative builder.)

M. W. Kellogg Co.
(subs. of Dresser
Industries)
3 Greenway Plz.
Houston, TX 77046
713/960-2000
(Heavy construction.)

**Kiewit Construction
Group, Inc.**
1000 Kiewit Plz.
Omaha, NE 68131
402/342-2052
(Nonresidential
builders.)

Lennar Corp.
700 NW 107th Ave.
Miami, FL 33172
305/559-4000
(Operative builder.)

William Lyon Co.
4490 Von Karmen Ave.
Newport Beach, CA
92660
714/833-3600
(Operative builder.)

MK—Ferguson Co.
(subs. of
Morrison-Knudsen)
1500 W. 3rd St.
Cleveland, OH 44114
216/523-5600
(Nonresidential builder,
engineering services.)

**Morrison-Knudsen
Corp.**
Morrison-Knudsen Plz.
Boise, ID 83729
208/386-5000
(Heavy construction.)

NVR L.P.
7601 Lewinsville Rd.,
No. 300

McLean, VA 22102
703/761-2000
(Residential builder.)

Parsons Corp.
100 W. Walnut St.
Pasadena, CA 91103
818/440-2000
(Heavy construction,
engineering services.)

Perini Corp.
73 Mount Wayte Ave.
Framingham, MA
01701
508/875-6171
(Commercial builder.)

PHM Corp.
33 Bloomfield Hills
Pky.
Bloomfield Hills, MI
48304
313/644-7300
(Residential builder.)

Ryland Group, Inc.
10221 Wisconsin Cir.
Columbia, MD 21044
410/715-7000
(Operative builder.)

Turner Corp.
375 Hudson St.
New York, NY 10014
212/229-6000
(Nonresidential
construction.)

**Wheelabrator
Technologies, Inc.**
3003 Butterfield Rd.
Oak Brook, IL 60521
708/218-1700
(Heavy construction,
eingeering services.)

TOP ENVIRONMENTAL SERVICES/
WASTE MANAGEMENT COMPANIES

Air & Water Technologies Corp.
Route 22 and Station Rd.
Branchburg, NJ 08876
201/685-4600

Browning-Ferris Industries, Inc.
757 N. Eldridge
Houston, TX 77079
713/870-8100

Chemical Waste Management, Inc.
(subs. of Waste Management, Inc.)

3003 Butterfield Rd.
Oak Brook, IL 60521
708/218-1500

ICF International, Inc.
9300 Lee Hwy.
Fairfax, VA 22031
703/934-3000

Thermo Electron Corp.
81 Wyman St.
Waltham, MA 02254
617/622-1000

Waste Management, Inc.
3003 Butterfield Rd.
Oak Brook, IL 60521
708/572-8800

Zurn Industries, Inc.
1 Zurn Pl.
Erie, PA 16505
814/452-2111

TOP CONSTRUCTION MATERIALS COMPANIES

American Standard, Inc.
1114 Ave. of the Americas
New York, NY 10036
212/703-5100

Armstrong World Industries, Inc.
313 W. Liberty St.
Lancaster, PA 17603
717/397-0611

Holnam, Inc.
65211 N. Ann Arbor Rd.
Dundee, MI 48131
313/529-2411

LaFarge
1130 Sunrise Valley Dr.
Reston, VA 22091
703/264-3600

Masco
21001 Van Born Rd.
Taylor, MI 48180
313/274-7400

Owens-Corning Fiberglas Corp.
Fiberglas Tower
Toledo, OH 43659
419/248-8000

PPG Industries
1 PPG Pl.
Pittsburgh, PA 15272
412/434-3131

Tecumseh Products
100 E. Patterson St.
Tecumseh, MI 49286
517/423-8411

USG Corporation
101 S. Wacker Dr.
Chicago, IL 60606
312/606-4000

Vulcan Materials Co.
P.O. Box 530187
Birmingham, AL 35253-0187
205/877-3000

York International Corp.
631 S. Richland Ave.
York, PA 17403
717/771-7890

WHERE TO GO FOR MORE INFORMATION

REAL ESTATE & CONSTRUCTION INDUSTRY ASSOCIATIONS

American Society of Professional Estimators
11141 Georgia Ave.,
Suite 412
Wheaton, MD 20902
301/929-8849

American Subcontractors Association
1004 Duke St.
Alexandria, VA 22314
703/684-3450

Asasociated Builders and Contractors
729 15th St., NW
Washington, DC 20005
202/637-8800

Associated General Contractors of America
1957 E St., NW
Washington, DC 20006
202/393-2040

Institute of Real Estate Management
430 N. Michigan Ave.
Chicago, IL 60611
312/329-6000
(Puts out publication *Journal of Property Management* for members only; includes good help-wanted section.)

International Association of Corporate Real Estate Executives; National Association of Corporate Real Estate Executives
440 Columbia Dr.,
Suite 100
West Palm Beach, FL 33409
407/683-8111
(Puts out newsletters for members only; contains job opportunities.)

National Association of Home Builders
15th and M Sts., NW
Washington, DC 20005
202/822-0200
(Puts out monthly magazine *Builder*, semimonthly *Nation's Building News*.)

National Association of Minority Contractors
1333 F St. NW,
Suite 500
Washington, DC 20004
202/347-8259

National Association of Realtors
430 N. Michigan Ave.

Chicago, IL 60611
312/329-8449
(Puts out ten-issue magazine *Real Estate Today*.)

National Association of Real Estate Appraisers
8383 E. Evans Rd.
Scottsdale, AZ 85260
602/948-8000

National Association of Women in Construction
3277 S. Adams St.
Fort Worth, TX 76104
817/877-5551
800/552-3506
(Publishes a monthly job openings listing for members.)

National Constructors Association
1730 M St.,
Suite 900
Washington, DC 20036
202/466-8880

Society of Industrial and Office Realtors
777 14th St., NW
Washington, DC 20005
202/383-1150

REAL ESTATE AND CONSTRUCTION INDUSTRY DIRECTORIES

*Executive Guide to
Specialists in Industrial
and Office Real Estate*
Society of Industrial
and Office Realtors
777 14th St. NW
Washington, DC 20005
202/383-1150

*National Real Estate
Investor Directory
Issue*
Communications

Channels Inc.
6255 Barfield Rd.
Atlanta, GA 30328
404/256-9800

The One List Directory
The Brenden Partners
16824 Kercheval Pl.
Grosse Point, MI 48230
313/882-2860
(Covers property and
facility developers.)

*The Real Estate
Sourcebook*
National Register
Publishing Company
3004 Glenview Rd.
Wilmette, IL 60091
708/441-2210
800/323-6772

REAL ESTATE AND CONSTRUCTION INDUSTRY PERIODICALS

*Building Design and
Construction*
P.O. Box 5080
Des Plaines, IL 60018
708/635-8800
(Monthly magazine for
those involved in
commercial building,
including engineers,
general contractors,
subcontractors, and
architects.)

Buildings
P.O. Box 1888
Cedar Rapids, IA
52406
319/364-6167
(Monthly magazine for
developers, building
managers and owners,
building management
firms, etc.)

*Engineering
News-Record*
1221 Ave. of the
Americas
New York, NY 10020

212/512-2000
(Weekly magazine
covering engineering,
heavy and industrial
construction, etc.,
aimed primarily at
construction executives,
engineers, architects,
and contractors. Good
help-wanted section.)

*Environmental
Protection*
Box 2573
Waco, TX 76702
817/776-9000
(Magazine for
professionals in
pollution control and
waste control
management and
hazardous waste
disposal.)

*Environmental Waste
Management*
243 W. Main St.
Kutztown, PA 19530
215/683-5098

(Monthly magazine for
environmental waste
professionals—transporters,
shippers, generators,
disposers, and
equipment
manufacturers.)

*Highway and Heavy
Construction*
Box 5080
Des Plaines, IA 60017
708/635-8800
(Monthly magazine for
contractors and
engineers involved in
highway and heavy
construction.)

*National Real Estate
Investor*
6255 Barfield
Atlanta, GA 30328
404/256-9800
(Monthly magazine
covering the real estate
industry. Annual "Top
Developers" survey
(January issue) includes

names, addresses, upcoming projects, and contact names for the top hundred real estate developers. An excellent source for an address list.)

Professional Builder/Remodeler
1350 E. Touhy Ave.
Des Plaines, IL 60018

708/635-8800
(Eighteen-issue magazine for professionals in construction, contracting, architecture, etc.)

Water Engineering & Management
380 Northwest Hwy.

Des Plaines, IL 60016
708/298-6622
(Monthly publication for designers, construction personnel, and others in waste water/water engineering.)

RETAILING

INDUSTRY OUTLOOK: Directly tied to the economy and consumer confidence, but generally expect long-term improvement.

With a bounce in the economy and consumers loosening their purse strings, retailers should strengthen. Watch as competition, always hot, intensifies. Looking strongest: category killers, specialty home-furnishings stores.

Over the short term, expect continued attention to cost containment—including adding more laborsaving automation. The bad news? This means jobs cut over the past few years may not be re-added, even as stores improve.

A LOOK BACK

▶ **The past five years have been volatile: First it was mergers and takeovers, then bankruptcies and price-slashing.**

Mergers and acquisitions changed the retailing industry, as long-standing chains were split up, venerable department stores were swallowed by newcomers to the American scene, and stores changed identity as quickly as they changed owners. A new type of retailer dominated the picture—one with primary expertise in real estate development, which was one of the prime reasons the industry began to founder. Real estate values were taking precedence over retail considerations, and the industry began paying the price.

Heavily leveraged retail companies ran stores with an eye to canceling debt, as opposed to long-range planning. Then came a drop in consumer spending, excess inventory, sluggish sales, and falling profits. Stores began entering a vicious cycle of price slashing and promotional sales. By the time the recession hit in 1990, retailers were already reeling. The result? In 1990 alone, a record number of retailers went bankrupt: fifty retailers, with nearly $24 billion in annual sales. But there were some strong performers even during the worst of times. Discount giant Wal-Mart consistently posted gains, as did specialty retailers The Limited and The Gap. There was an overall improvement at the end of 1992, with a robust fourth quarter. And in 1993, most retailers were facing the future with cautious optimism—expecting a slow recovery.

WHAT'S NEXT

▶ **Look for continued industry consolidation.**

A survival-of-the-fittest mode will continue changing the face of the retail industry. The strongest companies will keep getting stronger; the weaker ones will either be swallowed or will fall by the wayside. Department stores, in particular, will be feeling the squeeze, as customers continue to favor specialty stores and discount stores.

The result? A few companies will be controlling the majority of the retail business. For example, retail consultants predict that over the next ten years, the top ten specialty retailers will control 40% of the market, and the top ten discount chains will control a whopping 90% of their market.

Where employment is concerned, this trend paints a clear picture: Opportunities will remain strong for healthy retailers like Wal-Mart, while retailers that have been suffering (like Sears) will be less likely to offer jobs or will be more likely to institute hiring freezes or layoffs.

▶ **On the flip side, expect to see a long term increase in the number of specialty stores.**

The consolidation trend won't cancel out the emergence of new specialty stores aimed at specific customer niches. Specialization is hitting a number of other industries as well and is developing into one of the best ways for companies to stay competitive. Smaller stores will focus in on narrow market niches—in many cases, ones that until now have been filled by catalog sales. The result? Increased competition for mail-order companies and more competition for department stores as well.

In a related trend, expect to see a number of the stronger mail-order houses build on their popularity and name recognition and move into regular retail. Both trends point to increased employment opportunities over the long term in retail management and merchandising.

▶ **The three key words on retailers' minds:** *value, service, and positioning.*

It's the way of keeping old customers, attracting new ones, and beating the competition. As mentioned above, there were several standout performers who not only survived the shakeout but actually prospered. The key to their success? Attention to at least one of the three key words.

▶ **First watch for a decline in sales and a focus on providing "everyday value."**

In other words, retailers will be moving away from the traditional method of marking prices up, then slashing them during seasonal promotions or sales. The everyday-value method not only makes customers feel that they are getting the merchandise at a fair price, it also stabilizes the industry by steering it away from the damaging price wars of recent years. This method has worked successfully at Wal-Mart and at specialty stores like The Gap—which is now launching warehouse stores to tap more value-conscious consumers.

▶ **Second, watch for the different ways stores commit to customer service.**

Customer service means different things. On one hand, increased automation is part of the customer-service thrust, as stores offer such items as automated customer service kiosks that will place catalog orders or answer customer questions; and "smarter cash registers"—improved computerized checkouts that speed up the time spent at the cash register or that issue store credit cards and the like.

On the other hand, personalized attention is another customer-service trend at stores. Following in the successful footsteps of Nordstrom's and others, more stores will be stressing the personal touch: salespeople who call customers when certain items are in stock, personal shoppers, and the like. One result of this trend will be an increase in commission salespeople. As salesclerks become more important and require more skills, their compensation picture will change.

▶ **As for positioning: To compete with one another and with speciality stores, department stores will try to develop distinct images.**

Positioning to keep up with a changing customer has already made a number of specialty stores the big success stories of the past few years. For example, The Gap experienced a growth surge when it grew up with its customers and moved away from a jeans-only (primarily Levi's) image to become a fashion merchandiser.

Now department stores will be following suit. Facing still heavy competition, department stores will be forced to identify their key target markets and position themselves to attract these customers.

Watch as department stores determine ways to distinguish themselves from the competition. One method that more stores will be trying: managing the store as if it were a group of specialty stores. This makes the individual departments stronger and more focused to their particular customers.

▶ **Increasing at a rapid pace: The use of technological systems.**

Computerized sales and inventory systems are making retailers more efficient, better able to meet the demands of their customers, and more cost-effective.

The most commonly used: Quick Response or QR (also discussed in Fashion, page 331). QR computers analyze sales data, enabling retailers to track items, and to determine what's selling and what isn't, what modifications should be made on merchandise, and more. QR is typically used in conjunction with Electronic Data Interchange (EDI), which allows retailers to automatically record sales information at the point of sale. EDI can also automatically place orders, track shipments, and pay vendors for merchandise.

The bottom line of these systems: retailers can act more quickly, reordering merchandise without fear of time lags, adjusting merchandise orders according to consumer preferences (such as style changes, color changes, etc.), as demonstrated by sales, and trend-tracking.

▶ **A major employment result of this increasing use of technology: The job of buyer is changing—for the better, according to many insiders.**

With automated systems, basic items are automatically reordered and restocked. So buyers are freed from spending time on the basics, and can devote more time to the creative side of merchandising: shopping the vendors, planning ahead, fore-casting trends, and the like. And since automation cuts the time between ordering and the delivery date, buyers can buy merchandise closer to the season and so target their consumer more precisely.

Another offshoot of the increased use of technology: Centralized buying respon-sibility. Instead of being responsible for only one store, or one store chain, buyers at the larger department store companies will buy merchandise in their category for all the stores and chains nationwide. Then the buyers at the specific stores can adjust the merchandise mix according to the needs of their particular region. The result? The emergence of a new career path, and higher visiblity for certain buyer positions.

▶ **As with other industries, expect to see increased internationaliza-tion of retailing.**

U.S. retailers will be expanding overseas, not in a huge rush, but steadily. Among the areas targeted: Europe, Japan, and other Pacific Rim countries, and, over the long term, Eastern Europe and the former Soviet Union (both of which are particularly interesting to department stores).

Different companies will try different approaches. Watch as some retailers, particularly upscale specialty stores, open international subsidiaries. Some exam-ples: Tiffany & Co. already has subsidiaries in a number of countries and is planning moves into Spain and the Pacific Rim countries; the women's apparel store Talbot's has opened in Tokyo, as has the specialty housewares store Williams-Sonoma. Another tactic: entering into joint ventures with already-established for-eign retailers. This is the strategy employed by the clothing store Barney's, which, with Japanese retailer Isetan Co., has opened Barney's Japan.

EMPLOYMENT OUTLOOK: Short term is better than the recent past; long term will show more improvement.

It's been a rough period due to the recession and the number of stores going out of business. An example: from June 1990 to November 1992, 620,000 jobs were cut due to store closings. And even the stores that didn't close cut back on staffing. It's an obvious cause-and-effect situation: when the economy is weak, customers don't shop—and retailers streamline. When the economy is strong, consumers return—and retailers restaff . . . sometimes.

This is why the long-term picture looks much brighter but may not bounce back a great deal. Among the reasons: automation is cutting back on available staff positions; certain types of retailers will still be lagging. Best employment bets: strong stores in strong industry sectors, such as category killers (giants focusing on one single category, such as Toys 'R' Us) and certain specialty stores. It's slower growth ahead in department stores, especially general merchandise stores. Since 1990 Sears, the struggling giant, has eliminated or plans to eliminate 42,650 jobs. Among the reasons are increased use of technology and lagging sales.

Over the short term, the real key to hiring will be individual store strength. Over the long term, the retail industry will grow, making it the second largest source of employment in the United States by the end of the decade. The long-range outlook for managers is fairly good, with stable employment projected. Buyers and mer-chandisers may see stiffer competition because the move toward centralized buying and merchandising has eliminated certain positions. At some companies, however, the changeover has actually created jobs, and in many cases, salaries have improved along with the increased responsibility.

BEST BETS

Toys 'R' Us, Inc.
461 From Rd.
Paramus, NJ 07652
201/262-7800

One of the best-performing category killers, this chain now owns about 25% of the total U.S. toy market. It's also moving aggressively overseas and has expanded into children's clothes with the Kids "R" Us stores. Given the new baby boomlet, Toys "R" Us has staked out a strong niche. This, plus its strength in marketing, makes the company a solid bet for the future.

Wal-Mart Stores
702 SW Eighth St.
Bentonville, AR 72716
501/273-4000

Number 3 in *Fortune*'s 1993 Most Admired Corporations listing and a company that keeps coming on strong, Wal-Mart maintains a strong belief in employee motiviation and in innovation. It not only is considered one of the best managed companies in the industry, it also consistently performs—even during the recession, Wal-Mart was posting high sales. It encourages input from employees and is committed to automation.

TOP DEPARTMENT STORES

Abraham & Straus
420 Fulton St.
Brooklyn, NY 11201
718/875-7200

P. A. Bergner & Co.
331 W. Wisconsin Ave.
Milwaukee, WI 53203
414/347-4141

Bloomingdale's, Inc.
59th St. and Lexington Ave.
New York, NY 10022
212/705-2000

The Bon
1601 Third Ave.
Seattle, WA 98101
206/344-2121

Boscov's Department Store
4500 Perkiomen Ave.
Reading, PA 19606
215/779-2000

The Broadway
444 S. Flower St.
Los Angeles, CA 90071
213/620-0150

Burdine's, Inc.
7 W. 7th St.
Cincinnati, OH 45202
513/579-7000

Carson Pirie Scott & Co.
36 S. Wabash Ave.
Chicago, IL 60603
312/641-8000

Dayton-Hudson Corp.
777 Nicollet Mall
Minneapolis, MN 55402
612/370-6948

Dillard's Department Stores, Inc.
900 W. Capitol Ave.
Little Rock, AR 72201
501/376-5200

The Elder-Beerman Stores Corp.
3155 El-Bee Rd.
Dayton, OH 45401
513/296-2700

Famous-Barr
601 Olive St.
St. Louis, MO 63101
314/444-3111

Filene's
426 Washington St.
Boston, MA 02101
617/357-2100

Foley's, Inc.
1110 Main St.
Houston, TX 77002
713/651-7038

Gayfer's
3120 Airport Blvd.
Mobile, AL 36606
205/471-6000

Hecht's
685 N. Glebe Rd.
Arlington, VA 22203
703/558-1200

Hess's Department Stores, Inc.
Ninth and Hamilton Mall
Allentown, PA 18101
215/821-4377

Jacobson's
1200 N. West Ave.
Jackson, MI 49202
517-787-3600

Jordan Marsh Stores Corp.
450 Washington St.
Boston, MA 02107
617/357-3000

K Mart Corp.
3100 W. Big Beaver Rd.
Troy, MI 48084
313/643-1000

Kaufman's
400 Fifth Ave.
Pittsburgh, PA 15219
412/232-2000

Kohl's Department Stores, Inc.
N54 W13600 Woodale Dr.
Menomonee Falls, WI 53051
414/783-5800

Lazarus
690 Race St.
Cincinnati, OH 45202
513/369-7000

Liberty House
1450 Ala Moana Blvd., 1300
Honolulu, HI 96814
808/941-2345

Lord & Taylor
424 Fifth Ave.
New York, NY 10018
212/391-3344

Maas Brothers/Jordan Marsh
610 Franklin St.
Tampa, FL 33601
813/223-7525

Macy's California, Inc.
P.O. Box 7888
San Francisco, CA 94120
415/397-3333

Macy's Northeast, Inc.
151 W. 34th St.
New York, NY 10001
212/695-4400

Macy's South/Bullock's
180 Peachtree St., NW
Atlanta, GA 30303
404/221-7221

I. Magnin, Inc.
135 Stockton St.
San Francisco, CA 94108
415/362-2100

Maison Blanche, Inc.
1500–07 Main St.
Baton Rouge, LA 70802
504/389-7000

Marshall Field & Company
111 N. State St.
Chicago, IL 60690
312/781-5000

May Company California
6160 Laurel Canyon Blvd.
N. Hollywood, CA 91606
818/508-5226

May Company Ohio
158 Euclid Ave.
Cincinnati, OH 44114
216/664-6000

McAlpin Co.
2301 Richmond Rd.
Lexington, KY 40502
606/269-3611

McRae's
P.O. Box 20080
Jackson, MS 39209
601/968-4400

Mervyn's
25001 Industrial Blvd.
Hayward, CA 94545
415/785-8800

Neiman-Marcus
Main and Ervay Sts.
Dallas, TX 75201
214/741-6911

Nordstrom
1501 Fifth Ave.
Seattle, WA 98101
206/628-2111

Parisian, Inc.
200 Research Pkwy.
Birmingham, AL 35211
205/940-4000

JC Penney Company, Inc.
6501 Legacy Dr.
Plano, TX 75024
214/431-1000

Rich's
45 Broad St., SW
Atlanta, GA 30303
404/586-4636

Robinson's
600 W. Seventh St.
Los Angeles, CA 90017
213/488-5522

Saks Fifth Avenue
12 E. 49th St.
New York, NY 10017
212/753-4000

Sears Roebuck & Co.
Sears Tower
Chicago, IL 60684
312/875-2500

Stern's
Bergen Mall Shopping Center
Rte. 4
Paramus, NJ 07652
201/845-5500

Strawbridge & Clothier
801 Market St.
Philadelphia, PA 19107
215/629-6000

Woodward & Lothrop, Inc.
1025 F St., NW
Washington, DC 20013
202/879-8000

TOP SPECIALTY STORES

Best Buy Co., Inc.
4400 W. 78th St.
Minneapolis, MN 55435
612/896-2300
(Consumer electronics.)

Burlington Coat Factory Warehouse Corp.
Rte. 130 N.
Burlington, NJ 08016
609/386-3314
(Apparel.)

Charming Shoppes, Inc.
450 Winks Ln.
Bensalem, PA 19020
215/245-9100
(Apparel.)

Circuit City Stores, Inc.
9950 Maryland Dr.
Richmond, VA 23233
804/527-4000
(Consumer electronics.)

Consolidated Stores Corp.
300 Phillipi Rd.
Columbus, OH 43228
614/278-6800
(Closeout merchandise.)

B. Dalton Bookseller, Inc.
1400 Old Country Rd.
Westbury, NY 11590
516/338-8000
(Books.)

Eddie Bauer, Inc.
15010 NE 36th St.
Redmond, WA 98052
206/682-6100
(Apparel.)

Edison Apparel
501 N. Broadway
St. Louis, MO 63102
314/331-6000
(Apparel.)

Egghead Software, Inc.
22011 SE 51st
Isaquah, WA 98027
206/391-0800
(Software.)

Gap, Inc.
900 Cherry Ave.
San Bruno, CA 94066
415/952-4400
(Sportswear.)

Herman's Sporting Goods
2 Germak Dr.
Carteret, NJ 07008
201/541-1550
(Sporting goods.)

Highland Superstores, Inc.
909 N. Sheldon Ave.
Plymouth, MI 48170
313/451-3200
(Consumer electronics.)

Kay Jewelers, Inc.
320 King St.
Alexandria, VA 22314
703/683-3800
(Jewelry.)

Kay-Bee Toy Stores
100 West St.
Pittsfield, MA 01201
413/499-0086
(Toys.)

Kinney/Footlocker
233 Broadway
New York, NY 10279
212/270-3700
(Shoes, sporting apparel.)

Lechmere
275 Wildwood St.
Woburn, MA 01801
617/935-8320
(Hard goods.)

Levitz Furniture Corp.
611 Broken Sound Pkwy.
Boca Raton, FL 33487
407/994-6006
(Furniture.)

Limited Stores, Inc.
3 Limited Pkwy.
Columbus, OH 43230
614/479-2000
(Apparel.)

Marshall's
30 Harvard Mill Sq.
Box 1000–34
Wakefield, MA 01880
617/721-3001
(Apparel.)

Merry-Go-Round Enterprises
3300 Fashion Way
Joppa, MD 21085
301/538-1000
(Apparel.)

Musicland Group, Inc.
7500 Excelsior Blvd.
Minneapolis, MN 55426
612/932-7700
(Entertainment software.)

Petrie Stores Corp.
70 Enterprise Ave.
Secaucus, NJ 07094
201/866-3600
(Apparel.)

Pic N' Save Corp.
2430 E. Del Amo Blvd.
Dominguez, CA 90220
310/537-9220
(Closeout merchandise.)

Pier 1 Imports, Inc.
P.O. Box 961020
Fort Worth, TX 76161-0020
817/878-8000
(Home furnishings.)

Radio Shack
1800 1 Tandy Ctr.
Fort Worth, TX 76102
817/390-3700
(Consumer electronics.)

Ross Stores, Inc.
8333 Central Ave.
Newark, CA 94560
415/790-4400
(Apparel.)

Silo Electronics
6900 Lindbergh Blvd.
Philadelphia, PA 19142
215/365-2000
(Consumer electronics.)

T. J. Maxx
770 Cochituate Rd.
Framingham, MA 01701
508/390-1000
(Apparel.)

Tower Records
2500 Del Monte St.
West Sacramento, CA 95691
916/373-2500
(CDs, tapes, etc.)

Toys 'R' Us
461 From Rd.
Paramus, NJ 07652
201/262-7800
(Toys.)

U.S. Shoe
1 Eastwood Dr.
Cincinnati, OH 45227
513/527-7000
(Shoes.)

Volume Shoe Corp.
3231 E. 6th
Topeka, KS 66607
913/233-5171
(Shoes.)

Walden Books Co., Inc.
201 High Ridge Rd.
Stamford, CT 06905

203/352-2000
(Books.)

Woolworth
233 Broadway
Woolworth Bldg.
New York, NY 10279

212/553-2000
(Discount stores.)

Zale Corp.
901 W. Walnut Hill Ln.
Irving, TX 75038
214/580-4000
(Jewelry.)

WHERE TO GO FOR MORE INFORMATION

(Also see listings under "Fashion," page 331. For more general business information sources, see listings in "Managers," page 119, and "General Business Sources," page 504.)

RETAIL INDUSTRY ASSOCIATIONS

International Association of Chain Stores
3800 Moor Pl.
Alexandria, VA 22305
703/683-3136

International Council of Shopping Centers
665 Fifth Ave.
New York, NY 10022
212/421-8181

International Mass Retail Association
1901 Pennsylvania Ave.,
10th Fl.

Washington, DC 20006
202/861-0774

Menswear Retailers of America
2011 I Street, NW,
Suite 300
Washington, DC 20006
202/347-1932

National Retail Federation
100 W. 31st St.
New York, NY 10001
212/244-8780
(Publishes monthly magazine *Stores;* see below for more information.)

RETAIL INDUSTRY DIRECTORIES

Directory of Consumer Electronics, Photography, and Major Appliance Retailers and Distributors
Chain Store Guide Information Services
425 Park Ave.
New York, NY 10022
212/371-9400

Directory of Department Stores
Chain Store Guide Information Services
425 Park Ave.

New York, NY 10022
212/371-9400

Directory of General Merchandise/Variety Chains and Specialty Stores
Chain Store Guide Information Services
425 Park Ave.
New York, NY 10022
212/371-9400

Fairchild's Financial Manual of   7 E. 12th St.
Retail Stores   New York, NY 10001
Fairchild Publications   212/244-8780

RETAIL INDUSTRY PERIODICALS

Chain Store Age Executive
425 Park Ave.
New York, NY 10022
212/371-9400
(Monthly magazine aimed at retail
executives, managers, buyers, etc., at
general merchandise, department, and
specialty chain stores. Annual
roundups include rankings of top
stores in different retail categories.)

Children's Business
7 W. 34th St.
New York, NY 10001
212/630-4000
(Monthly tabloid covering children's
apparel and accessories.)

Discount Merchandiser
223 Park Ave. S.
New York, NY 10003
212/979-4860
(Monthly magazine for executives,
managers, buyers, etc., at discount
stores.)

Discount Store News
425 Park Ave.
New York, NY 10022
212/371-9400
(Biweekly for merchandisers, discount
store managers, and operators,
planners, etc., at discount stores.)

Drug Store News
425 Park Ave.
New York, NY 10022
212/371-9400
(Biweekly publication for chain and
independent drugstore executives,
managers, pharmacists, and
manufacturers.)

HFD Retailing Home Furnishings
7 W. 34th St.
New York, NY 10001
212/630-4800
(Weekly tabloid covering the home
furnishings retail industry.)

Kids Fashions Magazine
485 Seventh Ave.
New York, NY 10018
212/594-0880
(Monthly magazine for children's
clothing and accessories retailers and
manufacturers.)

Mass Market Retailers
220 Fifth Ave.
New York, NY 10001
212/213-6000
(Biweekly for headquarters executives
of chain drugstores, discount stores,
and supermarkets.)

Sportstyle
7 W. 34th St.
New York, NY 10001
212/630-4000
(Semimonthly publication for sporting
goods and activewear retailers,
wholesalers, and manufacturers.)

Stores
100 W. 31st St.
New York, NY 10001
212/244-8780
(Monthly magazine published by the
National Retail Federation; aimed at
retail executives; annual directory
issues offer listings of leading stores.)

TELECOMMUNICATIONS

INDUSTRY OUTLOOK: A period of change due to emerging technologies and regulation rollbacks.

The telecommunications industry is in for a volatile period, marked by intense competition and the emergence of new businesses, products and services. Key reasons: the rush to cash in on new technologies and to adapt to loosening FCC regulations. Hottest areas: wireless communications, including cellular phones and service and, even newer, PCs (pocket-sized wireless phones). Also emerging as a very hot spot: digital interactive telecommunications services—which will result in more partnerships between telecommunications companies and cable TV companies (such as the 1993 pairing of US West and Time-Warner). Local carriers face a flat short-term future; long distance stronger. Telecommunications equipment manufacturers are in for continued growth—with new services, companies and consumers need new equipment, but also face possible mergers-and-acquisitions activity, such as the recent AT&T–McCaw Cellular merger.

A LOOK BACK

▶ **The major trends since the 1984 breakup of Ma Bell: the long-distance industry consolidated; the growth of local-access lines slowed; local carriers increased their offering of private networking services.**

Since the divestiture of Bell Telephone—which resulted in seven Bell regional companies and about 1,500 independent local carriers, and the emergence of competing long-distance carriers—the telecommunications industry has been through a number of changes.

Among them: Hot competition between long-distance carriers led to consolidation, as weaker companies were swallowed by larger ones.

WHAT'S NEXT

▶ **Technological advances will continue having a major impact on the telecommunications industry.**

Experts predict that in five to ten years, both private and public telecommunications services will have changed dramatically.

The key trends that are emerging: the growth of high-speed data services, resulting from the range of broadband options now available, including fast-packet switching, high-speed frame-relay data services, and Switched Multimegabit Data Service (SMDS). An important area as the use of LANs (local area networks) increases the need for high-speed data communications is Integrated Services Digital Networks (ISDNs).

This area, in particular, has had an impact on the job market, creating opportunities for telecommunications professionals with experience in both voice and data communications and knowledge in both the telecommunications field and in other industries.

▶ **The effect of these technological trends on the telecommunications equipment industry? Increased R&D budgets, consolidation, and competition.**

Keeping up with technological advances has become the only way to survive in the telecommunications equipment industry. As such, companies will continue to pour money into R&D. This may point to continued employment opportunities for those involved in product and systems development.

Companies that previously only manufactured switches may be forced to expand their product lines, as the emerging technology requires that the new switches, software, and systems work together. One result of this climate will be industry consolidation. This should take place over the next decade, as smaller companies find themselves unable to keep up with the high cost of development and either fall by the wayside or are bought by other companies. The large companies with the financing capability will be the winners, but even they may be squeezed by price competition and the race to be on the cutting edge with new equipment.

▶ **Adding to the competition in the domestic telecommunications equipment area: the influx of foreign competitors.**

Already a number of international telecommunications equipment companies have expanded into the U.S. market, among them NEC, Fujitsu, Siemens, Alcatel, and Ericsson. The reason? The United States is deregulated and offers strong telecommunications services.

The flip side to this is the fact that U.S. equipment companies are pushing into foreign markets. Two examples: AT&T has already successfully penetrated the telecom equipment markets in the Netherlands, Spain, South Korea, and Japan; Motorola is one of the two leaders in the worldwide cellular market. This activity should continue.

▶ **Keep an eye on: The regional Bell companies' lobbying efforts to reverse the legislation barring them from making telephone equipment, among other things.**

If Congress drops the restrictions, competition in the telephone equipment area will even be hotter. AT&T, as the chief supplier to the Baby Bells, will be especially affected. Another possible outcome: The regional Bell companies may enter into joint ventures with foreign manufacturers to make entering the equipment business smoother and less costly. This, too, would increase competition and might give foreign competitors a push into other areas of the marketplace as a result of their partnership with the regional Bells.

▶ Telecommunications services companies will be aggressively expanding into a range of international markets.

This expansion is vital to stay competitive—and even alive—in today's telecommunications industry. The key reason? As corporations increasingly turn to international markets for business, they need international suppliers of telecommunications services.

As a result, U.S. telecommunications companies are targeting and penetrating international markets in a variety of ways, and this activity, while slower than in the past, will continue.

Some examples: Expect an increase in international private networks, such as U.S. Sprint's optical fiber network (linking Europe to Asia through its U.S. network), which was completed in 1991. Multinational corporations can use this type of private network to link their headquarters office with their foreign branches. Due to the increasing number of multinationals and the overall globalization of the corporate world, demand for private networks should be increasing. But there are problems, among them different technical standards between countries, government policies regulating the attachment of equipment to public networks, and difficulties in getting (and high costs of) leased line services or circuits.

The growth of private global networks will result in a corresponding growth in the services that support these networks. The major U.S. carriers have already introduced Virtual Private Network (VPN) services. AT&T has service agreements with six countries, and U.S. Sprint and Cable & Wireless have teamed up in service agreements with seven countries. Expect to see further increases in the next few years.

Also expect to see an increase in joint ventures and arrangements between U.S. and foreign telecommunications companies. For example, in 1991 MCI teamed up with fifteen foreign companies to offer Global Communications Service, which manages international private networks.

Because businesses dealing globally need to communicate across different time zones, there will be a great deal of growth in value-added data services and International Value Added Network Services (IVANS). This area encompasses such services as electronic mail, enhanced store-and-forward faxes, and on-line databases.

Another growing area: supplying services to the domestic international markets. The Baby Bells in particular are moving heavily into this area, investing in cellular and paging services. They have also been investing in foreign telephone companies. For example, Southwestern Bell bought part of Mexico's state-owned Telmex in 1991; before that, Bell Atlantic and Ameritech bought the New Zealand phone company. The region that looks especially interesting is Eastern Europe.

Other areas the Baby Bells have been targeting in the international marketplace are directory publishing, cable television, network management, voice mail, packet-switched data communications, and Personal Communications Networks.

► Local telephone business: Headed for increasing competition as the monopoly of Baby Bells starts crumbling?

Opening up local service to competition would be the final step to the complete deregulation of telecommunications services—and, as such, it would transform the telecommunications industry as much as the deregulation of AT&T did. For the short term, then, this is the area of telecommunications that many people are watching closely.

How it has developed: Recently, there has been a growth in the number of Metropolitan Area Networks (MANs), companies offering private communications services to corporations, usually over local fiber optics lines. State officials have begun loosening restrictions against allowing these smaller independents to connect their lines and switches to the existing public networks. The result? MANs are then able to access the entire phone system and so provide services to low-volume users (typically not the large corporations that use MANs).

The outcome of this? A completely deregulated local phone service system, in which a number of local telephone services providers form a phone network and compete for customers.

Local telephone services providers are already feeling the competition for corporate clients and are instituting such services as disaster avoidance which keeps telephone lines working even during black-outs and the like. This is especially important given the growing use of telephone lines for data transmission. But should the deregulation proceed, competition should get more intense, as the MANs typically offer high-technology service at a lower cost. The probable bottom line? A highly volatile industry with tough competition and a period of shakeouts, mergers, and consolidation, similar to what the long-distance services industry went through.

► Cellular telecommunications: still hot—and increasingly competitive.

Cellular telecommunications services is still on a roll—usage was up 40 percent in 1991 alone, in spite of the recession. But as the industry grows older, it is becoming more competitive. A sign of the increasing competition: The regional Bell telephone companies already have been scooping up cellular properties.

Even so, expect to see more companies entering the cellular services field as the market continues to grow. A recent development to keep abreast of: Motorola Inc. has proposed a global cellular network, called Iridium. It will use seventy-seven satellites and more than twenty ground stations to provide worldwide cellular telephone services. It has already received the radio frequencies it needs to operate and is scheduled to be operational in 1997.

► A potentially hot area in the long term—information services.

The 1989 ruling allowing AT&T to enter electronic publishing—transmitting financial and news information, videotex, audiotex, and other data over phone lines—will continue to have far-reaching implications. With enormous capital, heavy attention to R&D, and computer telecommunications capabilities, AT&T may succeed where others have failed. Watch for other telecommunications companies to begin eyeing and breaking into the field.

EMPLOYMENT OUTLOOK: Weak in some areas, stronger in others.

Since the breakup of AT&T and the layoffs that followed, the employment picture hasn't been that bright in the telecommunications field. And it still isn't going to be the best of times.

The U.S. government projects a drop of 1.8% annually in jobs for the next twelve years—in other words, a loss of 223,000 jobs. But not all the news is bad: The key to success in the '90s is combinining communications experience with computer knowledge. Areas that will see hiring activity include network management, telecom technician, fiber-optics technicians (especially as fiber optics is expected to re-revolutionize cable TV), local area network technicians (LAN), and satellite technicians.

Employment in the telecommunications equipment industry is projected to decline over the next five years. The reasons? Technological changes and increasing productivity will cut down on labor needs. Also, the consolidation the industry is going through will result in streamlining, cutbacks, and slow hiring.

JOBS SPOTLIGHT

For information on specific telecommunications positions, see Technical Careers, page 186.

BEST BETS

MCI Communications
1133 19th St., NW
Washington, DC 20036
202/872-1600

MCI is well known for encouraging innovation and flexibility. This free-spirited attitude comes from the top. Management wants its employees to come up with fresh ideas, rather than sticking with the tried and true. This, plus the fact that it hires extensively from *outside* the company to bring in new blood, makes MCI look like an interesting employment prospect.

U.S. West
7800 E. Orchard Rd.
Englewood, CO 80111
303/793-6500

The winner of a Corporate Conscience award in 1990 for sponsoring employee support programs for minorities and gays, U.S. West is comitted to management '90s style. Among its accomplishments: women hold 21% of the jobs at the company; it offers eight resource groups for workers to discuss concerns, problems, etc.; managers' compensation is tied to participation in diversity training (a program that teaches how to manage a diverse work force). Add to this its exciting plans for the future: It is building Eastern Europe's first cellular systems, is laying fiber optic-cable in the former Soviet Union, and more. All in all, U.S. West looks like an excellent choice for the future.

TOP TELECOMMUNICATIONS AND DATA COMMUNICATIONS EQUIPMENT COMPANIES

ADC Telecommunications, Inc.
4900 W. 78th St.
Minneapolis, MN 55435
612/835-6800

AT&T Paradyne Corp.
8545 126th Ave. N.
Largo, FL 34649
813/530-2000

Ameritech Information Systems
500 W. Madison
Chicago, IL 60606
312/906-4000

Comdial Corporation
1180 Seminole Trail
Box 7266
Charlottesville, VA 22906
804/978-2200

Communications Systems, Inc.
213 S. Main St.
Hector, MN 55342
612/848-6231

Contel IPC, Inc.
1 Station Pl.
Stamford, CT 06903
203/326-7000

DSC Communications Corp.
1000 Coit Rd.
Plano, TX 75075
214/519-3000

Dynatech Corporation
3 New England Executive Park
Burlington, MA 01803
617/272-6100

Executone Information Systems Inc.
6 Thorndal Cir.
Darien, CT 06820
203/655-6500

General Datacomm Industries, Inc.
1579 Straits Tpke.
Middlebury, CT 06762
203/574-1118

GTE Communications Systems Corp.
1 Stamford Forum
Stamford, CT 06904
203/965-2000

Harris Digital Telephone Systems
300 Bel Mana Keys Blvd.
Novato, CA 94949
415/382-5000

Infotron Systems Corp.
Cherry Hill Industrial Ctr.
Cherry Hill, NJ 08003
609/424-9400

Intellicall Inc.
2155 Chenault
Carrolton, TX 75006
214/416-0022

Motorola-Codex Corp.
20 Cabot Blvd.
Mansfield, MA 02048
508/261-4000

Network Systems Corporation
7600 N. Boone Ave. N.
Minneapolis, MN 55428
612/424-4888

Northern Telecom, Inc.
200 Athens Way
Nashville, TN 37228
615/734-4000

Northern Telecom, Inc.
Integrated Network Systems Group
P.O. Box 13010
Research Triangle Park, NC 27709
919/992-5000

Octel Communications Corp.
890 Tasman Dr.
Milpitas, CA 95035
408/942-6500

Racal Data Communications Inc.
1601 N. Harrison Pkwy.
Sunrise, FL 33323
305/475-1601

Reliance Electric Co.
29325 Chagrin Blvd.
Cleveland, OH 44122
216/266-7000

Ricoh Corp.
5 Dedrick Pl.
West Caldwell, NJ 07006
201/882-2000

Siemens Corp.
900 Broken Sound Pkwy.
Boca Raton, FL 33487
407/955-5000

Silicon General Inc.
85 W. Tasman Dr.
San Jose, CA 95134
408/943-9403

TIE/Communications, Inc.
4 Progress Ave.
Seymour, CT 06483
203/888-8252

Tellabs, Inc.
4951 Indiana Ave.
Lisle, IL 60532
312/969-8800

Universal Data Systems, Inc.
5000 Bradford Dr.
Huntsville, AL 35805
205/430-8000

TOP TELECOMMUNICATION SERVICES COMPANIES

(including local carriers, long-distance carriers, and cellular telephone services)

Alltel Corporation
1 Allied Dr.
Little Rock, AR 72202
501/661-8000

American Telephone & Telegraph (AT&T)
32 Ave. of the Americas
New York, NY 10013-2412
212/387-5400

Ameritech
(Bell Regional Holding Company)
30 S. Wacker Dr.
Chicago, IL 60606
312/750-5000

Ameritech Mobile Communications
(cellular subs. of Ameritech)
1515 Woodfield Rd.
Schaumburg, IL 60173
708/706-7600

Bell Atlantic Corporation
(Bell regional holding company)
1717 Arch St.
Philadelphia, PA 19103
215/963-6000

Bell Atlantic Mobil Systems
(cellular subs. of Bell Atlantic)
180 Mount Airy Rd.
Basking Ridge, NJ 07920
908/953-2200

Bell Atlantic Network Services, Inc.
(subs. of Bell Atlantic)
1310 N. Court House Rd.
Arlington, VA 22201
703/974-3000

Bell Communications Research (Bellcore)
(Bell research/engineering/support co.)
290 W. Mount Pleasant Ave.

Livingston, NJ 07039
201/740-3000

Bell of Pennsylvania/Diamond State Telephone
(subs. of Bell Atlantic)
1-16B Parkway
Philadelphia, PA 19102
215/466-9900

BellSouth Corporation
(Bell regional holding company)
1155 Peachtree St., NE
Atlanta, GA 30367-6000
404/249-2000

C&P Telephone of Maryland
(subs. of Bell Atlantic)
1 E. Pratt St.
Baltimore, MD 21202
410/539-9900

C&P Telephone of Viginia
(subs. of Bell Atlantic)
703 Grace St.
Richmond, VA 23219
804/772-2000

C&P Telephone of West Virginia
(subs. of Bell Atlantic)
1500 MacCorkle Ave., NE
Charleston, WV 25314
304/343-9911

C-Tec Corporation
46 Public Sq.
Box 3000
Wilkes-Barre, PA 18703
717/825-1100

CP National Corporation
2121 N. California Blvd.,
Suite 400
Walnut Creek, CA 94596
415/945-4900

Centel Corporation
O'Hare Plz.
8725 Higgins Rd.
Chicago, IL 60631
312/399-2500

Century Telephone Enterprises, Inc.
P.O. Box 4065
520 Riverside
Monroe, LA 71211
318/388-9500

Cincinnati Bell, Inc.
201 E. Fourth St.,
Suite 700
Cincinnati, OH 45202
513/397-9900

Citizens Utilities Company
High Ridge Pk.
Stamford, CT 06905
203/329-8800

Communications Satellite Corp.
950 L'Enfant Pl., SW
Washington, DC 20024
202/863-6000

Communications Systems, Inc.
213 Main St.
Box 777
Hector, MN 55342
612/848-6231

Contel Corporation
245 Perimeter Ctr. Pkwy.
P.O. Box 105194
Atlanta, GA 30348
404/391-8000

Fail, Inc.
236 E. Capital St.
Jackson, MS 39201
601/352-0966

GTE Corporation
1 Stamford Forum
Stamford, CT 06904
203/965-2000

Illinois Bell
(subs. of Ameritech)
225 W. Randolph St.
Chicago, IL 60606
312/727-9411

Indiana Bell
(subs. of Ameritech)
240 N. Meridian St.
Indianapolis, IN 46204
317/265-2266

MCI Communications Corp.
1801 Pennsylvania Ave., NW
Washington, DC 20006
202/872-1600

McCaw Cellular Communications
P.O. Box 97060
Kirkland, WA 98083-9760
206/827-4500

Michigan Bell
(subs. of Ameritech)
444 Michigan Ave.
Detroit, MI 48226
313/223-9900

Nevada Bell
(subs. of Pacific Telesis)
645 E. Plumb Ln.
Reno, NV 89502
702/789-6208

New England Telephone
(subs. of Nynex)
185 Franklin St.
Boston, MA 02107
617/743-9800

New Jersey Bell
(subs. of Bell Atlantic)
540 Broad St.
Newark NJ 07101
201/649-9900

New York Telephone
(subs. of Nynex)
1095 Ave. of the Americas
New York, NY 10036
212/395-2121

North-West Telecommunications, Inc.
First Bank Pl.
201 Main St.
LaCrosse, WI 54602
608/784-6920

Nynex Corp.
(Bell regional holding company)
335 Madison Ave.
New York, NY 10017
212/370-7400

Nynex Mobile Communications Co.
(cellular subs. of Nynex)
1 Blue Hill Plz.
Pearl River, NY 10965
914/577-5200

Ohio Bell
(subs. of Ameritech)
45 Erieview Plz.
Cleveland, OH 44114
216/822-9700

Ollig Utilities Company
Box 72
Ada, MN 56510
218/784-7272

PacTel Cellular
(cellular subs. of Pacific Telesis)
2355 Main St.
Irvine, CA 92714
415/394-3000

PacTel Personal Communications Companies
(subs. of Pacific Telesis)
950 Tower Ln.
Foster City, CA 94404
415/394-3000

Pacific Bell
(subs. of Pacific Telesis)
140 New Montgomery St.
San Francisco, CA 94105
415/542-1977

Pacific Telecom, Inc.
805 Broadway
P.O. Box 9901
Vancouver, WA 98668
206/696-0893

Pacific Telesis Group
(Bell regional holding company)
130 Kearny St.

468   INDUSTRY FORECASTS 1994

San Francisco, CA 94108
415/394-3000

Rochester Telephone Corporation
180 S. Clinton Ave.
Rochester, NY 14646
716/777-9800

SLT Communications, Inc.
150 Brooks St.
Sugar Land, TX 77478
713/491-2131

South Central Bell
(subs. of BellSouth)
600 N. 19th St.
Birmingham, AL 35203
205/321-1000

Southern Bell
(subs. of BellSouth)
675 W. Peachtree St., NE
Atlanta, GA 30375
404/529-8611

**Southern New England
Telecommunications**
227 Church St.
New Haven, CT 06506
203/771-5200

Southwestern Bell Corporation
(Bell regional holding company)
175 E. Houston
San Antonio, TX 78205
210/821-4105

**Southwestern Bell Mobile Systems,
Inc.**
(subs. of Southwestern Bell)
17330 Preston Rd.
Dallas, TX 75252
214/733-2000

Southwestern Bell Telephone Co.
(subs. of Southwestern Bell)
1010 Pine St.
St. Louis, MO 63101
314/235-9800

**Southwestern Bell Telephone
Co.—Arkansas Division**
(subs. of Southwestern Bell)
111 W. Capitol
Little Rock, AR 72201
501/373-9800

**Southwestern Bell Telephone
Co.—Kansas Division**
(subs. of Southwestern Bell)
220 E. Sixth St.
Topeka, KS 66603
913/276-1585

**Southwestern Bell Telephone
Co.—Missouri Division**
(subs. of Southwestern Bell)
100 N. Tucker St.
St. Louis, MO 63101
314/247-9800

**Southwestern Bell Telephone
Co.—Oklahoma Division**
(subs. of Southwestern Bell)
1 Bell Central/800 N. Harvey
Oklahoma City, OK 73102
405/236-6611

**Southwestern Bell Telephone
Co.—Texas Division**
(subs. of Southwestern Bell)
1 Bell Plz.
Dallas, TX 75202
214/464-4647

**Sprint International
Communications Corp.**
12490 Sunrise Valley
Reston, VA 22096
703/689-5664

Telephone & Data Systems, Inc.
79 W. Monroe St.,
Suite 905
Chicago, IL 60603
312/630-1900

Telephone Electronics Corporation
236 E. Central St.
Jackson, MS 39201
601/352-0966

US Sprint Communications
2330 Shawnee Mission Pkwy.
Westwood, KS 66209
913/624-3000

US West
(Bell regional holding company)
7800 E. Orchard St.
Englewood, CO 80111
303/793-6500

US West
Communications—Mountain Bell
(subs. of US West)
1801 California St.
Denver, CO 80202
303/869-2355

US West
Communications—Northwestern
Bell
(subs. of US West)
1314 Douglas on-the-Mall
Omaha, NE 68102
402/422-2000

US West Communications—Pacific
Northwest Bell
(subs. of US West)

1600 Bell Plz.
Seattle, WA 98191
206/345-2211

US West New Vector Group
(US West cellular subsidiary)
3350 161 Ave., SE
Box 7329
Bellevue, WA 98008
206/747-4900

United Telecommunications, Inc.
P.O. Box 11315
Kansas City, KS 64112
913/676-3000

Universal Telephone, Inc.
231 W. Wisconsin Ave.
Milwaukee, WI 53202
414/278-7000

Wisconsin Bell
(subs. of Ameritech)
722 N. Broadway
Milwaukee, WI 53202
414/549-7300

WHERE TO GO FOR MORE INFORMATION

(For more information sources in related areas, see "Engineers," page 41, "Technical Careers," page 186, and "Computers/Electronics," page 298.)

TELECOMMUNICATIONS INDUSTRY ASSOCIATIONS

Competitive Telecommunications
Association
1140 Connecticut Ave., NW,
Suite 220
Washington, DC 20036
202/296-6650

International Communications
Association
12750 Merritt Dr.,
Suite 710

Dallas, TX 75287
214/233-3889

Society of Telecommunications
Consultants
1 Rockefeller Plz.
New York, NY 10020
212/582-3909

Telecommunications Association
858 S. Oak Park Rd.,
Suite 102
Covina, CA 91724-3625
818/967-9411

United States Telephone Association
900 19th St., NW
Washington, DC 20006-2102
202/835-3100

TELECOMMUNICATIONS INDUSTRY DIRECTORIES

The Mobil Communications Directory
2000 M St., NW,
Suite 230
Washington, DC 20036
800/326-8638

Telecommunications Directory
Gale Research, Inc.
835 Penobscot Bldg.
Detroit, MI 48226
800/877-4253

Telephone Engineer & Management Directory
Edgell Communications, Inc.
1 E. First St.
Duluth, MN 55802
218/723-9470
800/346-0085

Telephone Industry Directory and Sourcebook
Phillips Publishing, Inc.
7811 Montrose Rd.
Potomac, MD 20854
301/340-2100

Statistics of the Local Exchange Carriers
United States Telephone Association
900 19th St., NW
Washington, DC 20006-2105
202/835-3263
(Lists top 150 U.S. telephone companies, and over 600 local exchange carriers.)

TELECOMMUNICATIONS INDUSTRY PERIODICALS

Communication News
12936 Falling Water St.
Strongsville, OH 44136
216/238-4556
(Monthly magazine for managers and supervisors in voice and signal data communications.)

Communications Magazine
6300 S. Syracuse Way,
Suite 650
Englewood, CO 80111
303/220-0600
(Monthly magazine for telecommunications professionals,

including those in sales, management, and technical positions.)

Telecommunications
685 Canton St.
Norwood, MA 02062
617/769-9750
(Monthly magazine for telecommunications engineers, and managers involved in telecommunications buying or specifications.)

Telephone Engineer & Management
225 N. Michigan Ave.
Chicago, IL 60601
312/938-2378
(Semimonthly magazine for telephone
company managers, engineers,
executives, etc.)

Telephony
55 E. Jackson Blvd.
Chicago, IL 60604
312/922-2435
(Weekly magazine for engineers,
specifiers, buyers, etc.)

TRANSPORTATION

INDUSTRY OUTLOOK: Linked with the economy. Improvements—and tight competition—likely.

Trucking: Watch for hot competition with other trucking firms and with railroads. Crucial to be able to compete—using information-systems applications to automate shipping, track vehicles, manage data, etc. Those companies that don't keep up with the technological breakthroughs will fall behind.

Railroads: Going full steam ahead in step with the economy. Expect increases in intermodal arrangements. Key challenge? Facing increasing competition from trucking and other modes of transportation.

Water: Generally fair, but the U.S. foreign water transportation industry may be affected by the reduction of U.S. military troops abroad. As for domestic shipping, as always it will mirror the national economy. Two key issues that may have an effect on the industry: environmental legislation and the need for capital improvements on the inland waterways system.

A LOOK BACK

▶ **Truckers were faced with several changes and challenges over the past few years.**

Deregulation in 1980 sent the trucking industry into a slump because of the high number of new entrants into the marketplace and the resulting oversupply of carriers. Then came price slashing, consolidation, and—for a while—improved earnings. Even the recession and the Persian Gulf War didn't hurt the industry all that much. While diesel prices rose, truck companies were able to pass the costs along to shippers. But 1991 saw a drop in shipments, a slump in operating and income levels, and a decline in earnings. It was a matter of waiting for other industries to improve before the trucking companies could pull out of the downslide.

▶ **While the railroad industry is still number two, it has been helped by favorable government legislation.**

In 1990 legislation from Congress helped rail companies in their mediation with unions. In 1991 provisions were added into congressional highway bills freezing the spread of double and triple trailer rigs beyond the seventeen states in which they were already allowed. The bottom line? Even during the recession, the railroad industry was feeling strong and better able to compete with the industry-leading trucking companies.

What's Next

▶ The trucking industry will continue to be highly competitive.

It's an inevitability. Expect competition in all four areas of service in the trucking industry: truckload (TL) carriers, less-than-truckload (LTL) carriers, small package, and package express. In both the LTL and TL areas, expect to see a continued dominance by the large carriers, with small and midsized carriers feeling the pinch. At the same time, in the TL area, expect to see the continuing emergence of small upstart carriers. Many of these will fail, especially as shippers cut back on the number of carriers used in an effort to simplify the freight process and cut costs. The bottom line? The trucking industry will continue on its typical intensely competitive track.

▶ To succeed in today's climate, trucking companies will turn to technological methods and applications.

The use of technology is crucial for success in today's trucking industry, for three reasons: first, international production of goods is creating a need for precise coordination between production and distribution; second, the growth of "just-in-time" manufacturing is creating a need for precisely timed delivery of components; third, automation improves efficiency and keeps costs in check.

As such, expect the use of technological applications and systems to grow over the next few years. The chief use of automation will continue to be freight-transport management and integration. Among the advances already being used in this area: bar-code technology, satellite tracking of individual trucks, shipment tracking, computerized route selection. Companies already using systems such as these will expand their use; those without automation will be forced to upgrade—or lose market share rapidly.

▶ Another way to beat the competition: positioning a company for a specific marketplace.

The large companies will be establishing a national presence through industrial advertising and marketing campaigns. Smaller companies will focus on specialized fields and niche markets. Two of the main growth areas are commodity-specific hauling, and "just-in-time" delivery services, in which a carrier guarantees a delivery time.

In general, this attention to marketing points to new opportunities for trucking-company sales representatives and marketing professionals. Both areas will be more visible than in the past.

▶ Railroads will compete with trucking and barge companies by stepping up rail intermodal service, double-stack trains, and computerized systems.

Like trucking companies, railroads will be coming up with ways of cutting costs, expediting shipments, and the like.

One of the most common of these methods will be intermodal transportation. The concept—trailers and containers are moved by more than one transport method—isn't new, but as competition in the transportation industry stays hot, intermodal transportation is heating up again. An example of how quickly it is growing: it doubled between 1990 and 1991, from 3.1 million trailers and containers to 6.2 million. As container shipments from the Far East increase, expect to see more rail companies increase the use of piggybacks, in which trailers or containers are placed on flatbed cars. Double-stack trains, which carry containers stacked two high, are also increasing in use; they now account for about 25% of all intermodal capacity.

To keep costs down and to enhance competitive reach, there should be a rise in cooperative ventures—marketing and joint-usage agreements between rail companies. Most commonly, companies share terminals and tracks. Among the companies already involved in cooperative ventures are Burlington Northern, Santa Fe Pacific, and Consolidated Rail.

Also watch for increasing computerization of the railroad industry. For example, both the U.S. and Canadian railroads have been developing integrated telecommunications and microelectronic systems that control train operations—Advanced Train Control Systems (ATCs). These systems can monitor a train's performance, manage maintenance crews, and more. When the systems are fully operational, they should create "smart trains"—trains that are more efficient and safer than regular trains and can detect any malfunctions and mechanical problems. The bottom line: Costs will be cut, productivity and efficiency increased, and customer service more easily ensured.

► **An interesting note: Because railroads cut into trucking's market share in the recent past, watch for more trucking companies to step up their intermodal operations.**

J.B. Hunt and Santa Fe Pacific have already set up an intermodal system. Expect to see more developments along these lines.

► **A related trend: the emergence of multimodal companies that encompass different types of transportation.**

It's a way of beating the competition, by being able to offer all forms of transportation to a customer. Multimodal companies—mergers of trucking, railroad, and water freight companies—first appeared in 1984, when CSX Corporation acquired controlling interest in American Commercial Lines and its subsidiary, American Barge Lines, and later, container ship company SeaLand Corporation. Rail companies in particular have been buying trucking companies while divesting themselves of nontransportation businesses.

Expect this type of across-the-board transportation merging to continue at a slower pace and to heat up when the national economy forces another industry shakeout.

► **Water transportation looks generally favorable in the long term, but there are several challenges ahead.**

Deep-sea foreign shipping will, as always, be dependent to a great degree on the performance of international shipping markets. The two keys to success: keeping shipping capacity in line with the supply of global merchandise that will be shipped by water; and keeping costs down—especially problematic because of the Oil Pollution Act of 1990, which will require the replacement of older tankers and tank barges.

Similarly, domestic carriers are tied to the health of the national economy—in particular, to the performance of steel, crude oil, coal, chemicals, and grain. The challenges ahead for this sector of the industry? The threat of more demanding government regulations regarding hazardous waste, waste disposal, and vessel inspection, among other things.

Overall, however, the picture is stable for water transportation, and employment opportunities should remain fair but limited.

EMPLOYMENT OUTLOOK: Variable.

The trucking industry is predicted to add about 410,000 new jobs by the year 2005. One reason for this is that the continued growth in foreign trade is increasing the number of truck shipments required to move imports and exports to and from seaports. Truck-driving jobs should grow anywhere from 16 to 30% over the next decade. Also looking strong: managers and logistics personnel with computer backgrounds.

The railroad industry doesn't offer as bright an employment picture. Available jobs have been declining since World War II, and it's unlikely that there will be a sharp reversal of this trend. The Bureau of Labor Statistics forecasts job growth over the next twelve years increasing by 2% at best. The strongest demand will be, again, for people with computer backgrounds, due to the increased computerization of the industry. Also looking better than other areas: locomotive and yard engineers. The weakest area: brake operators.

Water transportation isn't a hot growth industry either, where employment is concerned. The government estimates a 10% gain in jobs at best over the next ten years; at worst a 4% loss. The bulk of the jobs will be replacement positions.

JOBS SPOTLIGHT

TRANSPORTATION MANAGERS: This is an area that has been seeing an increasing need in recent years. While experience is generally necessary, a college degree isn't—but it is a big plus. Best background: a degree in logistics, and computer skills.

TRUCKING SALES REPRESENTATIVE: A high turnover rate in this area leads to continued opportunities, especially as trucking companies fight the competition. There has been a recent trend toward hiring more women and college graduates for sales positions. Salaries start at about $30,000.

BEST BETS

Norfolk Southern
3 Commercial Pl.
Norfolk, VA 23510
804/629-2600

Norfolk Southern has big plans for the future, chief among them, a push to globalize. One aspect of this: selling international transport services. It's all part of

Norfolk Southern's plan to provide comple transportation services. Closer to home, it has been a leader in intermodal transporation. This makes Norfolk Southern look like a long-term winner.

Schneider National Inc.
P.O. Box 2545
Green Bay, WI 54306
414/497-2201

A trucking company that has changed to fit the '90s, Schneider National has a number of strong points that make it a good choice for employment. First, the company has few layers of management and a belief in a democratic organization—one governed more by merit, less by titles. Employees (or "associates" as the company calls them) are encouraged to share ideas, critiques, and suggestions. Drivers receive an extra paycheck each month based on their performance. Add to this management style the fact that Schneider National has jumped onto the technology bandwagon in a big way—using a satellite computer system for delivery tracking, order transmission directly to trucks, and much more. All in all, Schneider looks like a real winner.

TOP TRANSPORTATION COMPANIES

ABF Freight System, Inc.
P.O. Box 48
Fort Smith, AR 72902
501/785-8700
(Trucking)

Alexander & Baldwin, Inc.
822 Bishop St.
Box 3440
Honolulu, HI 96801
808/525-6611
(Shipping.)

Allied Van Lines, Inc.
P.O. Box 4403
Chicago, IL 60680
708/717-3000
(Trucking.)

American President Lines
1111 Broadway
Oakland, CA 94607
510/272-8000
(Shipping.)

Arkansas Best Corp.
1000 S. 21st St.
Fort Smith, AR 72901
501/785-6000
(Trucking.)

Burlington Northern Inc.
777 Main St.
Fort Worth, TX 76102
817/878-2000
(Railroad.)

Carolina Freight Corp.
P.O. Box 545
Cherryville, NC 28021
704/435-6811
(Trucking.)

Chicago & North Western Transportation Company
1 North Western Ctr.
Chicago, IL 60606
312/559-7000
(Railroad.)

Consolidated Freightways, Inc.
3240 Hillview Ave.
Palo Alto, CA 94304
415/494-2900
(Trucking.)

Consolidated Rail Corp. (Conrail)
P.O. Box 41417
Philadelphia, PA 19101-1417
215/209-5099
(Railroad.)

CSX Transportation, Inc.
P.O. Box C-32222
Richmond, VA 23261
804/782-1400

Florida East Coast Railway Co.
1 Malaga St.
St. Augustine, FL 32084
904/829-3421
(Railroad.)

J. B. Hunt Transport Services, Inc.
P.O. Box 130
Lowell, AR 72745
501/820-0000
(Trucking.)

Illinois Central Railroad
455 N. Cityfront Plaza Dr.
Chicago, IL 60611-5504
312/755-7500
(Railroad.)

Kansas City Southern Industries, Inc.
114 W. 11th St.
Kansas City, MO 64105
816/556-0303
(Railroad.)

Leaseway Transportation Corp.
3700 Park East Dr.
Cleveland, OH 44122
216/765-5500
(Trucking.)

Mayflower Transit, Inc.
P.O. Box 107B
Indianapolis, IN 46206

317/875-1000
(Trucking.)

Norfolk Southern Corp.
3 Commercial Pl.
Norfolk, VA 23510
804/629-2600
(Railroad.)

North American Van Lines, Inc.
5001 U.S. Hwy 30 W.
Fort Wayne, IN 46801
219/429-2511
(Trucking.)

Overnite Transportation Co.
1000 Semmes Ave.
Richmond, VA 23224
804/231-8000
(Trucking.)

Preston Trucking Co., Inc.
151 Easton Blvd.
Preston, MD 21655
301/673-7151
(Trucking.)

Roadway Express, Inc.
P.O. Box 471
Akron, OH 44309
216/384-1717
(Trucking.)

Santa Fe Pacific Corp.
1700 E. Golf Rd.
Schaumburg, IL 60173
708/995-6000

TNT Red Star Express, Inc.
24 Wright Ave.
Auburn, NY 13021
315/253-2721
(Trucking.)

Union Pacific Railroad
Eighth & Eaton Aves.
Bethlehem, PA 18018
215/861-3200
(Railroad.)

United Van Lines, Inc.
1 United Dr.
Fenton, MO 63026
314/326-3100
(Trucking.)

Yellow Freight System, Inc.
10990 Roe Ave.
Box 7563
Overland Park, KS 66207
913/967-4300
(Trucking.)

WHERE TO GO FOR MORE INFORMATION

TRANSPORTATION INDUSTRY ASSOCIATIONS

American Bureau of Shipping
2 World Trade Ctr.
106th Fl.
New York, NY 10048
212/839-5000

American Institute of Merchant Shipping
1000 16th St., NW,
Suite 511
Washington, DC 20036
202/775-4399

American Maritime Association
485 Madison Ave.,
15th Fl.
New York, NY 10022
212/319-9217

American Trucking Association
2200 Mill Rd.
Alexandria, VA 22314
708/838-1700
(Publishes weekly publication
Transport Topics, which includes a
strong help-wanted section, available
to nonmembers as well as members.)

Association of American Railroads
American Railroad Building
50 F St., NW
Washington, DC 20001
202/639-2100

Industrial Truck Association
1750 K St., NW,
Suite 210

Washington, DC 20006
202/296-9880

**National Association of Fleet
Administrators; National
Association of Fleet Managers**
120 Wood Ave. S.
Iselin, NJ 08830
908/494-8100

**National Association of Marine
Services**
1900 Arch St.
Philadelphia, PA 19103
215/564-3484

National Association of Stevedores
2011 I St., NW
Washington, DC 2006
202/296-2810

**National Motor Freight Traffic
Association**
2200 Mill Rd.
Alexandria, VA 22314
703/838-1821

National Tank Truck Carriers
2200 Mill Rd.
Alexandria, VA 22314
703/838-1960

**National Private Truck Council of
America**
1320 Braddock Pl.,
Suite 720
Alexandria, VA 22314
703/683-1300

Transportation Institute
5201 Auth Way
Fall Springs, MD 20746
202/347-2590

TRANSPORTATION INDUSTRY DIRECTORIES

Air Freight Directory
Air Cargo, Inc.
1819 Bay Ridge Ave.
Annapolis, MD 21403
410/263-8054

American Motor Carrier Directory
K-111 Press, Inc.
424 W. 33rd St.
New York, NY 10001
212/714-3100

Directory of Truckload Carriers
Optimum Transportation Services
210 Teaberry Ln.
Clarks Summit, PA 18411
717/586-9023

Moody's Transportation Manual
Moody's Investors Service, Inc.
99 Church St.

New York, NY 10007
212/553-0300

National Tank Truck Carrier Directory
2200 Mill Rd.
Alexandria, VA 22314
703/838-1960

Official Motor Carrier Directory
3865 Wilson Blvd.
Arlington, VA 22203-1919
703/528-3100

Official Railway Guide–North American Freight Service Edition
K-111 Press Inc.
424 W. 33rd St.
New York, NY 10001
211/714-3100

TRANSPORTATION INDUSTRY MAGAZINES

American Shipper
P.O. Box 4728
Jacksonville, Fl 32201
904/355-2601
(Monthly magazine aimed at those involved in the shipping industry, including ship and barge operators, traffic and export managers, manufactures, service agencies, etc.)

Commercial Carrier Journal
201 King of Prussia Rd.
Radnor, PA 19089
215/964-4523
(Monthly publication for executives involved in truck fleets, long and short haul, volume buses, etc.)

Distribution
201 King of Prussia Rd.
Radnor, PA 19089
215/964-4384
(Monthly magazine for traffic and transportation managers and executives, shippers, packers, etc.)

Fleet Owner
342 Madison Ave.
New York, NY 10173
212/867-2350
(Monthly magazine for managers in fleet operations.)

Heavy Duty Trucking
P.O. Box W
Newport Beach, CA 92658
714/261-1636
(Monthly magazine aimed at
managers, maintenance and
specifications personnel, etc., at
companies with fleets over 26,000
pounds.)

Inbound Logistics
5 Penn Plz.,
8th Fl.
New York, NY 10001
212/629-1560
(Monthly magazine aimed at people
involved in inbound freight
transportation.)

*Owner-Operator: The Business
Magazine of Independent Trucking*
201 King of Prussia Rd.
Radnor, PA 19089
215/964-625
800/345-1214
(Nine-issue magazine for small-fleet
operators and independent truckers.)

Pro Trucker
610 Colonial Park Dr.
Roswell, GA 30075
404/587-0311
(Monthly magazine for professional
drivers, fleet operators, etc.)

Progressive Railroading
2 N. Riverside Plz.
Chicago, IL 60606
312/454-9155
(Monthly magazine aimed at railroad
operations and maintenance officials,
etc.)

Railway Age
345 Hudson St.
New York, NY 10014
212/620-7200
(Monthly magazine covering railroads
and rapid transit systems.)

Shipping Digest
51 Madison Ave.
New York, NY 10010
212/689-4411
(Weekly magazine aimed at
executives involved in overseas export
of U.S. goods.)

Trucks Magazine
765 Churchville Rd.
Southampton, PA 18966
215/355-1034
(Monthly magazine covering
long-haul, heavy-duty trucking.)

TRAVEL

INDUSTRY OUTLOOK: Hot competition for tourist dollars ahead.

Key challenges for the travel industry? Responding to the changing demands of the consumer and facing increasing competition. In line with this, watch companies aim at niche markets (such as the elderly, the environmentally aware or the health-conscious). Also watch for shifts in marketing strategies, promotion and advertising. A likely development—an increase in cooperative programs between travel industry companies (including agencies, tour operators, etc.), destinations, attractions, cities and states.

A LOOK BACK

▶ **The key factors affecting the travel industry in the past few years were record-breaking growth, the Persian Gulf War, and the recession.**

For three straight years—1989 to 1991—Americans took a record 1.3 billion trips per year. The chief problems in the initial phases of this period were stiff competition, much of it brought about by the high number of new businesses emerging, and the resulting business failures and consolidation brought about by this tough competition.

Then came the double whammy of the Gulf War—which caused international travel to drop—and the recession—which made all travel slump. Vacationers became value conscious and businesses cost conscious. The result? Travel companies saw a decline. The recession actually helped a number of cruise lines, however, because many people were interested in keeping costs down. To do this, they opted to stay closer to home and buy package deals that included airfare and meals. The result? Relatively smooth sailing for cruise lines, while other areas of the travel business sank. Fortunes changed in 1992 and travel increased again. The result—a new record, with Americans taking nearly 1.4 billion trips that year. The only dark spot, persisting through 1993: the weak dollar cut back on foreign travel. Overall, though, the future looked positive.

WHAT'S NEXT

▶ **Competition will stay hot across the board.**

Expect to see continued tight competition, not only between travel agencies but between agencies and suppliers and between the different segments of the travel industry.

The competition between agencies and suppliers—cruise lines, airlines, and the like—began following deregulation. It grew even hotter during the recent recession, as slumping airlines and other sectors geared up to attract customers any way they could and to avoid paying commissions to agents. Expect this type of activity to keep growing, with suppliers increasing their advertising, marketing, and promotional campaigns, and packages aimed directly at consumers.

The question many are asking in light of this: Will the '90s bring an end to the traditional commission structure? Keep abreast of any developments in this area, as industry insiders wait to see if airlines will start cutting commissions as a way of keeping costs down. This, clearly, will have a strong impact on travel agencies—and could spell real problems for the smaller agencies in particular.

▶ A continuing trend: industry consolidation.

The travel industry is increasingly being dominated by large agencies and agency networks—consortiums of smaller agencies that link up to remain competitive with the big guys like Carlson, Thomas Cook, and American Express.

This type of activity will continue as smaller independent agencies face stiffer competition from other agencies, particularly chains and franchises, and, as outlined above, from suppliers. By linking up with a network, even a small agency can gain the resources needed to stay alive in this competitive field. Among them: cooperative personnel recruiting, centralized computer systems, increased cooperative advertising and marketing and collective purchasing.

▶ Also increasing: specialization and targeted marketing.

This, too, is a result of competition in the field. Some developments to be on the lookout for: In the business travel segment, watch small and midsized corporate agencies target their services specifically to small and midsized corporations as the large chains will dominate much of the business travel segment.

Similarly, in the general travel field, local and regional agencies will rely on focused marketing to compete with the large agencies and chains. They will develop packages and services to meet the very specific needs of their so-called mini-markets.

An employment note: This emphasis on marketing and sales may translate into new opportunities for marketing and sales personnel in the travel industry.

▶ Similarly, the travel industry will be shifting focus and marketing to keep up with changing demographics.

It's the logical way for the industry to continue growing. And the general demographic picture is a positive one, chiefly because of the increasing number of older Americans and those with higher levels of education and income—all positive traits where travel is concerned.

Other key "people trends" that the travel industry will be tracking: The increase in two-income families will mean an increase in "short stay" travel—that is, trips of two to seven days. As a result, cruise lines and tour companies—even international tour companies—will emphasize shorter trip packages. The increasing number of baby boomers having babies—and so, the increase in the number of grandparents—will result in the growth of the family travel area. Again, tour operators and cruise lines will be developing special packages to accommodate these changes—and the related trend of families accompanying business travelers.

Another hot area: adventure-type trips, as the population ages and has more disposable income. Adventure trips—trekking, scuba diving, and other active trips—as well as trips to exotic locations are especially hot areas for entrepreneurs and small tour operators. A related travel segment that should remain strong in the short term is package tours or trips aimed at environmentally aware travelers: "ecotourism" or "low-environmental-impact-travel."

▶ The travel industry will continue strong in the international arena.

With an increase in international business—especially to Europe as a result of the EC and the changes in Eastern Europe—and the growing internationalization of U.S. companies, foreign business travel will remain strong over the long term. One result: corporations will beef up in-house travel operations to keep costs down and arrangements efficient. This points to increased opportunities for corporate travel managers (described in Jobs Spotlight, page 484).

Also pointing to growth in international travel: the changes in Eastern Europe and the former Soviet Union are opening up new markets. The U.S. already has bilateral tourism agreements with Poland, Hungary and Yugoslavia, and at the time of writing was negotiating one with many former Soviet Union nations. Watch more areas to open up to U.S. travel—including Cuba and Vietnam.

▶ Cruise lines: in for competition, some ups and downs, but still coming on strong.

North American cruise lines added nearly 50,000 new berths between 1981 and 1991. In the same period, demand increased nearly 10%. While there may be periods of softer sales, slower growth, and price cuts, the overall picture is one of long-term growth.

Again, demographic trends point to this. As mentioned above, the population is growing older—and the traditional cruise customer is over forty-five. Aging baby boomers and senior citizens are likely cruise customers. In addition, the growing value-consciousness of the American consumer fits in with the cruise industry as cruises are all-inclusive vacations.

Some developments to watch for: Expect the evolution of a two-tier industry, with larger lines offering diversified services and smaller cruise lines finding niche markets (such as windjammer cruises, hands-on cruising, or special destinations) and offering specialized services.

Also expect to see more cruise lines linking up with other travel companies. Some will buy up or enter joint ventures with resorts or hotels and offer "land-sea" packages. For example, Cunard already owns seven hotels. Other cruise lines will develop arrangements and packages with tour operators and airlines. These collaborative arrangements will increase competitive power and attract more customers.

As for employment: The cruise lines offer good employment prospects. Salespeople are in for a relatively bright future as cruise lines beef up sales forces. Similarly, advertising and marketing will be heating up. As the cruise industry matures, more lines are pumping money into advertising to establish brand identity.

EMPLOYMENT OUTLOOK: Positive.

The long-term picture is a good one where jobs are concerned. The travel and tourism industry already employs more than 9 million people, and that number should increase over the next ten years.

According the Bureau of Labor Statistics, travel agent is among the fastest-growing occupations of the decade, with employment forecast to grow 62.3%— which means the addition of 82,000 jobs by 2005. Many agencies are targeting women, minorities, senior citizens, and foreign-born people. And many are also starting to offer flexible work arrangements: seasonal work schedules, part-time schedules, temporary assignments, and the like.

Corporate travel managers and staffs should also be increasing as business becomes more internationalized. See the Jobs Spotlight below for more information.

JOB SPOTLIGHT

CORPORATE TRAVEL MANAGERS: A position that is becoming more visible and more important as corporate travel resurges. With corporations paying close attention to costs and with the increase in globalization leading to an increase in business travel, in-house travel managers are in demand. Specific duties vary, depending on the size and scope of the corporate travel department. While some corporations have complete in-house agencies, others work in conjunction with outside agencies. Average salaries usually fall in the $35,000–50,000 range.

BEST BETS

Ask Mr. Foster
(subsidiary of Carlson Cos., Inc.)
7833 Haskell Ave.
Van Nuys, CA 91406
818/988-0181

Downey office:
8520 E. Florence
Downey, CA 90240
818/988-01881

A leading travel agency with a reputation for customer service to corporations, Ask Mr. Foster provides an extensive six week in-house training program for agents. This program allows someone with no experience to become a travel counselor in a short time. The company also offers flexible schedules to attract nontraditional workers, such as single parents and the elderly.

Carnival Cruise Lines, Inc.
3915 Biscayne Blvd.
Miami, FL 33137
305/573-6030

Known for aggressive marketing and advertising, Carnival remains the top cruise line in the country and should keep coming on strong. There are expansion plans in the works, including zeroing in on a hot growth area: short-term cruises. A good bet for the future.

TOP TRAVEL COMPANIES

(including agencies, cruise lines, and tour operators)

Adventure Tours, Inc.
9818B Liberty Rd.
Randallstown, MD 21133
410/922-8661
(Tour operator, travel agency.)

American Express Travel Group, Inc.
American Express Tower
World Financial Ctr.
New York, NY 10285
212/640-2000
(Diversified travel services.)

American Hawaii Cruises
550 Kearny St.
San Francisco, CA 94108
415/392-9400
(Cruise line.)

Beehive Business and Leisure Travel
1130 W. Center St.
N. Salt Lake City, UT 04054
801/292-4445
(Travel agency.)

Carlson Travel Group, Inc.
P.O. Box 59159
Minneapolis, MN 55459
612/540-8159
(Travel agencies.)

Carnival Cruise Lines, Inc.
3655 NW 87th Ave.
Miami, FL 33178
305/599-2600
(Cruise line.)

Commodore Cruise Line
800 Douglas Rd.,
Suite 700
Coral Gables, FL 33134
305/529-3000
(Cruise line.)

Thomas Cook Travel
100 Cambridge Park Dr.
Cambridge, MA 02138
617/868-9800
(Travel agency.)

Cunard Line
555 Fifth Ave.
New York, NY 10017
212/880-7500
(Cruise line.)

Garber Travel Service, Inc.
1406 Beacon St.
Brookline, MA 02146
617/734-2100
(Travel agency.)

Holland America Line
300 Elliott Ave. W.
Seattle, WA 98119
206/281-3535
(Cruise line.)

IVI Travel, Inc.
400 Skokie Blvd.
Northbrook, IL 60062
708/480-8400
(Travel agency.)

Kloster Cruise Ltd.
95 Merrick Way
Miami, FL 33134
305/387-6000
(Cruise line.)

Lifeco Services Corp.
2901 Wilcrest Dr.
Houston, TX 77042
713/954-7500
(Travel agency.)

Morris Travel Express Corp.
240 E. Morris Ave.
Salt Lake City, UT 84115
801/487-9731
(Travel agency.)

Northwestern Travel Service, Inc.
7250 Metro Blvd.
Minneapolis, MN 55431
612/921-3700
(Travel agency.)

Omega World Travel, Inc.
5203 Leesburg Pike
Falls Church, VA 22041
703/998-7171
(Travel agency.)

PS Group, Inc.
4370 La Jolla Village
San Diego, CA 92122
619/546-5001
(Travel agency.)

Pleasant Travel Service, Inc.
2040 Townsgate Rd.
Wastlake Village, CA 91361
818/991-3390
(Travel agency.)

Princess Cruises
10100 Santa Monica Blvd.
Los Angeles, CA 90067
310/553-1770
(Cruise line.)

Rosenbluth Travel Agency, Inc.
1650 Market St.
Philadelphia, PA 19103
215/981-1710
(Travel agency.)

Royal Caribbean Corp.
903 S. America Way
Miami, FL 33132
305/379-2601

Scheduled Airline Traffic Offices, Inc.
1005 N. Glebe Rd.
Arlington, VA 22203
703/358-1200
(Travel agency.)

Travel, Inc.
3680 N. Peachtree Rd.
Atlanta, GA 30341
404/455-6575
(Travel agency.)

US Travel Systems, Inc.
1401 Rockville Pike
Rockville, MD 20852
301/251-9450
(Travel agency.)

Visatatours
1923 N. Carson St.,
Suite 105
Carson City, NV 89710
800/647-0800
(Tour operator.)

WHERE TO GO FOR MORE INFORMATION

TRAVEL INDUSTRY ASSOCIATIONS

American Society of Travel Agents
1101 King St.
Alexandria, VA 22314
202/965-7520

Association of Retail Travel Agents
25 South Riverside
Croton-on-Hudson, NY 10520
914/271-4357

Institute of Certified Travel Agents
148 Linden St.
P.O. Box 56
Wellesley, MA 02181
617/237-0280

International Association of Tour Managers
North American Region
1646 Chapel St.
New Haven, CT 06511
203/777-5994

Travel Industry Association of America
1899 L St., Suite 600
Washington, DC 20036
202/293-1433

TRAVEL INDUSTRY DIRECTORIES

Travel Industry Personnel Directory
Travel Agent Magazine
825 Seventh Ave.
New York, NY 10019
212/887-1900

World Travel Directory
Travel Weekly
Reed Travel Group
500 Plz. Dr.
Secaucus, NJ 07096
201/902-2000

TRAVEL INDUSTRY PERIODICALS

Business Travel News
600 Community Dr.
Manhasset, NY 11030
516/562-5511
(Thirty-six-issue periodical aimed at those involved in corporate travel, including corporate travel managers, agencies with a business travel practice, travel companies such as airlines, etc.)

Travel Agent
801 Second Ave.
New York, NY 10017
212/370-5050

(Weekly magazine aimed at travel agents and others in the travel industry, including tour operators, executives, etc.)

Travel Trade
15 W. 44th St.
New York, NY 10036
212/730-6600
(Weekly periodical for travel agency personnel—salespeople, executives, reservation clerks—as well as tour operators, resort personnel, etc.)

Travel Weekly
500 Plz. Dr.
Secaucus, NJ 07096
201/902-2000
(Weekly tabloid covering all aspects
of the travel industry, aimed at agency
personnel, sales and promotion
staffers, tour operators, hospitality
industry personnel, etc.)

Travelage MidAmerica
Official Airlines Guide, Inc.
320 North Michigan Ave., Suite 701

Chicago, IL 60601
312/346-4952
(For travel agents in the
mid-American states, Ontario, and
Manitoba.)

Travelage West
Official Airline Guides, Inc.
49 Stevenson, No. 460
San Francisco, CA 94105-2909
415/905-1155

UTILITIES

INDUSTRY OUTLOOK: Increased competition.

Utilities companies will be locked in a competitive battle with independents—non-utility generators (NUGs), both over power-plant construction and over customers. One possible development—an increase in agreements between utilities and independents.

A LOOK BACK

▶ **The most important factor in the utilities industry in the past—and the future: partial deregulation.**

Utilities had always existed in a regulated environment in which regulating authorities balanced the risks of energy production and distribution against the rewards and then established consumer and commercial rate structures based on their estimates of a fair return. In other words, utilities were classic, regulated monopolies.

Then, in the late '70s, came the changes. Some of the impetus came from the push to build and finance nuclear power plants. Building these huge and costly plants resulted in large losses for the utilities industry. This forced the industry and its state and federal regulators to reexamine the traditional operating environment. One conclusion: In some situations it would be necessary for power utilities to go beyond the regulatory systems and into the marketplace to obtain financing.

The Public Utilities Regulatory Act of 1978 opened another wedge in the regulated marketplace by allowing the creation of small power-production and cogeneration plants (which produce electricity from the steam released by factories and plants). The result? The beginning of competitive pressures in the industry—a trend that is continuing to affect the industry.

WHAT'S NEXT

▶ **A continuing trend: an increasing number of non-utility generators (NUGs).**

NUGs are independently owned generators, and their emergence has been changing the utility industry.

The chief factor leading the increase of independents is money. Because building power plants is so costly, many utility companies can't or won't risk the money to build them. But independents will.

NUGs will continue to play an increasingly important role, particularly where new capacity is concerned. One energy consultant predicts that independents will add more than six to seven thousand megawatts each year. Estimates are that by the year 2000, the amount of power produced by independents will double—from about 6% of the total power used to 12%.

The key reason for the continuing inroads being made by independents is low rates. Independents can afford to offer lower rates than the utilities because their overhead is lower and, perhaps the biggest advantage of all, because they are free of many of the regulations under which the large utilities must operate and so can raise capital more easily. As such, independents pass along the savings to their customers, usually industrial users.

▶ More large utilities will follow the "if you can't beat 'em, join 'em" strategy with independents.

In other words, expect to see a growing number of large utilities entering into agreements with the independent power companies.

With the need for power up, and the cost of building plants to add capacity extremely high, more utilities companies will be buying power from independents, then selling that power to their own customers. These contracts will become more common as customer usage continues on its upward path.

Along similar lines, watch for more utilities to buy smaller independents. One example: U.S. Generating Inc., a top independent, is owned by Pacific Gas & Electric Co. and construction company Bechtel Corp. The degree of ownership is limited by federal regulation; as of 1990, utilities could own only 10% of the independent power producers. And, in order to be exempt from regulations, these independents had to be environmentally desirable—for example, cogeneration or alternative fuel plants. But industry insiders expect these regulations to become less stringent and utilities to expand their ownership of independents.

▶ Environmental concerns and legislation will continue affecting the industry.

Electric utilities companies are the nation's largest consumer of coal—which, in turn, produces sulfur oxide and other hazardous air pollutants. According to the Clean Air Act Amendments, utilities plants must control their sulfur emissions. Some utilities companies can comply by burning low-sulfur coal. Others face a choice: either to install "scrubbers" (flue gas desulfurizers) or to retrofit their plants to run on natural gas. Either way, the cost is high.

▶ Over the long term, there should be a rise in natural gas usage.

Federal regulations passed in April 1992 changed the way in which gas pipelines sold natural gas to utilities. In brief, instead of being forced to pay pipelines one flat fee that included shipping and storage as well as the cost of the gas, utilities can now bargain directly with the producers and marketers of the natural gas. The result? Lower prices and less seasonal fluctuation. This, combined with the fact that natural gas is a clean fuel in line with the Clean Air Act Amendments, should lead to greater usage of natural gas by utilities.

▶ **Over the next five years, the building of new plants will increase.**

This will happen because the need for new capacity will increase by the end of the decade, and many of the utilities won't take up the slack by contracting with independents. This will clearly require a high capital outlay on the part of utilities—and, in conjunction with the high cost of adapting existing plants to meet new environmental standards, may result in a gradual increase in the number of mergers between utilities companies. Mergers will probably proceed very slowly, however, and some proposed mergers may be rejected.

▶ **There will be continued research into alternative forms of energy and use of renewable energy.**

Attempts to find alternative forms of energy are increasing as environmental pressures and legislation keep nuclear power from expanding in use and the use of high-sulfur coal is being phased out. While natural gas use may increase, many companies will still be looking into other energy sources. For example, there has recently been research into utility-scale applications of photovoltaic cells, which create solar-generated electricity. While the price of these is still too high for utility use, further research should result in a price drop. Watch for more developments along these and other lines.

EMPLOYMENT OUTLOOK: Variable—fair to good for electric, fair for gas.

The long-term employment picture looks fairly good for electric utilities, as power demand keeps growing. Over the next twelve years, electric power–generating plant operators, distributors, and dispatchers should see job growth of about 9% percent—or an additional 4,000 jobs added; job growth for power distributors and dispatchers should be about 6%, or an additional 1,000 jobs added. Another interesting note: According to *Electric Light and Power*, the electric utility work force is aging. In the long term, this means the opening of a large number of replacement positions.

It's not as bright for gas utilities. The Bureau of Labor Statistics projects a drop in jobs of about 11%—for a job loss of 3,000—over the same period.

JOBS SPOTLIGHT

MANAGEMENT INFORMATION SYSTEMS (MIS) PERSONNEL: The utilities industry is one of the best-paying fields for MIS staffers. Several recent studies show that utilities pay information-systems professionals the most of seven industries. And as utilities continue to emphasize cost control and automation, the need will remain constant. But there's a downside: Career advancement has been slowing. With automation, MIS positions have been cut, and entry-level openings are tighter. The general outcome: MIS people are needed, they're well paid, and their positions in utilities companies are secure—but competitive.

TOP ELECTRIC AND WATER UTILITY COMPANIES

Allegheny Power System
12 E. 49th St
New York, NY 10017
212/752-2121

American Electric Power
1 Riverside Plz.
Columbus, OH 43215
614/223-1000

Baltimore Gas & Electric
Charles Ctr.
Baltimore, MD 21203
410/783-5920

Boston Edison
800 Boylston St.
Boston, MA 02199
617/424-2000

CMS Energy
330 Towncenter Dr.
Dearborn, MI 48126
313/436-9200

Carolina Power & Light
411 Fayetteville St.
Box 1551
Raleigh, NC 27602
919/546-6111

Centerior Energy
P.O. Box 94661
Cleveland, OH 44101-4661
216/447-3100

Central & South West
2121 San Jacinto St.
Dallas, TX 75266
214/754-1000

Cincinnati Gas & Electric
139 E. Fourth St.
Cincinnati, OH 45202
513/381-2000

Commonwealth Edison
One 1st National Plz.
Chicago, IL 60603
312/294-4321

Consolidated Edison Co. of New York
4 Irving Pl.
New York, NY 10003
212/460-4600

DPL
1065 Woodman Dr.
Box 8825
Dayton, OH 45432
513/224-6000

DQE
1 Oxford Ctr.
301 Grant St.
Pittsburgh, PA 15279
412/393-6000

Detroit Edison
2000 Second Ave.
Detroit, MI 48226
313/237-8000

Dominion Resources
701 E. Byrd St.
Richmond, VA 23219
804/775-5700

Duke Power
422 S. Church St.
Charlotte, NC 28242
704/373-4011

Entergy
225 Baronne St.
New Orleans, LA 70112
504/529-5262

FPL Group
11770 U.S. Hwy. 1
Box 088801
North Palm Beach, FL 33408
407/694-6300

Florida Progress
1 Progress Plz.
St. Petersburg, FL 33701
813/824-6400

General Public Utilities
100 Interpace Pkwy.
Parsippany, NJ 07054
201/263-6500

Gulf States Utilities
285 Liberty Ave.
Beaumont, TX 77701
409/838-6631

Hawaiian Electric
900 Richards St.
Honolulu, HI 96813
808/548-7771

Houston Industries
P.O. Box 4567
Houston, TX 77210
713/629-3000

Idaho Power Co.
1220 Idaho St.
Box 70
Boise, ID 83707
208/383-2200

Illinois Power
500 S. 27th St.
Decatur, IL 62525
217/424-6600

Ipalco Enterprises
25 Monument Cir.
Box 1595B
Indianapolis, IN 46206
317/261-8261

Kansas Power & Light
818 Kansas Ave.
Topeka, KS 66612
913/296-6300

Kentucky Utilities Co.
1 Quality St.
Lexington, KY 40507
606/255-2100

LG&E Energy Corp.
P.O. Box 32010
Louisville, KY 40232
502/627-2000

Long Island Lighting Co.
175 E. Old Country Rd.
Hicksville, NY 11801
516/933-4590

Montana Power
40 E. Broadway
Butte, MT 59701
406/723-5421

New England Electric System
25 Research Dr.
Westborough, MA 01582
508/366-9011

New York State Electric & Gas
P.O. Box 287
Ithaca, NY 14851
607/347-4131

Niagara Mohawk Power
300 Erie Blvd. W.
Syracuse, NY 13202
315/474-1511

Nipsco Industries
5265 Hohman Ave.
Hammond, IN 46320
219/853-5200

Northeast Utilities
P.O. Box 270
Hartford, CT 06101
203/666-6911

Northern States Power
414 Nicollet Mall
Minneapolis, MN 55401
612/330-5500

Ohio Edison
76 S. Main St.
Akron, OH 44308
216/384-5100

Oklahoma Gas & Electric
321 N. Harvey Ave.
Oklahoma City, OK 73101
405/272-3000

PSI Resources
1000 E. Main St.
Plainfield, IN 46168
317/839-9611

Pacific Gas & Electric
77 Beale St.
San Francisco, CA 94106
415/972-7000

Pacificorp
700 NE Multnomah St.
Portland, OR 97232
503/731-2000

Pennsylvania Power & Light
2 N. Ninth St.
Allentown, PA 18101
215/774-5151

Philadelphia Electric
2301 Market St.
Philadelphia, PA 19101
215/841-4000

Pinnacle West Capital
400 E. Van Buren
Phoenix, AZ 85004
602/379-2500

Portland General Corp.
121 SW Salmon St.
Portland, OR 97204
503/464-8000

Potomac Electric Power
1900 Pennsylvania Ave., NW
Washington, DC 20068
202/872-2000

Public Service Co. of Colorado
550 15th St.
Denver, CO 80202
303/571-7511

Public Service Enterprise Group
80 Park Plz.
Newark, NJ 07101
201/430-7000

Puget Sound Power & Light Co.
Puget Power Bldg.
Bellevue, WA 98009
206/454-6363

SCEcorp
2244 Walnut Grove Ave.
Rosemond, CA 91770
818/302-2222

San Diego Gas & Electric
P.O. Box 1831
San Diego, CA 92112
619/696-2000

Scana
1426 Main St.
Box 764
Columbia, SC 29202
803/748-3000

Southern Co.
64 Perimeter Ctr. E.
Atlanta, GA 30346
404/393-0650

TECO Energy
702 N. Franklin St.
Tampa, FL 33602
813/228-4111

Texas Utilities
2001 Bryan Tower
Dallas, TX 75201
214/812-4600

Union Electric
P.O. Box 149
St. Louis, MO 63166
314/621-3222

Wisconsin Energy
231 W. Michigan St.
Milwaukee, WI 53201
414/221-2949

TOP GAS & TRANSMISSION UTILITY COMPANIES

Arkla
P.O. Box 21734
Shreveport, LA 71151
318/429-2700

Atlanta Gas Light
235 Peachtree St.
Atlanta, GA 30303
404/584-4000

Brooklyn Union Gas
195 Montague St.
Brooklyn, NY 11201
718/403-2000

The Coastal Corp.
9 Greenway Plz. E.
Houston, TX 77046
713/877-1400

The Columbia Gas System
20 Montchanin Rd.
Wilmington, DE 19807
302/429-5000

Consolidated Natural Gas
CNG Tower
Pittsburgh, PA 15222
412/227-1000

Enron
1400 Smith St.
Houston, TX 77002
713/853-6161

Enserch
300 S. St. Paul St.
Dallas, TX 75201
214/651-8700

MCN
500 Griswold St.
Detroit, MI 48226
313/256-5500

National Fuel Gas
30 Rockefeller Plz.
New York, NY 10112
212/541-7533

Nicor
1700 W. Ferry Rd.
Naperville, IL 60563
708/305-9500

Pacific Enterprises
633 W. Fifth St.
Los Angeles, CA 90071
213/895-5000

Panhandle Eastern
5400 Westheimer Ct.
Box 1642
Houston, TX 77251
713/627-5400

Peoples Energy
122 S. Michigan Ave.
Chicago, IL 60603
312/431-4000

Sonat
AmSouth-Sonat Tower
Birmingham, AL 35203
205/325-3800

Southwest Gas
P.O. Box 98510
Las Vegas, NV 89102
702/876-7011

Transco Energy
2800 Post Oak Blvd.
Houston, TX 77056
713/439-2000

The Williams Cos.
1 Williams Ctr.
P.O. Box 2400
Tulsa, OK 74102
918/588-2000

WHERE TO GO FOR MORE INFORMATION

UTILITIES INDUSTRY ASSOCIATIONS

American Public Gas Association
P.O. Box 11094D
Vienna, VA 22183
703/352-3890

American Public Power Association
2301 M St., NW
Washington, DC 20037
202/467-2970

National Rural Electric Cooperative Association
1800 Massachusetts Ave., NW
Washington, DC 20036
202/797-5441
(Maintains résumé listing service.)

National Utility Contractors Association
4301 N. Fairfax Dr.
Suite 360
Arlington, VA 22203
703/358-9300

UTILITIES INDUSTRY DIRECTORIES

American Public Gas Association Directory
American Public Gas Association
P.O. Box 1426
Vienna, VA 22180
703/281-2910

Directory of Gas Utility Companies
Midwest Oil Register, Inc.
P.O. Box 7248
Tulsa, OK 74105
918/742-9925

Electrical World Directory of Electric Utilities
McGraw-Hill
1 E. 19th St.
New York, NY 10011
212/337-4068

Moody's Public Utility Manual
Moody's Investors Service, Inc.
99 Church St.
New York, NY 10007
212/553-0300

UTILITIES INDUSTRY PERIODICALS

Electrical World
11 W. 19th St.
New York, NY 10011
212/337-3811
(Monthly magazine for electric utility

executives and managers, engineers, and other related areas, including students.)

Public Power
2301 M. St., NW
Washington, DC 20037
202/467-2900
(Bimonthly published by the
American Public Power Association.)

Public Utilities Fortnightly
211 Wilson Blvd.
Arlington, VA 22201
703/243-7000

(Semimonthly magazine for utility
executives, managers, engineers, and
other personnel.)

Transmission & Distribution
707 Westchester Ave.
White Plains, NY 10604
914/949-8500
(Monthly magazine for electric
utilities executives, engineers, etc.)

SECTION 3

REGIONAL ROUNDUP 1994

NATIONAL OUTLOOK

U.S. OUTLOOK: Improving across the board.

It's a mixed picture across the board, with some areas doing better than others. Generally, those areas that began recovering from the recession first are the strongest—as growth brings construction or home-buying increases. Weakest regions: those with heavy hiring in aerospace, defense, computers.

MAJOR TRENDS

▶ **Trend No. 1: Job growth will slow through the 1990s to about half the pace of the 1980s. But certain industries and occupations will offer excellent job opportunities.**

According to the Bureau of Labor Statistics, the nation is headed for a decade of slower job growth after the explosive growth in the 1980s, especially in the service industries. The recent recession was the first real sign of a slowdown. And now, with the recession past, the economy has picked up—but the momentum is gone. Instead, companies that have streamlined are often staying lean; industries that lost jobs have switched to automation and technology to keep costs down and productivity high.

One result of this slowdown: Some experts now say that the labor shortage that the government and other experts had predicted would hit the country between now and the year 2000 probably won't occur. The labor shortage that many economists thought would be occurring was based on the continued shift away from manufacturing jobs to service-industry jobs. The jobs that were predicted to have been created by the service economy were higher-skilled, higher-paying jobs. Instead, economists are noting that higher-paying manufacturing jobs are falling by the wayside due to automation, and they are being replaced by low-paid, low-skill service jobs.

Whether or not this is the case, both sides agree on one thing: Training is becoming increasingly important. Technical ability, computer skills, and higher education are all becoming vital to land a job in today's job market.

On a more general note, certain industries seem headed for quicker growth than others. To a great degree, those that are strong prospects fall into several major areas: Technology, Health Service, Health Care Products, and Services. Among the fastest growing industries:

1. Biotechnology

2. Computers and High Tech

3. Health Care Services

4. Information Services

5. Legal Services

6. Pharmaceuticals

There also are a number of specific occupations that are headed for strong performance:

1. Home health aides

2. Paralegals

3. Systems analysts and computer scientists

4. Personal and home care aides

5. Physical therapists

6. Medical assistants

7. Operations research analysts

8. Human services workers

9. Radiologic technologists and technicians

10. Medial secretaries

It's interesting to note the number of occupations related to the health care field. To a great degree, this is due to demographic changes in the nation's population. As people grow older, there is a rising need for and attention paid to health care and health services. As such, there will be a corresponding rise in jobs. *An important note:* Health care reform may affect hiring in the health services area, however.

▶ **Trend No. 2: Jobs are moving out of the cities into the exurbs, or small fringe cities near major metropolitan areas.**

Jobs of the '90s are moving closer to where most people live —that is, right next door to the suburbs.

Some writers call this the "Los Angelesization" of America. But whatever it is called, the implications are clear: More jobs will be found in the "fringe towns"— the small cities that border major cities throughout the U.S. Some of these communities already have mini-skylines, like Fairfax County, Virginia, outside Washington, D.C., or Marietta, Georgia, outside Atlanta.

Also called "urbanized suburbs," "exurban job centers," or "edge cities", fringe towns offer the right amenities to employers: They are located near a large pool of educated workers, good transportation, schools, and houses. Many are also hotbeds of entrepreneurial businesses. As for their pluses where employees are concerned, fringe towns often offer lower housing costs, safer neighborhoods, and fewer crowds.

Some of the leading fringe towns:

East Brunswick, NJ
Herndon/Manassas, VA
Lake County, IL
Marietta/Roswell, GA

▶ **A related trend: When jobs aren't moving to exurbs, they're moving to smaller cities.**

It's a best-of-both-worlds scenario. Many companies and their employees aren't willing to give up certain amenities that cities offer, such as cultural activities, universities, intellectual outlets, wider-based career opportunities, and larger employee pools. Yet, tired of high costs, crime, crowds, and the like, they don't want to stay in the traditional large cities either.

As a result, a number of companies are relocating to small cities—a second tier of cities that on the one hand offer the peace and quiet of a smaller town but on the other hand still offer the sophistication and cultural amenities that can only be found in a city.

Among the top smaller cities where jobs can be found:

Austin, TX
Charlottte, NC
Des Moines, IA
Naples, FL
Olympia, WA
Orlando/Kissimmee, FL
Peoria, IL
Portland, ME
Raleigh-Durham, NC
Scranton/Wilkes-Barre, PA

Certain industries, however, will continue to be based primarily in larger cities. It's an inevitability—certain industries rely upon the services only a large city can provide. Among them telecommunications, publishing, and financial services.

▶ **Trend No. 3: Employment continues to move to the Sunbelt—especially the South.**

This long-term trend will make these regions the top growth areas for employment in this decade, even though the pace slowed in 1991 and 1992 along with the national economy.

While growth has slowed in California and in the Pacific Northwest, the long-term trend remains: The Northeast will continue losing ground, and more people—and more jobs—will be moving west and south.

Mountain states like Utah and Colorado are seeing an influx of companies and workers. Further west, Las Vegas, Nevada, and Riverside, California, will continue growing. However, job growth on the West Coast in general looks slower over the short term. Much of the Southwest is growing as well, with states such as Texas coming on strong. As for the Southeast, while Florida slowed its explosive growth rate of a few years ago, it's still one of the prime employment spots in the country.

For more specific information on these and other areas, see information on each region.

GENERAL BUSINESS PERIODICALS

Barron's
Dow Jones & Co.
200 Liberty St.
New York, NY 10281
212/416-2759

Business Week
McGraw-Hill, Inc.
1221 Ave. of the Americas
New York, NY 10020
212/997-3608

Forbes
Forbes, Inc.
60 Fifth Ave.
New York, NY 10011
212/620-2200

Fortune
The Time, Inc., Magazine Company
Time & Life Bldg.
New York, NY 10020-1393
212/522-1212

INC.
38 Commercial Wharf
Boston, MA 02110
617/258-8000
(Invaluable for targeting the
fast-moving corporations that tend to
do the most hiring.)

Industry Week
1100 Superior Ave.
Cleveland, OH 44114

216/696-7000
(Semimonthly; covers industrial
management.)

InternAmerica
Ford Careerworks
800/456-7335
(Bimonthly newsletter with many
internships listed for liberal arts,
technical, and vocational grads.)

Nation's Business
U.S. Chamber of Commerce
1615 H St., NW
Washington, DC 20062
202/463-5650

**National Business Employment
Weekly**
420 Lexington Ave.
New York, NY 10170
212/808-6791
(Contains *Wall Street Journal*
help-wanted ads, articles on
job-hunting techniques, careers, etc.;
special weekly sections, including
"Engineering Weekly," "Computer,"
and "High Technology.")

Wall Street Journal
200 Liberty St.
New York, NY 10281
212/416-2000

GENERAL BUSINESS DIRECTORIES

(Most of the following directories are extremely comprehensive, extremely useful—and extremely expensive. In most cases you may be better off using them at your local library.)

AMA's Executive Employment Guide
Eileen Monahan, Editor
American Management Association
135 W. 50th St.
New York, NY 10020
FAX: 212/903-8163
(Free to AMA members; lists search firms, job registries, etc.)

AMBA's MBA Employment Guide
Association of MBA Executives
227 Commerce St.
East Haven, CT 06512
203/467-8870
(For $10 each, sends a listing of corporations in three states of choice for one functional area.)

American's Corporate Families and International Affiliates
Dun's Marketing Services
3 Sylvan Way
Parsippany, NJ 07054
1-800-526-0651
201/455-0900

Association Yellow Book
Monitor Publishing Co.
104 Fifth Ave.,
2nd Fl.
New York, NY 10011
212/627-4140
(Lists associations.)

Business Organizations, Agencies, and Publications Directory
Gale Research, Inc.
645 Griswold
835 Penobscot Bldg.
Detroit, MI 48226
800/877-4253

Business Publication Rates & Data
Standard Rate & Data Service, Inc.
3004 Glenview Rd.
Wilmette, IL 60091
708/256-6067
(Lists business, trade, and technical publications in the United States and abroad.)

Career & Job Fair Finder
College Placement Council, Inc.
62 Highland Ave.
Bethlehem, PA 18017
215/868-1421
800/544-5272 (for orders)
(Information on more than seventeen hundred career days, job fairs, etc., indexed geographically, functionally, etc. Designed for professional counselors.)

Directories in Print
Gale Research, Inc.
645 Griswold
835 Penobscot Bldg.
Detroit, MI 48226
800/877-4253

Directory of Corporate Affiliations
Reed Reference Publishing
P.O. Box 31
New Providence, NJ 07974
800/323-6772

Directory of Leading Private Companies
Reed Reference Publishing
P.O. Box 31
New Providence, NJ 07974
800/323-6772

Dun & Bradstreet Million-Dollar Directory
Dun's Marketing Services
3 Sylvan Way
Parsippany, NJ 07054
800/526-0651
(Expensive, but extensive listings of leading U.S. corporations.)

Dun & Bradstreet Reference Book of Corporate Managements
Dun's Marketing Services
3 Sylvan Way
Parsippany, NJ 07054
800/526-0651

Dun's Business Rankings
Dun's Marketing Services
3 Sylvan Way
Parsippany, NJ 07054
800/526-0651

Dun's Career Guide
Dun's Marketing Services
3 Sylvan Way
Parsippany, NJ 07054
800/526-0651
(Lists employers, hiring areas, contact names, etc.)

Dun's Directory of Service Companies
Dun's Marketing Services
3 Sylvan Way
Parsippany, NJ 07054
800/526-0651
(Covers range of service industries, including management consulting, executive search services, public relations, engineering and architecture, accounting, auditing and bookkeeping, health services, legal and social services, research, hospitality, motion pictures, amusement, and recreational services.)

Dun's Regional Business Directory
Dun's Marketing Services
3 Sylvan Way
Parsippany, NJ 07054

800/526-0651
(Different volumes covering different regions of the United States.)

Encyclopedia of Associations
Gale Research, Inc.
645 Griswold
835 Penobscot Bldg.
Detroit, MI 48226
800/877-4253

International Directory of Corporate Affiliations
Reed Reference Publishing
P.O. Box 31
New Providence, NJ 07974
800/323-6772

Job Hunter's Sourcebook
Gale Research, Inc.
645 Griswold
835 Penobscot Bldg.
Detroit, MI 48226
800/877-4253

Macmillan Directory of Leading Private Companies
Reed Reference Publishing
P.O. Box 31
New Providence, NJ 07974
800/323-6772
(An expensive but good source for hard-to-find private firms.)

Moody's Industrial Manual
(Lists about three thousand publicly traded U.S. and international companies. Moody's also puts out manuals for bank and finance, public utilities, transportation, and municipals.)

Moody's Industry Review
Moody's Investors Service, Inc.
99 Church St.
New York, NY 10007
212/533-0300
(Rankings of about four thousand major firms.)

National Trade and Professional Associations
Columbia Books
1212 New York, Ave., NW,
Suite 330
Washington, DC 20005
202/898-0662
(An inexpensive—$65 in
1992—directory listing thousands of
associations.)

Peterson's Job Opportunities for Business and Liberal Arts Graduates 1993
P.O. Box 2123
Princeton, NJ 08543-2123
609/243-9111
800/338-3282
(Inexpensive; lists hundreds of
corporations and organizations that are
hiring; includes detailed information.)

Source Directory
Predicasts
1101 Cedar Ave.

Cleveland, OH 44106
216/795-3000
(Lists publications—technical,
financial, business, trade.)

Standard & Poor's Register of Corporations, Directors, and Executives
Standard & Poor's Corp.
25 Broadway
New York, NY 10004
212/208-8702
(Three volumes covering over fifty
thousand firms, brief financials,
names, addresses of major executives,
directors, new firms.)

Thomas Register
Thomas Publishing Co.
1 Pennsylvania Plz.
New York, NY 10110
212/695-0500
(Twelve-volume directory of U.S.
manufacturers.)

DATABASES

Adnet Online
800/682-2901
317/579-6922
(Online database with approximately
1.5 million professional managerial
and technical candidates nationwide;
available on PRODIGY.)

Career Network
Available through college placement
office.
(Online service that links college
placement offices with employees
nationwide. If it's been years since
you graduated, or if you never have,
check your nearest college or past
college attended; chances are you can
use the network, possibly for a fee.
Network lists jobs nationally.)

Career Placement Registry (CPR)
800/338-3283
(Résumé bank of applicants in all
fields, all levels; accessible by
recruiters via DIALOG.)

Connexion
800/338-3282
(International job-listing database; all
levels, most fields; accessible via
Compuserve.)

HRIN: Human Resources Information Network
800/421-8884
(Includes general résumé database as
well as minority college graduate,
military departees, college grads, etc.
Also includes job description
database.)

Job Market, Inc.
801/484-3808
(Wide variety of listings.)

JobTRAK
213/474-3377
(The easiest way to use this database
is to go to a subscribing college
recruitment center. Corporations send
JobTRAK listings, and in turn sends
them to colleges of the corporation's
choice. Concentrated on the West
Coast, but expanding.)

KiNexus
800/828-0422
(Database of college and university
seniors and alumni—on more than
fifteen hundred campuses nationwide,
with more than 10 million students.
Employers can tap into this database
online and via CD-ROM.)

Prodigy
914/993-8000
(Lists Adnet—see above—as well as
want ads from *USA Today* and
*National Business Employment
Weekly.*)

ROC: Résumés on Computer
317/636-1000

Career Expo
513/721-3030
(Open-house recruitment; call for
locations and details.)

Job Bank USA
800/296-1USA
(Résumé bank covering all business
levels.)

NORTHEAST AND MIDDLE ATLANTIC REGION

OUTLOOK: Improving.

The picture is brightening in the Northeast and Middle Atlantic region, although some problems remain. Key industries were hit hard during the recession. Among them: insurance, aerospace and defense. This may keep recovery slower than hoped.

WHAT'S NEXT

▶ **After a bleak few years, the New York metropolitan area should be coming back.**

To a great degree, it is Wall Street that has spearheaded the region's improvement. Wall Street was the focal point of some of the first problems in the area—and it has also been one of the first industries to improve.

First, a quick rehash of how badly the region was hit by the recession: In the course of three years, New York lost more than 500,000 jobs. Among the industries that suffered the most were financial services, apparel manufacturing, retailing, banking, restaurants, advertising, and other communications industries. On the whole, the bulk of New York industries were battered.

With the national economy improving, however, the area should pull out of the slump slowly. The key to continued improvement in the region is the performance of communications and financial services industries, including insurance and real estate. One problem: over the short term, job growth is expected to stay relatively slow, as companies remain as streamlined as possible. With so much of the economy revolving around these fields, their health is vital.

New York has a great many strong points that should help keep it from falling back into a downslide. One of the most important, specially in the long term, is the city's ties to the international community. New York still draws a large number of international real estate investors. While the rapid pace of acquisition has declined, Japanese and other foreign investors are still snapping up New York office buildings. International companies are more inclined to set up shop in New York than in lesser-known, less cosmopolitan areas. In addition, about half of the U.S. exports in service come from New York.

But even with the recovery, one disturbing question remains: New York's position as an international business center depends on large U.S. businesses that have headquarters here. Will they stay in New York or will they opt for the lower taxes and better climates of the Sunbelt or other regions, as so many others have? To a great degree, the long-term health of New York rests on the answer to this question.

▶ New Jersey, Pennsylvania, Upstate New York—Mixed.

New Jersey, like New York City, was severely affected by the recession. The state lost 245,000 jobs between 1988 and 1991. The chief problem? A sharp decline in manufacturing jobs. But New Jersey does have one bright spot: biotechnology. An increasing number of biotech firms are settling in the state, making New Jersey number two in the nation in biotech, with 193 biotech companies as of 1992. This number should increase. Also providing growing employment opportunities: pharmaceutical and other health-product firms, such as Merck, Ortho Pharmaceutical, and Johnson & Johnson. A recent development: Sandoz Pharmaceuticals opened a research center in March 1992, which is expected to house more than 1,400 employees by the mid-1990s.

Pennsylvania will also be experiencing job growth due to its pharmaceutical industry. Upturns in both the foreign and domestic demand for steel, fabricated metals, machinery and chemicals, will also point to good prospects. All in all, the state is poised for stable growth and increasing job opportunities in the long term, especially as the national economy improves.

Upstate New York: Hopes are pinned on the newly created "Ceramics Corridor"—an area centering around Corning, NY, devoted to high-tech work in ceramics and electronics packaging, among other things. Formed through teamwork between Corning, IBM and three universities, the area is attracting attention and companies. Recently, 110 companies (including Corning, Westinghouse and Toshiba, as well as many small start-ups) have located here, bringing 31,500 jobs to the area. Also looking relatively promising: the Buffalo area, where an upsurge in manufacturing is expected to bring job gains of 3,000 to 5,000 over the next few years.

▶ New England—Should rebound after being hammered by recession.

In spite of a run of bad years, New England has a number of strengths, and these are helping it on the road to recovery. Among them: increasing numbers of software, communications and other high tech companies, and growing biotechnology and environmental industries—lured by low office prices, a skilled work force, venture capital ties, and the presence of top-notch universities.

More specifically: Vermont is seeing an upswing in tourism. In addition, in a trend similar to that affecting western New York, several Canadian companies have moved to the state, lured by lower taxes and labor costs. *Massachusetts* was hit early by the recession and, in some areas, took longer to emerge from the downslide. The state is improving now, however, and appears poised for further growth. Areas that are beginning to heat up once again: banking, brokerage, and other financial services plus biotech and high-tech R & D. Repair of aging infrastructure is also creating jobs—for example, a Boston project to bury an elevated highway is bringing in 20,000 new jobs. *New Hampshire* will see growth in tourism as well. Looking weakest? *Connecticut,* which will still be feeling the pinch from defense cutbacks and the real estate slump.

► **Washington, D.C., Maryland, and the Virginia suburbs: Still facing challenges brought about by recession and government budget cuts.**

The three largest problems for this area: defense budget cuts, a weak real estate market, and the poor performance of the financial services area. In the long term, however, the outlook is much brighter.

The main reason for this is the large number of government jobs, which bring an unusual degree of stability to the economy. In addition, the six regional universities, and the large number of associations, lobbying organizations, and consulting groups in the area, promise further growth. Maryland's Prince George County is growing into a regional commercial center. Throughout, the large number of relatively high-paying white-collar jobs promises a strong service and retail sector in the long term, although some experts still predict a slight shakeout in the next few years.

REGIONAL HOT SPOTS

PITTSBURGH, PA: Home to more than just big steel, Pittsburgh benefits from a number of large companies—including Bayer USA, Rockwell International, and Westinghouse—and a number of small, dynamic firms as well. This, plus strong cultural offerings and a pleasant life-style, make the area a good choice for the future.

SYRACUSE, NY: This was one of the few places in New York State to weather the recession with relatively little trouble. A key factor was its diversified economy. Another plus: Syracuse is well known for its excellent public school system.

CORNING, NY: As mentioned previously, this area—dubbed the Ceramics Corridor—should heat up with the influx of new ceramic companies. Another plus: housing costs remain relatively reasonable.

CONNECTICUT

LEADING CONNECTICUT EMPLOYERS

Aetna Life & Casualty Co.
151 Farmington Ave.
Hartford, CT 06156
203/273-0123
(Insurance: life, group, accident, and health, pensions, casualty and property.)

Ames Department Stores, Inc.
2418 Main St.
Rocky Hill, CT 06067
203/563-8234
(Discount department stores.)

Boehringer Ingleheim Corp.
90 East Ridge Rd.
Ridgefield, CT 06877
203/438-0311
(Pharmaceuticals.)

Caldor Corp.
20 Glover Ave.
Norwalk, CT 06856
203/849-2000
(Discount department stores.)

Champion International Corp.
1 Champion Plz.
Stamford, CT 06921
203/358-7000
(Paper mills.)

Connecticut General Life Insurance Corp.
900 Cottage Grove Rd.
Bloomfield, CT 06002
203/726-6000
(Insurance: life, accident, and health.)

Connecticut Light & Power Co.
P.O. Box 2010
Hartford, CT 06101
203/665-5000
(Utility company.)

Connecticut Mutual Life Insurance Co.
140 Garden St.
Hartford, CT 06154
203/987-6500
(Life insurance.)

Connecticut National Bank
(subs. of Shawmut National Corp.)
777 Main St.
Hartford, CT 06115
203/728-2000
(Banking.)

The Dexter Corporation
1 Elm St.
Windsor Locks, CT 06096
203/627-9051
(Chemicals.)

Echlin
100 Double Beach Rd.
Bramford, CT 06405
203/481-5751
(Automotive parts & equipment.)

GTE Corp
1 Stamford Forum
Stamford, CT 06904
203/965-2000
(Telephone operating;
telecommunications equipment and
services.)

General Datacomm Industries, Inc.
1579 Straits Tpke.
Middlebury, CT 06762
203/574-1118
(Data communication network and
subsystems.)

General Electric Capital Corp.
260 Long Ridge Rd.
Stamford, CT 06927
203/357-4000
(Credit institution.)

General Electric Co.
3135 Easton Tpke.
Fairfield, CT 06431
203/373-2211
(Conglomerate—aircraft engines,
broadcasting, electronics, appliances,
communications, etc.)

Gerber Scientific, Inc.
83 Gerber Rd. W.
South Windsor, CT 06074
203/644-1551
(Computer services and software.)

Hamilton Standard Company
(subs. of United Technologies)
1 Hamilton Rd.
Windsor Locks, CT 06096
203/654-6000
(Aerospace products.)

Hartford Fire Insurance Co.
(subs. of ITT Corp.)
Hartford Plz.
Hartford, CT 06155
203/547-5000
(Insurance.)

Hartford Life Insurance Co., Inc.
Hartford Plz.
Hartford, CT 06115
203/547-5000
(Insurance.)

Hubbell Incorporated
584 Derby-Milford Rd.
Orange, CT 06477
203/799-4100
(Electrical wiring devices, etc.)

Kaman Corp.
Blue Hills Ave.
Bloomfield, CT 06002
203/243-8311
(Aircraft parts, bearings, drive shafts.)

Loctite Corp.
Ten Columbus Blvd.
Hartford, CT 06106
203/520-5000
(Chemicals.)

Norden Systems, Inc.
Norden Pl.
P.O. Box 5300
Norwalk, CT 06856
203/852-5000
(Aeronautical systems and
instruments.)

Northeast Bancorp
Church and Elm St.
New Haven, CT 06510
203/929-5552
(Banking.)

Northeast Utilities
P.O. Box 270
Hartford, CT 06101
203/666-6911
(Utility.)

Olin Corp
120 Long Ridge Rd.
Stamford, CT 06904-1355
203/356-2000
(Chemicals.)

Otis Elevator Company
(subs. of United Technologies)
10 Farm Springs Rd.
Farmington CT 06032
203/674-4000
(Elevators, escalators, etc.)

People's Bank
850 Main St.
Bridgeport, CT 06604
203/338-7171
(Banking.)

Pepperidge Farm, Inc.
595 Westport Ave.
Norwalk, CT 06851

203/846-7000
(Food processing.)

Perkin-Elmer Corp.
761 Main Ave.
Norwalk, CT 06859
203/762-1000
(Scientific instruments.)

Phoenix Mutual Life Insurance Co.
1 American Row
Hartford, CT 06115
203/275-5000
(Insurance.)

Pitney Bowes, Inc.
World Headquarters
Stamford, CT 06926
203/356-5000
(Office machines.)

Pratt & Whitney Group
(subs. of United Technologies)
400 Main St.
East Hartford, CT 06108
203/565-4321
(Aircraft, marine, and industrial
engines.)

Remington Products, Inc.
60 Main St.
Bridgeport, CT 06602
203/367-4400
(Personal electric products.)

Savin Corp.
9 W. Broad St.
Box 10270
Stamford, CT 06904
203/967-5000
(Copiers, fax machines.)

Shawmut National Corp.
777 Main St.
Hartford, CT 06115
203/728-2000
(Banking.)

**Southern New England
Telecommunications**
227 Church St.
New Haven, CT 06506

203/771-5200
(Independent telephone company.)

Sprague Technologies, Inc.
4 Stamford Forum
Stamford CT 06903
203/964-8600
(Capacitators, resistors, networks, etc.)

Standard Fire Insurance Co.
(subs. of Aetna Life & Casualty Co.)
151 Farmington Ave.
Hartford, CT 06156
203/273-0123
(Insurance.)

Stanley Works, Inc.
1000 Stanley Dr.
New Britain, CT 06053
203/225-5111
(Hand tools, home hardware, garden products, etc.)

Tilling Thomas, Inc.
1000 1 Main Pl.
Stamford, CT 06902
203/324-3600
(General contractor, highway/street construction, etc.)

Torrington Co.
59 Field St.
Torrington, CT 06790
203/482-9511
(Ball and roller bearings; machine tool accessories.)

The Travelers Corp.
1 Tower Sq.
Hartford, CT 06183
203/277-0111

(Insurance.)
(subs. at the same address include: Travelers Indemnity Co. and Travelers Insurance Co.)

Union Carbide Corp.
39 Old Ridgebury Rd.
Danbury, CT 06817-0001
203/794-2000
(Chemicals, plastics, etc.)

United States Surgical Corp.
150 Glover Ave.
Norwalk, CT 06850
203/866-5050
(Surgical and medical instruments and apparatus.)

United Technologies Corp.
1 Financial Plz.
Hartford, CT 06101
203/728-7000
(Aircraft engines, electrical and electronic parts, systems, etc.)

Waldenbook Co., Inc.
201 High Ridge Rd.
Stamford, CT 06905
203/358-2000
(Chain bookstores.)

Xerox Corp.
Long Ridge Rd.
Box 1600
Stamford, CT 06904
203/968-3000
(Office machinery, copiers, computers, other electronic equipment.)

CONNECTICUT BUSINESS PERIODICALS

Business Digest of Greater Waterbury
Four Stars Publishing Co., Inc.
182 Grand St.
Waterbury, CT 06702
203/754-9922
(Mont   hly.)

New Haven Business Digest
Vought Communications, Inc.
1160 Oldfield Rd.
Fairfield, CT 06430-6314

CONNECTICUT DIRECTORIES

Connecticut Business Directory
American Business Directories
5711 S. 86th Cir.
P.O. Box 27347
Omaha, NE 68127
402/593-4600

Connecticut, Rhode Island Directory of Manufacturers
Commerce Register Inc.
190 Godwin Ave.
Midland Park, NJ 07432
201/445-3000

Connecticut Service Directory
George D. Hall Co.
50 Congress St.

Boston, MA 02109
617/523-3745

Directory of Connecticut Manufacturers
George D. Hall Co.
50 Congress St.
Boston, MA 02109
617/523-3745

MacRAE's State Industrial Directory—Connecticut–Rhode Island
MacRAE's Blue Book, Inc.
817 Broadway
New York, NY 10003
212/673-4700
800/MAC-RAES

CONNECTICUT GOVERNMENT EMPLOYMENT OFFICES

Office of Personnel Management
Federal Bldg., Rm. 613
450 Main St.
Hartford, CT 06103
203/240-3263
(Federal job-information center.)

Job Service
Connecticut Labor Dept.
200 Folly Brook Blvd.
Wethersfield, CT 06109

203/566-8818
(State job-service center; lists local state job offices.)

State Recruitment and Testing Center
1 Hartford Sq. W.,
Suite 101A
Hartford, CT 06106
203/566-2501

DELAWARE

LEADING DELAWARE EMPLOYERS

Cigna Holdings, Inc.
1 Beaver Valley Rd.
Wilmington, DE 19850
302/479-6800
(Financial holding company.)

Citicorp Banking Corp.
1 Perins Way
New Castle, DE 19720
302/323-3142
(Mortgage banking.)

Columbia Gas System, Inc.
20 Montchanin Rd.
Wilmington, DE 19807
302/429-5000
(Natural gas distribution.)

E. I. Du Pont De Nemours & Co.
1007 Market St.
Wilmington, DE 19898
302/774-1000
(Chemicals, environmental services,
petroleum products, etc.)

Du Pont-Merck Pharmaceuticals
Barley Mill Plz.
Wilmington, DE 19880
301/992-5000
(Pharmaceuticals.)

W. L. Gore and Associates
555 Paper Mill Rd.
Newark, DE 19711
302/738-4880
(Wire and cable, medical devices,
fixtures, laminated fabric, etc.)

Hercules, Incorporated.
Hercules Plz.
1313 N. Market St.
Wilmington, DE 19894
302/594-5000
(Electronic systems, propulsion
systems, etc.)

Himont, Inc.
2801 Centerville Rd.
Wilmington, DE 19850
302/996-6000
(Resins, compounds, and alloys.)

Holman Lend Lease Corp.
240 S. DuPont Hwy.
New Castle, DE 19720
302/322-3381
(Passenger car leasing.)

ICI Americas, Inc.
New Murphy Rd. and Concord Pike
Wilmington, DE 19897
302/886-3000
(Chemicals.)

MBNA America, Inc.
400 Christiana Rd.
Newark, DE 19713
302/453-9930
(Credit card services; collection;
commercial banks.)

Matlack, Inc.
1 Rollins Plz.
Wilmington, DE 19899
302/479-2700
(Trucking.)

Rollins Environmental Services
1 Rollins Plz.
Wilmington, DE 19803
302/479-2700
(Refuse systems, waste management.)

Rollins Truck Leasing Corp.
1 Rollins Plz.
Wilmington, DE 19899
302/773-5291
(Truck leasing.)

Star Building Services, Inc.
34 Blevins Dr.
Wilmington, DE 19850
302/324-1600
(Building cleaning and maintenance
services.)

Star States Corp.
838 Market St.
Wilmington, DE 19801
302/571-7000
(Bank holding company; passenger car
leasing; trailer rental.)

Townsend Farms, Inc.
Rte. 24
P.O. Box 468
Millsboro, DE 19966
302/934-9221
(Chickens.)

DELAWARE DIRECTORIES

Delaware Business Directory
American Business Directories
5711 S. 86th Cir.
P.O. Box 27347
Omaha, NE 68127
402/593-4600

Delaware Directory of Commerce & Industry
Manufacturers' News, Inc.
1633 Central St.
Evanston, IL 60201
708/864-7000

The Delaware Valley Corporate Guide
Corfacts Inc.
50 Route 9 N.
Morganville, NJ 07751
201/972-2500

Directory of Central Atlantic States Manufacturers
George D. Hall Company
50 Congress St.
Boston, MA 02109
617/523-3745
(Includes Maryland, Delaware, Virginia, West Virginia, North Carolina, and South Carolina.)

MacRAE's State Industrial Directory—Maryland/DC/Delaware
MacRAE's Blue Book, Inc.
817 Broadway
New York, NY 10003
212/673-4700
800/MAC-RAES

DELAWARE GOVERNMENT EMPLOYMENT OFFICES

Office of Personnel Management
(Federal job-service center—see Philadelphia, PA listing.)

Employment and Training Division
Delaware Department of Labor
P.O. Box 9029
Newark, DE 19711
302/368-6911
(State job-service center.)

WASHINGTON, DC

LEADING WASHINGTON, DC EMPLOYERS

Associated Press.
1825 K St., NW
Washington, DC 20006-1253
202/955-7200
(Media company; newswire, broadcast services, etc.)

The Bureau of National Affairs, Inc.
1231 25th St., NW
Washington, DC 20037
202/452-4200
(Direct mail advertising services, software, periodicals, etc.)

Chesapeake & Potomac Telephone Co.
2055 L St., NW
Washington, DC 20036
202/392-9900
(Telephone services.)

Communications Satellite Corp.
950 L'Enfant Plaza, SW
Washington, DC 20024
202/863-6000
(Communications, telecommunications.)

Danaher
1250 24th St., NW
Washington, DC 20037
202/828-0850
(Tools.)

The Donohoe Companies, Inc.
2101 Wisconsin Ave., NW
Washington, DC 20007
202/333-0880
(Real estate developer and contractor.)

Federal National Mortgage Association
3900 Wisconsin Ave., NW
Washington, DC 20016
202/752-7000
(Secondary mortgage market.)

First American Bankshares, Inc.
15th and H Sts., NW
Washington, DC 20005
202/383-1400
(Banking.)

GEICO Corp.
GEICO Plz.
Washington, DC 20076
301/986-3000
(Insurance.)

Harman International Industries, Inc.
1155 Connecticut Ave., NW
Washington, DC 20036
202/955-6130
(Consumer electronics.)

Hay Group, Inc.
1500 K St., NW
Washington, DC 20005
202/637-6600
(Management services.)

Host International, Inc.
1 Marriott Dr.
Washington, DC 20058
202/380-3677
(Food service.)

International Monetary Fund
19th and H Sts., NW
Washington, DC 20431
202/623-7000
(Federal and federally sponsored credit agencies.)

International Telecommunications Satellite Organization
3400 International Dr., NW
Washington, DC 20008
202/944-7800
(Communications services.)

The Kiplinger Washington Editors, Inc.
1729 H St., NW
Washington, DC 20006
202/887-6400
(Magazine and newsletter publishing.)

MCI Communications Corp.
1801 Pennsylvania Ave., NW
Washington, DC 20006
202/872-1600
(Telecommunications.)

Marriott Corp.
Marriott Dr.
Washington, DC 20058
202/897-9000
(Hotels.)

NHP Inc.
1225 I St., NW
Washington, DC 20005
202/347-6247
(Real estate agents, managers, developers, etc.)

National Geographic Society
1145 17th St., NW
Washington, DC 20036
202/857-7000
(Magazine, book publishing.)

National Public Radio
2025 M St., NW
Washington, DC 20036
202/822-2000
(Public radio broadcasting.)

National Railroad Passenger Corp.
(dba Amtrak)
400 N. Capitol St., NW
Washington, DC 20001
202/383-3000
(Railroads—terminals and operation.)

National Science Foundation
1800 G St., NW
Washington, DC 20550
202/357-7757
(Scientific research agency.)

Potomac Electric Power Co.
1900 Pennsylvania Ave., NW
Washington, DC 20068
202/872-2000
(Electric utility.)

Student Loan Marketing Association
1050 Thomas Jefferson St., NW
Washington, DC 20007
202/298-3075

(Guarantees student loans traded on
secondary market.)

Syscon Corp.
1000 Thomas Jefferson St., NW
Washington, DC 20007
202/342-4000
(Computer programming services.)

United Press International
1400 I St., NW
Washington, DC 20005
202/898-8000
(Media company–newswire, radio
network, broadcast services.)

Washington Gas Light Co.
1100 H St., NW
Washington, DC 20080
202/750-1500
(Natural gas utility.)

Washington Post Company
1150 15th St., NW
Washington, DC 20071
202/334-6000
(Newspaper and magazine publishing,
communications.)

**Woodward & Lothrop, Inc./John
Wanamaker**
1025 F St., NW
Washington, DC 20013
202/879-8000
(Department store.)

WASHINGTON, DC BUSINESS PERIODICALS

Regardie's Business Washington
1010 Wisconsin Ave., NW
Washington, DC 20007
202/342-0410
(Bimonthly.)

WASHINGTON, DC DIRECTORIES

*Dalton's Baltimore-Washington
Metropolitan Directory*
Dalton's Directory
410 Lancaster Ave.

Haverford, PA 19041
800/221-1050
215/649-2680

MacRAE's State Industrial Directory—Maryland/DC/Delaware
MacRAE's Blue Book, Inc.
817 Broadway
New York, NY 10003
212/673-4700
800/MAC-RAES

Washington, DC, Business Directory
American Business Directories
5711 S. 86th Cir.
P.O. Box 27347
Omaha, NE 68127
402/593-4600

WASHINGTON, DC GOVERNMENT EMPLOYMENT OFFICES

Office of Personnel Management
1900 E St., NW, Room 1416
Washington, DC 20415
202/653-8468
(Federal job-service center.)

Office of Job Service
Dept. of Employment Services
500 C St., NW, Room 317
Washington, DC 20001
202/639-115

MAINE

LEADING MAINE EMPLOYERS

ABB Environmental Services
261 Commercial St.
Portland, ME 04101
207/775-5401
(Environmental services.)

Bath Iron Works Corp.
700 Washington St.
Bath, ME 04530
207/443-3311
(Ship building and repairing.)

L. L. Bean, Inc.
Freeport, ME 04033
207/865-4761
(Sporting goods/clothing retailer and mail order house.)

Central Maine Morning Sentinel
25 Silver St.
Waterville, ME 04901207/873-3341
(Newspaper.)

Central Maine Power Co.
Edison Dr.
Augusta, ME 04336

207/623-3521
(Electric utility.)

Cianbro Corp.
Hunnewell Sq.
P.O. Box 1000
Pittsfield, ME 04967
207/487-3311
(Heavy construction.)

Dexter Shoe Co.
Railroad Ave.
Dexter, ME 04930
207/924-7341
(Shoes.)

Eastern Fine Paper, Inc.
P.O. Box 129
Brewer, ME 04412
207/989-7070
(Coated and printing paper.)

Emery-Waterhouse Co., Inc.
Rand Rd.
P.O. Box 659
Portland, ME 04104
207/775-2371
(Wholesale hardware.)

Forster Manufacturing Co., Inc.
Depot St.
Box 657
Wilton, ME 04294
207/645-2574
(Wood products—clothespins, rolling pins, etc.)

Fraser Paper Ltd.
Bridge St.
P.O. Box 160
Madawaska, ME 04756
207/728/3321
(Specialty papers.)

Hannaford Brothers
145 Pleasant Hill Rd.
Scarborough, ME 04074
207/883-2911
(Grocery stores.)

Key Bancshares of Maine, Inc.
286 Water St.
Augusta, ME 04330
207/623-5673
(Banking.)

Lincoln Pulp & Paper Co., Inc.
Katahdin Ave.
Lincoln, ME 04457 207/794-6721
(Tissue paper, pulp mills.)

Madison Paper Industries
Main St.
P.O. Box 129
Madison, ME 04950
207/696-3307
(Paper mills.)

McCain Foods, Inc.
Station Rd.
Easton, ME 04740
207/488-2561
(Potato products, vegetables, etc.)

Prime Tanning Co.
Sullivan St.
Berwick, ME 03901
207/698-1100
(Leather tanneries.)

Shape, Inc.
Biddeford Industrial Pk.
Biddeford, ME 04005
207/282-6155
(Audio- and videotapes.)

UNUM Life Insurance Co.
2211 Congress St.
Portland, ME 04122
207/770-2211
(Insurance.)

Webber Oil Co.
700 Main St.
Bangor, ME 04401
207/942-5501
(Fuel oil and petroleum product dealers.)

MAINE BUSINESS PERIODICAL

Maine Enterprise
60 Elm St.
Portland, ME 04104
207/761-0999
(Monthly.)

MAINE DIRECTORIES

Maine Business Directory
American Business Directories
5711 S. 86th Cir.
P.O. Box 27347
Omaha, NE 68127
402/593-4600

*MacRAE's State
Directories—Maine/New
Hampshire/Vermont*
MacRAE's Blue Book, Inc.
817 Broadway
New York, NY 10003
212/673-4700
800/MAC-RAES

*Maine, Vermont, New Hampshire
Directory of Manufacturers*
Commerce Register, Inc.
190 Godwin Ave.
Midland Park, NJ 07432
201/445-3000

MAINE GOVERNMENT EMPLOYMENT OFFICES

Office of Personnel Management
(Federal job-service center—see New
Hampshire listing.)

Job Service Division
Bureau of Employment Security
P.O. Box 309
Augusta, ME 04330
207/289-3431
(State job-service center.)

MARYLAND

LEADING MARYLAND EMPLOYERS

AAI Corp.
P.O. Box 126
Hunt Valley, MD 21030
410/666-1400
(Aerospace systems and instruments.)

ARC Professional Services Group
(div. of Atlantic Research
Corp.—Aerospace Group)
1375 Piccard Dr.
Rockville, MD 20850
301/670-2000
(Engineering and support for
aerospace systems, etc.)

Arinc Research Corp.
2551 Riva Rd.
Annapolis, MD 21401
410/266-4000
(Engineering and
telecommunications.)

Avis Car Leasing
307 International Circle
Hunt Valley, MD 21030
410/527-3200
(Car rentals and leasing.)

Baltimore Bancrop
P.O. Box 896
Baltimore, MD 21203
410/244-3360
(Banking.)

Baltimore Gas & Electric Co.
Gas & Electric Bldg.
P.O. Box 1475
Baltimore, MD 21203
410/234-5000
(Electric and gas utility.)

Bendix Field Engineering Corp.
(div. of Allied-Signal Aerospace Co.)
1 Bendix Rd.
Columbia, MD 21045
410/964-7000

(Integrated management and field engineering services.)

Black & Decker Corp.
701 E. Joppa Rd.
Baltimore, MD 21286
410/716-3900
(Power tools, accessories, outdoor and household products.)

CSX Transportation, Inc.
100 N. Charles St.
Baltimore, MD 21201
410/237-2000
(Railroad—line haul operating.)

Chesapeake & Potomac Telephone of Maryland
(subs. of Bell Atlantic)
1 E. Pratt St.
Baltimore, MD 21202
410/539-9900

Citizens Bank of Maryland
14401 Sweitzer Ln.
Laurel, MD 20707
301/206-6080
(Banking.)

Commercial Credit Co.
300 St. Paul Pl.
Baltimore, MD 21202
410/332-3000
(Consumer finance, financial services, business insurance.)

Computer Data Systems, Inc.
1 Curie Ct.
Rockville, MD 20850
301/921-7000
(Computer intergrated systems design.)

Equitable Bancorp
100 S. Charles St.
Baltimore, MD 21201
410/547-4000
(Banking—Equitable Bank NA.)

Fairchild Space & Defense Corp.
20301 Century Blvd.
Germantown, MD 20874
301/428-6000
(Spacecraft and aerospace electronics.)

Fidelity & Deposit Co. of Maryland
P.O. Box 1227
Baltimore, MD 21203
410/539-0800
(Banking.)

First Maryland Bancorp
25 Charles St.
Baltimore, MD 21201
410/244-4000
(Banking—First National Bank of Maryland.)

General Electric Information Services
401 N. Washington St.
Rockville, MD 20850
301/340-4000
(Computer services.)

Hechinger Co.
3500 Pennsy Dr.
Landover, MD 20785
301/341-1000
(Retail hardware and lumber stores.)

Legg Mason, Inc.
111 S. Calvert St.
Baltimore, MD 21203
410/244-4000
(Brokerage, investment banking, investment and real estate adviser.)

Legg Mason Wood Walker, Inc.
111 S. Calvert St.
Baltimore, MD 21203
410/539-3400
(Security brokers and dealers.)

Londontown Corp.
1332 Londontown Blvd.
Eldersburg, MD 21784
410/795-5900
(Rainwear.)

Manor Care, Inc.
10750 Columbia Pike
Silver Spring, MD 20901
301/681-9400
(Healthcare and lodging—retirement
communities.)

Martin Marietta Corp.
6801 Rockledge Dr.
Bethesda, MD 20817
301/897-6000
(Aerospace; electronics; information
systems and materials.)

Maryland National Bank
10 Light St.
Baltimore, MD 21201
410/244-5000
(Banking.)

McCormick & Co., Inc.
18 Loveton Circle
Sparks, MD 21152
410/771-7301
(Spices, flavorings, extracts, etc.)

Mercantile Bancshares Corp.
2 Hopkins Plz.
Baltimore, MD 21201
410/237-5900
(Banking.)

Miller & Long Co., Inc.
4824 Rugby Ave.
Bethesda, MD 20814
301/657-8000
(Construction—concrete work.)

Noxell Corp.
11050 York Rd.
Hunt Valley, MD 21030
410/785-7800
(Cosmetics, personal and household
products, specialty foods.)

Perdue Farms
P.O. Box 1537
Salisbury, MD 21802
410/543-3000
(Poultry processing.)

PHH Corp.
11333 McCormick Rd.
Hunt Valley, MD 21031
410/771-1900
(Integrated management services and
cost-control programs.)

PHH
11333 McCormick
Hunt Valley, MD 21030
410/771-3600
(Management services.)

Premier Management Group, Inc.
5247 Reisterstown Rd.
Baltimore, MD 21215
410/367-3300
(Real estate management.)

Preston Trucking Co., Inc.
151 Easton Blvd.
Preston, MD 21655
410/673-7151
(Motor carrier.)

Rouse Co.
10275 Little Patuxent Pkwy.
Columbia, MD 21044
410/992-6000
(Real estate
developer/owner/operation.)

The Ryland Group, Inc.
10221 Wisconsin Cir.
Columbia, MD 21044
410/715-7000
(Home construction, mortgages.)

SCM Chemicals Inc.
7 St. Paul St.,
Suite 1010
Baltimore, MD 21202
410/783-1120
(Chemicals.)

USF&G Corp.
100 Light St.
Baltimore, MD 21202
410/547-3000
(Insurance, financial services.)

Vitro Corp.
14000 Georgia Ave.
Silver Spring, MD 20906
301/231-2403
(Computer integrated system design.)

Westinghouse Electronic Systems
Box 1693
Baltimore-Washington International
Airport, MD 21203
410/765-1000

(Electronic systems; maintenance and
service.)

Whiting-Turner Contracting Co.
300 E. Joppa Rd.
Towson, MD 21204
410/821-1100
(General contracting, construction
management.)

MARYLAND BUSINESS PERIODICALS

Baltimore Business Journal
117 Water St.
Baltimore, MD 21202
410/576-1161

Warfield's Baltimore
11 E. Saratoga St.
Baltimore, MD 21202
410/528-0600
(Monthly.)

MARYLAND DIRECTORIES

Dalton's Baltimore-Washington
Metropolitan Directory
Dalton's Directory
410 Lancaster Ave.
Haverford, PA 19041
800/221-1050
215/649-2680

Directory of Central Atlantic States
Manufacturers
George D. Hall Company
540 Congress St.
Boston, MA 02109
617/523-3745
(Includes Maryland, Delaware,
Virginia, West Virginia, North
Carolina, and South Carolina.)

Harris Directory of Maryland
Manufacturers
Harris Publishing Company
2057 Aurora Rd.
Twinsburg, OH 44087
216/425-5900
800/888-5900

MacRAE's State
Directories—Maryland/DC/Delaware
MacRAE's Blue Book, Inc.
817 Broadway
New York, NY 10003
212/673-4700
800/MAC-RAES

Maryland Business Directory
American Business Directories
5711 S. 86th Cir.
P.O. Box 27347
Omaha, NE 68127
402/593-4600

MARYLAND GOVERNMENT EMPLOYMENT OFFICES

Office of Personnel Management
Garmatz Federal Bldg.
101 W. Lombard St.
Baltimore, MD 21201
410/962-3822
(Federal job-service center.)

Maryland Dept. of Employment and Economic Development
1100 N. Eutaw St., Room 701
Baltimore, MD 21201
410/383-5353
(State job-service center.)

MASSACHUSETTS

LEADING MASSACHUSETTS COMPANIES

Addison-Wesley Publishing Co.
South St.
Reading, MA 01867
617/944-3700
(Book publishing.)

Affiliated Publications, Inc.
135 Morrissey Blvd.
Boston, MA 02107
617/929-3300
(Newspaper publishing.)

Americare Health Services, Inc.
264 Monsignor O'Brien Hwy.
Cambridge, MA 02141
617/628-5300
(Health services.)

Analog Devices, Inc.
1 Technology Way
Norwood, MA 02062
617/329-4700
(High-tech products.)

Bank of Boston Corp.
100 Federal St.
Boston, MA 02110
617/434-2200
(Banking.)

Bank of New England Corp.
28 State St.
Boston, MA 02109
617/742-4000
(Banking.)

Baybanks, Inc.
175 Federal St.
Boston, MA 02110
617/482-1040
(Banking.)

Baystate Financial Services
100 N. Washington St.
Boston, MA 02114
617/638-2222
(Life insurance.)

Blue Cross & Blue Shield of Massachusetts
100 Summer St.
Boston, MA 02110
617/956-9700
(Health insurance.)

Bolt, Beranek & Newman, Inc.
10 Fawcett St.
Cambridge, MA 02238
617/873-2000
(Private wide area networks, software, etc.)

Bose Corp.
The Mountain
Framingham, MA 01701
508/879-7330
(Consumer audio equipment.)

The Boston Co., Inc.
1 Boston Pl.
Boston, MA 02108
617/722-7000
(Banking.)

Boston Edison Co.
800 Boylston St.
Boston, MA 02199
617/424-2000
(Electric utility.)

Boston Safe Deposit Trust Co.
1 Boston Pl.
Boston, MA 02106
617/722-7000
(Banking.)

Bradlee's New England, Inc.
1 Bradlee Cir.
Braintree, MA 02184
617/380-8000
(Discount department stores.)

Bull H N Information Systems
Technology Pk.
Billerica, MA 01821
508/294-6000
(Mainframes, personal computers.)

Cabot Corp.
75 State St.
Boston, MA 02109
617/345-0100
(Chemicals.)

Commercial Union Insurance Co.
1 Beacon St.
Boston, MA 02108
617/725-6000
(Insurance.)

Data General Corp.
4400 Computer Dr.
Westboro, MA 01580
508/366-8911
(Minicomputers.)

Dennison Manufacturing Co.
300 Howard St.
Framingham, MA 01701
508/879-0511
(Office supplies.)

Digital Equipment Corp.
146 Main St.
Maynard, MA 01754
508/493-5111
(Computers.)

EG&G, Inc.
45 William St
Wellesley, MA 02181
617/237-5100
(Engineering and construction sources.)

Federal Reserve Bank of Boston
600 Atlantic Ave.
Boston, MA 02110
617/973-3000
(Federal Reserve bank.)

Fidelity Congress Street Fund
82 Devonshire St.
Boston, MA 02109
617/570-7000
(Investments.)

Filene's
(div. of The May Department Stores Company)
426 Washington St.
Boston, MA 02101
617/357-2100
(Department store.)

First National Bank
100 Federal St.
Boston, MA 02110
617/434-2200
(Banking.)

The Foxboro Company
33 Commercial St.
Foxboro, MA 02035
508/543-8750
(Indicating, controlling and recording instruments, and control systems.)

Friendly Ice Cream Corp.
1855 Boston Rd.
Wilbraham, MA 01095
413/543-2400
(Restaurants.)

GenRad, Inc.
300 Baker Ave.
Concord, MA 01742
617/369-4400
(Electrical measuring instruments,
electronics.)

Gillette Co.
Prudential Tower Bldg.
Boston, MA 02199
617/421-7000
(Personal electronic products.)

GTE Government Systems Corp.
100 First Ave.
Waltham, MA 02254
617/890-9200
(Control, communication, command,
and intelligence systems.)

Hills Department Stores, Inc.
15 Dan Rd.
Canton, MA 02021
617/821-1000
(Department stores.)

H. P. Hood, Inc.
(subs. of Agway)
500 Rutherford Ave.
Boston, MA 02129
617/242-0600
(Food processing, dairy foods, citrus,
etc.)

Houghton Mifflin Co.
1 Beacon St.
Boston, MA 02108
617/725-5000
(Book publishing.)

**John Hancock Mutual Life
Insurance Co.**
John Hancock Plz.
Boston, MA 02117
617/572-6000
(Life insurance.)

Jordan Marsh Stores Corp.
450 Washington St.
Boston, MA 02107
617/357-3000
(Department stores.)

LTX Corp.
LTX Park at University Ave.
Westwood, MA 02090
617/461-1000
(Measuring instruments.)

Lechmere, Inc.
275 Wildwood St.
Woburn, MA 01801
617/935-8320
(Consumer electronics store.)

Liberty Mutual Insurance Co.
175 Berkeley St.
Boston, MA 02117
617/357-9500
(Insurance.)

Lotus Development Corp.
55 Cambridge Pkwy.
Cambridge, MA 02142
617/577-8500
(Computer software.)

**Massachusetts Mutual Life
Insurance Co.**
1295 State St.
Springfield, MA 01111
413/788-8411
(Insurance.)

Millipore Corp.
80 Ashby Rd.
Bedford, MA 01730
617/275-9200
(Electronic instruments and
measurement.)

Mitre Corp.
Burlington Rd.
P.O. Box 208
Bedford, MA 01730
617/271-2000
(Commercial physical and biological
research, systems engineering.)

NEC Technologies, Inc.
1414 Massachusetts Ave.
Foxboro, MA 01719
508/264-8000
(Computers, peripherals, etc.)

New England Electric System
25 Research Dr.
Westboro, MA 01582
508/366-9011
(Utility.)

New England Power Service Co.
25 Research Dr.
Westboro, MA 01582
508/366-9011
(Utility.)

**New England Telephone &
Telegraph Co.**
185 Franklin St.
Boston, MA 02107
617/743-9800
(Telephone services.)

Norton Co.
1 New Bond St.
Worcester, MA 01606
508/795-5000
(Abrasive products.)

Nynex Information Resources Co.
35 Village Rd.
Middletown, MA 01949
508/762-1000
(Directory publishing.)

Ocean Spray Cranberries, Inc.
1 Ocean Spray Dr.
Lakeville–Middleboro, MA 02349
508/946-1000
(Cranberry beverages and foods.)

Polaroid Corp.
549 Technology Sq.
Cambridge, MA 02139
617/577-2000
(Photographic equipment and
supplies.)

Raytheon Co.
141 Spring St.
Lexington, MA 02173
617/862-6600

(Electronic components, equipment,
and systems.)

Reebok International Ltd.
100 Technology Center Dr.
Stoughton, MA 02072
617/341-5000
(Athletic and leisure shoe
manufacturer.)

Reed Publishing USA, Inc.
275 Washington St.
Newton, MA 02185
617/964-3030
(Publishing.)

Shawmut Corp.
1 Federal St.
Boston, MA 02110
617/292-2000
(Banking.)

Smith & Wesson Corp.
2100 Roosevelt Ave.
Springfield, MA 01102
413/781-8300
(Weapons manufacturing.)

Stanhome Inc.
333 Western Ave.
Westfield, MA 01085
413/562-3631
(Direct sale of household items, etc.)

L. S. Starrett Co.
121 Crescent St.
Athol, MA 01331
508/249-3551
(Cutting tools.)

**State Mutual Life Assurance Co. of
America**
440 Lincoln St.
Worcester, MA 01605
508/852-1000
(Life insurance.)

State St. Boston Corp.
225 Franklin St.
Boston, MA 02110
617/786-3000
(Banking.)

State St. Growth Trust
State St. Investment Trust
1 Financial Ctr.
Boston, MA 02111
617/482-3920
(Investments.)

Stone & Webster Engineering Corp.
245 Summer St.
Boston, MA 02110
617/589-5111
(Engineering, power plant, chemical plant, and refining construction.)

Stop & Shop Cos., Inc.
1 Bradlees Cir.
Braintree, MA 02184
617/380-8000
(Convenience stores.)

Stratus Computers, Inc.
55 Fairbanks Blvd.
Marlboro, MA 01752
508/460-2000
(Computers.)

TJX Companies, Inc.
7700 Cochituate Rd.
Framingham, MA 01701
508/390-1000
(Retail clothing stores, inc. T. J. Maxx.)

Talbot's Inc.
175 Beal St.
Hingham, MA 02043
617/749-7600
(Women's clothing stores/catalog sales.)

Teradyne, Inc.
321 Harrison Ave.
Boston, MA 02118
617/482-2700
(Electrical measuring instruments.)

Thermo Electron Corp.
101 First Ave.
Waltham, MA 02254
617/622-1000
(Cogeneration systems, monitoring instruments, etc.)

Wang Laboratories, Inc.
1 Industrial Ave.
Lowell, MA 01851
508/459-5000
(Computers and office machines.)

MASSACHUSETTS BUSINESS PERIODICALS

Boston Business Journal
451 D St.
Boston, MA 02210
617/330-1000
(Weekly.)

New England Business
20 Park Plz.
Boston, MA 02216
617/426-6677
(Monthly magazine.)

MASSACHUSETTS DIRECTORIES

Directory of Massachusetts Manufacturers
George D. Hall Company
50 Congress St.
Boston, MA 02109
617/523-3745

Directory of New England Manufacturers
George D. Hall Company
50 Congress St.
Boston, MA 02109
617/523-3745

MacRAE's State Directories—Massachusetts/Rhode Island
MacRAE's Blue Book, Inc.
817 Broadway
New York, NY 10003
212/673-4700
800/MAC-RAES

Massachusetts Business Directory
American Business Directories
5711 S. 86th Cir.
P.O. Box 27347
Omaha, NE 68127
402/593-4600

Massachusetts Directory of Manufacturers
Commerce Register, Inc.
190 Godwin Ave.
Midland Park, NJ 07432
201/445-3000

Massachusetts Service Directory
George D. Hall Company
50 Congress St.
Boston, MA 02109
617/523-3745

MASSACHUSETTS GOVERNMENT EMPLOYMENT OFFICES

Office of Personnel Management
Thomas P. O'Neill Federal Bldg.
10 Causeway St.
Boston, MA 02222-1031
617/565-5900
(Federal job-service center.)

Div. of Employment Security
Charles F. Hurley Bldg.
Government Ctr.
Boston, MA 02114
617/727-6810
(State job-service center.)

NEW HAMPSHIRE

LEADING NEW HAMPSHIRE EMPLOYERS

Amoskeag Bank Shares, Inc.
875 Elm St.
Manchester, NH 03105
603/647-3200
(Banking.)

BankEast Corp.
1 Wall St.
Manchester, NH 03105
603/624-6000
(Banking.)

Bank of Ireland First Holdings, Inc.
1000 Elm St.
Manchester, NH 03105
603/668-5020
(Banking.)

Bank of New Hampshire Corp.
300 Franklin St.
Box 600
Manchester, NH 03105
603/624-6600
(Banking.)

Brookstone, Inc.
Voss Farm Rd.
Peterborough, NH 03458
603/924-7181
(Specialty stores.)

Cabletron Systems, Inc.
35 Industrial Way
Rochester, NH 03867
603/332-9400
(Local area network components.)

Chubb Life Insurance Co. of America
1 Granite Pl.
Concord, NH 03301
603/226-5000
(Life insurance.)

Ekco Group, Inc.
98 Spit Brook Rd.
Nashua, NH 03062
603/888-1212
(Housewares, kichenware, baking equipment, etc.)

Grinnell Corp.
3 Tyco Pk.
Exeter, NH 03833
603/778-9200
(General industrial machinery and equipment.)

Guilford Transportation Industries, Inc.
7 Executive Pk. Dr.
Merrimack, NH 03054
603/429-1685
(Railroads, line haul operating.)

Hadco Corp.
10 Manor Pkwy.
Salem, NH 03079
603/898-8000
(Circuit boards.)

Harris Graphics Corp.
121 Broadway
Dover, NH 03820
603/749-6600
(Printing machinery/equipment.)

Henley Properties, Inc.
Liberty Ln.
Hampton, NH 03842
603/926-5911
(Real estate.)

Indian Head Banks, Inc.
1 Indian Head Plz.
Nashua, NH 03060
603/880-5000
(Banking.)

Kollsman
(div. of Sequa Corp.)
220 Daniel Webster Hwy.
Merrimack, NH 03054
603/889-2500
(Advanced electro-optical and avionics systems.)

Lockheed Sanders, Inc.
P.O. Box 0868
Daniel Webster Hwy. S.
Nashua, NH 03061
603/885-4321
(Advanced electronics systems, etc.)

Lowell Shoe, Inc.
8 Hampshire Dr.
Hudson, NH 03051
603/880-8900
(Shoes.)

MPB Corp.
Precision Pk.
P.O. Box 547
Keene, NH 03431
603/352-0310
(Ball bearings.)

Markem Corp.
150 Congress St.
Keene, NH 03431
603/352-1130
(Printing machinery/equipment.)

Nashua Corp.
44 Franklin St.
Nashua, NH 03061
603/880-2323
(Photocopying supplies, paper, labels, computer disks, etc.)

New Hampshire Ball Bearings
Rte. 202
Peterborough, NH 03458
603/924-3311
(Ball bearings.)

New Hampshire Oak
Liberty Lane
Hampton, NH 03842
603/926-1340
(Chemical and industrial products.)

Omni Hotels Corp.
500 Layfayette Rd.
Hampton, NH 03842
603/926-8911
(Hotels.)

The Timberland Co.
11 Merrill Industrial Dr.
Box 5050
Hampton, NH 03842
603/926-1600
(Shoes.)

Tyco Laboratories
One Tyco Pk.
Exeter, NH 03833

603/778-9700
(Metal products.)

United Savings Bank
156 Hanover St.
Manchester, NH 03101
603/625-2600
(Banking.)

Wheelabrator Technologies, Inc.
Liberty Ln.
Hampton, NH 03842
603/929-3000
(Heavy construction.)

NEW HAMPSHIRE BUSINESS PERIODICAL

Business New Hampshire Magazine
404 Chestnut St.,
Suite 201
Manchester, NH 03101-1803
603/626-6354
(Monthly.)

NEW HAMPSHIRE DIRECTORIES

Maine Vermont, New Hampshire
Directory of Manufacturers
Commerce Register, Inc.
190 Godwin Ave.
Midland Park, NJ 07432
201/445-3000

MacRAE's State
Directories—Maine/New
Hampshire/Vermont
MacRAE's Blue Book, Inc.
817 Broadway
New York, NY 10003
212/673-4700
800/MAC-RAES

New Hampshire Business Directory
American Business Directories
5711 S. 86th Cir.

P.O. Box 27347
Omaha, NE 68127
402/593-4600

New Hampshire Manufacturing
Directory
Tower Publishing Co.
36 Diamond St.
Box 7720
Portland, ME 04112
207/774-9813
(also available from:
Manufacturers' News, Inc.
1633 Central St.
Evanston, IL 60201
708/864-7000)

NEW HAMPSHIRE GOVERNMENT EMPLOYMENT OFFICES

Office of Personnel Management
Thomas J. McIntyre Federal Bldg.,
Room 104
80 Daniel St.
Portsmouth, NH 03801-3879
603/431-7115
(Federal job-service center.)

Employment Service Bureau
Dept. of Employment Security
32 S. Main St.
Concord, NH 03301
603/224-3311
(State job-service center.)

NEW JERSEY

LEADING NEW JERSEY EMPLOYERS

AT&T Bell Labs
600 Mountain Ave.
Murray Hill, NJ 07974
908/582-3000
(Scientific research, engineering, development, and design.)

AT&T Communications of New Jersey
295 N. Maple Ave.
Basking Ridge, NJ 07920
908/221-2000
(Telephone communications.)

AT&T Technologies, Inc.
1 Oak Way
Berkeley Heights, NJ 07922
201/771-2000
(Telecommunications and data communications equipment.)

Allied-Signal, Inc.
101 Columbia Rd.
Morristown, NJ 07962
201/455-2000
(Conglomerate—inc. aerospace and advanced electronics.)

American Cyanamid Co.
1 Cyanamid Plz.
Wayne, NJ 07470
201/831-2000
(Pharmaceuticals.)

American Water Works Company, Inc.
1025 Laurel Oak Rd.
Box 1770
Vorhees, NJ 08043
609/346-8200
(Water.)

Armco Inc.
300 Interpace Pkwy.
Parsippany, NJ 07054
201/316-5200
(Bar and wire, oil and mine field equipment, steel and steel products, etc.)

Automatic Data Processing, Inc.
1 ADP Blvd.
Roseland, NJ 07068
201/994-5000
(Data processing services.)

BASF Corp.
8 Campus Dr.
Parsippany, NJ 07054
201/397-2700
(Chemicals.)

Bell Communications Research
290 W. Mount Pleasant Ave.
Livingston, NJ 07039
201/740-3000
(Software.)

Block Drug
257 Corneilson Ave.
Jersey City, NJ 07302
201/454-3000
(Health care products,
pharmaceuticals.)

Campbell Soup Co.
Campbell Pl.
Camden, NJ 08101
609/342-4800
(Food processing.)

Church & Dwight Co., Inc.
469 N. Harnson St.
Princeton, NJ 08543-5297
609/683-5900
(Soaps, detergents, baking soda, etc.)

The Chubb Corp.
P.O. Box 1615
Warren, NJ 07061-1615
908/580-2000
(Management services.)

Cosmair, Inc.
30 Terminal Ave.
Clark, NJ 07066
908/382-7000
(Personal care products.)

Engelhard Corp.
101 Wood Ave.
Iselin, NJ 08830
201/205-6000
(Industrial inorganic chemicals.)

GAF
1361 Alps Rd.
Wayne, NJ 07470
201/628-3000
(Chemicals.)

Hoechst Celanese Corp.
Rte. 202–206
Somerville, NJ 08876
908/231-2000
(Chemicals, manmade fibers, etc.)

Hoffman-LaRoche, Inc.
340 Kingsland St.
Nutley, NJ 07110
201/235-5000
(Pharmaceuticals.)

Ingersoll-Rand Company
200 Chestnut Ridge Rd.
Woodcliff Lake, NJ 07675
201/573-0123
(Compressors, pumps, etc.)

Johnson & Johnson
1 Johnson & Johnson Plz.
New Brunswick, NJ 08933
908/524-0400
(Pharmaceuticals, health care
products, etc.)

Lear Siegler
220 S. Orange Ave.
Livingston, NJ 07039
201/535-9522
(Industrial equipment.)

**Matsushita Electronics Corp. of
America**
1 Panasonic Way
Secaucus, NJ 07094
201/348-7000
(Appliances, television, radios, etc.)

Mennen
Hanover Ave.
Morristown, NJ 07960
201/631-9000
(Personal care products.)

Merck & Co.
P.O. Box 2000
Rahway, NJ 07065
908/574-4000
(Pharmaceuticals.)

Nabisco Brands, Inc.
Nabisco Brands Plaza
Hanover, NJ 07936
201/503-2000
(Food processing.)

New Jersey Bell Telephone Co.
540 Broad St.
Newark, NJ 07101
201/649-9900
(Telephone services.)

Ortho Pharmaceutical Corp.
Rte. 202
Raritan, NJ 08869
908/218-6000
(Pharmaceuticals.)

Public Service Enterprise Group, Inc.
80 Park Plz.
Newark, NJ 07101
201/430-7000
(Utility.)

Sandoz Pharmaceuticals Corp.
(subs. Sandoz Corp.)
Rte. 10
East Hanover, NJ 07936
201/503-7500
(Pharmaceuticals.)

Schering-Plough
1 Giraldo Farms
Madison, NJ 07940
201/882-7000
(Pharmaceuticals.)

Squibb Corp.
P.O. Box 4000
Princeton, NJ 08543
609/921-4000
(Pharmaceuticals, health care, and personal care products.)

Thomas & Betts
1001 Frontier Rd.
Bridgewater, NJ 08807
908/685-1600
(Electrical products.)

Trump Taj Mahal Associates, Inc.
1000 Boardwalk
Atlantic City, NJ 08401
609/449-1000
(Casino/hotel.)

Warner-Lambert Co.
201 Tabor Rd.
Morris Plains, NJ 07950
201/540-2000
(Pharmaceuticals.)

Wellman Inc.
1040 Broad St.
Shrewsbury, NJ 07702
908/542-7300
(Chemicals.)

NEW JERSEY BUSINESS PERIODICALS

Business Journal of New Jersey
50 U.S. Hwy. 9 N.
Morganville, NJ 07751
201/972-1170
(Monthly.)

New Jersey Business
New Jersey Business & Industry Assoc.
310 Passaic Ave.
Fairfield, NJ 07004
201/882-5004

NEW JERSEY DIRECTORIES

Business Journal's Directory of Manufacturing
Corfacts—Business Journal of New Jersey
Business Information Division
50 Rte. 9 N

Morganville, NJ 07751
800/678-2565

Directory of New Jersey Manufacturers
George D. Hall Company
50 Congress St.

Boston, MA 02109
617/523-3745

MacRAE's State Industrial Directory—New Jersey
MacRAE's Blue Book, Inc.
817 Broadway
New York, NY 10003
212/673-4700
800/MAC-RAES

New Jersey Business Directory
American Business Directories
5711 S. 86th Cir.
P.O. Box 27347

Omaha, NE 68127
402/593-4600

New Jersey Directory of Manufacturers
Commerce Register, Inc.
190 Godwin Ave.
Midland Park, NJ 07432
201/445-3000

New Jersey Service Directory
George D. Hall Company
50 Congress St.
Boston, MA 02109
617/523-3745

NEW JERSEY GOVERNMENT EMPLOYMENT OFFICES

Office of Personnel Management
Peter W. Rodino, Jr., Federal Bldg.
970 Broad St.
Newark, NY 07102
201/645-3673
(Federal job-service center; in Camden, call 215/597-7440.)

New Jersey Dept. of Labor
Labor and Industry Bldg.
CN 058
Trenton, NJ 08625
609/292-2400
(State job-service center.)

NEW YORK

LEADING NEW YORK EMPLOYERS

American Express Co.
American Express Tower
World Financial Ctr.
New York, NY 10285
212/640-2000
(Diversified financial services.)

American International Group, Inc.
70 Pine St.
New York, NY 10270
212/770-7000
(Insurance.)

American Telephone & Telegraph Co. (AT&T)
32 Ave. of the Americas

New York, NY 10013-2412
212/387-5400
(Telecommunications.)

Backer Spielvogel Bates, Inc.
405 Lexington Ave.
New York, NY 10174
212/297-7000
(Advertising.)

The Bank of New York
48 Wall St.
New York, NY 10286
212/495-1784
(Banking.)

Bankers Trust Co.
280 Park Ave.
New York, NY 10017
212/250-2500
(Commercial banking.)

The Bear Stearns Companies, Inc.
245 Park Ave.
New York, NY 10167
212/272-2000
(Diversified financial services.)

Bell Aerospace Textron
(div. of Textron, Inc.)
P.O. Box 1
Buffalo, NY 14240
716/297-1000
(Aerospace and electronic products
and systems.)

Booz Allen & Hamilton Inc.
101 Park Ave.
New York, NY 10178
212/697-1900
(Management consulting.)

Bristol-Myers Squibb Co.
345 Park Ave.
New York, NY 10154
212/546-4000
(Health-care products,
pharmaceuticals.)

Brown Brothers Harriman & Co.
59 Wall St.
New York, NY 10005
212/483-1818
(Commercial banking, brokerage,
investment advisory services.)

Bulova Corp.
1 Bulova Ave.
Woodside, NY 11377
718/204-3399
(Watches.)

CBS, Inc.
51 W. 52nd St.
New York, NY 10019
212/975-4321
(Broadcasting.)

Cablevision Systems Corp.
1 Media Crossways
Woodbury, NY 11797
516/364-8450
(Cable television.)

Capital Cities/ABC Inc.
77 W. 66th St.
New York, NY 10023-6298
212/456-7777
(Media communications.)

Chase Lincoln First Bank, N.A.
1 Lincoln First Sq.
Rochester, NY 14643
716/258-5000
(Banking.)

The Chase Manhattan Corp.
1 Chase Manhattan Plz.
New York, NY 10081
212/552-2222
(Commercial banking.)

Chemical Banking Corp.
270 Park Ave.
New York, NY 10017
212/270-6000
(Banking.)

Ciba-Geigy Corp.
444 Saw Mill River Rd.
Ardsley, NY 10502
914/478-3131
(Pharmaceuticals.)

Citibank, N.A.
399 Park Ave.
New York, NY 10043
212/559-1000
(Banking.)

Citicorp
399 Park Ave.
New York, NY 10043
212/559-1000
(Holding company.)

**Consolidated Edison Company of
New York, Inc.**
4 Irving Pl.

New York, NY 10003
212/460-4600
(Electric utility.)

Corning Incorporated
Houghton Pk.
Corning, NY 14831
607/974-9000
(Chemicals and chemical products,
diagnostic substances, glassware,
scientific instruments' telephone wire
and cable, fiber optics systems and
equipment, etc.)

**Dean Witter Financial Services
Group Inc.**
2 World Trade Ctr.
New York, NY 10048
212/392-2222
(Diversified financial services.)

Donaldson Lufkin & Jenrette
140 Broadway
New York, NY 10005
212/504-3000
(Investment brokers.)

Dow Jones & Co.
200 Liberty St.
New York, NY 10281
212/416-2000
(Newspaper publishing.)

Eastman Kodak Co.
343 State St.
Rochester, NY 14650
716/724-4000
(Photographic equipment and supplies,
etc.)

Ebasco Services Inc.
2 World Trade Ctr.
New York, NY 10048
212/839-1000
(Engineering services.)

Empire Blue Cross & Blue Shield
633 Third Ave.
New York, NY 10017
212/476-1000
(Health insurance.)

Equitable Life Assurance Society
787 Seventh Ave.
New York, NY 10019
212/554-1234
(Life insurance.)

**Fidelity & Casualty Co. of New
York**
180 Maiden Ln.
New York, NY 10038
212/440-3000
(Insurance.)

The First Boston Corp.
55 E. 52nd St.
New York, NY 10055
212/909-2000
(Underwriters, distributors, investment
dealers.)`

First Boston, Inc.
Park Ave. Plz.
New York, NY 10036
212/909-2000
(Stock and bond dealers.)

Goldman Sachs Group LP
85 Broad St.
New York, NY 10004
212/902-1000
(Investment banking.)

Grey Advertising Inc.
777 Third Ave.
New York, NY 10017
212/546-2000
(Advertising.)

Grumman Corp.
1111 Stewart Ave.
Bethpage, NY 11714
516/575-0574
(Holding company. At same address:
Grumman Aircraft Systems Division,
Grumman Data Systems Division,
Grumman Systems Group, Grumman
Electronic Systems Division,
Grumman Space Systems Division,
Grumman International, Inc., etc.)

Guardian Life Insurance Co. of America
201 Park Ave. S.
New York, NY 10003
212/598-8000
(Insurance.)

Hearst Corporation
959 8th Ave.
New York, NY 10019
212/649-2000
(Communications media—book publishing, magazine publishing, etc.)

Helmsley-Noyes Company, Inc.
22 Cortland St.
New York, NY 10007
212/693-4400
(Real estate.)

International Business Machines Corp. (IBM)
Old Orchard Rd.
Armonk, NY 10504
914/765-1900
(Computers, electronics systems, etc.)

Jordache Enterprises, Inc.
226 W. 37th St.
New York, NY 10018
212/279-7343
(Clothing.)

Kidder, Peabody & Co. Incorporated
10 Hanover Sq.
New York, NY 10005
212/520-3000
(Investment banking.)

Long Island Lighting Co.
175 E. Old Country Rd.
Hicksville, NY 11801
516/933-4590
(Electric utility.)

Loral Corp.
600 Third Ave.,
New York, NY 10016
212/697-1105
(Electronic systems and components.)

R. H. Macy & Co.
151 W. 34th St.
New York, NY 10001
212/695-4400
(Department store.)

Macy's Northeast, Inc.
Herald Sq.
New York, NY 10001
212/695-4400
(Retailing.)

Marine Midland Bank, N.A.
1 Marine Midland Ctr.
Buffalo, NY 14240
716/843-2424
(Banking.)

McGraw-Hill, Inc.
1221 Ave. of the Americas
New York, NY 10020
212/512-2000
(Magazine and book publishing.)

Merrill Lynch Pierce Fenner & Smith, Inc.
World Financial Ctr.
New York, NY 10281
212/449-1000
(Diversified financial services.)

Metro-North Commuter Railroad
347 Madison Ave.
New York, NY 10017
212/340-3000
(Railroad.)

Metropolitan Life Insurance Co.
1 Madison Ave.
New York, NY 10010
212/578-2211
(Insurance.)

Moog, Inc.
East Aurora, NY 14052
716/652-2000
(Electrohydraulic servovalves, servocativators, etc.)

J. P. Morgan & Co., Inc.
60 Wall St.
New York, NY 10260
212/483-2323
(Holding company.)

Morgan Guaranty Trust Company of New York
60 Wall St.
New York, NY 10260
212/483-2323
(Banking.)

Morgan Stanley Group, Inc.
1251 Ave. of the Americas
New York, NY 10020
212/703-4000
(Diversified financial services.)

National Broadcasting Company, Inc.
30 Rockefeller Plz.
New York, NY 10020
212/664-4444
(Broadcasting.)

New York Life Insurance Co.
51 Madison Ave.
New York, NY 10010
212/576-7000
(Life insurance.)

New York Newsday
2 Park Ave.
New York, NY 10016
516/ 454-2020
(Newspaper publishing.)

New York Telephone Company
1095 Ave. of the Americas
New York, NY 10036
212/395-2121
(Telephone services.)

The New York Times Company, Inc.
229 W. 43rd St.
New York, NY 10036
212/556-1234
(Newspaper publishing.)

Ogilvy & Mather Worldwide
309 W. 49th St.
New York, NY 10019
212/237-4000
(Advertising.)

Oneida Ltd.
Kenwood Station
Oneida, NY 13421
315/361-3000
(Silverware.)

Oppenheimer & Co., Inc.
Oppenheimer Tower
World Financial Ctr.
New York, NY 10281
212/667-7000
(Diversified financial services.)

PaineWebber Group Inc.
1285 Ave. of the Americas
New York, NY 10019
212/713-20000
(Diversified financial services.)

Pall Corp.
2200 Northern Blvd.
East Hills, NY 11548
516/484-5400
(Air intake filters; internal combustion engines, exc. auto.)

PepsiCo, Inc.
Anderson Hill Rd.
Purchase, NY 10577
914/253-2000
(Beverage, food, etc.)

Pfizer, Inc.
235 E. 42nd St.
New York, NY 10017
212/573-2323
(Pharmaceuticals.)

Philip Morris Companies, Inc.
120 Park Ave.
New York, NY 10017
212/880-5000
(Conglomerate—tobacco, food processing, etc.)

Primerica Corp.
65 E. 55th St.
New York, NY 10022
212/891-8900
(Consumer finance companies,
insurance brokerage, mutual funds,
etc.)

Prudential-Bache Securities
1 Seaport Plz.
New York, NY 10292
212/776-1000
(Securities brokerage.)

Readers Digest Association, Inc.
Reader's Digest Rd.
Pleasantville, NY 10570
914/238-1000
(Magazine publishing.)

Republic New York Corp.
452 Fifth Ave.
New York, NY 10018
212/525-6000
(Banking.)

Saatchi & Saatchi Advertising
375 Hudson St.
New York, NY 10014
212/463-2000
(Advertising.)

Saks Fifth Avenue
12 E. 49th St.
New York, NY 10017
212/753-4000
(Retailing.)

Salomon Brothers, Inc.
1 New York Plz.
New York, NY 10004
212/747-7000
(Diversified financial services.)

Shearson Lehman Brothers, Inc.
388 Greenwich St.
New York, NY 10013
212/298-2000
(Financial services.)

Shearson Lehman Hutton Holdings, Inc.
World Financial Ctr
New York, NY 10285
212/298-2000
(Security brokers and dealers.)

Smith Barney Harris Upham & Co. Inc.
1345 Ave. of the Americas
New York, NY 10105
212/399-6000
(Investment brokers.)

Sterling Drug Inc.
90 Park Ave.
New York, NY 10016
212/907-2000
(Pharmaceuticals.)

Teachers Insurance & Annuity Association of America
730 Third Ave.
New York, NY 10017
212/490-9000
(Pensions, insurance, and annuities for teachers and professors.)

Texaco, Inc.
2000 Westchester Ave.
White Plains, NY 10650
914/253-4000
(Petroleum exploration and refining, petrochemicals, etc.)

J. Walter Thompson Co.
466 Lexington Ave.
New York, NY 10017
212/210-7000
(Advertising.)

Time, Inc.
Time-Life Bldg.
Rockefeller Ctr.
New York, NY 10020
212/522-1212
(Magazine and book publishing, cable TV, etc.)

Time Warner Inc.
75 Rockefeller Plz.
New York, NY 10019
212/484-8000
(Broadcasting, publishing.)

Yonkers Contracting Co., Inc.
969 Midland Ave.
Yonkers, NY 10804
914/965-1500
(Highway and street construction.)

Young & Rubicam, Inc.
285 Madison Ave.
New York, NY 10017
212/210-3000
(Advertising.)

NEW YORK BUSINESS PERIODICALS

Business NY
152 Washington Ave.
Albany, NY 12210
518/465-7511
(Monthly.)

Crain's New York Business
220 E. 42nd St.
New York, NY 10017
212/210-0270
(Weekly: annual directory issue lists
the top companies in New York.)

Long Island/Business
2150 Smithtown Ave.
Ronkonkoma, NY 11779

516/737-1700
(Weekly; puts out annual special issue
"Long Island Executive Register,"
which lists area businesses and
includes contact names.)

Westchester Business Journal
Box 1311
Port Chester, NY 10573
914/258-4008
(Weekly.)

NEW YORK DIRECTORIES

*Dalton's New York Metropolitan
Directory*
Dalton's Directory
410 Lancaster Ave.
Haverford, PA 19041
800/221-1050
215/649-2680
(also includes Northern New Jersey)

Greater Buffalo Business Directory
Greater Buffalo Chamber of
Commerce
107 Delaware Ave.
Buffalo, NY 14203
716/852-7100

*MacRAE's State Industrial
Directory—New York State*
MacRAE's Blue Book, Inc.
817 Broadway
New York, NY 10003
212/673-4700
800/MAC-RAES

New York Business Directory
American Business Directories
5711 S. 86th Cir.
P.O. Box 27347
Omaha, NE 68127
402/593-4600

New York Manufacturers Directory
George D. Hall Company
50 Congress St.
Boston, MA 02109
617/523-3745

New York Metropolitan Directory of Manufacturers
Commerce Register, Inc.
190 Godwin Ave.
Midland Park, NJ 07432
201/445-3000

New York SOICC—Bureau of Labor Market Information
IPTA Services Office
Room 488, Bldg.12
State Campus
Albany, NY 12240

(Puts out two publications: *Occupations Licensed or Certified by New York State*, which covers sixty-five different occupations, lists licensing requirements, job descriptions, outlooks, salaries, etc.; and *Suggestions for Career Exploration and Job-Seeking/Suggestiones apra Exploración de Carreras y Busqueda de Empleo*, a bilingual career guide.)

New York Upstate Directory of Manufacturers
Commerce Register, Inc.
190 Godwin Ave.
Midland Park, NJ 07432
201/445-3000

NEW YORK GOVERNMENT EMPLOYMENT OFFICES

Office of Personnel Management
Jacob J. Javits Federal Bldg.
26 Federal Plz.
New York, NY 10278
212/264-0422
(Federal job-service center.)

Office of Personnel Management
James M. Hanley Federal Bldg.
100 S. Clinton St.
Syracuse, NY 13260

315/423-5660
(Federal job-service center.)

Job Service Division
New York State Dept of Labor
State Campus
Bldg. 12G
Albany, NY 12240
518/457-2612
(State job-service center.)

PENNSYLVANIA

LEADING PENNSYLVANIA EMPLOYERS

The ARA Group Inc.
ARA Tower
1101 Market St.
Philadelphia, PA 19107
215/238-3000
(Diversified services.)

Air Products & Chemicals, Inc.
P.O. Box 538
Allentown, PA 18105
215/481-4911
(Chemicals, industrial gases, engineering services.)

Allegheny Ludlum Corp.
1000 Six PPG Pl.
Pittsburgh, PA 15222
412/394-2800
(Steel.)

Aluminum Company of America
1501 Alcoa Bldg.
Pittsburgh, PA 15219
412/553-4545
(Aluminum mining and mills.)

Armstong World Industries, Inc.
Liberty and Charlotte Sts.
Lancaster, PA 17604
717/397-0611
(Floor coverings, building products,
furniture.)

Bell Atlantic Corp.
1717 Arch St.
Philadelphia, PA 19103
215/963-6000
(Telecommunications holding
company.)

**Bell Telephone Company of
Pennsylvania**
1–16B Pkwy.
Philadelphia, PA 19102
215/466-9990
(Telephone service.)

Bethlehem Steel
1170 Eighth Ave.
Bethlehem, PA 18016
215/694-2424
(Steel.)

Betz Laboratories, Inc.
4636 Somerton Rd.
Trevose, PA 19053
215/355-3300
(Design, treatment, and control of
water systems, etc.)

Carpenter Technology Corp.
P.O. Box 14662
Reading, PA 19612
215/371-2000
(Specialty metals.)

CIGNA Corp.
1 Liberty Pl.
Philadelphia, PA 19192
215/761-7000
(Insurance.)

Commodore International, Ltd.
1200 Wilson Dr.
West Chester, PA 19380
215/431-9100
(Computers.)

Consolidated Rail Corp. (Conrail)
P.O. Box 41417
Philadelphia, PA 19101-1417
215/209-5099
(Railroad.)

Corporate Data Systems
3700 Market St.
Philadelphia, PA 19104
215/222-7046
(Computer integrated systems design.)

Crown Cork & Seal Co., Inc.
9300 Ashton Rd.
Philadelphia, PA 19114
215/698-5100
(Packaging machinery, corks, etc.)

Day & Zimmerman
1818 Market St.
Philadelphia, PA 19103
215/299-8000
(Engineering services, consulting,
etc.)

Dick Corp.
P.O. Box 10896
Pittsburgh, PA 15236
412/384-1000
(Construction.)

Equibank
2 Oliver Plz.
Pittsburgh, PA 15222
412/288-5000
(Banking.)

Equitable Resources, Inc.
420 Blvd. of the Allies
Pittsburgh, PA 15219
412/261-3000
(Natural gas and oil.)

Ferranti International, Inc.
P.O. Box 3040
3750 Electronics Way
Lancaster, PA 17604-3040
717/285-3113
(Electronic systems.)

Fidelity Bank, N.A.
Broad & Walnut Sts.
Philadelphia, PA 19109
215/985-6000
(Banking.)

General Accident Insurance Co. of America
436 Walnut St.
Philadelphia, PA 19105
215/625-1000
(Insurance.)

H. J. Heinz
600 Grant St.
Pittsburgh, PA 15219
412/456-5700
(Food processing.)

Hershey Foods Corp.
100 Crystal A Dr.
Hershey, PA 17033
717/534-4000
(Food processing.)

Hess's Department Stores, Inc.
9th & Hamilton Mall
Allentown, PA 18101
215/821-4377
(Department stores.)

Insurance Company of North America
1600 Chestnut St.
Philadelphia, PA 19192
215/761-1000
(Insurance.)

Lukens, Inc.
50 S. First Ave.
Coatesville, PA 19320
215/383-2000
(Plate steel, plate products, materials handling equipment, etc.)

Mellon Bank Corp.
Mellon Bank Ctr.
500 Grant St.
Pittsburgh, PA 15258
412/234-5000
(Banking.)

Meridian Bancorp, Inc.
P.O. Box 1102
Reading, PA 19603
215/655-2000
(Banking.)

Metropolitan Edison Co.
P.O. Box 16001
Reading, PA 19640
215/929-3601
(Electric utility.)

PNC Financial Corp.
Fifth Ave. & Wood St.
Pittsburgh, PA 15222
412/762-2666
(Banking.)

PPG Industries
1 PPG Pl.
Pittsburgh, PA 15272
412/434-3131
(Glass, construction materials.)

Pennsylvania Power Co.
1 E. Washington St.
Box 891
New Castle, PA 16103
412/652-5531
(Electric utility.)

Pennsylvania Power & Light Co.
2 N. Ninth St.
Allentown, PA 18101
215/770-5151
(Utility.)

Philadelphia Electric Co.
2301 Market St.
Philadelphia, PA 19101
215/841-4000
(Utility.)

Philadelphia Newspapers, Inc.
400 N. Broad St.
Philadelphia, PA 19101
215/854-2000
(Newspaper publishing.)

Quaker State Corporation
255 Elm St.
Oil City, PA 16301
814/676-7676
(Lubricants, fuels, etc.)

Rhone-Poulenc Rorer, Inc.
500 Arcola Rd.
Box 1200
Collegeville, PA 19426
215/454-8000
(Pharmaceuticals.)

Rohm & Haas Co.
Independence Mall W.
Philadelphia, PA 19105
215/592-3000
(Industrial and agricultural chemicals,
plastics, polymers, etc.)

Scott Paper Co., Inc.
Scott Plz.
Philadelphia PA 19113
215/522-5000
(Paper products, printing and
publishing paper, forest products, etc.)

Shared Medical Systems Corp.
51 Valley Stream Pkwy.
Malven, PA 19355
215/296-6300
(Computer-based information systems
for health-care industry.)

Sharon Steel Corp.
Roemer Blvd.
Farrell, PA 16121

412/983-6000
(Steel.)

SmithKline Beecham Corp.
1 Franklin Plz.
Philadelphia, PA 19101
215/751-4000
(Pharmaceuticals, analytical products
for biomedical research.)

Strawbridge & Clothier
801 Market St.
Philadelphia, PA 19107
215/629-6000
(Department store.)

Sun Company, Inc.
1801 Market St.
Philadelphia, PA 19103
215/977-3000
(Oil and gas.)

USX Corp.
600 Grant St.
Pittsburgh, PA 15219
412/433-1121
(Steel, chemicals, petroleum, natural
gas, etc.)

Unisys Corp.
P.O. Box 500
Blue Bell, PA 19424
215/986-4011
(Information systems, electronic
systems, and services.)

Westinghouse Electric Corp.
Westinghouse Bldg.
6 Gateway Ctr.
Pittsburgh, PA 15222
412/244-2000
(Electronic systems and products.)

Woolrich, Inc.
Mill St.
Woolrich, PA 17779
717/769-6464
(Apparel.)

Wyeth-Ayerst Laboratories
Lancaster Ave.
P.O. Box 8299
Radnor, PA 19101
215/688-4400
(Pharmaceuticals.)

York International Corp.
631 S. Richland Ave.
York, PA 17403
717/771-7890
(Air conditioning, heating,
refrigeration equipment.)

PENNSYLVANIA BUSINESS PERIODICALS

Allegheny Business
471 Lincoln Ave.
Pittsburgh, PA 15202
412/734-2300
(Biweekly.)

Philadelphia Business Journal
718 Arch St.
Philadelphia, PA 19106
215/238-1450
(Weekly.)

Focus
1015 Chestnut St.
Philadelphia, PA 19107
215/925-6800
(Weekly newsmagazine covering the
Philadelphia area.)

Pittsburgh Business Times
4 Gateway Ctr.
Pittsburgh, PA 15222
412/391-7222
(Weekly.)

PENNSYLVANIA DIRECTORIES

*Dalton's Philadelphia Metropolitan
Directory*
Dalton's Directory
410 Lancaster Ave.
Haverford, PA 19041
800/221-1050
215/649-2680

*Harris Pennsylvania Industrial
Directory*
Harris Publishing Co.
2057 Aurora Rd.
Twinsburg, OH 44087
216/425-9000
800/888-5900

*MacRAE's State Industrial
Directory—Pennsylvania*
MacRAE's Blue Book, Inc.
817 Broadway
New York, NY 10003
212/673-4700
800/MAC-RAES

Pennsylvania Business Directory
American Business Directories
5711 S. 86th Cir.
P.O. Box 27347
Omaha, NE 68127
402/593-4600

*Pennsylvania Directory of
Manufacturers*
Commerce Register, Inc.
190 Godwin Ave.
Midland Park, NJ 07432
201/445-3000

Pennsylvania Manufacturers Register
Manufacturers' News, Inc.
1633 Central St.
Evanston, IL 60201
708/864-7000

PENNSYLVANIA GOVERNMENT EMPLOYMENT OFFICES

Office of Personnel Management
Federal Bldg.
600 Arch St.
Philadelphia, PA 19106
(Regional OPM office.)

Office of Personnel Management
Federal Bldg., Room 168
P.O. Box 761
Harrisburg, PA 17108
717/782-4494
(Federal job-service center.)

Office of Personnel Management
William J. Green, Jr. Federal Bldg.
600 Arch St., Room 1416
Philadelphia, PA 19106

215/597-7440
(Federal job-service center.)

Office of Personnel Management
Federal Bldg.
1000 Liberty Ave., Room 119
Pittsburgh, PA 15222
412/644-2755
(Federal job-service center.)

Bureau of Job Service
Labor 7 Industry Bldg.
Seventh and Forster Sts.
Harrisburg, PA 17121
717/787-3354
(State job-service center.)

RHODE ISLAND

LEADING RHODE ISLAND EMPLOYERS

American Insulated Wire Corp.
36 Freeman St.
Pawtucket, RI 02862
401/726-0700
(Insulated wire and cable.)

American Tourister, Inc.
91 Main St.
Warren, RI 02885
401/245-2100
(Luggage.)

Amica Mutual Insurance Co.
10 Weybosset St.
Providence, RI 02940
401/521-9100
(Insurance.)

Amtrol, Inc.
1400 Division Rd.
West Warwick, RI 02893
401/884-6300
(Fabricated platework.)

Brooks Drug, Inc.
75 Sabin St.
Pawtucket, RI 02860
401/724-9500
(Drug stores.)

Brown & Sharpe Manufacturing Co.
Precision Park
North Kingston, RI 02852
401/886-2000
(Machine tool accessories.)

Carol Cable Co., Inc.
249 Roosevelt Ave.
Pawtucket, RI 02860
401/728-7000
(Wire and cable.)

Citizens Savings Bank
870 Westminster St.
Providence, RI 02903
401/456-7000
(Savings bank.)

Cranston Print Works Co.
1381 Cranston St.
Cranston, RI 02920
401/943-4800
(Textile printing, finishing, converting.)

A. T. Cross Co., Inc.
1 Albion Rd.
Lincoln, RI 02865
401/333-1200
(Pens, pencils, desk sets, etc.)

Davol, Inc.
100 Sockanosset Crossrd.
Cranston, RI 02920
401/463-7000
(Orthopedic, prosthetic, and surgical appliances and devices.)

Fleet/Norstar Financial Group, Inc.
50 Kennedy Plz.
Providence, RI 02903
401/278-5800
(Banking.)

Gilbane Building
7 Jackson Walkway
Providence, RI 02940
401/456-5800
(Commercial and industrial construction.)

Hasbro, Inc.
1027 Newport Ave.
Pawtucket, RI 02861
401/431-8697
(Toys.)

Mark Steven Service Merchandisers
1 CVS Dr.
Woonsocket, RI 02895
401/765-1500
(Wholesale drug store supplies.)

Narragansett Electric Co., Inc.
280 Melrose St.
Providence, RI 02901
401/941-1400
(Utility.)

Nortek Inc.
50 Kennedy Plz.
Providence, RI 02903
401/751-1600
(Building materials.)

PlaySkool Inc.
1027 Newport Ave.
Box 1059
Pawtucket, RI 02862
401/431-8697
(Toys.)

Providence Energy Corporation
100 Weybosset St.
Providence, RI 02901
401/272-9191
(Natural gas distribution, real estate.)

Providence Journal Co.
75 Fountain St.
Providence, RI 02902
401/277-7000
(Newspaper publishing.)

Royal Electric Inc.
95 Grand Ave.
Pawtucket, RI 02861
401/722-8600
(Wire and cable.)

Sheaffer Eaton, Inc.
1 Crown Mark Dr.
Lincoln, RI 02865
401/333-0303
(Pens, pencils, desk accessories.)

Stanley-Bostitch, Inc.
Rte. 2
East Greenwich, RI 02818
401/884-2500
(Office equipment.)

Teknor Apex Co.
505 Central Ave.
Pawtucket, RI 02861
401/725-8000
(Plastics materials.)

Textron, Inc.
40 Westminister St.
Providence, RI 02903

401/421-2800
(Aerospace, helicopters, defense
systems, engines, etc.)

RHODE ISLAND BUSINESS PERIODICAL

Providence Business News
Herald Press, Inc.
300 Richmond St.
Providence, RI 02903
401/273-2201

RHODE ISLAND DIRECTORIES

*Connecticut, Rhode Island Directory
of Manufacturers*
Commerce Register, Inc.
190 Godwin Ave.
Midland Park, NJ 07432
201/445-3000

*MacRAE's State Industrial
Directory—Massachussetts/Rhode
Island*
MacRAE's Blue Book, Inc.
817 Broadway
New York, NY 10003
212/673-4700
800/MAC-RAES

Rhode Island Business Directory
American Business Directories
5711 S. 86th Cir.
P.O. Box 27347
Omaha, NE 68127
402/593-4600

*Rhode Island Directory of
Manufacturers*
Dept. of Economic Development
7 Jackson Walkway
Providence, RI 02903
401/277-2601

RHODE ISLAND GOVERNMENT EMPLOYMENT OFFICES

Office of Personnel Management
John O. Pastore Federal Bldg.
Room 310, Kennedy Plz.
Providence, RI 02903
401/528-5251
(Federal job-service center.)

Job Service Division
Dept. of Employment Security
24 Mason St.
Providence, RI 02903
401/277-3722
(State job-service center.)

VERMONT

LEADING VERMONT EMPLOYERS

Bank of Vermont
148 College St.
Burlington, VT 05401
802/658-1810
(Banking.)

BankNorth Group, Inc.
300 Financial Plz.
Burlington, VT 05401
802/658-9959

Ben & Jerry's Homemade, Inc.
Rte. 100
Box 240
Waterbury, VT 05676
802/244-5641
(Ice cream.)

C & S Wholesale Grocers, Inc.
Ferry Rd.
Brattleboro, VT 05301
802/257-4371
(Wholesale grocery distributor.)

Cabot Farmers' Co-op Creamery Co., Inc.
130 Main St.
Cabot, VT 05647
802/563-2231
(Cheese and dairy products.)

Carris Reels, Inc.
P.O. Box 696
Rutland, VT 05702
802/773-9111
(Plywood, pressboard, metal and plastic reels for wire/cordage industry.)

Champlain Cable Corp.
P.O. Box 7
Winooski, VT 05404
802/665-2121
(Wire and cable.)

Chittenden Bank
2 Burlington Sq.
Burlington, VT 05401
802/658-4000
(Banking.)

EHV-Weidmann Industries, Inc.
Memorial Dr.
Industrial Pk.
St. Johnsbury, VT 05819
802/748-8106
(Electronic and electrical equipment.)

Engelberth Construction, Inc.
2000 Mountain View Dr.
Colchester, VT 05446
802/655-0100
(Construction.)

Fonda Group, Inc.
15–21 Lower Newton St.
St. Albans, VT 05478
802/524-5966
(Paper food containers, etc.)

Green Mountain Power Corp.
25 Green Mountain Dr.
South Burlington, VT 05402
802/864-5731
(Electric utility.)

IDX Corp.
1400 Shelburne Rd.
South Burlington, VT 05403
802/862-1022
(Medical software development.)

Killington Ltd.
Killington Rd.
Killington, VT 05751
802/422-3333
(Ski resort.)

Lane Press, Inc.
P.O. Box 130
Burlington, VT 05402
802/863-5555
(Commercial printing.)

Mack Molding Co., Inc.
E. Arlington Rd.
Arlington, VT 05250
802/375-2511
(Molded plastics.)

Merchants Bankshares, Inc.
123 Church St.
Burlington, VT 05401
802/658-3400
(Banking.)

National Life Insurance Co.
National Life Dr.
Montpelier, VT 05604
802/229-3333
(Insurance.)

**National Life Investment
Management Co., Inc.**
National Life Dr.
Montpelier, VT 05604
802/229-9300
(Securities brokers and dealers,
investment advisors.)

Orvis, Inc.
U.S. Rte. 7A
Manchester, VT 05254
802/362-3622
(Mail order catalog house—sporting
goods, apparel, etc.)

Pizzagalli Construction Co.
55 Joy Dr.
Burlington, VT 05403
802/658-4200
(General contractor.)

Rock of Ages Corp.
Box 482
Barre, VT 05641
802/476-3115
(Dimension stone mining/quarrying.)

John A. Russell Corp.
117 Strongs Ave.
Rutland, VT 05701
802/775-3325
(Construction.)

Stratton Corp.
Stratton Mountain
S. Londonderry, VT 05155
802/297-2200
(Ski resort.)

Velan Valve Corp.
Ave. C
Griswold Industrial Park
Williston, VT 05495
802/863-2561
(Valves.)

Vermont Financial Services Corp.
100 Main St.
Brattleboro, VT 05301
802/257-7151
(Bank holding company.)

Vermont National Bank
100 Main St.
Brattleboro, VT 05301
802/257-7151
(Banking.)

**Vermont Yankee Nuclear Power
Corp.**
Ferry Rd.
RFD 5
Box 169
Brattleboro, VT 05301
802/257-5271
(Electrical generator.)

VERMONT BUSINESS PERIODICAL

Vermont Business
Box 6120
Brattleboro, VT 05302
802/257-4100
(Monthly.)

VERMONT DIRECTORIES

MacRAE's State Directories—Maine/New Hampshire/Vermont
MacRAE's Blue Book, Inc.
817 Broadway
New York, NY 10003
212/673-4700
800/MAC-RAES

Maine, Vermont, New Hampshire Directory of Manufacturers
Commerce Register, Inc.

190 Godwin Ave.
Midland Park, NJ 07432
201/445-3000

Vermont Business Directory
American Business Directories
5711 S. 86th Cir.
P.O. Box 27347
Omaha, NE 68127
402/593-4600

VERMONT GOVERNMENT EMPLOYMENT OFFICES

Office of Personnel Management (Federal job-service center—see New Hampshire listing.)

Employment Service
Dept. of Employment and Training
P.O. Box 488
Montpelier, VT 05602
802/229-0311
(State job-service center.)

THE SOUTHEAST, TEXAS, AND THE GULF STATES

OUTLOOK: Poised for long-term growth.

The overall region should be coming on strong relative to the rest of the country. The key reason? The South has been diversifying—moving into high-tech industries, services, and international trade, and away from old-line businesses like paper, pulp, and textiles. This makes the area stronger in general and better able to grow as the national economy continues to strengthen. In a late 1993 national survey, southern companies were expected to hire more than the national norm. Especially strong: Florida, Georgia, the Carolinas.

WHAT'S NEXT

▶ **Southeast: Mixed, but generally positive.**

In general, the Southeast will be benefiting from the upsurge in consumer confidence and the resulting uptrend in the auto, home furnishings and housing industries. This is a function of the many auto-related companies, textile and home furnishings manufacturers, and appliance manufacturers in the region. In addition, the increase of high-tech firms in the area will continue to spur growth and job creation, particularly in the Research Triangle Park area in North Carolina.

The downside: Defense cutbacks have hurt the defense and related service industries. Also, low wages—which made the region a low-cost manufacturing center—are now near the national average, and the special incentives used to lure corporations South are now also offered in the North. But perhaps the most important problem in the area is the fact that outside cities, much of the South is still poor—and poorly educated.

▶ **Some specifics for several Southeastern states.**

While the boom days appear to be over for the time being, *Florida* is in for steady long-term growth. One area in particular that will continue to expand is health care. While health care is a hot industry throughout the country, it's especially strong in Florida, a key reason being the number of senior citizens who retire to Florida. Other strong industries: Tourism, import/export, international banking (Miami is the number-two foreign banking center in the U.S.), and biomedical technology.

Tennessee will be steadily improving and growing. As home to the Saturn auto plant and growing in importance as an auto center, Tennessee will reap the benefits of an improved national economy—and resurgence in car sales. So too will *Kentucky,* with its Georgetown Toyota plant and its GE Appliance factory. Also benefiting will be *Mississippi* and *Alabama*. The latter will be seeing growth in its forestry industry as well, due to environmental legislation limiting timber-cutting in the Pacific Northwest, and emerging high-tech industry. *West Virginia* is weaker, suffering from the downsizing of the coal industry.

Georgia has come out of the downturn with a bang. With a turnaround in process, it is adding jobs in a range of sectors. The greatest activity is in real estate, with more than 32,000 jobs slated to be added, according to Georgia State University data. Another plus for the region: having Atlanta as host city of the 1996 Olympics. This should increase construction and, ultimately, tourism.

A regional best bet: *North Carolina* is growing in importance as a banking center. One reason: the NCNB-Sovran merger, which thrust the state into the spotlight. And the repercussions are very positive. In fact, some experts are pointing to Charlotte as the Atlanta of the future—that is, a focal point for new business and corporate relocations. Keep an eye on this area as it may really heat up.

And *South Carolina* is benefitting from the low cost of doing business in the state. An influx of new businesses, such as the $625 million BMW plant being built in 1993, is translating into increased employment opportunities.

▶ **Texas and the oil-patch states: Growing and going strong.**

Texas, in particular, is on a fast track. It fell into the economic downslide early, and now it's reaping the benefits of being one of the first states to pull out. For the last few years, its economy has performed better than the rest of the country, and this trend should continue. Among the reasons—a diversified economy; an influx of new businesses, including such large companies as Exxon, GTE, and J.C. Penney; and world-class universities. Particularly hot: Austin (see below), Richardson, a Dallas suburb recently dubbed "Telecom Corridor" due to its growing telecommunications industry, and Houston, which has attracted a number of heavy-hitting companies and, as a port, should benefit from the North America Free Trade Agreement.

The outlook for the oil patch states is, as always, tied to a degree to the performance of the energy industry. More specifically:

Oklahoma is aggressively targeting California businesses that intend to relocate, focusing its efforts on the aviation and food industries. In addition, it has set up economic development offices in Pacific Rim countries, India, and Europe—all in an effort to draw new business. The outlook? Could be very interesting and very ripe for employment prospects.

Louisiana should rebound when the price of oil begins another cyclical rise, and once it has tackled its budgetary problems. Also a contributor to a bright long-term outlook: Louisiana's role as a gateway to the United States. More than one-third of domestic water-borne commerce and one-sixth of foreign sea trade moves through six deep-water ports in Louisiana. The bottom line, then, is simple: As U.S. trade exports continue to increase, so will port activity.

REGIONAL HOT SPOTS

AUSTIN, TX: Home of the University of Texas as well as four other colleges and two seminaries, Austin has a reputation for being a great place to live. It's also shaping up into a great place to work—between the state university and the state government, there is typically little unemployment. Adding to the city's bright employment prospects is a recent proposal to convert a closing local military base into a commercial airport. This would result in the creation of a large number of new jobs and would also help the local economy.

CORINTH, MS: Aerospace manufacturers Lockheed and Aerojet are building a high-tech center here to manufacture space-shuttle motors, making this relatively unknown city a good employment bet. Slated for a 1994 opening, the center will create 1,000 new jobs. In addition, there has already been a flurry of growth as California transplants have moved to the area to work on the plant.

ALABAMA

LEADING ALABAMA EMPLOYERS

Alabama Power Company
600 N. 18th St.
Birmingham, AL 35291
205/250-1000
(Utilities company.)

AmSouth Bancorp
20th St. and Fifth Ave. N.
Birmingham, AL 35288
205/320-7151
(Banking.)

American Cast Iron Pipe Co.
Box 2727
Birmingham, AL 35202
205/325-7701
(Iron foundries.)

Avex Electronics, Inc.
4807 Bradford Dr., NW
Huntsville, AL 35805
205/722-6000
(Semiconductors and related devices.)

B E & K, Inc.
2000 International Pk. Dr.
Birmingham, AL 35243
205/969-3600
(Engineering services.)

BellSouth Services, Inc.
3535 Colonade Pkwy. S.
Birmingham, AL 35243
205/977-1590
(Telephone services.)

Blount, Inc.
4520 Executive Pk. Dr.
Montgomery, AL 36116
205/244-4000
(Industrial and commercial construction; manufacturing. Also at same address: Blount Construction Division, Blount International Ltd.)

Boone Newspapers, Inc.
P.O. Box 2370
Tuscaloosa, AL 35403
205/752-3381
(Newspaper publishing.)

Brunos Inc.
800 Lakeshore Pkwy.
Birmingham, AL 35211
205/940-9400
(Supermarkets.)

Buffalo Rock Co.
P.O. Box 10048
Birmingham, AL 35202
205/952-3435
(Soft drinks.)

Central Bancshares of the South, Inc.
701 S. 20th St.
Birmingham, AL 35233
205/933-3000
(Bank holding co.)

Coca-Cola Bottling Company United, Inc.
4600 E. Lake Blvd.
Birmingham, AL 35217
205/841-2653
(Soft drink bottling.)

Courtaulds Fibers Inc.
P.O. Box 141
Axis, AL 36505
205/679-2200
(Manmade fibers.)

Diversified Products Corp.
309 Williamson Ave.
Opelika, AL 36803
205/749-9001
(Sporting goods and recreational products.)

Drummond Co., Inc.
530 Beacon Pkwy.
Birmingham, AL 35209
205/387-0501
(Coal mining.)

Ebsco Industries, Inc.
P.O. Box 1943
Birmingham, AL 35201
205/991-6600
(Magazine subscription sales/service, display fixtures, etc.)

First Alabama Bancshares, Inc.
P.O. Box 10247
Birmingham, AL 35202
205/326-7060
(Banking.)

Gulf States Paper Corp.
P.O. Box 48999
Tuscaloosa, AL 35404
205/553-6200
(Paper and paper products, lumber and other forest products.)

Gayfer's
3120 Airport Blvd.
Mobile, AL 36606
205/471-6000
(Department stores.)

Harbert Corporation
P.O. Box 1297
Birmingham, AL 35201
205/987-5500
(Construction and engineering, cogeneration, real estate.)

Intergraph Corp.
One Madison Industrial Pk.
Huntsville, AL 35807
205/730-2000
(Workstations and applications.)

Kinder-Care, Inc.
2400 Presidents Dr.
Montgomery, AL 36116
205/277-5090
(Daycare centers, etc.)

Liberty National Life Insurance Co.
2001 Third Ave. S.
Birmingham, AL 35233
205/325-2722
(Life insurance.)

Morrison Inc.
P.O. Box 160266
Mobile, AL 36625
205/344-3000
(Cafeterias, restaurants, etc.)

Parisian, Inc.
200 Research Pkwy.
Birmingham, AL 35211
205/940-4000
(Apparel stores.)

Russell Corporation
P.O. Box 272
Alexander City, AL 35010
205/329-4000
(Apparel manufacturer.)

Rust International Corp.
100 Corporate Pkwy.
Box 101
Birmingham, AL 35201
205/995-7878
(Industrial design, engineering, construction.)

SCI Systems, Inc.
2101 Clinton Ave.
Huntsville, AL 35805
205/882-4800
(Computer and communications
systems.)

Sonat, Inc.
AmSouth-Sonat Tower
Birmingham, AL 35203
205/325-3800
(Utility.)

Sony Magnetic Products, Inc.
Hwy. 84 W.
Dothan, AL 36301
205/793-7655
(Magnetic recording tapes.)

**South Central Bell Telephone
Company**
(subs. of BellSouth)
P.O. Box 771
Birmingham, AL 35201
205/321-1000
(Telephone services.)

Southern Company Services, Inc.
800 Shades Creek Pkwy.
Birmingham, AL 35209
205/870-6011
(Accounting, engineering, and
technical services for Atlanta's
Southern Co.)

Southern Natural Gas Co.
1900 Fifth Ave. N.
Birmingham, AL 35203
205/325-7410
(Utilities company.)

SouthTrust Bank of Alabama
920 N. 20th St.
Box 2554
Birmingham, AL 35290
205/254-5600
(Banking.)

SouthTrust Corporation
420 N. 20th St.
Birmingham, AL 35290
205/254-5509
(Banking.)

Torchmark Corp.
2001 Third Ave. S.
Birmingham, AL 35233
205/325-4000
(Insurance, financial planning
services, management services.)

Vulcan Materials Co.
P.O. Box 530187
Birmingham, AL 35253-0187
205/877-3000
(Chemicals, construction materials.)

Jim Wilson & Associates
300 Water St.
Montgomery, AL 36104
205/263-1500
(Real estate developers.)

Wolverine Tube, Inc.
2100 Market St., NE
Decatur, AL 35602
205/353-1310
(Metal tubing.)

ALABAMA BUSINESS PERIODICAL

Business Alabama Monthly
PMT Publishing
2465 Commercial Park Dr.
Mobile, AL 36606
205/473-6269

(Monthly magazine; puts out annual
"Top Public Companies," listing
leading area companies.)

ALABAMA DIRECTORIES

Alabama Business Directory
American Business Directories
5711 S. 86th Cir.
P.O. Box 27347
Omaha, NE 68127
402/593-4600

Alabama Directory of Mining and Manufacturing
available from: Harris Publishing Company
2057 Aurora Rd.
Twinsburg, OH 44087
216/425-9000
800/888-5900

Alabama Industrial Directory
Alabama Development Office
c/o State Capitol

Montgomery, AL 36130
205/263-0048

Alabama Manufacturers Register
Manufacturers' News, Inc.
1633 Central St.
Evanston, IL 60201
708/864-7000

Southeastern Regional Manufacturers Directory
George D. Hall Company
50 Congress St.
Boston, MA 02109
617/523-3745
(Includes Alabama, Georgia, and Mississippi.)

ALABAMA GOVERNMENT EMPLOYMENT OFFICES

Office of Personnel Management
Bldg. 600, Suite 347
3322 Memorial Pkwy. S.
Huntsville, AL 35801-5351
205/544-5803
(Federal job-service center.)

Employment Service
Dept. of Industrial Relations
649 Monroe St.
Montgomery, AL 36130
205/261-5364
(State job-service center.)

FLORIDA

LEADING FLORIDA EMPLOYERS

John Alden Financial
7300 Corporate Center Dr.
Miami, FL 33126
305/470-3100
(Insurance.)

AT&T Paradyne Corp.
8545 126th Ave. N.
Largo, FL 34649
813/530-2000
(Telecommunications equipment.)

Barnett Banks
50 N. Laura St.
Jacksonville, FL 32203
904/791-7720
(Banking.)

Barnett Bank of Central Florida, N.A.
201 S. Orange Ave.
Orlando, FL 32801
407/646-3501
(Banking.)

Barnett Bank of Pinellas County
P.O Box 12288
St. Petersburg, FL 33733
813/535-0711
(Banking.)

Barnett Bank of South Florida, N.A.
701 Brickell Ave.
Miami, FL 33131
305/350-1832
(Banking.)

Bendix/King Air Transport Avionics Division
(div. of Allied-Signal Aerospace Co.)
P.O. Box 9327
Fort Lauderdale, FL 33310
305/928-2100
(Avionics systems manufacturer.)

Burger King Corp.
17777 Old Cutler Rd.
Miami, FL 33157
305/378-7011
(Fast food restaurants.)

Carnival Cruise Lines, Inc.
3655 NW 87th Ave.
Miami, FL 33178
305/599-2600
(Cruise lines.)

EG&G Florida, Inc.
412 High Point Dr.
Cocoa, FL 32926
407/639-3530
(Engineering services.)

FPL Group, Inc.
P.O. Box 08801
11770 U.S. Hwy. 1
North Palm Beach, FL 33408
407/694-6300
(Utility holding company.)

First Florida Banks
P.O. Box 31265
Tampa, FL 33631
813/224-1455
(Banking.)

First Union National Bank of Florida
200 Forsyth St.
Box 2080
Jacksonville, FL 32231
904/632-6565
(Banking.)

Florida Power & Light Co.
P.O. Box 078768
W. Palm Beach, FL 33407
405/640-2602
(Utility.)

Florida Progress Corp.
1 Progress Plz.
St. Petersburg, FL 33701
813/824-6400
(Utility.)

GTE Florida Incorporated
Tampa City Ctr.
Tampa, FL 33602
813/224-4011
(Telecommunications.)

Gates Energy Products, Inc.
U.S. Hwy. 441 N.
Box 147114
Gainesville, FL 32614
904/462-3911
(Storage batteries.)

General Mills Restaurants, Inc.
6770 Lake Elienor Dr.
Orlando, FL 32809
407/851-0370
(Chain restaurants, inc. Red Lobster Inns.)

W. R. Grace
One Town Center Rd.
Boca Raton, FL 33486
407/362-2000
(Chemicals.)

Harcourt Brace Jovanovich, Inc.
6277 Sea Harbor Dr.
Orlando, FL 32887
407/345-2000
(Book and periodical publishing.)

Harris Corp.
1025 NASA Blvd.
Melbourne, FL 32919
407/727-9100
(Electronic systems, semiconductors,
communications, and office
equipment.)

Home Shopping Network, Inc.
12000 25th Ct. N.
St. Petersburg, FL 33716
813/572-8585
(Cable television network.)

Independent Insurance Group
1 Independent Dr.
Jacksonville, FL 32276
904/358-5151
(Insurance.)

Kloster Cruise Ltd.
95 Merrick Way
Miami, FL 33134
305/447-9660
(Cruise line.)

Knight-Ridder, Inc.
1 Herald Plz.
Miami, FL 33132
305/376-3800
(Newspaper publishing.)

**Martin Marietta Electronics &
Missiles Group**
P.O. Box 5837
Orlando, FL 32855
407/356-2000
(Patriot missiles; other electronics and
defense systems.)

P-I-E Nationwide, Inc.
2050 Kings Rd.
Jacksonville, FL 32209
904/798-2000
(Motor freight carrier.)

**Pratt & Whitney Group—
Government Engine Business**
(unit of Pratt & Whitney Group)
P.O. Box 1096000
W. Palm Beach, FL 33410-9600

407/796-2000
(Military aircraft and rocket engines.)

Publix Super Markets, Inc.
1936 George Jenkins Blvd.
Lakeland, FL 33802
813/688-1188
(Supermarkets.)

Rascal Data Communications, Inc.
1601 N. Harrison Pkwy.
Sunrise, FL 33323
305/475-1601
(Telecommunications equipment.)

Royal Caribbean Corp.
903 S. America Way
Miami, FL 33132
305/379-2601
(Cruise line.)

Ryder System, Inc.
3600 NW 82nd Ave.
Miami, FL 33166
305/593-3726
(Truck leasing, jet engine repair,
aircraft components sale and leasing.)

Sentinel Communications Co.
633 N. Orange Ave.
Orlando, FL 32801
407/420-5000
(Newspaper publishing.)

Southeast Banking Corporation
1 Southeast Financial Ctr.
Miami, FL 33131
305/375-7500
(Banking.)

Universal Studios—Florida
1000 Universal Studio Plz.
Orlando, FL 32819
407/363-8000
(Entertainment company.)

Walt Disney World, Inc.
1675 Buena Vista Dr.
Lake Buena Vista, FL 32830
407/824-2222
(Amusement park, etc.)

Walter Industries
1500 N. Dale Mabry Hwy.
Tampa, FL 33607
813/871-4811
(Home building and financing, etc.)

Jim Walter Inc.
4010 Boy Scout Blvd.
Tampa, FL 33607
813/873-4194
(Building materials.)

FLORIDA BUSINESS PERIODICALS

Florida Business/Southwest
P.O. Box 9859
Naples, FL 33941
813/263-7525
(Monthly; covers southwestern
Florida.)

Florida Trend
Box 611
St. Petersburg, FL 33731
813/821-5800
(Monthly.)

Miami Today
Box 1368
Miami, FL 33101
305/579-0211
(Weekly.)

Orlando Magazine
Box 2207
341 N. Maitland Ave.
Orlando, FL 32802
407/539-3939
(Monthly.)

South Florida Business Journal
7950 NW 53rd St.
Miami, FL 33166
305/594-2100
(Weekly.)

Tampa Bay Business
Box 24185
Tampa, FL 33623
813/289-8225
(Weekly.)

FLORIDA DIRECTORIES

Florida Business Directory
American Business Directories
5711 S. 86th Cir.
P.O. Box 27347
Omaha, NE 68127
402/593-4600

Florida Manufacturers Register
Manufacturers' News, Inc.
1633 Central St.
Evanston, IL 60201
708/864-7000

FLORIDA GOVERNMENT EMPLOYMENT OFFICES

Office of Personnel Management
Commodore Bldg., Suite 125
3444 McCrory Pl.
Orlando, FL 32803-3701
407/648-6148
(Federal job-service center.)

**Dept. of Labor and Employment
Security**
1320 Executive Ctr. Cir.
300 Atkins Bldg.
Tallahassee, FL 32301
904/488-7228
(State job-service center.)

GEORGIA

LEADING GEORGIA EMPLOYERS

American Family Corp.
1932 Wynton Rd.
Columbus, GA 31999
706/323-3431
(Insurance.)

Bank South, N.A.
55 Marietta St., NW
Atlanta, GA 30303
404/529-4111
(Banking.)

BellSouth Corporation
1155 Peachtree St., NE
Atlanta, GA 30367-6000
404/249-2000
(Bell regional holding company.)

Cable News Network, Inc.
(part of Turner Broadcasting System)
1 CNN Ctr.
Atlanta, GA 30335
404/827-1500
(Cable television all-news network.)

Ciba Vision Care Corp.
2910 Amwiler Ct.
Atlanta, GA 30360
404/448-1200
(Optical care products.)

Citizens & Southern Corp.
35 Broad St.
Atlanta, GA 30303
404/581-2121
(Banking.)

The Coca-Cola Company
1 Coca-Cola Plz., NW
Atlanta, GA 30313
404/676-2121
(Beverages and food.)

Coca-Cola Enterprises Inc.
One Coca-Cola Plz., NW
Atlanta, GA 30313
404/676-2100
(Soft drinks, extracts and syrups.)

Contel Cellular Inc.
245 Perimeter Center Pkwy.
Atlanta, GA 30346
404/391-8000
(Cellular telephone service.)

Coronet Industries, Inc.
Coronet Dr.
Dalton, GA 30722
706/259-4511
(Carpeting.)

Cox Enterprises
1400 Lake Hearn Dr.
Atlanta, GA 30319
404/843-5000
(Communications media.)

Crawford & Co.
5620 Glenridge Dr., NE
Atlanta, GA 30342
404/256-0830
(Insurance agents; brokers and
service.)

Delta Airlines, Inc.
Hartsfield-Atlanta International Airport
Atlanta, GA 30320
404/715-2600
(Airline.)

Digital Communications Associates
1000 Alderman Dr.
Alpharetta, GA 30201
404/442-4000
(Computer peripherals.)

Equifax, Inc.
1600 Peachtree St., NW
Atlanta, GA 30302
404/885-8000
(Credit information.)

Federal Reserve Bank of Atlanta
P.O. Box 1731
Atlanta, GA 30301

404/586-8500
(Federal Reserve bank.)

First Atlanta Bank
2 Peachtree St., NW
Box 4148
Atlanta, GA 30303
404/332-5000
(Banking.)

First Financial Management
3 Corporate Sq.
Atlanta, GA 30329
404/321-0120
(Financial data processing.)

First Union National Bank of Georgia
55 Park Pl.
Atlanta, GA 30303
404/827-7100
(Banking.)

Flowers Industries, Inc.
200 U.S. Hwy. 19 S.
Thomasville, GA 31799
912/226-9110
(Food processing.)

Forstmann & Co., Inc.
Nathaniel Dr.
P.O. Box 1049
Dublin, GA 31021
912/275-5400
(Wool fabric mills.)

Georgia Federal Bank
20 Marietta St., NW
Atlanta, GA 30303
404/330-2400
(Banking.)

Georgia Gulf Corp.
400 Perimeter Ctr. Terr.
Atlanta, GA 30346
404/395-4500
(Chemicals.)

Georgia-Pacific Corp.
133 Peachtree St., NE
Atlanta, GA 30303

404/521-4000
(Forest products.)

Georgia Power Co.
333 Piedmont Ave., NE
Atlanta, GA 30308
404/526-6526
(Utility.)

Georgia U.S. Corp.
5780 Powers Ferry Rd., NW
Atlanta, GA 30327
404/980-5100
(Life insurance.)

Gold Kist, Inc.
244 Perimeter Ctr. Pkwy., NE
Atlanta, GA 30346
404/393-5000
(Poultry processing.)

Gulfstream Aerospace Corp.
Box 2206
Savannah International Airport
Savannah, GA 31402-2206
912/964-3000
(Aircraft manufacturing, support, and services.)

HBO & Co.
301 Perimeter Ctr. N.
Atlanta, GA 30346
404/393-6000
(Computer software.)

Home Depot, Inc.
2727 Paces Ferry Rd.
Atlanta, GA 30339
404/433-8211
(Building supply retailer.)

Kemira, Inc.
President St. Ext.
Savannah, GA 31404
912/236-6171
(Inorganic pigments.)

Lanier Worldwide, Inc.
2300 Parklake Dr., NE
Atlanta, GA 30345
404/496-9500

(Dictating machines, fax machines, etc.)

Life Insurance Co. of Georgia
5780 Powers Ferry Rd., NW
Atlanta, GA 30327
404/980-5100
(Insurance.)

Macy's South, Inc.
180 Peachtree St., NW
Atlanta, GA 30303
404/221-7221
(Department stores.)

National Data Corp.
1 National Data Plz.
Atlanta, GA 30329
404/728-2000
(Electronic services.)

Rollins, Inc.
2170 Piedmont Rd., NE
Atlanta, GA 30324
404/888-2000
(Pest control and lawn care.)

Roper Corp.
1507 Broomtown Rd.
La Fayette, GA 30728
706/638-5100
(Household cooking products.)

Scientific Atlanta, Inc.
1 Technology Pk.
Atlanta, GA 30348
404/441-4000
(Equipment for telecommunications and cable industries, etc.)

Southern Bell
675 W. Peachtree St., NE
Atlanta, GA 30375
404/529-8611
(Telephone services.)

The Southern Company
64 Perimeter Ctr. E.
Atlanta, GA 30346

404/393-0650
(Electric utility.)

Southwire Co.
1 Southwire Dr.
Carrolton, GA 30117
404/832-4242
(Extruded shapes and wire, copper and copper alloy.)

SunTrust Banks
25 Park Pl., NE
Atlanta, GA 30303
404/588-7711
(Banking.)

Swift Textiles, Inc.
P.O. Box 1400
Columbus, GA 31994
706/324-3623
(Textile mills.)

Trammel Crow Residential
2859 Paces Ferry Rd.
Suite 2100
Atlanta, GA 30339
404/433-2000
(Real estate developers.)

Turner Broadcasting System
1 CNN Ctr.
Box 105366
Atlanta, GA 30348
404/827-1700
(Broadcasting.)

West Point-Pepperell
400 W. 10th St
West Point, GA 31833
706/645-4000
(Textiles, home furnishings.)

A. L. Williams & Co.
3120 Breckenridge Blvd.
Duluth, GA 30136
404/381-1674
(Insurance.)

GEORGIA BUSINESS PERIODICALS

Atlanta Business Chronicle
1801 Peachtree St., NE
Atlanta, GA 30309
404/249-1000
(Weekly.)

Georgia Trend
133 Peachtree St., NE
Atlanta, GA 30303
404/522-7200
(Monthly.)

GEORGIA DIRECTORIES

Georgia Business Directory
American Business Directories
5711 S. 86th Cir.
P.O. Box 27347
Omaha, NE 68127
402/593-4600

Georgia Manufacturers Register
Manufacturers' News, Inc.
1633 Central St.
Evanston, IL 60201
708/864-7000

Georgia Manufacturing Directory
Dept. of Industry, Trade and Tourism
Marquis II Tower

Ste. 1100
285 Peachtree Center Ave.
Box 56706
Atlanta, GA 30343
404/656-3607

*Southeastern Regional
Manufacturers Directory*
George D. Hall Company
50 Congress St.
Boston, MA 02109
617/523-3745
(Includes Alabama, Georgia, and
Mississippi.)

GEORGIA GOVERNMENT EMPLOYMENT OFFICES

Office of Personnel Management
75 Spring St., SW
Atlanta, GA 30303-3109
(Regional federal OPM office.)

Richard B. Russell Federal Bldg.
75 Spring St., SW, Room 960
Atlanta, GA 30303-3309
404/331-4315
(Federal job-service center.)

Employment Service
148 International Blvd. N.,
Room 400
Atlanta, GA 30303
404/656-0380
(State job-service center.)

KENTUCKY

LEADING KENTUCKY EMPLOYERS

Accuride Corp.
(subs. Phelps Dodge Corp.)
2315 Adams Ln.
Henderson, KY 42420
502/826-5000
(Wheels.)

Appalachian Computer Services
U.S. Hwy. 25 S.
P.O. Box 140
London, KY 40741
606/878-7900
(Data processing/data entry services; computer peripherals; software.)

Arco Aluminum, Inc.
101 S. Fifth St.
Louisville, KY 40202
502/566-5700
(Aluminum bars, rods, ingots, etc.)

Ashland Oil, Inc.
P.O. Box 391
Ashland, KY 41114
606/329-3333
(Oil refining, transportation and marketing, chemicals, gasoline, etc.)

Blue Cross & Blue Shield of Kentucky
9901 Linn Station Rd.
Louisville, KY 40223
502/423-2011
(Health insurance.)

Brown & Williamson Tobacco Corp.
1500 Brown & Williamson Tower
Louisville, KY 40202
502/568-7000
(Tobacco products.)

Brown-Forman Corp.
P.O. Box 1080
Louisville, KY 40201
502/585-1100
(Liquors.)

Capital Holding Corp.
680 Fourth Ave.
Box 32830
Louisville, KY 40202
502/560-2000
(Holding company—insurance companies.)

Chi-Chi's, Inc.
10200 Linn Station Rd.
Box 32338
Louisville, KY 40223
502/426-3900
(Chain restaurants.)

Citizens Fidelity Corp.
500 W. Jefferson St.
Louisville, KY 40296
502/581-2100
(Banking.)

Commonwealth Life Insurance Co.
680 Fourth Ave.
Louisville, KY 40202
502/587-7371
(Life insurance.)

First Kentucky National Corp.
3700 First National Tower
Box 36000
Louisville, KY 40233
502/581-4200
(Banking.)

First National Bank of Louisville
101 S. Fifth St.
Louisville, KY 40202
502/581-4200
(Banking.)

First Security Corp. of Kentucky
1 First Security Plz.
Lexington, KY 40507
606/231-1000
(Banking.)

Humana, Inc.
500 W. Main St.
Box 1438
Louisville, KY 40201
502/580-1000
(Hospitals.)

I.C.H. Corp.
100 Mallard Creek Rd.
Box 400
Louisville, KY 40207
502/894-2100
(Insurance; holding company.)

Island Creek Coal Co.
P.O. Box 11430
Lexington, KY 40575
606/288-3000
(Coal.)

Jerrico, Inc.
101 Jerrico Dr.
Lexington, KY 40579
606/263-6000
(Chain restaurants, restaurant supplies.)

Kentucky Central Life Insurance Co.
Kincaid Towers
Lexington, KY 40507
606/253-5111
(Life insurance.)

Kentucky Fried Chicken Corp.
1411 Gardiner Ln.
Louisville, KY 40213
502/456-8300
(Chain restaurants.)

Kentucky Utilities Co.
1 Quality St.
Lexington, KY 40507
606/255-1461
(Utility.)

Liberty National Bancorp, Inc.
416 W. Jefferson St.
Louisville, KY 40202
502/566-2000
(Banking.)

Link Belt Construction Equipment Co.
3001 Todds Rd.
Lexington, KY 40509
606/263-5200
(Construction machinery and equipment.)

Mazak Corp.
8025 Production Dr.
Florence, KY 41402
606/727-5700
(Wholesale industrial equipment and machinery.)

National Processing Co.
1231 Durrett Ln.
Louisville, KY 40285
502/364-2000
(Data processing services.)

National Southwire Aluminum Co.
Junction of Hwys. 271 and 334
Hawesville, KY 42348
502/927-6921
(Secondary aluminum smelting/refining.)

Peabody Coal Company
1951 Barrett Ct.
Box 1990
Henderson, KY 42420
520/827-0800
(Coal mining and handling.)

Publishers Printing Co.
1 Fourth Ave.
Shepherdswood, KY 40165
502/543-2251
(Commercial printing.)

Toyota Motor Manufacturing USA
1001 Cherry Blossom
Georgetown, KY 40324
502/868-2000
(Automobiles.)

Union Underwear Co., Inc.
1 Fruit of the Loom Dr.
Bowling Green, KY 42103
502/781-6400
(Underwear manufacturing.)

Valvoline, Inc.
P.O. Box 14000
Lexington, KY 40512
606/268-7777
(Oils and greases.)

Henry Vogt Machine Co.
10th & Ormsby Sts.
Louisville, KY 40210
502/634-1500
(Fabricated platework.)

KENTUCKY BUSINESS PERIODICALS

Business First
111 W. Washington St.
P.O. Box 40201
Louisville, KY 40202-1311
(Weekly.)

Kentucky Business Ledger
Kentucky Communications, Inc.
Box 470867
Charlotte, NC 28247
(Monthly.)

KENTUCKY DIRECTORIES

Harris Kentucky Industrial Directory
Harris Publishing Company
2057 Aurora Rd.
Twinsburg, OH 44087
216/425-9000
800/888-5900

Kentucky Business Directory
American Business Directories
5711 S. 86th Circle
P.O. Box 27347
Omaha, NE 68127
402/593-4600

Kentucky Directory of Manufacturers
Department of Business & Industry
Capital Plaza Tower
Frankfort, KY 40601
502/564-4886

Kentucky Manufacturers Register
Manufacturers' News, Inc.
1633 Central St.
Evanston, IL 60201
708/864-7000

KENTUCKY GOVERNMENT EMPLOYMENT OFFICES

Office of Personnel Management
(For federal job service centers see
Ohio listing.)

Dept. for Employment Services
275 E. Main St., 2nd Fl.
Frankfort, KY 40621
502/564-5331
(State job-service center.)

LOUISIANA

LEADING LOUISIANA EMPLOYERS

Arkla, Inc.
Arkla Bldg.
525 Milam St.
Shreveport, LA 71151
318/429-2700
(Gas transmission and distribution.)

Avondale Industries, Inc.
P.O. Box 50280
New Orleans, LA 70150
504/436-2121
(Shipbuilding and repair.)

The Babcock & Wilcox Company
1010 Common St.
Box 61038
New Orleans, LA 70161
504/587-5700
(Power generation systems &
equipment, etc.)

Al Copeland Enterprises, Inc.
1333 S. Clearview
Jefferson, LA 70121
504/733-4300
(Chain restaurants—Popeye's Famous
Fried Chicken.)

**Copolymer Rubber & Chemical
Corp.**
P.O. Box 2591
Baton Rouge, LA 70821
504/355-5655
(Synthetic rubber.)

Entergy Corp.
225 Baronne St.
New Orleans, LA 70112
504/529-5262
(Electric services, natural gas
distribution.)

Ethyl Corp. Chemicals Group
451 Florida
Baton Rouge, LA 70801
504/388-7755
(Industrial organic chemicals.)

Exxon Chemical Americas
3825 Plz. Tower Dr.
Baton Rouge, LA 70816
504/293-9933
(Industrial inorganic chemicals.)

First Commerce Bank
210 Baronne St.
Box 60279
New Orleans, LA 70160
504/561-1371
(Banking.)

Freeport Minerals Co.
1615 Poydras St.
Box 61119
New Orleans, LA 70112
504/582-4000
(Sulphur, phosphoric acid, etc.)

**Freeport-McMoran Copper & Gold
Inc.**
1615 Poydras St.
New Orleans, LA 70112
504/582-4000
(Copper, gold and silver mines.)

Freeport-McMoran Inc.
1615 Poydras St.
New Orleans, LA 70112
504/582-4000
(Agricultural mineral mining oil &
gas, etc.)

**Freeport-McMoran Resource
Partners**
1615 Poydras St.
New Orleans, LA 70112
504/582-4000
(Fertilizer chemicals, oil and natural
gas development, etc.)

Hibernia National Bank
313 Carondelet St.
New Orleans, LA 70130
504/586-5552
(Banking.)

Louisiana Power & Light Co.
317 Baronne St.
New Orleans, LA 70160
504/595-3100
(Electric utility.)

Lykes Brothers Steamship Co., Inc.
Lykes Ctr.
300 Poydras St.
New Orleans, LA 70130
504/523-6611
(Steamships.)

Maison Blanche, Inc.
1500–07 Main St.
Baton Rouge, LA 70802
504/389-7000
(Department store.)

Manville Forest Products Corp.
P.O. Box 35800
West Monroe, LA 71291
318/362-2000
(Paperboard, paper bags, other paper products.)

Martin Marietta Manned Space Systems
P.O. Box 29304
13800 Old Gentilly Rd.
New Orleans, LA 70189
504/257-3700
(Shuttle external tanks.)

Martin Mills, Inc.
Hwy. 31 N.
P.O. Box 129
St. Martinville, LA 70112
504/587-5400
(Apparel—men's and boys' briefs and T-shirts.)

McDermott International, Inc.
1010 Common St.
New Orleans, LA 70112
504/587-5400
(Heavy construction offshore platforms, engineering, etc.)

New Orleans Public Service
317 Baronne St.
New Orleans, LA 70160
504/587-5439
(Utility.)

Ocean Drilling and Exploration Co.
P.O. Box 61780
New Orleans, LA 70161
504/561-2811
(Petroleum and natural gas drilling and exploration.)

Pan American Life Insurance
601 Poydras St.
New Orleans, LA 70130
504/566-1300
(Life insurance.)

Picadilly Cafeterias, Inc.
3232 Sherwood Forest Blvd.
Baton Rouge, LA 70821
504/293-9440
(Restaurant food services.)

Premier Bancorp, Inc.
P.O. Box 1511
Baton Rouge, LA 70821
504/332-4011
(Banking—owns Premier Bank, N.A.)

Shell Offshore, Inc.
1 Shell Sq.
701 Poydras St.
New Orleans, LA 70139
504/588-6161
(Petroleum exploration and drilling.)

Turner Investments Co.
2865 Mason St.
Baton Rouge, LA 70805
504/356-1301
(Industrial buildings/warehouses, machinery/equipment repair, rental and leasing.)

Wiener Enterprises, Inc.
5725 Powell St.
Harahan, LA 70123
504/733-7055
(Retail shoes and apparel, etc.)

LOUISIANA BUSINESS PERIODICALS

Baton Rouge Business Report
Louisiana Business, Inc.
P.O. Box 1949
Baton Rouge, LA 70821
504/928-1700

New Orleans Business
111 Veterans Blvd.
Metairie, LA 70005
504/834-0202

LOUISIANA DIRECTORIES

**Directory of Louisiana
Manufacturers**
Department of Economic Development
Box 94185
Capitol Station
Baton Rouge, LA 70804-9185
504/342-5383

**Greater Baton Rouge Manufacturers
Directory**
Greater Baton Rouge Chamber of
Commerce
564 Laurel St.
Box 3217

Baton Rouge, LA 70821
504/381-7125
Louisiana Business Directory
American Business Directories
5711 S. 86th Cir.
P.O. Box 27347
Omaha, NE 68127
402/593-4600

Louisiana Manufacturers Register
Manufacturers' News, Inc.
1633 Central St.
Evanston, IL 60201
708/864-7000

LOUISIANA GOVERNMENT EMPLOYMENT OFFICES

Employment Service
Office of Employment Security
P.O. Box 94094
Baton Rouge, LA 70804-9094
504/342-3016
(State job-service center.)

Office of Personnel Management
1515 Poydras St.,
Suite 600
New Orleans, LA 70130
504/589-2764
(Federal job-service center.)

MISSISSIPPI

LEADING MISSISSIPPI EMPLOYERS

Bancorp of Mississippi Inc.
1 Mississippi Plz.
Tupelo, MS 38801
601/680-2000
(Banking.)

Bill's Dollar, Inc.
P.O. Box 9407
Jackson, MS 39286
601/981-7171
(Discount stores.)

Bryan Foods, Inc.
Church Hill Rd.
P.O. Box 1177
West Point, MS 39773
601/494-3741
(Meat packing.)

Cortelco USA, Inc.
Fulton Dr.
P.O. Box 831
Corinth, MS 38834
601/287-3771
(Telecommunications equipment.)

Croft Metals, Inc.
24th St.
McComb, MS 39648
601/684-6121
(Aluminum and plastic plumbing
fixtures.)

Delta Pride Catfish, Inc.
Indianola Industrial Pk.
Hwy. 495
Indianola, MS 38751
601/887-5401
(Catfish processing.)

Deposit Guaranty
P.O. Box 730
Jackson, MS 39205
601/968-4794
(Banking.)

Ergon, Inc.
202 E. Pearl St.
Jackson, MS 39205
601/948-3472
(Oil and gas, transportation,
manufacturing.)

First Mississippi Corp.
700 North St.
Box 1249
Jackson, MS 39215
601/948-7550
(Organic crudes and intermediates,
dyes and pigments.)

Hancock Fabrics, Inc.
3406 W. Main St.
Tupelo, MS 38801

601/842-2834
(Sewing/needlework stores.)

Ingall's Shipbuilding, Inc.
1000 W. River Rd.
Box 149
Pascagoula, MS 39563
601/935-1122
(Shipbuilding.)

Irby Construction Co.
P.O. Box 1819
Jackson, MS 39215
601/969-1822
(Construction electric power lines,
etc.)

Jitney-Jungle Stores of America
451–57 N. Mill St.
Jackson, MS 39207
601/948-0361
(Food stores.)

KLLM Transport Services Inc.
3475 Lakeland Dr.
Box 6098
Jackson, MS 39208
601/939-2545
(Trucking.)

McCarty Farms, Inc.
Industrial Park Dr.
Magee, MS 39111
601/849-3351
(Poultry processing, feed mills.)

McCarty Processors, Inc.
238 Wilmington
Jackson, MS 39204
601/372-7441
(Poultry processing.)

McRae's, Inc.
3455 Hwy. 80 W.
Jackson, MS 39209
601/968-4400
(Department stores.)

Mississippi Chemical Corp.
P.O. Box 388
Yazoo City, MS 39194
601/746-4131
(Fertilizers.)

Mississippi Power Co.
2992 W. Beach
Gulfport, MS 39501
601/864-1211
(Utility.)

Mississippi Power & Light Co.
P.O. Box 1640
Jackson, MS 39215
601/969-2311
(Electric utility.)

Mississippi Valley Gas Co.
711 W. Capitol St.
Jackson, MS 39203
601/961-6900
(Natural gas distribution.)

Mobile Communications Corp. of America
(subs. BellSouth)
1800 E. County Line Rd.
Ridgeland, MS 39157
601/977-0888
(Radio communications, holding company.)

National American Corp.
2012 Hwy. 90
Gautier, MS 39553
601/497-4100
(Real estate developer.)

Peavey Electronics Corp.
711 A St.
P.O. Box 2898
Meridian, MS 39301
601/483-5365
(Commercial sound equipment.)

South Mississippi Electric Power Association
Hwy. 49 N.
Hattiesburg, MS 39401
601/268-2083
(Electric services.)

Southern Farm Bureau Casualty Insurance Co.
1401 Livingston Ln.
Jackson, MS 39213
601/982-7777
(Insurance.)

Southern Farm Bureau Life Insurance Co.
P.O. Box 78
Jackson, MS 39205
601/981-7422
(Insurance.)

System Energy Resources, Inc.
P.O. Box 23070
Jackson, MS 39225
601/960-9600
(Electric services.)

Trustmark National Bank
248 E. Capitol St.
Jackson, MS 39201
601/354-5111
(Banking.)

United Technologies Motor Systems
McCrary Rd.
PO Box 2228
Columbus, MS 39701
601/328-4150
(Auto and aircraft motors.)

MISSISSIPPI BUSINESS PERIODICAL

Mississippi Business Journal
Venture Publications
P.O. Box 4566
Jackson, MS 39296
601/352-9035
(Monthly.)

MISSISSIPPI DIRECTORIES

Mississippi Business Directory
American Business Directories
5711 S. 86th Cir.
P.O. Box 27347
Omaha, NE 68127
402/593-4600

Southeastern Manufacturers
Directory
George D. Hall Company
50 Congress St.
Boston, MA 02109
617/523-3745
(Includes Alabama, Georgia, and
Mississippi.)

MISSISSIPPI GOVERNMENT EMPLOYMENT OFFICES

Office of Personnel Management
(See Alabama listing.)

Employment Service Division
Employment Service Commission
P.O. Box 1699
Jackson, MS 39215-1699
601/354-8711

NORTH CAROLINA

LEADING NORTH CAROLINA EMPLOYERS

BarclaysAmerican Corporation
201 S. Tryon St.
Charlotte, NC 28231
704/339-5000
(Business credit institution.)

Burlington Industries, Inc.
3330 W. Friendly Ave.
Greensboro, NC 27410
919/379-2000
(Textiles.)

Biggers Brothers, Inc.
920 Black Satchel Dr.
Charlotte, NC 28216
704/394-7121
(Wholesale institutional foods.)

Burroughs Wellcome Co.
3030 Cornwallis Rd.
Research Triangle Park, NC 27709
919/248-3000
(Pharmaceuticals.)

Branch Banking & Trust Co.
223 W. Nash St.
Wilson, NC 27893
919/399-4111
(Banking.)

Carolina Freight Carriers Corp.
P.O. Box 697
Cherryville, NC 28021
704/435-6811
(Motor carrier.)

Broyhill Furniture Industries, Inc.
Broyhill Pk.
Lenoir, NC 28633
704/758-3111
(Furniture.)

Carolina Power & Light Co.
411 Fayetteville St.
Raleigh, NC 27602
919/546-6111
(Utility.)

Carolina Telephone & Telegraph Co.
122 E. St. James St.
Tarboro, NC 27886
919/823-9900
(Telephone services.)

Century Furniture Co.
408 12th St., NW
Hickory, NC 28601
704/328-1851
(Furniture.)

Cone Mills
1201 Maple St.
Greensboro, NC 27405
919/379-6220
(Textiles.)

Drexel Heritage Furnishings
101 Main St.
Drexel, NC 28619
704/433-3000
(Furniture.)

Duke Power Co.
422 S. Church St.
Charlotte, NC 28242
704/594-0887
(Utility.)

Exide Electronics Group, Inc.
3201 Spring Forest Rd.
Raleigh, NC 27604
919/872-3020
(Electrical apparatus.)

Fieldcrest Cannon, Inc.
725 N. Regional Rd.
Greensboro, NC 27409
919/665-4000
(Household furnishings—rugs, sheets, etc.)

First Citizens Bancshares, Inc.
20 E. Martin St.
Box 151
Raleigh, NC 27602
919/755-7000
(Banking.)

First Union Corp.
First Union Plz.
Charlotte, NC 28288
704/374-6565
(Banking.)

First Union Mortgage Corp.
First Union Plz.
Charlotte, NC 28288
704/374-6787
(Mortgage banking, real estate, etc.)

Food Lion, Inc.
2110 Executive Dr.
Salisbury, NC 28144
704/633-8250
(Supermarkets.)

Glaxo, Inc.
5 Moore Dr.
Research Triangle Park, NC 27709
919/248-6811
(Pharmaceuticals.)

GTE South Incorporated
4100 Roxboro Rd.
Durham, NC 27704
919/471-5000
(Telecommunications.)

Guilford Mills, Inc.
4925 W. Market St.
Greensboro, NC 27407
919/292-7550
(Textile mills, yarn, dyes.)

Hampton Industries, Inc.
2000 Greenville Hwy.
Kinston, NC 28501
919/527-8011
(Apparel.)

Hardees Food Systems, Inc.
1233 Hardees Blvd.
Rocky Mount, NC 27804
919/977-2000
(Fast food restaurants.)

Harriet & Henderson Yarns, Inc.
Alexander Ave.
Henderson, NC 27536
919/438-3101
(Yarn spinning mill.)

Henredon Furniture Industries
Henredon Rd.
P.O. Box 70
Morganton, NC 28655
704/437-5261
(Furniture.)

Hoechst-Celanese Corp.
Fibers & Film Division
6000 Carnegie Blvd.
Charlotte, NC 28209
704/554-2000
(Manmade fibers, etc.)

Integon Corp.
500 W. Fifth St.
Box 3199
Winston-Salem, NC 27152
919/770-2000
(Insurance.)

Jefferson-Pilot Corp.
100 N. Greene St.
Greensboro, NC 27401
919/691-3000
(Insurance.)

Lance, Inc.
P.O. Box 32368
8600 South Blvd.
Charlotte, NC 28232
704/554-1421
(Cookies, crackers, snack foods.)

L'Eggs Products, Inc.
P.O. Box 2495
Winston-Salem, NC 27102
919/768-9540
(Hosiery.)

Lowe's Companies, Inc.
P.O. Box 1111
N. Wilkesboro, NC 28656
919/651-4000
(Windows, doors.)

Medical Personnel Pool Metrolina
118 Colonial Ave.
Charlotte, NC 28207
704/372-8230
(Medical employment agency.)

Mitsubishi Semiconducter America
3 Diamond Ln.
Durham, NC 27704
919/479-3333
(Semiconductors.)

NationsBank
One NationsBank Plz.
Charlotte, NC 28255
704/386-5000
(Commercial banking.)

Nucor Corp.
4425 Randolph Rd.
Charlotte, NC 28211
704/366-7000
(Steel.)

Planters Lifesavers Co.
1100 Reynolds Blvd.
Winston-Salem, NC 27102
919/741-2000
(Nuts, candy, etc.)

Research Triangle Institute
3040 W. Cornwallis Rd.
Research Triangle Park, NC 27705
919/541-6000
(Commercial physical research, etc.)

R. J. Reynolds Tobacco Co.
401 N. Main St.
Winston-Salem, NC 27102
919/741-5000
(Tobacco.)

Rose's Stores, Inc.
P.O. Box 947
Henderson, NC 27536
919/430-2600
(Discount stores.)

Royal Group, Inc.
9300 Arrowpoint Blvd.
Charlotte, NC 28217
704/522-2000
(Insurance.)

SAS Institute, Inc.
SAS Campus Dr.
P.O. Box 8000
Cary, NC 27513
919/677-8000
(Computer software development.)

Volvo GM Heavy Truck Corp.
7825 National Service Rd.
Greensboro, NC 27409
919/279-2000
(Trucks.)

Wachovia Bank
301 N. Main St.
Winston-Salem, NC 27101
919/770-5000
(Banking.)

NORTH CAROLINA BUSINESS PERIODICAL

Business NC
77 Ctr. Dr.
Charlotte, NC 28217
704/523-6987
(Monthly.)

NORTH CAROLINA DIRECTORIES

Directory of Central Atlantic States Manufacturers
George D. Hall Company
50 Congress St.
Boston, MA 02109
617/523-3745
(Includes Maryland, Delaware, Virginia, West Virginia, North Carolina, and South Carolina.)

Directory of North Carolina Manufacturers
George D. Hall Company

50 Congress St.
Boston, MA 02109
617/523-3745

North Carolina Business Directory
American Business Directories
5711 S. 86th Cir.
P.O. Box 27347
Omaha, NE 68127
402/593-4600

NORTH CAROLINA GOVERNMENT EMPLOYMENT OFFICES

Office of Personnel Management
P.O. Box 25069
4505 Falls of the Neuse Rd.,
Suite 445
Raleigh, NC 27611-5069
919/856-4361
(Federal job-service center.)

Employment Security Commission of North Carolina
P.O. Box 27625
Raleigh, NC 27611
919/733-7522
(State job-service center.)

OKLAHOMA

LEADING OKLAHOMA EMPLOYERS

C. R. Anthony & Co.
701 N. Broadway
Oklahoma City, OK 73102
405/235-3711
(Department stores.)

Citgo Petroleum Corp.
P.O. Box 3758
Tulsa, OK 74102
918/495-4000
(Petroleum refining, marketing,
transportation.)

Fleming Companies, Inc.
6301 Waterford Blvd.
Box 26647
Oklahoma City, OK 73126
405/840-7200
(Food distribution.)

Flintco Companies, Inc.
1624 W. 21st St.
Tulsa, OK 74101
918/587-8451
(Construction.)

Hale-Halsell Co.
P.O. Box 582898
Tulsa, OK 74158
918/835-4484
(Wholesale groceries.)

Helmerich & Payne, Inc.
1579 E. 21st St.
Tulsa, OK 74114
918/742-5531
(Oil/gas wells drilling, exploration,
chemicals manufacturing, real estate.)

Hilti, Inc.
5400 S. 122nd Ave.
Tulsa, OK 74146
918/252-6000
(Power tools.)

Kerr-McGee Corp.
Kerr-McGee Ctr.
P.O. Box 25861

Oklahoma City, OK 73125
405/270-1313
(Petroleum/natural gas exploration,
processing, marketing
petrochemicals.)

Macklanburg-Duncan Co.
4041 N. Santa Fe
Oklahoma City, OK 73125
405/528-4411
(Building specialty products.)

Mapco, Inc.
1800 S. Baltimore Ave.
Tulsa, OK 74119
918/581-1800
(Integrated natural resources.)

McDonnell Douglas Tulsa
2000 N. Memorial Dr.
Tulsa OK 74115
918/836-1616
(Subassemblies for aircraft and
missiles, etc.)

Memorex Telex Corp.
6422 E. 41st St.
Box 1526
Tulsa, OK 74101
918/627-2333
(Computer terminals and other
peripherals.)

Noble Affiliates, Inc.
110 W. Broadway
Ardmore, OK 73401
405/223-4110
(Petroleum services.)

**Northrop Worldwide Aircraft
Services, Inc.**
P.O. Box 108
21 NW 44th St.
Lawton, OK 73505-0108
405/353-2733
(Aircraft maintenance and support
services.)

Northwest Energy Co.
1 Williams Ctr.
Suite 4800
Tulsa, OK 74172
918/588-2000
(Pipeline transmission of natural
gas/petroleum products.)

Oklahoma Gas & Electric Co.
321 N. Harvey Ave.
Oklahoma City, OK 73101
405/272-3000
(Utility.)

Oklahoma Publishing Co.
550 N. Broadway
Box 25125
Oklahoma City, OK 73125
405/475-3311
(Newspaper publishing.)

Parker Drilling Co.
8 E. Third St.
Tulsa, OK 74103
918/585-8221
(Oil/gas wells drilling and
exploration.)

Philips 66 Co.
Philips Bldg.
Fourth & Keeler Sts.
Bartlesville, OK 74004

918/661-4400
(Petroleum marketing; convenience
stores.)

Philips Petroleum Co.
Philips Bldg.
Fourth & Keeler Sts.
Bartlesville, OK 74004
918/661-6600
(Petroleum exploration, production,
refining, marketing.)

Purolator Products Co.
6120 S. Yale
Tulsa, OK 74136
918/492-1800
(Motor vehicle parts and accessories.)

Scrivner, Inc.
5701 N. Shartel
Box 26030
Oklahoma City, OK 73126
405/841-8500
(Wholesale foods.)

The Williams Companies, Inc.
1 Williams Ctr.
Tulsa, OK 74172
918/588-2000
(Pipeline transmission of natural gas,
etc.; digital telecommunications.)

OKLAHOMA BUSINESS PERIODICAL

Tulsa Business Chronicle
World Publishing Co.
315 S. Boulder
P.O. Box 1770

Tulsa, OK 74102
918/581-8560
(Weekly.)

OKLAHOMA DIRECTORIES

Oklahoma Business Directory
American Business Directories
5711 S. 86th Cir.
P.O. Box 27347
Omaha, NE 68127
402/593-4600

*Oklahoma Directory of
Manufacturers and Processors*
Oklahoma Dept. of Commerce
Box 26980
Oklahoma City, OK 73126
405/521-2401

OKLAHOMA GOVERNMENT EMPLOYMENT OFFICES

Office of Personnel Management
200 NW Fifth St.,
2nd Fl.
Oklahoma City, OK 73102
405/231-4948
(Federal job-service center.)

**Employment Service Employment
Security Commission**
Will Rogers Memorial Office Bldg.
Oklahoma City, OK 73105
405/521-3652
(State job-service center.)

SOUTH CAROLINA
LEADING SOUTH CAROLINA EMPLOYERS

Bi-Lo, Inc.
Industrial Blvd.
Mauldin, SC 29662
803/243-1600
(Supermarkets.)

Clinton Mills, Inc.
600 Academy St.
Clinton, SC 29325
803/833-5500
(Textiles.)

Coats & Clark, Inc.
30 Patewood Dr.
Greenville, SC 29615
803/234-0331
(Thread, trim, etc.)

Delta Woodside Industries
233 N. Main St.
Greenville, SC 29601
803/232-8301
(Textiles.)

Evening Post Publishing Co.
134 Columbus St.
Charleston, SC 29403
803/577-7111
(Newspaper publishing, television
stations.)

**First Citizens Bancorporation of
South Carolina, Inc.**
1230 Main St.
Columbia, SC 29201
803/771-8700
(Banking.)

Graniteville Co.
Main St.
Graniteville, SC 29829
803/663-7231
(Textiles.)

Greenwood Mills, Inc.
Greenwood Bldg.
P.O. Box 1017
Greenwood, SC 29648
803/229-2571
(Textiles.)

Klear Knit, Inc.
510 Sunset Dr.
Clover, SC 29710
803/222-3011
(Apparel.)

Liberty Corp.
Wade Hampton Blvd.
Greenville, SC 29602
803/268-8111
(Insurance.)

Lockwood-Greene Engineers, Inc.
1500 International Dr.
Spartanburg, SC 29303
803/578-2000
(Engineering and architectural
services.)

George J. Meyer Manufacturing
(Div. Figgie International Inc.)
300 Eagle Rd.
Goose Creek, SC 29445

803/572-6640
(Beverage processing products.)

Michelin Tire Corp.
1 Pkwy. S.
Greenville, SC 29615
803/458-5000
(Tires, inner tubes.)

Milliken and Company
P.O. Box 1926
Spartanburg, SC 29304
803/573-2020
(Textiles.)

Multimedia
305 S. Main St.
P.O. Box 1688
Greenville, SC 29602
803/298-4373
(Newspaper publishing, television
production, and syndication.)

Oneita Industries, Inc.
Conifer St.
P.O. Box 24
Andrew, SC 29510
803/264-5225
(Knit outer- and underwear.)

Policy Management Systems Corp.
P.O. Box 10
Columbia, SC 29202
803/735-4000
(Computer software, support and
services.)

SCANA Corp.
1426 Main St.
Columbia, SC 29201
803/748-3000
(Utility.)

SSI Medical Services Inc.
4349 Corporate Rd.
Charleston Heights, SC 29405
803/747-8002
(Medical equipment rental and
leasing.)

Sonoco Products Co.
N. Second St.
P.O. Box 160
Hartsville, SC 29550
803/383-7000
(Paper and plastic tubes, containers,
paperboard, etc.)

South Carolina Electric & Gas Co.
1426 Main St.
Columbia, SC 29201
803/748-3000
(Utility.)

South Carolina National Bank
101 Greystone Blvd.
Columbia, SC 29226
803/765-3000
(Banking.)

Springs Industries, Inc.
205 N. White St.
Box 70
Fort Mill, SC 29715
803/547-3650
(Textiles.)

U.S. Shelter Corporation
1 Shelter Pl.
Box 1089
Greenville, SC 29602
803/239-1000
(Real estate managers.)

SOUTH CAROLINA BUSINESS PERIODICAL

Carolina Business
Box 1088
New Bern, SC 28563
919/633-5106

SOUTH CAROLINA DIRECTORIES

Directory of Central Atlantic States
Manufacturers
George D. Hall Company
50 Congress St.
Boston, MA 02109
617/523-3745
(Includes Maryland, Delaware,
Virginia, West Virginia, North
Carolina, and South Carolina.)

MacRAE's State Industrial
Directory—North Carolina/South
Carolina/Virginia
MacRAE's Blue Book, Inc.
817 Broadway
New York, NY 10003
212/673-4700
800/MAC-RAES

South Carolina Business Directory
American Business Directories
5711 S. 86th Cir.
P.O. Box 27347
Omaha, NE 68127
402/593-4600

SOUTH CAROLINA GOVERNMENT EMPLOYMENT OFFICES

Office of Personnel Management
(federal job-service center.) (See
North Carolina listing.)

Employment Service
P.O. Box 995
Columbia, SC 29202
803/737-2400
(State job-service center.)

TENNESSEE

LEADING TENNESSEE EMPLOYERS

AMCA International Construction
Co.
6000 Poplar Ave.
Memphis, TN 38119
901/685-5899
(Construction.)

Acme Boot Company, Inc.
1002 Stafford St.
Clarksville, TN 37040
615/552-2000
(Boots.)

Aladdin Industries, Inc.
703 Murfreesboro Rd.
Nashville, TN 37210
615/748-3000
(Thermalware.)

American General Life & Accident
Insurance
American General Ctr.
Nashville, TN 37250
615/749-1000
(Life, health, and accident insurance.)

American Uniform Co.
Parker St. NE
Box 2130
Cleveland, TN 37320
615/476-6561
(Uniforms.)

Arcadian Corp.
6750 Poplar Ave, #600
Memphis, TN 38138
901/758-5200
(Fertilizers, etc.)

Astec Industries, Inc.
4101 Jerome Ave.
Chattanooga, TN 37407
615/867-4210
(Asphalt plants, construction
equipment, etc.)

Autozone, Inc.
3030 Poplar Ave.
Memphis, TN 38111
901/325-4600
(Auto and home supply stores.)

Baddour, Inc.
4300 New Getwell Rd.
Memphis, TN 38118
901/365-8880
(Department stores.)

Berkline Corp.
1 Berkline Dr.
P.O. Box 100
Morristown, TN 37814
615/586-1500
(Furniture.)

Better-Bilt Aluminum Products Co.
Smyrna Industrial Pk.
Box 277
Smyrna, TN 37167
615/459-4161
(Metal doors, etc.)

Buster Brown Apparel, Inc.
2001 Wheeler Ave.
Chattanooga, TN 37406
615/629-2531
(Children's apparel/shoes.)

Constar International, Inc.
1 Central Plz.
Chattanooga, TN 37402
615/267-2973
(Plastic containers, etc.)

Delta Beverage Group, Inc.
860 Ridge Lake Blvd.
Memphis, TN 38120
901/682-4700
(Bottled and canned soft drinks.)

Dixie Yarns, Inc.
P.O. Box 751
Chattanooga, TN 37401
615/698-2501
(Yarn spinning mills.)

Dunavant Enterprises
P.O. Box 443
Memphis, TN 38101
901/369-1500
(Cotton merchant.)

Equicor Holdings Inc.
1801 W. End Ave.
Nashville, TN 37203
615/320-7608
(Insurance.)

Federal Express Corp.
2005 Corporate Ave.
Memphis, TN 38132
901/369-3600
(Air freight.)

First American Corp.
First American Ctr.
Nashville, TN 37237
615/748-2100
(Banking.)

First Tennessee National Corp.
165 Madison Ave.
Memphis, TN 38103
901/523-4444
(Banking.)

GKN/Parts Industries Corp.
601 S. Dudley St.
Memphis, TN 38104
901/523-7711
(Wholesale motor vehicle supplies and
parts.)

Genesco, Inc.
Genesco Pk.
Nashville, TN 37202
615/367-7000
(Men's footwear.)

Guardsmark, Inc.
22 S. Second St.
Memphis, TN 38103
901/522-6000
(Security services, etc.)

Health Trust
4525 Harding Rd.
Nashville, TN 37205
615/383-4444
(Hospitals.)

Holiday Inns, Inc.
3796 Lamar Ave.
Memphis, TN 38195
901/369-5895
(Hotels and motels.)

Hospital Corp. of America
1 Park Plz.
Nashville, TN 37202
615/327-9551
(Hospitals.)

Ingram Industries, Inc.
4400 Harding Rd.
Nashville, TN 37205
615/298-8200
(Inland marine transportation,
insurance, consumer products
distribution, etc.)

**Johnstown Coca-Cola Bottling
Group**
Krystal Bldg., 600
Chattanooga, TN 37402
615/756-1202
(Soft drinks.)

Martin Marietta Energy Systems
Bearcreek and Scarboro Rds.
Oak Ridge, TN 37830
615/574-3764
(Radioactive isotopes, nuclear fuels,
etc.)

McKee Baking Co.
Apison Pike
Collegedale, TN 37315
615/238-7111
(Baked goods.)

**Nissan Motor Manufacturing Corp.
USA**
812 Nissan Dr.
Smyrna, TN 37167
615/459-1400
(Automobile manufacturing.)

Northern Telecom, Inc.
200 Athens Way
Nashville, TN 37228
615/734-4000
(Telephone equipment.)

Opryland U.S.A., Inc.
2802 Opryland Dr.
P.O. Box 2138
Nashville, TN 37214
615/889-6600
(Entertainment/amusement park.)

Philips Consumer Electronics
(subs. North American Philips)
1 Philips Dr.
Knoxville, TN 37914
615/521-4316
(Consumer electronics.)

Plasti-Line, Inc.
623 Emory Rd.
Powell, TN 37950
615/938-1511
(Sign and advertising specialists.)

**Provident Life and Accident
Insurance Co. of America**
Fountain Sq.
Provident Bldg.
Chattanooga, TN 37402
615/755-1011
(Life and accident insurance; financial
services.)

Reemay Inc.
70 Old Hickory Blvd.
Old Hickory, TN 37138
615/847-7000
(Yarn spinning mills.)

Service Merchandise Co., Inc.
7100 Service Merchandise Blvd.
Brentwood, TN 37027
615/660-6000
(Discount department stores.)

Shoney's, Inc.
1727 Elm Hill Pike
Nashville, TN 37210
615/391-5201
(Restaurant chain.)

Horace Small Manufacturing Co.
P.O. Box 1269
Nashville, TN 37209
615/320-1000
(Men's and boys' apparel.)

Smith & Nephew Richards, Inc.
1450 E. Brooks Rd.
Memphis, TN 38116
901/396-2121
(Medical supplies.)

State Industries, Inc.
Ashland City, TN 37015
615/792-4371
(Water heaters, pump tanks, etc.)

Sullivan Graphics
100 Winners Circle
Brentwood, TN 37027
615/377-0377
(Printing.)

Textron Aerostructures
P.O. Box 210
Nashville, TN 37202
615/361-2000
(Structures for aircraft and space vehicles.)

Third National Corp.
Third National Financial Ctr.
Nashville, TN 37244
615/748-4000
(Banking.)

Union Planters Corp.
P.O. Box 387
Memphis, TN 38147
901/383-6000
(Banking.)

TENNESSEE BUSINESS PERIODICALS

Memphis Business Journal
Mid-South Communications, Inc.
88 Union, Suite 102
Memphis, TN 38103
901/523-0437
(Weekly tabloid; covers business, agriculture, and industry issues in Memphis area—western Tennessee, northern Mississippi, eastern Arkansas.)

Nashville Business Journal
Mid-South Communications
Box 23229
Nashville, TN 37202
615/254-9154
(Weekly tabloid.)

TENNESSEE DIRECTORY

Tennessee Business Directory
American Business Directories
5711 S. 86th Cir.
P.O. Box 27347

Omaha, NE 68127
402/593-4600

TENNESSEE GOVERNMENT EMPLOYMENT OFFICES

Office of Personnel Management
200 Jefferson Ave.,
Suite 1312
Memphis, TN 38103-2335
901/521-3956
(Federal job-service center.)

Employment Service
Dept. of Employment Security
503 Cordell Hull Bldg.
Nashville, TN 37219
615/741-0922
(State job-service center.)

TEXAS

LEADING TEXAS EMPLOYERS

American Airlines, Inc.
Box 619616
Dallas-Fort Worth Airport, TX
75261-9616
817/967-1234
(Airline.)

American General Corp.
2929 Allen Pkwy.
Houston, TX 77019
713/522-1111
(Insurance and financial services.)

American National Insurance Co.
1 Moody Plz.
Galveston, TX 77550
409/763-4661
(Insurance.)

Baker Hughes, Inc.
3900 Essex Ln.
Houston, TX 77207
713/439-8600
(Oil field production and services.)

Bank One, Texas, N.A.
1717 Main St.
Box 655415
Dallas, TX 75265
214/290-2000
(Holding company, financial
services.)

Bank One, Dallas
1717 Main St.
Box 655415
Dallas, TX 75265
214/290-2000
(Banking.)

Bank One, Houston
P.O. Box 2629
Houston, TX 77002
713/751-6100
(Banking.)

Bell Helicopter Textron, Inc.
(subs. of Textron)
Box 482
Fort Worth, TX 76101
817/280-2011
(Rotary-wing aircraft.)

Blue Cross & Blue Shield of Texas
901 Central Expwy.
Richardson, TX 75080
214/669-6900
(Health insurance.)

Brown & Root, Inc.
4100 Clinton Dr.
Houston, TX 77020
713/676-3011
(Construction, engineering,
maintenance.)

Cameron Iron Works, Inc.
P.O. Box 1212
Houston, TX 77251
713/939-2211
(Petroleum services.)

The Coastal Corporation
9 Greenway Plz. E.
Houston, TX 77046
713/877-1400
(Natural gas extraction, transportation and distribution, etc.)

Compaq Computer Corp.
20555 State Hwy. 249
Box 69-2000
Houston, TX 77069-2000
713/370-0670
(Computers.)

Conoco Inc.
600 N. Dairy Ashford Rd.
Houston, TX 77079
713/293-1000
(Petroleum refining.)

Convex Computer Corp.
3000 Waterview Pkwy.
Richardson, TX 75080
214/497-4000
(Computers.)

Daniel Industries, Inc.
9753 Pine Lake Dr.
Houston, TX 77055
713/467-6000
(Oil and gas field equipment.)

Diamond Shamrock, Inc.
P.O. Box 696000
San Antonio, TX 78269-6000
210/641-6800
(Petroleum.)

Digicon, Inc.
3701 Kirby Dr.
Houston, TX 77098
713/526-5611
(Oil and gas field exploration services.)

Dresser Industries, Inc.
1600 Pacific Bldg.
Box 718
Dallas, TX 75221
214/740-6000
(Energy industry equipment and services.)

E-Systems
Greenville Division
Box 6056
Greenville, TX 75403
903/455-3450
(Electronic systems.)

E-Systems, Inc.
P.O. Box 660248
Dallas, TX 75266-0248
214/661-1000
(Electronic systems.)

El Paso Natural Gas Co.
P.O. Box 1492
El Paso, TX 79978
915/541-2600
(Natural gas transmission.)

Electronic Data Systems Corp.
7171 Forest Ln.
Dallas, TX 75230
214/604-6000
(Data processing.)

Electrospace Systems, Inc.
1301 E. Collins Blvd.
Richardson, TX 75081
214/470-2000
(Electronic equipment.)

Enron Corp.
1400 Smith St.
Houston, TX 77002
713/853-6161
(Pipelines, energy exploration.)

Enserch Corp.
300 S. St. Paul St.
Dallas, TX 75201
214/651-8700
(Diversified energy operations.)

Epic Healthcare Group
P.O. Box 650398
Dallas, TX 75265
214/443-3333
(Hospitals.)

Exxon Corp.
225 E. Carpenter Fwy.
Irving, TX 75062
214/444-1000
(Petroleum.)

Fairchild Aircraft
Box 790490
San Antonio, TX 78279-0490
210/824-9421
(Aircraft manufacturing.)

Family Service Life Insurance Co.
9430 Old Katy Rd.
Houston, TX 77055
713/827-0458
(Life insurance.)

Farah Inc.
8889 Gateway Blvd.
El Paso, TX 79925
915/593-4444
(Men's trousers.)

First City Bancorporation of Texas
P.O. Box 2557
Houston, TX 77252
713/658-6011
(Banking.)

First Interstate Bank Texas, N.A.
1000 Louisiana
Houston, TX 77002
713/224-6611
(Banking.)

Foley's
1110 Main St.
Houston, TX 77002
713/651-7038
(Department store.)

Frito Lay, Inc.
7701 Legacy Dr.
Plano, TX 75024
214/353-2000
(Food processing.)

GSC Enterprises, Inc.
130 Hillcrest Dr.
Sulphur Springs, TX 75482
903/885-7621
(Wholesale groceries.)

GTE Southwest Inc.
2701 S. Johnson St.
San Angelo, TX 76902
915/944-5511
(Telephone services.)

General Dynamics Corp.
Fort Worth Division
Box 748
Fort Worth, TX 76101
817/777-2000
(F-111 spares and support, F-16 airframe, radar, etc.)

Grocers Supply Co.
3131 E. Holcombe Blvd.
Houston, TX 77021
713/747-5000
(Wholesale groceries, drugs, hardware.)

Gulf State Utilities Co.
285 Liberty Ave.
Beaumont, TX 77701
409/838-6631
(Electric utility.)

Halliburton Co.
500 N. Akard St.
Dallas, TX 75201
214/978-2600
(Petroleum services.)

Hoechst Celanese
Chemicals Division
1250 Mockingbird Ln.
Dallas, TX 75247
214/689-4000
(Chemicals.)

Houston Industries Incorporated
P.O. Box 4567
Houston, TX 77210
713/629-3000
(Holding company—utilities; cable television; etc.)

Houston Lighting & Power Co.
P.O. Box 1700
Houston, TX 77251
713/228-9211
(Utility.)

Houston Pipe Line Co.
1400 Smith St.
Houston, TX 77251
713/654-6161
(Natural gas transmission and sales.)

Houston Post Co.
P.O. Box 4747
Houston, TX 77210
713/840-5600
(Newspaper publishing.)

Intermedics, Inc.
4000 Technology Dr.
Angleton, TX 77515
409/848-4000
(Electromagnetic and
electrotherapeutic apparatuses.)

International Maintenance Corp.
2005 Industrial Pk.
Nederland, TX 77627
409/722-8031
(General contractors.)

International Telecharge, Inc.
108 S. Akard
Dallas, TX 75202
214/744-0240
(Telephone communications.)

Kaiser Aluminum Corp.
5847 San Felipe
Houston, TX 77057
713/267-3777
(Aluminum, etc.)

M. W. Kellogg Co.
3 Greenway Plz.
Houston, TX 77046
713/960-2000
(Chemical plant and refinery
construction; engineering services.)

**LTV Aerospace and Defense
Company**
Box 655003
2001 Ross Ave.
Dallas, TX 75265
214/979-7711
(Military aircraft, missiles, etc.)

LTV Aircraft Products Group
P.O. Box 655907
Dallas, TX 75265-5907
214/266-2011
(Aircraft manufacturing subs. of The
LTV Corp.)

The LTV Corp.
Box 655003
2001 Ross Ave.
Dallas, TX 75265-5003
214/979-7711
(Conglomerate.)

LTV Missiles & Electronics Group
P.O. Box 6500003
1701 Marshall Dr.
Grand Prairie, TX 75051
214/266-2011
(Missiles and electronics subs. of The
LTV Corp.)

Lincoln Property
500 N. Alkard, Suite 3300
Dallas, TX 75201
214/740-3300
(Real estate development and
management.)

J. D. Linder & Associates
1705 Capital of Texas Hwy.
Austin, TX 78746
512/328-4220
(Insurance agents.)

**Lockheed Engineering & Sciences
Co.**
2625 Bay Area Blvd.
Houston, TX 77058
713/333-5411
(Engineering services.)

Lufkin Industries, Inc.
601 S. Raquet
Lufkin, TX 75902
409/634-2211
(Oil and gas field machinery and
equipment.)

**Manufacturing Auditing
Redemption Service**
6936 Commerce Ave.
El Paso, TX 79915
915/772-4415
(Coupon redemption services.)

**Marathon Manufacturing
Companies**
P.O. Box 2307
Longview, TX 75606
214/753-4411
(Mining machinery and equipment.)

Marathon Oil Co.
P.O. Box 3128
Houston, TX 77253
713/629-6600
(Oil and gas.)

Mary Kay Cosmetics, Inc.
8787 Stemmons Fwy.
Dallas, TX 75247
214/630-8787
(Cosmetics.)

Maxus Energy Corp.
717 N. Harwood St.
Dallas, TX 75201
214/953-2000
(Oil and gas exploration and
production.)

Mitchell Energy & Development Co.
P.O. Box 4000
The Woodlands, TX 77387
713/377-5500
(Crude petroleum and natural gas.)

NCH Corp.
2727 Chemsearch Blvd.
Irving, TX 75062
214/438-0211

(Cleaning, sanitation and maintenance
chemicals, etc.)

Neiman-Marcus
Main and Ervay Sts.
Dallas, TX 75201
214/741-6911
(Department stores.)

Otis Engineering Corp.
2601 Belt Line Rd.
Carrollton, TX 75006
214/418-3000
(Oil and gas field machinery and
equipment.)

Panhandle Eastern Corp.
5400 Westheimer Ct.
Houston, TX 77056
713/627-5400
(Natural gas and pipeline holding
company.)

J.C. Penney Company, Inc.
6501 Legacy Dr.
Plano, TX 75024
214/431-1000
(Department stores.)

Pennzoil Co.
700 Milam
Pennzoil Pl.
Houston, TX 77002
713/546-4000
(Petroleum refining.)

Rexene Corp.
5005 LBJ Fwy.
Occidental Tower
Dallas, TX 75244
214/450-9000
(Chemicals.)

S&B Engineers and Constructors
7809 Park Pl.
Houston, TX 77087
713/645-4141
(Heavy construction.)

Sakowitz, Inc.
5000 Westheimer Ct.
Houston, TX 77002
713/759-1111
(Clothing stores.)

Schlumberger Technologies Corp.
5000 Gulf Fwy.
Houston, TX 77023
713/928-4000
(Oil field services.)

Serv-Air, Inc.
9315 FM Rd. 1570
Greenville, TX 75403
903/454-2000
(Organizational and field maintenance;
repair of aircraft.)

Shell Oil Company
1 Shell Plz.
Houston, TX 77001
713/241-6161
(Petroleum refining.)

Shell Pipe Line Corp.
2 Shell Plz.
P.O. Box 2648
Houston, TX 77252
713/241-6161
(Pipeline transportation, petroleum,
etc.)

Southwest Airlines Co.
Box 36611
Love Field
Dallas, TX 75235
214/904-4000
(Airline.)

Sun Energy Partners LP
5656 Blackwell
Dallas, TX 75231
214/890-6207
(Oil and gas field exploration
services.)

Tandy Corp.
1800 One Tandy Ctr.
Fort Worth, TX 76102
817/390-3700
(Electronics.)

Tenneco Inc.
101 Milam
Houston, TX 77002
713/747-2131
(Petroleum, pipelines, land
management.)

Texas Commerce Bancshares, Inc.
712 Main St.
Houston, TX 77002
713/236-4865
(Banking.)

Texas Eastern Transmission Corp.
5400 Westheimer Ct.
Houston, TX 77251
713/627-5400
(Pipelines, oil/gas exploration, and
distribution.)

Texas Instruments Inc.
13500 N. Central Expy.
Dallas, TX 75243
214/995-2011
(Computers and electronics.)

Texas Utilities Co.
2001 Bryan Tower
Dallas, TX 75201
214/812-4600
(Electric utility.)

Tracor, Inc.
6500 Tracer Ln.
Austin, TX 78725
512/926-2800
(Engineering services.)

Trammel Crow Co.
2001 Ross Ave.
Suite 3500
Dallas, TX 75201-2997
214/979-5100
(Real estate developer.)

Transco Energy Co.
P.O. Box 1396
Houston, TX 77251
713/439-2000
(Pipelines, oil, coal, etc.)

USX-Marathon Oil Company
P.O. Box 3128
Houston, TX 77253
713/629-6600
(Oil and gas.)

Union Texas Petroleum Holdings, Inc.
1330 Post Oak Blvd.
Houston, TX 77252
713/623-6544
(Oil and gas exploration and development, etc.)

Valhi Inc.
3 Lincoln Ctr.
5430 LBJ Fwy.

Suite 1700
Dallas, TX 75240
214/233-1700
(Chemicals.)

Varo Inc.
2203 Walnut St.
Box 461426
Garland, TX 75046
214/487-4100
(Night-vision systems and components, weapons delivery systems, etc.)

TEXAS BUSINESS PERIODICALS

Dallas Business Journal
4131 N. Central Expy.
Dallas, TX 75204
214/520-1010
(Weekly.)

Houston Business Journal
1 W. Loop S.
Houston, TX 77027
713/688-8811
(Weekly.)

TEXAS DIRECTORIES

Directory of Texas Manufacturers
University of Texas at Austin
Bureau of Business Research
Box 7459
Austin, TX 78713
512/471-1616

Texas Business Directory
American Business Directories
5711 S. 86th Cir.

P.O. Box 27347
Omaha, NE 68127
402/593-4600

Texas Manufacturers Register
Manufacturers' News, Inc.
1633 Central St.
Evanston, IL 60201
708/864-7000

TEXAS GOVERNMENT EMPLOYMENT OFFICES

Office of Personnel Management
1100 Commerce
Dallas, TX 75250
(Regional OPM office.)

Office of Personnel Management
1100 Commerce St., Room 6812
Dallas, TX 75242
214/767-8035
(Federal job-service center—mail or phone only.)

Office of Personnel Management
8610 Broadway, Room 305
San Antonio, TX 78217
512/229-6611
(Federal job-service center—mail or
phone only.)

Employment Service
Texas Employment Commission
12th and Trinity, 504BT
Austin, TX 78778
512/463-2820
(State job-service center.)

VIRGINIA

LEADING VIRGINIA EMPLOYERS

Advanced Technology, Inc.
12005 Sunrise Valley Dr.
Reston, VA 22091
703/620-8000
(Computer services.)

American Furniture Co., Inc.
Hairstan St. off Starling
Martinsville, VA 24112
703/632-2061
(Furniture.)

American Management Systems, Inc.
1777 N. Kent St.
Arlington, VA 22209
703/841-6000
(Business data processing.)

Atlantic Research Corp.
(sub. of Sequa Corp.)
5390 Cherokee Ave.
Alexandria, VA 22312
703/642-4000
(Aerospace.)

BDM International, Inc.
7915 Jones Branch Dr.
McLean, VA 22102
703/848-5000
(Business services, government
consulting.)

Bassett Furniture Industries, Inc.
Hwy. 57
Bassett, VA 24055
703/629-6000
(Furniture, housewares.)

Bell Atlantic Network Services, Inc.
(subs. of Bell Atlantic)
1310 N. Court House Rd.
Arlington, VA 22201
703/974-3000
(Telecommunications network
services.)

**Blue Cross & Blue Shield of
Virginia**
2015 Staples Mill Rd.
Richmond, VA 23230
804/359-7000
(Health insurance.)

British Aerospace, Inc.
13873 Park Center Rd. #500
Herndon, VA 22071
703/478-9420
(Sale of aircraft, spare parts, and
product support.)

C&P Telephone of Virginia
(subs. of Bell Atlantic)
703 Grace St.
Richmond, VA 23219
804/772-2000
(Telephone services.)

Cable & Wireless Communications
1919 Gallows Rd.
Vienna, VA 22182
703/790-5300
(Long distance telephone services.)

Canon Virginia Inc.
12000 Canon Blvd.
Newport News, VA 23606
804/281-2000
(Office machines.)

Central Fidelity Banks
1021 E. Cary St.
Richmond, VA 23219
804/782-4000
(Banking.)

Colonial Williamsburg Foundation, Inc.
Goodwin Bldg.
P.O. Box C
Williamsburg, VA 23185
804/229-1000
(Hotel, gift shops, etc.)

Contel Federal Systems Inc.
15000 Conference Ctr. Dr.
Chantilly, VA 22021
703/818-4000
(Telephone communications.)

Crestar Financial
919 E. Main St.
Richmond, VA 23219
804/782-5000
(Banking.)

Dan River, Inc.
2291 Memorial Dr.
Danville, VA 24543
804/799-4876
(Textiles.)

Dominion Bankshares Corp.
231 S. Jefferson St.
Roanoke, VA 24040
703/563-7000
(Banking.)

Dyn Corp
2000 Edmund Halley Dr.
Reston, VA 22091
703/264-0330
(Technical and professional services.)

Ericsson-GE Mobile Communications
Mountainview Rd.
Lynchburg, VA 24502
804/528-7000
(Cellular telephone equipment, etc.)

Ethyl Corp.
P.O. Box 2189
Richmond, VA 23217
804/788-5000
(Chemicals.)

The Fairchild Corporation
300 W. Service Rd.
Box 10803
Chantilly, VA 22021
703/478-5800
(Aerospace.)

Federal Home Loan Mortgage Corp.
8200 Jones Branch Dr.
McLean, VA 22102
703/903-2000
(Secondary mortgages.)

First Virginia Banks, Inc.
1 First Virginia Plz.
6400 Arlington Blvd.
Falls Church, VA 22042-2336
703/241-4000
(Banking.)

Gannett Co., Inc.
1100 Wilson Blvd.
Arlington, VA 22209
703/284-6000
(Newspaper publishing.)

Genicom Corp.
1 Genicom Dr.
Waynesboro, VA 22980
703/949-1000
(Business data processing.)

Honeywell Federal Systems, Inc.
7900 W. Pk. Dr.
McLean, VA 22102
703/827-3000
(Electrical power systems contractors; computer installation.)

ITT Defense
(subs. ITT Corp.)
1000 Wilson Blvd.
Arlington, VA 22209
703/247-2942
(Defense electronics.)

Interbake Foods, Inc.
P.O. Box 27487
Richmond, VA 23261
804/257-7497
(Cookies and crackers.)

James River Corp. of Virginia
Tredegar St.
P.O. Box 2218
Richmond, VA 23217
804/644-5411
(Paper and packaging.)

Landmark Communications, Inc.
150 W. Brambleton Ave.
Norfolk, VA 23510
804/446-2000
(Publishing, broadcasting.)

Lane Co., Inc.
E. Franklin Ave.
P.O. Box 151
Altavista, VA 24517
804/369-5641
(Furniture.)

Life Insurance Company of Virginia
6610 W. Broad St.
Richmond, VA 23230
804/281-6000
(Life insurance.)

Mars Inc.
6885 Elm St.
McLean, VA 22101
703/821-4900
(Food processing.)

Media General Inc.
333 E. Grace St.
Richmond, VA 23219
804/649-6000
(Publishing.)

Mobil Corporation
3225 Gallows Rd.
Fairfax, VA 22037
703/846-3000
(Holding company, oil and gas
exploration and refining. At same
address: Mobil Oil Corp.)

O'Sullivan Corp.
1944 Valley Ave.
Winchester, VA 22601
703/667-6666
(Plastic, vinyl sheeting, molded
plastics.)

Overnite Transportation Co.
1000 Semmes Ave.
Richmond, VA 23224
804/231-8000
(Trucking.)

Pannill Knitting Co., Inc.
202 Cleveland Ave.
Martinesville, VA 24115
703/638-8841
(Textiles, apparel.)

Perpetual Financial Corp.
2034 Eisenhower Ave.
Alexandria, VA 22314
703/838-6000
(Savings institutions.)

Planning Research Corp.
1500 Planning Research Dr.
McLean, VA 22102
703/556-1000
(Computer programming services,
etc.)

Pulaski Furniture Corp.
1 Pulaski Sq.
Pulaski, VA 24301
703/980-7330
(Furniture.)

Reynolds Metals Co.
6601 Broad St.
Richmond, VA 23261
804/281-2000
(Aluminum.)

Richfood Holdings Inc.
2000 Richfood Rd.
Mechanicsville, VA 23111
804/746-6000
(Wholesale groceries.)

A. H. Robins Co., Inc.
1407 Cummings Dr.
Richmond, VA 23220
804/257-2000
(Pharmaceuticals, health and beauty
aids.)

Signet Banking
7 N. Eighth St.
Richmond, VA 23219
804/747-2000
(Banking.)

Smithfield Foods, Inc.
501 N. Church St.
Smithfield, VA 23430
804/357-4321
(Meat packing and processing.)

**Sprint International
Communications Corp.**
12490 Sunrise Valley
Reston, VA 22096

703/689-5664
(Telecommunications.)

**Stanley Acquisition Corp.; Stanley
Holding Corp.; Stanley Interiors**
Hwy. 57
P.O. Box 30
Stanleytown, VA 24168
703/629-7561
(Furniture.)

Thalhimer's
615 E. Broad St.
Richmond, VA 23261
804/643-4211
(Department stores.)

USAir, Inc.
2345 Crystal Dr.
Arlington, VA 22227
703/418-7000
(Airline.)

Virginia Electric & Power Co.
1 James River Plz.
Richmond, VA 23219
804/771-3000
(Utility.)

VIRGINIA BUSINESS PERIODICAL

Virginia Business
411 E. Franklin St.
Richmond, VA 23219
804/649-6899
(Monthly.)

VIRGINIA DIRECTORIES

*Directory of Central Atlantic States
Manufacturers*
George D. Hall Company
50 Congress St.
Boston, MA 02109
617/523-3745
(includes Maryland, Delaware,
Virginia, West Virginia, North
Carolina, and South Carolina.)

*MacRAE's State Directories—North
Carolina/South Carolina/Virginia*
MacRAE's Blue Book, Inc.
817 Broadway
New York, NY 10003
212/673-4700
800/MAC-RAES

Virginia Business Directory
American Business Directories
5711 S. 86th Cir.

P.O. Box 27347
Omaha, NE 68127
402/593-4600

VIRGINIA GOVERNMENT EMPLOYMENT OFFICES

Office of Personnel Management
Federal Bldg., Room 220
200 Granby St.
Norfolk, VA 23510-1886
804/441-3355
(Federal job-service center.)

Employment Service
Virginia Employment Commission
P.O. Box 1258
Richmond, VA 23211
804/786-7097
(State job-service center.)

WEST VIRGINIA

LEADING WEST VIRGINIA EMPLOYERS

Ames Co.
P.O. Box 1774
Parkersburg, WV 26101
304/424-3000
(Lawn and garden tools.)

Arch of West Virginia
156 Yolyn
Yolyn, WV 25654
304/792-8200
(Coal mining.)

Ashland Coal Inc.
2205 5th St. Rd.
Box 6300
Huntington, WV 25771
304/526-3333
(Coal mining.)

C&P Telephone of West Virginia
1500 MacCorkle Ave., S.E.
Charleston, WV 25314
304/343-9911
(Telephone services—subs. of Bell Atlantic.)

CNG Transmission Corp.
445 W. Main St.
Clarksburg, WV 26301
304/623-8000
(Natural gas transmission and production.)

CSX Hotels Inc.
Rte. 60
White Sulpher Springs, WV 24986
304/536-1110
(Resort hotel.)

Cannelton Holding Co.
315 70th St.
Charleston, WV 25304
304/925-1222
(Iron ore mining.)

Columbia Gas Transmission Corp.
1700 MacCorkle Ave., SE
Charleston, WV 25314
304/357-2000
(Natural gas transmission and distribution.)

Dixie-Narco Inc.
(subs. Maytag Corporation)
Lawrence St.
Ranson, WV 25438
304/725-3481
(Automatic vending machines.)

Eastern Associated Coal Corp.
800 Laidley Tower
Box 1233
Charleston, WV 25324
304/340-0300
(Coal mining.)

Elk Run Coal Co., Inc.
State Rte. 3
P.O. Box 497
Sylvester, WV 25193
304/854-1890
(Coal mining.)

Gabriel Brothers Inc.
55 Scott Ave.
Morgantown, WV 26505
304/292-6965
(Family clothing stores.)

Marrowbone Development Co.
State Rte. 65
P.O. Box 119
Naugatuck, WV 25685
304/235-7650
(Coal mining.)

McJunkin Corp.
835 Hillcrest Dr.
Charleston, WV 25311
304/348-5211
(Industrial carbon.)

Monongahela Power Co.
1310 Fairmont Ave.
Fairmont, WV 26544
304/366-3000
(Electric utility.)

Mountaineer Gas Co.
414 Summers St.
Charleston, WV 25301
304/347-0595
(Natural gas transmission.)

National Banc of Commerce Co.
1 Commerce Sq.
Charleston, WV 25322
304/348-5000
(Banking; does business as Commerce Bank.)

Ogden Newspapers, Inc.
1500 Main St.
Wheeling, WV 26003
304/233-0100
(Newspaper publishing.)

One Valley Bancorp of West Virginia, Inc.
P.O. Box 1793
Charleston, WV 25326
304/348-7000
(Banking.)

Ravenswood Aluminum Corp.
P.O. Box 98
Ravenswood, WV 26164
304/273-6000
800/258-6686
(Aluminum.)

Retail Acquisition Corp.
Hub Industrial Park
Nitro, WV 25143
304/759-2200
(Family clothing stores.)

Steel of West Virginia Inc.
17th St. and 2nd Ave.
Huntington, WV 25726
304/529-7171
(Steel products.)

Stone & Thomas
1030 Main St.
Wheeling, WV 26003
304/232-3344
(Department stores.)

Vecellio & Grogran, Inc.
P.O. Drawer V
Beckley, WV 25802
304/252-6575
(Highway and street construction.)

Cecil I. Walker Machinery Co.
Rte. 60 E.
Belle, WV 25015
304/949-6400
(Construction and mining machinery and equipment.)

Weirton Steel Corp.
400 Three Springs Dr.
Weirton, WV 26062
304/797-2000
(Steel.)

Wheeling-Pittsburgh Steel Corp.   304/234-2400
1134 Market St.   (Steel.)
Wheeling, WV 26003

WEST VIRGINIA DIRECTORIES

Directory of Central Atlantic States   216/425-9000
Manufacturers   800/888-5900
George D. Hall Company
50 Congress St.   *West Virginia Business Directory*
Boston, MA 02109   American Business Directories
617/523-3745   5711 S. 86th Circle
(Includes Maryland, Delaware,   P.O. Box 27347
Virginia, West Virginia, North   Omaha, NE 68127
Carolina, and South Carolina.)   402/593-4600

Harris West Virginia Manufacturing   *West Virginia Manufacturers*
Directory   *Register*
Harris Publishing Company   Manufacturers' News Inc.
2057 Aurora Rd.   1633 Central St.
Twinsburg, OH 44087   Evanston, IL 60201
    708/864-7000

WEST VIRGINIA GOVERNMENT EMPLOYMENT OFFICES

Office of Personnel Management   **Employment Service Division**
(Federal job-service center—see Ohio   Dept. of Employment Security
listing; call 513/225-2866.)   112 California Ave.
    Charleton, WV, 25305
    304/348-9180
    (State job-service center.)

THE MIDWEST

OUTLOOK: Strong over the long term.

Much of the Midwest did better than the rest of the country during the past few years—and the future looks fairly bright, although some areas may lag in job growth as manufacturers streamline. A good sign: of the top twenty cities in the U.S. in terms of job growth, nine were from the Midwest. In fact, during the recession, the Midwest was the only region that actually gained jobs. The bottom line? This kind of performance in the worst of times points to an even brighter picture in better times.

WHAT'S NEXT

▶ **The Great Lakes region: Improving as manufacturing becomes stable, and service industries begin expanding into the area. Overall, the Great Lakes states should be headed for a period of stability.**

Two reasons for this positive outlook: 1. Exports of capital goods and industrial components should stay strong, meaning the manufacturing sector will stay healthy. 2. A growing number of service companies is diversifying the regional economy—and increasing employment opportunities. Areas that look especially promising where job growth is concerned: *Illinois, Indiana, Ohio.*

Michigan, with its health directly tied to the auto industry, is coming on relatively strong. After a two-year slump, its economy grew 3% in 1992, 3.5% in 1993. Many economists are forecasting growth in this state to *exceed* that of the rest of the country.

▶ **Plains states: Expect steady growth.**

Thanks to increasing global demand for crops and decreasing farm debt, the farm belt states are in for fairly smooth sailing.

Coming on strong: *Indianapolis,* which has an increasingly diversified economy—including healthy telecommunications and services companies. Perhaps the best example of its growing economy: while much of the rest of the nation was laying people off, Indianapolis added over 13,000 new jobs.

Two other good bets: *Nebraska,* which has been seeing strong growth in telemarketing. Omaha ranked number 2 in the nation in terms of job growth, adding

16,200 new jobs in 1991. Among the industries expanding there: credit-card operations, direct mail, education, construction, food processing. *Iowa* is also home to a number of new industries as well—including plastics, and ethanol production.

▶ Looking strong: Arkansas.

Home to retail giant Wal-Mart as well as to a number of other companies that proved to be virtually recession-proof, *Arkansas* is developing into one of the region's strongest performers. In 1992, it had an unemployment rate of only 3%—and has been posting impressive job growth numbers. Industries that are poised for long term growth include: textiles, machinery, and business services.

Missouri was affected by the defense cutbacks, as military contractor McDonnell Douglas and others laid off about 11,000 workers. But there is a positive development in the area: Second counties in the state have teamed up to create business "incubators"—industrial parks that are designed to attract biotech and health care companies, and commercial and industrial aviation. Already a number of entreprenerial firms are moving in. This may develop into an interesting area for long-term prospects. As for *Minnesota,* long-term outlook seems favorable, with growth visible in retail trade, tourism, medical instruments and health care.

REGIONAL HOT SPOTS

CEDAR RAPIDS, IA: A good bet for laid-back types—chiefly because Cedar Rapids was chosen the nation's least stressful city. Perhaps one reason people aren't stressed out is the low unemployment rate—only 4.3%, which is far below the national average. This, plus a diversified economy, make Cedar Rapids a good choice for employment.

COLUMBUS, OH: Relatively low unemployment and a strong job growth rate plus a diversified economy—divided among government, manufacturing, finance, and services—make Columbus a city with good employment prospects and a stable future. It's also a major center for insurance, warehousing, and distribution facilities. Leading area companies include: specialty store owner The Limited, fast-food chain Wendy's International, Inc.

LOUISVILLE, KY: Ranked 14th in the country in job growth, Louisville is coming on strong. It's one of the regional leaders in the trend away from a strict manufacturing base, and has added a number of service companies in recent years. This growth, plus its move toward a more diversified economy, makes Louisville look like a good choice for the future.

MINNEAPOLIS/ST. PAUL, MN: The Twin Cities consistently appear on best places to live and best places to locate a business surveys. Making them look good where employment is concerned: revived manufacturing, expansion of insurance, and publishing. This, plus the fact that Minneapolis/St. Paul is home to industry giants in a range of industries—including 3M, Honeywell, General Mills, and Northwest Airlines—point to continued prospects.

ARKANSAS

LEADING ARKANSAS EMPLOYERS

ABF Freight System, Inc.
301 S. 11th St.
Fort Smith, AR 72901
501/785-6000
(Trucking.)

Acxiom Corp.
301 Industrial Blvd.
Conway, AR 72032
501/336-1000
(Information retrieval services.)

Alltel Corporation
One Allied Dr.
Little Rock, AR 72202
501/661-8000
(Independent telephone company.)

Arkansas Best Corp.
1000 S. 21st St.
Fort Smith, AR 72901
501/785-6000
(Trucking; computer services; real estate.)

Arkansas Blue Cross & Blue Shield
601 S. Gaines St.
Little Rock, AR 72201
501/378-2000
(Group hospitalization and medical insurance plans.)

Arkansas Freightways Corp.
2200 Forward Dr.
Harrison, AR 72601
501/741-9000
(Trucking.)

Arkansas Power & Light Co.
P.O. Box 551
Little Rock, AR 72203
501/377-4000
(Utilities.)

Baldor Electric Company
5711 S. 7th St.
Fort Smith, AR 72901
501/646-4711
(Electric motors.)

Beverly Enterprises, Inc.
P.O. Box 3324
Fort Smith, AR 72913
501/452-6712
(Long term health care, retirement facilities, etc.)

Dillard Department Stores Inc.
900 W. Capitol Ave.
Little Rock, AR 72201
501/376-5200
(Department stores.)

Donrey Media Group
920 Rogers Ave.
P.O. Box 1359
Fort Smith, AR 77902-1359
501/785-7827
(Media company—daily newspapers, cable tv, etc.)

Fairfield Communities, Inc.
2800 Cantrell Rd.
Little Rock, AR 72202
501/664-6000
(Residential and commercial construction and development.)

Harvest Foods
8109 I-30
Little Rock, AR 72209
501/562-3583
(Supermarkets.)

Hudson Foods Inc.
1125 Hudson Rd.
Rogers, AR 72756
501/636-1100
(Poultry processing.)

J.B. Hunt Transport Services Inc.
Highway 71 N.
Lowell, AR 72745
501/820-0000
(Trucking.)

Jones Truck Lines Inc.
610 E. Emma Ave.
Springdale, AR 72764
501/751-4806
(Trucking.)

Mass Merchandisers, Inc.
P.O. Box 790
Harrison, AR 72601
501/741-3425
(Service merchandising.)

Munro & Co. Inc.
Hwy. 270 E. 5 Miles
P.O. Box 1157
Hot Springs Nation, AR 71901
501/262-1440
(Men's shoes.)

Murphy Oil Corp.
200 Peach St.
El Dorado, AR 71730
501/862-6411
(Oil and gas exploration.)

Nucor-Yamato Steel Co.
Hwy. 18 & 137
P.O. Box 1228
Armorel, AR 72310
501/762-5500
(Steel.)

Pace Industries Inc.
62-65 By-Pass
P.O. Box 1198
Harrison, AR 72601
501/741-8255
(Aluminum die-castings.)

Peterson Industries, Inc.
Main St.
Decatur, AR 72722
501/752-3211
(Poultry hatcheries, feedlot cattle.)

Producers Rice Mill Inc.
N. Anna St.
Box 461
Stuttgart, AR 72160
501/673-4444
(Rice processing and marketing.)

Riceland Foods
2120 Park Ave.
Stuttgart, AR 72160
501/673-5500
(Rice milling, sales, soybean meal and oil, etc.)

Southland Racing Corp.
1550 N. Ingram Blvd.
West Memphis, AR 72301
501/735-2757
(Greyhound racing.)

Southwestern Bell Corporation—Arkansas Division
(operating subsidiary of Southwestern Bell Corp.)
1111 W. Capitol
Little Rock, AR 72201
501/373-9800
(Telephone services.)

Stephens Inc.
114 E. Capitol Ave.
Little Rock, AR 72201
501/374-4361
(Underwriter, broker.)

Systematics, Inc.
4001 Rodney Parham Rd.
Little Rock, AR 72212
501/223-5100
(Data processing services, software.)

TCBY Enterprises, Inc.
425 W. Capitol Ave.
Little Rock, AR 72201
501/688-8229
(Frozen yogurt manufacturing, retail and franchise.)

Tyson Foods Inc.
2210 W. Oaklawn Dr.
Springdale, AR 72764
501/756-4000
(Poultry processing.)

Wal-Mart Stores, Inc.
702 SW 8th St.
Bentonville, AR 72716
501/273-4000
(Discount department stores.)

ARKANSAS BUSINESS PERIODICAL

Memphis Business Journal
Mid-South Communications, Inc.
88 Union
Suite 102
Memphis, TN 38103
901/523-0437

(Weekly tabloid, covers business,
agriculture and industry issues in
Memphis area—western Tennessee,
northern Mississippi, eastern
Arkansas.)

ARKANSAS DIRECTORIES

Arkansas Business Directory
American Business Directories
5711 S. 86th Cir.
P.O. Box 27347
Omaha, NE 68127
402/593-4600

Directory of Arkansas
Manufacturers
Arkansas Industrial Development
Foundation
Box 1784
Little Rock, AR 72203
501/371-1121

ARKANSAS GOVERNMENT EMPLOYMENT OFFICES

Office of Personnel Management
(Federal job-service center—see
Oklahoma listing.)

Employment Security Division
P.O. Box 2981
Little Rock, AR 72203
501/371-1683
(State job-service center.)

ILLINOIS
LEADING ILLINOIS EMPLOYERS

Abbott Laboratories
One Abbott Park Rd.
Abbott Park, IL 60064
708/937-6100
(Chemicals, food processing.)

Acme Steel Co.
13500 S. Perry Ave.
Riverdale, IL 60627
708/849-2500
(Steel works.)

Allied Van Lines Inc.
P.O. Box 4403
Chicago, IL 60680
708/717-3000
(Motor carrier.)

Allstate Insurance Co.
Allstate Plz.
Northbrook, IL 60062
708/402-5000
(Insurance.)

**American Manufacturers Mutual
Insurance Co.**
Kemper Ctr.
Long Grove, IL 60049
708/540-2000
(Insurance.)

Ameritech
(Bell regional holding company)
30 S. Wacker Dr.
Chicago, IL 60606
312/750-5000
(Telephone services.)

Amoco Corp.
200 E. Randolph Dr.
Box 87703
Chicago, IL 60680
312/856-6111
(Oil and natural gas exploration,
refining, marketing, distribution.)

Amoco Chemical Co.
200 E. Randolph Dr.
Box 87759
Chicago, IL 60680
312/856-3200
(Chemicals.)

Amoco Oil Co.
P.O. Box 87707
Chicago, IL 60680
312/856-5111
(Gasoline, motor oils, etc.)

Aon Corp.
123 N. Wacker Dr.
Chicago, IL 60606
312/701-3000
(Insurance, brokerage, financial
services holding co.)

Archer-Daniels-Midland Co.
4666 Fairs Pkwy.
Decatur, IL 62525
217/424-5200
(Flours, grains, soybean oil, etc.)

Bankers Life & Casualty Co.
4444 W. Lawrence Ave.
Chicago, IL 60630
312/777-7000
(Insurance.)

Baxter Healthcare Corp.
One Baxter Pkwy.
Deerfield, IL 60015
708/948-2000
(Healthcare products.)

Baxter International Inc.
One Baxter Pkwy.
Deerfield, IL 60015
708/948-2000
(Medical care products and services.)

Borg-Warner
200 S. Michigan Ave.
Chicago, IL 60604
312/322-8500
(Automotive parts.)

CNA Financial Corp.
CNA Plz.
Chicago, IL 60685
312/822-5000
(Insurance.)

Caterpillar Inc.
100 NE Adams St.
Peoria, IL 61629
309/675-1000
(Construction, earth-moving and
materials handling equipment mfr.)

Centel Corp.
8725, W. Higgins Rd.
Chicago, IL 60631
312/399-2500
(Telephone services, products.)

Chicago Title & Trust Co.
111 W. Washington St.
Chicago, IL 60602
312/630-2000
(Title insurance, trust services.)

Chicago Tribune Co.
435 N. Michigan Ave.
Chicago, IL 60611
312/222-3232
(Newspaper publishing.)

Citibank, Federal Savings Bank, Illinois
1 S. Dearborn St.
Chicago, IL 60603
312/977-5000
(Federal savings and loan
association.)

Coldwell Banker & Co.
55 W. Monroe St.
Chicago, IL 60603
312/875-5200
(Real estate brokerage and agents.)

Commonwealth Edison Co.
One First National Plz.
Chicago, IL 60603
312/294-4321
(Utility.)

Continental Bank Corp.
231 S. LaSalle St.
Chicago, IL 60697
312/828-2345
(Owns Continental Bank N.A.)

Continental Casualty Co.
CNA Plz.
Chicago, IL 60685
312/822-5000
(Insurance.)

Deere & Co.
John Deere Rd.
Moline, IL 61265
309/765-8000
(Farm, industrial and grounds care
equipment, financing.)

Dominick's Finer Foods, Inc.
505 N. Railroad Ave.
Melrose Park, IL 60164
708/562-1000
(Retail food stores, food and drug
combo stores.)

R. R. Donnelly & Sons Co.
77 W. Wacker Dr.
Chicago, IL 60601-1696
312/326-8000
(Commercial printing.)

FMC Corp.
200 E. Randolph Dr.
Chicago, IL 60601
312/861-6000
(Machinery, chemicals.)

First Chicago Corp.
One First National Plz.
Chicago, IL 60670
312/732-4000
(Banking.)

Franklin Life Insurance Co.
Franklin Sq.
Springfield, IL 62713
217/528-2011
(Insurance.)

General Instrument Corp.
181 W. Madison
Chicago, IL 60602
312/541-5000
(Electronics.)

Harris Trust & Savings Bank
111 W. Monroe St.
Chicago, IL 60603
312/461-2121
(Banking.)

Household International Inc.
2700 Sanders Rd.
Prospect Heights, IL 60070
708/564-5000
(Financial services.)

Illinois Bell
(subsidiary of Ameritech)
225 W. Randolph St.
Chicago, IL 60606
312/727-9411
(Telephone service.)

IMC Fertilizer Group, Inc.
2100 Sanders Rd.
Northbrook, IL 60062
312/272-9200
(Chemicals.)

Kemper Corp.
Kemper Ctr.
Long Grove, IL 60049
708/540-2000
(Investment, investment services,
insurance, etc.)

Kemper Securities Group, Inc.
333 W. Wacker Dr.
Chicago, IL 60606
312/553-8500
(Investment services and products.)

Kraft General Foods
Kraft Ct.
Glenview, IL 60025
708/998-2000
(Food processing.)

Leo Burnett Co.
35 W. Wacker Dr.
Chicago, IL 60601
312/565-5959
(Advertising.)

**Lutheran General Health Care
System**
1775 Dempster St.
Park Ridge, IL 60068
708/696-5113
(Commercial and general building
operation.)

Marmon Group
225 W. Washington St.
Chicago, IL 60606
312/372-9500
(Industrial materials, etc.)

Marshall Field & Company
111 N. State St.
Chicago, IL 60690
312/781-5000
(Department stores.)

McDonald's Corporation
1 McDonald's Plz.
Oak Brook, IL 60521
708/575-3000
(Fast food restaurant chain.)

Midway Airlines Inc.
5700 S. Cicero Ave.
Chicago, IL 60638
312/838-0001
(Regional airline.)

Montgomery Ward & Co., Inc.
Montgomery Ward Plz.
Chicago, IL 60671
312/467-2000
(Retail and catalog sales.)

Morton International Inc.
100 N. Riverside Plz.
Chicago, IL 60606
312/807-2000
(Specialty chemicals.)

Motorola, Inc.
1303 E. Algonquin Rd.
Schaumburg, IL 60196
708/576-5000
(Electronics.)

Northern Trust Co.
50 S. LaSalle St.
Chicago, IL 60675
312/630-6000
(Banking.)

Outboard Marine Corp.
100 Sea Horse Dr.
Waukegan, IL 60085
708/689-6200
(Marine products, lawn care
products.)

Quaker Oats Co.
321 N. Clark St.
Quaker Tower
Chicago, IL 60610
312/222-7111
(Food processing.)

Joseph T. Ryerson & Son
2621 W. 15th Pl.
Chicago, IL 60608
312/762-2121
(Carbon steel bars, plates, etc.)

Sargent & Lundy
55 E. Monroe St.
Chicago, IL 60603
312/269-2000
(Engineering services.)

G. D. Searle & Co.
5200 Old Orchard Rd.
Skokie, IL 60077
708/982-7000
(Pharmaceuticals.)

Sears Consumer Financial Group.
2500 Lake Cook Rd.
Deerfield, IL 60015
708/405-0900
(Financial services, real estate.)

Sears, Roebuck & Co.
Sears Tower
Chicago, IL 60684
312/875-2500
(Retailing, financial services,
insurance, real estate.)

Speigel Inc.
3500 Lacey Rd.
Dauners Grove, IL 60515
708/986-8800
(Mail-order retailer, chain stores.)

**State Farm Mutual Automobile
Insurance Co.**
1 State Farm Plz.
Bloomington, IL 61710
309/766-2311
(Also at this address: State Farm Fire
& Casualty Co.; State Farm Life
Insurance Co.—insurance.)

Sun Times Co.
401 N. Wabash Ave.
Chicago, IL 60611
312/321-3000
(Newspaper publishing.)

Sundstrand Corp.
P.O. Box 7013
Rockford, IL 61125-7003
815/226-6000
(Aerospace and defense parts.)

Sweetheart Cup Co. Inc.
7575 S. Kostner Ave.
Chicago, IL 60652
312/767-3300
(Paper cups, etc.)

Tang Industries
1965 Pratt Blvd.
Elk Grove Village, IL 60007
708/806-7600
(Metal fabricating and distribution.)

Tribune Company
435 N. Michigan Ave.
Chicago, IL 60611
312/222-9100
(Communications media.)

UAL Corp.
(parent of United Airlines)
P.O. Box 66919
Chicago, IL 60666
708/952-4000
(Airline.)

Unitrin Inc.
1 E. Wacker Dr.
Chicago, IL 60601
312/661-4600
(Insurance.)

Walgreen Co.
200 Wilmot Rd.
Deerfield, IL 60015
708/940-2500
(Drug stores.)

Waste Management Inc.
3003 Butterfield Rd.
Oak Brook, IL 60521
708/572-8800
(Waste collection and disposal
services.)

Westwood One Inc.—Chicago office
111 E. Wacker Dr.
Chicago, IL 60601
312/938-0222
(Radio network.)

Wheelabrator Technologies, Inc.
3003 Butterfield Rd.
Oak Brook, IL 60521
708/218-1700
(Heavy construction, etc.)

Wm. Wrigley Jr. Co.
410 N. Michigan Ave.
Chicago, IL 60611
312/644-2121
(Chewing gum.)

World Color Press Inc.
401 Industrial Dr.
Effingham, IL 62401

217/342-9241
(Commercial printing.)

Zenith Electronics Corp.
1000 Milwaukee Ave.
Glenview, IL 60025-2423
708/391-7000
(Consumer Electronics.)

Zurich Insurance Co.
1400 American Ln.
Schaumburg, IL 60196
708/605-6000
(Insurance.)

ILLINOIS BUSINESS PERIODICALS

Crain's Chicago Business
740 North Rush St.
Chicago, IL 60611
312/649-5370
(Weekly; publish yearly directory of
leading companies.)

*The Wall St. Journal (Midwest
Edition)*
Dow Jones & Co.
1 S. Wacker Dr.
Chicago, IL 60606
312/750-4000

ILLINOIS DIRECTORIES

Harris Illinois Industrial Directory
Harris Publishing Company
2057 Aurora Rd.
Twinsburg, OH 44087
216/425-9000
800/888-5900

Illinois Business Directory
American Business Directories
5711 S. 86th Cir.
P.O. Box 27347
Omaha, NE 68127
402/593-4600

Illinois Manufacturers Register
Manufacturers' News, Inc.
1633 Central St.
Evanston, IL 60201
708/864-7000

Illinois Services Register
Manufacturers' News, Inc.
1633 Central St.
Evanston, IL 60201
708/864-7000

ILLINOIS GOVERNMENT EMPLOYMENT OFFICES

Office of Personnel Management
John C. Kluczynski Bldg.
230 S. Dearborn St.
Chicago, IL 60604-1687
(Regional federal OPM office.)

Office of Personnel Management
175 W. Jackson Blvd.
Rm. 530
Chicago, IL 60604
312/353-6192

(Federal job-service center; for
Madison and St. Clair, see MO
listing.)

Employment Services
Employment Security Division
910 S. Michigan Ave.

Chicago, IL 60605
312/793-6074
(State job-service center.)

INDIANA

LEADING INDIANA EMPLOYERS

American General Finance Inc.
601 NW 2nd St.
Evansville, IN 47701
812/424-8031
(Consumer loans, life and casualty
insurance.)

Anacomp, Inc.
P.O. Box 40888
Indianapolis, IN 46240
317/844-9666
(Computer systems and services.)

Arvin Industries, Inc.
P.O. Box 3000
Columbus, IN 47202
812/379-3000
(Automobile exhaust systems, metal
parts, etc.)

Associated Insurance Companies
120 W. Market St.
Indianapolis, IN 46204
317/263-8000
(Insurance.)

Ball Corp.
345 S. High St.
Muncie, IN 47305
317/747-6100
(Packaging products.)

Banc One Indiana
111 Monument Cir.
Indianapolis, IN 46277
317/321-3000
(Banking.)

Bendix Engine Controls Division
(div. of Allied-Signal Aerospace Co.)
717 N. Bendix Dr.
South Bend, IN 46620
219/231-3000
(Aircraft engine controls and
subsystems, electronic systems and
equipment.)

Boehringer Mannheim Corp.
9115 Hague Rd.
Indianapolis, IN 46250
317/845-2000
(Medical and surgical instruments,
equipment and supplies.)

Central Newspapers, Inc.
307 N. Pennsylvania St.
Indianapolis, IN 46204
317/231-9201
(Newspaper publishing.)

Central Soya Co, Inc.
1033 Fort Wayne National Bank Bldg.
Fort Wayne, IN 46802
219/425-5100
(Soy proteins, lecithins, feed
manufacturing.)

Clark Equipment Co.
100 N. Michigan St.
South Bend, IN 46634
219/239-0100
(Heavy equipment.)

Conseco Inc.
P.O. Box 1911
Carmel, IN 46032
317/573-6100
(Life and health insurance.)

Cummins Engines Co., Inc.
500 Jackson St.
Box 3005
Columbus, IN 47202
812/377-6000
(Diesel engines and components.)

Delco Electronics Corp.
1 Corporate Ctr.
Kokomo, IN 46902
317/451-2384
(Avionics equipment.)

GTE North Incorporated
19845 N. US 31
Westfield, IN 46074
817/896-6464
(Telecommunications.)

Great Lakes Chemical
P.O. Box 2200
Highway 52 NW
West Lafayette, IN 47906
317/497-6100
(Chemicals.)

Hillenbrand Industries, Inc.
Highway 46 E.
Batesville, IN 47006
812/934-7000
(Hospital beds, medical equipment rental, burial caskets, etc.)

Indiana Bell Telephone Co. Inc.
240 N. Meridian St.
Indianapolis, IN 46204
317/265-2266
(Telephone services.)

Indiana Gas Company, Inc.
1630 N. Meridian St.
Indianapolis, IN 46202
317/926-3351
(Natural gas distribution.)

Indiana Michigan Power Co.
One Summit Sq.
Fort Wayne, IN 46801
219/425-2111
(Utility.)

Indiana National Bank (INB)
One Indiana Sq.
Indianapolis, IN 46266
317/266-6000
(Banking.)

Inland Container Corp.
4030 Vincennes Rd.
Indianapolis, IN 46268
317/879-4222
(Boxes.)

Kimball International, Inc.
1600 Royal Rd.
Jasper, IN 47549
812/482-1600
(Office and home furnishings, etc.)

Eli Lilly & Co.
Lilly Corporate Ctr.
Indianapolis, IN 46285
317/276-2000
(Pharmaceuticals.)

Lincoln National Corp.
1300 S. Clinton St.
Fort Wayne, IN 46801
219/455-2000
(Insurance, pension investment management.)

Magnavox Government & Industrial Electronics Co.
1313 Production Rd.
Fort Wayne, IN 46808
219/429-6000
(Aerospace and electronics systems.)

Mead Johnson & Co.
2400 W. Lloyd Exwy.
Evansville, IN 47721
812/429-5000
(Pharmaceuticals, etc.)

Merchants National Corp.
One Merchants Plz.
Indianapolis, IN 46255
317/267-7000
(Banking.)

Miles Inc.
1127 Myrtle St.
Elkhart, IN 46515
219/264-8111
(Pharmaceuticals, diagnostics,
cleaning products.)

North American Van Lines, Inc.
5001 US Highway 30 W.
Fort Wayne, IN 46818
219/429-2511
(Motor carrier.)

**Northern Indiana Public Service
Co.**
5265 Hohman Ave.
Hammond, IN 46320
219/853-5200
(Utility.)

PSI Energy Inc.
1000 E. Main St.
Plainfield, IN 46168
317/839-9611
(Utility.)

Thompson Consumer Electronics
600 N. Sherman Dr.
Indianapolis, IN 46201
317/267-5000
(Consumer electronics.)

Zimmer, Inc.
727 N. Detroit St.
Warsaw, IN 46580
219/267-6131
(Orthopedic, prosthetic and surgical
appliances and devices.)

INDIANA BUSINESS PERIODICAL

Indiana Business
6502 East Westfield Blvd.
Indianapolis, IN 46620
317/252-2737
(Monthly.)

INDIANA DIRECTORIES

Harris Indiana Industrial Directory
Harris Publishing Company
2057 Aurora Rd.
Twinsburg, OH 44087
216/425-9000
800/888-5900

Indiana Business Directory
American Business Directories
5711 S. 86th Cir.

P.O. Box 27347
Omaha, NE 68127
402/593-4600

Indiana Manufacturers Directory
Manufacturers' News, Inc.
1633 Central St.
Evanston, IL 60201
708/864-7000

INDIANA GOVERNMENT EMPLOYMENT OFFICES

Office of Personnel Management
575 N. Pennsylvania St.
Indianapolis, IN 46204
317/226-7161

(Federal job-service center; for Clark,
Dearborn, and Floyd counties, see OH
listing.)

E.S., Employment Security Division
10 N. Senate Ave.
Indianapolis, IN 46204

317/232-7680
(State job-service center.)

IOWA

LEADING IOWA EMPLOYERS

AUSA Life Insurance Co., Inc.
4333 Edgewood Rd., NE
Cedar Rapids, IA 52402
319/398-8511
(Life insurance.)

Aegon USA Inc.
4333 Edgewood Rd., NE
Cedar Rapids, IA 52402
319/398-8511
(Insurance.)

Allied Group
701 Fifth Ave.
Des Moines, IA 50309
515/280-4211
(Insurance.)

Amana Refrigeration, Inc.
Main St.
Amana, IA 52204
319/622-5511
(Appliances.)

Amco Insurance Co.
701 Fifth Ave.
Des Moines, IA 50309
515/280-4211
(Insurance.)

Bandag, Inc.
Bandag Ctr.
Muscatine, IA 52761
319/262-1400
(Tread rubber, other rubber products.)

Collins General Aviation Division
(subs. of Rockwell)
400 Collins Rd., NE
Cedar Rapids, IA 52498
319/395-1000

(Communications, navigation and flight control equipment.)

Delong Sportswear Inc.
733 Broad St.
Grinnell, IA 50112-0189
515/236-3106
(Sportswear.)

EMC Insurance Group
717 Mulberry St.
Des Moines, IA 50309
515/280-2511
(Insurance.)

Equitable of Iowa Cos.
P.O. Box 1635
Des Moines, IA 50306
515/245-6911
(Insurance.)

FDL Marketing Inc.
701 East 16th St.
Dubuque, IA 52001
319/588-5400
(Pork products.)

Flexsteel Industries, Inc.
Brunswick Industrial Block
Dubuque, IA 52001
319/556-7730
(Furniture.)

Hon Industries, Inc.
P.O. Box 1109
Muscatine, IA 52761
319/264-7400
(Office furniture.)

Hubinger Co.
One Progress St.
Keokuk, IA 52632
319/524-5757
(Corn starch and syrup.)

Hy-vee Food Stores Inc.
1801 Osceola Ave.
Chariton, IA 50049
515/774-2121
(Food stores.)

Inspiration Resources Corp.
600 Fourth St.
Terra Ctr.
Sioux City, IA 51101
712/277-1340
(Holding company—chemicals,
minerals, etc.)

Interstate Power Co.
1000 Main St.
Dubuque, IA 52001
319/582-5421
(Utility.)

Iowa-Illinois Gas & Electric Co.
206 E. 2nd St.
Davenport, IA 52801
319/326-7111
(Utility.)

Iowa Southern Inc.
300 Sheridan Ave.
Centerville, IA 52544
515/437-4400
(Utility.)

Lee Enterprises Inc.
130 East 2nd St.
Davenport, IA 52801
319/383-2100
(Newspaper publishing.)

Maytag Corp.
One Dependability Sq.
Newton, IA 50208
515/792-8000
(Appliances.)

Meredith Corp.
1716 Locust St.
Des Moines, IA 50312
515/284-3000
(Magazine publishing.)

Norwest Financial Services Inc.
206 8th St.
Des Moines, IA 50309
515/243-2131
(Consumer and commercial finance,
insurance and reinsurance, etc.)

Pioneer Teletechnologies Inc.
102 Sergeant Square Dr.
Sergeant Bluff, IA 51054
712/943-1000
(Telemarketing services.)

The Principal Financial Group
711 High St.
Des Moines, IA 50392
515/247-5111
(Insurance, financial services, etc. At
same address: Principal National Life
Insurance Co., Principal Casualty
Insurance Co.)

Statesman Group
1400 Des Moines Bldg.
Des Moines, IA 50309
515/284-7500
(Insurance.)

Teleconnect Co.
500 Second Ave., SE
Cedar Rapids, IA 52401
319/366-6600
(Telephone communications.)

United Fire & Casualty Co.
118 Second Ave., NW
Cedar Rapids, IA 52407
319/399-5700
(Insurance.)

Younker's Inc.
7th & Walnut Sts.
Des Moines, IA 50397
515/244-1112
(Department stores.)

IOWA BUSINESS PERIODICALS

Business & Industry
Business Magazine, Inc.
1720 28th St.
West Des Moines, IA 50265
515/255-2545

Business Record
100 Fourth St.
Des Moines, IA 50309
515/288-3336
(Weekly.)

IOWA DIRECTORIES

Directory of Iowa Manufacturers
Harris Publishing Company
2057 Aurora Rd.
Twinsburg, OH 44087
216/425-9000
800/888-5900

Iowa Business Directory
American Business Directories
5711 S. 86th Cir.

P.O. Box 27347
Omaha, NE 68127
402/593-4600

Iowa Manufacturers Register
Manufacturers' News, Inc.
1633 Central St.
Evanston, IL 60201
708/864-7000

IOWA GOVERNMENT EMPLOYMENT OFFICES

Office of Personnel Management
(Federal job-service center—see
listing for MO; phone 816/426-7757.)

Job Service Program Bureau
Department of Job Service
1000 E. Grand Ave.
Des Moines, IA 50319
515/281-5134
(State job-service center.)

KANSAS

LEADING KANSAS EMPLOYERS

Air Midwest Inc.
6810 W. Kellogg
P.O. Box 7724
Wichita, KS 67277
316/942-8137
(Regional air carrier.)

Associated Wholesale Grocers, Inc.
5000 Kansas Ave.
Kansas City, KS 66106
913/321-1313
(Wholesale groceries.)

Beech Aircraft Corp.
(subs. of Raytheon)
Box 85
Wichita, KS 67201-0085
316/681-7111
(Aircraft, aerospace systems.)

**Bendix/King Mobile
Communications Division**
2920 Haskell Ave.
Lawrence, KS 66046
913/842-0402
(Two-way mobile communications
and base stations and accessories.)

**Boeing Commercial
Airplanes—Wichita Division**
P.O. Box 7730
3801 S. Oliver
Wichita, KS 67277-7730
316/526-3153
(Aircraft manufacturer.)

Cessna Aircraft Co.
P.O. Box 1521
Wichita, KS 67201
316/685-9111
(Aircraft.)

**Coca-Cola Bottling Mid-America
Inc.**
9000 Marshall Dr.
Shawnee Mission, KS 66215
913/492-8100
(Beverage bottler.)

Doskocil Companies, Inc.
P.O. Box 1570
South Hutchison, KS 67501
316/663-1005
(Precooked meat, dry sausage
producer.)

Duckwall-Alco Stores Inc.
401 Cottage St.
Albilene, KS 67410
913/263-3350
(Discount stores.)

Fourth Financial Corp.
100 N. Broadway
Wichita, KS 67201
316/261-4444
(Multibank holding co.)

Health Care Lodges Inc.
512 W. 11th
Coffeyville, KS 67337
316/251-6780
(Nursing homes.)

Kansas Gas & Electric Co.
120 E. 1st St.
Wichita, KS 67202
316/261-6611
(Utility.)

Kansas Power & Light Co.
818 Kansas Ave.
Topeka, KS 66612
913/296-6300
(Utility.)

King Radio Corp.
400 N. Rogers Rd.
Olathe, KS 66062
913/782-0400
(Broadcasting.)

Koch Industries Inc.
4111 E. 37th N. St.
Wichita, KS 67220
316/832-5500
(Oil and gas exploration, chemicals,
minerals, etc.)

Learjet Inc.
P.O. Box 7707
Wichita-Mid-Continent Airport
Wichita, KS 67277-7707
316/946-2000
(Business jets.)

The Lee Apparel Company Inc.
9001 W. 67th St.
Merriam, KS 66202
913/384-4000
(Apparel.)

Marley Co.
1900 Shawnee Mission Pkwy.
Mission Woods, KS 66205
913/362-5440
(Cooling towers, boilers, etc.)

Mast Advertising & Publishing Inc.
7500 W. 110th St.
Overland Park, KS 66210
913/451-6278
(Telephone directories.)

National Co-op Refinery Association
2000 S. Main St.
McPherson, KS 67460
316/241-2340
(Gasoline blending plants, diesel
fuels, oil.)

Pizza Hut Inc.
9111 E. Douglas
Wichita, KS 67207
316/681-9000
(Chain restaurants.)

Puritan-Bennett Corp.
9401 Indian Creek Pkwy.
Box 25905
Overland Park, KS 66225
913/661-0444
(Medical and surgical instruments.)

Southwestern Bell—Kansas Division
220 East 6th St.
Topeka, KS 66603
913/276-1585
(Telephone company.)

US Sprint Communications
2330 Shawnee Mission Pkwy.
Westwood, KS 66209
913/624-3000
(Long-distance telecommunications.)

Yellow Freight System Inc.
10990 Roe Ave.
Box 7563
Overland Park, KS 66207
913/967-4300
(Trucking.)

KANSAS BUSINESS PERIODICALS

Kansas Business News
P.O. Box 490
Augusta, KS 67010
316/775-3201
(Monthly.)

Wichita Business Journal
American City Business Journals, Inc.
138 Ida Street
Wichita, KS 67211
316/267-6406
(Weekly.)

KANSAS DIRECTORY

Kansas Business Directory
American Business Directories
5711 S. 86th Cir.
P.O. Box 27347
Omaha, NE 68127
402/593-4600

KANSAS GOVERNMENT EMPLOYMENT OFFICES

Office of Personnel Management
120 S. Market St. Rm. 101
Wichita, KS 67202
316/269-6794
(Federal job-service center; in
Johnson, Leavenworth, and
Wyandotte counties, see Kansas City
MO listing.)

Division of Employment & Training
Dept. of Human Resources
401 Topeka Ave.
Topeka, KS 66603
913/296-5317
(State job-service center.)

MICHIGAN

LEADING MICHIGAN EMPLOYERS

ALC Communications Corp.
30300 Telegraph Rd.
Bingham Farms, MI 48025
313/647-6920
(Telephone services.)

ANR Pipeline Co.
500 Renaissance Ctr.
Detroit, MI 48243
313/496-0200
(Natural gas transmission.)

American Natural Resources Co.
1 Woodward Ave.
Detroit, MI 48226
313/496-0200
(Natural gas transmission.)

Amway Corp.
7575 East Fulton Rd.
Ada, MI 49355
616/676-6000
(Cleaning and other consumer products [direct sales].)

Auto Owners Insurance Co.
6101 Anacapri Blvd.
Lansing, MI 48917
517/323-1200
(Automobile insurance.)

Bissell Inc.
2345 Walker Rd., NW
Grand Rapids, MI 49504
616/453-4451
(Vacuum cleaners.)

Blue Cross & Blue Shield of Michigan
600 Lafayette East
Detroit, MI 48226
313/225-9000
(Insurance.)

Brunswick Bowling & Billiards Corp.
525 West Laketon Ave.
Muskegon, MI 49441

616/725-3300
(Sporting and athletic goods.)

Chrysler Corp.
12000 Chrysler Dr.
Detroit, MI 48288
313/956-5252
(Automobile manufacturer.)

Chrysler Financial Corp.
27777 Franklin Rd.
Southfield, MI 48034
313/948-2890
(Finance company.)

Citizens Banking Corp.
One Citizens Banking Ctr.
Flint, MI 48502
313/766-7500
(Banking.)

Comerica Inc.
211 West Fort St.
Detroit, MI 48226
313/222-3300
(Banking.)

Consumers Power Co.
212 West Michigan Ave.
Jackson, MI 49201
517/788-0550
(Utility.)

Detroit Edison Co.
2000 2nd Ave.
Detroit, MI 48226
313/237-8000
(Electric utility.)

Donnelly Corp.
414 East 40th St.
Holland, MI 49423
616/786-7000
(Glass products.)

Dow Chemical Co.
2030 Willard H. Dow Ctr.
Midland, MI 48674

517/636-1000
(Diversified chemicals.)

Dow Corning Corp.
Box 994
Midland, MI 48686
517/496-4000
(Chemicals.)

Federal-Mogul Corp.
P.O. Box 1966
Detroit, MI 48235
313/354-7700
(Motor vehicle parts and accessories.)

Fireman's Fund Mortgage Corp.
27555 Farmington Rd.
Farmington Hill, MI 48334
313/661-7000
(Mortgage bankers.)

First of America Bancorp
211 S. Rose St.
Kalamazoo, MI 49007
616/376-9000
(Banking.)

First Fed Michigan
1001 Woodward Ave.
Detroit, MI 48226
313/965-1400
(Banking.)

Ford Motor Company
The American Rd.
Dearborn, MI 48121
313/322-3000
(Automobile manufacturer.)

Ford Motor Credit Co.
The American Rd.
P.O. Box 1732
Dearborn, MI 48121
313/322-3000
(Credit institution.)

General Dynamics Land Systems
38500 Mound Rd.
Sterling Heights, MI 48310
313/825-4000
(Tanks and tank components.)

General Motors Acceptance Corp.
3044 West Grand Blvd.
Detroit, MI 48202
313/556-5000
(Credit institution.)

General Motors Corp.
3044 West Grand Blvd.
Detroit, MI 48202
313/556-5000
(Automobile manufacturer.)

Gerber Products Co.
445 State St.
Fremont, MI 49412
616/928-2000
(Food processor.)

Haworth Inc.
One Haworth Ctr.
Holland, MI 49423
616/393-3000
(Office furniture.)

Heath Co.
Hilltop Rd.
P.O. Box 1288
St. Joseph, MI 49085
616/982-3200
(Computers.)

Herman Miller Inc.
8500 Byron Rd.
Zeeland, MI 49464
616/772-3300
(Office furniture.)

Highland Superstores Inc.
909 N. Sheldon Ave.
Plymouth, MI 48170
313/451-3200
(Consumer electronics stores.)

K Mart Corp.
3100 West Big Beaver Rd.
Troy, MI 48084
313/643-1000
(Discount department stores.)

KH Corp.
38481 Huron River Dr.
Romulus, MI 48174
313/941-2000
(Motor vehicle parts and accessories.)

Kellogg Co.
1 Kellogg Sq.
Battle Creek, MI 49016
616/961-2000
(Food processor.)

Kelly Services Inc.
999 West Big Beaver Rd.
Troy, MI 48084
313/362-4444
(Temporary employment agencies.)

MCN Corp.
500 Griswold St.
Detroit, MI 48226
313/256-5500
(Natural gas, data processing, etc.)

Manufacturers National Corp.
Manufacturers Bank Tower
Detroit, MI 48243
313/222-4000
(Banking.)

Mejier Inc.
2929 Walker Ave. NW
Grand Rapids, MI 49504
616/453-6711
(Department stores.)

Michigan Bell Telephone Co.
444 Michigan Ave.
Detroit, MI 48226
313/223-9900
(Telephone services.)

Michigan Consolidated Gas Co.
500 Griswold St.
Detroit, MI 48226
313/965-2430
(Utility.)

Michigan National Corp.
Box 9065
Farmington Hills, MI 48333

313/473-3000
(Banking.)

NBD Bancorp, Inc.
611 Woodward Ave.
Detroit, MI 48226
313/225-1000
(Banking.)

National-Standard Co.
1618 Terminal Rd.
Niles, MI 49120
616/683-8100
(Steel wiredrawing, nails, etc.)

Old Kent Financial Corp.
1 Vandenburg Ctr.
Grand Rapids, MI 49503
616/771-5000
(Bank holding co.)

Penske
13400 Outer Dr. W
Detroit, MI 48239
313/592-5000
(Diesel manufacturing, truck leasing,
dealerships.)

Spartan Stores Inc.
850 76th St. SW
Grand Rapids, MI 49508
616/878-2000
(Grocery stores.)

Standard Federal Bank
2600 West Big Beaver Rd.
Troy, MI 48084
313/643-9600
(Banking.)

Steelcase Inc.
901 44th St. SE
Grand Rapids, MI 49508
616/247-2710
(Office furniture.)

Tecumseh Products Co.
100 East Patterson St.
Tecumseh, MI 49286
517/423-8411
(Auto & truck OEM.)

United Technologies Automotive
5200 Auto Club Dr.
Dearborn, MI 48126
313/593-9600
(Motor vehicle parts and accessories.)

University Microfilms Inc.
300 North Zeeb Rd.
Ann Arbor, MI 48103
313/761-4700
(Microfilms—div. Bell & Howell
Company.)

Upjohn Co.
7000 Portage Rd.
Kalamazoo, MI 49001

616/323-4000
(Pharmaceuticals.)

Volkswagen of America Inc.
3800 Hamlin Rd.
Auburn Hills, MI 48326
313/340-5000
(Automobile manufacturer.)

Whirlpool Corp.
2000 M63 North
Benton Harbor, MI 49022
616/923-5000
(Appliance manufacturer.)

MICHIGAN BUSINESS PERIODICALS

Corporate Detroit
26111 Evergreen Rd.
Southfield, MI 48076
313/357-8300
(Monthly.)

Crain's Detroit Business
1400 Woodbridge St.
Detroit, MI 48207
313/446-6032
(Weekly.)

Detroit Marketplace
2701 Troy Ctr.
Troy, MI 48084

313/362-0490
(Monthly.)

Michigan Business
2611 Evergreen Rd.
Suite 303
Southfield, MI 48076-4499
313/357-8300
(Monthly.)

MICHIGAN DIRECTORIES

Harris Michigan Industrial Directory
Harris Publishing Co.
2057 Aurora Rd.
Twinsburg, OH 44087
216/425-9000

Michigan Business Directory
American Business Directories
5711 S. 86th Cir.
P.O. Box 27347
Omaha, NE 68127
402/593-4600

Michigan Distributors' Directory
Pick Publications, Inc.
28715 Greenfield Rd.
Southfield, MI 48076
313/443-1799

MICHIGAN GOVERNMENT EMPLOYMENT OFFICES

Office of Personnel Management
477 Michigan Ave.
Rm. 565
Detroit, MI 48226
313/226-6950
(Federal job-service center.)

Bureau of Employment Service
Employment Security Division
7310 Woodward Ave.
Detroit, MI 48202
313/876-5309
(State job-service center.)

MINNESOTA

LEADING MINNESOTA EMPLOYERS

Bemis Company, Inc.
625 Marquette Ave.
Minneapolis, MN 55402
612/340-6000
(Packaging, industrial products.)

Carlson Hospitality Group, Inc.
(subs. of Carlson Companies, Inc.)
Carlson Pkwy.
P.O. Box 59159
Minneapolis, MN 55441
612/540-5275
(Hotels and motels.)

Carlson Marketing Group Inc.
12755 Hwy. 55
Minneapolis, MN 55459
612/540-5000
(Management consulting.)

Carlson Travel Group Inc.
12755 Hwy. 55
Minneapolis, MN 55441
612/449-1900
(Travel agencies.)

Control Data Corp.
8100 34th Ave. S.
Minneapolis, MN 55440
612/853-8100
(Electronic components, computer products.)

Data Card Corp.
11111 Bren Rd. W.
Minnetonka, MN 55343
612/933-1233
(Office machines.)

Dayton-Hudson Corp.
777 Nicollet Mall
Minneapolis, MN 55402
612/370-6948
(Department stores.)

Deluxe Corp.
1080 W. County Rd. F
St. Paul MN 55126
612/483-7111
(Commercial printing.)

Diversified Energies Inc.
201 S. 7th St.
Minneapolis, MN 55402
612/342-5101
(Natural gas distribution.)

Donaldson Co., Inc.
1400 W. 94th St.
Minneapolis, MN 55431
612/887-3131
(Industrial and commercial equipment and machinery.)

Ecolab Inc.
Ecolab Ctr.
St. Paul, MN 55102
612/293-2233
(Specialty chemicals.)

Federal Hoffman Inc.
900 Ehlen Dr.
Anoka, MN 55303
612/421-7100
(Small arms ammunition.)

Fingerhut Companies, Inc.
4400 Baker Rd.
Hopkins, MN 55343
612/932-3100
(Mail order.)

First Bank System
601 Second Ave. S.
Minneapolis, MN 55402
612/973-1111
(Banking.)

General Mills Inc.
One General Mills Blvd.
Minneapolis, MN 55426
612/540-2311
(Food processor.)

George A. Hormel & Co.
501 16th Ave. NE
Austin, MN 55912
507/437-5611
(Food products.)

Green Tree Acceptance
345 St. Peter St.
St. Paul, MN 55102
612/293-3400
(Mobile manufactured housing
financing.)

Honeywell, Inc.
Honeywell Plz.
Minneapolis, MN 55408
612/870-5200
(Aerospace and electronics systems
and products.)

Hutchinson Technology Inc.
40 W. Highland Park
Hutchinson, MN 55350
612/587-3797

(Computer peripherals, electronics and
defense equipment.)

Imprimis Technology Inc.
12501 Whitewater Dr.
Hopkins, MN 55343
612/936-6515
(Computer storage devices.)

Inter-Regional Financial Group, Inc.
100 Dain Tower
Minneapolis, MN 55402
612/371-7750
(Securities broker and dealer,
investment banking.)

International Multifoods Corp.
Multifoods Tower
P.O. Box 2942
Minneapolis, MN 55402
612/340-3300
(Food products.)

Jostens, Inc.
5501 Norman Ctr. Dr.
Minneapolis, MN 55437
612/830-3300
(Class rings, yearbooks, caps and
gowns, etc.)

Land O'Lakes Inc.
4001 Lexington Ave. N.
Arden Hills, MN 55112
612/481-2222
(Dairy products.)

MTS Systems Corp.
14000 Technology Dr.
Eden Prairie, MN 55344
612/937-4000
(Measuring and controlling devices.)

Medtronic Inc.
7000 Central Ave. NE
Minneapolis, MN 55432
612/574-4000
(Medical equipment.)

**Minnesota Mining & Manufacturing
Co. (3M)**
3M Ctr.
St. Paul, MN 55144
612/733-1110
(Diversified conglomerate.)

Minnesota Mutual Life Insurance Co.
400 N. Robert St.
St. Paul, MN 55101
612/298-3500
(Life insurance.)

Minnesota Power & Light Co.
30 W. Superior St.
Duluth, MN 55802
218/722-2641
(Utility.)

M.A. Mortenson Cos.
700 Meadow Ln. N.
Minneapolis, MN 55422
612/522-2100
(Construction.)

NCR Corp.—NCR Network Products
2700 Snelling Ave. N.
Roseville, MN 55113
612/638-7777
(Computers, prepackaged software.)

National Car Rental System
7700 France Ave. S.
Minneapolis, MN 55435
612/830-2121
(Car rentals.)

Northern States Power Co.
414 Nicollet Mall
Minneapolis, MN 55401
612/330-5500
(Utility.)

Northwest Airlines, Inc.
Minneapolis-St. Paul Airport
St. Paul, MN 55111
612/726-2111
(Airline.)

**Northwestern National Life
Insurance Co.**
20 Washington Ave. S.
Minneapolis, MN 55401
612/372-5432
(Insurance.)

Norwest Corporation
Sixth St. & Marquette Ave.
Minneapolis, MN 55479
612/667-1234
(Banking.)

Onan Corp.
1400 73rd Ave. NE
Minneapolis, MN 55432
612/574-5000
(Motors and generators.)

Pillsbury Co.
Pillsbury Ctr.
200 S. 6th St.
Minneapolis, MN 55402
612/330-4966
(Food processing.)

Piper, Jaffrey, and Hopwood Inc.
222 S. Ninth St.
Minneapolis, MN 55402
612/342-6000
(Securities broker.)

Sheldahl, Inc.
1150 Sheldahl Rd.
Northfield, MN 55057
507/663-8000
(Printed circuit boards, graphic
displays, plastic processing.)

Smead Manufacturing Co.
600 East Smead Blvd.
Hastings, MN 55033
612/437-4111
(Filing folders, manila folders, index
cards, etc.)

Soo Line Corp.
1000 Soo Line Bldg.
Box 530
Minneapolis, MN 55440
612/347-8000
(Railroad.)

St. Paul Companies, Inc.
385 Washington St.
Minneapolis, MN 55102
612/221-7911
(Insurance, financial services.)

Starkey Laboratories Inc.
6700 Washington Ave. S.
Hopkins, MN 55344
612/941-6401
(Orthopedic, prosthetic and surgical
appliances and devices.)

Super Valu Stores, Inc.
P.O. Box 990
Minneapolis, MN 55440
612/828-4000
(Food wholesaler.)

TCF Financial
801 Marquette Ave.
Minneapolis, MN 55402
612/370-7000
(Banking, financial services.)

Tennant Co.
701 North Lilac Dr.
Minneapolis, MN 55440
612/540-1200
(Dirt sweepers, floor
washing/polishing machines, wax,
sealants and detergents.)

Thermo King Corp.
314 W. 90th St.
Minneapolis, MN 55420
612/887-2200
(Air conditioning and refrigeration
equipment.)

The Toro Company
8111 Lyndale Ave. S.
Minneapolis, MN 55420
612/888-8801
(Lawn and garden equipment.)

Valspar Corp.
1101 E. Third St., S.
Minneapolis, MN 55415
612/332-7371
(Paint, etc.)

Waldorf Corp.
2250 Wabash Ave.
St. Paul, MN 55114
612/641-4938
(Folding boxboard, corrogating
medium.)

West Publishing Co.
50 West Kellogg Blvd.
St. Paul, MN 55102
612/228-2500
(Textbook publishing, data
communications.)

MINNESOTA BUSINESS PERIODICALS

Corporate Report Minnesota
5500 Wayzata Blvd.
Minneapolis, MN 55416
612/591-2700
(Monthly.)

Minneapolis/St. Paul Business
5500 Wayzata Blvd.
Minneapolis, MN 55416
612/591-2701
(Weekly.)

MINNESOTA DIRECTORIES

Minnesota Business Directory
American Business Directories
5711 S. 86th Cir.
P.O. Box 27347
Omaha, NE 68127
402/593-4600

Minnesota Manufacturers Directory
George D. Hall Company
50 Congress St.

Boston, MA 02109
617/523-3745

Minnesota Manufacturers Register
Manufacturers' News, Inc.
1633 Central St.
Evanston, IL 60201
708/864-7000

MINNESOTA GOVERNMENT EMPLOYMENT OFFICES

Office of Personnel Management
Federal Bldg. Room 501
Ft. Snelling
Twin Cities, MN 55111
612/725-3430
(Federal job-service center.)

Job Service and UI Operations
690 American Ctr. Bldg.
150 E. Kellogg
St. Paul, MN 55101
612/296-3627
(State job-service center.)

MISSOURI

LEADING MISSOURI EMPLOYERS

Anheuser-Busch Companies, Inc.
1 Busch Place
St. Louis, MO 63118
314/577-2000
(Brewery, food and beverage products.)

Black & Veatch
8400 Ward Pkwy.
Kansas City, MO 64114
913/339-2000
(Engineering services.)

Boatmen's Bancshares Inc.
800 Market St.
St. Louis, MO 63102
314/466-6000
(Banking.)

Brown Group Inc.
8400 Maryland Ave.
St. Louis, MO 63105
314/854-4000
(Footwear, specialty retailing.)

Citicorp Mortgage Inc.
670 Mason Ridge Ctr.
St. Louis, MO 63141
314/851-1400
(Mortgage banking.)

Commerce Bancshares Inc.
1000 Walnut St.
Kansas City, MO 64106
816/234-2000
(Banking.)

Edison Brothers Stores, Inc.
501 N. Broadway
St. Louis, MO 63102
314/331-6000
(Stores [including Bakers, Chandlers (shoes), Jeans West, J. Riggings].)

A. G. Edwards & Sons, Inc.
1 N. Jefferson
St. Louis, MO 63103
314/289-3000
(Security brokers, dealers.)

Electronics & Space Corp.
(subs. of Emerson Electric Co.)
8100 W. Florissant Ave.
St. Louis, MO 63136
314/553-2000
(Armament, communications, testing and other electronic systems.)

Emerson Electric Co.
8000 W. Florissant Blvd.
St. Louis, MO 63136
314/553-2000
(Electronic and consumer products, defense products and systems.)

Farmland Industries, Inc.
3315 N. Oak Trafficway
Kansas City, MO 64116
816/459-6000
(Petroleum refining.)

General Dynamics Corp.
Pierre Laclede Centre
St. Louis, MO 63105
314/889-8200
(Defense systems, aviation mfr.,
space systems, etc.)

Graybar Electric
P.O. Box 7231
St. Louis, MO 63177
314/727-3900
(Electrical equipment wholesaling.)

Hallmark Cards Inc.
2501 McGee Trafficway
Kansas City, MO 64108
816/274-5111
(Greeting cards.)

Harbour Group Ltd.
7701 Forsyth Blvd., Suite 600
St. Louis, MO 63105
314/727-5550
(Medical products, cutting tools, etc.)

Hussmann Corp.
12999 St. Charles Rock Rd.
Hazelwood, MO 63044
314/291-2000
(Air conditioning, heating and
refrigeration equipment.)

Kansas City Power & Light Co.
1330 Baltimore Ave.
Kansas City, MO 64141
816/556-2200
(Utility.)

The Kansas City Star Co.
1729 Grand Ave.
Kansas City, MO 64108
816/234-4141
(Newspaper publishing—subs. of
Capital Cities/ABC, Inc.)

Marion Merrell Dow Inc.
9300 Ward Pkwy.
Kansas City, MO 64114
816/966-4000
(Pharmaceuticals.)

Maritz, Inc.
1375 N. Hwy. Dr.
Fenton, MO 63026
314/827-4000
(Motivation, communication, market
research training, business travel.)

The May Department Stores Co.
611 Olive St.
St. Louis, MO 63101
314/342-6300
(Department stores.)

McDonnell Aircraft Co.
(division of McDonnell Douglas
Corp.)
P.O. Box 516
St. Louis, MO 63166
(Aircraft, [F-15 Eagle, AV-8B
Harrier, FA-19 Hornet].)

McDonnell Douglas Corp.
P.O. Box 516
St. Louis, MO 63166
314/232-0232
(Aerospace products and systems.)

**McDonnell Douglas Missile Systems
Co.**
P.O. Box 516
St. Louis, MO 63166
314/232-0232
(Missiles and combat weapons.)

Memc Electronic Materials Inc.
501 Pearl Old Hwy. 79
O'Fallon, MO 63376
314/279-5000
(Semi-conductors and related
devices.)

Mercantile Bank of St. Louis N.A.
7th & Washington Sts.
St. Louis, MO 63101
314/425-2525
(Banking.)

Monsanto Chemical Co.
800 N. Lindbergh Blvd.
St. Louis, MO 63167
314/694-1000
(Chemical, agricultural products,
pharmaceuticals, plastics, etc.)

Pulitzer Publishing Co.
515 N. 6th St.
St. Louis, MO 63101
314/231-5950
(Newspaper publisher, radio, and
television station owner.)

Ralston Purina Co.
Checkerboard Sq.
St. Louis, MO 63164
314/982-1000
(Food products.)

Sigma-Aldrich Corp.
3050 Spruce St.
St. Louis, MO 63103

314/771-5765
(Chemicals supplier.)

Sverdrup
13723 Riverport Dr.
Maryland Heights, MO 63043
314/436-7600
(Engineering, architectural services,
etc.)

Union Electric Co.
P.O. Box 149
St. Louis, MO 63166
314/621-3222
(Utility.)

United Missouri Bankshares
1010 Grand Ave.
Kansas City, MO 64141
816/860-7000
(Banking.)

MISSOURI BUSINESS PERIODICALS

Kansas City Business Journal
324 East 11th St.
Kansas City, MO 64106
816/561-5900
(Weekly.)

St. Louis Business Journal
Box 647
St. Louis, MO 63188
314/421-6200
(Weekly.)

MISSOURI DIRECTORIES

Harris Missouri Directory of
Manufacturers
IDC (div. of Harris Publishing Co.)
2057 Aurora Rd.
Twinsburg, OH 44087
216/425-9000
800/888-5900

Missouri Business Directory
American Business Directories
5711 S. 86th Cir.

P.O. Box 27347
Omaha, NE 68127
402/593-4600

Missouri Manufacturers Directory
Manufacturers' News Inc.
1633 Central St.
Evanston, IL 60201
708/864-7000

MISSOURI GOVERNMENT EMPLOYMENT OFFICES

Office of Personnel Management
Federal Bldg. Rm. 134
601 E. 12th St.
Kansas City, MO 64106
816/426-5702
(Federal job-service center—for
counties west of and including
Mercer, Grundy, Livingston, Carroll,
Saline, Pettis, Benton, Hickory,
Dallas, Webster, Douglas, and
Ozark.)

Office of Personnel Management
Old Post Office Bldg.
815 Olive St. Rm. 400
St. Louis, MO 63101
314/539-2285
(Federal job-service center—for all
other MO counties not listed under
Kansas City, MO.)

Employment Service
Division of Employment Security
P.O. Box 59
Jefferson City, MO 65104
314/751-3790

NEBRASKA

LEADING NEBRASKA EMPLOYERS

Ag Processing Inc.
11717 Burt St.
Omaha, NE 68154
402/496-7809
(Soybean oil.)

BeefAmerica Inc.
5600 Harry Anderson Ave.
Omaha, NE 68137
402/896-2400
(Meat packing.)

Berkshire Hathaway Inc.
1440 Kiewit Plz.
Omaha, NE 68131
402/346-1400
(Fire, property, and casualty
insurance.)

Commercial Federal Corp.
2120 S. 72nd St.
Lincoln, NE 68124
402/554-9200
(Savings and loan.)

ConAgra Inc.
1 Con Agra Dr.
Omaha, NE 68102
402/595-4000
(Meat packing.)

Cushman Inc.
900 N. 21st St.
Lincoln, NE 68503
402/475-9581
(Transportation equipment.)

Data Documents, Inc.
4205 S. 96th St.
Omaha, NE 68127
402/339-0900
(Computer paper.)

Drivers Management Inc.
14507 Frontier Rd.
Omaha, NE 68138
402/895-6640
(Automobile recovery and help supply
services.)

First Data Resources
(subs. American Express)
10825 Farnam Dr.
Omaha, NE 68154
402/399-7050
(Bank credit card processing, etc.)

First National of Nebraska
16th & Dodge St.
Omaha, NE 68102
402/341-0500
(Banking.)

IBP Inc.
IBP Ave.
P.O. Box 515
Dakota City, NE 68731
402/494-2061
(Meat processing.)

Kawasaki Motor Manufacturing Corp. USA
6600 Northwest 27th St.
Lincoln, NE 68524
402/476-6600
(Motorcycles, all-terrain vehicles, etc.)

Kiewit Construction Group Inc.
3555 Farnam St.
Omaha, NE 68131
402/342-2052
(Hwy. and street construction, commercial and office building contractors, etc.)

Kiewit Mining Group Inc.
3555 Farnam St.
Omaha, NE 68131
402/342-2052
(Coal mining.)

Peter Kiewit Sons' Inc.
1000 Kiewit Plz.
Omaha, NE 68131
402/342-2052
(Metal cans, plastic bottles, etc.)

Lozier Corp.
6336 Pershing Dr.
Omaha, NE 68110
402/457-8000
(Store display fixtures.)

Mid-America Webpress Inc.
3700 NW 12th
Lincoln, NE 68501
402/474-5825
(Commercial printing.)

Mutual of Omaha Insurance Co.
Mutual of Omaha Plz.
Omaha, NE 68175
402/342-7600
(Accident and health insurance.)

Omaha Public Power District
444 S. 16th Mall
Omaha, NE 68102
402/636-3213
(Utility.)

Omaha World-Herald Co.
World-Herald Sq.
Omaha, NE 68102
402/444-1000
(Newspaper publishing.)

Pamida Inc.
8800 F St.
Omaha, NE 68127
402/339-2400
(General merchandise store.)

Union Pacific Railroad Co.
1416 Dodge St.
Omaha, NE 68179
402/271-5000
(Railroad.)

Valmont Industries, Inc.
Hwy. 275
Valley, NE 68064
402/359-2201
(Irrigation systems, steel tubing, poles, etc.)

Werner Enterprises Inc.
I-80 & Hwy. 50
Box 37308
Omaha, NE 68137
402/895-6640
(Trucking.)

West Telemarketing Corp.
9910 Maple St.
Omaha, NE 68134

402/571-7700
(Telemarketing services.)

Woodmen Accident & Life Co.
1526 K St.
Lincoln, NE 68508
402/476-6500
(Insurance.)

Woodmen of the World Life Insurance Society
1700 Farnam St.
Omaha, NE 68102
402/342-1890
(Insurance.)

NEBRASKA DIRECTORIES

Directory of Nebraska Manufacturers
Department of Economic Development
Box 94666
Lincoln, NE 68509
402/471-3111

Nebraska Business Directory
American Business Directories
5711 S. 86th Cir.
P.O. Box 27347
Omaha, NE 68127
402/593-4600

NEBRASKA GOVERNMENT EMPLOYMENT OFFICES

Office of Personnel Management
(Federal job-service center—see
Kansas listing.)

Job Service
NE Dept. of Labor
Lincoln, NE 68509
402/475-8451
(State job-service center.)

NORTH DAKOTA

LEADING NORTH DAKOTA EMPLOYERS

Basin Electric Power Co-op
1717 E. I Ave.
Bismarck, ND 58501
701/223-0441
(Utility.)

Blue Cross & Blue Shield of North Dakota
4510 13th Ave. SW
Fargo, ND 58121
701/282-1100
(Group hospitalization plans.)

Diagnostic Medical Systems
2101 N. University Dr.
Fargo, ND 58102

701/237-9073
(Medical equipment and supplies.)

Federal Beef Processors Inc.
Stockyard Rd.
240 West Fargo, ND 58078
701/282-9570
(Meat packing.)

Forum Publishing Co.
P.O. Box 2020
Fargo, ND 58102
701/235-7311
(Newspaper publishing, broadcasting.)

Hornbachers Food Inc.
2510 Broadway
Fargo, ND 58102
701/293-5444
(Grocery stores.)

MDU Resources Group Inc.
400 N. 4th St.
Bismarck, ND 58501
701/222-7900
(Utility.)

Metropolitan Federal Bank
215 N. Fifth St.
Fargo, ND 58102
701/293-2600
(Savings banks.)

Minnkota Power Co-op
1822 State Mill Rd.
Grand Forks, ND 58201
701/795-4000
(Utility.)

Sioux Manufacturing Corp.
Main St.
P.O. Box 400

Fort Totten, ND 58335
701/766-4211
(Plastic products, molding.)

Valley Markets Inc.
P.O. Box 1675
Grand Forks, ND 58203
701/772-5531
(Grocery stores.)

Vanderhave USA Inc.
1214 Prairie Pkwy.
West Fargo, ND 58078
701/282-7338
(Farm supplies.)

Vanity Shop of Grand Forks
1001 25th St.
Fargo, ND 58102
701/237-3330
(Women's clothing stores.)

Willston Basin Interest Pipeline
304 E. Rosser Ave.; No. 200
Bismarck, ND 58501
701/222-7609
(Crude petroleum and natural gas.)

NORTH DAKOTA DIRECTORIES

MacRAE's State Directories—North Dakota/South Dakota
MacRAE's Blue Book Inc.
817 Broadway
New York, NY 10003
800/MAC-RAES

North Dakota Business Directory
American Business Directories
5711 S. 86th Cir.
P.O. Box 27347
Omaha, NE 68127
402/593-4600

NORTH DAKOTA GOVERNMENT EMPLOYMENT OFFICES

Office of Personnel Management
(Federal job-service center—see
Minnesota listing.)

Employment & Job Training Division
Job Service North Dakota
P.O. Box 1537
Bismarck, ND 58502
701/224-2842
(State job-service center.)

OHIO

LEADING OHIO EMPLOYERS

ABX Air Inc.
145 Hunter Dr.
Airborne Air Park
Wilmington, OH 45177
513/382-5591
(Cargo express airline.)

American Financial Corp.
1 E. Fourth St.
Cincinnati, OH 45202
513/579-2121
(Insurance.)

American Greetings Corp.
10500 American Rd.
Cleveland, OH 44144
216/252-7300
(Greeting cards.)

Ameritrust Co. N.A.
900 Euclid Ave.
Cleveland, OH 44115
216/737-5000
(Banking.)

BP America Inc.
200 Public Sq.
Cleveland, OH 44114
216/586-4141
(Holding company.)

Bailey Controls Co.
29801 Euclid Ave.
Wickliffe, OH 44092
216/585-8500
(Industrial instruments.)

Banc One
100 East Broad St.
Columbus, OH 43271
614/248-5800
(Banking.)

Battelle Memorial Institute
505 King Ave.
Columbus, OH 43201
614/424-6424

(Non-profit scientific research and
development.)

Brenlin Group
670 W. Market St.
Akron, OH 44303
216/762-2420
(Metal fabricating, steel.)

Bridgestone/Firestone Inc.
1200 Firestone Pkwy.
Akron, OH 44317
216/379-7000
(Tires, inner tubes, etc.)

Chiquita Brands International, Inc.
250 E. Fifth St.
Cincinnati, OH 45202
513/784-8000
(Food, food processing.)

Cincinnati Financial Corp.
P.O. Box 14567
Cincinnati, OH 45214
513/870-2000
(Insurance holding company.)

Cincinnati Gas & Electric Co. Inc.
139 East 4th St.
Cincinnati, OH 45202
513/381-2000
(Utility.)

Cincinnati Milacron Inc.
4701 Marburg Ave.
Cincinnati, OH 45209
513/841-8100
(Machine tools.)

Cincom Systems Inc.
2300 Montana Ave.
Cincinnati, OH 45211
513/662-2300
(Computer systems.)

The Cleveland Electric Illuminating Co.
55 Public Sq.
Cleveland, OH 44113
216/622-9800
(Utility.)

Comair Inc.
P.O. Box 75021
Greater Cincinnati Airport
Cincinnati, OH 45275
606/525-2550
(Regional air carrier.)

Cooper Tire & Rubber Co.
Western & Lima Aves.
Findlay, OH 45840
419/423-1321
(Tires, inner tubes.)

Copeland Corp.
1675 Campbell Rd.
Sidney, OH 45365
513/498-3011
(Air conditioning, heating and refrigeration equipment.)

Crown Equipment Corp.
40 South Washington St.
New Bremen, OH 45869
419/629-2311
(Industrial trucks, trailers, etc.)

Dana Corp.
P.O. Box 1000
Toledo, OH 43697
419/535-4500
(Mobile fluid power products, etc.)

Diebold, Incorporated
818 Mulberry Rd., SE
Canton, OH 44711
216/489-4000
(Automated transaction systems [ATMs], security equipment.)

Eaton Corp.
1111 Superior Ave., NE
Cleveland, OH 44114
216/523-5000
(Vehicle power train components, etc.)

The Elder-Beerman Stores Corp.
3155 El-Bee Rd.
Dayton, OH 45401
512/296-2700
(Department stores.)

Ferro Corp.
1000 Lakeside Ave.
Cleveland, OH 44114
216/641-8580
(Chemicals.)

Fifth Third Bankcorp
38 Fountain Sq. Plz.
Cincinnati, OH 45263
513/579-5300
(Banking.)

GE Aircraft Engines
1 Neumann Way
Cincinnati, OH 45215-6301
513/243-2000
(Gas turbine engines.)

Gencorp Inc.
175 Ghent Rd.
Fairlawn, OH 44333
216/869-4400
(Industrial rubber products.)

Gibson Greetings Inc.
2100 Section Rd.
Cincinnati, OH 45237
513/841-6600
(Greeting cards.)

BF Goodrich Company
3925 Embassy Pkwy.
Akron, OH 44333
216/374-2000
(Chemicals.)

The Goodyear Tire & Rubber Company
1144 East Market St.
Akron, OH 44316
216/796-2121
(Tires, inner tubes.)

Hobart Corp.
Hobart Sq.
Troy, OH 45373
513/332-3000
(Arc welding equipment, metals, etc.)

LTV Steel Co.
(subs. of the LTV Corp.)
25 W. Prospect Ave.
Cleveland, OH 44115
216/622-5000
(Stainless steel, alloy steels, other
steels and steel products.)

Lazarus Division
Federated Department Stores, Inc.
690 Race St.
Cincinnati, OH 45202
513/369-7000
(Department stores.)

The Limited, Inc.
2 Limited Pkwy.
Columbus, OH 43216
614/479-7000
(Speciality stores [Limited, Express,
Victoria's Secret, etc.].)

Lincoln Electric Co.
22801 St. Clair Ave.
Cleveland, OH 44117
216/481-8100
(Welding equipment.)

Loral Defense Systems—Akron
1210 Massilion Rd.
Akron, OH 44315
216/796-4929
(Undersea and anti-submarine defense
systems.)

Lubrizol Corp.
29400 Lakeland Blvd.
Wickliffe, OH 44092
216/943-4200
(Automotive lubricants.)

Marathon Oil Co.
539 South Main St.
Findlay, OH 45840
419/422-2121
(Oil and petroleum products.)

May Company Ohio
158 Euclid Ave.
Cincinnati, OH 44114
216/664-6000
(Department stores.)

Mead Corp.
10 W. Second St.
Dayton, OH 45463
513/222-6323
(Paper.)

Mead Data Central Inc.
9443 Springboro Pike
Dayton, OH 45342
513/865-6800
(Computerized legal, accounting and
research services.)

NCR Corp.
1700 S. Patterson Blvd.
Dayton, OH 45479
513/445-5000
(Computers, peripherals, computerized
cash registers, other business
machines.)

National City Bank
1900 East Ninth St.
Cleveland, OH 44114
216/575-2000
(Banking.)

Nationwide Mutual Insurance Co.
One Nationwide Plz.
Columbus, OH 43216
614/249-7111
(Insurance.)

Ohio Bell Telephone Co.
45 Erieview Plz.
Cleveland, OH 44114
216/822-9700
(Telephone company.)

Ohio Casualty Corp.
136 N. Third St.
Hamilton, OH 45025
513/867-3000
(Insurance.)

Ohio Edison Co.
76 South Main St.
Akron, OH 44308
216/384-5100
(Utility.)

Owens-Corning Fiberglas Corp.
Fiberglas Tower
Toledo, OH 43659
419/248-8000
(Fiberglass, other industrial products.)

Owens-Illinois, Inc.
1 Seagate
Toledo, OH 43666
419/247-5000
(Glass containers, etc.)

Parker Hannifin Corp.
17325 Euclid Ave.
Cleveland, OH 44112
216/531-3000
(Fluid power systems.)

Procter & Gamble Co.
One Procter & Gamble Plz.
Cincinnati, OH 45202
513/983-1100
(Consumer products, foods, etc.)

Reliance Electric
6065 Parkland Blvd.
Cleveland, OH 44124
216/266-5800
(Telecommunications and industrial
equipment.)

Reynolds & Reynolds Company
115 S. Ludlow St.
Dayton, OH 45402
513/443-2000
(Computer systems and system
supports, forms, etc.)

Rubbermaid Inc.
1147 Akron Rd.
Wooster, OH 44691
216/264-6464
(Household products.)

Scripps Howard Inc.
1100 Central Trust Tower
Cincinnati, OH 45202
513/977-3000
(Newspaper publishing, cable
television, other media-related field.)

Sealy
1228 Euclid Ave.
Cleveland, OH 44115
216/522-1310
(Mattresses.)

Sherwin-Williams Co.
101 Prospect Ave. NW
Cleveland, OH 44115
216/566-2000
(Paints and coatings manufacturing
and distribution.)

Society
127 Public Sq.
Cleveland, OH 44114
216/689-3000
(Banking.)

Standard Register Co.
600 Albany St.
Dayton, OH 45408
513/443-1000
(Business forms.)

The Stouffer Corp.
29800 Bainbridge Rd.
Solon, OH 44139
216/248-3600
(Frozen foods, etc.)

Trinova Corp.
3000 Strayer
Maumee, OH 43537
419/867-2200
(Fluid conveying components and
systems, etc.)

TRW Inc.
1900 Richmond Rd.
Cleveland, OH 44124
216/291-7000
(High-tech products and services for
electronics, auto, defense.)

The Timken Company
1835 Dueber Ave. SW
Canton, OH 44706
216/438-3000
(Ball bearings.)

United States Shoe Corp.
One Eastwood Dr.
Cincinnati, OH 45227
513/527-7000
(Retail stores.)

Western & Southern Life Insurance
400 Broadway
Cincinnati, OH 45202

513/629-1800
(Insurance.)

Worthington Industries, Inc.
1205 Dearborn Dr.
Columbus, OH 43085
614/438-3210
(Flat-rolled steel, etc.)

OHIO BUSINESS PERIODICALS

Business Cleveland
Business Journal Publishing
1720 Euclid Ave.
Cleveland, OH 44115
216/621-1644
(Monthly.)

Crain's Cleveland Business
700 St. Clair Ave. West
Cleveland, OH 44113
216/522-1383
(Weekly.)

OHIO DIRECTORIES

Harris Ohio Industrial Directory
Harris Publishing Co.
29057 Aurora Rd.
Twinsburg, OH 44087
216/425-9000

Ohio Business Directory
American Business Directories
5711 S. 86th Cir.
P.O. Box 27347
Omaha, NE 68127
402/593-4600

Ohio Directory of Manufacturers
Commerce Register, Inc.
190 Godwin Ave
Midland Park, NJ 07432
201/445-3000

Ohio Manufacturers Register
Manufacturers' News, Inc.
1633 Central St.
Evanston, IL 60201
708/864-7000

OHIO GOVERNMENT EMPLOYMENT OFFICES

Office of Personnel Management
200 W. Second St. Rm. 506
Dayton, OH 45402
513/225-2720
(Federal job-service center; but for
counties north of and including: Van
Wert, Auglaize, Hardin, Marion,
Crawford, Richland, Ashland, Wayne,
Stark, Carroll, and Columbiana, see
Michigan listing.)

Employment Service Division
Bureau of Employment Services
145 S. Front St. Rm. 640
Columbus, OH 43215
614/466-2421
(State job-service center.)

SOUTH DAKOTA

LEADING SOUTH DAKOTA EMPLOYERS

Austad Co.
4500 East 10th St.
Sioux Falls, SD 57103
605/336-3135
(Mail order golf equipment.)

Black Hills Corp.
625 9th St.
Rapid City, SD 57104
605/348-1700
(Utility.)

Citibank South Dakota N.A.
701 60th St. N.
Sioux Falls, SD 57104
605/331-2626
(Commercial banking, credit card
operations.)

First Bank of South Dakota
141 N. Main Ave.
Sioux Falls, SD 57102
605/339-8600
(National trust companies.)

Gateway 2000
610 Gateway Dr.
North Sioux, City SD 57049
605/232-2000
(Mail-order computers.)

Hub City Inc.
2914 Industrial Ave.
Aberdeen, SD 57401
605/225-0360
(Mechanical power transmission
equipment.)

Kesslers Inc.
615-621 6th Ave. SE
Aberdeen, SD 57401
605/225-1692
(Grocery stores.)

Norwest Bank South Dakota
101 N. Phillips Ave.
Sioux Falls, SD 57102

605/339-7300
(National trust companies.)

Northwestern Public Service Co.
3rd St. & Dakota Ave.
South Huron, SD 57350
605/352-8411
(Utility.)

Randalls Stores Inc.
1705 North Main St.
Mitchell, SD 57301
605/996-5593
(Grocery stores.)

Raven Industries Inc.
205 East 6th St.
Sioux Falls, SD 57102
605/336-2750
(Plastic, electronic, and apparel
products.)

Sunshine Food Markets
815 South 6th Ave.
Sioux Falls, SD 57104
605/336-2505
(Grocery stores.)

Super 8 Enterprises Inc.
1910 8th Ave. NE
Aberdeen, SD 57401
605/229-5945
(Franchises, hotel equipment, and
supplies.)

Super 8 Motels Inc.
1910 8th Ave. NE
Aberdeen, SD 57401
605/225-2272
(Motels.)

Telelect Inc.
600 Oakwood Rd.
Watertown, SD 57201
605/882-4000
(Derricks, truck bodies, hydraulic
cylinders.)

Trail King Industries Inc.
300 East Norway
Mitchell, SD 57301
605/996-6482
(Truck trailers.)

SOUTH DAKOTA DIRECTORIES

South Dakota Business Directory
American Business Directories
5711 S. 86th Cir.
P.O. Box 27347
Omaha, NE 68127
402/593-4600

South Dakota Manufacturers &
Processors Directory
Governor's Office of Economic
Development
711 Wells Ave.
Pierre, SD 57501-3369
605/773-5032

SOUTH DAKOTA GOVERNMENT EMPLOYMENT OFFICES

Office of Personnel Management
(Federal job-service center—see
Minnesota listing.)

South Dakota Dept. of Labor
700 Governors Dr.
Pierre, SD 57501
605/773-3101
(State job-service center.)

WISCONSIN

LEADING WISCONSIN EMPLOYERS

Air Wisconsin, Inc.
203 Challenger Dr.
Appleton, WI 54915
414/739-5123
(Passenger and cargo air carrier.)

American Foods Group
544 Acme St.
Green Bay, WI 54308
414/437-6330
(Meat packing.)

Ashley Furniture Industries
1 Ashley Way
Arcadia, WI 54612
608/323-3377
(Furniture.)

Beloit Corp.
1 St. Lawrence Ave.
Beloit, WI 53511
608/365-3311
(Paper industries machinery.)

Briggs & Stratton Corp.
12301 W. Wirth St.
Wauwatosa, WI 53222
414/259-5333
(Internal combustion engines.)

CUNA Mutual Insurance Society
5910 Mineral Point Rd.
Madison, WI 53705
608/238-5851
(Insurance.)

Consolidated Papers Inc.
231 1st Ave. N.
Wisconsin Rapids, WI 54495
715/422-3111
(Paper mills.)

Employers Health Insurance Co.
Weg Blvd.
De Pere, WI 54115
414/336-1100
(Insurance.)

Employers Insurance of Wausau
2000 Westwood Dr.
Wausau, WI 54401
715/845-5211
(Insurance.)

First Wisconsin National Bank
777 E. Wisconsin Ave.
Milwaukee, WI 53202
414/765-4321
(Banking.)

Firststar Corp.
777 E. Wisconsin Ave.
Milwaukee, WI 53202
414/765-4321
(Banking.)

Ft. Howard Corp.
1919 S. Broadway
Green Bay, WI 54304
414/435-8821
(Paper products [food containers, etc.].)

Johnson Controls Inc.
5757 N. Green Bay Ave.
Milwaukee, WI 53209
414/228-1200
(Electronic control systems, automotive batteries, sealing, containers, etc.)

S.C. Johnson Wax
1525 Howe St.
Racine, WI 53403
414/631-2000
(Household products.)

Journal Communications Inc.
333 W. State St.
Milwaukee, WI 53203
414/224-2000
(Newspaper publishing.)

Kohler Co.
444 Highland Dr.
Kohler, WI 53044
414/457-4441
(Plumbing products, engines, etc.)

Ladish Co., Inc.
5481 S. Packard Ave.
Cudahy, WI 53110
414/747-2611
(Iron and steel forgings.)

Land's End Inc.
Land's End Lane
Dodgeville, WI 53595
608/935-9341
(Catalog sales.)

Manitowoc Co., Inc.
500 S. 16th St.
Manitowoc, WI 54220
414/684-0066
(Liftcranes, ice-making equipment.)

Marshall & Illsley
770 N. Water St.
Milwaukee, WI 53202
414/765-7801
(Banking.)

Menasha
P.O. Box 367
Neenah, WI 54957
414/751-1000
(Packaging, forest products, plastics, etc.)

Miller Brewing Co.
3939 W. Highland Blvd.
Milwaukee, WI 53208
414/931-2000
(Beer, ale brewing.)

Miller Group Ltd., Inc.
1635 W. Spencer St.
Appleton, WI 54914
414/734-9821
(Welding and soldering equipment.)

Nekoosa Papers Inc.
100 Wisconsin River Dr.
Port Edwards, WI 54469
715/887-5111
(Paper mills.)

North-West Telecommunications, Inc.
First Bank Place
201 Main St.
LaCrosse, WI 54602
608/784-6920
(Telecommunications.)

Northwestern Mutual Life Insurance Co.
720 E. Wisconsin Ave.
Milwaukee, WI 53202
414/271-1444
(Life insurance.)

Oscar Mayer Foods Corp.
910 Mayer Ave.
Madison, WI 53704
608/241-1444
(Food processing.)

Oshkosh B'Gosh, Inc.
112 Otter Ave.
P.O. Box 300
Oshkosh, WI 54902
414/231-8800
(Clothing.)

Oshkosh Truck Corp.
2307 Oregon St.
Oshkosh, WI 54901
414/235-9150
(Heavy duty all-wheel drive vehicles.)

Quad Graphics Inc.
W. 224 N. 3322 Duplainville Rd.
Pewaukee, WI 53072
414/246-9200
(Commercial printing.)

Schneider International
P.O. Box 2545
Green Bay, WI 54306
414/497-2201
(Trucking.)

Schreiber Foods
P.O. Box 19010
Green Bay, WI 54307
414/437-7601
(Cheese and meat processing.)

Snap-On Tools Corp.
2801 80th St.
Kenosha, WI 53141
414/656-5200
(Hand tools, automotive mechanic equipment.)

Time Insurance Co., Inc.
515 W. Michigan St.
Milwaukee, WI 53203
414/271-3011
(Insurance.)

Wasau Service Corp.
2000 Westwood Dr.
Wausau, WI 54401
715/845-5211
(Life insurance.)

Western Publishing Co.
1220 Mound Ave.
Racine, WI 53404
414/633-2431
(Book publishing.)

Wisconsin Bell Inc.
17950 W. Corporate Dr.
Brookfield, WI 53045
414/792-8277
(Telephone services [subs. of Ameritech].)

Wisconsin Electric Power Co.
231 W. Michigan St.
Milwaukee, WI 53290
414/221-2345
(Electric utility.)

Wisconsin Energy Corp.
231 W. Michigan St.
Milwaukee, WI 53290
414/221-2345
(Utility, investment holding company.)

WISCONSIN BUSINESS PERIODICALS

*The Business Journal Serving
Greater Milwaukee*
American City Business Journals
2025 N. Summit Ave.
Milwaukee, WI 53202
414/278-7788
(Weekly.)

Corporate Report Wisconsin
Box 878
Memomonee Falls, WI 53052
414/255-9077

WISCONSIN DIRECTORIES

*Classified Directory of Wisconsin
Manufacturers*
WMC Service Corporation
501 E. Washington Ave.
Box 352
Madison, WI 53701-0352
608/258-3400

Wisconsin Business Directory
American Business Directories
5711 S. 86th Cir.
P.O. Box 27347
Omaha, NE 68127
402/593-4600

Wisconsin Manufacturers Register
Manufacturers' News, Inc.
1633 Central St.
Evanston, IL 60201
708/864-7000

Wisconsin Services Directory
W M C Service Corporation
501 E. Washington Ave.
Box 352
Madison, WI 53701-0352
608/258-3400

WISCONSIN GOVERNMENT EMPLOYMENT OFFICES

Office of Personnel Management
(Federal job-service center—in
counties of Grant, Iowa, Lafayette,
Dane, Green, Rock, Jefferson,
Walworth, Waukesha, Racine,
Kenosha, and Milwaukee, see Illinois
listing and dial 312/353-6189; for all
other Wisconsin listings and phone the
Minnesota number listed.)

Job Service
P.O. Box 7905
Madison, WI 53707
608/266-8561
(State job-service center.)

THE WEST

OUTLOOK: Mixed—with certain areas stronger than others.

WHAT'S NEXT

▶ **California: No longer superhot, but still strong in the long term.**

The recession is taking its toll on California. By the fall of 1993, well over 300,000 jobs had been cut, over 25% of them in defense. Other industries that were hard hit included real estate—victim to increased migration, the shaky job market, and commercial overbuilding; agriculture—due to a long-standing drought; and banking—suffering from the weak real estate market. In late 1993, job growth in California was projected to be below the national average.

But California has a number of factors on the plus side that make it one of the regions best poised for long-term strength. A key factor is its proximity to the Pacific Rim and its role as hub for Japan and other Pacific Rim countries. Other important strengths: the high percentage of high-technology industries and companies making California their home; the entertainment industry; a diverse manufacturing base; and the state's top-ranked university system. So, in spite of some short-term slumps, California's long-term prospects should be better.

▶ **The Pacific Northwest is seeing two trends at once: on one hand, weak industries are cutting jobs; on the other, stronger industries are adding.**

Cutbacks in logging and timber due to environmental pressures have resulted in heavy job losses. For example, over 11,000 people lost jobs due to mill closings. And the timber industry estimates that by the year 2000, Oregon, Washington and Northern California will lose up to 45,000 more jobs. In addition, cutbacks in the aerospace industry—both defense and commercial—have resulted in job cuts. On the other hand, however, certain sectors have been performing relatively well. Computers and high tech have been one of the fastest-growing industries in the area and should continue to do well in the long term. Leisure and recreation also should continue to grow over the long term.

In addition, *Oregon* is showing a great deal of activity in real estate, construction, and education. Activity in forest products is slower, due in part to increasing environmental pressures.

As for *Washington,* it, too, can expect slowdowns in the forestry industry due to environmental pressures and regulations. The biggest concern, however, is Boeing. The aircraft giant cut 6,000 jobs and may cut thousands more. Will this cause a regional recession over the short term? Hopes are that it will not, due to the presence of high-tech firms such as Microsoft, which still dominates the computer software industry, Japanese firms such as Matsushita and Fujitsu, and the area's growing presence in Far East trade, particularly through Seattle/Tacoma. One interesting note: With Seattle residents concerned about overdevelopment and city managers trying to steer away would-be relocators, Yakima, Spokane, Bellingham and Olympia may wind up the beneficiaries. The result? These four cities may offer increasing employment opportunities.

▶ Mountain and Southwestern states will stay strong, as well, making this region one of the best in the nation.

One sign of the region's strength: Mountain states lead the country in terms of homebuilding. One of the reasons for this is the large number of people relocating here from California. Slated for growth due to the high number of California migrants are Nevada and Utah.

More specifically: *Arizona* is still growing, with activity especially visible in the Scottsdale/Sun City area. Job growth is expected in construction and real estate, among other areas. *Nevada* isn't seeing the hot growth of a few years ago, as its construction industry takes a breather from its overexpansion. But gambling remains a growth area.

Colorado will continue to benefit from a diversified economy, in particular from the high-tech and biotechnology firms that have moved here. The state is already home to about 5,000 high-tech companies. Other areas that are in for a growth period are construction, business services, and, as the energy industry continues to improve, petroleum.

Utah is particularly strong, fueled to a great degree by computer software firms such as WordPerfect and Novell. Transportation, legal services, and construction are also growing. One downside: The pay in Utah isn't that great, with salaries typically about 15% less than the national average.

Montana is also growing because of an influx of ex-Californians and other ex-city dwellers seeking natural beauty. Since 1990, more than 1,000 new business opened in the state. While the recession brought a bit of a slowdown, Montana remains a long-term growth spot. An industry area to keep an eye on is tourism.

Another good bet is *Idaho*. Even during the recession, Idaho was coming on strong, with job growth in business services, recreation, and government especially notable. Called the hottest housing market by Century 21 Real Estate Corp. in 1993, Boise looks very promising, with job growth up 5% in 1993—a trend that looks like it will continue.

New Mexico will be weaker, due to defense cuts and uranium-mine shutdowns. In the long term, however, Albuquerque may develop into a regional hot spot, attracting people disenchanted with California and big-city life. *Wyoming* is also slated for long-term improvement, especially as environmental legislation increases the use of low-sulfur coal.

▶ Alaska and Hawaii— fairly stable.

Hawaii has been relatively strong, even through recessionary periods, and should remain so. One potential problem here is high real estate prices due to Japanese investment.

As for *Alaska,* improvement in the energy industry will fuel an improved outlook and eventual job growth.

REGIONAL HOT SPOTS

DENVER, CO: Denver has pulled out of its nine-year run of real estate problems and seen a flurry of job creation over the past two years. Among the reasons are the construction of Stapleton Airport and improved energy businesses. All in all, Denver looks like a very strong performer for the '90s—and a good prospect for employment opportunities.

OREM & PROVO, UT: Employment prospects here have been good—and have been improving in recent years. Other pluses: Provo was chosen the most livable city in the U.S. in the 1991 *Money* magazine survey. Nearly half of the residents are between eighteen and forty-nine, making this area appealing to young people. The downside: As mentioned before, salaries in Utah tends to be lower than in the country as a whole.

PORTLAND, OR: A city that is known for its natural beauty, good public school system, and friendly citizens, Portland is also a good bet because of the stable growth it will be enjoying. Over the past few years its strongest job growth has been in services and government. In addition, it is a port of growing importance, from which agricultural commodities are shipped to the Far East, and a gateway city for airline passengers.

ALASKA

LEADING ALASKA EMPLOYERS

Alascom Inc.
210 East Bluff Rd.
Anchorage, AK 99501
907/264-7000
(Telephone communications.)

Alaska Commercial Co.
1577 C St.
Anchorage, AK 99501
907/276-2226
(General merchandise stores.)

Alaska International Industries
4100 W. International Airport
Anchorage, AK 99502
907/243-1414
(Air cargo and passenger carrier.)

Alaska Railroad Corp.
421 W. First Ave.
Anchorage, AK 99501
907/265-2403
(Railroads, line haul operating.)

Arco Alaska Inc.
700 G St.
Anchorage, AK 99501
907/276-1215
(Oil and gas exploration services, drilling, production.)

Arctic Slope Regional Corp.
1230 Aguik
Barrow, AK 99723
907/852-8633
(Oil field services, etc.)

Arctic Slope Regional Construction Co.
1230 Natchiq
Barrow, AK 99723
907/852-8633
(Pipeline construction.)

Carr-Gotstein Inc.
6411 A St.
Anchorage, AK 99518
970/561-1944
(Groceries, residential real estate developer.)

Era Aviation Inc.
6160 South Airpark Dr.
Anchorage, AK 99502
907/248-4422
(Air transportation.)

General Communication Inc.
2550 Denali St.
Anchorage, AK 99503
907/265-5600
(Telephone Communications.)

Ketchikan Pulp Co.
7559 North Tongass Hwy.
Ketchikan, AK 99901
907/225-2151
(Pulp.)

Markair
4100 West International Airport Rd.
Anchorage, AK 99502
907/243-1414
(Passenger and cargo air carrier.)

Martech USA Inc.
300 East 54th Ave.
Anchorage, AK 99518
907/561-1970
(Sanitary services—oil spill cleanup, etc.)

Natchiq Inc.
6000 C St.
Suite B
Anchorage, AK 99518
907/563-3419
(Oil and gas field services.)

Reeve Aleutian Airways Inc.
4700 West International Airport Rd.
Anchorage, AK 99502-1091
907/243-1112
(Regional air carrier.)

Veco International, Inc.
813 W. Northern Lights
Anchorage, AK 99503
907/277-5309
(Construction and oilfield services.)

ALASKA BUSINESS PERIODICAL

Alaska Business
P.O. Box 241288
Anchorage, AK 99524
907/276-4373
(Monthly.)

ALASKA BUSINESS DIRECTORY

Alaska Business Directory
American Business Directories
5711 S. 86th Cir.
P.O. Box 27347
Omaha, NE 68127
402/593-4600
(Lists 26,000 businesses.)

ALASKA GOVERNMENT EMPLOYMENT OFFICES

Office of Personnel Management
222 W. Seventh Ave. Box 22
Anchorage, AK 99513
907/271-5821
(Federal job-service center.)

Employment Service
Employment Security Div.
P.O. Box 3-7000
Juneau, AK 99802
907/465-2712
(State job-service center.)

ARIZONA

LEADING ARIZONA EMPLOYERS

AG Communications Systems Corp.
2500 W. Utopia Rd.
Phoenix, AZ 85027
602/582-7000
(Switchboards.)

America West Airlines Inc.
4000 E. Sky Harbor Blvd.
Phoenix, AZ 85034
601/693-0800
(Passenger and cargo carrier.)

APAC-Arizona Inc.
701 N. 44th St.
Phoenix, AZ 85008
602/220-5000
(Concrete, highway and street
construction, etc.)

Arizona Public Service Co.
400 N. 5th St.
Phoenix, AZ 85004
602/250-1000
(Utilities.)

Armour & Co.
1850 N. Central Ave.
Phoenix, AZ 85004
602/207-2800
(Foreign marketing of consumer
products made by The Dial Corp.)

Bryant/Universal Roofing Inc.
1245 S. 7th St.
Phoenix, AZ 85034

602/258-7941
(Roofing.)

Burr-Brown Corp.
6730 S. Tucson Blvd.
Tucson, AZ 85706
602/746-1111
(Microcomputer and electronics
systems and products.)

Cir. K Corp.
1601 N. 7th St.
Phoenix, AZ 85006
602/253-9600
(Convenience stores.)

Citibank Arizona
330 N. Central Ave.
Phoenix, AZ 85012
602/248-2225
(Banking.)

Del Webb Corp.
2231 E. Camelback Rd.
Phoenix, AZ 85016
602/468-6800
(Real estate, adult community
management and development.)

Dial Corp.
Dial Tower
Phoenix, AZ 85077
602/207-4000
(Personal care, food, household, and
laundry products.)

First Interstate Bank
100 W. Washington
Phoenix, AZ 85003
602/528-6000
(Banking.)

Garrett Engine Division
(div. of Allied /Signal Aerospace)
111 S. 34th St.
Phoenix, AZ 85034
602/231-1000
(Aircraft and missile engine and
components manufacturer.)

Jostens Learning Corp.
7878 16th St.
Phoenix, AZ 85020
602/678-7272
(Computer integrated systems design.)

Karsten Manufacturing Corp.
2201 W. Desert Cove
Phoenix, AZ 85029
602/943-7243
(Golf equipment, aluminum
die-castups, etc.)

Magma Cooper Co., Inc.
7400 N. Oracle, No. 200
Tucson, AZ 85704
602/575-5600
(Copper mining.)

McCarthy Western Constructors, Inc.
120 N. 44th St.
Phoenix, AZ 85034
602/267-8811
(Hotel/motel, commercial, and office
construction, etc.)

McDonnell Douglas Helicopter Co.
5000 E. McDowell Rd.
Mesa, AZ 85205
602/891-3000
(Helicopter manufacturer.)

Microchip Technologies, Inc.
2355 W. Chandler Blvd.
Chandler, AZ 85224
602/963-7373
(Computer chips.)

Motorola Inc.—Government Electronics Group
Box 1417
8201 E. McDowell Rd.
Scottsdale, AZ 85252-1417
602/441-3905
(R&D and production of advanced
electronic systems and equipment.)

Phelps Dodge Corp.
2600 N. Central Ave.
Phoenix, AZ 85004
602/234-8100
(Metals.)

Phoenix Newspapers, Inc.
120 E. Van Buren
Phoenix, AZ 85004
602/271-8000
(Newspaper Publishing.)

Phoenix Resort Corp.
6000 E. Camelback
Scottsdale, AZ 85251
602/941-8200
(Hotels, resort, etc.)

Pinnacle West Capital Corp.
2828 N. Central Ave., #800
Phoenix, AZ 85004
602/234-1142
(Utility.)

Ramada International Hotels & Resorts
3838 E. Van Buren St.
Phoenix, AZ 85008
602/273-4000
(Hotels, restaurants, etc.)

Reinalt-Thomas Corp.
14631 N. Scottsdale Rd.
Scottsdale, AZ 85254
602/951-1938
(Retail tires and accessories.)

Rural/Metro Corp.
8401 E. Indian School Rd.
Scottsdale, AZ 85251
602/994-3886
(Fire protection, ambulance, security,
and other services.)

Salt River Project Agricultural Improvement & Power District
P.O. Box 52025
Tempe, AZ 85072
602/236-5900
(Electric utility.)

Scott Container Products Group
(subs. Scott Paper Co.)
2501 E. Magnolia St.
Phoenix, AZ 85034
602/275-4711
(Disposable cups and plates, etc.)

Security Pacific Bancorp
101 N. First Ave.
Phoenix, AZ 85003
602/262-2000
(Banking.)

Shamrock Foods Co.
2228 N. Black Canyon Hwy.
Phoenix, AZ 85009

602/272-6721
(Food distributor.)

Sundt Corporation
4101 E. Irvington
Tucson, AZ 85714
602/748-7555
(Construction.)

Talley Industries Inc.
2800 N. 44th St.
Phoenix, AZ 85008
602/957-7711
(Defense electronics, agricultural machinery, etc.)

Valley National Bank of Arizona
241 N. Central Ave.
Phoenix, AZ 85004
602/261-2900
(Banking.)

ARIZONA BUSINESS PERIODICALS

Arizona Business Gazette
Box 1950
Phoenix, AX 85004
602/271-7304
(Weekly.)

The Business Journal
3737 N. 7th St
Phoenix, AZ 85014
602/230-8400
(Weekly; covers Phoenix and Valley of the Sun.)

ARIZONA BUSINESS DIRECTORIES

Arizona Business Directory
American Business Directories
5711 S. 86th Cir.
P.O. Box 27347
Omaha, NE 68127
402/593-4600

Arizona Industrial Directory
Manufacturers' News, Inc.
1633 Central St.
Evanston, IL 60201
708/864-70000

ARIZONA GOVERNMENT EMPLOYMENT OFFICES

Office of Personnel Management
US Postal Office Bldg.
Room 120
522 N. Central Ave.

Phoenix, AZ 85004
602/261-4736
(Federal job-service center.)

**Department of Employment
Security**
P.O. Box 6123
Site Code 730A

Phoenix, AZ 85005
602/542-4016
(State job-service center.)

CALIFORNIA

TOP CALIFORNIA EMPLOYERS

ABC
2040 Ave. of the Stars
Century City, CA 90067
213/557-7777
(Broadcasting.)

ALZA Corp.
950 Page Mill Rd.
Palo Alto, CA 94304
415/494-5000
(Research laboratory,
pharmaceuticals.)

AST Research Inc.
16215 Alton Pkwy.
Box 19658
714/727-4141
(Computers.)

Acura Division
American Honda Motor Co.
1919 Torrance Blvd.
Torrance, CA 90501-2746
213/783-2000
(Car manufacturer.)

Advanced Micro Devices Inc.
901 Thompson Pl.
Sunnyvale, CA 94086
407/732-2400
(Semiconductors and related devices.)

H. F. Ahmanson & Co.
4900 Rivergrade Rd.
Irwindale, CA 91706
818/960-6311
(Savings and loan holding company.)

Allergan Inc.
2525 Dupont Dr.
Irvine, CA 92715
714/752-4500
(Optical healthcare products.)

Allied-Signal Aerospace Co.
2525 W. 190th St.
Torrance, CA 90504-6009
213/321-5000
(Aerospace manufacturer [avionics,
electronics, engines, etc.].)

Amdahl Corp.
1250 E. Arques Ave.
Sunnyvale, CA 94088
408/746-6000
(Computers.)

**American Honda Motor Car Co.,
Inc.**
1919 Torrance Blvd.
Torrance, CA 90501-2746
213/783-2000
(Automotive manufacturer.)

Amgen Inc.
1840 DeHavilland Dr.
Thousand Oaks, CA 91320
805/499-5725
(Biotechnology.)

Ampex Corp.
401 Broadway
Redwood City, CA 94063
415/967-2011
(Recording tapes, video recording
systems, etc.)

Apple Computer
20525 Mariani Ave.
Cupertino, CA 95014
408/996-1010
(Computers.)

Atlantic Richfield Co.
515 S. Flower St.
Los Angeles, CA 90071
213/486-3511
(Petroleum products.)

BankAmerica
555 California St.
San Francisco, CA 94104
415/622-3456
(Commercial banking.)

Beatrice/Hunt Wesson Inc.
1645 W. Valencia Dr.
Fullerton, CA 92634
714/680-1000
(Food processing.)

Bechtel Group Inc.
50 Beale St.
San Francisco, CA 94119
415/768-1234
(Construction engineering, advanced
systems, etc.—at same address:
Bechtel Power Corporation, Bechtel
National Inc., Bechtel Corporation,
Bechtel Enterprises, Bechtel Civil
Inc., and Bechtel, Inc.)

Beckman Instruments Inc.
2500 Harbor Blvd.
Fullerton,CA 92634
714/871-4848
(Automated systems and supplies for
life science research.)

Bergen Brunswig Corp.
4000 Metropolitan Dr.
Orange, CA 92668
714/385-4000
(Medical products.)

CBS
7800 Beverly Blvd.
Los Angeles, CA 90036

213/852-2345
(Broadcasting.)

CalFed Inc.
5700 Wilshire Blvd.
Los Angeles, CA 90036
213/932-4200
(Thrift institution.)

Chevron Corp.
225 Bush St.
San Francisco, CA 94104
415/894-7700
(Petroleum products.)

The Chronicle Publishing Co.
901 Mission St.
San Francisco, CA 94103
415/777-7444
(Newspaper publishing.)

City National Bank
400 N. Roxbury Dr.
Beverly Hills, CA 90210
310/550-5400
(Banking.)

Copley Newspapers
P.O. Box 1530
La Jolla, CA 92038
619/454-0411
(Newspaper publishing.)

The Disney Channel
3800 W. Alameda Ave.
Burbank, CA 91505
818/569-7701
(Pay cable television services and
programming.)

Walt Disney Company
500 S. Buena Vista St.
Burbank, CA 91521
818/560-1000
(Entertainment.)

Douglas Aircraft Co.
(div. of McDonnell Douglas Corp.)
3855 Lakewood Blvd.
Long Beach, CA 90846
213/593-8611
(Aircraft manufacturing.)

Firemans Fund Insurance Co.
777 San Marin Dr.
Novato, CA 94998
415/899-2000
(Insurance company.)

First Interstate Bank of California
707 Wilshire Blvd.
Los Angeles, CA 90017
213/614-4111
(Bank.)

Fluor Corp.
3333 Michelson Dr.
Irvine, CA 92730
714/975-2000
(Engineering, construction.)

Fox Broadcasting Company
10201 W. Pico Blvd.
Los Angeles, CA 90035
213/203-3266
(Broadcasting.)

The Gap, Inc.
1 Harnson St.
San Francisco, CA 94105
415/952-4400
(Apparel retailer.)

Genentech
460 Point San Bruno Blvd.
S. San Francisco, CA 94080
415/225-1000
(Biotechnology.)

GlenFed Inc.
700 N. Brand Blvd.
Glendale, CA 91203
818/500-2000
(Thrift institution.)

Golden West Financial Corp.
1901 Harrison St.
Oakland, CA 94612
510/446-6000
(Savings and loan associations.)

Great Western Financial Corp.
9200 Oakdale Ave.
Chatsworth, CA 91311
818/775-3411
(Savings and loan associations.)

Hewlett Packard Co.
3000 Hanover St.
Palo Alto, CA 94304
415/857-1501
(Computers.)

HomeFed
625 Broadway
San Diego, CA 92101
619/699-7679
(Savings and loan association.)

Hughes Aircraft Co.
(subs. of GM Hughes Electronics
Corp.)
P.O. Box 45066
7200 Hughes Terr.
Los Angeles, CA 90045
310/568-7200
(Aircraft manufacturer.)

Infiniti Division
Nissan Motor Co.
18701 S. Figueroa St.
Carson, CA 90248
213/532-3111
(Car manufacturer.)

Intel Corp.
3065 Bowers Ave.
Santa Clara, CA 95052
408/987-8080
(Semiconductors.)

Kaiser Foundation Health Plan
1 Kaiser Plz.
Oakland, CA 94612
415/271-5910
(Health maintenance organization.)

LSI Logic Corp.
1551 McCarthy Blvd.
Milpitas, CA 95035
408/433-8000
(Semiconductors.)

Levi Strauss & Co.
1155 Battery St.
San Francisco, CA 94111
415/544-6000
(Apparel.)

Lexus Division
Toyota Motor Sales U.S.A:, Inc.
19001 S. Western Ave.
Torrance, CA 90509
213/618-4000
(Car manufacturer.)

Litton Industries
360 N. Crescent Dr.
Beverly Hills, CA 90210-4867
310/859-5000
(Electrical and electronics equipment.)

Lockheed Corp.
4500 Park Granada Blvd.
Calabasas, CA 91399
818/876-2000
(Aerospace manufacturer.)

Lockheed Missiles and Space Co.
1111 Lockheed Way
Sunnyvale, CA 94089
408/742-4321
(Aerospace.)

MAI Systems Corp.
14101 Myford Rd.
Tustin, CA 92680
714/731-5100
(Software.)

Mattel Inc.
333 Continental Blvd.
El Segundo, CA 90245
310/524-2000
(Toy manufacturer.)

Mazda Motors of America, Inc.
7755 Irvine Center Dr.
Irvine, CA 92718
714/727-1990
(Car manufacturer.)

MCA, Inc.
100 Universal City Plz.
Universal City, CA 91608
818/777-1000
(Entertainment company [film,
records, etc.].)

McClatchy Newspapers
2100 Q St.
Sacramento, CA 95816
916/321-1000
(Newspaper publishing.)

McDonnell Douglas Space Systems
(div. of McDonnell Douglas Corp.)
5301 Balsa Ave.
Huntington Beach, CA 92647
714/896-3311
(Delta rocket, space station work
package, strategic systems.)

McKesson Corp.
One Post St.
San Francisco,CA 94104
415/983-8300
(Drugs, chemicals, liquor.)

Mervyn's
25001 Industrial Blvd.
Hayward, CA 94545
415/785-8800
(Speciality apparel stores.)

MGM/UA Communications Co.
10000 W. Washington Blvd.
Culver City, CA 90230
310/280-6000
(Film, etc.)

NBC
3000 Alameda Ave.
Burbank, CA 91523
818/840-4444
(Broadcasting.)

National Health Laboratories, Inc.
7590 Fay Ave.
La Jolla, CA 92037
619/454-3314
(Health services.)

National Semiconductor Corp.
2900 Semiconductor Dr.
Santa Clara, CA 95051
408/721-5000
(Semiconductors.)

Nissan Motor Corp.
18501 Figueroa St.
Carson, CA 90248
213/532-3111
(Car manufacturer.)

North American Aircraft
(div. of Rockwell International)
201 N. Douglas St.
Box 92098
El Segundo, CA 90245
310/647-1000
(Aircraft assemblies.)

Northrop Corp.
1840 Century Park East
Century City
Los Angeles, CA 90067-2199
310/553-6262
(Aerospace manufacturing.)

Occidental Petroleum Corp.
10889 Wilshire Blvd.
Los Angeles, CA 90024
213/879-1700
(Petroleum products.)

Oracle Systems Corp.
500 Oracle Pkwy.
Redwood Shores, CA 94065
415/506-7000
(Software.)

Pacific Bell
140 New Montgomery St.
San Francisco, CA 94105
415/542-9000
(Telephone services.)

Pacific Enterprises
633 W. Fifth St.
Los Angeles, CA 90071
213/895-5000
(Diversified holding co.)

Pacific Gas & Electric Co.
77 Beale St.
San Francisco, CA 94106
415/972-7000
(Utilities co.)

Pacific Mutual Life Insurance Co.
700 Newport Center Dr.
Newport Beach, CA 92660
714/640-3011
(Life insurance.)

The Parsons Corp.
100 W. Walnut St.
Pasadena, CA 91124
310/440-2000
(Construction and engineering
services.)

Raychem Corp.
300 Constitution Dr.
Menlo Park, CA 94025
415/361-3333
(Electronics, automatic systems, etc.)

Rockwell International Corp.
2201 Seal Beach Rd.
Box 4250
Seal Beach, CA 90740
310/797-3311
(Aerospace, electronics systems, etc.)

**Rockwell International Space
Systems Division**
12214 Lakewood Blvd.
Box 7009
Downey, CA 90241
310/922-2111
(Space shuttle contractors.)

Rohr Industries, Inc.
P.O. Box 878
Chula Vista, CA 92012-0878
619/691-4111
(Major structural components for
aircraft.)

SCECorp.
2244 Walnut Grove Ave.
Rosemead, CA 91770
818/302-1212
(Electric and gas services.)

Safeway Inc.
201 Fourth St.
Oakland, CA 94660

510/891-3000
(Supermarkets.)

San Diego Gas & Electric
P.O. Box 1831
San Diego, CA 92112
619/696-2000
(Utility.)

Charles Schwab & Co., Inc.
101 Montgomery St.
San Francisco, CA 94104
415/627-7000
(Financial services.)

Science Applications International Corp.
10260 Campus Point Dr.
San Diego, CA 92121
619/546-6000
(Scientific technical services and products, defense systems.)

Seagate Technology Inc.
920 Disc Dr.
Scotts Valley, CA 95066
408/438-6550
(Disk drives, storage devices.)

Security Pacific Corp.
333 S. Hope St
Los Angeles, CA 90071
213/345-6211
(Banking.)

Southern California Edison Co.
2244 Walnut Grove Ave.
Rosemead, CA 91770
818/302-1212
(Electric utility.)

Southern California Gas Co.
555 W. Fifth St.
Los Angeles, CA 90013
213/689-2333
(Gas company.)

Southern Pacific Transportation Co.
1 Market Plz.
San Francisco, CA 94105
415/541-1000
(Railroad transportation.)

Sun Microsystems Inc.
2550 Garcia Ave.
Mountain View, CA 94043
415/960-1300
(Computers—workstations, etc.)

Syntex Corp.
3401 Hillview Ave.
Palo Alto, CA 94304
415/855-5050
(Biotechnology.)

Tandem Computers Inc.
19333 Vallco Pkwy.
Cupertino, CA 95014
408/285-6000
(Computers.)

Tandon Corp.
301 Science Dr.
Moorpark, CA 93021
805/523-0304
(Computers.)

The Times Mirror Company
Times-Mirror Sq.
Los Angeles, CA 90053
213/237-3700
(Communications media [newspapers, etc.].)

Toyota Motor Sales U.S.A., Inc.
19001 S. Western Ave.
Torrance, CA 90509
213/618-4000
(Car manufacturer.)

Transamerica Corp.
600 Montgomery St.
San Francisco, CA 94111
415/983-4000
(Diversified financial services.)

Transamerica Finance Corp.
1150 S. Olive St.
Los Angeles, CA 90015
213/742-2111
(Consumer lending, commercial finance, etc.)

Union Bank
350 California St.
San Francisco, CA 94104-1476
415/445-0200
(Bank.)

Universal City Studios Inc.
100 Universal City Plz.
Universal City, CA 91608
818/777-1000
(Film production.)

Unocal Corp.
Unocal Ctr.
Los Angeles, CA 90017
213/977-7600
(Petroleum products.)

Varian Associates
3050 Hansen Way
Palo Alto, CA 94301
415/493-4000
(Electronic products.)

Warner Brothers Inc.
4000 Warner Blvd.
Burbank, CA 91522

818/954-6000
(Entertainment company.)

Wells Fargo & Co.
420 Montgomery St.
San Francisco, CA 94163
415/396-0123
(Bank holding co.)

Wells Fargo Bank, N.A.
464 California St.
San Francisco, CA 94163
415/477-1000
(Banking.)

Western Digital Corp.
2445 McCabe Way
Irvine, CA 92714
714/863-0102
(Computer peripherals.)

Westwood One Inc.
9540 Washington Blvd.
Culver City, CA 90230
310/840-4000
(Broadcasting.)

CALIFORNIA BUSINESS PERIODICALS

California Business
4221 Wilshire Blvd.
Los Angeles, CA 90010
213/937-5820
(Monthly magazine.)

Long Beach Business
2599 East 28th St.
Long Beach, CA 90806
213/988-1222
(Bi-weekly.)

Los Angeles Business Journal
3345 Wilshire Blvd.
Los Angeles, CA 90010

213/385-9050
(Weekly.)

San Diego Business Journal
4909 Murphy Canyon Rd.
San Diego, CA 92123
619/277-6359
(Weekly.)

San Francisco Business Times
325 5th St.
San Francisco, CA 94107
415/777-9355
(Weekly.)

CALIFORNIA DIRECTORIES

California Business Directory
American Business Directories
5711 S. 86th Cir.

P.O. Box 27347
Omaha, NE 68127
402/593-4600

(Two-volume set—North [includes San Francisco area] and South [includes Los Angeles area]. Each volume also available singly.)

California Manufacturers Register
Database Publishing Co.
523 Superior Ave.
Newport Beach, CA 92663
800/888-8434

San Diego County Business Directory
Database Publishing Co.
523 Superior Ave.

Newport Beach, CA 92663
800/888-8434

Southern California Business Directory and Buyers Guide
Database Publishing Co.
523 Superior Ave.
Newport Beach, CA 92663
800/888-8434

CALIFORNIA GOVERNMENT EMPLOYMENT OFFICES

Office of Personnel Management
211 Main St.
San Francisco, CA 94105
(Regional OPM headquarters.)

Office of Personnel Management
Linder Bldg. Third Fl.
845 S. Figueroa St.
Los Angeles, CA 90017
213/894-3360
(Federal job-service center.)

Office of Personnel Management
1029 J St. Second Fl.
Sacramento, CA 95814
(Mail only.)
located at:
4695 Watt Ave.
North Highlands, CA
(Federal job-service center.)

Office of Personnel Management
Federal Bldg. Rm. 4-S-9
880 Front St.

San Diego, CA 92188
619/557-6165
(Federal job-service center.)

Office of Personnel Management
P.O. Box 7405
San Francisco, CA 94120
(Mail only.)
located at:
211 Main St.
2nd Fl. Rm 235
San Francisco, CA 94105
415/744-5627
(Federal job-service center.)

Job Service Division
Empl. Dev. Dept.
800 Capitol Mall
Sacramento, CA 95814
916/322-7318
(State job-service center.)

COLORADO

LEADING COLORADO EMPLOYERS

ANR Freight System
P.O. Box 5070
Denver, CO 80217

303/278-9900
(Holding company, trucking.)

Adolph Coors Co.
311 Tenth St.
Golden, CO 80401
303/279-6585
(Beer brewer.)

Affiliated Bankshares of Colorado
1125 17th St.
Denver, Co 80202
303/296-7788
(Banking.)

Amax Gold Inc.
350 Indiana
Golden, CO 80401
303/273-0600
(Mining.)

Anschutz
555 17th St., Suite 2400
Denver, CO 80202
303/298-1000
(Oil, mining, railroads, real estate.)

Aspen Airways, Inc.
3980 Quebec St.
Denver, CO 80207
303/320-4747
(Regional air carrier.)

C F & I Steel Corp.
P.O. Box 316
225 Canal St.
Pueblo, CO 81002
719/561-6000
(Steel production.)

COBE Laboratories Inc.
1185 Oak St.
Lakewood, CO 80215
303/232-6800
(Medical products.)

Coast to Coast Stores
501 S. Cherry St.
Denver, CO 80222
303/377-8400
(Housewares/giftwares retailer.)

Current Inc.
1005 East Woodmen Rd.
Colorado Springs, CO 80920

719/594-4100
(Greeting cards, stationery, etc.)

Cyprus Minerals Co.
9100 East Mineral Cir.
Englewood, CO 80112
303/643-5000
(Mining.)

Gates Corp.
P.O. Box 5887
Denver, CO 80217
303/744-1911
(Auto and industrial rubber products,
batteries, other auto products.)

Gates Rubber Co.
999 S. Broadway
Denver, CO 80209
308/744-1911
(Belts, hoses, mechanical rubber
goods.)

Hensel Phelps Construction
420 Sixth Ave.
P.O. Box O
Greeley, CO 80632
303/352-6565
(Commercial construction.)

ITT Federal Services Corp.
1 Gateway Plz.
Colorado Springs, CO 80910
719/574-5850
(Ops & mtn. of communications,
surveillance, radar detection sys.)

Keystone Resorts Management
22010 Hwy. 6
Dillon, CO 80435
303/468-2316
(Resort/hotel.)

Manville Corp.
P.O. Box 5108
Denver, CO 80217
303/978-2000
(Building materials.)

Miniscribe Corp.
1871 Lefthand Cir.
Longmont, CO 80501

303/651-6000
(Hard disk drives.)

Multi-Financial Group
5350 S. Roslyn St.
Suite 310
Englewood, CO 80111
303/694-6710
(Insurance and securities brokers,
etc.)

Newmont Mining Corp.
1700 Lincoln St.
Denver, CO 80203
303/863-7414
(Mining.)

Pace Membership Warehouse Inc.
5680 Greenwood Plz. Bldg.
Englewood, CO 80111
303/834-8000
(Membership price club/hypermarket
operator.)

**Public Service Company of
Colorado**
550 15th St.
Denver, CO 80202
303/571-7511
(Utility.)

Rocky Mountain Airways, Inc.
Hangar 6
Stapleton International Airport
Denver, CO 80207
303/388-8585
(Regional air carrier [subs. of
Continental].)

**Rocky Mountain Hospital &
Medical Services**
700 Broadway
Denver, CO 80203
303/831-2131
(Group hospital plans.)

Samsonite Corp.
11200 East 45th Ave.
Denver, CO 80239
303/373-2000
(Luggage.)

Storage Technology
2270 S. 88th St.
Louisville, CO 80027
303/673-5151
(Information storage and retrieval.)

**Total Petroleum Ltd.—North
America**
999 18th St.
Box 500
Denver, CO 80201
303/291-2000
(Oil and gas.)

US West
7800 E. Orchard Rd.
Englewood, CO 80111
303/793-6500
(Bell regional holding company.)

**US West
Communications—Mountain Bell**
(subs. of US West)
1801 California St.
Denver, CO 80202
303/869-2355
(Telephone services.)

United Artists Entertainment Co.
2930 East 3rd Ave.
Denver, CO 79296
303/321-4242
(Movie theaters [owns, operates],
cable system operation.)

Vicorp Restaurants
400 W. 48th Ave.
Denver, CO 80239
303/296-2121
(Restaurant franchises.)

Western Capital Investment Corp.
1675 Broadway
Denver, CO 80202
303/623-5577
(Financial services.)

COLORADO BUSINESS PERIODICALS

Boulder County Business Report
1830 N. 55th St.
Boulder, CO 80301
301/440-4950
(Magazine covering Boulder County
business issues.)

Denver Business Journal
1700 Broadway
Denver, CO 80290
303/837-3500
(Weekly.)

COLORADO DIRECTORY

Colorado Business Directory
American Business Directories
5711 S. 86th Cir.
P.O. Box 27347
Omaha, NE 68127
402/593-4600

COLORADO GOVERNMENT EMPLOYMENT OFFICES

Office of Personnel Management
P.O. Box 25167
Denver, CO 89225
(Mail only.)
located at:
12345 W. Alameda Pkwy.
Lakewood, CO
303/236-4160
(Federal job-service center.)

Employment Program
Div. of Employment & Training
251 E. 12th Ave.
Denver, CO 80203
303/866-6180
(State job-service center.)

HAWAII

LEADING HAWAII EMPLOYERS

Alexander & Baldwin Inc.
822 Bishop St.
Honolulu, HI 96813
808/525-6611
(Water transportation.)

Azabu USA Corp.
410 Atkinson Dr.
Honolulu, HI 96814
808/955-4811
(Hotel, shopping center operation.)

Aloha Airlines, Inc.
Honolulu International Airport
Honolulu, HI 96819
808/836-4101
(Airline.)

Bancorp Hawaii Inc.
111 South King St.
Honolulu, HI 96813
808/537-8111
(Bank.)

Buyco Inc.
827 Fort St. Mall
Honolulu, HI 96813
808/536-4461
(Sugar cane, etc.)

Castle & Cooke Properties Inc.
650 Iwilei Rd.
Honolulu, HI 96817
808/548-6611
(Real estate sub-dividers, developers, etc.)

Daiei USA Inc.
801 Kaheka St.
Honolulu, HI 96814
808/949-6155
(Department stores.)

Dillingham Construction Pacific, Ltd
614 Kapahula Ave.
Honolulu, HI 96815
808/735-3211
(Construction—nonresidential buildings.)

Dole Co. Hawaiian Division
650 Iliwei Rd.
Honolulu, HI 96817
808/536-3411
(Canned fruits.)

First Hawaiian Bank
165 South King St.
Honolulu, HI 96813
808/525-7000
(Bank.)

GTE Hawaiian Telephone Inc.
P.O. Box 2200
Honolulu, HI 96841
808/546-3000
(Telephone company.)

Hawaii Electric Light Co.
1200 Kilauea Ave.
Hilo, HI 96720
808/935-1171
(Utility.)

Hawaiian Airlines Inc.
P.O. Box 30008
Hawaiian International Airport
Honolulu, HI 96820
808/525-5511
(Airline.)

Hawaiian Electric Co. Inc.
900 Richards St.
Honolulu, HI 96813
808/543-7771
(Utility.)

Hilton Hawaiian Village
2005 Kalia Rd.
Honolulu, HI 96815
808/949-4321
(Resort hotel.)

Kyo-Ya Co. Ltd.
2255 Kalakaua Ave.
Honolulu, HI 96815
808/922-4422
(Hotel, restaurants, etc.)

Liberty House, Inc.
1450 Ala Moana Blvd. #1300
Honolulu, HI 96814
808/941-2345
(Department stores.)

Maui Electric Co., Ltd.
210 Kamehameha Ave.
Kahului, HI 96732
808/871-8461
(Utility.)

Maui Land & Pineapple Co.
120 Kane St.
Kahului, HI 96732
808/877-3351
(Canned fruits.)

Outrigger Hotels Hawaii
2375 Kuhio Ave.
Honolulu, HI 96815
808/924-6018
(Resort hotel.)

HAWAII BUSINESS PERIODICALS

Hawaii Business
Box 913
Honolulu, HI 96808
808/946-3978
(Monthly.)

Pacific Business News
Box 833
Honolulu, HI 96808
808/521-0021
(Weekly.)

HAWAII DIRECTORIES

Directory of Manufacturers
Chamber of Commerce of Hawaii
735 Bishop St.
Honolulu, HI 98613
808/531-4111

Hawaii Business Directory
American Business Directories
5711 S. 86th Cir.
P.O. Box 27347
Omaha, NE 68127
402/593-4600

HAWAII GOVERNMENT EMPLOYMENT OFFICES

Office of Personnel Management
Federal Bldg, Rm. 5316
300 Ala Moana Blvd.
Honolulu, HI 96850
808/541-2791
808/541-2784 (For outer islands and
Pacific area.)
(Federal job-service center.)

Employment Service Division
Dept. of Labor & Ind. Rel
1347 Kapiolani Blvd.
Honolulu, HI 96814
808/548-6468
(State job-service center.)

IDAHO

LEADING IDAHO EMPLOYERS

Albertson's Inc.
250 Parkcenter Blvd.
Boise, ID 83726
208/385-6200
(Supermarkets.)

American Microsystems Inc.
2300 Buckskin Rd.
Pocotello, ID 83201
208/233-4690
(Semiconductors and related devices.)

Boise Cascade Corp.
111 W. Jefferson St.
Boise, ID 83702
208/384-6161
(Paper mills.)

Conda Mining Inc.
40 Miles NE of Hwy. 34
Soda Springs, ID 83276
208/547-2525
(Phosphate mining.)

First Interstate Bank of Idaho
877 Main
Boise, ID 83702
208/327-2000
(National trust companies with deposits.)

Hagadone Corporation
111 N. First St.
Coeur D'Alene, ID 83814
208/667-3431
(Newspaper publishing, hotels and motels.)

Idaho Power Co.
1220 W. Idaho St.
Boise, ID 83702
208/383-2200
(Utility.)

Micron Technology, Inc.
2805 East Columbia Rd.
Boise, ID 83706
208/383-4000
(Semiconductors and other equipment.)

Morrison-Knudsen Co., Inc.
Morrison-Knudsen Plz.
Boise, ID 83729
208/386-5000
(Heavy construction, engineering, real estate development.)

Ore-Ida Foods, Inc.
220 W. Park Center Blvd.
Boise, ID 83706
208/383-6100
(Frozen foods.)

J.R. Simplot Co.
1 Capital Ctr.
Boise, ID 83702
208/336-2110
(Frozen and dehydrated potatoes, fertilizers, livestock.)

Universal Frozen Foods Co.
856 Russett St.
Twin Falls, ID 83301
208/733-5664
(Frozen foods.)

Waremart Inc.
4550 Overland Rd.
Boise, ID 83705
208/377-0110
(Supermarkets.)

West One Bancorp
101 S. Capitol Blvd.
Boise, ID 83702
208/383-7000
(Banking.)

IDAHO BUSINESS PERIODICAL

Idaho Business Review
4218 Emerald St.
P.O. Box 7193
Boise, ID 83707
208/336-3768
(Weekly.)

IDAHO DIRECTORIES

Idaho Business Directory
American Business Directories
5711 S. 86th Cir.

P.O. Box 27347
Omaha, NE 68127
402/593-4600

Idaho Manufacturing Directory
Center for Business Development and
Research
College of Business and Economics
University of Idaho
Moscow, ID 83843
208/885-6611

*Inland Northwest Manufacturing
Directory*
Spokane Area Economic Development
Council
N. 221 Well
Ste. 310
Box 203
Spokane, WA 99210
309/624-9285
(Covers western Montana, northern
Idaho and Oregon, and eastern
Washington.)

IDAHO GOVERNMENT EMPLOYMENT OFFICES

Office of Personnel Management
(Federal job-service center—see
Washington listing.)

**Operations Div. Employment
Services**
Department of Employment
317 Main St.
Boise, ID 83735
208/334-3977
(State job-service center.)

MONTANA

LEADING MONTANA EMPLOYERS

Coca-Cola Bottling Co. West, Inc.
4151 1st Ave. S.
Billings, MT 59101
406/245-6286
(Soft drink bottling.)

Columbia Falls Aluminum Co.
2000 Aluminum Dr.
Columbia Falls, MT 59912
406/892-3261
(Aluminum.)

Entech Inc.
16 E. Granite
Butte, MT 59701
406/782-4233
(Coal mining.)

First Bank Montana
P.O. Box 30678
Billings, MT 59101
406/657-8000
(Banking.)

4Bs Restaurants Inc.
Bud Lake Village
Missoula, MT 59802
406/543-8265
(Restaurant.)

Hennessey Co., Inc.
140 S. 24th St. W.
Billings, MT 59102
406/656-0100
(Department stores.)

Industrial Constructors Inc.
101 International Dr.
Missoula, MT 59802
406/523-1205
(Heavy construction.)

Montana Power Co., Inc.
401 E. Broadway
Butte, MT 59701
406/723-5421
(Utility.)

Montana Rail Link Inc.
101 International Dr.
Missoula, MT 59802
406/523-1500
(Railroads.)

Pacific Hide & Fur Depot
1401 3rd St. NW
Great Falls, MT 59404
406/727-6222

(Furs, steel service center, farm equipment, etc.)

Stillwater Mining Co.
Off Hwy. 420
Nye, MT 59061
406/328-6400
(Mining.)

Tractor & Equipment Co.
1835 Harnish Blvd.
Billings, MT 59101
406/656-0202
(Construction and mining machinery and equipment.)

Washington Corps
101 International Way
Missoula, MT 59802
406/523-1200
(Construction.)

MONTANA BUSINESS PERIODICAL

Montana Business Quarterly
University of Montana
Bureau of Business and Economic Research
Missoula, MT 59812
406/243-5113

MONTANA DIRECTORIES

Inland Northwest Manufacturing Directory
Spokane Area Economic Development Council
N. 221 Well
Ste. 310
Box 203
Spokane, WA 99210
309/624-9285
(Covers western Montana, northern Idaho and Oregon, and eastern Washington.)

Montana Business Directory
American Business Directories
5711 S. 86th Cir.
P.O. Box 27347
Omaha, NE 68127
402/593-4600

Montana Manufacturers Directory
Montana Dept. of Commerce
Small Business Development Center
1424 Ninth Ave.
Helena, MT 59620
406/443-3923

MONTANA GOVERNMENT EMPLOYMENT OFFICES

Office of Personnel Management
(Federal job-service center—see
Colorado listing; call 303/236-4162.)

**Job Service/Employment and
Training Division**
P.O. Box 1728
Helena, MT 59624
406/444-4524
(State job-service center.)

NEW MEXICO

LEADING NEW MEXICO EMPLOYERS

Advanced Sciences Inc.
2620 San Mateo NE
Albuquerque, NM 87110
505/883-0959
(Commercial scientific research.)

Albuquerque Publishing Co.
7777 Jefferson St., NE
P.O. Drawer J-T
Albuquerque, NM 87109
505/823-7777
(Newspaper publishing.)

American Furniture Co., Inc.
Carlisle & Menaul NE
Albuquerque, NM 87110
505/883-2015
(Furniture stores.)

Chino Mines Co.
210 Cortez
Hurley, NM 88043
505/537-3381
(Copper ores.)

Hondo Oil & Gas Co.
410 East College Blvd.
Roswell, NM 88201
505/625-8700
(Petroleum refining.)

**Honeywell Defense Avionics Systems
Division**
9201 San Mateo Blvd. NE
Albuquerque, NM 87113-2227
505/822-5000
(Electronic systems for military
aircraft.)

Mesa Airlines Inc.
2325 East 30th St.
Farmington, NM 87401
505/327-0271
(Regional air carrier.)

Navajo Refining Co.
501 East Main St.
Artesia, NM 88210
(Petroleum refining.)

**Plains Electric Generation
Transmission Co-op**
2401 Aztec Ave. NE
Albuquerque, NM 87107
505/884-1881
(Utility.)

Prepared Foods Inc.
5701 North McNutt
Santa Teresa, NM 88008
505/589-0100
(Prepared meat products.)

**Public Service Company of New
Mexico**
Alvarado Sq.
Albuquerque, NM 87102
505/848-2700
(Electric and water utility.)

Roadrunner Trucking Inc.
501 Industrial Ave. NE
Albuquerque, NM 87107
505/345-8856
(Motor carrier.)

Sandia Corp.
Kirtland Air Force Base
Albuquerque, NM 87185
505/844-5678
(Research laboratory.)

Sunwest Bank New Mexico
303 Roma NW
Albuquerque, NM 87102

505/765-2211
(Banking.)

Sunwest Financial Services Inc.
303 Roma NW
Albuquerque, NM 87102
505/765-2403
(Banking.)

NEW MEXICO BUSINESS PERIODICAL

New Mexico Business Journal
2323 Aztec Rd. NE
Albuquerque, NM 87107
505/889-2911
(Monthly.)

NEW MEXICO DIRECTORIES

New Mexico Business Directory
American Business Directories
5711 S. 86th Cir.
P.O. Box 27347
Omaha, NE 68127
402/593-4600

New Mexico Manufacturing Directory
Economic Development & Tourism Dept.
1100 St. Francis Dr.
Santa Fe, NM 87503
505/827-6217

NEW MEXICO GOVERNMENT EMPLOYMENT OFFICES

Federal Building
421 Gold Ave. SW
Albuquerque, NM 87102
505/766-5583
(Federal job-service center.)

Employment Service Employment Security Dept.
P.O. Box 1928
Albuquerque, NM 87103
305/841-8437
(State job-service center.)

NEVADA

LEADING NEVADA EMPLOYERS

Amerco
1325 Airmotive Way, Suite 100
Reno, NV 89502
702/688-6300
(U-Haul rentals.)

Bently Nevada Corp.
1617 Water St.
Minden, NV 89423
702/782-3611
(Measuring and controlling devices.)

Caesar's Palace, Inc.
3570 Las Vegas Blvd.
Las Vegas, NV 89109
702/731-7110
(Hotel/casino.)

California Hotel & Casino
3000 Las Vegas Blvd. S.
Las Vegas, NV 89109
702/456-7777
(Hotel/casino.)

Circus Circus Enterprises
2880 Las Vegas Blvd.
Las Vegas, NV 89109
702/734-0410
(Casino.)

Desert Palace Inc.
3570 Las Vegas Blvd. S.
Las Vegas, NV 89109
702/731-7110
(Casino.)

El Dorado Hotel Associates
345 N. Virginia
Reno, NV 89501
702/786-5700
(Hotel/casino.)

**First Interstate Bank of Nevada
N.A.**
1 E. First St.
Reno, NV 89501
702/784-3397
(Banking.)

Ginji Corp.
3667 Las Vegas Blvd. S.
Las Vegas, NV 89109
702/736-0111
(Casino.)

Gold Coast Hotel
4000 W. Flamingo Rd.
Las Vegas, NV 89103
702/367-7111
(Casino.)

Golden Nugget Inc.
129 Fremont St.
Las Vegas, NV 89101
702/385-7111
(Casino.)

Harrah's
300 E. 2nd St.
Reno, NV 89501
702/786-3232
(Casino.)

Harvey's Wagon Wheel Inc.
Hwy. 50
P.O. Box 120
Stateline, NV 89449
702/588-2411
(Casino.)

Holiday Casino Inc.
3475 Las Vegas Blvd. S.
Las Vegas, NV 89109
702/369-5000
(Casino.)

Imperial Palace Inc.
3535 Las Vegas Blvd. S.
Las Vegas, NV 89109
702/731-3311
(Casino.)

Las Vegas Hilton Corp.
3000 Paradise Rd.
Las Vegas, NV 89109
702/732-5111
(Hotel/casino.)

MGM Desert Inn, Inc.
3145 Las Vegas Blvd. S.
Las Vegas, NV 89109
702/733-4444
(Hotel/casino.)

Mare-Bear Inc.
3000 Las Vegas Blvd. S.
Las Vegas, NV 90109
702/732-6111
(Casino.)

Minami Nevada Inc.
3650 Las Vegas Blvd. S.
Las Vegas, NV 89109
702/737-4668
(Casino.)

Mirage Resorts
3400 Las Vegas Blvd. S.
Las Vegas, NV 89109
702/791-5627
(Casino.)

Nevada Bell
(subs. of Pacific Telesis)
645 E. Plumb Ln.
Reno, NV 89502
702/789-6000
(Telephone company.)

Nevada Power Co.
6226 W. Sahara Ave.
Las Vegas, NV 89102
702/367-5000
(Utility.)

Porsche Cars North America
1000 W. Liberty St.
Reno, NV 89501
702/348-3000
(Automobiles, auto supplies and parts,
aircraft engines.)

Ramada Hotel of Nevada
3801 Las Vegas Blvd. S.
Las Vegas, NV 89109
702/739-222
(Casino.)

Sahara Casino Partners LP
2535 Las Vegas Blvd. S.
Las Vegas, NV 89109
702/737-2111
(Casino.)

Showboat Inc.
2800 Fremont
Las Vegas, NV 89104
702/385-9123
(Casino.)

Sierra Construction Corp.
5255 S. Valley View
Las Vegas, NV 89118
702/739-9413
(Hotel/motel construction.)

Sierra Pacific Power Co.
6100 Neil Rd.
Reno, NV 89511
702/689-4011
(Utility.)

Southwest Gas Company
5241 Spring Mountain Rd.
Las Vegas, NV 89102
702/876-7011
(Utility.)

United Gaming Inc.
4380 Boulder Hwy.
Las Vegas, NV 89121
702/435-4200
(Slot machines, etc.)

NEVADA BUSINESS PERIODICALS

Las Vegas Business
5300 West Sahara Ave.
Las Vegas, NV 89102
702/871-6780
(Semi-monthly.)

Nevada Business Journal
3800 Howard Hughes Pkwy.
Las Vegas, NV 89109
702/735-7003
(Bimonthly.)

NEVADA DIRECTORY

Nevada Business Directory
American Business Directories
5711 S. 86th Cir.
P.O. Box 27347
Omaha, NE 68127
402/593-4600

NEVADA GOVERNMENT EMPLOYMENT OFFICES

Office of Personnel Management
(Federal job-service center—see
Sacramento, California listing.)

Employment Service
Employment Security Dept.
500 E. Third St.
Carson City, NV 89713
702/885-4510
(State job-service center.)

OREGON

LEADING OREGON EMPLOYERS

Bank of America Oregon
121 SW Morrison
Portland, OR 97204
503/275-1234
(Savings and loan associations.)

Bear Creek Corp.
2518 S. Pacific Hwy.
Medord, OR 97501
503/776-2362
(Fruit orchard.)

Blue Cross & Blue Shield of Oregon
100 SW Market St.
Portland, OR 97201
503/225-5221
(Health insurance.)

CH2M Hill Companies Ltd.
2300 NW Walnut Blvd.
Coryallis, OR 97330
503/752-4271
(Engineering services.)

Evergreen International Airlines, Inc.
3850 Three Mile Ln.
McMinnville, OR 97128-9496
503/472-0011
(Cargo airline.)

Fred Meyer Inc.
3800 SE 22nd Ave.
Portland, OR 97202
503/232-8844
(Chain stores.)

Freightliner Corp.
4747 North Channel Ave.
Portland, OR 97217
503/283-8662
(Truck trailers.)

Graphic Arts Center Inc.
2000 NW Wilson St.
Portland, OR 97209
503/224-7777
(Commercial printing.)

Kaiser Foundation Health Plan of the Northwest
3600 N. Interstate
Portland, OR 97227
503/280-2050
(Hospital and medical service plans.)

Mentor Graphics Corp.
8005 SW Creekside Pl.
Beaverton, OR 97005
503/626-7000
(Computer software.)

Nike, Inc.
1 Bowerman Dr.
Beaverton, OR 97005
503/671-6453
(Athletic shoes, apparel.)

Oeco Corp.
4607 SE International Way
Milwaukie, OR 97222
503/659-5999
(Electronic components.)

Pay Less Drug Stores Northwest
9275 Peyton Ln.
Wilsonville, OR 97070
503/682-4100
(Drug stores.)

Precision Castparts Corp.
4600 SE Harney Dr.
Portland, OR 97206
503/777-3881
(Aerospace parts.)

RLC Industries Co.
1 Mile S. on Hwy. 99
Dillard, OR 97432
503/679-3311
(Softwood veneer and plywood.)

Roseburg Forest Products
P.O. Box 1088
Roseburg, OR 97470
503/679-3311
(Forest products.)

Sequent Computer Systems Inc.
15450 SW Koll Pkwy.
Beaverton, OR 97006
503/626-5700
(Mainframe computers.)

Standard Insurance Co.
1100 SW Sixth Ave.
Portland, OR 97204
503/248-2700
(Insurance.)

Tektronix, Inc.
Tektronix Industrial Park
14150 SW Karl Braun Dr.
Beaverton, OR 97577
503/627-7111
(Electronic control and display systems.)

U.S. Bancorp
11 SW Fifth Ave.
Portland, OR 97204
503/225-6111
(Banking.)

United Grocers Inc.
6433 SE Lake Rd.
Milwaukie, OR 97222
503/653-6330
(Wholesale groceries.)

Wacker Siltronic Corp.
7200 NW Front St.
Portland, OR 97210
503/243-2020
(Semiconductors and related devices.)

OREGON BUSINESS PERIODICALS

The Business Journal
American City Business Journals
P.O. Box 14490
Portland, OR 97214
503/274-8733
(Weekly.)

Oregon Business
921 SW Morrison
Suite 407
Portland, OR 97205
503/223-0304
(Monthly.)

OREGON DIRECTORIES

Directory of Oregon Manufacturers
Economic Development Department
595 Cottage St., N.E.
Salem, OR 97310
503/373-1200

Inland Northwest Manufacturing Directory
Spokane Area Economic Development
Council
N. 221 Well
Ste. 310
Box 203

Spokane, WA 99210
309/624-9285
(Covers western Montana, northern
Idaho and Oregon, and eastern
Washington.)

Oregon Business Directory
American Business Directories
5711 S. 86th Cir.
P.O. Box 27347
Omaha, NE 68127
402/593-4600

OREGON GOVERNMENT EMPLOYMENT OFFICES

Office of Personnel Management
Federal Bldg. Rm. 376
1220 S.W. Third Ave.
Portland, OR 97204
503/326-3141
(Federal job-service center.)

Employment Service
875 Union St. NE
Salem, OR 97311
503/378-3213
(State job-service center.)

UTAH

LEADING UTAH EMPLOYERS

Alta Health Strategies
2610 Decker Ln.
Salt Lake City, UT 84119
801/973-7300
(Insurance agents, brokers and
service.)

Amalgamated Sugar Co.
2040 Washington Blvd.
Ogden, UT 84401
801/399-3431
(Sugar.)

American Stores Co.
709 E. South Temple
Salt Lake City, UT 84226
801/539-0112
(Grocery stores.)

Associated Food Stores Inc.
1812 Empire Rd.
Salt Lake City, UT 84104
801/973-4400
(Grocery stores.)

Deseret Medical Inc.
9450 South State St.
Sandy, UT 84070
801/565-2300
(Surgical and medical instruments and apparatus.)

Evans and Sutherland Computer Corp.
6000 Komas Dr.
Salt Lake City, UT 84108
801/582-5847
(Computer peripherals.)

First Security Corp.
79 South Main St.
Salt Lake City, UT 84111
801/350-5000
(Banking.)

Flying J Inc.
P.O. Box 678
Brigham City, UT 84302
801/734-6400
(Petroleum products.)

Geneva Steel
10 S. Geneva Rd.
Orem, UT 84058
801/227-9000
(Steel.)

Huntsman Chemical Corp.
2000 Eagle Gate Tower
Salt Lake City, UT 84111
801/532-5200
(Plastics materials, synthetic resins.)

Iomega Corp.
1821 West 4000 South
Roy, UT 84067
801/778-1000
(Computer storage devices.)

Ireco Inc.
Crossroads Tower
11th Fl.
Salt Lake City, UT 84114
801/364-4800
(Explosives.)

JB's Restaurants, Inc.
1010 West 2610 South
Salt Lake City, UT 84119
801/974-4300
(Restaurants.)

Kennecott Corp.
10 East S. Temple St.
Salt Lake City, UT 84147
801/322-7000
(Copper mining.)

Ralph K. Little Co.
2681 Parleys Way
Salt Lake City, UT 84109
801/484-2200
(Business credit institution.)

Longyear Co.
2340 West 1700 South
Salt Lake City, UT 84104
801/972-6430
(Mining machinery.)

Mountain Fuel Supply Co.
180 East 1st South
Salt Lake City, UT 84111
801/364-7402
(Natural gas transmission and distribution.)

Northwest Pipeline Corp.
295 Chipeta Way
Salt Lake City, UT 84108
801/583-8800
(Gas transmission and distribution.)

Norton Enterprises
1945 South Redwood Rd.
Salt Lake City, UT 84104
801/972-6690
(Truck rental and leasing.)

Novell Inc.
122 East 1700 South
Provo, UT 84606
801/429-7000
(Computer software and services.)

Price Savers Wholesale Club Inc.
310 Bearcat Dr.
Salt Lake City, UT 84115
801/466-777
(Discount stores.)

Quaker State Minit-Lube Inc.
1385 West 200 South
Salt Lake City, UT 84119
801/972-6667
(Automotive services.)

Questar Corp.
180 East 1st South
Salt Lake City, UT 84111
801/534-5600
(Natural gas distribution.)

Questar Pipeline Co.
79 South State St.
Salt Lake City, UT 84111
801/530-2400
(Gas transmission and distribution.)

Skywest Airlines
Suite 201
50 East 100 South St.
St. George, UT 84770
801/628-2655
(Regional airline.)

Smith's Food & Drug Centers, Inc.
1550 South Redwood Rd.
Salt Lake City, UT 84104

801/974-1400
(Food and drug stores.)

Steiner Corp.
505 East South Temple
Salt Lake City, UT 84102
801/328-8831
(Linen supply.)

Swire Pacific Holdings Inc.
875 South West Temple
Salt Lake City, UT 84110
801/530-5300
(Soft drinks.)

O. C. Tanner Manufacturing Inc.
1930 South State St.
Salt Lake City, UT 84115
801/486-2430
(Jewelry, precious metal.)

Thiokol Corp.
2475 Washington Blvd.
Ogden, UT 84401
801/629-2000
(Rocket motors for space shuttle, etc.)

WordPerfect Corp.
1555 North Technology Way
Orem, UT 84057
801/222-4000
(Software.)

Zion's Co-op Mercantile Institution
2200 South 900 West
Salt Lake City, UT 84119
801/321-6179
(Department stores.)

Zions Bancorp
1380 Kennecott Building
Salt Lake City, UT 84133
801/524-4787
(Banking.)

UTAH DIRECTORIES

Utah Business Directory
American Business Directories
5711 S. 86th Cir.
P.O. Box 27347

Omaha, NE 68127
402/593-4600

Utah Directory of Business and Industry
Department of Employment Security
Division of Economic Development

324 S. State St.
Ste. 200
Salt Lake City, UT 84111
801/538-8700

UTAH GOVERNMENT EMPLOYMENT OFFICES

Office of Personnel Management
(Federal job-service center—see
Colorado listing; call 303/236-4165.)

Employment Services/Field Oper.
Department of Employment Security
164 Social Hall Ave.
Salt Lake City, UT 84147
801/533-2201
(State job-service center.)

WASHINGTON

LEADING WASHINGTON COMPANIES

Ackerley Communications Inc.
800 Fifth Ave.
Seattle, WA 98104
206/624-2888
(Outdoor advertising services, etc.)

Advanced Technologies Laboratories, Inc.
22100 Bothell Hwy. SE
Bothell, WA 98021
206/487-7000
(Surgical and medical instruments.)

Airborne Freight Corp.
3101 Western Ave.
Seattle, WA 98121
206/285-4600
(Express package delivery, freight forwarding.)

Alaska Airlines Inc.
19300 Pacific Hwy. South
Seattle, WA 98188
206/433-3200
(Airline.)

Aldus Corp.
411 First Ave. S.
Suite 200
Seattle, WA 98104
206/622-5500
(Software.)

Alpac Corp.
2300 26th Ave. S.
Seattle, WA 98144
206/323-2932
(Bottled/canned soft drinks.)

Associated Grocers Inc.
2201 S. Norfolk St.
Seattle, WA 98118
206/762-2100
(Wholesale groceries.)

Eddie Bauer Inc.
15010 NE 36th St.
Redmond, WA 98052
206/882-6100
(Retail stores.)

Bayliner Marine Corp.
17825 59th Ave. NE
Arlington, WA 98223
206/435-5571
(Fiberglass pleasure boats.)

Boeing Co.
P.O. Box 3707
7755 E. Marginal Way S.
Seattle, WA 98124
206/655-2121
(Aerospace.)

Boeing Commercial Airplanes
Box 3707
7755 E. Marginal Way
Seattle, WA 98124
206/655-2121
(Commercial aircraft division of
Boeing Co.)

Boeing Military Airplanes Division
Box 3707
7755 E. Marginal Way
Seattle, WA 98124
206/655-2121
(Strategic systems.)

The Bon
1601 Third Ave.
Seattle, WA 98101
206/344-2121
(Department store.)

Burlington Resources Inc.
999 Third Ave.
Seattle, WA 98104
206/467-3838
(Oil and gas.)

Costco Wholesale Corp.
10809 120th Ave. NE
Kirkland, WA 98033
206/828-8100
(Membership warehouse store.)

Egghead Inc.
22011 SE 51st
Issaquah, WA 98027
206/391-0800
(Software stores.)

Eldec Corp.
16700 13th Ave. W.
Lynnwood, WA 98027
206/743-1313
(Electronic and electromechanical
products for aerospace use.)

EHC Cos. Inc.
1511 Sixth Ave.
Seattle, WA 98101
206/938-6500
(Lumber/building materials dealers.)

Frederick & Nelson
5th & Pine
Seattle, WA 98111
206/682-5500
(Department stores.)

**First Interstate Bank of Washington
N.A.**
999 Third Ave.
Seattle, WA 98104
206/292-3111
(Banking.)

John Fluke Manufacturing Co., Inc.
6920 Seaway Blvd.
Everett, WA 98203
206/347-6100
(Electronic test and measurement
equipment.)

Food Services of America Inc.
18430 East Valley Hwy.
Kent, WA 98032
206/251-3800
(Wholesale groceries.)

General Insurance Co. of America
Safeco Plz.
Seattle, WA 98185
206/545-5000
(Insurance.)

**Group Health Cooperative of Puget
Sound**
521 Wall St.
Seattle, WA 98121
206/448-6565
(Health maintenance organization,
hospital operator.)

GTE West Coast Inc.
1800 41st St.
Everett, WA 98207
206/261-5321
(Telephone service.)

Holland American Line
300 Elliot Ave. W.
Seattle, WA 98119
206/281-3535
(Cruise ships, travel services, etc.)

ISC-Bunker Ramo Corp.
East 22425 Appleway
Liberty Lake, WA 99019
509/927-5600
(Microprocessor data terminal systems
and software.)

Intalco Aluminum Corp.
Mountain View Rd.
Ferndale, WA 98248
206/382-7061
(Aluminum.)

Intermec Corp.
6001 36th Ave. W.
Everett, WA 98203
206/348-2600
(Bar code printers and related
products.)

Kaiser Engineers Hanford Co.
1200 Jadwin Ave.
Richland, WA 99352
509/376-9253
(Engineering and architectural
services.)

Key Tronic Corp.
4424 N. Sullivan Rd.
Spokane, WA 99216
509/928-8000
(Computer keyboards.)

Lamb-Weston Inc.
8701 Glade Rd. N.
Kennewick, WA 99301
509/735-4651
(Frozen fruits, juices, produce.)

Longview Fibre Co.
End of Fibre Way
Longview, WA 98632
206/425-1550
(Tree farming, logging, paper mill
operator.)

McCaw Cellular Communications
P.O. Box 97060
Kirkland, WA 98083-9760
206/827-4500
(Cellular telephone services.)

Microsoft Corp.
One Microsoft Way
Redmond, WA 98052
206/882-8080
(Computer software.)

Nintendo of America Inc.
4820 150th Avenue NE
Redmond, WA 98052
206/882-2040
(Computer/video games.)

Nordstrom Inc.
1501 Fifth Ave.
Seattle, WA 98101
206/628-2111
(Department stores.)

Paccar Inc.
777 106th Ave. NE
Bellevue, WA 98004
206/455-7400
(Heavy-duty truck manufacturing.)

Pacific First Federal Savings Bank
1420 Fifth Ave.
Seattle, WA 98101
206/224-3000
(Banking.)

Pacific Telecom Inc.
805 Broadway
Vancouver, WA 98660
206/696-0983
(Telephone communications.)

Pay 'n Save Drug Stores Inc.
4045 Deleridge Way, SW
Seattle, WA 98106
206/938-6500
(Retail drug stores.)

Puget Sound Bancorp
1119 Pacific Ave.
Tacoma, WA 98402
206/593-3600
(Banking.)

Safeco Corp.
Safeco Plz.
Seattle, WA 98185
206/545-5000
(Health and life insurance, financial
management.)

Safeco Properties Inc.
900 4th Ave., #800
Seattle, WA 98164
206/223-4500
(Building operation, developers, etc.)

Seafirst Corp.
Columbia Seafirst Ctr.
1001 4th Ave.
Seattle, WA 98154
206/358-3000
(Banking and financial services.)

Seattle Times Co.
1120 John St.
Seattle, WA 98109
206/464-2111
(Newspaper publishing.)

Security Pacific Bancorp Northwest
1301 Fifth Ave.
Seattle, WA 98101
206/621-5280
(Banking.)

Sundstrand Data Control Inc.
15001 NE 36th St.
Redmond, WA 98052
206/885-3711
(Avionic systems.)

Todd Shipyards Corp.
1801 16th Ave. S.
Seattle, WA 98134
206/223-1560
(Shipbuilding, ship repair and
conversion.)

U R M Stores Inc.
North 7511 Freya
Spokane, WA 99207
509/467-2620
(Groceries.)

U.S. Bank of Washington
1414 4th Ave.
Seattle, WA 98101
206/344-2300
(Savings and loans.)

**US West Communications—Pacific
Northwest Bell**
(subs. of US West)
1600 Bell Plz.
Seattle, WA 98191
206/345-2211
(Telephone services.)

US West New Vector Group
3350 161 Ave. SE—Box 7329
Bellevue, WA 98008
206/747-4900
(Cellular telephone services.)

Washington Mutual Savings Bank
1201 Third Ave.
Seattle, WA 98101
206/461-2000
(Savings bank.)

Westin Hotel Co.
2001 Sixth Ave.
Seattle, WA 98121
206/443-5000
(Hotels.)

Weyerhauser Co.
Weyerhauser Bldg.
Tacoma, WA 98477
206/924-2345
(Forest products.)

WASHINGTON BUSINESS PERIODICAL

Sound Business
3000 Northrup Way
Bellevue, WA 98004
206/827-9900
(Monthly, covers the greater Seattle metropolitan area.)

WASHINGTON DIRECTORIES

Inland Northwest Manufacturing Directory
Spokane Area Economic Development Council
N. 221 Well
Ste. 310
Box 203
Spokane, WA 99210
309/624-9285
(Covers western Montana, northern Idaho and Oregon, and eastern Washington.)

Washington Business Directory
American Business Directories
5711 S. 86th Cir.
P.O. Box 27347
Omaha, NE 68127
402/593-4600

Washington Manufacturers Register
Database Publishing Co.
523 Superior Ave.
Newport Beach, CA 92663
800/888-8434

WASHINGTON GOVERNMENT EMPLOYMENT OFFICES

Office of Personnel Management
Federal Bldg. Rm 110
915 Second Ave.
Seattle, WA 98174
206/442-4365
(Federal job-service center.)

Employment Security Dept.
212 Maple Pk.
Olympia, WA 98504
206/753-0747
(State job-service center.)

WYOMING

LEADING WYOMING EMPLOYERS

Bridger Coal Co.
35 Miles E. of City
P.O. Box 2068
Rock Springs, WY 82901
307/382-9741
(Coal mining.)

Cheyenne Newspapers, Inc.
702 W. Lincoln Way
Cheyenne, WY 82001
307/634-3361
(Newspaper publishing.)

Coastal Chemical Inc.
8305 Otto Rd.
Cheyenne, WY 82007

307/637-2700
(Fertilizers.)

Cordero Mining Co.
748 T-7 Rd.
Gillette, WY 82716
307/682-8005
(Coal mining.)

FMC Wyoming Corp.
P.O. Box 872
Westvaco Rd.
Green River, WY 82935
307/875-2580
(Chemicals: soda, phosphate, etc.)

Jackson Hole Ski Corp.
Teton Village, WY 83025
307/733-2292
(Ski resort.)

Key Bank of Wyoming
18th & Carey Ave.
Box 1227
Cheyenne, WY 82003
307/634-5961
(Banking.)

Maverick Country Stores
1 Mile S. Hwy. 89
P.O. Box 457
Afton, WY 83110
307/886-3861
(Convenience stores, filling stations.)

Mini Mart Inc.
907 N. Poplar St.
Casper, WY 82601
307/266-1230
(Filling stations, convenience stores.)

North Antelope Coal Co.
Caller Box 3032
Gillette, WY 82717
307/464-0012
(Coal mining.)

Rhone-Polence of Wyoming, Ltd.
LaBarge Rd.
P.O. Box 513
Green River, WY 82935
307/875-2600
(Mineral mining.)

SST Energy Corp.
7000 W. Yellowstone Hwy.
Casper, WY 82604
307/235-3529
(Oil and gas field exploration
services.)

Sinclair Oil Corp.
2800 W. Lincolnway
Cheyenne, WY 82001
307/632-4862
(Oil and gas, etc.)

T G Soda Ash Inc.
30 Miles NW of Green River
Granger, WY 82934
307/875-2700
(Soda, phosphate.)

Thunder Basin Coal Co.
13 Miles SE on Hwy. 450
Wright, WY 82732
307/939-1300
(Coal mining.)

**University of Wyoming Research
Corp.**
365 N. 9th
Laramie, WY 82070
307/721-2219
(Research.)

**Western Oil Tool & Manufacturing
Co.**
415 1st St.
Mills, WY 82644
307/235-1591
(Fabricated structural metal.)

Wyoming Machinery Co.
5300 W. Old Yellowstone
Casper, WY 82604
307/472-1000
(Construction and mining equipment
and machinery.)

Wyoming National Bank
152 N. Durbin St.
Casper, WY 82602
307/235-7797
(Banking.)

WYOMING DIRECTORY

Wyoming Business Directory
American Business Directories
5711 S. 86th Cir.
P.O. Box 27347
Omaha, NE 68127
402/593-4600

WYOMING GOVERNMENT EMPLOYMENT OFFICES

Office of Personnel Management
(Federal job-service center—see
Colorado listing, call 303/236-4166.)

Employment Service
Employment Security Commission
P.O. Box 2760
Casper, WY 82602
307/235-3611
(State job-service center.)